Multicultural Law Enforcement

Strategies for Peacekeeping
in a Diverse Society

Fourth Edition

Robert M. Shusta
Deena R. Levine
Herbert Z. Wong
Aaron T. Olson
Philip R. Harris

PEARSON

Prentice
Hall

Upper Saddle River, New Jersey 07458

Library of Congress Cataloging-in-Publication Data

Multicultural law enforcement : strategies for peacekeeping in a
diverse society / Robert M. Shusta. — 4th ed.
    p. cm.
  Includes bibliographical references and index.
  ISBN-13: 978-0-13-157131-0
  ISBN-10: 0-13-157131-1
  1. Police-community relations—United States. 2. Discrimination in
law enforcement—United States. 3.   Multiculturalism—United States.
4.   Intercultural communication—United States.   I. Shusta, Robert M.
  HV7936.P8M85 2007
  363.2'3—dc22

                                        2006101992

Publisher: Vernon R. Anthony
Executive Editor: Tim Peyton
Managing Editor: Mary Carnis
Editorial Assistant: Jillian Allison
Production Management: Pine Tree Composition, Inc.
Production Editor: Jessica Balch
Production Liaison: Ann Pulido
Manufacturing Buyer: Cathleen Petersen
Senior Design Coordinator: Miguel Ortiz
Printer/Binder: R. R. Donnelley & Sons, Harrisonburg, VA
Cover Printer: Coral Graphics
Cover Design: Jill Little, iDesign
Cover Image: Corbis

Pearson Education LTD.
Pearson Education Singapore, Pte. Ltd
Pearson Education, Canada, Ltd
Pearson Education–Japan

Pearson Education Australia PTY, Limited
Pearson Education North Asia Ltd
Pearson Educación de Mexico, S.A. de C.V.
Pearson Education Malaysia, Pte. Ltd.

10 9 8 7 6 5 4 3 2 1

ISBN-13 978-0-13-157131-0
ISBN-10   0-13-157131-1

To all our family members

Midge
Phyllis, Michele
Michael, Ilana, Kara
Susan, Michael, Brett, Eric, Hannah, Paige
Janet

For their support and understanding of the value of this work

CONTENTS

Foreword xiii

Preface xv

Acknowledgments xvii

PART 1: Impact of Cultural Diversity on Law Enforcement 1

CHAPTER 1: Multicultural Communities: Challenges for Law Enforcement 3

Overview 3
Commentary 3
Introduction 4
Diverse Society 8
Interplay between Police Incidents and Culture 19
Dimensions of Diversity 24
Police Knowledge of Cultural Groups 26
Prejudice in Law Enforcement 26
Community-Based Policing 31
Summary 35
Eight Tips for Improving Law Enforcement in Multicultural Communities 35
Discussion Questions and Issues 36
Website Resources 37
References 38

CHAPTER 2: The Changing Law Enforcement Agency: A Microcosm of Society 41

Overview 41
Commentary 41
Introduction 42
Changing Workforce 43
Ethnic and Racial Issues within the Workforce 46
Women in Law Enforcement 53
Gay Men and Lesbians in Law Enforcement 64
The Chief Executive 73
Summary 77
Discussion Questions and Issues 77
Website Resources 78
References 79

**CHAPTER 3: Multicultural Representation in Law Enforcement:
Recruitment, Retention, and Promotion   83**

Overview   83
Commentary   83
Introduction   84
Recruitment of a Diverse Workforce   84
Selection Processes   93
Retention and Promotion of a Diverse Workforce   99
Summary   101
Discussion Questions and Issues   102
Website Resources   103
References   104

CHAPTER 4: Cross-Cultural Communication for Law Enforcement   106

Overview   106
Commentary   106
Language Barriers and Law Enforcement   107
Attitudes toward Non- or Limited-English Speakers   110
Cross-Cultural Communication in the Law Enforcement Context   111
Cross-Cultural Communication Attempts   114
Interviewing and Data-Gathering Skills   119
Nonverbal Communication   121
Male–Female Communication in Law Enforcement   125
Summary   127
Discussion Questions and Issues   128
Website Resources   130
References   131

PART 2: Cultural Specifics for Law Enforcement   133

CHAPTER 5: Law Enforcement Contact with Asian/Pacific Americans   135

Overview   135
Commentary   135
Introduction   136
Asian/Pacific American Defined   136
Typology of Asian/Pacific Americans   140
Historical Information   140
Demographics: Diversity among Asian/Pacific Americans   143
Asian/Pacific Americans' Key Motivating Perspectives   145
Labels and Terms   149
Myths and Stereotypes   149
The Asian/Pacific American Family   154
Cultural Influences on Communication: Verbal and Nonverbal Styles
   of Asian/Pacific Americans   157

Key Issues in Law Enforcement   159
Summary of Recommendations for Law Enforcement   164
Discussion Questions and Issues   166
Website Resources   167
References   168

CHAPTER 6: Law Enforcement Contact with African Americans   171

Overview   171
Commentary   171
African American Culture   172
Historical Information   172
Demographics: Diversity among African Americans   174
Issues of Identity   176
Group Identification Terms   177
Myths and Stereotypes   177
Cross-Racial Perceptions in Law Enforcement   179
The African American Family   180
Language and Communication   183
Key Issues in Law Enforcement   187
Summary of Recommendations for Law Enforcement   194
Discussion Questions and Issues   197
Website Resources   198
References   199

CHAPTER 7: Law Enforcement Contact with Latino/Hispanic Americans   202

Overview   202
Commentary   202
Introduction   203
Latino/Hispanic Americans Defined   204
Historical Information   205
Demographics: Diversity among Latino/Hispanic Americans   207
Labels and Terms   209
Typology of Latino/Hispanic Americans   209
Myths and Stereotypes   210
The Latino/Hispanic American Family   213
Cultural Influences on Communication: Verbal and Nonverbal Styles
    of Latino/Hispanic Americans   217
Key Issues in Law Enforcement   219
Summary of Recommendations for Law Enforcement   229
Discussion Questions and Issues   230
Website Resources   231
References   232

CHAPTER 8: Law Enforcement Contact with Arab Americans and Other Middle Eastern Groups   235

Overview   235
Commentary   235
Middle Easterners and Related Terminology Defined   236
Historical Information   238
Demographics   239
Differences and Similarities   240
Stereotypes   242
Islamic Religion   244
Family Structure   247
Cultural Practices   250
Key Issues in Law Enforcement   254
Summary of Recommendations for Law Enforcement   261
Discussion Questions and Issues   264
Website Resources   265
References   266

CHAPTER 9: Law Enforcement Contact with Native Americans   268

Overview   268
Commentary   268
Historical Information and Background   269
The Question of Native American Identity   272
Native American Populations, Reservations, and Tribes and Related History   273
Language and Communication   279
Family-Related Issues   282
Key Issues in Law Enforcement   284
Summary of Recommendations for Law Enforcement   294
Discussion Questions and Issues   297
Website Resources   297
References   298

PART 3: Multicultural Law Enforcement Elements in Terrorism and Homeland Security   301

CHAPTER 10: Multicultural Law Enforcement and Terrorism: Overview, Response Strategies, and Multicultural Communities   303

Overview   303
Commentary   303
Definitions   304
Historical Information and Background   305
Myths and Stereotypes about Terrorists   307

Local Community Issues and Global, National, and Regional Issues 311
The First-Response Challenge for Law Enforcement 313
Response Strategies 314
Key Issues in Law Enforcement 322
Summary 324
Discussion Questions and Issues 324
Website Resources 325
References 325

CHAPTER 11: Multicultural Law Enforcement in Homeland Security and Disaster Preparedness 328

Overview 328
Commentary 329
Historical Information and Background 330
Ensuring Multicultural Considerations in Homeland Security and Disaster
    Preparedness Strategies 332
Working with Multicultural Communities on Prevention and Response 344
Key Issues in Law Enforcement 346
Summary 349
Discussion Questions and Issues 350
Website Resources 351
References 352

PART 4: Response Strategies for Crimes Motivated by Hate/Bias and Racial Profiling 355

CHAPTER 12: Hate/Bias Crimes: Victims, Laws, Investigations, and Prosecutions 357

Overview 357
Commentary 357
The Hate/Bias Crime Problem 358
Definition of Hate Crime and Hate Incident 364
Hate Crime Source Theories 366
Jews and Anti-Semitism 368
Lesbian, Gay, Bisexual, and Transgender Victimization 373
Hate Crime Laws 385
Hate/Bias Crime and Incident Investigations 386
Hate/Bias Crime Prosecution 389
Hate/Bias Crime and Incident Victimology 393
Summary 396
Discussion Questions and Issues 396
Website Resources 397
References 399

CHAPTER 13: Hate/Bias Crimes: Reporting, Monitoring, and Response Strategies   402

Overview   402
Commentary   402
Introduction   403
Hate/Bias Crimes Reporting   404
Hate/Bias Crimes Monitoring   405
Organized Hate Groups   406
Response Alternatives to Organized Hate Groups   411
Trends and Predictions for Organized Hate Groups   412
Hate/Bias Crime and Incident Control   414
Trends to Monitor: STEEP Typology   416
Law Enforcement Response Strategies   418
Summary   424
Discussion Questions and Issues   424
Website Resources   426
References   427

CHAPTER 14: Racial Profiling   428

Overview   428
Commentary   428
Definitions   430
Historical Background of the Term *Racial Profiling* in Law Enforcement   432
Profiling Challenges in the War on Terrorism   434
Police and Citizen Perceptions of Racial Profiling   436
Profiling as a Legal Tool of Law Enforcement   446
Prevention of Racial Profiling in Law Enforcement   451
Professional Police Traffic Stops   459
Data Collection on Citizens' Race/Ethnicity   460
Summary   466
Discussion Questions and Issues   467
Website Resources   468
References   470

PART 5: Cultural Effectiveness for Peace Officers   473

CHAPTER 15: Emerging Strategies, Roles, and Technology for Peace Officers in Multicultural Law Enforcement   475

Overview   475
Commentary   475
The Future of Peacekeeping Strategies in Multicultural Communities   477
Crime Prevention among Minority and Immigrant Youth   482
Police Encounters among People with Mental Illness   486

Curtailing Litigation Against Police Agencies and Officers   488
Emerging Technology and Multicultural Law Enforcement Innovations   490
Summary   493
Discussion Questions and Issues   495
Website Resources   495
References   496

Appendix A: Multicultural Community and Workforce: Attitude Assessment Survey   499

Appendix B: Cultural Diversity Survey: Needs Assessment   505

Appendix C: Listing of Consultants and Resources   512

*Appendix D: Self-Assessment of Communication Skills in Law Enforcement:
Communications Inventory   518*

Glossary   520

Index   525

FOREWORD

Over the last 15 years, communities in the United States have witnessed a remarkable decline in the rate of crime. Years of effective and aggressive efforts by federal, state, and local law enforcement agencies, along with strong support for victim's rights and sentencing reform initiatives, have helped transform our neighborhoods from places of fear to safer, more secure communities.

Our success in reducing the level of crime can be traced to several factors: The typical police officer of today is better trained, better educated, and better equipped than his or her predecessors. In addition, advances in communication and information technologies have allowed law enforcement administrators to develop comprehensive, integrated crime-reduction strategies. Further, today's police officers have benefited from the dedicated and loyal contributions of the men and women before them who have since retired or given their lives in the line of duty.

No factor has been more crucial to the reduction in crime levels than the partnership between law enforcement agencies and the communities they serve. By embracing the philosophy of community policing, law enforcement agencies have been able to work with citizens to create safer towns and cities. We have learned that to be effective, police cannot operate alone; they require the active support and assistance of their communities.

Central to maintaining that support is the recognition that law enforcement agencies must reflect the diversity of the communities they serve. Every day, our officers come into contact with individuals from different cultural backgrounds, socioeconomic classes, religions, sexual orientations, and physical and mental abilities. Each of these groups brings a different perspective to police-community relations and, as a result, our officers must be prepared to respond to each group in the appropriate fashion. Failure to recognize and adjust to community diversity can foster confusion and resentment among citizens and quickly lead to a breakdown in the critical bond of trust between a law enforcement agency and its community.

Yet there are new critical issues in the nation impacting the criminal justice system. In the aftermath of the September 11, 2001, attacks, law enforcement agencies at all levels of government, including the new Department of Homeland Security, have had to reassess their responsibilities and duties. We face new challenges and must meet the increased expectations of the public and our elected officials. But terrorism has also brought the state and local law enforcement community face to face with a critical and fundamental question that will likely shape the way we police our communities: What role should state and local law enforcement play in the enforcement of federal immigration laws? All of these new challenges are taking place in times of federal, state, and local budget cuts impacting staffing, recruitment, and retention of officers nationwide.

The publication of this fourth edition of *Multicultural Law Enforcement: Strategies for Peacekeeping in a Diverse Society* is significant. Over 95 percent of published books never enter into their second edition. Clearly, the authors have filled a gap in the law enforcement literature, and we readers are fortunate to now have access to the fourth edition. Since the book was first printed in 1995, this volume has established itself as a classic in the criminal justice field. Its adoption by police and corrections academies and criminal justice courses at universities and colleges, is testimony to its far-reaching acceptance. *Multicultural Law Enforcement*'s major sections effectively address the key multicultural needs of law enforcement, as practitioners in increasing numbers have discovered for themselves. The practical contents of the book provide critical information and insight that will improve police performance and professionalism. The subject matter herein, especially on cultural-specific information, continues to be on the leading edge. Finally, instructors and trainers will welcome *Multicultural Law Enforcement* as a complete learning system that offers the following supplements to the main text: an Instructor's Manual, chapter quizzes, a student study guide, and PowerPoint presentations for each chapter.

This fourth edition of *Multicultural Law Enforcement* will enable agencies to prepare officers to form partnerships for effective community-based policing and to develop resources within criminal justice services for multicultural communities. Many of us have learned from the lessons of the past in terms of racial profiling, urban demonstrations, equal employment opportunity, terrorism, and homeland security, and we have developed strategies and implemented procedures to address, correct, and prevent the issues that caused them.

I am impressed by the diversity and competencies of the authors of *Multicultural Law Enforcement*. In addition to the vast and cumulative experience of the five co-authors, now consisting of a combined 53 years of active state and local law enforcement experience, each has sought additional cultural information and input from contributors from various other diverse backgrounds. This is why I feel confident in recommending this text. I encourage all who use it to take what you learn from the authors and put into action the strategies, information, and tools of this exceptional work for the betterment of your agencies, communities, and the larger society.

Mary Ann Viverette, Chief of Police
Gaithersburg, Maryland Police Department
2006 President, International Association of Chiefs of Police

PREFACE

This fourth edition of *Multicultural Law Enforcement: Strategies for Peacekeeping in a Diverse Society* is a continuing tribute to all our readers who enthusiastically received the first three editions. It is a textbook for police departments and academies as well as colleges and universities. Our text, with accompanying instructional tools, is a complete learning package designed to assist all levels of criminal justice representatives in understanding the pervasive influences of culture, race, and ethnicity in the workplace and in multicultural communities. The text focuses on the cross-cultural contact that police officers and civilian employees have with coworkers, victims, suspects, and citizens from diverse backgrounds. The fourth edition includes new sections on immigration and unauthorized migrants in the United States; the multifaceted dimensions of diversity; issues of multiracial census groups; recruitment and retention of women and minorities; Native American tribal police; information on contact with the mentally ill; multicultural issues related to terrorism, homeland security, and disaster preparedness; and expanded information on cultural groups that is relevant to law enforcement.

Throughout the text we stress the need for awareness, understanding of cultural differences, and respect toward those of different backgrounds. We encourage all representatives of law enforcement to examine preconceived notions they might hold of particular groups. We outline for police executives why they should build awareness and promote cultural understanding and tolerance within their agencies.

An increasing number of leaders in law enforcement agencies and their employees have accepted the premise that greater cross-cultural competency must be a key objective of all management and professional development. Demographic changes have had a tremendous impact not only on the types of crimes committed but also on the composition of the law enforcement workforce and the people with whom officers make contact. To be effective, police executives must understand and be responsive to the diversity in their workforces and in their changing communities. Professionalism today includes the need for greater consideration across cultures and improved communication with members of diverse groups.

In an era when news is processed and accessed immediately, the public is exposed almost daily to instances of cross-cultural and interracial contact between law enforcement agents and citizens. So, too, have community members become increasingly sophisticated and critical with regard to how members of diverse cultural and racial groups are treated by public servants. Employees of police departments and other agencies entrusted with law enforcement find that they are now serving communities that carefully observe them and hold them accountable for their actions.

This edition has been updated and expanded to provide practical information and guidelines for law enforcement managers, supervisors, officers, and instructors. With cross-cultural knowledge, sensitivity, and tolerance, those who are charged with the responsibility of peacekeeping will improve their image while demonstrating greater professionalism within the changing multicultural workforce and community. Our focus has primarily been on peace officers—in addition to police, this text also applies to issues and challenges faced by correctional officers, border patrol agents, marshals, federal agents, and military police.

With this fourth edition, our writing team welcomes a fifth author—retired Oregon State Police Sergeant Aaron T. Olson, who has considerable experience teaching from *Multicultural Law Enforcement* in community college and public safety classrooms. The authors now offer readers a complete learning package to supplement the main text. This includes an Instructor's Manual, Student Study Guide, PowerPoint presentations, and chapter quizzes. We hope that you find our revised and updated text, along with the additional learning tools, an enhancement to your criminal justice and law enforcement programs.

Robert M. Shusta, MPA
Deena R. Levine, MA
Herbert Z. Wong, PhD
Aaron T. Olson, MEd
Philip R. Harris, PhD

ACKNOWLEDGMENTS

This fourth edition has benefited from expert content contributions by the following people and organizations: David Barlow, PhD, Associate Professor, Fayetteville State University, North Carolina; Danilo Begonia, JD, Professor, Asian American Studies, San Francisco State University, San Francisco, California; Ondra Berry, retired Deputy Chief, Reno Police Department, Reno, Nevada; Peggy Bowen, PhD, Assistant Professor of Criminal Justice, Alvernia College, Reading, Pennsylvania; John Brothers, Executive Director, Quincy Asian Resources, Inc., Quincy, Massachusetts; Patricia DeRosa, President, ChangeWorks Consulting, Randolph, Massachusetts; Ronald Griffin, Pastor and Community Leader, Detroit, Michigan; Mitchell Grobeson, retired Sergeant, Los Angeles Police Department, Los Angeles, California; Ronald Haddad, Senior Deputy Chief, Detroit Police Department, Detroit, Michigan; Lubna Ismail, President, Connecting Cultures, Washington, D.C.; Sari Karet, Executive Director, Cambodian American Foundation, San Francisco, California; Marilyn Loden, Organizational Diversity Consultant with Loden Associates, Inc., Tiburon, California; Paula Parnagian, World View Services, Revere, Massachusetts; Oscar Ramirez, PhD, Police and Court Expert Consultant, San Antonio, Texas; Jose Rivera, retired Peace Officer, Education Director—Native American Museum, Sausalito, California; Greg Patton, Supervisor, Parole and Probation, Clackamas County Community Corrections, Clackamas, Oregon; Lourdes Rodriguez-Nogues, EdD, President, Rasi Associates, Boston, Massachusetts; Helen Samhan, Executive Director, Arab American Institute Foundation, Washington, D.C.; Margaret D. Shorter, Sgt., Royal Canadian Mounted Police and officer of the International Association of Women and Policing; Victoria Santos, President, Santos & Associates, Newark, California; George Thompson, President of Verbal Judo Institute, Auburn, New York; Reverend Onasai Veevau, Pastor and Pacific Islander Community Leader, San Mateo, California; Norita Jones Vlach, PhD, Professor, School of Social Work, San Jose State University, San Jose, California; James Zogby, PhD, Director, Arab American Institute Foundation, Washington, D.C.; John Zogby, PhD, President, Zogby International, New York, New York.

We owe special thanks to the following individuals for their helpful insights: Kim Ah-Low, Georgia; Corporal Mohamed Berro, Michigan; Joe Canton, PhD, California; Chung H. Chuong, California; Captain S. Rob Hardman, USCG (Ret.), Virginia; Wilbur Herrington, Massachusetts; Jim Kahue, Hawaii; Chief Susan Jones, California; Ilana Lipsett, Washington, D.C.; Charles Marquez, Colorado; Lieutenant Darryl McAllister, California; Sarah Miyahira, PhD, Hawaii; Margaret Moore, Washington, D.C.; Dinh Van Nguyen, California; JoAnne Pina, PhD, Washington, D.C.; Eduardo Rodela, PhD, Washington, D.C.; Chief Darrel Stephens, North Carolina; George Thompson, New York.

We would also like to thank the following reviewers: Shaun L. Gabbidon, Penn State University, Middletown, Pennsylvania; Arnold Waggoner, Rose State College, Midwest City, Oklahoma; and Stephen M. Hennessy, St. Cloud State, St. Cloud, Minnesota.

Part 1

IMPACT OF CULTURAL DIVERSITY ON LAW ENFORCEMENT

1 Multicultural Communities: Challenges for Law Enforcement

2 The Changing Law Enforcement Agency: A Microcosm of Society

3 Multicultural Representation in Law Enforcement: Recruitment, Retention, and Promotion

4 Cross-Cultural Communication for Law Enforcement

Part One of *Multicultural Law Enforcement* introduces readers to the implications of a multicultural society for law enforcement, both within and outside the police agency. Chapter 1 discusses aspects of the changing population and presents views on diversity.

The three case studies in Chapter 1 exemplify how the presence of different cultures can affect the very nature and perception of crime itself. We present the subject of prejudice and its effect on police work, providing specific examples of its consequences in law enforcement. We also discuss community-based policing and provide examples of departments with and without community partnerships. The chapter ends with suggestions for improving law enforcement in multicultural communities.

Chapter 2 discusses demographic changes taking place within law enforcement agencies, as well as reactions to diversity in the law enforcement workplace and responses to it. In addition to data on ethnic and racial groups, this chapter provides information on women and on gay men and lesbians in law enforcement organizations across the country. We illustrate the realities of the new workforce and the corresponding need for flexibility in leadership styles.

Chapter 3 discusses challenges in recruitment, retention, and promotion of police personnel from the perspectives of racial, ethnic, sexual orientation, and cultural diversity. We present strategies for recruitment, emphasizing the commitment required by law enforcement chief executives and the need to look inward—that is, to assess the level of comfort and inclusion that all employees experience in a given agency. If the levels are not high, hiring, retention, and promotion will be difficult. Chapter 3 describes the pressing need facing all agencies to build a workforce of highly qualified individuals of diverse backgrounds and in which all people have equal access to the hiring, retention, and promotion processes. It also presents a creative model for recruitment using community policing.

Chapter 4 provides practical information highlighting the dynamics of cross-cultural communication in law enforcement. The chapter includes a discussion of the special problems involved when officers must communicate with speakers of other languages. We present typical styles of communication that people may display when they are uncomfortable with cross-cultural contact. The chapter now includes a section on the need for communication sensitivity post-9/11. In addition, it covers nonverbal differences across cultures and addresses some of the communication issues that arise between men and women in law enforcement agencies. Finally, we present skills and techniques for officers to apply in situations of cross-cultural contact.

Each chapter ends with discussion questions and a list of references, including websites. The following appendices correspond to the chapter content in Part One:

A Multicultural Community and Workforce: Attitude Assessment

B Cultural Diversity Survey: Needs Assessment

C Listing of Consultants and Resources

D Self-Assessment of Communication Skills in Law Enforcement: Communications Inventory

Chapter 1

Multicultural Communities: Challenges for Law Enforcement

OVERVIEW

In this chapter we discuss law enforcement challenges related to the growing multicultural population in the United States. Chapter 1 begins by explaining the need for an increased understanding of the diverse populations with which law enforcement officials interact. The discussion of our mosaic society incorporates a brief historical perspective on immigration. Three mini case studies illustrate the points of contact between a person's culture and a particular crime or offense. We present practical reasons why officers should have an understanding of the cultural backgrounds of the groups they commonly encounter. We discuss how prejudice interferes with, but can be overcome by, the professional behavior of law enforcement officers. Next, we examine community-based policing, along with its implications for positive relations and contact with diverse immigrant and ethnic communities. The chapter ends with tips for improving law enforcement in multicultural communities.

COMMENTARY

The 21st century will be the century in which we redefine ourselves as the first country in world history that is literally made up of every part of the world.

—*Kenneth Prewitt, Director of the U.S. Census Bureau, 1998–2001*

Multiculturalism and diversity are at the very heart of America and describe accurately the demographics of our nation. The word *multiculturalism* does not refer to a movement or political force, nor is it an anti-American term. A multicultural community is simply one that is comprised of many different ethnic and racial groups. The United States, compared to virtually all other nations, has experienced unparalleled growth in its multicultural population. Reactions to these changes range from appreciation and even celebration of diversity to an absolute intolerance of differences. In its extreme form, intolerance resulting in crimes of hate is a major law enforcement and criminal justice concern.

Law enforcement officials—those whose professional ideal is to protect and serve people equally from all backgrounds—must face the challenges and complexities of a diverse society. Although our nation has been enriched by diversity, many police procedures and interactions with citizens can be complicated by diversity. A lack of knowledge of cultural differences can result in inadvertent violation of individuals' rights as well as officer safety and risk issues. Officers, even more than others, must ensure that their prejudices are in check and that they refrain from acting on any biased thought—after all, bias is common to all human beings. The following quotes provide a national perspective on the mandate of law enforcement:

Initial Report of the United States of America to the United Nations Committee on the Elimination of Racial Discrimination

As a functioning, multi-racial [and multicultural] democracy, the United States seeks to enforce the established rights of individuals to protection against discrimination based upon race, color, national origin, religion, gender, age, disability status, and citizenship status in virtually every aspect of social and economic life. . . . The federal government has established a wide-ranging set of enforcement procedures to administer these laws, with the U.S. Department of Justice exercising a major coordination and leadership role on most critical enforcement issues. (Convention on the Elimination of All Forms of Racial Discrimination, 2000)

Interview with Retired Assistant Chief Ondra Berry, Reno, Nevada, Police Department

Law enforcement is under a powerful microscope in terms of how citizens are treated. Minority and ethnic communities have become increasingly competent in understanding the role of law enforcement, and expectations of law enforcement for professionalism have been elevated from previous years. In an age when information about what happens in a police department on the East Coast speeds across to the West Coast in seconds, law enforcement officials must be aware. They must be vigilant. They must do the right thing. (Berry, 2006)

INTRODUCTION

The United States has always been a magnet for people from nearly every corner of the earth, and, consequently, U.S. demographics continue to undergo constant change. In efforts to be both proactive and responsive to diverse communities, police officers and groups from many backgrounds around the country are working to become more closely connected in direct relationships promoted in community-based policing models. Leaders from both law enforcement agencies and the community have realized that both groups benefit when each group seeks mutual assistance and understanding. The job of law enforcement requires a certain level of comfort and professionalism in interacting with people from all backgrounds whether one is working with community members to build trust or dealing with suspects, victims, and coworkers.

Through increased awareness, knowledge, and skills, law enforcement as a profession can increase its "cultural competence." Developing cultural competence is a process that evolves over time, requiring that individuals and organizations place a high value on the following (adapted from Cross, Bazron, Dennis, & Isaacs, 1989):

- Developing a set of principles, attitudes, policies, and structures that will enable all individuals in the organization to work effectively and equitably across all cultures

- Developing the capacity to:
  - acquire and apply cross-cultural knowledge
  - respond to and communicate effectively within the cultural contexts that the organization serves

The strategies an individual uses to approach and build rapport with his or her own cultural group may result in unexpected difficulties with another group. The acts of approaching, communicating, questioning, assisting, and establishing trust with members of culturally diverse groups require special knowledge and skills that have nothing to do with the fact that "the law is the law" and must be enforced equally. Acquiring knowledge and skills that lead to sensitivity does not imply preferential treatment of any one group; rather it contributes to improved communication with members of all groups.

Individuals must seek a balance between, on the one hand, downplaying and even denying the differences of others, and on the other hand, distorting the roles of culture, race, and ethnicity. In an effort to simply "respect all humans equally," we may inadvertently diminish the influence of culture or ethnicity, including the role it has played historically in our society.

The Melting Pot Myth and the Mosaic

Multiculturalism, also called cultural pluralism, violates what some consider to be the "American way of life." However, from the time our country was founded, we were never a homogeneous society. The indigenous peoples of America (the ancestors of the American Indians) were here long before Christopher Columbus "discovered" them. There is even strong evidence that the first Africans who set foot in this country came as free people, 200 years before the slave trade from Africa began (Rawlins, 1992). Furthermore, the majority of people in America can claim to be the children, grandchildren, or great-grandchildren of people who have migrated here. Americans did not originate from a common stock. Until fairly recently, America has been referred to as a melting pot, a term depicting an image of people coming together and forming a unified culture. One of the earliest usages of the term was in the early 1900s, when a famous American playwright, Israel Zangwill, referring to the mass migration from Europe, said, "America is God's crucible, the great Melting-Pot where all the races of Europe are melting and re-forming. . . . Germans and Frenchmen, Irishmen and Englishmen, Jews and Russians—into the Crucible with you all! God is making the American!" (Zangwill, 1908).

This first use of the term melting pot was not designed to incorporate anyone except Europeans. Did the melting pot ever exist, then, in the United States? No, it never did. Yet people still refer to the belief, which is not much more than a romantic myth about the "good old days." African Americans, brought forcibly to this country between 1619 and 1850, were never part of the early descriptions of the melting pot. Likewise, Native American peoples were not considered for the melting pot. It is not coincidental that these groups were nonwhite and were therefore not "meltable." Furthermore, throughout our past, great efforts have been made to prevent any additional diversity. Most notable in this regard was the Chinese Exclusion Act in 1882, which denied Chinese laborers the right to enter America. Early in the 20th century organized labor formed the Japanese and Korean Exclusion League "to protest the influx of 'Coolie' labor and in fear of threat to the living standards of American workingmen" (Kennedy, 1986, p. 72). Immigration was discouraged or prevented if it did not add strength to what already existed as the European-descended majority of the population (Handlin, 1975).

Even at the peak of immigration (late 1800s), New York City exemplified how different immigrant groups stayed separate from each other, with little of the "blending" that people often imagine took place (Miller, 2006). Three-fourths of New York City's population consisted of first- or second-generation immigrants (including Europeans and Asians); 80 percent did not speak English, and there were 100 foreign-language newspapers in circulation. The new arrivals were not accepted by those who had already settled, and newcomers found comfort in an alien society by choosing to remain in ethnic enclaves with people who shared their culture and life experiences.

The first generation of every immigrant and refugee group seeing the United States as the land of hope and opportunity has always experienced obstacles in acculturation (i.e., integration) into the new society. In many cases, people resisted Americanization and kept to themselves. Italians, Irish, eastern European Jews, Portuguese, Germans, and virtually all other groups tended to remain apart when they first came. Most previously settled immigrants were distrustful and disdainful of each newcomer group. "Mainstreaming" began to occur only with children of immigrants (although some people within certain immigrant groups tried to assimilate quickly). For the most part, however, society did not permit a quick shedding of previous cultural identity. History has never supported the metaphor of the melting pot, especially with regard to the first and second generations of most groups of newcomers. Despite the reality of past multicultural disharmony and tension in the United States, however, the notion of the melting pot prevailed.

The terms *mosaic* and *tapestry* more accurately and idealistically portray a view of diversity in America. They describe a society in which all colors and backgrounds contribute their parts to form society as a whole, but one in which groups are not required to lose their characteristics in order to "melt" together. The idea of a mosaic portrays a society in which all races and ethnic groups are displayed in a form that is attractive because of the very elements of which it is made. Each group is seen as separate and distinct in contributing its own color, shape, and design to the whole, resulting in an enriched society.

Reactions to Diversity: Past and Present

Accepting diversity has always been a difficult proposition for most Americans (Miller, 2006). Typical criticisms of immigrants, now and historically, include "They hold on to their cultures," "They don't learn our language," "Their customs and behavior are strange," and "They form cliques." Many newcomers, in fact, have historically resisted Americanization, keeping to ethnic enclaves. They were not usually accepted by mainstream society.

Are the reactions to newcomers today so different from people's reactions to earlier waves of immigrants? Let's look at reactions to the Irish, who by the middle of the 19th century constituted the largest group of immigrants in the United States, making up almost 45 percent of the foreign-born population. Approximately 4.25 million people left Ireland, mainly because of the potato famine. Many of these immigrants had come from rural areas but ended up in cities on the East Coast. Most were illiterate; some spoke only Gaelic (Kennedy, 1986). Their reception in America was anything but welcoming, exemplified by the plethora of signs saying, "Jobs available, no Irish need apply."

> The Irish . . . endure[d] the scorn and discrimination later to be inflicted, to some degree at least, on each successive wave of immigrants by already settled "Americans." In speech and in dress, they seemed foreign; they were poor and unskilled and they were arriving in overwhelming numbers. . . . The Irish found many doors closed to them, both socially and economically. When their earnings were not enough . . . their wives and daughters obtained employment as servants. (Kennedy, 1986, p. 18)

If this account were rewritten without specific references to time and cultural group, it would be reasonable to assume it describes contemporary reactions to newcomers. We could take this passage and substitute Jew, Italian, or Polish at various points in history. Today, it could be used in reference to Cubans, Somalis, Afghans, Mexicans, Haitians, Serbs, or Ethiopians. If we compare immigration today with that during earlier periods in U.S. history, we find similarities as well as significant differences. In the past few decades, we have received people from cultures more dramatically different than those from western Europe. For example, many of our "new Americans" from parts of Asia or Africa bring values and languages not commonly associated with or related to mainstream American values and language. Middle Easterners bring customs unknown to many U.S.-born Americans. (For cultural specifics, refer to Chapters 5 through 9.) Many refugees bring scars of political persecution or war trauma, the nature of which the majority of Americans cannot even fathom. The relatively mild experiences of those who came as voluntary migrants do not compare with the tragedies of many of the more recent refugees. True, desperate economic conditions compelled many early European immigrants to leave their countries (and thus their leaving was not entirely voluntary). However, their experiences do not parallel, for example, war-torn eastern European refugees who came to the United States in the 1990s.

Disparaging comments were once made toward the very people whose descendants would, in later years, constitute much of mainstream America. Many fourth- and fifth-generation immigrants have forgotten their history (Miller, 2006) and are intolerant of the "foreign ways" of emerging immigrant groups. Every new group seems to be met with some suspicion and, in many cases, hostility. Adjustment to a new society is and has always been a long and painful process, and the first-generation immigrant group suffers, whether Irish, Jewish, Polish, Afghani, Laotian, Filipino, or Russian. It must also be remembered that many groups did not come to the United States of their own free will but rather were victims of a political or economic system that forced them to abruptly cut their roots and escape their homelands. Although grateful for their welcome to this country, such newcomers did not want to be uprooted. Many new Americans did not have any part in the creation of events that led to the flight from their countries.

DIVERSE SOCIETY

In *One America in the 21st Century: Forging a New Future* (1998), data showed that although racially and ethnically diverse groups have made progress with respect to the indicators used to measure the quality of life, they still face barriers to full inclusion in American life. In the area of civil rights enforcement, the Advisory Board to the President's Initiative on Race made the following recommendations:

- Strengthen civil rights enforcement
- Improve data collection on racial and ethnic discrimination
- Strengthen laws and enforcement against hate crimes

A diverse society obviously makes any law enforcement officer's or manager's job more difficult. Racial tensions, cultural background, and ethnicity are bound to complicate many police procedures and encounters with citizens. It would be naive to preach to law enforcement officers, agents, and managers about the value of diversity when day-to-day activities are complicated by diversity. But the longer it takes to understand the influences of culture and ethnicity on behavior, the longer every police procedure and encounter between the police and the multicultural public will remain complicated. At a minimum, there must be a basic acceptance of diversity on the part of all criminal justice representatives as a precursor to improving interpersonal relations and contact across cultural, ethnic, and racial lines.

The Overlap of Race, Culture, and Ethnicity

Before we discuss the demographics of various minority and immigrant groups, we must mention how, in the 21st century, demographic estimates and projections are likely to fall short of counting the true mix of people in the United States. In the culture-specific chapters (Chapters 5 to 9) of this book, we discuss characteristics and law enforcement–related issues of Asian and Pacific Americans, African Americans, Latino and Hispanic Americans, Arab Americans and other Middle Eastern groups, and Native Americans. This categorization is merely for the sake of convenience; an individual may belong to two or more groups. For example, a black Latino, such as a person from the Dominican Republic or Brazil, may identify himself or herself as both black and Latino. Race and ethnic background (e.g., in the case of a black Latino) are not necessarily mutually exclusive. Hispanic is considered an ethnicity, not a race. Therefore, people of Latino descent can count themselves as part of any race. An individual who in the 1990 census counted himself or herself as black and now chooses both black and white is considered one person with two races in the 2000 census ("Multiracial Data in Census" 2000).

Law enforcement officials need to be aware of the overlap between race and ethnicity and that many individuals consider themselves to be multiracial. "Everyday, in every corner of America, we are redrawing the color lines and are redefining what race really means. It's not just a matter of black and white anymore; the nuances of brown and yellow and red mean more—and less than ever" ("The Changing Face of Race in America," 2000).

The United States, a heterogeneous society, is an amalgam of races, cultures, and ethnic groups. The first photo in the mentioned *Newsweek* article shows a child whose ethnicity is Nigerian, Irish, African American, Native American, Russian Jewish, and Polish Jewish (from parents and grandparents). Her U.S. census category may be simply "other." When we interpret population statistics, we have to understand that the face of America is changing. In 1860 there were only three census categories: black, white, and quadroon (a person who has one black grandparent, or the child of a mulatto and a white). In the 2000 census, there were 63 possible options for marking racial identity, or twice that if people responded to whether or not they were of Hispanic ethnicity. As the 2000 census director, Kenneth Prewitt, wrote, the concept of classification by race is human-made and endlessly complex.

> What is extraordinary is that the nation moved suddenly, and with only minimal public understanding of the consequences, from a limited and relatively closed racial taxonomy to one that has no limits. In the future, racial categories will no doubt become more numerous. And why not? What grounds does the government have to declare "enough is enough"? When there were only three or even four or five categories, maybe "enough is enough" was plausible. But how can we decide, as a nation, that what we allow for on the census form of today—63 racial groups or 126 racial/ethnic ones—is the "right" number? It can't be, nor can any other number be "right." There is no political or scientifically defensible limit. (Prewitt, 2001)

Changing Population

Changes in population characteristics between 1990 and 2000 have been dramatic. Exhibits 1.1 and 1.2 graphically presents the relative sizes of various ethnic populations. According to population projections, by 2050, the non-Hispanic white population will decline to 53 percent from 70 percent in 2000. In 2050, 25 percent of the population will be of Hispanic origin, 15 percent will be black, 9 percent Asian and Pacific Islander, and 1 percent American Indian, Eskimo, and Aleut. The non-Hispanic white

	1990	*2000*	*DIFFERENCE*	*PERCENT DIFFERENCE*
Hispanic Origin	22.4	35.3	13	58%
White, non-Hispanic	188.1	194.6	6.4	3.40%
Black, non-Hispanic	29.2	34	4.7	16.20%
Asian	6.6	10.1	3.5	52.40%
American Indian and Alaska Native	1.8	2.1	0.3	15.30%
Native Hawaiian and Other Pacific Islander	0.3	0.3	0	8.50%
Other Race	0.3	0.5	0.2	87.80%
Total	248.7	281.4	32.7	13.20%

Exhibit 1.1   Difference in Population by Race and Hispanic Origin: 1990 to 2000 (rounded to the nearest hundred thousand).
Source: U.S. Census Bureau, 2001
Notes: The 2000 data does not include persons who described themselves as being of more than one of the above racial categories, as the 1990 data did not include this option.

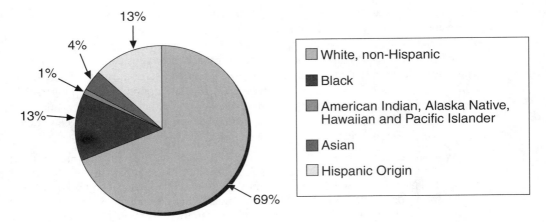

Exhibit 1.2   Resident Population by Race and Hispanic Origin: 2000.
Source: U.S. Census Bureau, Statistical Abstract of the United States: 2002.

population will be the slowest-growing race group (see Exhibit 1.3). This demographic shift has already occurred in some large cities across the country and in a number of areas in California, where the minority has become the majority. This change has had a huge impact on many institutions in society, not the least of which is law enforcement.

Immigrants

Immigration is not a new phenomenon in the United States. Virtually every citizen, except for indigenous peoples of America, can claim to be a descendent of someone who migrated (whether voluntarily or not) from another country. Immigration levels per

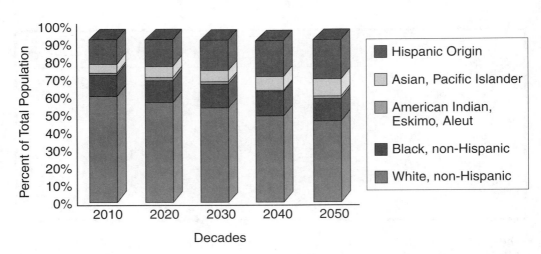

Exhibit 1.3   Resident Population by Race and Hispanic Origin Status—Projections: 2010 to 2050.
Source: U.S. Statistical Abstract of the United States: 2002.

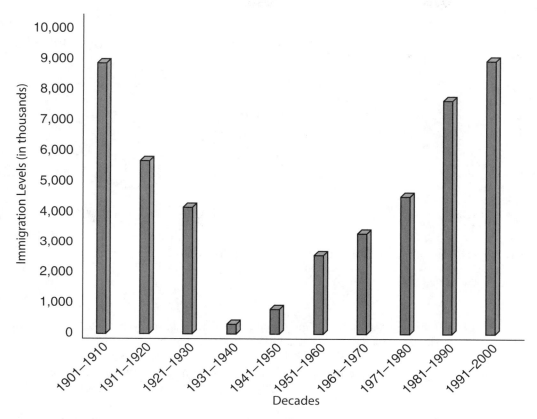

Exhibit 1.4   Immigration to America in the 20th Century.
Source: U.S. Census Bureau, Statistical Abstract of the United States: 2002.

decade reached their highest absolute numbers ever at the end of the last century, when the number of immigrants surpassed 9 million from 1991 to 2000 (see Exhibit 1.4). In addition, immigrants from 1980 to the present have come from many more parts of the world than those who arrived at the turn of the 20th century (Exhibit 1.5). The U.S. Census Bureau reported in March 2002 that approximately 32.5 million U.S. residents (11.5 percent of the population) had been born in other countries.

Among the foreign born in 2002, 52.2 percent were from Latin America, 25.5 percent from Asia, 14.0 percent from Europe, and the remaining 8.3 percent from other regions of the world. The foreign-born population from Central America, including Mexico, made up more than two thirds of the foreign born from Latin America and more than one third of the total foreign born (see Exhibit 1.5). In terms of geographic distribution within the country, 11 percent of the foreign-born population lived in the Midwest, 23 percent lived in the Northeast, 28 percent in the South, and 38 percent in the West (see Exhibit 1.6). (U.S. Census, 2002)

Even though most Americans, with the exception of the indigenous peoples, have been immigrants at some time in their lineage, anti-immigrant sentiment is common. Especially in a time of recession, many people perceive that immigrants are taking jobs

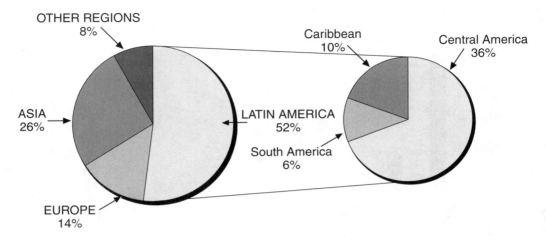

Exhibit 1.5   Emigration to America by World Region, 2002.
Source: U.S. Census Bureau, Current Population Reports, February 2003: "The Foreign Born Population in the United States: March 2002."

away from "real Americans" (forgetting that legal immigrants are also "real" Americans). However, the issues surrounding immigration are not as clear-cut as they may at first appear. Despite the problems that are inevitably created when large groups of people have to be absorbed into a society, some immigrant groups stimulate the economy, revitalize neighborhoods, and eventually become fully participatory and loyal American citizens. Nevertheless, if an officer has an anti-immigrant bias, negative attitudes may surface when that officer interacts with immigrants, especially under stressful circumstances. When officers are under pressure, negative attitudes become apparent, and their communication may become unprofessional. Indeed, some citizens have claimed

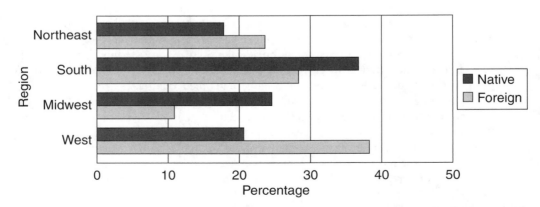

Exhibit 1.6   Distribution of Native and Foreign-Born Populations by Regional Percentages of Each Population.
Source: U.S. Census Bureau, Current Population Reports, February 2003: "The Foreign Born Population in the United States: March 2002."

that officers with whom they have been in contact do not attempt to understand them or that they demonstrate little patience in communicating or finding a translator. (See Chapter 4 for a discussion of communication issues and law enforcement.)

In addition, officers must be aware of "racial flash points" that are created when immigrants move into economically depressed areas with large and diverse populations. Some people feel that immigrants' moving into certain urban areas displaces economically disadvantaged groups or deprives them of access to work. (It is beyond the scope of this chapter to discuss the validity, or lack thereof, of this sentiment.) Thus law enforcement representatives may see hostility between, for example, blacks and Korean or Arab immigrants in such cities as Los Angeles, New York, and Detroit. Although officers cannot be expected to solve these deep-seated problems, they may find themselves in situations in which they can serve as cultural mediators, helping each group to increase understanding and toleration of the other. For example, police can point out that the absence of a Korean grocer's smile or greeting of a customer is not necessarily a sign of hostility but rather a cultural trait. (The behavior may also be an expression of distrust, but that is not always the case.) When a person complains that an Arab liquor-store owner does not hire outside his or her community, officers can explain that it is usually because the business is a small, family-run operation in which employees are family members. Of course, not all problems are cultural, but with an understanding of immigrants' backgrounds, officers can help explain points of tension to members of other ethnic groups.

Furthermore, some behaviors may be common to more than one immigrant population, yet unfamiliar to officers working with these groups. As part of his community policing outreach, one of the authors established an ongoing police outreach to Portland area immigrants and refugees in May 2002. The organization, called IRCO (Immigrant Refugee Community Organization), sponsors classes in which new immigrants and refugees are oriented on interaction with American police and on how to use 911. What is learned from the immigrant community is shared with police officers in various police departments (Olson, 2006). For example:

- In the U.S., most police departments don't want the driver or passengers to exit their car and walk back to the police car.

- In other countries, like Cuba, Japan, Mexico, and Russia, it is expected that motorists exit their car and walk back to the police officer.

- Translators, court interpreters, and new immigrants are an excellent source of information on customs from their country.

- Men from Eastern Europe and South America find it difficult to believe that a man can be arrested for touching a woman and find it silly that the U.S. police do prostitution-sting decoy operations.

- The police in Eastern Europe and South America expect bribes when they stop a motorist.

- Domestic violence laws in Eastern European countries are basically nonexistent because their governments view family matters as personal and private.

The more direct contact officers have in ethnic and immigrant communities, the more knowledge they will gain about cultural differences that may have an impact on law enforcement (see Exhibit 1.7 on workshops provided to immigrants and refugees).

To better serve new immigrants and refugees to the United States from all countries in the world, Organization and Training Services offers public safety and basic law workshops to I.R.C.O. (Immigrant Refugee Community Organization) http://www.irco.org. The workshops consist of an orientation on America's police, laws, and emergency services.

The immigrants and refugees usually have been in the United States for one month and have had no previous orientation on the American police, laws, or emergency services. The two-hour sessions are offered in the morning and afternoon and are part of the sixteen-week training and employment services program for new immigrants and refugees. The classes are held at I.R.C.O.'s office at 10301 N.E. Glisan, Portland, Oregon.

Interpreters translate during the presentation, which offers basic information on the following:

- Oregon State Police
- Oregon's 36 sheriff's departments and 124 city police departments
- Traffic and criminal laws
- Domestic violence
- What to do if stopped by a police officer
- How to use 9-1-1 for emergencies and alternatives for nonemergencies
- Question and answers

Exhibit 1.7   Workshops for Immigrants and Refugees on U.S. Police, Laws, and Emergency Services.
Source: Aaron T. Olson (2006). Used with permission.

European Americans In learning about diversity in U.S. society, focus is often centered on the diversity among immigrants from cultures very different from "mainstream" U.S. culture. However, there is also a great deal of diversity among European Americans. One of the myths about European Americans is that "they are all alike." Indeed, the majority of people in the United States are of European descent, but most Europeans are not of the same ethnicity or nationality, nor do they even have the same physical characteristics. Europe is a continent that is divided into four regions, east, west, north, and south, and has a population of 730 million people (Population Reference Bureau, 2005). Europe has 45 different countries, each with a unique national character, government, and, for the most part, language. To illustrate Europe's diversity and heterogeneity, the European Union has 20 official different languages for its European Parliament compared to the United Nations (which has six official languages). The European Union is the world's largest translation operation and has 60 interpreters in use when its 25-member state Parliament is in session (Owen, 2005). The countries listed in Exhibit 1.8 represent the continent of Europe.

Undocumented Immigrants

There are two major groups of undocumented immigrants: those who cross U.S. borders without having been "inspected" and those who enter the country with legal documents as temporary residents but have violated their legal admission status by extending their stay. Initially, Mexicans and other Latin Americans come to most people's minds when they hear the terms *illegal alien* and *undocumented worker.* Additionally, however, people from the Dominican Republic enter through Puerto Rico; since Puerto Ricans are U.S. citizens, they are considered legal. Therefore, officers

1. Albania	16. Greece	31. Norway
2. Andorra	17. Holy City (Vatican City)	32. Poland
3. Austria	18. Hungary	33. Portugal
4. Belarus	19. Iceland	34. Romania
5. Belgium	20. Ireland	35. Russia
6. Bosnia and Herzegovina	21. Italy	36. San Marino
	22. Latvia	37. Serbia and Montenegro
7. Bulgaria	23. Liechtenstein	38. Slovakia
8. Croatia	24. Lithuania	39. Slovenia
9. Cyprus	25. Luxembourg	40. Spain
10. Czech Republic	26. Macedonia, the former Yugoslav Republic	41. Sweden
11. Denmark		42. Switzerland
12. Estonia	27. Malta	43. Turkey
13. Finland	28. Moldova	44. Ukraine
14. France	29. Monaco	45. United Kingdom
15. Germany	30. Netherlands	

Exhibit 1.8   The Countries of Europe.

may be in contact with "Puerto Ricans" who are actually from the Dominican Republic and have therefore come to the United States under an illegal pretext. (Asians are also smuggled into the United States, including women brought in for the sex trade.) People from other parts of the world may come to the United States on a tourist visa and then decide to remain permanently (e.g., Canadians).

Some undocumented "aliens" come to the United States hoping to remain legally by proving that they escaped their homeland because of political repression, claiming that if they were to return, they would face persecution or death (i.e., they are seeking asylum). People who are often deported as undocumented arrivals are those who come as "economic refugees" (i.e., their economic status in their home country may be desperate). Undocumented aliens generally have few occupational skills and are willing to take menial jobs that many American citizens will not accept. They fill economic gaps in various regions where low-wage labor is needed.

Outer appearances are not an accurate guide to who has legal status and who does not. Both illegal and legal immigrants may live in the same neighborhoods. In addition, the U.S. government has occasionally legalized significant numbers of some populations of formerly illegal immigrants, usually in recognition of special circumstances in those persons' home countries, such as large-scale natural disasters or serious political instability.

Illegal immigrants lack documents that would enable them to obtain legal residence in the United States. The societal consequences are far-reaching. Law enforcement officials, politicians, and social services providers, among others, have had to deal with many concerns related to housing, education, safety, employment, spousal violence, and health care. The illegal segment of the immigrant population poses some difficult challenges for law enforcement officials. Trojanowicz and Bucqueroux (1990) found that:

> [Illegal immigrants] pose a difficult challenge for police, because fear of de-
> portation often makes them reluctant to report crimes committed against
> them—which also makes them easy prey. They can also fall victim to crimes
> related to their vulnerability—scams including extortion, fees for phony docu-
> mentation. Because so many arrive with little or no money and have difficulty
> making a living, undocumented aliens often cluster in low-income, high-crime
> areas. (p. 246)

The principal barrier to establishing trust with undocumented immigrants concerns their
fears about being reported to the U.S. Immigration and Customs Enforcement (ICE), the
largest investigative arm of the Department of Homeland Security (DHS). On March 1,
2003, the former Immigration and Naturalization Service (INS) was transitioned to
DHS and the enforcement side of the INS was given to ICE. The service and benefit
functions of the former INS were given to the newly developed U.S. Citizenship and
Immigration Services (USCIS). The USCIS is responsible for the administration of immigration and naturalization adjudication functions and establishing immigration services policies and priorities.

The argument supporting leaving illegal immigrants alone (unless they have committed a criminal act or are creating a disturbance) is based on the perspective that
tracking down and deporting illegal workers is technically the job of the ICE and not
the police. Police department managements have to create policies related to turning in
illegal immigrants to ICE. Sometimes the trust of the entire community (illegal and
legal immigrants) is at stake. Donya Fernandez, a language rights attorney in San Francisco, California, suggests that police departments make it known to immigrant communities when they have decided not to turn in illegal immigrants to the ICE (then the
former INS). When this is known, there may be less fear of the police when it comes to
reporting crimes (Fernandez, 2000).

Undocumented Immigrants: Demographic Information

In its 2003 report on undocumented immigrants, the former INS, now the USCIS,
places the growth of this population at 350,000 annually. This figure is 75,000 per year
higher than was estimated before the 2000 census, primarily because of improved
means of counting this hard-to-track population. In May 2006, it was estimated that 12
million undocumented people were living in the United States (Ferraro, 2006).

According to the INS report, California was estimated to have the highest number
of unauthorized residents, with 2.2 million, 32 percent of the national total. After California, Texas, New York, Illinois, and Florida had the largest numbers of unauthorized
immigrants (see Exhibit 1.9). Mexico provided the majority of them, with 4.8 million
or 69 percent of the national total. Over 100,000 unauthorized persons came from El
Salvador, Guatemala, Colombia, Honduras, China, and Ecuador (INS, 2003).

Immigrant Women: Victims of Domestic Violence and Fear of Deportation

In a 2003 report to a Congressional Subcommittee on Immigration, Leslye E. Orloff,
director of the Immigrant Women's Program (National Organization of Women's Legal
Defense and Education Fund), presented a full account of problems that continue to

Exhibit 1.9   Estimates of the Unauthorized Immigrant Population in the Top Ten States: January 1990 to January 2002.
Source: U.S. Immigration and Naturalization Services, Office of Policy and Planning, January, 2003.

beset battered immigrant women. Even though the frequency of domestic violence is consistent across socioeconomic classes, racial groups, and geographic areas, according to Orloff, immigrant women still face additional challenges in seeking help from their communities.

> [The] Violence Against Women Act (VAWA), passed by Congress in 1994 and improved in 2000, set out to reform the manner in which officers responded to domestic violence calls for help. Although significant improvement following the passage of VAWA has been noted, the response continues to be lacking. Some police officers' personal attitudes regarding domestic violence (i.e., it is a private problem) and how it should be handled (through mediation rather than arrest or formal charges), in essence, marginalizes victims of domestic violence. In extreme cases, victims' requests for help are disregarded. The lack of appropriate response to domestic violence from the police is further compounded when the battered woman is an immigrant. The police often do not have the capacity to communicate effectively with the immigrant victim in her own language. The police may use her abuser or her children to translate for her, and/or police may credit the statements of her citizen spouse or boyfriend over her statements to the police due to gender, race or cultural bias. (Orloff, 2003)

Jang (1994) offers the following explanations for the high rate of domestic violence experienced by immigrant women. This information appears to be as relevant now as it was when this statement was made:

1. Immigrant women may suffer higher rates of battering than U.S. citizens because they come from cultures which accept domestic violence, or because they have less access to legal and social services than U.S. citizens. In addition, immigrant batterers and victims may believe that the penalties and protections of the U.S. legal system do not apply to them.

2. A battered woman who is not a legal resident, or whose immigration status depends on her partner, is isolated by cultural dynamics which may prevent her from leaving her husband or seeking assistance from the legal system. These factors contribute to the higher incidence of abuse among immigrant women.

3. Some obstacles faced by battered immigrant women include: a distrust of the legal system arising from their experiences with the system in their native countries; cultural and language barriers; and fear of deportation.

4. A battered immigrant woman may not understand that she can personally tell her story in court, or that a judge will believe her. Based on her experience in her native country, she may believe that only those who are wealthy or have ties to the government will prevail in court. Batterers often manipulate these beliefs by convincing the victim he will prevail in court because he is a male, a citizen or that he has more money (p. 313).

Orloff told the house subcommittee that a survey of battered immigrant women revealed that only 27 percent of respondents were willing to call the police for help in a domestic violence incident. Specifically, concerning women who were physically and/or sexually abused versus emotionally abused, 31 percent said they called the police for help. Orloff compared these numbers to a 1998 Department of Justice survey in which 53 percent of domestic violence victims said they reported the crime to police. (Orloff, 2003)

The phenomenon of new immigrants, women or men, legal or illegal, presents challenges to law enforcement officers working the streets. Immigrants must learn a great deal about U.S. laws, the law enforcement system in general, and the role of police officers. Many immigrants fear the police because in their native countries police engaged in arbitrary acts of brutality in support of repressive governments (e.g., in Central America). In other countries, citizens disrespect police because they are poorly educated, inefficient, and corrupt and have a very low occupational status (e.g., in Iran). The barriers immigrants bring to the relationship with police suggest that American officers have to double their efforts to communicate and to educate. A further challenge for law enforcement is that for the reasons mentioned, new immigrants often become victims of violent crimes. In part, the acculturation and success of immigrants in this society depend on how they are treated while they are still ignorant of the social norms and laws. Law enforcement officials who have contact with new Americans will need extraordinary patience at times. Adaptation to a new country can be a long and arduous process.

INTERPLAY BETWEEN POLICE INCIDENTS AND CULTURE

With community changes have come shifts in the concerns of law enforcement and criminal justice, as well as the nature of some crime and reactions to police tactics. Without knowledge of citizens' cultural and national backgrounds, law enforcement officers in today's society are likely to experience baffling incidents and to observe citizens' surprising reactions to police tactics.

Expert in cultural diversity and the law, Alison Renteln (a University of Southern California political science professor) was cited in the following case in an article entitled "Cultural Sensitivity on the Beat," from the *Los Angeles Times.*

> The City of Spokane, Washington, agreed to pay a Gypsy family $1.43 million to settle a civil rights suit over an illegal police search. The most controversial element of the case was the body search of the 13 family members, male and female, including a number of people who were not targets of the investigation. The family claimed that the unmarried girls who were searched were now considered defiled and unclean in the Gypsy culture. As a result, they could never marry another Gypsy. In fact, the entire household was considered contaminated, a family patriarch testified, and was soon after ostracized and unwelcome at weddings and funerals. ("Cultural Sensitivity," 2000)

> A Danish woman was jailed for leaving her baby in a stroller outside a Manhattan restaurant—a case that focused international attention on New York City Police Tactics. . . . The woman and the baby's father were charged with endangering a child and were jailed for two nights. The 14-month-old baby girl was placed in foster care for four days before she was returned to her mother. The incident precipitated a war of words between Danish newspapers and city administrators. Copenhagen columnists called New York police "Rambo cops." Pictures wired from Denmark showed numerous strollers [with babies] parked outside cafes in view of their parents. ("Cultural Sensitivity," 2000)

An understanding of accepted social practices and cultural traditions in citizens' countries of origin can provide officers with the insight needed to understand and even predict some of the reactions and difficulties new immigrants will have in America. However, some customs are simply unacceptable in the United States, and arrests must be made in spite of the cultural background. Regardless of the circumstances, immigrant suspects need to be treated with respect; officers and all others in the criminal justice system must understand the innocent state of mind the citizen was in when committing the "crime." For example, female circumcision is illegal under all circumstances in the United States but is still practiced in certain African countries. The Hmong, mountain people of Southeast Asia, and particularly Laos, have a tradition considered to be an acceptable form of eloping. "Marriage by capture" translates into kidnap and rape in the United States. This Hmong tradition allows a male to capture and take away a female for marriage; even if she resists, he is allowed to take her to his home, and it is mandated that he consummate the union. Perpetrators of such crimes in the United States must be arrested.

In interviews with a deputy public defender and a deputy district attorney, a legal journal posed the following question: Should our legal system recognize a "cultural" defense when it comes to crimes? The deputy district attorney's response was, "No.

You're treading on shaky ground when you decide something based on culture, because our society is made up of so many different cultures. It is very hard to draw the line somewhere, but [diverse cultural groups] are living in our country, and people have to abide by [one set of] laws or else you have anarchy." The deputy public defender's response to the question was: "Yes. I'm not asking that the [various cultural groups] be judged differently, just that their actions be understood according to their own history and culture" (Sherman, 1986, p. 33).

If law enforcement's function is to protect and serve citizens from all cultural backgrounds, it becomes vital to understand the cultural dimensions of crimes. Obviously, behaviors or actions that may be excused in another culture must not go unpunished if they are considered crimes in this country (e.g., spouse abuse). Nevertheless, there are circumstances in which law enforcement officials at all levels of the criminal justice system would benefit by understanding the cultural context in which a crime or other incident occurred. Law enforcement professionals must use standard operating procedures in response to specific situations, and the majority of these procedures cannot be altered for different groups based on ethnicity. In a multicultural society, however, an officer can modify the way he or she treats a suspect, witness, or victim given knowledge of what is considered "normal" in that person's culture. When officers suspect that an aspect of cultural background is a factor in a particular incident, they may earn the respect of—and therefore cooperation from—ethnic communities if they are willing to evaluate their arrests in lesser crimes. (See the section "Police Knowledge of Cultural Groups" later in this chapter.)

Many officers say that their job is to uphold the law, but it is not up to them to make judgments. Yet discretion when deciding whether to take a citizen into custody for a lesser crime may be appropriate. When officers understand the cultural context for a crime, the crime will and should be perceived somewhat differently. Consider the Sikh religion (a strict religious tradition followed by a minority of people from northern India), which requires that its followers wear a ceremonial dagger, a sacred symbol, at all times, even during sleep. Consider Pacific Islanders having barbecues in their garages, where they roast whole pigs. And consider a Vietnamese family who eats dog. When officers understand the cultural context within which a "crime" takes place, then it is much easier to understand a citizen's intent. Understanding the cultural dimensions of a crime may result, for example, in not taking a citizen into custody. With lesser crimes, this may be the appropriate course of action and can result in the preservation of good police–community relations. Before looking at specific case studies of incidents and crimes involving cultural components, we present the concept of culture and its tremendous impact on the individual.

All people (except for very young children) carry cultural do's and don'ts, which some might also refer to as cultural baggage. The degree of this "baggage" is determined by their own conscious and unconscious identification with their group and their relative attachment to their cultural group's traditional values. Being influenced by cultural baggage is a natural human phenomenon. Much of who we are is sanctioned and reinforced by the society in which we have been raised. According to some experts, culture has a far greater influence on people's behavior than does any other variable such as age, gender, race, and socioeconomic status (Hall, 1959), and often this influence is unconscious. It is virtually impossible to lose one's culture completely when interacting in a new environment, yet change will inevitably take place.

The Definition of Culture

Although there are many facets of culture, the term is defined as beliefs, values, patterns of thinking, behavior, and everyday customs that have been passed on from generation to generation. Culture is learned rather than inherited and is manifested in largely unconscious and subtle behavior. With this definition in mind, consider that most children have acquired a general cultural orientation by the time they are five or six years old. For this reason, it is difficult to change behavior to accommodate a new culture. Many layers of cultural behavior and beliefs are subconscious. Additionally, many people assume that what they take for granted is taken for granted by all people ("all human beings are the same"), and they do not even recognize their own culturally influenced behavior. Anthropologist Edward T. Hall (1959) said, "Culture hides much more than it reveals and, strangely enough, what it hides, it hides most effectively from its own participants." In other words, people are blind to their own deeply embedded cultural behavior.

To further understand the hidden nature of culture, picture an iceberg (Ruhly, 1976). The only visible part of the iceberg is the tip, which typically constitutes only about 10 percent of the mass. Like most of culture's influences, the remainder of the iceberg is submerged beneath the surface. What this means for law enforcement is that there will be a natural tendency to interpret behavior, motivations, and criminal activity from the officer's cultural point of view. This tendency is due largely to an inability to understand behavior from alternative perspectives and because of the inclination toward **ethnocentrism** (i.e., an attitude of seeing and judging all other cultures from the perspective of one's own culture). In other words, an ethnocentric person would say there is only one way of being "normal" and that is the way of his or her own culture. When it comes to law enforcement, there is only one set of laws to which all citizens must adhere, whether native-born or not. However, the following case studies illustrate that culture does affect interpretations, meaning, and intention.

MINI CASE STUDIES: CULTURE AND CRIME[1]

The following mini case studies involve descriptions of crimes or offenses with a cultural component. If the crime is a murder or something similarly heinous, most people will not be particularly sympathetic, even with an understanding of the cultural factors involved. However, consider that understanding other cultural patterns gives one the ability to see and react in a different way. The ability to withhold judgment and to interpret a person's intention from a different cultural perspective is a skill that will ultimately enable a person to identify his or her own cultural blinders. Each case study describes an increasingly serious crime—from driving under the influence to child abuse to murder.

[1]Chapter 5, "Law Enforcement Contact with Asian/Pacific American's" includes several other examples regarding the involvement of police and child protective services and coining cases. Please note that, regarding the case above (A Tragic Case of Cross-Cultural Misinterpretation), we have no further facts about the case regarding what the police officers knew.

Mini Case Study 1: Driving under the Influence?

The following case, among others, was the subject of discussion in an officers' course in ethnic understanding in a San Francisco Bay Area police department ("Officers being trained," 2000).

> A Tongan man living in [the Bay Area] was arrested on Highway 101 on the Peninsula for driving under the influence of kava, a relaxing elixir popular with Pacific Islanders. But a hung jury effectively acquitted [this man] in October. The jury determined, in part, that police didn't fully understand the effect and the importance of the drink. Tongans, Samoans, and Fijians say the kava ritual is an integral part of life, a way to share information and reinforce traditions. And they say it doesn't affect their ability to drive any more than soda pop.

Mini Case Study 2: A Tragic Case of Cross-Cultural Misinterpretation

In parts of Asia, there are medical practices unfamiliar to many law enforcement officials (as well as medical practitioners) in the West. A number of these practices result in marks on the skin that can easily be misinterpreted as abuse by people who have no knowledge of these culturally based medical treatments. The practices include rubbing the skin with a coin ("coining," "coin rubbing," or "wind rubbing"), pinching the skin, touching the skin with burning incense, or applying a heated cup to the skin ("cupping"). Each practice leaves highly visible marks, such as bruises and even burns. The following is an account of a serious misreading of some very common Southeast Asian methods of traditional folk healing on the part of U.S. school authorities and law enforcement officials.

> A young Vietnamese boy had been absent from school for a few days with a serious respiratory infection. His father, believing that coining would help cure him, rubbed heated coins on specific sections of his back and neck. The boy's condition seemed to improve and he was able to return to school. Upon noticing heavy bruising on the boy's neck, the teacher immediately informed the school principal, who promptly reported the "abuse" to the police (who then notified Child Protective Services). When the police were notified, they went to the child's home to investigate. The father was very cooperative when questioned by the police and admitted, in broken English, that he had caused the bruising on his son's neck. The man was arrested and incarcerated. While the father was in jail, his son, who was under someone else's custody, apparently relapsed and died of his original illness. On hearing the news, the father committed suicide in his jail cell. Of course, it is not known whether the father would have committed suicide as a response to his son's death alone. The tragic misinterpretation on the part of the authorities involved, including the teacher, the principal, and the arresting police officers, provides an extreme case of what can happen when people attribute meaning from their own cultural perspective.
>
> Cultural understanding would not have cured the young boy, but informed interaction with the father could have prevented the second tragedy. All of the authorities were interpreting what they saw with "cultural filters" based on their

own belief systems. Ironically, the interpretation of the bruises (i.e., child abuse) was almost the opposite of the intended meaning of the act (i.e., healing). Even after some of the parties involved learned about this very common Southeast Asian practice, they still did not accept that it existed as an established practice, and they could not fathom how others could believe that coining might actually cure illness. Their own conception of medical healing did not encompass what they perceived as such "primitive treatment."

Ethnocentrism is a barrier to accepting that there is another way, another belief, another communication style, another custom, or another value that can lead to culturally different behavior. Ethnocentrism often causes a person to assign a potentially incorrect meaning or attribute an incorrect motivation to a given act. Consider how the outcome could have differed if only one person in the chain of authorities had viewed the bruises as something other than abuse. The tragic outcome of serious cultural misunderstandings might have been averted. (Personal communication with social worker, 1992, who wishes to remain anonymous)

Mini Case Study 3: Latino Values as a Factor in Sentencing

In a court of law, a cultural explanation or rationalization (i.e., a cultural defense) rarely affects a guilty or not-guilty verdict. Nevertheless, culture may affect sentencing. Consider the following case, in which, according to retired Judge Lawrence Katz (2006), cultural considerations lessened the severity of the sentence.

A Mexican woman living in the United States became involved in an extramarital affair. Her husband became outraged when the wife bragged about her extramarital activities at a picnic at which many extended family members were present. At the same time, the wife also made comments about her husband's lack of ability to satisfy her and how, in comparison, her lover was far superior. On hearing his wife gloat about her affair, the husband left the picnic and drove five miles to purchase a gun. Two hours later, he shot and killed his wife. In a case such as this, the minimum charge required in California would be second-degree murder. However, because the jury took into consideration the cultural background of this couple, the husband received a mitigated sentence and was found guilty of manslaughter. It was argued that his wife's boasting about her lover and her explicit comments made specifically to emasculate him created a passion and emotion that completely undermined his machismo, masculine pride and honor. To understand the severity of the wife's offense, the law enforcement officer and the prosecutor had to understand what it means to be humiliated in such a manner in front of one's family, in the context of Latino culture (Katz, 2006).

The purpose of these three mini case studies is not to discuss the "rightness" or "wrongness" of any group's values, customs, or beliefs but to illustrate that the point of contact between law enforcement and citizens' backgrounds must not be ignored. Officers must be encouraged to consider culture when investigating and presenting evidence regarding an alleged crime or incident involving people from diverse backgrounds. This consideration does not mean that standard operating procedures should be changed, nor does it imply that heinous crimes such as murder or rape should be excused on cultural grounds. However, as a matter of course, officers need to include culture as a variable in understanding, assessing, and reporting certain kinds of incidents and crimes.

DIMENSIONS OF DIVERSITY

To make sense of the different groups in our workplace and society, we need to have functional categories and terms. Marilyn Loden, organizational diversity consultant, describes and outlines the primary and secondary dimensions of diversity (Loden, 2006). The specific categories within the dimensions of diversity are not new but rather provide a functional construction of individual and group characteristics for understanding the people in the workforce and our society. This awareness and the ability to view differences as sources of strength often results in improved interpersonal relationships and improved citizen contacts.

Primary Dimensions of Diversity

A primary dimension is a core characteristic with which a person is born that remains with the individual in all stages of his or her life. According to Loden, people have a minimum of six primary dimensions (Loden, 2006):

1. Age
2. Ethnicity
3. Gender
4. Mental/physical abilities and characteristics
5. Race
6. Sexual orientation

Most people are aware of the meaning of these categories; however, for the sake of clarity, the following terms are included in the category "sexual orientation": heterosexual, homosexual, lesbian, gay, bisexual, and transgender. All of the six primary dimensions are characteristics that contribute to being advantaged or disadvantaged in the workforce and in society. Victims of hate bias crimes have been targeted because of these six dimensions of diversity—age, ethnicity, gender, disability status, race, and sexual orientation.

Secondary Dimensions of Diversity

A secondary dimension is a characteristic a person acquires as the result of a choice he or she made or a choice someone else made for him or her (Loden, 2006). Nearly all of the secondary dimensions' characteristics contribute to the microlevel demographic data. The secondary dimensions of diversity include, but are not limited to:

1. Communication style
2. Education

3. Family status
4. Military experience
5. Organizational role and level
6. Religion
7. First language
8. Geographic location
9. Income
10. Work experience
11. Work style
12. Others

Both primary and secondary dimensions of diversity influence the personal and professional lives of law enforcement personnel. Police officers need to be cognizant of these dimensions with their coworkers, and leaders with their subordinates. Tensions between supervisors and coworkers are often caused by the differences in secondary dimensions. Similarly, a police officer's ability to establish rapport with citizens can also be related to either the actual or perceived degree to which dimensions are shared.

Exhibit 1.10 shows how the primary and secondary dimensions of diversity influence people in the workforce and society. "While each dimension adds a layer of complexity, it is the dynamic interaction among all the dimensions of diversity that

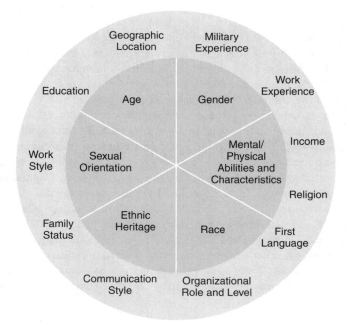

Exhibit 1.10   Dimensions of Diversity
Models such as the diversity wheel, designed by Loden Associates, facilitate understanding of a broad range of primary and secondary dimensions of diversity.
Source: Loden, 1996, p. 16. Reproduced with permission of Marilyn Loden.

influences one's self-image, values, opportunities, and expectations. Together, the primary and secondary dimensions give definition and meaning to our lives by contributing to a synergistic, integrated whole—the diverse person." (Loden, 2006).

POLICE KNOWLEDGE OF CULTURAL GROUPS

Law enforcement representatives have the ultimate authority to arrest or admonish someone suspected of a crime. According to Judge Katz, "Discretion based on cultural knowledge at the police level is much more significant than what happens at the next level in the criminal justice system (i.e., the courts)." Individual police officers have the opportunity to create positive public relations if they demonstrate cultural sensitivity and respect toward members of an ethnic community. Katz cited the example of police contact with the San Francisco Bay Area Samoan community, in which barbecues and parties can include a fair amount of drinking, resulting in fights. In Katz's opinion, the police, responding to neighbors' complaints, could come in with a show of force and the fighting would cool down quickly. However, word would spread that the police officers had no cultural understanding or respect for the people involved. This would widen the gap that already exists between police and many Pacific Islander and other Asian groups and would not be a way to foster trust in the Samoan community. Alternatively, the police could locate the leader, or the "chief," of this group and let that person deal with the problem in the way that he would have handled the conflict in Samoa. There is no question about the chief's ability to handle the problem. He has a prominent role to play and can serve as a bridge between the police and the community. The *matai* is also a resource; he is an elder who has earned the respect of the community.

The heads of Samoan communities are traditionally in full control of members' behavior, although this is changing somewhat in the United States. Furthermore, according to traditional Samoan values, if a family member assaults a member of another family, the head of the family is required to ensure punishment. Given the power entrusted to the chiefs, it is reasonable to encourage officers first to go through the community and elicit assistance in solving enforcement problems. This recommendation does not imply, in any way, that groups should be left to police themselves; instead, understanding and working with the leadership of a community represents a spirit of partnership.

The awareness of and sensitivity to such issues can have a significant impact on the criminal justice system, in which police have the power to either inflame or calm the people involved in a particular incident. According to Katz, "Many cases, especially those involving lesser offenses, can stay out of court." He asks, "Do you always need a show of force? Or can you counsel and admonish instead?" In certain situations, such as the one described earlier, officers can rethink traditional police methods in order to be as effective as possible. Doing so involves knowledge of ethnic communities and a desire to establish a positive and trustworthy image in those communities (Katz, 2006).

PREJUDICE IN LAW ENFORCEMENT

The following questions were asked of police officers participating in a cultural diversity program:

"Raise your hand if you are a racist." Not a single officer raised a hand.

"Raise your hand if you think that prejudice and racism exist outside this agency." Most officers raised their hands.

The instructor then asked with humor: "Then where were you recruited from?" (Berry, 2006).

When discussing the implications of multicultural diversity for police officers, it is not enough simply to present the need to understand cultural background. Whenever two groups are from entirely different ethnic or racial backgrounds, there is the possibility that prejudice exists (because of fear, lack of contact, ignorance, and stereotypes). To deny the existence of prejudice or racism in any given law enforcement agency would be to deny that it exists outside the agency.

What Is Prejudice?

Prejudice is a judgment or opinion formed before facts are known, usually involving negative or unfavorable thoughts about groups of people. Discrimination is action based on prejudiced thought. It is not possible to force people to abandon their own prejudices in the law enforcement workplace or when working in the community. Because prejudice is thought, it is private and does not violate any law. However, because it is private, a person may not be aware when his or her judgments and decisions are based on prejudice. In law enforcement, the expression of prejudice as bias discrimination and racism is illegal and can have tragic consequences. All police must consider the implications of prejudice in their day-to-day work as it relates to equal enforcement and professionalism.

It is not uncommon in diversity or cross-cultural workshops for officers to hear sentiments such as the following: "We've already had this training on prejudice. Why do we need to go over it again and again?"

As with other training areas in law enforcement, such as self-defense tactics, the area of prejudice needs to be reviewed on a regular basis. (It's like working out at the gym; doing it once is not enough to keep a person in shape.) A person has only to read the headlines periodically to see that the problem of prejudice and racism in law enforcement is not yet solved. Although police chiefs cannot mandate that their officers banish prejudicial thoughts, this subject should be dealt with seriously. While some police officers say they have every right to believe what they want, the chiefs of all departments must be able to guarantee, with as much certainty as possible, that no officer will ever act on his or her prejudices. All officers must understand where the line is between prejudice and discrimination, whether in the law enforcement agency with coworkers or with citizens. It becomes eminently clear that prejudice in the law enforcement agency must be addressed before it turns into racism and discrimination. Indeed, an agency cannot be expected to treat its multicultural population fairly if people within the agency are likely to act on their prejudiced thoughts.

How Prejudice Influences People

Prejudice is encouraged by stereotyping, which is a shorthand way of thinking about people who are different. The stereotypes that form the basis of a person's prejudice can be so fixed that he or she easily justifies his or her racism, sexism, or other bias and

even makes such claims as, "I'm not prejudiced, but let me tell you about those———
I had to deal with today." Coffey, Eldefonson, and Hartinger (1982) discuss the relationship between selective memory and prejudice:

> A prejudiced person will almost certainly claim to have sufficient cause for his
> or her views, telling of bitter experiences with refugees, Koreans, Catholics,
> Jews, Blacks, Mexicans and Puerto Ricans, or Indians. But in most cases, it is
> evident that these "facts" are both scanty and strained. Such a person typically
> resorts to a selective sorting of his or her own memories, mixes them up with
> hearsay, and then overgeneralizes. No one can possibly know all refugees, Ko-
> reans, Catholics, and so on. (p. 8)

Indeed, individuals may be so convinced of the truths of their stereotypes that they
claim to be experts on "those people." One of the most dangerous types of prejudice can
be subconscious. Subconscious prejudice (sometimes called character-conditioned prejudice) usually runs deep; the person with this character deficiency may hold hostile attitudes toward many ethnic groups, not just one or two. People who tend to mistreat or
oppress others because of their prejudices often were mistreated themselves, and this experience can leave them extremely distrustful of all others. In addition, people who have
strong prejudices can be insecure and frustrated because of their own failures. Consequently, they blame or scapegoat others. They have a great deal of stored-up anger that
frequently began to build in childhood because of dysfunctional relationships with their
parents. Quite often, people in racial supremacist organizations fit the description of the
extremely prejudiced person for whom mistrust and hate of all others is a way of life.

Another type of prejudice is acquired during "normal" socialization. This type of
prejudice results when a person belongs to a group that holds negative views of other
specific groups (e.g., southern whites and blacks, Arabs and Jews, Chinese and Japanese, Puerto Ricans and Mexicans). When there is a pattern of prejudice within a particular group, the "normal" person is the one who conforms to the prejudice. From
childhood, parents pass on stereotypes of the out-group in the child's mind because of
their "normal" prejudices. By adulthood, the person who has learned prejudice against
a particular group can justify the prejudice with rationalizations (Coffey et al., 1982).

However, not everyone in a given group holds prejudices common among the rest
of the members of the group. According to Coffey and his colleagues, some people are
more susceptible than others to learned (or culture-conditioned) prejudice. Those more
likely to be prejudiced include (1) older people, (2) less educated people, (3) farmers
and unskilled or semiskilled workers, (4) residents of rural areas or small towns,
(5) people uninterested in civic affairs, and (6) people of low socioeconomic status.

Police Prejudice

Ondra Berry conducts diversity training for law enforcement and repeatedly conveys this
message to officers: If you are normal, you have cultural blind spots that will give you an
unbalanced view of people who are different from you. Officers must look at themselves
first before getting into situations in which they act upon their biases (Berry, 2006).

Police prejudice received a great deal of attention in the latter half of the 1990s—
so much so that it was addressed as a topic of concern in the President's Initiative on
Race (*One America,* 1998):

Racial disparities and prejudices affect the way in which minorities are treated by the criminal system. Examples of this phenomenon can be found in the use of racial profiling in law enforcement and in the differences in the rates of arrest, conviction, and sentencing between whites and minorities and people of color. Law enforcement professionals have recognized, especially as they enter the twenty-first century, that prejudices unchecked and acted on can result in not only citizen humiliation, lawsuits, loss of jobs, and long-term damage to police–community relations but in personal tragedy as well. Sometimes, training can be successful in changing behavior and possibly attitudes. Consider the example of firing warning shots. Most officers have retrained themselves to refrain from this action because they have been mandated to do so. They have gone through a process of "unfreezing" normative behavior (i.e., what is customary) and have incorporated desired behavior. Thus explicit instruction and clear directives from the top can result in profound changes of police actions. The success of mandated change is supported by Fletcher Blanchard, a social psychologist at Smith College, who conducted and published research findings on fighting acts of bigotry (*New York Times,* September 16, 1991, pp. C-1 and C-8). His contention is that clear policies that unequivocally condemn racist acts or forms of speech will prevent most manifestations of prejudice. Asking a citizen, "What are you doing here?" just because he or she is of a different background than those of a particular neighborhood is not acceptable. Officers will listen to these specific and unambivalent directives coming from the top, even if their personal biases do not change. As Blanchard explains: "A few outspoken people (e.g., in an organization/agency) who are vigorously antiracist can establish the kind of social climate that discourages racist acts. It may be difficult to rid an officer of his or her stereotypes, but not acting upon prejudices become[s] the mandate of the department."

Peer Relationships and Prejudice

Expressions of prejudice in police departments may go unchallenged because of the need to conform or to fit into the group. Police officers do not make themselves popular by questioning peers or challenging their attitudes. It takes a leader to voice an objection or to avoid going along with group norms. Some studies have shown that peer behavior in groups reinforces acts of racial bias. For example, when someone in a group makes ethnic slurs, others in the group may begin to express the same hostile attitudes more freely. This behavior is particularly relevant in law enforcement agencies given the nature of the police subculture and the strong influence of peer pressure. Thus law enforcement leaders must not be ambiguous when directing their subordinates to control their expressions of prejudice, even among peers. Furthermore, according to some social scientists, the strong condemnation of any manifestations of prejudice can at times affect a person's feelings. Authorities or peers who keep prejudiced people from acting on their biases can, in the long run, weaken the prejudice itself, especially if the prejudice is not virulent. People conform and can behave differently, even if they hold the same prejudicial thoughts. Even if they are still prejudiced, they will be reticent to show it. National authorities have become much more vocal about dealing directly with racism and prejudice in law enforcement as an institution, especially in light of the quantity of allegations of racial profiling in police departments across the country.

A process of socialization takes place when change has been mandated by top management and a person is forced to adopt a new standard of behavior. When a mistake is made and the expression of prejudice occurs, a police department will pay the price (in adverse media attention, lawsuits, citizen complaints, human relations commissions involvement, or dismissal of the chief or other management). Government officials' public expressions are subject to a great deal of scrutiny. Berry-Wilkinson, a lawyer and expert on harassment issues, cited the case of a prosecutor who was publicly reprimanded for a hallway comment to another lawyer during a murder trial: "I don't believe either of those chili-eating bastards." The court stated: "Lawyers, especially . . . public officials, [must] avoid statements as well as deeds . . . indicating that their actions are motivated to any extent by racial prejudice" (*People* v *Sharpe,* 789 p.2d 659 [1989], Colorado, in Berry-Wilkinson, 1993, p. 2d). Berry-Wilkinson's concluding statement following the reporting of this case reads: "What once may have been acceptable is now definitely not and may bring discipline and monetary sanctions. While public employees may be free to think whatever they like, they are not free to say whatever they think. A public employee's right to free speech is not absolute" (Berry-Wilkinson, 1993, p. 2d).

When officers in a police department are not in control of their prejudices (in either their speech or in their behavior) the negative publicity affects the reputation of all police officers (by reinforcing the popular stereotype that police are racists or bigots). Yet because of publicized instances of discrimination, officers become increasingly aware of correct and incorrect behavior toward ethnic minorities.

Beginning in 1990, a California police department was besieged by the press and outraged citizens for over two years because six police officers had exchanged racist messages on their patrol car computers, using the word *nigger* and making references to the Ku Klux Klan. The citizens of the town in which the incident took place ended up conducting an investigation of the department to assess the degree of racism in the institution. In their report, the committee members wrote that the disclosure of the racial slurs was "an embarrassment and a crushing blow" to the image and credibility of the city and police department. In addition, citizens demanded the chief's resignation. In a cultural diversity workshop (April 13, 1993), some of the officers said they believed that the entire incident was overblown and that there was no "victim." These officers failed to understand that the use of derogatory terms alone is offensive to citizens. Officers who do not grasp the seriousness of the matter may not realize that citizens feel unprotected knowing that those entrusted with their safety and protection are capable of using such hateful language. While the language is offensive, the problem is more with the attitudes it conveys. Such incidents are extremely costly from all points of view; it may take years for a department to recover from one incident connected to an officer's prejudice or racism.

Officers need to be aware that anything they say or do with citizens of different backgrounds that even hints at prejudice automatically creates the potential for an explosive reaction. Here the experience of the minority and the nonminority do not even begin to approach each other. An officer can make an unguarded casual remark and not realize it is offensive. For example, an officer can offend a group member by saying "You people" (accentuating a we–they division) or by implying that if a member of a minority group does not fit a stereotype, he or she is exceptional (e.g., "She's Hispanic, but she works hard" or "He's African American, but very responsible").

Members of culturally diverse groups are up against the weight of history and tradition in law enforcement. Ethnic groups have not traditionally been represented in police work (especially in top management), nor have citizens of some ethnic groups had reasons to trust the police. The prejudice that might linger among officers must be battled constantly if they are to increase trust with ethnic communities. The perception of many ethnic group members is that police will treat them more roughly, question them unnecessarily, and arrest them more often than they arrest whites. Awareness of this perception is not enough, though. The next step is to try harder with ethnic groups to overcome these barriers. Officers should go out of their way to show extra respect to those citizens who least expect it. It is important to create nondefensiveness in citizens who have traditionally been the object of police prejudice and who expect rude or uncivil behavior from the officer.

Beyond eliminating the prejudice manifested in speech, police management can teach officers how to reduce or eliminate acts of bias and discrimination. A large metropolitan police department hired several human relations consultants to help assess community–police problems. The chief insisted that they ride in a police car for four weekends so that they would "appreciate the problems of law officers working in the black ghetto." Every Friday through Sunday night, the consultants rode along with the highway patrol, a unit other officers designated as the "Gestapo police." When the month ended and the chief asked what the consultants had learned, they replied, "If we were black, we would hate the police." The chief, somewhat bewildered, asked why. "Because we have personally witnessed black citizens experiencing a series of unjust, unwarranted intimidations, searches, and series of harassments by unprofessional police." Fortunately, that chief, to his credit, accepted the feedback and introduced a successful course in human relations skills. After this training, the officers demonstrated greater professionalism in their interactions with members of the black community.

When it comes to expressions of prejudice, people are not powerless. No one has to accept sweeping stereotypes (e.g., "You can't trust an Indian," "All whites are racists," "Chinese are shifty," and so on). To eliminate manifestations of prejudice, people have to begin to interrupt biased and discriminatory behavior at all levels. Officers have to be willing to remind their peers that ethnic slurs and offensive language, as well as differential treatment of certain groups of people, is neither ethical nor professional. Officers need to change the aspect of police culture that discourages speaking out against acts or speech motivated by prejudice. An officer or civilian employee who does nothing in the presence of racist or other discriminatory behavior by his or her peers becomes a silent accomplice. Law enforcement organizations across the country have used community-based policing to help overcome cultural barriers between officers and the different groups whom they come into contact with.

COMMUNITY-BASED POLICING

We need to open up dialogue with officers—we need a dialogue of critique. Let's look at what is working and what needs improvement. We need to work together to create a blueprint of cooperation.

—Pastor Ronald Griffin, Detroit-based clergyman and African American community leader, 2003

Today's officers are increasingly comfortable with contemporary community-based policing described as a problem-solving approach. Community-based policing enables officers to work with civilians outside the conventional channels by meeting with community groups and learning of their concerns. It also allows community members to understand the "culture" of law enforcement and to help them grasp the reasons for which officers make the decisions they do. It encourages unconventional and creative ways of dealing with crime and peacekeeping at the neighborhood level, and allows for a change of image of the traditional officer. This is especially true in certain immigrant neighborhoods or ethnic conclaves where citizens have traditionally feared the police.

Community-based policing for the majority of local police and sheriff's departments around the country has become a fact of life. As of June 2003, the Bureau of Justice Statistics (BJS) showed that there were 452,000 full-time sworn officers for local police departments and 174,000 for sheriff's offices throughout the United States. Overall, 58 percent of city police departments, employing 82 percent of all officers, had full-time sworn personnel serving as community policing officers, totaling about 55,000. Fifty-one percent of sheriff's offices, employing 70 percent of all officers, had full-time sworn personnel as community policing officers, totaling 14,900. In all population categories, ranging from under 10,000 people to 1,000,000 or more, the percentage of sheriff's offices and city police departments using community policing officers in 2003 is significantly greater than in 1997. To illustrate this change, among city police departments serving 50,000 to 249,999 residents in 1997, only 76 percent used community policing officers compared to 88 percent in 2003. Among sheriff's departments serving a population of 100,000 to 499,999 residents, in 1997, only 44 percent used community policing officers compared to 59 percent in 2003 (U.S. Department of Justice, 2006).

One of the authors (Olson, 2006) shares the following observations based on his personal experiences with community policing and, in particular, "storefront offices":

- If the police take the initiative to reach out into the community—it could be to a minority group or any neighborhood—the community appreciates it, but the relationship has got to be ongoing.

- The storefront office, for example, which is not a new concept, whereby police work at a desk in an office in a neighborhood location during day or swing shifts, serves this purpose.

- When the police officer shows up to that facility (school, business, or apartment complex) and parks his or her patrol vehicle, it is visible to the public. Inside, the officer will complete reports, return telephone calls, or visit with the facility's staff or occupants.

- At the storefront office, people in the community see the police on a frequent basis. This creates a more positive and personal interaction.

- The police at storefront offices provide interventions for problem students, resources for counselors, and safety-related classes to students and neighborhood organizations.

- The use of storefront offices is one example of an extremely productive style of community policing.

Community-based policing is one of several terms that police agencies across the nation use to refer to working partnerships with communities A few of the more commonly used terms are problem-oriented policing (POP), community policing (CP), and community-oriented policing (COP). The concept of and practices associated with community-based or community-oriented policing are central to any discussion on minority groups and immigrant populations. The legislative basis of what became known as Community Oriented Policing Services (COPS, Title 1 of the Violent Crime Control and Law Enforcement Act of 1994) listed four specific goals intended to change the level and practice of policing in the United States. The first two goals link directly to our discussion of police interaction and professionalism with community members, including those from diverse racial, cultural, ethnic, religious, and lifestyle backgrounds. These two goals are as follows (National Institute of Justice, 2000):

1. To increase the number of officers deployed in American communities
2. To foster problem solving and interaction with communities by police officers

A great deal of literature is available to law enforcement agencies on community-based policing. Community-based policing depends on a strong partnership with the various communities that make up a city or jurisdiction. The partnership ensures dialogue and provides the mechanism by which a police department is aware of current relevant issues in the community. The following description of a police department without a community-based approach, while dated, is a graphic example of how world events and the influx of refugees have to be monitored in a community-based partnership format.

This dramatic example involves the case of a medium-sized police department in southern California that exemplifies the problems associated with not using community-based policing. Neither the management of the department nor the city was aware that the ethnic community had been changing significantly. Only two years after dramatic events began to take place did patrol officers start to pay attention to the changes, most of which had occurred suddenly following the fall of Saigon in 1975. After the withdrawal of American forces from Vietnam, the United States changed its immigration policy to relocate peoples in jeopardy from Southeast Asia. Police officers were performing their "crime fighter" role, but because there was no partnership with the community, there was no reason or incentive to monitor and report the changes they were noticing. This particular community, therefore, was not prepared for the increase in racial disputes and violence on the streets and in the schools, nor was it prepared for increasing needs in government, infrastructures, and social services. Officers experienced that it took much longer answering calls involving Vietnamese citizens than those in the Anglo community because of language and cultural differences. Officer and management frustrations resulted. Community-based policing would have had a plan in place for that neighborhood transition. Why? The answer is because the department, including all local government institutions, and the neighborhoods would have been working together closely.

Community-based policing allows for collaboration with the community. Berry (2006) says, "We don't know the community as well as the community does." Community-based policing represents a more democratic style of policing. It allows for openness and dialogue. The police department is not cut off or insulated from the community (Skolnick, 1999). It has proven to be a contributing factor to the decrease in crime in certain areas. Berry shared the following firsthand account of how the implementation of community-based policing in his community (Reno, Nevada) was the definitive factor in the decrease in gang-related activities, including homicide.

Berry spoke of the alarming homicide rates in Reno, Nevada, in 1992, which included the deaths of two Hispanic children—a 13-year-old girl killed at a soccer game and a 3-year-old boy, both victims of Hispanic gang-related shootings. The dissension between the community and the police department was growing rapidly. The police department had no choice but to address the homicide rate in the community from an enforcement point of view; the community's needs were to address basic issues of survival and quality of life. Berry's dedication to the community resulted in the ultimate collaborative effort in community-based policing. Berry, with the help of the ethnic communities as well as the community at large, brought together representatives from the police department (and especially the gang task units), officials from the school districts, government, and nonprofit sectors of the community, and business representatives. Together they devised a plan for combating gang activity in Reno. The community had a strong voice; the police department valued and listened to community members' input. As a result of the collaboration, the police–community partnership created the Gang Alternative Partnership Center, which includes (1) gyms open until 1 A.M., (2) officers helping to coach basketball teams consisting of gang members, (3) drill teams and after-school programs, (4) community assistance to youth in finding jobs, and (5) organized tattoo removal available to gang members. In addition, the community and the police directed nonprofit organizations (such as United Way) in channeling funds to provide programs for youth. The police department also increased its gang units.

According to Berry, because of the successful collaboration of police department and community, lives have been saved. Since 1995 there have been one or two gang-related shootings. Drive-by shootings went down from an average of 140 shots-fired calls a month to an average of 20 calls per month. Gangs are still present in the city, but activity has decreased in Reno.

The Police Executive Research Forum (PERF) looked for commonalities among various community-policing programs across the country and conducted thorough research on community policing. The researchers outlined five different perspectives on community policing within agencies throughout the United States. Though this report was published in 1992, these principles are just as important and applicable today.

1. *Deployment perspective:* Placing officers in closer proximity to members of the community and thereby improving their knowledge of the area in which they work.

2. *Community revitalization perspective:* Focusing on preventing deterioration of neighborhoods by police paying closer attention to fear-inducing characteristics of neighborhoods.

3. *Problem-solving perspective:* Maintaining that the most critical element of community policing is the problem-solving efforts in which the police and community (residents, other government agencies, and private businesses) participate.

4. ***Customer perspective:*** Developing proactive mechanisms for determining the needs of the public relative to the police function; the approach uses routine surveys of citizen and advisory groups to accomplish this goal.

5. ***Legitimacy perspective:*** Striving, via community policing, for officers to be more equitable in their relationships with the minority community.

Such perspectives require opening a dialogue between the police and diverse community groups so that groups can identify their peacekeeping concerns and the police can respond to them. Departments typically mix varieties of community policing perspectives; however, the common thread within all approaches is that the police assist the community in policing and protecting itself. To do so, the police must engage the community in the task of policing. The police are actually dependent on a relationship and partnership (some call it "building bridges") with the community to perform these tasks. The community identifies problems with the encouragement, direction, and participation of the police.

SUMMARY

Dramatic changes in the ethnic and racial makeup of the population have created new challenges at all levels of police work. Willingness to gain cultural information about the new communities that they serve will ultimately benefit officers in their interactions with people of different backgrounds. Officers' knowledge of cultural differences, coupled with an ability to demonstrate respect for those differences, can result in increased rapport and effective communication with people from various ethnic and racial backgrounds. Trust in many ethnic communities has to be earned because of the cultural "baggage" that community members bring to their relationships with the police. Members of the law enforcement profession have to examine their words, behaviors, and actions to evaluate whether they are conveying professionalism and respect to all people, regardless of their race, culture, religion, or ethnic background. Law enforcement agencies must be free of all expressions of prejudice on the part of their officers and civilian employees. Finally, law enforcement agencies in partnership and collaboration with communities are likely to experience decreased crime rates and increased trust and cooperation with citizens of all backgrounds.

EIGHT TIPS FOR IMPROVING LAW ENFORCEMENT IN MULTICULTURAL COMMUNITIES*

- Make positive contact with community group members from diverse backgrounds. Don't let them see you only when something negative has happened.

- Allow the public to see you as much as possible in a nonenforcement role.

- Make a conscious effort in your mind, en route to every situation, to treat all segments of society objectively and fairly.

- Remember that all groups have some bad, some average, and some good people within them.

*Tips and quotes are from retired Assistant Chief Ondra Berry, Reno Police Department, 2006.

- Go out of your way to be personable and friendly with minority-group members. Remember, many don't expect it.

- Don't appear uncomfortable with or avoid discussing racial and ethnic issues with other officers and citizens.

- Take responsibility for patiently educating citizens and the public about the role of the officer and about standard operating procedures in law enforcement. Remember that citizens often do not understand "police culture."

- Don't be afraid to be a change agent in your organization when it comes to improving cross-cultural relations within your department and between police and community. It may not be a popular thing to do, but it is the right thing to do.

- Remember the history of law enforcement with all groups and ask yourself the question, Am I part of the past, or a part of the future?

DISCUSSION QUESTIONS AND ISSUES*

1. *Views on the Multicultural Society.* The following viewpoints regarding our increasingly multicultural population reflect varying levels of tolerance, understanding, and acceptance. Discuss these points of view and their implications for law enforcement:

   - Diversity is acceptable if there is not too much of it, but the way things are going today, it is hard to absorb and it just may result in our destruction.

   - They are here now and they need to do things our way.

   - To advance in our diverse society, we need to accept and respect our differences rather than maintain the myth of the melting pot.

2. *Police Work and Multiculturalism.* Describe three reasons police officers need to show multicultural respect to their coworkers and citizens in their community. Also list three ways to demonstrate this respect and the benefits that will result.

3. *Dealing with Illegal Immigrants.* Does the police department in which you work have a policy regarding undocumented immigrants? Are officers instructed not to inquire into their status unless a crime has been committed? How do you think police officers should deal with illegal immigrants?

4. *Mini Case Study 1.* Reread, then discuss.

   Driving under the Influence?

   a. Has this issue (kava drink and its use among Pacific Islanders) been identified as an issue or problem in your jurisdiction? If so, what has the prosecuting attorney said about dealing with these cases?

   b. What would the officer's and police department liability be if he released the driver and the erratic driving continued?

---

*See the Instructor's Manual accompanying this text for additional activities, role-play activities, questionnaires, and projects related to the content of this chapter.

5. ***Mini Case Study 2.*** Reread, then discuss.

   A Tragic Case of Cross-Cultural Misinterpretation

   a. Do you think this case would have proceeded differently if all the authorities involved understood the cultural tradition of the medical practice ("coin rubbing") that caused the bruising? Explain your answer.

   b. Discuss whether you think Southeast Asian refugees should give up this medical practice because it can be misinterpreted.

6. ***Mini Case Study 3.*** Reread, then discuss.

   Latino Values as a Factor in Sentencing

   a. Discuss whether culture should play any part in influencing the sentencing of a criminal convicted of violent crimes such as murder and rape. Was the lighter verdict in this case justified? Explain your answer.

   b. According to retired Superior Court Judge Katz, culture influenced the sentencing in this case. In your opinion, if the husband involved were not Latino, would the sentence have been the same?

7. ***Prejudice and Discrimination in Police Work.*** In your own words, define prejudice and discrimination. Give examples of (a) discrimination in society in general, (b) discrimination against police officers, and (c) discrimination toward minorities by police officers. Discuss two strategies for each one to help eradicate the discrimination and the benefits that will result.

8. ***Community-Based Policing.*** Why is community-based policing in minority, ethnic, and immigrant communities especially crucial to the success of law enforcement in any given city? Discuss the two cases presented in this section of the chapter (i.e., the case of the police department without community policing in place [at the time of the fall of Saigon] and the case of the police department whose community policing efforts resulted in a dramatic decline of the homicide rate in the city). What lessons can you extract from these two examples that may be applicable to your jurisdiction?

WEBSITE RESOURCES

Visit these websites for additional information related to the content of Chapter 1.

The Community Policing Consortium: http://www.communitypolicing.org

The website presents a consortium of organizations that work to improve community-based law enforcement; the site has a wealth of materials and links related to the topic.

The Population Reference Bureau: http://www.prb.org

The website informs people around the world about population, health, and the environment, and empowers them to use that information to advance the well-being of current and future generations. PRB analyzes complex demographic data and research to provide the most objective, accurate, and up-to-date population information in a format that is easily understood by advocates, journalists, and decision makers alike.

Vera Institute of Justice: http://www.vera.org

The Vera Institute of Justice works closely with leaders in government and civil society to improve the services people rely on for safety and justice. It creates innovative programs, studies social problems, and provides practical advice and assistance to government officials around the world. The Vera Institute has publications on many topics of interest to law enforcement.

The International Association of Chiefs of Police: http://www.theiacp.org

This comprehensive website provides a wide variety of information on police-related topics. It includes research, publications, and such topics as leadership and training. It also contains selected publications on community policing from the viewpoints of Chiefs of Police.

U.S. Census Bureau: http://www.census.gov

This website provides comprehensive information about changing demographics in the United States.

The U.S. Government's Official Web Portal: http://firstgov.gov

The official U.S. Government website connects to millions of web pages from federal government, state, local and tribal governments, and to foreign nations around the world. Most of these pages are not available on commercial websites. FirstGov has the most comprehensive search of government anywhere on the Internet.

REFERENCES

Berry, Ondra. (2006, July). Deputy Chief, Reno, Nevada, Police Department, personal communication.

Berry-Wilkinson, Alison. (1993). "Be Careful What You Say When . . . ," *Labor Beat,* 5(1), 16.

Coffey, Alan, Edward Eldefonson, and Walter Hartinger. (1982). *Human Relations: Law Enforcement in a Changing Community,* 3rd ed. Englewood Cliffs, N.J.: Prentice-Hall.

Convention on the Elimination of All Forms of Racial Discrimination: Initial Report of the United States of America to the United Nations Committee on the Elimination of Racial Discrimination, September 2000. Available: http://www.state.gov/www/global/human_rights/cerd_report/cerd_intro.html.

Cross, T., Bazron, B. J., Dennis, K. W. and Isaacs, M. R. (1989). *Toward a Culturally Competent System of Care.* Volume 1: Monograph on Effective Services for Minority Children who are Severely Emotionally Disturbed. Washington, DC: CASSP Technical Assistance Center, Georgetown University Child Development Center.

"Cultural Sensitivity on the Beat." (2000, January 10). *Los Angeles Times,* p. A12.

Fernandez, Donya. (2000, December 20). Language Rights Attorney for the Language Rights Project, Employment Law Center/Legal Aid Society, San Francisco, California, personal communication.

Ferraro, Thomas. (2006, May 1). "Immigrants set for massive rallies." ABC News. Retrieved June 24, 2006, from http://abcnews.go.com/US/wireStory?id=1908521

Griffin, Ronald Pastor. (2003). Detroit-based pastor and community leader, personal communication, October, 2003).

Hall, Edward T. (1959). *The Silent Language.* Greenwich, Conn.: Fawcett.

Handlin, Oscar. (1975). *Out of Many: A Study Guide to Cultural Pluralism in the United States.* Anti-Defamation League of B'nai B'rith, published through Brown & Williamson Tobacco Corporation.

Immigration and Naturalization Service (2003). Yearbook of Immigration Statistics: "Estimates of the Unauthorized Immigrant Population Residing in the United States: 1990 to 2000." Washington, D.C.: U.S. Government Printing Office. Available: http://www.immigration.gov/graphics/shared/aboutus/statistics/Illegals.htm

Jang, D. L. (1994). "Caught in a Web: Immigrant Women and Domestic Violence," National Clearinghouse Review (Special Issue 1994).

Katz, Lawrence. (2006, July). Retired Presiding judge, Juvenile Court of Contra Costa (California) County, personal communication.

Kennedy, John F. (1986). *A Nation of Immigrants.* New York: Harper & Row.

Loden, Marilyn. (1996). *Implementing Diversity.* New York: McGraw-Hill.

Loden, Marilyn (2006). Organizational diversity consultant with Loden Associates, Inc., Tiburon, Calif., personal communication, July 2006.

"Multiracial Data in Census Adds Categories and Controversies." (2000, December 10). *San Francisco Chronicle,* p. A-14.

Miller, Char. (2006, July). Professor of history, Trinity College, San Antonio, Texas, personal communication.

National Institute of Justice. (2000, August). *The COPS Program after 4 Years: National Evaluation,* by Jeffrey A. Roth and Joseph F. Ryan. Washington, D.C.: U.S. Department of Justice.

"Officers Being Trained in Ethnic Understanding." (2000, November 29). *San Jose Mercury News,* p. A3.

Olson, Aaron T. (2006). Workshops to Immigrants and Refugees on USA Police, Laws, and Emergency Services. Organization and Training Services. Retrieved June 23, 2006, from http://www.pcc.edu/staff/index.cfm/174,2200,30.html

Olson, Aaron T. (2006). Criminal justice instructor at Portland Community College and retired patrol supervisor with the Oregon State Police, personal communication.

One America in the 21st Century: Forging a New Future, Executive Summary, Advisory Board to the President's Initiative on Race, September 1998. Available: http//www.whitehouse.gov/Initiatives/OneAmerica/cevent.html

Orloff, Leslye. (2003, February 27). Testifying as the director of the Immigrant Women Program, NOW Legal Defense and Education Fund, before the Subcommittee on Immigration, Border Security, and Claims House Judiciary Committee.

Owen, James. (2005). "With 20 Official Languages, Is EU Lost in Translation?" National Geographic News, February 22, 2005. Retrieved June 23, 2006, from http://news.nationalgeographic.com/news/2005/02/0222_050222_translation.html

Police Executive Research Forum (PERF). (1992). *Revisiting Community Policing: A New Typology.* Washington, D.C.: Author.

Population Reference Bureau. (2005). 2005 World Population Data Sheet. Retrieved June 23, 2006, from http://www.prb.org/pdf05/05WorldDataSheet_Eng.pdf

Prewitt, Kenneth. (2001, Fall). "Beyond Census 2000: As a Nation, We Are the World." *The Carnegie Reporter,* 1(3), p. 1.

Rawlins, Gary H. (1992, October 8). "Africans Came 200 Years Earlier," *USA Today,* p. 2a.

"The Changing Face of Race in America." (2000, September 18). *Newsweek,* p. 38.

Ruhly, Sharon. (1976). *Orientations to Intercultural Communication: Modules in Speech Communication.* Chicago: Science Research Associates.

Sherman, Spencer. (1986). "When Cultures Collide." *California Lawyer,* 6(1), 33.

Skolnick, Jerome H. (1999). *On Democratic Policing.* Washington, D.C.: Police Foundation.

Trojanowicz, Robert, and Bonnie Bucqueroux. (1990). *Community Policing: A Contemporary Perspective.* Lansing: Michigan State University, Cincinnati, Ohio: Anderson Publishing.

U.S. Census Bureau. (2002). "The Foreign Born Population in the United States," the U.S. Census Bureau Current Population Survey, March 2002.

U.S. Census Bureau. (2003). Current Population Survey: "The Foreign Born Population in the United States: March 2002." Washington, D.C.: U.S. Government Printing Office.

U.S. Department of Justice. (2000). Office of Justice Programs, Bureau of Justice Statistics: "Community Policing." Available: http://www.ojp.usdoj.gov/bjs/sandlle .htm#policing

U.S. Department of Justice. (2006). Office of Justice Programs, Bureau of Justice Statistics: "Law Enforcement Management and Administrative Statistics—Sheriff's Offices," 2003 Report, May 2006, NCJ211361.

U.S. Department of Justice. (2006). Office of Justice Programs, Bureau of Justice Statistics: "Law Enforcement Management and Administrative Statistics—Local Police Departments," 2003 Report, May 2006, NCJ210118.

Zangwill, Israel. (1908). *The Melting Pot: Drama in Four Acts.* New York: Macmillan.

Chapter 2

The Changing Law Enforcement Agency: A Microcosm of Society

OVERVIEW

The ethnic, racial, gender, and sexual orientation composition of law enforcement agencies is changing in the United States. In this chapter we address the increasingly pluralistic workforce and provide examples of racism and cultural insensitivity within the law enforcement agency. We present suggestions for defusing racially and culturally rooted conflicts and address issues related to women, gay men, and lesbians in law enforcement. The chapter ends with recommendations for all employees who work within a diverse workforce and particularly emphasizes the role of the chief executive. In this chapter, when the authors use the term *officer,* it is intended to mean city police officer, sheriff's deputy, and state police.

COMMENTARY

There is striking evidence of the changing law enforcement environment, both internal and external, in today's diverse society, as the following articles illustrate:

> It would be naïve to say women have completed the gender battle in law enforcement. Women make up a scant 13 percent of major police agencies nationwide, according to the National Center for Women and Policing. Women still face some unique challenges, including overcoming the attitudes of society and of some of their male coworkers and bosses. ("Women Still Underrepresented," 2003, p. A32)

> Workers who quit because of "intolerable" sexual harassment may sue their employers as though they had been fired—even if they did not formally complain about any abuse [according to the Supreme Court decision]. The decision clarifies the law on sexual harassment and makes it somewhat easier for victims to bring their claims in court. . . . In particular, it cleared the way for a jury to hear a sexual harassment suit brought by a woman who quit after working for a few months at a Pennsylvania State Police barracks in McConnellsburg. ("Harassed Workers Who Quit," 2004, p. A13)

Central to maintaining that support is the recognition that law enforcement agencies must reflect the diversity of communities they serve. Every day, our officers come into contact with individuals from different cultural backgrounds, socioeconomic classes, religions, sexual orientations, and physical and mental abilities. Each of these groups brings a different perspective to police–community relations and, as a result, our officers must be prepared to respond to each group in the appropriate fashion. Failure to recognize and adjust to community diversity can foster confusion and resentment among citizens and quickly lead to breakdown in the critical bond of trust between a law enforcement agency and its community. ("President's Message: Diversity on the Force," 2006, p. 1)

INTRODUCTION

In Chapter 1, we reviewed the evolution of multicultural communities and the demographic changes that the United States has experienced in recent decades. The most notable demographic changes mentioned involve the increases in racial, ethnic, and immigrant populations in our country. Diversity is becoming so commonplace in communities that terms such as *majority group* and *minority group* are almost obsolete. There has been a negative reaction to the term *minority,* which critics find not just outmoded but offensive. The term leaves nonwhites feeling diminished—almost second-class. The word carries overtones of inferiority and inequity. The word, technically, is used to describe numerical designations, but over the years it has come to have much larger implications.

The range of reactions to these changes by society as a whole is no different from the range within law enforcement agencies. Members of police communities across the country have demonstrated both tolerance of and resistance to the changing society and workforce. Some officers dislike the multicultural workforce and the involvement of women in policing, although the latter is becoming a nonissue. They may resent diversity because of their own prejudices or biases. This resentment is due in part to perceived or actual advantages others receive when competing for law enforcement positions, either entry level or promotional. In addition, because of past inept affirmative action hiring (i.e., management rushed to fill quotas but did not focus on competence), some officers perceive that affirmative action (where still being used) means lowering standards. Indeed, where standards have been lowered, everyone suffers, especially less-qualified employees hired because of affirmative action. (This issue is discussed further in Chapter 3.)

Leading positively and valuing the diversity within an agency are the keys to meeting the challenge of policing multicultural communities. As discussed in Chapter 1, racial and ethnic tensions still exist in the law enforcement community. Agency personnel must address the conflicts in their own organizations before dealing with community racial and ethnic problems. For example, if there are allegations of harassment, a hostile work environment, or differential treatment within the agency, these allegations must be addressed on a timely basis, or they fester and result in lawsuits, court injunctions, and unhappy employees who do not remain with the organization.

Law enforcement agencies, by their action or inaction, determine whether social problems that manifest themselves within their agencies are resolved. Across the United States, the national press has reported numerous cases in which law enforcement agencies did nothing or took the wrong action. Whether they like it or not, police officers are primary role models for citizens and are judged by a higher standard of behavior than are others. While supervision of police officers is important to ensure that this higher standard of behavior is maintained, no supervision of officers working with the public, no matter how thorough and conscientious, will prevent some officers from violating policies; there simply are too many police officers and too few supervisors. Thus, it is important that police officers demonstrate integrity and a stable set of core virtues. These virtues must include the ability to remain professional in protecting and serving a diverse public.

As stated in Chapter 1, those concerned with peacekeeping and enforcement must accept the realities of a diverse society as well as the heterogeneity within their workforce. The irony is that the peacekeepers sworn to uphold laws pertaining to acts of bias sometimes themselves become perpetrators, even against their peers. If police departments are to be representative of the populations served, police executives must effect changes. These changes have to do with the treatment of peers as well as recruitment, selection, and promotion of employees who have traditionally been underrepresented in law enforcement. The argument (Chapter 1) that the United States has never really been a melting pot applies also to the law enforcement community. In some cases, relationships within the law enforcement workplace, especially as diversity increases, are characterized by disrespect and tension. Although many in the police subculture would argue that membership implies brotherhood (and therefore belonging), this membership has traditionally excluded certain groups in both subtle and obvious ways.

CHANGING WORKFORCE

As microcosms of their communities, law enforcement agencies increasingly include among their personnel more women, members of ethnic and racial minorities, and gay males and lesbians. Although such groups are far from achieving parity in most law enforcement agencies in the United States, advances have been made. Exhibit 2.1 shows the percentages of women and minorities in the U.S. labor force for 1995 and 2005, and makes predictions for the year 2020.

This profound shift in demographics has resulted in notable changes in law enforcement. In many regions of the country, today's law enforcement workforce differs greatly from the workforce of the past. An article by the Office of Community Oriented Police discusses one dilemma for law enforcement.

	1995	2005	2020
Whites, Non-Hispanic	76%	73%	68%
Women	46%	48%	50%
Hispanic	9%	11%	14%
African American	11%	11%	11%
Asian American	4%	5%	6%

Exhibit 2.1   Percentage of Women and Minorities in U.S. Labor Force, 1995, 2005, 2020
Source: Workforce 2020, Hudson Institute, 2005

Good community policing practice encourages the recruitment and hiring of officers that reflect the diversity of their communities so that communication and trust can be built between officers and citizens who have a common background and ethnic heritage. The Hispanic population in many communities, however, is growing at rates of up to 450 percent per year. This makes it very difficult for any public sector organization, but especially law enforcement agencies, to even approach that rate of hiring and organizational change ("Closing the Communications Gap," 2002, p. 1).

Law Enforcement Diversity: A Microcosm of Society

According to the most recent Bureau of Justice Statistics (BJS) report, as of June 2003, local police departments had about 452,000 sworn personnel; sheriffs' offices had about 174,000 sworn personnel. The same report established the overall percentage of racial and ethnic minority-group representation among full-time sworn personnel nationwide. The percentage change of sworn personnel in minority representation between 2000 and 2003 was as follows (U.S. Department of Justice, 2006):

- Among local police officers, minority representation increased from 22.6 percent to 23.6 percent.

- Among sheriffs' offices, minority representation increased from 17.1 percent to 18.8 percent.

With increases came a corresponding reduction in the number of white officers and deputies in law enforcement workforces. Exhibits 2.2 and 2.3 provide more details on the percentages of women and ethnic and racial groups in local police and sheriffs' departments between 1987 and 2003.

Some major law enforcement agencies have achieved parity in terms of the percentage of diverse groups in their workforce compared to the percentage in the com-

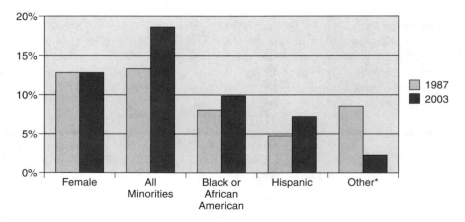

Exhibit 2.2   Female and Minority Officers in Sheriff's Offices, 1987–2003
Source: Sheriffs' Offices 2003. May 2006, U.S. Department of Justice, BJS 211361.
*Includes Asians, Native Hawaiians or other Pacific Islanders, American Indians, Alaska Natives, and any other racial or ethnic minority.

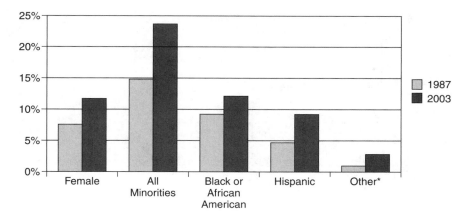

Exhibit 2.3   Female and minority local police officers, 1987–2003
Source: Local Police Departments 2003. May 2006, U.S. Department of Justice, BJS 210118.
*Includes Asians, Native Hawaiians or other Pacific Islanders, American Indians, Alaska Natives, and any other racial or ethnic minority.

munity; most have not, but the numbers are improving. In local police departments and sheriffs' offices, from 2000 to 2003, the percentage of

- Black or African American police officers increased by 3 percent; black or African American deputies increased 13 percent.
- Hispanic or Latino police officers increased by 13 percent: Hispanic or Latino deputies increased by 20 percent.
- Officers and deputies from other minority groups increased by 7 percent.
- Women police officers and deputies comprised 11.3 percent of officers in 2003, up from 10.6 in 2000.

When looking at minority female representation in U.S. law enforcement, the percentages are much lower with

- 2.7 percent African American female officers; 2.6 percent deputies.
- 1.3 percent Latina police officers; 0.9 percent deputies.
- 0.3 percent of those identified as "other" (Asian, Native Hawaiian, American Indian, and Alaska Natives) are women officers in local police departments; 0.2 percent deputies (U.S. Department of Justice, 2006).

A study in 2001 by the National Center for Women and Policing (NCWP) confirms that in the majority of law enforcement agencies, women of color are underrepresented (see Exhibit 2.4). Their study determined that women of color hold only 4.8 percent of sworn positions in contrast with their 8.2 percent representation in the overall labor force over age 16. The study and Department of Justice statistics reveal that women of color are virtually absent from the highest ranks, holding only 1.6 percent of top command positions in sworn law enforcement (NCWP survey, 2001, p. 10). Law enforcement is still a predominantly white male occupation, and there must be an expansion of

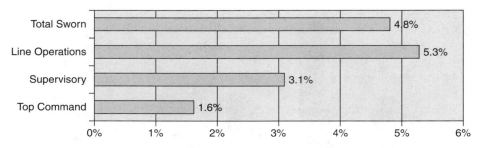

Exhibit 2.4   Women of Color as Percentage of Sworn Law Enforcement by Rank: Large Police Agencies, 2001
Source: NCWP Survey, 2001, p.10

efforts in the recruitment, hiring, and promotion of women and people of other races and ethnicities nationwide. This issue is discussed further in Chapter 3.

Measuring Responsiveness to Diversity

A manual produced by the Canadian Association of Chiefs of Police includes a 10-question checklist and scoring method for law enforcement organizations to determine how responsive they are in adapting to diversity. It is reproduced here (Exhibit 2.5) for use in rating your own agency.

ETHNIC AND RACIAL ISSUES WITHIN THE WORKFORCE

What Is Racism?

The American Heritage Dictionary provides two definitions of the word *racism.*

   1. The belief that race accounts for differences in human character or ability and that a particular race is superior to others.

   2. Discrimination or prejudice based on race.

Examples of the first definition are found not only in the words and actions of white supremacist groups but also, unfortunately, in the words and actions of some nonhate-group members of society. Racism in the first definition involves the underlying assumption that one race, almost always the white race, is superior to all others. *Racist* is the term applied to those who subscribe to this belief. The second, broader definition involves the term *discrimination* (treatment or consideration based on class or category rather than on individual merit) or *prejudice* (a preconceived preference or idea) and allows that people of any race can be labeled as racist and any biased act (an unfair act or policy stemming from prejudice) to be categorized as racism. With these terms in mind, let's discuss racism within the criminal justice system.

Racism within law enforcement agencies has been documented for decades. An African American history display at the New York Police Academy, observed by one of the authors, contains the following written account of the experiences of one of the first black officers in the New York Police Department:

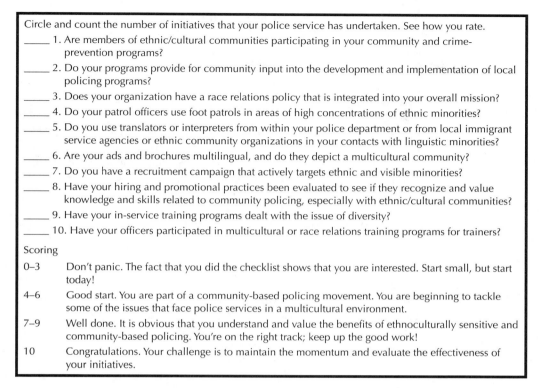

Circle and count the number of initiatives that your police service has undertaken. See how you rate.

_____ 1. Are members of ethnic/cultural communities participating in your community and crime-prevention programs?

_____ 2. Do your programs provide for community input into the development and implementation of local policing programs?

_____ 3. Does your organization have a race relations policy that is integrated into your overall mission?

_____ 4. Do your patrol officers use foot patrols in areas of high concentrations of ethnic minorities?

_____ 5. Do you use translators or interpreters from within your police department or from local immigrant service agencies or ethnic community organizations in your contacts with linguistic minorities?

_____ 6. Are your ads and brochures multilingual, and do they depict a multicultural community?

_____ 7. Do you have a recruitment campaign that actively targets ethnic and visible minorities?

_____ 8. Have your hiring and promotional practices been evaluated to see if they recognize and value knowledge and skills related to community policing, especially with ethnic/cultural communities?

_____ 9. Have your in-service training programs dealt with the issue of diversity?

_____ 10. Have your officers participated in multicultural or race relations training programs for trainers?

Scoring

0–3   Don't panic. The fact that you did the checklist shows that you are interested. Start small, but start today!

4–6   Good start. You are part of a community-based policing movement. You are beginning to tackle some of the issues that face police services in a multicultural environment.

7–9   Well done. It is obvious that you understand and value the benefits of ethnoculturally sensitive and community-based policing. You're on the right track; keep up the good work!

10   Congratulations. Your challenge is to maintain the momentum and evaluate the effectiveness of your initiatives.

Exhibit 2.5   How Responsive Is Your Organization?
Source: Canadian Association of Chiefs of Police. (1992). *Police Race Relations: Raising Your Effectiveness in Today's Diverse Neighborhoods through Community Policing.* Place de Ville, Tower B, 112 Kent St., Suite 1908, Ottawa, Ontario K1P 5P2, Canada.

> Seven years before the adoption of the charter creating New York City, Brooklyn, then an independent city, hired the first black policeman. Wiley G. Overton was sworn in March 6, 1891. . . . His first tour of duty was spent in civilian clothing because fellow officers breaking with tradition refused to furnish him with a temporary uniform. . . . Officers in his section refused to sleep in the same room with him. . . . The officers in the precinct ignored him and spoke only if it was necessary in the line of duty.

The New York Police Department is not alone. Racism can occur in police departments regardless of size or region. Unfortunately, racism has been an issue for decades. In 2004, a University of Florida graduate research professor in sociology, Joe Feagin, conducted a study that concluded that "black police officers in the South still face racism." In a book he co-authored, *Black in Blue: African-American Police Officers and Racism,* Feagin and Kenneth Bolton Jr., a criminal studies professor at Southeastern Louisiana University, reported:

> Racial discrimination is a routine, recurring and everyday reality for black police officers. Many lament how white officers continually underestimate their

abilities, treating them as less intelligent and less able to perform their policing duties.

The book is based on personal interviews conducted in the late 1990s with 50 black officers—38 men and 12 women—in 16 law enforcement agencies throughout the South, from Texas to Virginia, and at city, county, and federal levels. Notably, the researchers said respondents provided anecdotal examples wherein white officers in positions of authority tried to discourage them [black officers] from taking promotional exams or routinely passed them over for special assignments that were given to less qualified white officers. Some of those interviewed also reported a disparity or contradiction in how black and white officers were disciplined. One respondent said, "A white officer will do something that is a fairly serious infraction of police regulations and is given a slap on the wrist, and a black officer is fired" ("Black Police Officers," 2004).

We spoke with several officers from different states about racism in their departments. Those interviewed requested that their names not be included, because they felt they might face repercussions. One African American officer recalled almost coming to blows with a white officer who used a racial slur against him; the use of such slurs was commonplace for the white officer and his friends. A Cuban American officer recounted the story of a nonresistant Latino suspect who was caught in the commission of a minor crime and beaten by the white arresting officers, who used racial epithets. One major city in Massachusetts suspended a deputy superintendent of police for using the word "nigger" directed toward one of his own officers. An African American officer in a large city in Florida was fired after using racial epithets against other blacks in violation of a strict citywide policy. In this particular case, the African American officer's conduct was reported by another officer at the scene. In yet another city, an African American officer was overheard telling a white prisoner, "Wait until you get to central booking and the niggers get a hold of you."

Defusing Racially and Culturally Rooted Conflicts

Racism exists within our law enforcement organizations; police are not immune to social ills. One of the greatest challenges for police officers is dealing with their own racism. The first step in addressing the problem is for police department personnel, on all levels, to admit rather than deny that racism exists. Police researcher David Shipler, after two years of interviews across the country, maintained that he encountered very few black officers who had not been "hassled by white cops." He was quick to point out, however, that not every white police officer is a bigot and not every police force a bastion of racism; in fact, some agencies have made great strides in improving race relations.

Shipler recommends that law enforcement should combat and defuse racism by using the U.S. Army model developed during a time of extreme racial tension in the military in the early 1970s ("Report Recommends Using Military Model," 1992). Obviously, no model of training will bring guaranteed success and alleviate all acts of prejudice and racism. However, professional groups can build on each other's attempts, especially when these efforts have proven to be fairly successful. Shipler recognizes that police officers are not identical to soldiers, because the former have constant contact with the public (where they see the worst) and must use personal judgment in dangerous and ambiguous situations. Nevertheless, he suggests that some military approaches are adaptable to law enforcement. According to Shipler, the basic framework for combating and defusing racism in the military has been:

- ***Command commitment:*** The person at the top sets the tone all the way down to the bottom. Performance reports document any bigoted or discriminatory behavior. A record of racial slurs and discriminatory acts can derail a military career.

- ***Training of advisers:*** Military personnel are trained at the Defense Equal Opportunity Management Institute in Florida as equal opportunity advisers. The advisers are assigned to military units with direct access to commanders. They conduct local courses to train all members of the unit on race relations.

- ***Complaints and monitoring:*** The advisers provide one channel for specific complaints of racial and gender discrimination, but they also drop in on units unannounced and sound out the troops on their attitudes. Surveys are conducted and informal discussions are held to lessen racial tensions. ("Report recommends," 1992)

Sondra Thiederman (1991), cultural diversity consultant and author, provides nine tips, still applicable today, that will help organizational managers or leaders identify and resolve conflicts that arise because of cultural (not only racial) differences in the workplace. She states that the following guidelines are applicable no matter what cultures, races, religions, or lifestyles are involved:

1. Give each party the opportunity to voice his or her concerns without interruption.

2. Attempt to obtain agreement on what the problem is by asking questions of each party to find out specifically what is upsetting each person.

3. During this process, stay in control and keep employees on the subject of the central issue.

4. Establish whether the issue is indeed rooted in cultural differences by determining:
   a. If the parties are from different cultures or subcultures.
   b. If the key issue represents an important value in each person's culture.
   c. How each person is expected to behave in his or her culture as it pertains to this issue.
   d. If the issue is emotionally charged for one or both of the parties.
   e. If similar conflicts arise repeatedly and in different contexts.

5. Summarize the cultural (racial, religious, or lifestyle) differences that you uncover.

6. State the negative outcomes that will result if the situation is not resolved (be specific).

7. State the positive outcomes that will result if the situation is resolved (be specific).

8. Negotiate terms by allowing those involved to come up with the solutions.

9. Provide positive reinforcement as soon as the situation improves.

Thiederman's approach is based on conflict resolution and crisis intervention techniques training that many police and correctional officers receive in either their academy or in-service training. Police department command must encourage the use of conflict resolution techniques by officers of all backgrounds as a way of handling issues prior to their becoming flash points. With professionalism and patience, the use of conflict resolution techniques to reduce racial and ethnic problems will work within both the workforce and the neighborhoods.

As a result of allegations of racism against it, the Alameda, California, Police Department developed a series of general orders as one approach to remedy the problem. Violation of the department general orders (DGOs) carries progressive disciplinary ramifications up to and including termination. The general orders deal with control of prejudicial conduct based on race, religion, ethnicity, disability, sex, age, or sexual orientation and are as follows:

1. ***Code of ethics:*** Commits to personal suppression of prejudice, animosities, malice, and ill will, as well as respect for the constitutional rights of all persons.

2. ***DGO 80-1:*** Specifically addresses discrimination and racial remarks and requires courtesy and respect for all persons. It states: "Discrimination or racism in any form shall never be tolerated."

3. ***DGO 80-1:*** Requires impartiality toward all persons and guarantees equal protection under the law. Prohibits exhibition of partiality due to race, creed, or influence.

4. ***DGO 90-3:*** Deals with harassment in the workplace based on race, religion, color, national origin, ancestry, disability, marital status, sex, age, or sexual preference.

The Alameda Police Department also produced an in-service training guide listing "mortal sins" or actions not condoned, which include:

1. Racism, racial slurs, racial discrimination.

2. Sexism, offensive sexual remarks, sexual harassment, sexual discrimination.

3. Discrimination or harassment for sexual orientation.

4. Religious discrimination.

This department sent a clear message to its employees that its leaders will not tolerate discriminatory behavior. The same department adapted a San Diego Police Department attitude assessment survey instrument on perceptions regarding contact with the multicultural community and workforce. The survey instrument is reproduced in Appendix A.

Police Fraternal Organizations

Police fraternal, religious, and ethnic organizations offer their members social activities, fellowship, counseling, career development, resources, and networking opportunities with persons of common heritage, background, or experience. The New York Police Department, for example, has many clubs, societies, and associations to address the needs of its pluralistic organization. The Irish are represented by the Emerald Society, African Americans by the Guardians Association, Christian officers by Police Officers for Christ, those of Asian or Pacific Islander heritage (which includes Chinese, Japanese, Korean, Filipino, and Asian Indian officers) by the Asian Jade Society, Italian officers by the Columbia Association, and so on. The police subculture can be a stressful environment, so it is only natural that persons different from the majority workforce members seek emotional comfort zones with those of similar background. Membership in these groups provides emotional sanctuary from the stereotypes, hostility, indifference, ignorance, or naïveté that members encounter within their organizations and communities.

Occasionally, we hear of criticism within a department or by the public that such organizations actually highlight the differences between groups of people. At a National Organization of Black Law Enforcement Executives (NOBLE) conference, a white female (nonattendee) asked the meaning of the acronym NOBLE. When given the answer, she asked: "Is it ethical for blacks to have their own organization? Could whites have an organization called the 'National Organization of White Law Enforcement Executives' without being referred to as racists? Why can't the multicultural, social, and professional organizations that already exist satisfy the needs of everyone?"

The woman's concern was brought up directly with one of the conference participants, Sergeant Thomas Hall, an African American who at the time was a Virginia state trooper. Sergeant Hall explained:

> In America, we need independent black institutions . . . to foster cultural pride, and have a place where we can go and feel comfortable. We cannot express ourselves in society. We cannot assimilate in society. We cannot even assimilate like some Hispanic groups can because of their complexions. I can't assimilate on a bus. As soon as I step on the bus, you are going to realize there is a black guy on the bus. I can't assimilate in a police organization . . . so without these black institutions, I cannot survive. We all have survival mechanisms. I have cultural needs and I have to be around people that share my needs and frustrations. I cannot do that in organizations that are predominantly white. The whites don't suffer from the racial pressures and tensions that I suffer from. So how can they [mostly white organizations] meet my interests and needs? It is impossible. (Hall, 1992)

Hall stressed that African American law enforcement organizations provide him with a network of persons with similar interests, concerns, and backgrounds.

The racial, ethnic, religious, and lifestyle organizations within law enforcement are not meant to divide but rather to give support to groups that traditionally were not accepted in law enforcement fully and had no power within the organization. Yet the sentiment expressed by the white female who inquired into the meaning of NOBLE is not uncommon among police officers. Police command officers and supervisors must not ignore this debate (whether expressed or not). They must address the issues underlying the need for the support groups within the department. They must also foster dialogue and shared activities between all formalized groups within the organization. All officers must hear an explanation of the benefit they receive from membership in the groups of different ethnic, racial, and lifestyle perspectives. Officers must be willing to discuss ways to guard against divisiveness, either real or perceived, within their agencies.

Assignments Based on Diversity

There has been limited research on the assumption that an increase in the proportion of any underrepresented group in a police agency would have a positive effect in the community. Some believe that an increase in Hispanic, African American, or Asian officers in a neighborhood of the same race or ethnicity would improve police–community relations. The same argument could be made regarding gay and lesbian officers. We might speculate that there would be a more sensitive response of "like folks" who are aware of needs and issues of "their kind." In fact, historically, immigrants (Irish, Italians, and Germans) were hired by police departments because they could communicate and operate more effectively than could nonimmigrant officers in neighborhoods with large concentrations of immigrants.

Although citizens appreciate having officers of their own color or national origin work their area, this deployment strategy may result in unfairness. Studies have concluded that this practice can result in a career path for minorities that may be very different from that of white officers in agencies that follow this practice (Benson, 1992; Ross, Snortum, & Beyers, 1982; Wells, 1987). For example, instead of receiving specialized assignments in traffic, investigations, special weapons and tactics (SWAT) team, and so on, the minority officer who is working effectively in the minority community may have an extended tour of duty in that function. In addition, the area to which this officer is assigned is often a tougher, high-crime area, which means that he or she is exposed more frequently to violence.

Officers of the same background as the predominant ethnicity or race in the neighborhood do not necessarily make the best crime fighters or problem solvers there. Not all racially or ethnically diverse officers may have the skills or desire to work with their own cultural or racial group. Assignments based on diversity alone, therefore, are generally unfair and may be a disservice to both the officer and the neighborhood. Officers should not be restricted to working in specific areas based on the notion that police–community relations will improve automatically. In addition, it cannot be assumed that an officer of the same background as the citizens will always show sensitivity to their particular needs.

Ronald Hampton, a retired Washington, D.C., Metropolitan police officer and executive director of the National Black Police Officers Association since 1989, illustrated this point at a NOBLE conference when he discussed the reasons why a new African American recruit wanted to work the black areas of Washington, D.C. The recruit said that he could tell people of his own race what to do and could not always do so in predominantly white neighborhoods. Hampton noted, however, that the young recruit "called people from his neighborhood 'maggots.'" Hampton made the point that supervisors must hold subordinates accountable for their conduct, and the chief executive must make it known that inappropriate behavior will be disciplined no matter what the neighborhood (Hampton, 2006). We present this example to illustrate that some officers may have internalized the hatred society has directed toward them and consequently are not automatically the most effective officers in certain neighborhoods.

When Chief Robert Burgreen was the top executive of the San Diego Police Department, he, like many other law enforcement managers, did not deploy officers according to color, sexual orientation, or ethnicity. Deployment was based on the best fit for the neighborhood and was related to an officer's competence and capabilities. However, Chief Burgreen had four community relations sergeants, one acting as a liaison for each major group in the city: Hispanic, African American, Asian, and gays and lesbians. He described these sergeants as his "eyes and ears" for what was going on in the various communities. Some cities use cultural affairs committees made up of people from diverse groups in the community and the officers who provide them service to perform a similar function.

WOMEN IN LAW ENFORCEMENT

Women have always been part of the general workforce in American society, although for many years in primarily traditional female employment roles, such as nurses, secretaries, schoolteachers, waitresses, and flight attendants. In 1845, New York City hired its first police "matron." In 1888, Massachusetts and New York passed legislation requiring communities with a population over 20,000 to hire police matrons to care for female prisoners. According to More (1992), during the first half of the 19th century, a number of police practices were challenged, thus allowing for the initial entry of women into the police field. In 1922, the International Association of Chiefs of Police passed a resolution supporting the use of policewomen; however, no women worked patrol or as detectives.

The first major movement of women into the general workforce occurred during World War II. With men off to war, women entered the workforce in large numbers and successfully occupied many nontraditional employment roles. A nontraditional occupation for women is defined as one in which women comprise 25 percent or less of total employment. After the war, 30 percent of all women continued working outside the home ("History of Woman in Workforce," 1991). By 2003, almost 60 percent of women in the United States worked outside the home, a 5 percent increase from 1990 ("Women in the Labor Force," 2005). Women continue to make inroads into nontraditional occupations (i.e., traditionally male-dominated occupations) such as detectives, architects, chefs, clergy, truck drivers, firefighters, aircraft pilots, and construction occupations, to name a few. ("Quick Facts on Nontraditional Occupations for Women, 2006). According to the Bureau of Labor Statistics, between 1983 and 2002, in the male-dominated occupations of police detectives and supervisors, the number of female workers in those jobs increased 360 percent ("Many U.S. Jobs," 2005).

Women hired as police officers during the early years were given duties that did not allow or require them to work street patrol. Assignments and roles were limited to positions such as juvenile delinquency and truancy prevention, child abuse, crimes against women, and custodial functions (Bell, 1982). It was not until 1968 that the Indianapolis Police Department made history by assigning the first two female officers to patrol on an equal basis with their male colleagues (Schulz, 1995). This delay was due, in part, to role perceptions. The predominant belief that law enforcement agencies function to exercise authority and use force is accompanied by the idea that women are not capable of performing these functions.

In 1972, the passage of the Equal Employment Opportunity (EEO) Act applied to state and local governments the provisions of Title VII of the Civil Rights Act of 1964. The EEO Act prohibited employment discrimination on the basis of race, color, religion, sex, or national origin. The law played an important role in opening up police departments to women. Adoption of affirmative action policies, now illegal in many states, along with court orders and injunctions, also played a role in bringing more women into law enforcement. Although more women were entering law enforcement, they still encountered blatant and open skepticism, resentment, and hostility from male officers.

Historically, law enforcement agencies' requirements or standards pertaining to minimum height and weight, strength, and agility posed one of many barriers to female entry into the police field (Polisar & Milgram, 1998). Most civil service tests modified these requirements in order to comply with court-ordered legal mandates and injunctions by the early 1980s (Balkin, 1988). However, a study published by the National Center for Women and Policing (NCWP) in 2003 concluded that there is still an adverse impact on women due to entry-level physical agility testing that eliminates a large number of women. NCWP suggests that there are other options that will yield the benefits of qualified women entering the profession and eliminate this obstacle to their being hired ("Tearing Down the Wall," 2003). This study is discussed more fully in Chapter 3.

In 2004, women made up 46.4 percent of the U.S. labor force and 50.3 percent of managerial, professional, and related positions. According to the Bureau of Labor Statistics (2005), of those in managerial, professional, and related positions,

- **African American women** made up 6.0 percent, with 2,447,000 (5 percent of all people employed in those occupations).

- **Asian American women** made up 2.0 percent, with 1,204,000 (2.5 percent of all people employed in those occupations).

- **Latinas** made up 5.2 percent, with 1,588,000 (3.3 percent of all people employed in those occupations).

In 2004, the U.S. labor force included these numbers and percentages (Bureau of Labor Statistics, 2005; Toosi, 2004):

- *African Americans:* 16,638,000 (11.3 percent). In 1992, they were 11.1 percent; 2012 projected to be 12.2 percent of labor force.

- *Asian Americans:* 6,271,000 (4.3 percent). In 1992, they were 4 percent; 2012 projected to be 5.5 of labor force.

- *Latinos/Latinas:* 19,272,000 (13.1 percent). In 1992, they were 8.9 percent; 2012 projected to be 14.7 percent of labor force.

- *Native American/Alaska Native:* 6.5 percent of the U.S. labor force; 50.2 percent were women.

The number of women in law enforcement remains small and is increasing very slowly (see earlier discussion and exhibits 2.2 and 2.3). Researchers in the late 1980s had made various predictions of the numbers of women expected to be in law enforcement professions by the turn of the 21st century, ranging from 47 to 55 percent of the workforce, but those predictions never materialized.

The Law Enforcement Management and Administrative Statistics (LEMAS) report, issued by the U.S. Department of Justice in 2006, established that, as of 2003:

- Of the 174,251 full-time sworn personnel in sheriffs' offices, an estimated 12.9 percent were women. The percentage of female officers ranged from about 15 percent in sheriffs' offices serving 500,000 or more residents to 5 percent in those serving fewer than 10,000 residents.

- Of the 451,737 full-time sworn personnel in local police departments, approximately 11 percent were women. The percentage of female officers ranged from about 17 percent in departments serving 1 million or more residents to about 6 percent in those serving fewer than 10,000 residents.

The number of females in sheriffs' offices or police departments has not changed substantially since 1987 when female sheriff deputies were at 12.6 percent and female police officers were at 7.6 percent. Women were gaining in numbers at approximately half a percentage point per year in their representation within large police agencies from 1972 to 1999, but the trend halted or even reversed in 2000 and 2001. During this period, there was a 5.5 percent (1,200 deputies) drop in the numbers of female sheriffs' deputies. The representation of women in large police agencies also declined—from 14.3 percent in 1999 and 13 percent in 2000 to 12.7 percent in 2001. A 2001 study by the NCWP addressed this issue:

> One possible explanation for the stall or even decline in women's representation within law enforcement is the decrease in the number of consent decrees mandating the hiring and/or promotion of women and/or minorities. Among surveyed agencies, eight consent decrees expired in the period of time from 1999 to 2002, yet only two consent decrees were implemented since 1995, and only six were implemented in the entire decade. Without the consent decrees imposed to remedy discriminatory hiring and employment practices by law enforcement agencies, even the marginal gains women have made in policing would not have been possible. (NCWP, 2002a, p. 3)

A review of the statistics makes it clear that women are underrepresented in law enforcement. Recall that the participation of women in the whole of the labor force in 2004 was 46.4 percent.

However, women do not constitute the only group that saw a numbers reduction in law enforcement, as the following statement from an article based on a study by the Federal Reserve of Dallas, Texas, indicates: ". . . since the start of this decade, the workforce participation of women in prime working years—between 25 and 54—has experienced its largest sustained decline since World War II" ("More Women Leaving Labor Market," 2005). This particular research found that the women who are dropping out have been mostly educated and married with children and higher incomes, and that many were leaving to go back to school or to have families. The study did not focus on women in law enforcement, so further research is needed to verify if retention problems are occurring in this occupation for the same reasons.

The integration of women into policing and the problems with their retention have led many law enforcement chief executives, managers, and supervisors to grapple with workplace issues within their departments.

Workplace Issues

Workplace issues confronting law enforcement agencies, and especially women in law enforcement, involve sexual harassment, gender discrimination, role barriers, the "brotherhood," a double standard, differential treatment, and career versus family.

Sexual Harassment. The following is considered sexual harassment in the workplace:

- ***Hostile Environment,*** which consists of unwelcome sexual behavior, such as "jokes," cartoons, posters, banter, repeated requests for dates, requests for sexual favors, references to body parts, or physical touching that has the purpose or effect of unreasonably interfering with an individual's work performance or creating an intimidating, hostile, or offensive working environment.

- ***Quid pro quo sexual harassment,*** which means one is asked to perform sexual acts in return for a job benefit. For example, you are told you will pass probation, get a promotion, get a good performance evaluation, or not be written up for doing something wrong if you will engage in some type of sexual behavior.

- ***Gender harassment,*** which is behavior that is not based on sexual behavior but is based on gender. It is also known as sex-based harassment. Examples include comments such as "women are not brave enough to be police officers," "women should stay home and have babies and leave policing to real men," and the like. (Workplace Issues, 2005).

The U.S. Equal Employment Opportunity Commission in 2005 received 12,679 complaints (from public and private sectors) alleging sexual harassment (14.3 percent of the charges were by males), down from 15,836 in the year 2000, or a decrease of 19.9 percent. Although sexual harassment exists in both private and public sectors, we believe it is particularly problematic in law enforcement—an occupation that is still mostly male. Since 1976, harassment on the basis of sex has been a violation of Section 703 of Title VII of the Civil Rights Act (29CFR Section 1604.11[a][1]).

The majority of women officers interviewed for each edition of this book (who requested that their names not be used) said they had been sexually harassed in the workplace. There have been few national studies on sexual harassment in law enforcement agencies, but the findings of those few indicate that the problem is pervasive. In a 1995 survey of female officers in a medium-sized department, 68 percent responded "yes" to the question, "Have you ever been sexually harassed while on duty by a member of your agency?" (Nichols, 1995). Most of the women indicated that when they were exposed to offensive behavior by male officers, they remained quiet for fear of negative male backlash. This lack of reporting can also be directly attributed to the code of silence in law enforcement agencies and the severe retaliation that occurs when women report misconduct. Those interviewed revealed that sexual harassment occurs at all levels of an organization and is not limited to male harassment of women. In 2003, Seklecki and Allen (2004) of the University of Minot, North Dakota, administered a survey to 2,000 female police officers, selected at random, in departments across the United States. The survey contained questions designed to collect information about employment motivations, experiences, and attitudes of women who became law enforcement officers. The response rate was approximately 27 percent (531 female police officers and deputies). The summary of their findings is:

> When examining sexual harassment, it appears as though the situations most frequently encountered by female officers were: putting women down, being insulted and called homosexual by citizens, someone trying to have a sexual relationship with an officer despite her objections, someone making sexually suggestive remarks at or about the officer, and hearing dirty jokes and/or stories being told. What is most amazing is, there was not one situation presented which no female officer had never encountered This becomes extremely interesting given that 377 officers reported that they had never been sexually harassed (72.8%). That is, this sample of female officers reported frequencies for

experiencing every sexual harassment situation, yet the majority of officers reported that they had never been sexually harassed. (p. 38)

Department executives must institute a zero-tolerance sexual harassment policy and send that message throughout the department. Police-specific training must also be provided on sexual harassment and its prevention. Some departments have revised their promotional exam to include questions on the department's sexual harassment policies and procedures. The Albuquerque, New Mexico, Police Department went so far as to move the investigation of sexual harassment complaints from within the department to an external city agency with expert Equal Employment Opportunity investigators on staff. According to the Albuquerque PD, this approach tends to speed up the process, ensure impartiality, and increase confidence in the procedures. Officers who make a complaint do not have to go through the chain of command. An 8-hour police-specific training course for sworn supervisors on preventing sexual harassment, developed by the Institute for Women in Trades, Technology and Science (IWITTS), is also of value. It is presented in a case-study format that analyzes police legal cases, and it has been highly rated by those who have attended. Information on IWITTS can be found on its website, listed in the Website Resources section of this chapter.

When harassment takes place, the results can be devastating in terms of the involved employees' careers, the internal environment of the organization, and the department's public image. The importance of training all law enforcement employees (sworn and nonsworn) on the issues of sexual harassment cannot be stressed enough. With policies and procedures as well as training, sexual harassment is expected to decrease in the law enforcement workforce as the once male-dominated occupation makes its transition to a mixed-gender, multiethnic, multiracial, and multilifestyle one—a microcosm of the society served. Discrimination and sexual harassment training should deal not only with legal and liability issues but also with deep-seated attitudes about differences based on gender.

Gender Discrimination. Gender discrimination occurs when a person is subjected to unequal treatment in the workplace on the basis of the sex. A few examples of what might constitute workplace gender discrimination are:

- Assignments to jobs or programs that are considered "traditionally women's" instead of the nontraditional positions such as SWAT teams, K9, gang units, and narcotics.

- Tests for promotions or other job opportunities that are not job related or represent a small part of the job duties that result in women not getting promoted at the same rate that men are promoted.

- Women are held to a higher or different level on performance evaluations.

- Women are not given equal consideration for specialized training, conferences, specialty job assignments, and the like.

- Pregnant women are not given light duty, but men who are injured off-duty are given these assignments. (Workplace Issues, 2005)

Some agencies have unlawfully discriminated against pregnant employees. One of the biggest complaints from pregnant female sworn officers is that when they notify their department that they are pregnant, they are removed from their position and there is little or no effort to find a light-duty position (Workplace Issues, 2005). Discrimination on the basis of pregnancy, childbirth, or a related medical condition is discrimination on the basis of gender. The U.S. Equal Employment Opportunity Commission in 2005 received 23,094 private and public sector complaints alleging sex-based (gender) discrimination, down 8.3 percent from 25,194 in the year 2000 (EEOC, 2006).

Role Barriers. Barriers and hostility toward women in the workplace based on gender have diminished, both in the general population and within law enforcement. For example, ideas about protection differ by gender—who protects whom? In American society, women may protect children, but it has been more socially acceptable and traditional for men to protect women. In the act of protecting, the protectors become dominant and the protected become subordinate. Although this gender-role perception has not completely broken down, especially in the law enforcement and corrections workforce, it is subsiding because of the number of women and young male officers in those professions today. There are now fewer veteran male officers who have never worked with women. Many veteran police and correctional officers initially had difficulty with the transition as women came into the dangerous, male-dominated, nontraditional occupations that men felt required "male" strength and abilities. The result has been described as a clash between cultures—the once male-dominated workforce versus the new one in which women are integral parts of the organizational environment. The veteran male police or correctional officers, socially conditioned to protect women, often feel that in addition to working with inmates or violent persons on the streets, they have the added responsibility of protecting the women officers with whom they work.

These feelings, attitudes, and perceptions can make men and women in law enforcement positions uncomfortable with each other. Women sometimes feel patronized, overprotected, or merely tolerated rather than appreciated and respected for their work. Again, these attitudes and perceptions are diminishing as many in the new generation of male officers are more willing to accept women in law enforcement. In our numerous interviews with veteran officers, we found that, with few exceptions, women were generally accepted by men, but the acceptance was related to how well a specific woman performed her duties. The National Survey of Female Police Officers 2003 study, previously cited, questioned those participating about how they were treated, and:

> the majority of respondents felt they were treated equally and were made to feel as welcomed as their male counterparts upon entering the field of law enforcement. However, 39 percent of respondents indicate they were made to feel less welcomed than males, and almost 32 percent indicated they were treated worse than male officers when they first began their careers in law enforcement. Thus, there are a large number of respondents who feel they were treated less favorably than male officers upon beginning their careers in policing. (Seklecki & Allen, 2004, p. 31)

The Brotherhood. Women who are accepted into the "brotherhood" of police or correctional officers have generally had to become "one of the guys." (Refer to Chapter 4 for more information on how language used in the brotherhood excludes women.) According to Susan Jones, Chief of Police of the Healdsburg, California, Police Department, and other women interviewed, the term *brotherhood* still exists today along with the associated behaviors. Chief Jones hopes that one day there will be just the "family of law enforcement" (Jones, 2006).

Often, a woman who tries to act like one of the guys (be part of the brotherhood) on the street or in a jail or prison is considered too hard, too coldhearted, or too unemotional and may be criticized by peers and supervisors. Although perhaps this is a little exaggerated, some women have been described as "Jane Waynes" because they swagger, swear, spit, and are highly aggressive. Yet if a female officer is too feminine or not sufficiently aggressive, men will not take her seriously and she will not do well in either police or correctional work. So women are confronted with a dilemma: they must be aggressive enough to do the job but feminine enough to be acceptable to male peers, and they must also be able to take different approaches to problems.

When women feel compelled to behave like men in the workplace, the results can be counterproductive and can even result in disciplinary action. To succeed, women may feel that they have to stay within narrow bands of acceptable behavior and exhibit only certain traditionally masculine and feminine qualities. Walking this fine line is difficult. This phenomenon is not unique to law enforcement, as women in construction trades, historically male-dominated turf, have asserted. One example is a woman ironworker who reported that she and her coworkers feel that no matter how skilled they are, they still have to prove themselves over and over again.

Most women police officers have a different style of policing—"service-oriented style"—and they see their roles as peace restorers (Skolnick & Bayley, 1986). Male officers typically view their roles as crime fighters also involved in maintaining the brotherhood. The following is a summary of research related to policing styles and gender conducted both in the United States and internationally:

> [W]omen police officers rely on a style of policing that uses less physical force. They are better at defusing and de-escalating potentially violent confrontations with citizens and less likely to become involved in problems with use of excessive force. Additionally, women officers often possess better communication skills than their male counterparts and are better able to facilitate the cooperation and trust required to implement a community-policing model. In an era of costly litigation, hiring and retaining more women in law enforcement is likely to be an effective means of addressing the problems of excessive force and citizen complaints. As an additional benefit, female officers often respond more effectively to incidents of violence against women—crimes that represent one of the largest categories of calls to police departments. Increasing the representation of women on the force is also likely to address another costly problem for police administrators—the pervasive problem of sex discrimination and sexual harassment—by changing the climate of modern law enforcement agencies. Because women frequently have different life experiences than men, they approach policing with a different perspective, and the very presence of women in the field will often bring about changes in policies and procedures that benefit both male and female officers. All of these factors can work to the advantage of those in the police profession and the communities they serve. (NCWP, 2002a)

Another study by the same organization in 2002 had similar findings. The executive summary provides a concise overview:

> Research from seven major U.S. police agencies has documented what many police and community leaders have known for a long time: women officers are

substantially less likely than their male counterparts to be involved in problems of excessive force. Whether citizen complaints, sustained allegations, or civil liability payouts are used as the measure, women officers are dramatically underrepresented in excessive force incidents. (NCWP, 2002b, p. 2)

The same report also reflected the following:

Given that women currently comprise 12.7% [2001] of sworn personnel in big city police agencies, we would expect that female officers in these agencies should be involved in approximately 12.7% of the citizen complaints, sustained allegations, or payouts for excessive force. Yet the data indicate that only 5% of the citizen complaints for excessive force and 2% of the sustained allegations of excessive force in large agencies involve female officers. Women also account for only 6% of the dollars that are paid out in court judgments and settlements for excessive force among these large agencies. (p. 2)

Captain Foster, 19-year veteran of the Fresno, California, Police Department, researched this issue, and his findings suggest that the differences in an officer's willingness to use force to resolve conflict may be explained by men being, in most cases, inherently stronger than women.

Some might suggest that male officers are more concerned with improving their physical characteristics [i.e., strength training and tactical skills] rather than their intellectual capacities [i.e., persuasion and negotiation skills]. This notion may be due to the belief that strength counts when persuasion and negotiation fail. Generally speaking, female police officers often rely on negotiation, persuasion, and effective communication to resolve conflict. ("Women in Policing," 2006, p. 8)

Foster's study suggests that most women who come into law enforcement with limited upper body strength or knowledge of arrest and control techniques develop physical strength and become proficient in the tactics of arrest over time. He asserts, however, that "female police officers never forget how to use their most valuable tool in law enforcement—their ability to prevent and/or defuse conflict rather than provoking it and/or responding to it" (pp. 8–9).

A Double Standard. Interviews with women officers for each of the editions of this book showed clearly that the majority felt they had to perform better than male officers just to be considered equal—a double standard. These women spoke of how they imposed pressures on themselves to perform up to or exceed the expectations of their male peers. (Note that minority, gay, and lesbian employees often express the same sentiment.) One woman officer explained that many women were using a community policing philosophy long before it became the practice of their agency. She mentioned that when she tried to do problem solving, she was criticized in her evaluations. Her supervisor rated her negatively for "trying too hard to find solutions to complainants' problems" and said she "spends too much time on calls explaining procedures" and "gets too involved" (Jones, 1993). Today, however, women police officers report that the double standard is less common because of the emphasis that law enforcement places on Community-Oriented Policing. Now this approach is seen as the norm and is expected of all officers (Jones, 2006).

Differential Treatment. Many women in law enforcement, when interviewed for prior editions of this text, indicated that they were treated differently than men by staff members and that they were frequently held back from promotions or special assignments in areas like special weapons and tactics, homicide investigations, and motorcycles because of the perception that these are "male" jobs. They reported feeling that they were also held back from training for these assignments and were not promoted at the same rate as men. Over the years, some change has occurred: more women officers are now serving in special assignment and showing no special problems with performance. Women are also being promoted to executive, managerial, and supervisory positions; however, their numbers in these positions are still low. Recall that the U.S. Department of Labor indicated that women in the workforce held half of all management, professional, and related occupations in 2004 (Women in the Labor Force, 2005). This is far from the case in U.S. law enforcement. According to data collected by the NCWP (2001, p. 3):

- Within large police agencies, sworn women currently [2001] hold 7.3 percent of Top Command positions and 9.6 percent of Supervisory positions. Sworn women of color hold 1.6 percent of Top Command positions and 3.1 percent of Supervisory positions.

- Within small and rural agencies, sworn women hold only 3.4 percent of all Top Command positions and 4.6 percent of all Supervisiory positions. Women of color represent less than 1 percent of both Top Command positions (0.3 percent) and Supervisory positions (0.4 percent).

Police executives must determine if their female officers are receiving equal opportunities for assignments and training that will provide the groundwork and preparation for their eventual promotion. They need to determine if female officers are applying for promotions in numbers proportionate to their representation in the department. If not, perhaps women officers need encouragement from their supervisors, mentors, and informal network associates. It is also possible that the promotion process disproportionately screens out female officers. Research shows that the more subjective the process is, the less likely women are to be promoted. The use of assessment center, "hands-on" testing is said to offer some safeguards against the potential for the perception of bias against women. Utilizing structured interviews and selecting interview board members who represent different races and both sexes can also minimize this risk. Many departments are now training interview board members on interviewing techniques. The *IWITTS* has developed a well-received half-day training session for supervisors, "Creating a Supportive Work Environment," to address issues of integration and retention of women. See the Website Resources at the end of this chapter.

Career versus Family. Women in law enforcement are faced with another dilemma—trying to raise a family and have a successful career, two goals that are often difficult to combine. Women, especially single parents, who had children when they entered law enforcement frequently find that they have difficulty balancing their commitments to family and work. If they had children after entering the occupation, they may be confronted with inadequate pregnancy and maternity-leave policies (see earlier discussion). In both cases, women often feel a sense of guilt, stress, and frustration in trying to both do well in a job and maintain a family. Progressive criminal law enforcement organizations offer innovative work schedules, modified duty assignments during pregnancy, child care programs, mentoring and support groups, and a positive work atmosphere for women. Such programs benefit all employees within the organization. Today, men are taking a more active role in parenting and family; therefore, child care, creative work schedules, and even maternity leave should be of importance to them as well.

Mentor and Informal Networking Programs for Women

Women's performance and attitudes can be enhanced if they have access to support and mentoring programs. There is a great deal of research on the topic of mentoring and networking for women as well as for minorities. Law enforcement management is well advised to consult these studies, the information from which will contribute to the successful creation of programs for women.

A *mentor* is described as an experienced, productive supervisor or manager (usually 8 to 10 years older than the employee) who relates well to a less experienced employee and facilitates his or her personal development for the benefit of both the individual and the organization. Usually, mentoring occurs in a one-on-one coaching context over a period of time through suggestions, advice, and support on the job. There are many reasons for law enforcement agencies to provide for or encourage the use of mentor and support programs. Studies over the years have found that women who had one or more mentors reported greater job success and job satisfaction than women who did not have a mentor.

A 2001 *Catalyst* (the newsletter of a nonprofit group by the same name that studies women's issues and business trends) reported on a study wherein women and men were surveyed on what they perceived as barriers to their advancement. Exhibit 2.5 shows that 70 percent of the women responding to the survey (compared to 38 percent of men) believed the lack of mentoring opportunities was a barrier to their advancement. A report ("Advancing Asian Women in the Workplace") released in 2003 by *Catalyst* stated that Asian American women also face difficult challenges in the workplace. "Many have trouble finding mentors or feel their managers don't understand their culture" ("Obstacles Hinder Minority Women," 2003, p. C1). The report mirrors one released earlier in 2003 about Latinas in business. Latinas and Asian American women are among the fastest-growing groups in the U.S. labor force.

Informal networks involve influential colleagues who can, because of their position or power within an organization, connect the employee with information, resources, or other contacts helpful to their promotion or special assignment prospects. The *Catalyst* Barriers series focuses on women's perception that lack of access to networks of influential colleagues is a key barrier to promotions and special assignments to women in the workforce. The report states:

> This issue is particularly pronounced for women of color who face "double exclusion" in the workplace, based on both their gender and race/ethnicity. In fact, lack of access to networks of influential colleagues underlies all major barriers identified by women of color, including lack of influential mentors or sponsors (as one needs connections with others to obtain mentors and sponsors); lack of company role models of the same racial/ethnic group (reflecting a shortage of similar others who might form part of an influential network); and lack of high-

	WOMEN	MEN
Lack of mentoring opportunities	70%	38%
Commitment to personal and family responsibilities	69%	53%
Exclusion from informal networks of communication	67%	25%
Lack of women role models	65%	35%
Failure of senior leadership to assume accountability for women's advancement	62%	22%
Stereotyping and preconceptions of women's roles and abilities	61%	27%
Lack of opportunities to take on visible and/or challenging assignments	54%	12%
Lack of significant general management or line experience	51%	47%

Exhibit 2.6   Barriers to Women's Advancement
Source: Catalyst Newsletter, July 2001.

> visibility assignments (which are often facilitated by personal relationships with those wielding influence). ("Connections that Count," 2006, p. 1)

Exhibit 2.6 shows that 67 percent of women identified exclusion from informal networks of communication (compared to 25 percent of men) as a barrier to advancement

Several associations provide an organized voice for the interests of women in policing: the International Association of Women Police (IAWP), the National Association of Women Law Enforcement Executives (NAWLEE), and the National Center for Women and Policing (NCWP). The NAWLEE focuses on helping women to strengthen their leadership roles in policing, while the NCWP focuses on growth and leadership. However, while these organizations provide excellent resources, they cannot take the place of departmental, in-house mentoring programs or informal networks for women.

In both *Catalyst* Barriers surveys, Latinas and Asian American women said they encounter stereotypes in the workplace. Asian women said they often feel overlooked by their companies' diversity programs, in part, because they are labeled "overachievers" who don't require specific diversity efforts. Both reports suggest managers should encourage more experienced Asian American women and Latinas to serve as mentors for younger women, as well as make more of an attempt to understand the cultural background of their diverse workforce.

The Transition of Women into Law Enforcement

The survey administered by Seklecki and Allen (2004), mentioned earlier, reports interesting findings pertaining to the transition of women into law enforcement:

> Our research indicates that female law enforcement officers have made a promising transition from their professional status some thirty years ago. While still a minority, they view themselves quite often as equally, if not more capable than their male peers, and upon completion of training, the overwhelming majority of women officers are intent to stay on their present career path. In addition, we

must note the perception of working conditions has clearly improved as agencies have become more harassment conscious, while remaining undeniably male influenced. The study respondents confirm the continued presence of the traditional "male behaviors"; however, most female officers, surprisingly, do not take great exception to them. This suggests the female officers entered the profession expecting to encounter these behaviors and consider such behavior normal to the work setting. (p. 39).

GAY MEN AND LESBIANS IN LAW ENFORCEMENT

The terms *lesbian, gay, bisexual,* and *transgender* are used in our discussion of sexual orientation. These terms are defined here as follows: gay: a male homosexual; homosexual: characterized by sexual attraction to those of the same sex as oneself; lesbian: a homosexual woman; bisexual: the ability to be sexually attracted to both men and women. The term transgender covers a range of people, including heterosexual cross-dressers, homosexual drag queens, and transsexuals who believe they were born in the wrong body. There are also those who consider themselves to be both male and female, or intersexed, and those who take hormones and believe that is enough to complete their gender identity without a sex change. The acronym LGBT is used throughout this section to stand for lesbian, gay, bisexual, and transgender.

Most authors and police administrators group "gay" and "lesbian" together as if the experiences of the two groups are identical. However, nowhere is the dichotomy more visible than within law enforcement. Stemming from persistent sexism, many officers still assume that "macho" women are lesbians and that stereotypically "feminine" women are heterosexual, although such mapping of gender roles onto sexual orientation is frequently erroneous. This topic is discussed later in this chapter.

Policy versus Practice

As the issue of sexual orientation has come of age in the public consciousness due in part to movies and television shows (such as *Will & Grace* and HBO's *Six Feet Under,* which featured a gay police officer), so have gay and lesbian individuals become more willing to stand up against discrimination.

The past decade and a half has seen the removal of the explicit ban against employing gay men and lesbians by most law enforcement agencies. Some agencies did so out of fear of litigation and negative publicity, some because research indicated gay men and lesbians should not be excluded from law enforcement professions. Despite this apparently dramatic paradigm shift, the reality remains that the vast majority of law enforcement agencies, including many of those within urban areas with large, openly gay populations, find ways to surreptitiously avoid hiring or retaining openly gay men. To a lesser extent, this includes openly lesbian individuals. The rejection of homosexuals in law enforcement by some agencies continues despite studies that have shown that the presence of openly LGBT personnel enhanced service and did not negatively impact morale or unit cohesion in integrated police departments (e.g., San Diego Police Department; Belkin & McNichol, 2002) and armed forces (e.g., Israel, Britain, and Australia; Belkin & McNichol, 2002). However, a study by Amnesty International USA published in 2005 found:

Anecdotal evidence suggests there are relatively few LGBT officers who are in a position to be open about their sexual orientation or gender identity, although LGBT police officer associations exist in some larger cities; for example, GOAL in New York. However, Amnesty International is only aware of a fairly small number of LGBT officers who serve on police forces in the U.S. . . . Only four of 29 responding departments in Los Angeles; New York, New York; Fargo, North Dakota; and Salt Lake City, Utah, reported any kind of affirmative action hiring practice for LGBT individuals. ("Stonewalled," 2005, p. 81)

A deputy chief of a large department, one of the highest-ranking openly gay officers, told *Frontiers* that in terms of how gay and lesbian officers are treated currently, "The discrimination is much more sophisticated than discrimination in the past . . ." (*Brooke,* 2005, p. 18). Lawsuits and judgments also seem to verify discrimination as well as covert bans against employing LGBT persons, as evidenced by the following:

- "Lesbian gets $2.8 million for harassment at sheriff's office" (2004, p. 33.)
- "Verdicts and Settlements: Discrimination, Police Negligence, $490,000, *Alan Weiner v. Los Angeles Police Department.*" Weiner sued the police department for harassment and discrimination, claiming he was discriminated against because of his sexual orientation. He contended that the department had a policy and practice of treating gay officers differently from its straight officers. ("Verdicts and Settlements," 2005 p. 18).

Public Relations versus Recruitment

According to Mitchell Grobeson (2003, 2006), a retired Los Angeles Police Department sergeant who is gay, many urban law enforcement agencies engage in public relations campaigns as substitutes for actual recruitment efforts. His observation is that many city or county personnel departments place recruitment advertisements in the gay and lesbian media or assign officers to attend gay and lesbian events such as gay pride festivals. However, he believes that these agencies are only providing "lip service," while avoiding actual recruitment. Law enforcement administrators seeking to have a workforce on parity with their community need to be cognizant of artificial barriers. To ensure equal opportunity, it is important to conduct applicant tracking, in which applicant information is taken at an event and contact with the applicant is maintained to determine if the applicant is hired or at which point in the process he or she is disqualified. If a disproportionate number of these applicants are failing during a specific part of the hiring process, such as oral interviews, background investigations, or polygraph exams, then administrators must be able to capture this information starting from the original point of contact. Further, this approach can help determine if committing resources for LGBT events or advertisements is an effective use of public funds. Another area to monitor to determine if a department provides equal opportunity is the number of openly gay and lesbian officers who voluntarily participate in events with the LGBT communities and the number who are willing to be named when interviewed by the mainstream media.

Department personnel who cite numbers of gays and lesbians on a police force are usually viewed skeptically by LGBT officers and by LGBT community organizations. While the trend between 2001and 2006 has been for many gay and lesbian officers to become more comfortable being open to select coworkers, for most gay male police officers, it is still clear that choosing to be open about their sexual orientation places both their career and their lives in jeopardy. A *Los Angeles Times* reporter, in an exhaustive investigative study, spent two years attempting to interview the "250 openly gay officers" cited by the Los Angeles Police Department as being members of the department. She was able to locate and interview only 16 officers, most of whom were not openly gay and virtually all of whom stated that "being openly gay jeopardizes careers" and subjects them to discrimination and harassment ("LAPD Still Biased," 2004).

The Controversy

Some police officers view openly gay and lesbian individuals as extremist militant types who publicly display their sexuality in offensive or socially unacceptable ways. This is a stereotype; most heterosexuals do not draw attention to their sexual preference, and neither do most homosexuals. Concerns about homosexuals in the military or in law enforcement include beliefs that gay soldiers or police officers will walk hand in hand, dance together at clubs, make passes at non-gay colleagues, and display aspects of their private lives (as well as seek benefits for gay marriages). These arguments for bans are not based in reality, however, since most gays in the military and the criminal justice system are as work-oriented as their heterosexual colleagues. They do not wish to provoke anyone in the system; rather, like most other officers, homosexual officers want to accomplish their missions, work special assignments, be promoted, and avoid confrontation. In fact, gay and lesbian officers and military personnel are much less likely than their heterosexual counterparts to engage in even such mundane acts as putting a picture of their partner on their desk or posted inside their locker. Gay and lesbian officers are no different from others in wanting to support the disciplinary processes, and they believe that any inappropriate conduct should be handled with proper discipline. Research on the subject of homosexuals in the military and in law enforcement at the beginning of the 21st century concluded that the presence of gays and lesbians has not caused morale to drop in either setting. The research also determined that there were no negative consequences within urban police departments that adopt nondiscrimination statutes and actively recruit and hire homosexual officers. One comprehensive study of gays and lesbians in a large police agency was designed to discover whether the integration of self-disclosed gay and lesbian officers has undermined the organizational effectiveness of the San Diego Police Department (SDPD).

> Based on an analysis of prior research and a 3-day site visit, our findings are that a quiet process of normalization has reduced much of the emotional charge that heterosexual officers originally anticipated. Although integration has proceeded largely uneventfully, subtle forms of discrimination do persist, and gay officers who do not already enjoy respect may face challenges. Despite these uneven effects, integration has enhanced cohesion as well as the SDPD's standing with the communities it serves. (Belkin & McNichol, 2002, p. 63)

The report indicates that the integration of gay men and lesbians into law enforcement has been similar to the earlier experiences of women and minorities. Initial reactions among officers within the organization and some prominent community members were often negative, and longstanding work cultures were slow to change (Belkin & McNichol, 2002). Research on police culture through the early 1990s depicts a work environment that was seeking to reinforce traditional notions of masculinity and describes casual remarks ridiculing or stereotyping homosexuals as being commonplace in formal and informal settings (Belkin & McNichol, 2002, p. 64). The report's key finding is that:

> the increasing participation of self-disclosed homosexuals in the SDPD has not led to any overall negative consequences for performance, effectiveness, recruiting, morale, or other measures of well-being. Even though incidents of harassment and discrimination continue and new internal tensions have arisen concerning the integration of homosexuals, self-disclosed gay personnel, their peers and commanders, and outside observers all agree that disruptive incidents continue to decline in frequency and are usually handled effectively through both informal and formal channels. (Belkin & McNichol, 2002, p. 65)

The researchers noted that complaints by gay and lesbian officers at the San Diego Police Department about harassment or discrimination are extremely low, resulting in underestimates of the actual number of occurrences. They hypothesize that the low number is related to the fact that closeted personnel fear being identified as gay and are reluctant to complain. The study also suggests, however, that another reason might be that, as in most departments, the work culture of the San Diego Police Department strongly emphasizes the informal and discreet resolution of problems at the unit level. According to the study, the number of self-described gay and lesbian officers in the department has grown from about five in 1992 to 50 out of 2,100 in 2003, scattered among patrol, investigations, the SWAT team, community relations, and training. The report concludes that:

> concern over working with openly gay men and lesbians has subsided as day-to-day interactions with gay colleagues become more commonplace. In many divisions, for straight and gay people alike, sexual orientation issues are relatively unimportant vis-à-vis the daily challenges of being a cop. Although isolated comments and misconduct may occur, the professional working environment and strong support for equal treatment from headquarters tend to diffuse their frequency and significance. . . . Virtually all respondents believe that the increasing, taken-for-grantedness [sic] of gay cops reflects in part the more tolerant values of new recruits coming into the department. Younger cohorts of recruits have brought with them more diverse views and greater comfort levels with gay issues than in years past, and EEO policies and training programs are allowing for more candid give-and-take as recruits wrestle with uncertainties over how to work with gay people. (Belkin & McNichol, 2002, p. 76)

Differences in Treatment of Gay versus Lesbian Officers

Many law enforcement professionals have voiced opinions that because of the "macho" requirements of police work, a double standard exists with respect to the way gay and lesbian officers are viewed. The traditional male dominance of the profession has made it difficult for many male officers to accept that women or gay men are equally able to perform the same tasks they do. They view their work as an occupation for only the "strongest and the toughest." Male officers' self-esteem can be threatened by the ability of women and gay men to do "their" job. (This issue is discussed further in this chapter under "Women in Law Enforcement.")

According to Grobeson, there has been a trend of acceptance of "macho" lesbians into law enforcement. Many male officers are more accepting of lesbian officers, particularly those who are not openly homosexual, than they are of heterosexual women. It appears that male officers are more fearful that "feminine" women will not provide them with sufficient backup where physicality is required. They are more willing to rely on lesbian officers, whom they stereotype as being macho and athletic. Grobeson believes that there is still a great deal of discrimination directed toward women who break the cultural mores and choose to be open or apparent about their sexual orientation.

In addition, the pervasive stereotype of gay men as effeminate remains a factor in most officers' bias against the hiring of and working with gay men. Allowing openly gay men to serve as officers is perceived by many as threatening to the macho image of police work: if a gay man can successfully complete the necessary tasks, their job is therefore less macho. Further, those officers whose self-image is based on their job, perceiving themselves as "John Wayne," are generally the most uncomfortable with the concept of working with gay officers.

Grobeson asserts that gay men are relegated to the least desirable status of any minority group in terms of acceptance in police culture. Homophobic jokes and nicknames, for example, are still prevalent locker room banter, whereas racial epithets have been mostly eliminated. One stereotype characterizes effeminate men as unworthy of trust as partners, despite that many gay officers are military combat veterans with awards and accolades for bravery, heroism, and service under fire. There are also many homosexual officers in agencies of all sizes who have received medals or citations for their valor. Officers suspected of being homosexual are often teased, belittled, or openly harassed with little or no intervention from supervisors or managers. Some newly hired homosexual officers have reported that they believe it is important to stay "in the closet" until they have proven to their peers and supervisors that they are effective officers.

Gay and lesbian officers often identify more readily with their fellow officers than they do with members of the LGBT community. Many gay and lesbian individuals still view law enforcement as society's arm of social control. With many law enforcement officers still hostile toward gay men and lesbians, LGBT officers feel forced to choose a side, particularly when it comes to the issue of vice enforcement. Therefore, gay and lesbian officers are often accepted by neither the gay community nor their peers.

Gay male officers also assert that management in some law enforcement agencies serving large LGBT populations gives preferential treatment to lesbian officers. Although the trend was first noted in the 1980s, between 2000 and 2006 it became more apparent. Law enforcement managers who were willing to be honest about the subject have admitted that lesbian officers are chosen for specific specialized assignments over both their heterosexual counterparts (male and female) and gay male officers. These assignments have included recruitment, background investigation, internal affairs/ management control, community relations, and liaisons from the chief's office. There have been two reasons cited for this reverse discrimination: first, managers get a "3-for" in which their selection is approved by personnel departments and policymakers because it fulfills affirmative action obligations in as many as three protected categories: gender, sexual orientation, and, often, ethnicity or race. Second, law enforcement managers believe that by involving lesbian officers in both the disqualification of gay male applicants and in disciplinary actions against gay officers, they have decreased their liability with regard to claims of bias based upon sexual orientation. In short, lesbian officers are used against gay men, as well as their fellow lesbian officers, to avoid claims of sexual orientation discrimination or harassment (Grobeson, 2006).

The Transition of LGBT Individuals into Law Enforcement

Problems will inevitably surface within law enforcement agencies as gay and lesbian officers "come out of the closet." Many organizations and employees will be hesitant to welcome such a major change and may resist it unless measures are taken to allay their fears. Officers thought to be or who are openly gay or lesbian may encounter discriminatory treatment and/or hostility because of other employees' negative stereotypes and attitudes. People without proper education on acquired immune deficiency syndrome (AIDS), for example, may be afraid of AIDS transmission. This and other fears may mean that gay men will have an even more difficult time in assimilating into departments than ethnic or racial minorities, heterosexual women, or lesbians.

As more openly gay and lesbian officers are recruited and hired, the organizational atmosphere will undoubtedly become more tolerant. Individual and group prejudices and assumptions, for example, will be challenged. Because of the small number of openly gay and lesbian officers in law enforcement today, there are currently no policies dealing specifically with inappropriate displays of sexuality; obviously, discipline would have to be applied equally to both gay and lesbian and heterosexual officers who behave unprofessionally. Among gay and lesbian law enforcement officers, however, there is a strong desire to conform to the norms of the organization and to prove their worth as members of that organization. They seldom engage in behaviors that would challenge those norms or shock or offend fellow officers. Law enforcement agencies should have written policies to assist gay and lesbian officers' transition into the department as well as operational plans to promote employee acceptance of these officers.

With notable exceptions such as the San Francisco Sheriff's Department, the San Francisco Police Department, and the New York Police Department, the presence of openly gay and lesbian officers within law enforcement is relatively new. As such, it is still critically important that agency officials establish openly gay and lesbian liaisons to the LGBT community. This assignment provides role models to qualified LGBT persons who may desire a career in law enforcement. Critically, with the increasing prevalence of hate crimes, it also gives an agency the ability to provide victims with LGBT officers, whose expertise and compassion will likely elicit both cooperation and information that could impact the outcome of the investigation. Police officials realized years ago the invaluable service of providing women rape victims the comfort of female officers in conducting the interview. That need is duplicated when it comes to LGBT hate crime victims. Moreover, with the reticence of LGBT crime victims to come forward due to the real or perceived bias of law enforcement personnel, the availability of an LGBT officer helps negate the fear of "double victimization." In the end, the community as a whole, as well as the law enforcement agency, benefit from the presence of such forthright and honest personnel.

Policies against Discrimination and Harassment

Unfortunately, there have been many incidents in which gay and lesbian officers have been subjected to discrimination or harassment by fellow officers or supervisors. Many of these incidents of discrimination and harassment, in large and small law enforcement agencies across the nation, have resulted in lawsuits, and some ended in large monetary judgments against the agency. One of the country's top law enforcement executives, William J. Bratton, who has been the chief executive of police agencies in New York, Boston, and Los Angeles, admitted that gay and lesbian officers have been forced to sue to end discrimination ("L.A. May Settle," 2004, p. 25).

The chief executive must establish departmental policies and regulations regarding LGBT officers. These policies must clearly state that discrimination, harassment, and failure to assist fellow LGBT officers are unacceptable and will result in severe discipline. The chief executive must obtain the support of his or her supervisors and managers to ensure that the intent of these rules, policies, and procedures is clear and that all employees adhere to these regulations. All employees must be held accountable, and those who do not support these antidiscrimination policies should not be promoted or awarded special assignments. Department executives must be aware that gay and lesbian officers might not report victimization by other employees. For example, one independent investigation determined that 64 percent of gay and lesbian employees stated they would fear retaliation if they made a complaint against another officer for discrimination or harassment. A gay law enforcement officer told Amnesty International:

> If someone were to use words like "n——r" or "spic," they would be immediately disciplined. However, if they use the word "faggot," generally nothing happens to them. Discipline only happens if someone steps forward, complains, and says they are offended. Jokes and innuendoes in the locker room are still tolerated. This still happens rampantly across law enforcement. Racial jokes and slurs are immediately dealt with, regardless if there is a "complaining party" or not, but with gay jokes, if no one complains, no one is disciplined ("Stonewalled," 2005, p. 96).

If the state does not have one, the city, county, or law enforcement agency should adopt an antidiscrimination policy with regard to gays and lesbians in the workplace. As of June 2006, 17 states and Washington, D.C., along with 180 cities and counties, have passed laws prohibiting discrimination based on sexual orientation. Eight states and 82 cities and counties have also passed laws that prohibit discrimination based upon gender identity or expression (Human Rights Campaign Fund, 2006; Transgender Law & Policy Institute, 2006). City or county officials must support and possibly even champion such legislation. The policy should establish that:

- Sexual orientation is not a hindrance in hiring, retention, or promotion.
- Hiring is based solely on merit and all individuals meet objective standards of employment.
- Hiring is done on the basis of identical job-related standards and criteria for all individuals.

Law enforcement managers and supervisors must routinely check to ensure that this policy is being carried out as intended.

Training on Gay, Lesbian, and Transgender Issues

Cultural awareness programs that train department personnel on diversity within communities and in the workforce must also educate employees on LGBT issues. The training should address and demonstrate the falsehoods of stereotypes and myths. It must also cover legal rights, including a discussion of statutes and departmental policies on nondiscrimination and the penalties for violating them. These penalties include liability for acts of harassment and discrimination. Often, involving openly gay or lesbian officers (from other agencies, if necessary) in these training programs provides the best outcome. Ideally, this training will enable employees to know the gay or lesbian officers they work with as human beings, reduce personal prejudices, and dispel false assumptions, and thus change behavior. This type of training furthers the ideal of respect for all people. A secondary benefit of this training is the decreased likelihood of personnel complaints and lawsuits by gay or lesbian employees or community members against a city, county, or individual officer.

For a nondiscrimination policy to be implemented effectively, managers must provide regular and ongoing training at all levels of their department (see curricula in Instructor's Manual). The RAND National Defense Research Institute conducted a historic study on the compatibility of homosexuality within the U.S. military, which was published in 1993 and is still the best resource on this subject today. The RAND study addressed the efficacy of types of training on LGBT issues relative to both military and paramilitary (law enforcement) organizations. The finding was one which had been supported by many law enforcement trainers, including those in the San Francisco Police Department, and was contrary to the positions maintained by LGBT community and professional groups. The report stated that because homophobic attitudes are present among the rank and file, and because sensitivity training and similar programs usually provoke resentment rather than tolerance, the emphasis on training is most successful when it focuses on strict standards of professional conduct and behavior. This is the strategic difference between "diversity" training (which is marked by role playing and command officer disciplinary statements) versus "sensitivity" training (which is what is usually presented by LGBT groups within the business and professional community) (Grobeson, 2006). Grobeson also points out that localized surveys have shown that due to the media, tolerance toward gay men and lesbians is increasing among the younger generations. The increasing tolerance may impact the ability to host effective recruit academy training on many LGBT issues, especially as young gay or lesbian recruit officers are gradually becoming more willing to be open about their orientation. Grobeson is quick to point out that such is not the case for in-service training for officers, with tenured veterans tending to be the most vocal opinion leaders. In time, Grobeson states, this tendency will even prove true for military veterans, who often comprise the primary hiring pool for law enforcement agencies. Our service members work alongside multinational troops that have now removed the barrier and allow openly gay and lesbian persons to serve in their country's military. These include NATO countries such as Britain, Canada, Australia, the Netherlands, and Israel (Center for the Study of Sexual Minorities in the Military, 2006).

Cultural diversity training, which is much more confrontational than sensitivity training but is not abrasive, challenges officers' current attitudes without being condescending. In measuring officers' attitudes, beliefs, feelings, and knowledge, this type of training has been shown to have a positive impact. The training uses simulated situations in which officers deal with partners who are gay. Managers and supervisors are required to handle situations in which a fellow officer is being harassed for perceived homosexuality. Such presentations are most successful when conducted by gay or lesbian officers who are experienced diversity trainers, but this is not to suggest that trainers will be qualified or successful merely because of their sexual orientation.

It is recommended that the training include discussion panels made up of local LGBT community members, business owners, service providers, and community groups, as well as gay youth and gay youth services providers. For supervisors and managers, additional panels comprising attorneys, including municipal attorneys who prosecute hate crimes and who specialize in defense work dealing with homosexual arrestees, HIV issues, and sexual orientation employment discrimination, should be provided.

In a recent nationwide study conducted throughout 2003 and 2004, Amnesty International contacted law enforcement agencies in large cities to determine specifically what training, if any, was done on LGBT issues and the type and results of the training. Training in question included academy recruit officer training as well as in-service (after graduation) training of law enforcement officers in each of the agencies contacted. As a follow-up, Amnesty International attempted to interview individuals involved with overseeing and providing the training, including law enforcement officials and community members and organizations. Sixty-nine percent (20 out of 29) of police departments responding to the survey reported that they provide training on issues relating to LGBT individuals or communities. Twenty-eight percent (8 out of 29) of police departments reported that they do not have any training on LGBT issues. It is important to note that the police departments surveyed are located in the largest cities and are more likely than smaller departments to develop training. Thus the problem may be more widespread than indicated by Amnesty International's survey, and their follow-up also determined that some agencies reported having had training on LGBT issues when that might not actually have been the case or that the training was inconsistent. In many of the agencies surveyed, the training provided was only during "roll call," which is probably the least effective manner to provide any type of training for anything except policy-specific management directives. The survey also discovered that, within those agencies responding, most did not cover such rudimentary training topics as (1) same-sex domestic violence, (2) LGBT hate crimes, (3) sexual assult of LGBT individuals, and (4) searches of transgender individuals ("Stonewalled," 2005, p. 92).

The police departments that stated they provided LGBT training were Birmingham, Alabama; Anchorage, Alaska; Los Angeles, California; Jacksonville, Florida; Honolulu, Hawaii; Chicago, Illinois; Lexington, Kentucky; Boston, Massachusetts; Jackson, Mississippi; Kansas City, Missouri; Las Vegas, Nevada; Manchester, New Hampshire; Albuquerque, New Mexico; New York, New York; Fargo, North Dakota; Portland, Oregon; Philadelphia, Pennsylvania; San Antonio, Texas; Salt Lake City, Utah; and Seattle, Washington. Amnesty International noted that in Washington, D.C., a liaison unit is staffed by four full-time officers and 10 volunteers. This Gay and Lesbian Liaison Unit (GLLU) is involved in the academy training and offers one hour per year of mandated in-service training.

Police officers are the protectors of individuals in a diverse society that includes LGBT people. Although we recognize that police officers are human and entitled to their own personal beliefs, they cannot display biased behavior or engage in discriminatory actions. Police officers who are prejudiced against LGBT people must still uphold their rights. When prejudice or bias by an officer results in an overt discriminatory act, he or she must be appropriately punished. Officers also cannot remain silent if they witness a harassing or discriminatory act or crime of any kind committed by fellow employees. These same officers must maintain a good working relationship with peers who may be different than themselves. Police officers represent the entire community. Any act they commit while on duty (or off) can bring dishonor not only to them but also to their agency, the community they serve, and the entire profession of law enforcement.[1]

Support Groups for Lesbian, Gay, Bisexual, and Transgender Officers

LGBT officers benefit from support groups and peer counselors in their own or neighboring police agencies. In the early 1980s, openly gay and lesbian officers formed networks of support within the San Francisco Sheriff's Department. In the late 1980s, the San Francisco and New York City police departments, along with other agencies, assisted gay and lesbian officers in forming support groups. In the early 1990s, chapters of the Golden State Peace Officers Association (founded in San Francisco) and the Gay Officers Action League (founded in New York) were established in southern California to assist officers there. In addition to networking opportunities, the groups provide mentoring and support for their members. Heterosexual employees who support the rights of LGBT personnel have also joined as members and associate members of these organizations. It is important that agency executives and managers provide opportunities for LGBT individuals to not only enter into law enforcement careers but also assimilate comfortably into the organization.

THE CHIEF EXECUTIVE

The chief law enforcement executive should follow specific guidelines to meet the challenge of policing a pluralistic community. As emphasized previously, he or she must first effectively manage the diversity within his or her own organization. Progressive law enforcement executives are aware that before employees can be asked to value diversity in the community, it must be clear that diversity is valued within the organizations. Managing differences in the law enforcement workplace is therefore of high priority.

> Perhaps the biggest challenge facing police executives of the 21st century will be to develop police organizations that can effectively recognize, relate and assimilate the global shifts in culture, technology and information. Changing community expectations, workforce values, technological power, governmental arrangements, policing philosophies, and ethical standards are but a sample of the forces that must be understood and constructively managed by the current

---

[1]For more information on conducting diversity training, refer to the Instructor's Manual for this textbook, which offers suggestions for a cultural diversity training program that includes LGBT awareness.

and incoming generation of chief executives. ("Police Leadership in the 21st Century," 1999)

Executive leadership and team building are crucial to managing a pluralistic workforce and establishing good minority–community relations. The chief executive must take the lead in this endeavor by:

- Demonstrating commitment.
- Developing strategic, implementation, and transition management plans.
- Managing organizational change.
- Developing police–community partnerships (community-based policing).
- Providing new leadership models.

Demonstrate Commitment

The organization must adopt and implement policies that demonstrate a commitment to policing a diverse society. These policies must be developed with input from all levels of the organization and community. The chief executive must reflect the imperative to value diversity and treat all persons with respect. His or her personal leadership and commitment are the keystones to implementing policies and awareness training within the organization and to successfully building bridges to the community. One of the first steps is the development of a "macro" mission statement for the organization; it should elaborate the philosophy, values, vision, and goals of the department to foster good relationships within a diverse workforce and community. All existing and new policies and practices of the department must be evaluated to determine how they may affect women, members of diverse ethnic and racial groups, gay men, lesbians, bisexuals, and transgender employees on the force. Recruitment, hiring, and promotional practices must be reviewed to ensure that there are no institutional barriers to particular groups in an agency. The chief executive must stress, via mission and values statements, that the agency will not tolerate discrimination, abuse, or crimes motivated by hate against protected classes within the community or within the agency itself. The policy statements should also include references to discrimination or bias based on physical disability or age.

The executive must use every opportunity to speak out publicly on the value of diversity and to make certain that people both inside and outside the organization know that upholding those ideals is a high priority. He or she must actively promote policies and programs designed to improve community relations and use marketing techniques to sell these programs, both internally and externally. Internal marketing is accomplished by involving senior management and the police association in the development of the policies and action plans. The chief or sheriff can use this opportunity to gain support for these policies by demonstrating the value of community support to increasing both the department's effectiveness and the officers'. External marketing is accomplished by involving representatives of community-based organizations in the process.

Police leaders must institute policies that develop positive attitudes toward a pluralistic workplace and community even as early as the selection process (see discussion in Chapter 3). During background interviews, polygraphs, and psychological exams, candidates for law enforcement employment must be carefully screened. The questions and processes can help determine candidates' attitudes and beliefs and, at the same time, make them aware of the agency's strong commitment to a diverse workforce.

Develop Strategic, Implementation, and Transition Management Plans

Textbooks and courses that teach strategic, implementation, and transition management planning are available to law enforcement leaders. The techniques, although not difficult, are quite involved and are not the focus of this book. Such techniques and methodologies are planning tools, providing the road map that the organization uses to implement programs and to guide the agency through change. Action plans that identify specific goals and objectives form an essential component. These plans include budgets and timetables and establish accountability—who is to accomplish what by when. Multiple action plans involving the improvement of police–community relations in a diverse society would be necessary to cover such varied components as policy and procedures changes; affirmative action recruitment (where legal), hiring, and promotions; cultural awareness training; and community involvement (i.e., community-based policing).

Manage Organizational Change

The department leadership is responsible for managing change processes and action plans. This is an integral part of implementation and transition management, as discussed previously. The chief executive must ensure that any new policies, procedures, and training result in increased employee responsiveness and awareness of the diversity in the community and within the organization's workforce. He or she must require that management staff continually monitor progress on all programs and strategies to improve police–community relations. Additionally, the chief must ensure that all employees are committed to those ideals. Managers and supervisors need to ensure application of these established philosophies and policies of the department, and they must lead by example. When intentional deviation from the system is discovered, retraining and discipline should be quick and effective. Employees (especially patrol officers) must be rewarded and recognized for their ability to work with and within a pluralistic community. The reward systems for employees, especially first- and second-line supervisors, would recognize those who foster positive relations with individuals of different gender, ethnicity, race, or sexual orientation both within and outside the organization. As we have illustrated, the chief executive, management staff, and supervisors are role models and must set the tone for the sort of behavior and actions they expect of employees.

Develop Police–Community Partnerships

Progressive police organizations have adopted community-based policing as one response strategy to meet the needs and challenges of a pluralistic workforce and society. The establishment of community partnerships is a very important aspect of meeting today's challenges. For example, a cultural awareness training component will not be as effective if police–community partnerships are not developed, utilized, and maintained. The chief executive must establish and maintain ongoing communication with all segments of the community. These lines of communication are best established by community-based policing (discussed in detail in Chapter 1).

Provide New Leadership Models

Leadership is exercised when one takes initiative, guides or influences others in a particular direction, and demonstrates how a process or procedure is performed. Leaders should possess a good balance of conceptual, technical, and professional competence and demonstrate good judgment and excellent people skills. Good leaders are not only creative change agents but also practical futurists, exercising foresight and the capacity to see the "big picture" and the "long view" (see McGregor, 1991; Sullivan, 2000; Tamayo, 1999). Today, as we transition into a new information age and multicultural work environment, leaders need to be both transformational and culturally sensitive. That is, such high performers innovate by:

- Transforming workplaces from the status quo to appropriate environments.
- Renewing organizations and becoming role models by transmitting intellectual excitement and vision about their work.
- Helping personnel to manage change by restructuring their mindsets and values.

Leaders help to improve their organizations by preparing the next generation of supervisors and professionals. They do this primarily through the human resource development program that they initiate and/or supervise (Harris, 2005). At a more personal level, they become mentors and coaches to high-performing personnel with potential to rise within the organization.

In terms of the intercultural aspect, such leaders deal with all persons fairly, regardless of gender, race, color, religion, sexual orientation, or cultural differences. A leader seeks to empower a more diverse workforce in law enforcement to be reflective of the communities served. Furthermore, culturally sensitive leaders cut across cultural barriers while combating prejudice, bigotry, and racism wherever found in the organization and the community. Police supervisors, for example, exercise this leadership through anticipatory thinking, strategic planning, creative decision making, and effective communication (Harris, 2005).

In the past, all methods or models of management and organizational behavior were based on implicit assumptions of a homogeneous, white male workforce. Even bestsellers such as *The One-Minute Manager* (Blanchard & Johnson, 1983) and *In Search of Excellence* (Thomas & Waterman, 1984) that continue to be useful management tools are based on that traditional assumption. Managers must learn to value diversity and overcome personal and organizational barriers to effective leadership, such as stereotypes, myths, unwritten rules, and codes (one of those being that the organizational role model is a white male). New models of leadership must be incorporated into law enforcement organizations to manage the diverse workforce.

Good leaders not only acknowledge their own ethnocentrism but also understand the cultural values and biases of the people with whom they work. Consequently, such leaders can empower, value, and communicate more effectively with all employees. Developing others involves acquiring or developing mentoring and coaching skills, important tools for modern managers. To communicate responsibly, leaders must understand the diverse workforce from a social and cultural context and be able to use a variety of verbal and nonverbal communication strategies with employees. Modern leaders are also familiar with conflict mediation in cross-cultural disputes.

To be leaders in the new workforce, most managers will have to unlearn practices rooted in old mindsets, change the way their organization operates, shift organizational culture, revamp policies, create new structures, and redesign human resource systems. The vocabulary of the future involves leading employees rather than simply managing them. People want to be led, not managed, and the more diverse the working population becomes, the more leadership is needed. This approach to leadership was echoed in the introduction to *Transcultural Leadership—Empowering the Diverse Workforce.* Transcultural leadership addresses a new global reality. Today productivity must come from the collaboration of culturally diverse women and men. It insists that leaders change organizational culture to empower and develop people. It demands that employees be selected, evaluated, and promoted on the basis of *performance and competency,* regardless of sex, race, sexual orientation, religion, or place of origin. Beyond that, leaders must learn the skills to enable men and women of all backgrounds to work together effectively (Simons, Vazquez, & Harris, 1993).

Management, to build positive relationships and show respect for a pluralistic workforce, must be aware of differences, treat all employees fairly (and not necessarily in identical ways), and lead. The differing needs and values of a diverse workforce require flexibility by organizations and their leaders. Modern leaders of organizations recognize not only that different employees have different needs but also that these needs change over time. To bridge cultural and racial gaps within their organizations must be a goal of law enforcement leaders.

SUMMARY

Officers who traditionally worked in predominantly white male workforces must learn to work with increasing numbers of women, gay men and lesbians, blacks, Hispanics, Asians, and others within our diverse society. In this chapter, we have suggested that to be effective in this new environment, officers must have knowledge of conflict resolution techniques to reduce racial and ethnic problems.

The chapter focused on concerns and issues of members of underrepresented ethnically and racially diverse groups as well as women and gay men and lesbians in law enforcement. The importance of support and mentoring programs for women and diverse groups was stressed. Such programs help them make transitions into new organizations, cope with stress, and meet their workplace challenges more effectively.

We also provided suggestions for law enforcement executives whose jurisdictions and workforce are pluralistic. Law enforcement leaders must be committed to setting an organizational tone that does not permit bigoted or discriminatory acts and must act swiftly against those who violate these policies. They must monitor and deal quickly with complaints both from within their workforce and from the public they serve.

DISCUSSION QUESTIONS AND ISSUES

1. ***Measuring Responsiveness to Diversity.*** Using the check-off and scoring sheet (Exhibit 2.3), determine how responsive your police department has been to the diversity of the jurisdiction it serves. If you are not affiliated with an

agency, choose a city or county police department and interview a command officer to determine the answers and arrive at a score. Discuss with the command officer what initiatives his or her department intends to undertake to address the issues of community diversity.

2. ***Defusing Racially and Culturally Rooted Conflicts.*** What training does the police academy in your region provide on defusing racially and culturally rooted conflicts? What training of this type does your local city or county law enforcement agency provide to officers? What community (public and private) agencies are available as referrals or for mediation of such conflicts? Discuss what training should be provided to police officers to defuse, mediate, and resolve racially and culturally rooted conflicts. Discuss what approaches a law enforcement agency should utilize.

3. ***Women in Law Enforcement.*** How many women officers are there in your local city or county law enforcement agency? How many of those women are in supervisory or management positions? Are any of the women assigned to nontraditional roles such as special weapons and tactics teams, motorcycle enforcement, bomb units, hostage negotiations, or community relations? Have there been incidents of sexual harassment or gender discrimination against women employees? If so, how were the cases resolved? Has the agency you are examining implemented any programs to increase the employment of women, such as flextime, child care, mentoring, awareness training, or career development? Has the agency been innovative in the recruitment efforts for women applicants? Discuss your findings in a group setting.

4. ***Diversity in Law Enforcement.*** Comment on the diversity in your local city or county law enforcement agency. What is the breakdown in your agency's hierarchy? For example, who holds supervisory or management positions? Have there been reported acts of discrimination against people of diverse backgrounds? Has the agency you are examining implemented any programs to increase the employment of minorities? Discuss your findings in a group setting.

WEBSITE RESOURCES

Visit these websites for additional information related to the content of Chapter 2.

Catalyst: http://www.catalyst.org

A research and advisory, nonprofit membership organization working with businesses and the professions to build inclusive environments and expand opportunities for women at work. Catalyst conducts research on all aspects of women's career advancement and provides strategic and web-based consulting services globally.

International Association of Chiefs of Police: http://www.theiacp.org

An online resource for law enforcement issues publications including "Recruitment/ Retention of Qualified Police Personnel: A Best Practices Guide," December 7, 2001.

International Association of Women Police (IAWP): http://www.iawp.org

A website for information about training conferences, careers, jobs, publications, and research pertinent to women in law enforcement.

Institute for Women in Trades, Technology and Science (IWITTS):
http://www.womenpolice.com

This website features fact sheets, news articles, and publications for departments on women and policing, including a free women in policing e-newsletter, which provides best practice information.

National Center for Women and Policing (NCWP): http://www.feminist.org

This website provides information concerning regional training seminars on recruiting and retaining women. It also is a resource for the latest research about women in policing and other critical issues. The organization has consultants to help agencies identify and remove obstacles to recruiting and retaining women.

National Association of Women Law Enforcement Executives (NAWLEE):
http://www.nawlee.com

The website contains resources, news, member directory, conference and training information, seminars, and an information exchange for women executives in law enforcement.

Vera Institute of Justice: http://www.vera.org

The Vera Institute of Justice works closely with leaders in government and civil society to improve the services people rely on for safety and justice. Vera develops innovative, affordable programs that often grow into self-sustaining organizations, studies social problems and current responses, and provides practical advice and assistance to government officials around the world. They have publications on many law enforcement subjects.

REFERENCES

Balkin, J. (1988). "Why Policemen Don't Like Policewomen." *Journal of Police Science and Administration, 16*(1).

Barriers to Women's Advancement. (2001, July). *Catalyst Newsletter.*

Belkin, Aaron, and Jason McNichol. (2002, March). "Pink and Blue: Outcomes Associated with the Integration of Open Gay and Lesbian Personnel in the San Diego Police Department." *Police Quarterly, 5*(1), 63–96.

Bell, Daniel. (1982). "Policewomen: Myths and Reality." *Journal of Police Science and Administration, 10*(1), 112.

Benson, Katy. (1992, August). "Black and White on Blue." *Police,* p. 167.

"Black Police Officers in the South Still Face Racism, UF Researcher says." (2004, March 18). *UF News.*

Blanchard, Kenneth H., and Spencer Johnson. (1983). *The One-Minute Manager.* New York: Berkeley.

Brooke, Aslan. (2005, March 1). "Gay Officers Allege Ongoing Sexual Orientation Discrimination at LAPD; Others Find Acceptance." *Frontiers,* p. 18.

Center for the Study of Sexual Minorities in the Military. (2006). Available: http://www.gaymilitary.ucsb.edu.

"Closing the Communications Gap Between the Hispanic Community and Law Enforcement." (2002, November 20). Office of Community Oriented Police.

"Connections that Count: The Informal Networks of Women of Color in the United States." (2006). *Catalyst.*

Equal Employment Opportunity Commission (2006). "Sex-based charges, FY1992–FY2005," http://www.eeoc.gov/stats/sex.html. Accessed 6/4/2006.

"Gender and excessive force complaints. (2006, Aug.). *Law and Order* (2006, July). *Law and Order*

Grobeson, Mitchell. (2003, 2006). Sergeant-retired, Los Angeles Police Department, California, personal communication.

Hall, Thomas. (1992). Sergeant, Virginia State Troopers, personal communication, October, 1992.

Hammond, Teresa, and Brian Kleiner. (1992). "Managing Multicultural Work Environments." *Equal Opportunities International, 11*(2).

Hampton, Ron. (2006, June). "Unfinished Business: Racial and Ethnic Issues Facing Law Enforcement II." Paper presented at a conference sponsored by the National Organization of Black Law Enforcement Executives and the Police Executive Research Forum, Reno, Nevada.

"Harassed Workers Who Quit Can Later Sue, Justices Rule." (2004, June 15). *Contra Costa Times,* p. A13.

Harris, Philip. (2005). *High Performance Leadership.* Amherst, Mass: HRD Press.

Hartmann Report (2000, August). City of Los Angeles Police Department Study. Independent Commission on the Los Angeles Police Department (1991). Summary: Racism and Bias. Los Angeles: Independent Commission, pp. 7–8.

"History of Woman in the Workforce." (1991, September 19). *Business Week,* p. 112. Human Rights Campaign Fund. (2006). Available: http://www.hrc.org.

Jones, Susan. (1993). Sergeant, Concord, California Police Department, personal communication.

Jones, Susan. (2003, 2006). Chief of Police, Healdsburg, California Police Department, personal communication.

"L.A. May Settle Discrimination Lawsuits Filed by Gay Police Officers." (2004, Dec. 30). *Gay & Lesbian Time,* p. 25.

"LAPD Still Biased, Gays Allege: Homosexual Officers Say That Despite a 1993 Pledge to End Discrimination, They Face Hostility, Slow Promotions, Stalled Careers." (2004, Nov. 25). *Los Angeles Times.*

"Lesbian Gets $2.8 Million for Harassment at Sheriff's Office." (2004, Nov 25) *Gay and Lesbian Times,* p. 33.

"Many U.S. Jobs Have Become Less Male-Dominated." (2005, April). Department of Labor, Bureau of Labor Statistics.

McGregor, E. B. (1991). *Strategic Management of Human Knowledge, Skills, and Abilities.* San Francisco: Jossey-Bass.

More, Harry. (1992). *Male-Dominated Police Culture: Reducing the Gender Gap.* Cincinnati, Ohio: Anderson Publishing, pp. 113–137.

"More Women Leaving the Labor Market." (2005, December 21). *Dallas Morning News,* p. C5.

National Center for Women and Policing. (2002a). *Equality Denied: The Status of Women in Policing.* Los Angeles: Author, pp. 1–17.

National Center for Women and Policing. (2002b). *Men, Women, and Police Excessive Force: A Tale of Two Genders.*

National Center for Women and Policing. (2002c). Survey on the Status of Women in Policing, 1997, 2000, 2001.

Nichols, D. (1995, Summer). "The Brotherhood: Sexual Harassment in Police Agencies." *Women Police,* pp. 10–12.

"Obstacles Hinder Minority Women." (2003, August 7). *Contra Costa Times,* p. C1.

RAND's National Defense Research Institute. (1993). *Sexual Orientation and U.S. Military Personnel. Policy, Options and Assessment.* Santa Monica, Calif.: RAND Institute.

Report recommends using military model to defuse racism in police departments. (1992, May 26). *New York Times,* p. A17.

Ross, Ruth, John Snortum, and John Beyers. (1982). "Public Priorities and Police Policy in a Bicultural Community." *Police Studies,* 5(1), 18–30.

Schulz, Dorothy M. (1995). *From Social Worker To Crime Fighter: Women in United States Municipal Policing.* Westport, Conn.: Praeger, p. 5.

Simons, George, Carmen Vazquez, and Philip Harris (1993). *Transcultural Leadership—Empowering the Diverse Workforce.* Houston, Texas: Gulf Publishing.

"Police Leadership in the 21st Century: Achieving and Sustaining Executive Success." (1999). Bobby D. Moody, President IACP.

Polisar, J., and Milgram, D. (1998). "Recruiting, integrating and retaining women police officers: Strategies that work". *Police Chief,* October, pp. 46–60.

President's Message: Diversity on the Force, (2006, May 31), International Association of Chiefs of Police, Chief Mary Ann Viverette President's Message, p.1

"Quick Facts on Nontraditional Occupations for Women". (2006, May 30). U.S. Department of Labor, Women's Bureau, p. 1.

Seklecki, Richard, and Rebecca Allen. (2004, March). *"A National Survey of Female Police Officers: An Overview of Findings."* A paper presented at the Academy of Criminal Justice Sciences Conference in Las Vegas, Nevada.

Skolnick, J., and Bayley, D. (1986). "The New Blue Line". *Police Innovation,* New York, Free Press.

Stonewalled: Police Abuse and Misconduct against Lesbian, Gay, Bisexual and Transgender People in the U.S. (2005). Amnesty International.

Sullivan, S. (2000). *Mastering Leadership* [Audiovisual workshop]. Amherst, Mass.: Human Resource Development Press.

Tamayo, R. (1999). "What Will Be the Leadership Training Subject Delivery System for Middle Managers by the Year 2003?" (Order 26-0539). Sacramento, Calif.: Post Commission.

Tearing Down the Wall: Problems with Consistency, Validity, and Adverse Impact of Physical "Agility Testing in Police Selection." (2003, Spring). National Center for Women & Policing, pp. 1–10.

Theiderman, Sondra. (1991). *Bridging Cultural Barriers for Corporate Success.* San Francisco: Jossey-Bass.

Toosi, Mitra. (2004, February). "Labor Force Projections to 2012: The Graying of the U.S. Workforce." *Monthly Labor Review.*

Transgender Law & Policy Institute. Available: http://www.transgenderlaw.org. Retrieved: June 2, 2006.

U.S. Department of Justice, Bureau of Justice Statistics: Census of Local Law Enforcement Agencies and Sheriffs Offices, 2003: May 2006, NCJ 194066. Washington D.C.

U.S. Bureau of Labor Statistics. (2005). Current Population Survey, Annual Averages (unpublished data).

"Verdicts and Settlements: Discrimination, Police Negligences, $490,000. Alan Weiner v. Los Angeles Police Department." (2005; June 6) *Dailey Journal,* p. 18.

Wells, James. (1987). "Crime and the Administration of Criminal Justice," in Gerald D. Jaynes and Robin M. Williams, eds., *A Common Destiny: Blacks and American Society,* Washington, DC: The National Academies Press, pp. 491–497.

"Women Land More Top Jobs, but Not Top Pay." (2003, March 25). *Contra Costa Times,* p. A16.

Women in the Labor Force: A Databook. (2005, May 13). U.S. Department of Labor, Bureau of Labor Statistics.

"Women Still Underrepresented in Law Enforcement." (2003, March 16). *Contra Costa Times,* p. A32.

"Workplace Issues" (2005). National Center for Women and Policing.

Chapter 3

Multicultural Representation in Law Enforcement: Recruitment, Retention, and Promotion

OVERVIEW

In this chapter we discuss recruitment trends and the probability that recruitment of women and minorities will be an ongoing challenge for law enforcement agencies. We also provide a brief historical perspective of women and minorities in law enforcement. We offer reasons for recruitment difficulties and strategies for success. The chapter includes a discussion of one of the most important paradigm shifts in law enforcement recruiting processes, Hiring in the Spirit of Service, considered an innovative tool for use in seeking, attracting, and hiring minorities and women. The retention and promotion of minorities and women are addressed in the final section of the chapter.

COMMENTARY

The following quotes draw attention to the recruitment crisis for law enforcement occupations and illustrate the importance of recruitment, hiring, retention, and promotion of women and minorities.

> The nature of policing has broadened to a more diverse range of missions requiring a complex set of skills from officers. Population shifts, particularly those that result in greater cultural diversity, create demand for police officers who have the ability to work with different types of people. The adoption of the community policing model requires departments to be more representative of and responsive to the communities served.
>
> In addition, responsibilities for law enforcement agencies at all levels are changing in the wake of the September 11, 2001, terrorist attacks. A new homeland security mission increases the demand for local police in many jurisdictions in the country.
>
> In short, the expanded responsibilities for local police require an expanded set of police skills, and perhaps a different type of officer. The population from which police agencies recruit has also changed in the past several decades. Some trends may restrict the potential labor pool while others may increase it. (Raymond, 2004)

> The law enforcement profession needs intelligent, not just educated, officers who can solve problems and accept racial and cultural diversity. In short,

agencies prefer smarter over tougher. Law enforcement is moving away from the "big tough cops" in favor of candidates, regardless of size, who possess qualities that mirror the tenets of the COP (community-oriented policing) and POP (problem-oriented policing) philosophies. Also, more and more, communities want service-oriented people with interpersonal skills as their guardians of justice. (Vest, 2001, p. 13)

When I became a law enforcement officer in 1979, women were severely underrepresented in policing. Unfortunately, despite the fact that 26 years later a woman is president of the IACP, only 12 to13 percent of the nation's police officers are women. These numbers represent an improvement over those of 30 years ago, but they are still far from where they need to be. The same can be said of many other underrepresented racial and ethnic groups. Things have gotten better, but we still have a long way to go. ("President's Message," 2006, pp. 1–2)

The Hiring in the Spirit of Service initiative explores ways to change the process of recruiting and hiring law enforcement officers. Most current applicants are drawn to law enforcement because of the spirit of adventure associated with the profession, and applicants who do not fit this model are often discouraged. "Hiring in the Spirit of Service" requires law enforcement to develop a selection process that not only attracts but also reaches out to other service-minded candidates. (COPS, 2006)

INTRODUCTION

Our society is becoming increasingly diverse. To recruit and retain a representative staff and provide effective services, therefore, law enforcement executives must have a clear understanding of their community and their own workforce. The recruitment and retention of qualified employees, and especially of women, blacks, Asians, Hispanics, and other diverse groups, continues to be a concern and a priority of law enforcement agencies nationwide. Many agencies are having difficulty finding qualified applicants, resulting in a general recruitment crisis, and it appears that this is the case regardless of the economic condition of state or local governments. The recruitment pool of eligible and qualified candidates is diminishing. The crisis is multidimensional and is discussed in detail in this chapter.

RECRUITMENT OF A DIVERSE WORKFORCE

The recruitment of women and members of diverse groups has been a concern and a priority of law enforcement agencies nationwide for a few decades. This is not a new issue in the history of U.S. law enforcement. A President's Crime Commission Report in 1967 recommended that more minorities be hired and that they receive opportunities for advancement. Soon after the Watts riot in Los Angeles, the 1968 Kerner Commission Report identified the underrepresentation of blacks in law enforcement as a serious problem. The report recommended improved hiring and promoting policies and procedures for minorities. The Warren Christopher Commission report on the Los Angeles Police Department, released soon after the 1992 riots following the first Rodney King trial, cited the problems of racism and bias within the LAPD. The commission recommended, among other things, improved hiring and promotions processes that would benefit all groups.

The U.S. Department of Justice collects information from criminal justice organizations and produces a report every three years. One part of the report profiles the demographic makeup of law enforcement agencies in the United States. Students interested in this makeup can contact the U.S. Department of Justice via their website listed in Website Resources at the end of this chapter. Information pertaining to the numbers of women and minorities in law enforcement is presented in Chapter 2.

Recruitment Crisis

Recruitment problems are affecting urban police departments nationwide and also in Canada. For a period of time during the late 1990s and into 2000, the United States experienced the lowest unemployment rate in 30 years (3.9%) because of a robust economy. There were plenty of jobs in law enforcement, but the number of applicants was substantially lower than in the past. Due to the employees' market, those seeking jobs could be very selective. Many jobs in private industry, especially high-tech jobs, came with high salaries, stock options, signing bonuses, company cars, year-end bonuses, and broader opportunities for advancement. Public-sector employers have difficulty competing with such incentives and opportunities in the private sector; thus public safety occupations seem less attractive. Court decisions (and pretrial settlements) against such companies as Coke, Texaco, and Wall Street's Smith Barney in race bias lawsuits also factored in to recruitment difficulties. U.S. firms scrambled to recruit and promote talented women and minorities. Many large companies, aware that the populations within their recruitment areas were diversifying, knew that their employee demographics had to match those of the world outside or they, too, would be subject to lawsuits and/or criticism. This is particularly true of companies that sell products or services to the public. Their recruitment efforts, therefore, focused on women and members of diverse groups. The wide-open market also made for transitory employees, causing retention problems for employers, especially those of trained employees. During this period, smaller law enforcement agencies lost their employees as larger agencies lured experienced officers away with promises of benefits. The effort was compared to the National Football League draft, in which everyone was competing for the same pool of qualified candidates.

The highly publicized scandals involving police departments in some major cities over the years also had a negative effect on law enforcement recruitment. Such scandals or actions of rogue officers tarnish the image of law enforcement and may discourage potential applicants. Also, because of a history of acrimonious relationships between members of the diverse community and the police, persons from those communities, the very people whom law enforcement seeks to attract, may shy away. These people may fear active disapproval from community peers for joining with the perceived enemy ("Innovations in Police Recruitment," 2001).

Another reason that young people are not applying for careers in law enforcement is related to the paramilitary organizational structure of most agencies. It has been suggested that the independent-minded youth of today are less tolerant of the rigid paramilitary hierarchy to which most police agencies still adhere. In addition, most young people do not like being micro-managed. For these reasons, fewer young people find policing an attractive profession.

Adding to the shortage of eligible candidates is the fact that almost one-third of high school students nationwide will drop out before graduating and that "lacking a diploma, dropouts are more likely to end up jobless, on welfare or behind bars" ("High School Dropout Rates," 2006). This is according to a report published by *Education Week.* The study also highlights the disparity between graduation rates among different ethnic groups. About 55 percent of Latino and half of black students do not earn a high school diploma as determined by the research. The minimum education requirement in law enforcement agencies across the country is a high school diploma, with some agencies requiring 2 years of college or more; thus the pool of applicants is reduced even further.

At the same time, departments in the United States and Canada are not fully staffed because many employees who had been hired in the police expansion wave of the 1960s and 1970s (the baby boomers) are retiring. As the baby-boom-era officers begin retiring at an accelerated rate, due in part to improved retirement benefits that became an industry standard during the early 2000s, the result is a shortage of people. An aging workforce puts pressure on the public agencies to find ways to attract and retain experienced professionals. Incentives must be provided, and they must be competitive with those offered by private industry.

Serious budget shortfalls in most local and state governments, which started in 2002 and extended into 2006, are another problem. Budget problems forced cities and counties to reduce law enforcement personnel through layoffs, attrition, and not increasing department size. Cities and counties in financial difficulty also had to reduce salaries and benefits (or the amount they paid toward same) and, in many cases, seasoned officers moved to other agencies or employers that met their financial needs. Since they are not at full strength, many cities and counties have had to use extensive amounts of overtime to cover shifts. Since 2001, and continuing to the present, shortages of law enforcement personnel within many agencies (and their recruitment pool) have been due in part to the call-up of military reserves to serve in Afghanistan and Iraq.

Whenever there is a recession causing layoffs, it creates a problem in maintaining a diverse workforce because cities and counties must layoff or fire those employees who were hired most recently. Women and people of diverse ethnic and racial groups, therefore, are usually the first to lose their jobs, canceling any gains made in achieving a multicultural and multiracial workforce, including women.

Another factor reducing the number of women entering law enforcement is their use of drugs. A 2004 National Survey on Drug Use and Health determined that teenage girls have caught up with their male counterparts in illegal drug use and alcohol consumption; thus fewer can pass public agency background investigations. Some agencies have had to ease limits on how often and how many years ago an applicant for law enforcement could have used certain drugs.

More women are also being incarcerated for offenses that make them ineligible for law enforcement careers. A report by the New York–based Women's Prison Association is the most comprehensive state-by-state breakdown of the huge increase in incarceration of women over the past 30 years. The report indicates that the number of female state inmates serving sentences of more than a year grew by 757 percent between 1977 and 2004, nearly twice the 388 percent increase for men during the same period of time ("States Vary on Imprisoning Women," 2006).

MINI CASE STUDY: OAKLAND, CALIFORNIA, POLICE DEPARTMENT

In 2006, the Oakland Police Department's chief of police, Wayne Tucker, indicated in an online website report that they were significantly under strength. With an authorized strength of 802, the agency was 100 short (12 percent below its budgeted allotment) and did not expect to be able to fill all the vacancies by the target date of early 2007. They were suffering an attrition rate of about 3.5 officers per month due to service and disability retirements. To combat this problem, they were conducting continuous recruiting and testing and overlapping police academies in order to recruit, hire, and train enough new police officers.

The chief said, "We are aggressively increasing our sworn strength, and we are competing in the hottest job market for law enforcement in the modern history of the state. The entire state is experiencing a shortage of police officers as the 'baby boomer' generation of police officers retires. This has been caused in large part by adoption of the 3 percent at 50 retirement program, which has become the standard in much of California.

"In this climate, the Office of Personnel and the Police Department have partnered in statewide recruiting efforts to attract the next generation of police officers. At the same time, the job of policing has become far more complex over the years. As a result, our recruiting efforts have a new focus in the education and healthcare fields, community organizations, 'homegrown' candidates and national resources" (Oakland PD, 2006, pp. 5–6).

Recruitment Difficulties

Cultural Diversity at Work, a newsletter addressing multicultural issues, presented a list of the 10 most frequent causes of the failure to attract and retain high-level minority and female employees. The following is a brief synopsis, still valid today, of those most pertinent to law enforcement:

1. ***Senior management is not sending the "diversity message" down the line.*** Senior management does not always demonstrate commitment in the form of value statements and policies emphasizing the importance of a diverse workforce.

2. ***Informal networking channels are closed to outsiders.*** Women and minorities often experience discomfort within the traditional all-white, all-male informal career networks, including extracurricular activities. For example, some women police officers are uncomfortable participating in police association activities that involve recreational gambling, fishing, sports activities, or the roughhousing that can take place at meetings.

3. ***In-house recruiters are looking in the wrong places.*** Recruiters must use different methods and resources than those they have traditionally used to find diverse candidates.

4. ***Differences in life experience are not taken into account.*** Some applicants, both women and minorities, will have had life experiences that differ from those of the traditional job candidate. For example, the latter has typically had some college experience, with a high grade point average, and is often single (and thus does not have the many responsibilities associated with marriage and children). On the other hand, many minority job candidates have had to work through school and are married and may have children. Therefore, their grade point averages may have suffered.

5. ***Negative judgments are made based on personality or communications differences.*** Although not everybody's style reflects cultural, racial, or gender characteristics, there are distinct differences in communication style and personality between women and minorities and traditional white-male job applicants. Communication style differences are especially apparent when English is the applicant's second language. Generally speaking, women are not as assertive as men in communication. Sometimes these factors can affect the outcome of a pre-employment interview and become barriers to a job offer.

6. ***The candidate is not introduced to people who are like him or her.*** It is important that the candidate or new hire meet people of the same gender, race, or ethnicity within the agency. A mentor or support group may be crucial to a successful transition into the organization.

7. ***Organizations are not able or willing to take the time to do a thorough search.*** Recruitment specialists indicate that searches for qualified minority and women candidates take 4 to 6 weeks longer than others. These searches take commitment, resources, and time.

8. ***Early identification is missing from the recruitment program.*** Programs that move students into the proper fields of study early on and that provide the education required for the job are essential. Examples of these programs include internships, scholarships, and police programs (e.g., police athletic league) that bring future job candidates into contact with the organization (Micari, 1993).

Recruitment Strategies

To build a diverse workforce, recruitment strategies used in the past will no longer be sufficient and will not provide agencies with high-quality applicants. In fact, a study, still useful today, commissioned by the International Association of Chiefs of Police (IACP) and completed in 1998, The Future of Women in Policing: Mandates for Action, (1998), reached the conclusion that "unfocused, random recruiting is unlikely to attract diversity. Targeted programs are more likely to do so." The study determined that approximately one in four departments (26 percent) have had policies and strategies in place to recruit women and that larger departments are about three times more likely than smaller ones to actively recruit female applicants. According to Kim Lonsway, research director for the National Center for Women and Policing (NCWP), women really need a special invitation to consider a career in law enforcement. In an article for the Center, she wrote that the message from agencies must be: "Yes, we want you, come apply" ("Woman Recruits," 2003). Agencies with the most success in recruiting women and minorities have had specific goals, objectives, and timetables in place; these policies must be established at the top level of the organization. At the same time, management must commit to not lowering standards for the sake of numbers and deadlines. The philosophy and procedures required are discussed in the following sections.

Commitment. Recruiting minority and women applicants, especially in highly competitive labor markets, requires commitment and effort. Police executives must communicate that commitment to their recruiting staff and devote the resources necessary to achieve recruitment goals. This genuine commitment must be demonstrated both inside and outside the organization. Internally, chief executives should develop policies and procedures that emphasize the importance of a diverse workforce. Affirmative action and/or programs that target certain applicants (where legal) will not work in a vacuum. Chief executives must integrate the values that promote diversity and affirmative action into every aspect of the agency, from its mission statement to its roll-call training. Externally, police executives should publicly delineate the specific hiring and promotion goals of the department to the community through both formal (e.g., media) and informal (e.g., community-based policing, networking with organizations representing the diverse groups) methods. While chief executives promote the philosophy, policies, and procedures, committed staff members, who are sensitive to the needs for affirmative hiring and promotions, carry them out. Executives should also build partnerships with personnel officials so that decisions clearly reflect the hiring goals of the department. It is recommended that police executives audit the personnel selection process to ensure that neither the sequencing of the testing stages nor the length of the selection process is hindering the objective of hiring women and minorities.

Although chiefs may be genuine in their efforts to champion diversity and affirmative action hiring, care must be taken that their policies and procedures do not violate Title VII of the Civil Rights Act of 1964. Also, agencies in states that have enacted laws prohibiting affirmative action hiring programs and the targeting of "protected classes" (e.g., California's Proposition 209, passed in 1996, which is discussed later in this chapter) must adhere to these regulations. A knowledgeable personnel department or legal staff should review policies and procedures prior to implementation.

Planning. A study by the NCWP, published in 2001 by the Bureau of Justice Assistance of the Department of Justice, offers recommendations for greatly increasing the pool of qualified female applicants. Among other suggestions, the study stressed the importance of making an assessment of your department's current recruitment practices and developing a strategic marketing plan. A strategic marketing plan would include the action steps that commit the objectives, goals, budget, accountability, and timetables for the recruitment campaign to paper. Demographic data should form one of the foundations for the plan, which must also take into account the current political, social, and economic conditions of the department and the community. To avoid losing qualified applicants to other agencies or private industry, the plan should provide for fast tracking the best candidates through the testing and screening processes. Fast tracking is an aggressive recruitment process wherein a preliminary, qualifying check quickly takes place concerning the driving, credit, and criminal history of the applicant before any other screening process occurs. Applicants who do not meet established standards are immediately notified. The remaining applicants are then interviewed by a trained, ranking officer or civilian holding the position for which he or she is applying.

Applicants earning a passing score on the personal interview immediately receive a letter advising them that they passed, thereby giving them tangible evidence that the agency is seriously considering hiring them. The letter also informs them that they must pass additional qualifying steps, including a background investigation, which must be commenced immediately. The applicant must complete the final testing within 10 days, or the agency may withdraw the offer. To streamline the process, background investigators have established blocks of time for other testing such as polygraphs and psychological and medical evaluations. Streamlining is important because in today's labor market, the best-qualified applicants will not wait for months while the testing proceeds at a slow pace; they will have been hired elsewhere.

The strategic recruitment plan should include an advertising campaign that targets:

- Colleges and universities
- Military bases and reserve units
- Churches, temples, synagogues, and other places of worship
- Gymnasiums, fitness and martial arts studios, athletic clubs, and the like

Participation of women and minority officers within the department in recruitment efforts is crucial (see "Recruiting incentives"), as is the involvement of groups and organizations that represent the target groups. If within the community there are high-profile minorities and women, such as athletes and business executives, they should be enlisted to promote police work as a career through media releases and endorsements on flyers and brochures.

The Fulton, New York, Police Department offers one example of how such planning can be accomplished. For them, newspaper advertising proved the most significant medium through which candidates learned about their department's police test, followed closely by television advertising. The department went a step further, however. They learned that 45 percent of candidates obtained police test packages from the police station and 33 percent from the personnel office, so they made test packages available 24 hours a day, 7 days a week at the station because the personnel office is only open 8:00 to 5:00 Monday through Friday (Spawn, 2003).

Resources. Adequate resources, including money, personnel, and equipment, must be made available to the recruitment effort. Financial constraints challenge almost every organization's recruitment campaign. The size or financial circumstances of an agency may necessitate less expensive—and perhaps more innovative—approaches. For example, many small law enforcement jurisdictions can combine to implement regional testing. One large county on the West Coast successfully formed a consortium of agencies and implemented regional testing three times per month for law enforcement candidates. To participate, each agency pays into an account based on the population of its jurisdiction. Alternatively, each agency can pay according to how many applicants it hired from the list. The pooled money is then used for recruitment advertising (e.g., billboards, radio, television, newspapers) and the initial testing processes (e.g., reading, writing, and agility tests, including proctors). The eligibility list is then provided to each of the participating agencies, which continue the screening process for applicants in whom they have an interest. Police agencies should not see other agencies as competitors with respect to recruiting. By combining their efforts, they may be able to:

- Save money (consolidate resources)
- Develop a larger pool of applicants
- Become more competitive with private industry and other public agencies
- Test more often
- Reduce the time it takes from application to hire

In terms of recruiting a diverse workforce, the second benefit listed—developing a larger pool of applicants—is central to reaching beyond the traditional applicant pool. Law enforcement agencies, in taking advantage of the Internet's global coverage, can post position openings in the effort to recruit individuals with a wide variety of backgrounds and skills. Agencies now commonly maintain their own websites describing their departments and offering information on jobs available, testing dates, and how to obtain applications. Department websites have been found to be valuable recruiting tools when used to highlight the work of women and minorities within an agency.

Selection and training of recruiters. A recruiter is an ambassador for the department and must be selected carefully. Police recruiters should reflect the diversity within the community and include women. Full-time recruiters are a luxury most often found only in large agencies. The benefit of a full-time recruiter program is that frequently the employees in this assignment have received some training in marketing techniques. They have no other responsibilities or assignments and can therefore focus on what they do and do it well. They develop the contacts, resources, and skills to be effective. Whether recruiters are full time, part time, or assigned on an as-needed basis, however, the following criteria should be considered when selecting them:

- Commitment to the goal of recruiting
- Belief in a philosophy that values diversity
- Ability to work well in a community policing environment
- Belief in and ability to market a product: law enforcement as a career
- Comfort with people of all backgrounds and ability to communicate this comfort
- Ability to discuss the importance of entire community representation in police work and the advantages to the department without sounding patronizing

Recruiters must be given resources (e.g., budget and equipment) and must have established guidelines. They must be highly trained with respect to their role, market research methods, public relations, and cultural awareness. They must also understand, appreciate, and be dedicated to organizational values and ethics. They must be aware and in control of any biases they might have toward individuals or groups of people who might be different from themselves.

Almost every state's Commission on Peace Officer Standards and Training (POST) has developed a course on the techniques and methods of recruitment. Large, progressive agencies (or a consortium of agencies) could develop an in-house program patterned after these model courses. The Institute for Women in Trades, Technology and Science (IWITTS) can provide resources and training programs on recruiting and retaining women. The organization conducts national workshops and also provides technical assistance to departments via personal contact or via the Internet. Their materials include a law enforcement environmental assessment tool (LEEAT) involving institutional checklists and data collection methods to help determine the best recruiting strategies for a particular law enforcement agency.

Recruiting incentives. It is recommended that police executives consider using financial and other incentives to recruit women and minorities where such programs are lawful (monetary incentive programs may be adversely affected by Fair Labor Standards Act considerations). Financial and other incentive programs are especially useful to agencies that cannot afford full-time recruiters. They are used to encourage officers to recruit bilingual whites, women, and ethnically and racially diverse candidates, informally, while on or off duty. One possible program would give officers overtime credit for each person they recruit in those categories who makes the eligibility list, additional credit if the same applicant is hired, and additional credit for each stage the new officer passes until the probation period ends. Some departments offer officers (not assigned to recruiting) up to 20 hours compensatory time for recruiting a lateral police officer. Department members can also receive an additional 40 hours of compensatory time for recruiting a lateral who is bilingual or from a protected class.

An East Coast agency awards $250 to employees who recruit applicants (of any racial or ethnic group) who are hired, complete all phases of the background process, and start the academy. The same department awards $250 to employees who recruit lateral police officer candidates once they complete all phases of the background process, are hired, and report for duty. When these recruits make it through probation, the employee who recruited them receives $250 as an additional incentive. The Boise, Idaho, Police Department developed a unique incentive program that rewards officers for bringing in a recruit who is qualified to perform the duties of a community law enforcement officer. Encouraging all department members to be involved in the recruitment effort, including the promotion of law enforcement as a career, is usually effective. To be competitive in recruiting employees, especially minorities and women, agencies must offer incentives just as corporations do.

Community involvement. A pluralistic community must have some involvement early in the effort to recruit candidates for police work. Representatives from different ethnic and racial backgrounds should be involved in initial meetings to plan a recruitment campaign. They can assist in determining the best marketing methods for the groups they represent and can help by personally contacting potential candidates. They should be provided with recruitment information (e.g., brochures and posters) that they can disseminate at religious institutions, civic and social organizations, schools, and cultural events. Community-based policing also offers the best opportunity for officers to put messages out regarding agency recruiting.

Community leaders representing the diversity of the community should also be involved in the selection process, including sitting on oral boards for applicants. The San Francisco Police Department utilizes community leaders in all the processes mentioned. Many progressive agencies have encouraged their officers to join community-based organizations, in which they interact with community members and are able to involve the group in recruitment efforts for the department.

High school police academy. Another innovative recruitment tool was launched in San Jose, California, in 2002. Called the Santa Teresa High School Police and Fire

Academy, it is a year-long academy program that helps students prepare for careers in fire services or law enforcement. The Academy provides recruiters a pool of candidates. The program is offered to about 60 students at a time from six school districts in Santa Clara County, California. The students spend half of each day at the academy and the other half at their own schools. Students, who wear uniforms, learn police and fire job skills, which help prepare them for those vocations. Another purpose of the Academy is to instill a sense of community service and spirit in the youth who attend and to provide positive mentor/role model guidance from professional law officers, firefighters, graduate students, and community members. Cadets perform 6,000 to 8,000 hours a year of community service ("High School Police Academy," 2003).

MINI CASE STUDY: RICHMOND, CALIFORNIA, POLICE DEPARTMENT

[Police Chief Chris Magnus of the Richmond, California, Police Department] has repeatedly stressed his intention to hire more locals to help fill a deficit in staffing that, in 2004, left vacant a quarter of Richmond's authorized contingent of officers. That new emphasis on finding local recruits, and those who reflect the region's diversity, has noticeably increased the flow of applicants through Richmond's recruitment office this year [2006] for its two dozen officer vacancies. "We are looking at a greater pool of people, and we are tapping pools of talent where we did not previously recruit," said Sgt. Lori Curran, the department's recruitment supervisor. Richmond is not just using traditional police recruitment tactics, which include visiting undeclared regional academy cadets, college students enrolled in criminal justice courses, and recently discharged military veterans. The department is seeking recruits in new venues, which include churches and temples of various faiths across the region, private-sector job fairs, and the city's extensive network of neighborhood councils. They are also seeking applicants from the private sector within the community—store clerks, office workers, and the like ("Department Finds Recruits," 2006, p. A27).

SELECTION PROCESSES

Prior to initiating any selection processes, law enforcement agencies must assess the satisfaction level of current employees and the workplace environment of the department.

Satisfaction Level for Employees

The first step before outreach recruitment can take place is for the department to look inward. Are any members, sworn or nonsworn, experiencing emotional pain or suffering because of their race, ethnicity, nationality, gender, or sexual orientation? A department seeking to hire applicants from these groups cannot have internal problems, either real or perceived, related to racism, discrimination, or hostility toward females, gay males, or lesbian officers. A department with a high turnover rate or a reputation for not promoting women, minorities, or gays and lesbians will also deter good people from applying. The department must resolve any internal problems before meaningful recruitment can occur. To determine the nature and extent of any such problems, law enforcement agencies can perform an assessment of all their employees through anonymous surveys about their work environment. There should be a review of policies and procedures (especially those related to sexual harassment and gender discrimination) and an examination of statistical information, such as the number of officers leaving the department and their reasons for doing so, as well as which employees are promoted. The goal is not only to evaluate the workplace environment for women and minorities but also to determine what steps need to be taken to dissolve barriers confronting them. See Appendix A for a sample survey that can be used for this purpose.

Supervisors and managers must talk with all members of their workforce on a regular basis to find out if any issues are disturbing them. They must then demonstrate that they are taking steps to alleviate the sources of discomfort, whether this involves modifying practices or simply discussing behavior with other employees.

The field-training program for new recruits should also be reviewed and evaluated to ensure that new officers are not being arbitrarily eliminated or subjected to prejudice or discrimination. By the time a recruit has reached this stage of training, much has been invested in the new officer; every effort should be made to see that he or she completes the program successfully. Negligent retention, however, is a liability to an organization. When it is well documented that a trainee is not suitable for retention, release from employment is usually the best recourse regardless of race, ethnicity, lifestyle, or gender.

Role models, networking, and mentoring programs should be established to give recruits and junior officers the opportunity to receive support and important information from senior officers of the same race, ethnicity, gender, or sexual orientation. Many successful programs, however, include role models of different backgrounds than the recruits.

Applicant Screening

Law enforcement agencies must assess applicants along a range of dimensions that include, but are not limited to:

- Basic qualifications such as education, requisite licenses, and citizenship
- Intelligence and problem-solving capacity
- Psychological fitness
- Physical fitness and agility
- Current and past illegal drug use
- Character as revealed by criminal record, driving record, work history, military record, credit history, reputation, and polygraph examination
- Aptitude and ability to serve others (see "Hiring in the Spirit of Service")
- Racial, ethnic, gender, sexual orientation, and cultural biases

The last dimension, testing for biases, deserves particular attention. An agency whose hiring procedures screen for unacceptable biases demonstrates to the community that it seeks police officers who will carry out their duties with fairness, integrity, diligence, and impartiality—officers who will respect the civil rights and dignity of the people they serve and with whom they work. Such screening should include not only the use of psychometric testing instruments developed to measure attitudes and bias but also careful background investigation of the candidate by personnel staff. The investigation should consider the applicant's own statements about racial issues, as well as interviews with references who provide clues about how the applicant feels about and treats members of other racial, ethnic, gender, and sexual-orientation groups. These interviews would include questions on:

- How the applicant has interacted with other groups
- What people of diverse groups say about the applicant
- Whether the applicant has ever experienced conflict or tension with members of diverse groups or individuals and how he or she handled the experience

Because of the emphasis on community-oriented policing, law enforcement recruiters must also seek applicants who demonstrate the mentality and ability to serve others (not just fight crime). Recruiters therefore are looking for candidates who are adaptable, analytical, communicative, compassionate, courageous (both physically and morally), culturally sensitive, decisive, disciplined, ethical, goal-oriented, incorruptible, mature, responsible, and self-motivated. Agencies also expect officers to have good interpersonal and communication skills, as well as sales and marketing abilities, so applicants should be screened for these attributes and for their desire for continued learning and ability to work in a rapidly evolving environment. Officers more and more are encountering the challenges of different language(s), cultural and generational differences, and the diverse opinions of members of the communities they serve. Agencies must develop means of generating trust among the diverse groups. The importance of bilingual officers and officers with cultural understanding is paramount in today's communities.

The search for recruits should focus on those who demonstrate an ability to take ownership of problems and work with others toward solutions. These potential officers must remain open to people who disagree with them or have opinions that differ from their own. Law enforcement agencies should make their goals and expectations clear to candidates for employment, recognizing that some will not match the department's vision, mission, and values and therefore should be screened out at the beginning of the process.

Robert Jones, professor of psychology at Southwest Missouri State University, says that recruiters can get a clear appraisal of applicants in service-related jobs, such as law enforcement, by applying the five basic traits of human behavior: (1) emotional stability, (2) extroversion versus introversion, (3) openness to experience, (4) agreeableness versus toughness, and (5) conscientiousness. Today, effective law enforcement agents work closely with neighborhood groups, social welfare agencies, housing code officials, and a host of others in partnerships to control crime and improve quality of life. Law enforcement agents must be eager to understand a task, draw up a plan, and follow it through to completion in concert with others. Without an agreeable nature, officers and deputies faced with today's changing attitude toward crime fighting would not have a chance.

It is in the best interest of law enforcement agencies, before implementing tests, to complete a job analysis. Although a time-consuming process, the final result is a clear description of the job for which applicants are applying and being screened. Utilizing the job analysis data, tests and job performance criteria can be developed and become part of the screening process. Applicants, when provided a copy of the job analysis, can decide in advance if they fit the criteria.

Aptitude for a law enforcement career can also be determined from structured oral interviews. The oral interview panel should be gender and racially diverse and include members of the local community to reduce the possibility of bias. The panel should also include both sworn and civilian law enforcement employees. It is important that all raters are supportive of women and minorities in policing and thoroughly trained in the rules of the interview process. Questions should be developed in advance for the oral interview and should test for the skills and abilities needed for community policing, including the ability to work with all types of people, to de-escalate violence, to mediate disputes, and to solve problems. The same questions should be asked of each candidate, regardless of whether the candidate is male or female.

The authors believe that one of the most useful new tools for law enforcement (a paradigm shift in recruitment philosophy) comes from the findings of the federally funded project Hiring in the Spirit of Service (HSS). The project's recommendations represent a major change in recruitment strategy as agencies using HSS are seeking and hiring service-oriented law enforcement personnel.

Hiring in the Spirit of Service. The HSS program, developed in the late 1990s, suggests ways of recruiting applicants who are not drawn to a law enforcement career because of the spirit of adventure ("crime fighter") associated with the profession but are attracted because they are service-minded. The HSS program targets persons whose qualifications are consistent with other service-oriented professions, like teaching, nursing, and counseling, as long as they are able to meet strict physical training demands. Historically, candidates who did not fit the "crime fighter" mentality were discouraged from applying or disqualified at some point of the testing processes. Those departments using the HSS selection process reach out to service-minded candidates, attracting them to law enforcement professions they might not have considered. The HSS project involved a cooperative agreement awarded to the Community Policing Consortium (CPC) by the U.S. Department of Justice Office of Community-Oriented Police Services (the COPS Office). The CPC examined the components of traditional screening procedures in order to find creative ways to revise traditional practices to make them consistent with the principles of community (service-oriented) policing.

> The CPC was particularly interested in a strong emphasis on community engagement—the core of community policing—which enables the building of trust, the development of collaborative problem-solving partnerships, and greater accountability to the community. These emphases set community policing apart from the professional model of policing and have been instrumental in introducing change to the police culture. ("Innovations in Police Recruitment," 2001, p. 1)

Through a competitive process, five law enforcement agencies were selected to serve as demonstration sites for the study. The five agencies were selected because they represent the gamut of law enforcement challenges in the United States. The sites were Burlington, Vermont, a small department with a growing multicultural community;

Sacramento, California; Detroit, Michigan; Hillsborough County, Florida; and King County, Washington (both of the latter are full-service sheriffs' offices).

The HSS project report noted the great lengths to which the agencies went to involve citizens in substantive ways in the processes and how the communities influenced strategies and outcomes. The report also stressed that the complicated processes of HSS are neither easy nor quick, especially the involvement of community members. Each agency encountered many challenges during the study. The study findings and recommendations resulted in revisions to each agency's recruitment and hiring practices, which are now based on the identified personal characteristics and required competencies necessary to perform the community policing function.

A study by the NCWP produced a self-assessment guide to assist agencies seeking to recruit and retain more women in sworn law enforcement positions. The resulting publication, *Recruiting and Retaining Women: A Self-Assessment Guide for Law Enforcement,* provides assistance to federal, state, and local law enforcement agencies on examining their policies and procedures to identify and remove obstacles to hiring and retaining women at all levels of the organization. The guide also provides a list of resources for agencies to use when they plan or implement changes to their current policies and procedures. The guide promotes increasing the number of women at all ranks of law enforcement as a strategy to strengthen community policing, reduce police use of force, enhance police response to domestic violence, and provide balance to the workforce. It is also recommended that chiefs of police, police recruiters, and city and county personnel department employees review *Recruitment and Retention of Qualified Police Personnel—A Best Practices Guide,* published by the International Association of Chiefs of Police. The National Institute of Justice (NIJ) has available *Hiring and Keeping Police Officers,* the findings of a study that examined recent experiences of police agencies nationwide in hiring and retaining sworn officers (Koper, 2004). This report is available online at http://www.ojp.usdoj.gov/nij/pubs-sum/202289.htm or by calling the Criminal Justice Reference Service. Another study, Tearing Down the Wall by NCWP also provides insights on physical agility testing (NCWP, 2003).

Examples of Successful Recruiting Programs

Successful recruitment programs vary by community. If recruitment efforts result in a large enough pool of qualified applicants, the pool will contain individuals of all backgrounds. The following agencies have had success in recruiting female and minority applicants, and might be contacted to determine the strategies they used:

- *Portland, Oregon:* The percentage of women is higher than in many other agencies its size nationwide.

- *Madison, Wisconsin:* The number of women officers, greater than 30 percent of the force, is well above the national average for agencies their size.

- *Pittsburgh, Pennsylvania:* One of the nation's most diverse police departments, with women making up more than 25 percent of the force.

- *Albuquerque, New Mexico:* Police executives point to Albuquerque as a potential model for other departments regarding recruitment.

- **Tucson, Arizona:** Due to a New Workplace for Women Project and its recommendations, the department was able to recruit many more women.

- **The five agencies involved in the HSS project study:** Burlington, Vermont; Sacramento, California; Detroit, Michigan; Hillsborough County, Florida; and King County, Washington.

To assist law enforcement agencies that wish to increase the number of women employees in their workforce, the NCWP offers the following services:

- A regional training seminar on recruiting and retaining women. This 2-day seminar helps law enforcement agencies develop effective recruiting programs to increase the number of female employees.

- Online updates to the self-assessment guide. New programs in law enforcement agencies across the country are described on the website, where readers can access the latest research about women in policing and other critical issues.

- Onsite consulting by a team of professional law enforcement experts to help agencies identify and remove obstacles to recruiting and retaining women.

For additional information on these services, contact the NCWP; see their website address at the end of this chapter.

Legal Issues and Affirmative Action

The authors acknowledge that there may be some controversial and even legal aspects, in some states or jurisdictions, to recruitment efforts that target women, as well as ethnically and racially diverse candidates, for law enforcement jobs. Federal law prohibits programs that require meeting specific hiring goals for any particular group except when necessary to remedy discrimination.

In California, Proposition 209, which outlawed governmental discrimination and preferences based on race, sex, color, ethnicity, or national origin, was passed in 1996. In September 2000, justices of the California Supreme Court affirmed that the proposition was legal. The justices, in their decision, placed strict limits on employers regarding the types of outreach programs they can legally use to recruit employees; any outreach program that gives minorities and women a competitive advantage is a violation of Proposition 209. Many other states followed California's example by enacting similar legislation. Agencies need to research what strategies are legal and appropriate within their state and jurisdiction.

Affirmative action and consent decrees have enjoyed only moderately successful attempts toward achieving parity in the hiring of women and individuals from ethnically and racially diverse backgrounds. There has been even less success with promotions of members of these groups to command ranks. In fact, studies have found that affirmative action has produced uneven results by race, gender, and occupation across the nation.

An unfortunate problem that can be associated with the promotion of women and nonwhites is that doubts are raised about their qualifications: Are they qualified for the job, or are they products of affirmative action? Peers may subtly or even explicitly express to each other that the promotion was not the result of competence, and the promoted candidate may feel that his or her success is not based entirely on qualifications. Consequently, employees may experience strained relationships and lowered morale. There is no denying the potential for a strong negative internal reaction in an organization when court orders have mandated promotions. Some white employees feel anger or frustration with consent decrees or affirmative action–based promotions. Clearly, preventive work must be done to avoid these problems.

MINI CASE STUDY: WHAT WOULD YOU DO?

You are the new personnel sergeant responsible for a department with 50 sworn officers. The department has one African American man, two Hispanic men, and two women officers. There has never been a large number of minority or women candidates applying for sworn positions in the department, and your agency does not reflect the demographics of the city. Your city has an affirmative action program, but to date, no outreach programs have been initiated to recruit women and minorities. Your chief has asked that you provide a proposal on what strategies you would suggest to recruit women and minorities. Develop a list of what you would propose. Make a list of what other departmental processes should take place prior to applicant testing.

RETENTION AND PROMOTION OF A DIVERSE WORKFORCE

Recruiting officers who reflect the gender, racial, ethnic, and sexual orientation demographics of the community is one important challenge of law enforcement agencies. Retention and promotion are equally important. The U.S. Labor Department closely watches the so-called quit rate, a sort of barometer of workers' ability to change jobs. The Department reported a steady 2 years of job-switching growth that reached a 4-year high in September 2005 when voluntary resignations totaled 2.3 percent (it was 1.7 percent in 2003) of total employment. Increasing numbers of employees were emboldened to look around and move to other jobs. The Labor Department indicated that nearly two-thirds of human resources professionals reported being concerned about the number of voluntary resignations in 2005, according to a recent poll of 435 executives by the Society for Human Resource Management. The Labor Department indicated that more companies are tuning up retention measures such as competitive raises, promotions, and other career opportunities as they face keener competition for workers ("Retention Tops Employers' Concerns," 2006). The same was true of law enforcement agencies during this period of time.

Retention of any employee is usually the result of good work on the part of the employee and a positive environment wherein all employees are treated with dignity and respect. A high rate of retention is most likely in organizations that meet the basic needs of employees, offer reasonable opportunities for career development, and have mentoring and networking programs. In fact, once an agency earns a reputation for fairness, talented men and women of all ethnicities and races will seek out that agency and will remain longer.

The lack of promotions of protected classes and women to supervisor and command ranks has been cited as a severe problem in policing for over three decades by scholars and police researchers alike. Authors and advocates for the promotion of women have used the term *glass ceiling* to describe an unacknowledged barrier that inhibits those officers from reaching ranks above entry level. Whether there is a glass ceiling or not, women still constitute only a small proportion of police supervisors and managers (see Exhibit 3.1). Within organizations, women and others of diverse backgrounds are frustrated when promotional opportunities seem more available to white males than to them. The disenchantment that often accompanies frustration frequently leads to low productivity and morale, early burnout, and resignation; to those individuals, opportunities appear better elsewhere. Lack of attention to equal opportunity promoting practices at some law enforcement agencies has resulted in court-ordered promotions. These have a negative impact on a department's operations and relationships, both internally and externally, and often lead to distrust and dissatisfaction.

Police executives and city or county managers cannot afford to minimize the consequences of poor retention and inadequate promotional opportunities for women and diverse members of their organizations. Some departments have done very well in recruiting and hiring women, but, for reasons that have yet to be studied, women have left departments more quickly than men. A 1998 study by the IACP found that about 60 percent of the women who leave law enforcement occupations do so between their second and fifth year on the job. The reasons vary, but family pressures are the most frequently cited cause. The report recommended fairer screening procedures, tougher sexual harassment policies, and sustained drives designed to attract women and keep them on the job. A more recent study (2004) by Catalyst (see Website Resources) determined the top three reasons for which senior-level women would leave their current organization, with 42 percent citing increased compensation, 35 percent to accept the

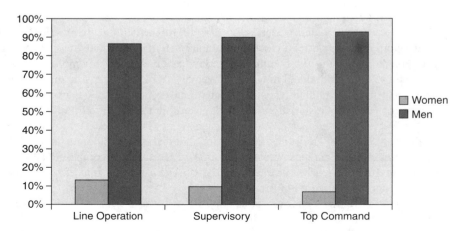

Exhibit 3.1   Percentage of Sworn Law Enforcement Officers by Rank and Gender: Large Police Agencies, 2001
Source: NCWP Survey, 2001

opportunity to develop new skills or competencies, and 33 percent to pursue greater advancement opportunities ("Women and Men in U.S. Corporate Leadership," 2004).

Chief executives need to determine if female officers are applying for promotions in numbers that are proportional to their numbers in the department. If not, perhaps female officers need encouragement from their supervisors, mentors, or informal network associates. It is also possible that the promotional process disproportionately screens out female officers. Research shows that the more subjective the process is, the less likely women are to pass it. Some safeguards against bias include weighting the process toward "hands-on" tasks (e.g., assessment center testing), conducting structured interviews, selecting board members who represent different races and both sexes, and training the board members on interviewing techniques.

Failure to promote qualified candidates representative of the diverse populations agencies serve, including women, can result in continued distrust of the police by the communities. Underrepresentation within police departments also aggravates tensions between the police and the community. Some scholars and criminal justice experts argue that underrepresentation at all levels within law enforcement agencies hurts the image of the department in the eyes of the community.

MINI CASE STUDY: HOW WOULD YOU HANDLE IT?

You are a male lieutenant in charge of the special weapons and tactics unit. The first female officer will be assigned to your specialized unit shortly. The special weapons and tactics team members are voicing negative opinions about a female officer being assigned to the unit. They are complaining that standards will be lowered in the unit because women are not as physically fit as men for this assignment. When you have overheard these conversations, or when they have been addressed to you directly, you have refuted them by pointing to the women in the department who are in outstanding physical shape. This strategy has not been effective, as the squad members continue to complain that women officers can't do the job and that their personal safety might be in jeopardy. What would you do?

SUMMARY

Recruiting, hiring, retaining, and promoting a diverse workforce will remain important issues in law enforcement for a long time. Too many of the issues of equity and diversity have not been resolved in the law enforcement workplace, by the courts, or even in the legislative and executive branches of the U.S. government. The number of people available and qualified for entry-level jobs will continue to decrease; more employers, both public and private, will be vying for the best candidates. This seems to be true regardless of the economic condition of federal, state, or local government.

Hiring and promoting women and minorities for law enforcement careers are achievable goals when agencies use strategies outlined in this chapter. Most departments in the United States utilize community policing; thus the need to recruit and retain female and minority officers, who are also service oriented (HSS), is critical.

With the changes in the hiring, screening, and promotional policies and practices of law enforcement agencies comes an unprecedented opportunity to build a future in which differences are valued and respected in our communities and our workforces. Progressive law enforcement executives must strive to secure the most qualified employees to serve the public: those who have the skills and tools to understanding various languages, cultures, and lifestyles. To do so, they must not only be committed to the challenges of affirmative hiring (where legal) but also be capable of educating and selling their workforce on the legitimate reasons, both legal and ethical, for such efforts. Law enforcement agencies, to be competitive in the market for qualified employees, must develop new ways to recruit targeted people or risk losing highly skilled potential employees to other occupations.

In this chapter, we presented effective strategies and successful programs for implementing changes in recruitment and promotion of a diverse workforce. Law enforcement will have to use innovative and sophisticated marketing techniques and advertising campaigns to reach the population of desired potential applicants, and it must develop fast-track processes for hiring these candidates.

A transition is taking place as police continue to move from the aggressive, male-dominated (and predominantly white) police departments and culture of the past. Most law enforcement observers agree that with the shift to community policing, women can thrive. Law enforcement agencies must overcome the common perception that policing is a male-oriented profession that requires only physical strength. Departments are looking for people who are community and service oriented and who have good interpersonal skills, and they are finding increasingly that women meet these qualifications. Law enforcement executives should seek minority employees for the same reasons.

Although it contributes to better police–community relations, improvement in protected class representation in law enforcement and other criminal justice professions will not alone resolve misunderstandings. Increased numbers of diverse staff members provide only the potential for improved dialogue, cooperation, and problem-solving within both the organization and the community the organization serves. Community and law enforcement officials should remember that serving multicultural and multiracial neighborhoods can never be the sole responsibility of workforce members from diverse ethnic and racial groups. In most jurisdictions, their limited numbers make this level of responsibility unrealistic. All staff should be prepared to understand and relate to diverse groups in a professional and sensitive manner, whether the people contacted are perpetrators, victims, or witnesses.

DISCUSSION QUESTIONS AND ISSUES*

1. ***Institutional Racism in Law Enforcement.*** Law enforcement agencies typically operate under the pretense that all their members are one color and that the uniform or job makes everyone brothers or sisters. Many members of diverse ethnic and racial groups, particularly African Americans, do not agree

---

*See the Instructor's Manual accompanying this text for additional activities, role-play activities, questionnaires, and projects related to the content of this chapter.

that they are consistently treated with respect and believe that there is institutional racism in law enforcement. Caucasians clearly dominate the command ranks of law enforcement agencies. Discuss with other students in your class whether you believe this disparity is the result of subtle forms of institutional racism or actual conscious efforts on the part of the persons empowered to make decisions. Consider whether tests and promotional processes give unfair advantage to white applicants and whether they discriminate against department employees of other races and ethnicities. Do officers from diverse groups discriminate against members of other, different cultures?

2. ***Employment of a Diverse Workforce and Police Practices.*** How has the employment of a diverse workforce affected police practices in your city or county? Is there evidence that significant changes in the ethnic or racial composition of the department alter official police policy? Can the same be said of gay male and lesbian employment? Does employment of protected classes have any significant effect on the informal police subculture and, in turn, police performance? Provide examples to support your conclusions.

WEBSITE RESOURCES

Visit these websites for additional information about recruitment and related issues.

Bureau of Justice Statistics (BJS): http://www.ojp.us.doj.bjs

A resource of crime statistics collected and analyzed by the Federal Bureau of Investigation.

Catalyst: http://www.catalyst.org

A research and advisory nonprofit membership organization working with businesses and the professions to build inclusive environments and expand opportunities for women at work. Catalyst conducts research on all aspects of women's career advancement and provides strategic and web-based consulting services globally.

Community Policing Consortium (CPC): http://www.cops.usdoj.gov

The Community Policing Consortium, also known as COPS, is a partnership of five police organizations: International Association of Chiefs of Police (IACP); National Organization of Black Law Enforcement Executives (NOBLE); National Sheriffs' Association (NSA); Police Executive Research Forum (PERF); and Police Foundation. Community Policing Consortium is administered and funded by the U.S. Department of Justice, Office of Community Oriented Policing Services (COPS).

International Association of Chiefs of Police (IACP): http://www.theiacp.org

An online resource for law enforcement issues and publications, including "Recruitment and Retention of Qualified Police Personnel: A Best Practices Guide."

International Association of Women Police (IAWP): http://www.iawp.org

A website for information about training conferences, careers, jobs, publications, and research pertinent to women in law enforcement.

Institute for Women in Trades, Technology and Science (IWITTS):
http://www.womenpolice.com

> This website features fact sheets, news articles, and publications for departments on women and policing, including a free women-in-policing e-newsletter, which provides best practice information.

National Career Academy Coalition (NCAC): http://www.ncacinc.org

> A website for information concerning career academies.

National Center for Women and Policing (NCWP): http://www.feminist.org

> This website provides information concerning regional training seminars on recruiting and retaining women. It also is a resource for the latest research about women in policing and other critical issues. The organization has consultants to help agencies identify and remove obstacles to recruiting and retaining women.

National Association of Women Law Enforcement Executives (NAWLEE):
http://www.nawlee.com

> The website contains resources, news, member directory, conference and training information, seminars, and an information exchange for women executives in law enforcement.

REFERENCES

"Department Finds Recruits from Community." (2006, April 16). *Contra Costa Times,* p. A27.

"High School Dropout Rates on the Rise." (2006, June 21). *Contra Costa Times,* p. A1.

"High School Police Academy." (2003, January 5). *Contra Costa Times,* p. A37.

Future of Women in Policing: Mandates for Action. (1998). International Association of Chiefs of Police. Washington, D.C.

"Innovations in Police Recruitment and Hiring: Hiring in the Spirit of Service." (2001). U.S. Department of Justice, Office of Community Oriented Policing Service. Project #2001-CK-WX-K094, pp.1, 10–11.

Koper, Christopher. (2004). *Hiring and Keeping Police Officers.* U.S. Department of Justice, Office of Justice Programs. Available online: www.ojp.usdoj.gov/nij.

Micari, Marina. (1993, September). "Recruiters of Minorities and Women Speak Out: Why Companies Lose Candidates," *Cultural Diversity at Work, 6*(1), 1.

Oakland Police Department. (2006) Vision and Plan of Action of Chief Wayne Tucker. Retrieved March 2006 from www.oaklandpolice.com.

National Center for Women and Policing. (2003, Spring). *Tearing Down the Wall: Problems with Consistency, Validity, and Adverse Impact of Physical Agility Testing in Police Selection,* pp. 1–10.

National Center for Women and Policing. (2002, April). *Equality Denied—The Status of Women in Policing: 2001.* Available online: www.womenandpolicing.org/publications.asap.

President's Message: Diversity on the Force. (2006, May 31). International Association of Chiefs of Police, Chief Mary Ann Viverette, p. 1–2.

Raymond, Barbara, Laura Hickman, Laura Miller, and Jennifer Wong. (2004). *Police Personnel Challenges Post September 11: Anticipating Expanded Duties and a Changing Labor Pool.* Rand Corporation. Available online: order@rand.org.

Recruiting and Retaining Women: A Self-Assessment Guide for Law Enforcement. (2001). Department of Justice, Bureau of Justice Statistics, Washington, D.C.

Recruitment and Retention of Qualified Police Personnel—A Best Practices Guide. Big Ideas for Smaller Department. (2000). A quarterly publication of the IACP available online @ www.thelacp. International Association of Chiefs of Police, *1*(2), 3–7.

"Retention Tops Employers' Concerns." (2006, January 30). *Contra Costa Times,* p. D5.

Spawn, Mark. (2003, March). "Recruitment Strategies—A Case Study in Police Recruitment." *FBI Law Enforcement Bulletin,* p. 2.

"States Vary on Imprisoning Women." (2006, May 21). *Contra Costa Times,* p. A17.

Vest, Gary. (2001, November). "Closing the Recruitment Gap—A Symposium's Findings." *FBI Law Enforcement Bulletin,* pp. 13–17.

"Women and Men in U.S. Corporate Leadership: Same Workplace, Different Realities?" (2004). *Catalyst.*

"Women Recruits Meet High Standards." (2003 March 16). *Contra Costa Times,* p. A32

Chapter 4

Cross-Cultural Communication for Law Enforcement

OVERVIEW

This chapter begins with a discussion of language barriers and their implications for law enforcement and gives examples of police departments' efforts to work with limited English-speaking populations. We discuss commonly held attitudes about nonnative English speakers and explain the challenges involved in second-language acquisition. The section on language barriers and law enforcement ends with a list of tips for communicating in situations in which English is an individual's second language. Next, the chapter provides an overview of specific issues that law enforcement professionals face with regard to communication in a diverse environment. We discuss several common reactions that people have when communicating with people from different backgrounds, including defensiveness, overidentification, denial of biases, and the creation of "we–they" attitudes. In addition, we discuss responses to citizens' accusations of racial profiling as well as communication post-9/11. We then present information on key issues and skills required for interviewing and gathering data, particularly across cultures. The next section covers cross-cultural nonverbal differences, emphasizing areas of contrast of which officers should be aware. The final section presents male–female communication issues, particularly within law enforcement agencies.

COMMENTARY

The challenge of communication across cultures for law enforcement personnel is multifaceted. Officers not only have to consider how communicating with speakers of other languages affects their day-to-day work but also have to deal with the changing culture within their agencies and the sensitivities required in a multicultural workforce.

In many parts of Asia, Africa and the Middle East, people often show respect by not making eye contact. Some officers think of this behavior as defiant, but first generation refugees or immigrants from these parts of the world are communicating respect. These officers totally miss the intended meaning behind this behavior. In addition, if the citizen has a certain tone of speech or is talking loudly, an officer may assume him to be out of control or aggressive. I often hear my fellow officers making judgments about citizens by the way they talk. The tone, the accent, the pace of speaking is not supposed to be the same as ours. This is their second language. This is ethnocentrism on the part of an officer and just a lack of awareness. (Personal communication with Arab American police officer [who wishes to remain anonymous], Cultural Awareness Session, 2003)

In dealing with a population whose second language is English, it is of key importance to keep these three points in mind:

- A listener can easily misinterpret speech patterns; intonation, in particular, carries emotion and intentionality; what one hears is not always what is intended

- A listener can easily misunderstand spoken words when a speaker is not fluent in English.

- A listener should use several indicators for interpreting correctly what a citizen is attempting to say.

It is not only the police officer who experiences frustration in an encounter with someone who is not fluent in English. The following is a personal account of a Vietnamese police officer's struggles with English when he first came to the United States.

For the first few months of being here, I was always tired from speaking the language. I had to strain my ears all day long and all my nerves were bothered. It was hard work to make people understand my broken English and to listen to them. Sometimes, I just could not anymore and I just stopped speaking English. Sometimes I had to pretend I understood what they said and why they were laughing. But inside I felt very depressed. I am an adult and my language sounded worse than a child's. Sometimes it was better not to say anything at all. (Personal communication with Vietnamese police officer [who wishes to remain anonymous], 2006).

Language barriers can lead to serious problems for non-English speakers. In one case, a man was in jail for agreeing that he molested his daughter. It turned out that the man had agreed that his drinking bothered his daughters. In Spanish, the word for bother, or annoy, is "molestar." After this was explained [by the court interpreter], the man was released ("Helping People Who Lack English," 1999). This event is an invaluable example to show limited Spanish speaking police officers and other criminal justice professionals the need to learn Spanish.

LANGUAGE BARRIERS AND LAW ENFORCEMENT

Nationwide, changing demographics have resulted in the need for law enforcement to deal increasingly with a multicultural population who are speakers of other languages and do not have the equivalent skills with English. From citizens who report crimes in limited English to crime suspects and victims, there are no absolute assurances that officers will understand them. Officers are justifiably frustrated by language barriers and find it difficult to do their jobs the way they have been trained to do them. On a "good day" some officers make a point to modify their English so that they will be better understood; on a stressful day, many officers are frustrated at having to slow down and listen more patiently. Some law enforcement officers are noticeably impatient when they deal with nonnative English speakers. Citizens who do not speak English know when police are not listening to their side of the story. As a result, a citizen with a language barrier is not successful at communicating even the minimum amount of necessary information. Perhaps most difficult is the situation in which a person with limited English skills is traumatized, further affecting the victim's ability to speak English. Officers need to be aware of the potential for inadvertent discrimination based on a citizen's language background, which could fall under "language and national origin discrimination" (Fernandez, 2000).

Clearly, the more bilingual officers a department has, the more efficient and effective the contact is with non-English-speaking citizens. Many agencies subsidize foreign-language training for their personnel or seek recruits with multiple-language skills. When the resources are not available for such programs, however, there can be serious and sometimes tragic consequences. Non-English-speaking citizens may not understand why they are being arrested or searched. They may not know their rights if they are unfamiliar with the legal system, as is the case with many recently arrived immigrants and refugees. Using the wrong translator can mislead officers, so much so that a victim and his or her translator may give two completely different versions of a story—for example, using the friend of a suspected child abuser to translate the allegations of the child who has been abused.

In some cases there is no sensitivity when it comes to language obstacles. For example, within a largely Spanish-speaking area in Los Angeles, a deputy, according to witnesses, asked a Hispanic male to get out of his car. The man answered in Spanish, "I'm handicapped," and he reached down to pull his left leg out of the car. The deputy apparently believed that the man was reaching for a weapon and consequently "struck him on the head with the butt of his gun" ("The Troubled LA County Sheriff's Department," 1992). This incident, while dated, is a lesson for all existing and future generations of police officers not to overreact on a motorist traffic stop.

Intolerance to language differences is sometimes voiced by veteran police officers in cultural diversity in-service training workshops; similarly, recruit police officers attending cultural diversity classes in police academies echo this sentiment. It is not uncommon to hear: "Why do I have to learn about their language and their customs?" In response to these questions, students need to be challenged and asked, Who benefits in citizen–police contacts when the police officer is able to communicate with limited English-speaking citizens? The response is that the police officer benefits.

Communication across cultures and with people for whom English is a second language can be frustrating and exacts a great deal of patience from officers. Exhibit 4.1 lists tips for communication with others when English is their second language. Sensitivity to the difficulties of those who do not speak English is in order, but that is only a partial solution to the problem. In attempting to cope with the problem of non-English-speaking citizens, suspects, and criminals, many departments have not only increased the number of bilingual officers in their forces but have also begun to utilize translation services, some of which provide translation in over 150 languages, 24 hours a day. The 911 emergency line has interpreters available 24 hours a day for some languages. Having access to translation services and referrals is a first step in addressing the challenge of communication with those who speak no or limited English, but it is not a long-term solution. Having bilingual officers or nonsworn personnel, however, constitutes a more direct method of addressing the problem. Many departments across the country offer language classes on the job with tuition reimbursement for classes and extra pay for second-language pro-

1. Speak slowly and enunciate clearly.
2. Face the person and speak directly even when using a translator.
3. Avoid concentrated eye contact if the other speaker is not making direct eye contact.
4. Do not use jargon, slang, idioms, or reduced forms (e.g., "gonna," "gotta," "wanna," "couldja").
5. Avoid complex verb tenses (e.g., "If I would have known, I might have been able to provide assistance").
6. Repeat key issues and questions in different ways.
7. Avoid asking questions that can be answered by yes or no; rather, ask questions so that the answer can show understanding.
8. Use short, simple sentences; pause between sentences.
9. Use visual cues such as gestures, demonstrations, and brief written phrases.
10. Use active rather than passive verbs (e.g., "I expect your attention" [active] rather than "Your attention is expected" [passive]).
11. Have materials duplicated in bilingual format.
12. Pause frequently and give breaks. Monitor your speed when you speak.
13. Use only one idea per sentence.
14. Respect the silence that nonnative English speakers need to formulate their sentences and translate them in their minds.
15. Check comprehension by having the other speaker repeat material or instructions, and summarize frequently.
16. Encourage and provide positive feedback on the person's ability to communicate.
17. Listen even more attentively than you do when communicating with a native speaker of English.
18. Be patient. Every first generation of immigrants struggles with the acquisition of English.
19. Do not speak louder. It will not help

Exhibit 4.1   Tips for communicating when English is a second language.

ficiency. Police department training personnel are encouraged to look for classes specially designed for law enforcement. If they do not exist, a few selected officers and language educators should form a partnership so that officers can guide language teachers in the development of police-specific second-language curricula (i.e., to meet the specialized needs of officers on the street). In "Policing a Multicultural Community," DeGeneste and Sullivan (1997) provided practical suggestions for police departments approximately one decade ago. With the increase of immigrant communities in both metropolitan and nonmetropolitan areas, their advice is as relevant today as it was then.

> Since a degree of ethnic or racial distrust is undoubtedly the result of frustration stemming from language and communication difficulties, enhanced language training during initial entry-level police academies, with subsequent refresher courses throughout an officer's career, should be strongly considered. [And, on a practical level] developing language skills for a police agency can be a costly undertaking. Initial training would extend the length of academy training, leading to additional costs for instructors, training space and course development. Agencies in large urban areas would need to craft curricula for multiple languages (for example, Spanish, Mandarin, Cantonese, etc.). Refresher training would require replacing officers while they receive updated or perhaps even initial instruction in a new language if demographic shifts warrant. Limiting these

costs requires close monitoring of demographic trends to match language skills with community needs.

Increasing bilingual hires is the most practical direction in which to go; in addition, bilingual officers often have a better understanding of the communities they serve. Some community-based police programs use trained community volunteers to assist them in situations in which English is not spoken. When translation is not available, officers have no choice but to rely on English. In doing so, the tips listed in Exhibit 4.1 on modifying one's language will be helpful.

ATTITUDES TOWARD NON- OR LIMITED-ENGLISH SPEAKERS

Most officers are aware that a citizen with few or no English skills is not necessarily an illegal immigrant. However, sometimes officers have seen English difficulties as a sign that a person is an illegal immigrant, and the consequences have been unfortunate. Donya Fernandez (2000), a language rights attorney, cited the case of a Spanish speaker with extremely limited English skills whom police turned over to the former Immigration and Naturalization Services (INS), now the U.S. Immigration and Customs Enforcement (ICE). The INS held him for 48 hours, despite that the man was a U.S. citizen who was born in the United States but had spent most of his life in Mexico.

Citizens' constant use of a second language and the accompanying frustrations for officers can be overwhelming. In general, whether the society at large (or police as a microcosm of society) is concerned about a particular group's use of their native language seems to be directly related to the population size of that group. For example, when large groups of Cubans or Puerto Ricans speak Spanish, there is often a higher level of anxiety among the dominant white population than when a few Armenians speak their native language. Virtually every immigrant group is said to resist learning English, yet the pattern of language acquisition among the generations of immigrants follows a predictable course. Members of the second and third generations of an immigrant family almost always become fluent in English, while many of the first-generation immigrants (the grandparents and the parents) struggle, sometimes partly learning English and sometimes not learning it at all. Many immigrants, however, are extremely motivated to learn English and become productive members of society. In urban areas, access to English classes is often limited (e.g., there have been known to be 4- and 5-year waiting lists for English programs at Los Angeles community colleges). Newcomers are fully aware that without English, they will never be able to integrate into the society.

Nevertheless, some people, including established immigrants, have a tendency to overgeneralize their observations about newcomers. It is true that some people do not want to learn English, and even some middle-class U.S.-born Americans do not make efforts to improve their language abilities. How often do we hear that high school graduates who are native English speakers have not learned to write or speak well? In such cases, laziness or lack of high-quality education (or both) may have contributed to this aspect of illiteracy. In fairness, all groups have a percentage of lazy people, but sometimes people tend to stereotype others. Although not all first-generation immigrants learn English, there is a great deal of mythology around the "masses" of immigrants who hold on to their native language.

The native language for an immigrant family is the language of communication for that family. It is not uncommon to hear comments such as, "They'll never learn English if they insist on speaking their native tongues at home." Imagine having been away from your family all day and coming home and interacting in a foreign language. Is it reasonable to expect that you could express affection, resolve conflicts, show anger, and simply relax in another language? Language is an integral part of a person's identity. During the initial months and even years of communicating in a second language, a person does not truly feel like himself or herself. Initially, an individual often has a feeling of play acting or taking on another identity when communicating in a second language.

In a physiological perspective, communicating in a foreign language can be fatiguing on the psychomotor and cognitive domains of learning or behavior. In speaking any given language, a person uses a set of muscles to articulate the sounds of that language. Changing to another language, particularly as an adult, requires the use of an entirely new set of muscles. Doing so causes mental strain and facial tension, which can result in a person "shutting down"—the result being an inability to communicate in English (or whatever the new language is). It is no wonder that in the multicultural workforce, clusters of people from different ethnic groups can be seen having lunch together, taking breaks together, and so on. Simply put, it is more relaxing to be able to speak one's own language than to struggle with a new one all day.

Sometimes police officers say: "I know they speak English because they speak it among themselves (i.e., when the group is culturally mixed). The minute I'm on the scene, it's 'No speak English.' Why do they have to play dumb? What do they think I am—stupid?" It would be naïve to say that this situation does not occur. There will always be some people who try to deceive others and use or not use English to their own advantage. However, there may be other reasons that people "feign" not knowing English. Several factors affect an immigrant's ability to use English at any given moment. A few of these are of particular significance to law enforcement officers. Generally speaking, an immigrant's ability to express himself or herself in English is best when that person is comfortable with the officer. So, the more intimidating an officer is, the higher the likelihood that anxiety will affect the speaker's ability in English. Language breakdown is one of the first signs that a person is ill at ease and stressed to the point of not being able to cooperate and communicate. It is in the officer's best interest to increase the comfort level of the citizen, whether a victim, a suspect, or simply a person requiring help. Language breakdown in a person who is otherwise fairly conversationally competent in English can also occur as a result of illness, intoxication, fatigue, and trauma.

Finally, officers must realize that their attitudes about immigrants and nonnative English speakers, whether positive or negative, may very well affect their interaction with them. This is especially true when an officer is under pressure and negative attitudes are more likely to surface in communication.

CROSS-CULTURAL COMMUNICATION IN THE LAW ENFORCEMENT CONTEXT

To understand the need for skillful communication with members of culturally and ethnically diverse groups, including women, officers should recognize some of the special characteristics of cross-cultural communication in the law enforcement context (Exhibit 4.2). To best protect and serve communities made up of individuals from

- Officers have traditionally used styles of communication and language that at one time were considered acceptable. Now, because of diverse groups within the police agency and within our cities, the unspoken rules about appropriate and inappropriate communication are changing.
- For officers, communication can be tense in crises and in culturally unfamiliar environments.
- Officers' perceptions of a cultural group may be skewed by the populations they encounter.
- Officers' communication will be enhanced when they are aware of
  1. Perceptions
  2. Cultural filters
  3. High- and low-context communication (see explanation in text)
  4. Possible biases and stereotypes
- Through communication, officers have tremendous power to influence the behavior and responses of the citizens they contact. A lack of knowledge of the dynamics of cross-cultural communication will diminish this power.
- Improved communication with all citizens will also result in safer interactions for officers

Exhibit 4.2   Key cross-cultural areas in communication for officers to consider.

many different racial and cultural backgrounds, officers as peacekeepers, crime fighters, and law enforcement representatives need to look beyond the "mechanics" of policing and examine what takes place in the process of cross-cultural communication. Communication, in general, is a challenge because "although the words are the same the meaning can be completely different. The same expression can easily have a different connotation or emotional emphasis. Misinterpretation is so common and consistent that eventually we develop limiting perspectives of each other" (Gray, 2002, p. 23). Does communication pose this much of a challenge? Talking to others, making one's points, and giving explanations should not be so difficult.

Every communication act involves a message, a sender, and a receiver; given that any two human beings are fundamentally different, there will always be a psychological distance between the two involved (even if they have the same cultural background). Professional police officers have learned ways of bridging the gap, or psychological distance, between the two very different worlds of sender and receiver. In instances of cross-cultural communication, including cross-racial and cross-ethnic interactions, in which the sender and receiver are from different cultures, officers have an even greater gap to try to bridge. Exhibit 4.2 summarizes key factors that can potentially contribute to cross-cultural and cross-racial communication challenges. Psychological distance exists between any two human beings because every individual is "wired" differently from the next. Styles of communication that differ across cultures can contribute to perceptions or misperceptions and incorrect filtering of communication "data."

High- and Low-Context Communication

Edward Hall, author of two dated but seminal books in the field of cross-cultural communication (*The Silent Language* and *The Hidden Dimension*), coined terms to describe very different frameworks of communication across cultures and individual styles. An understanding of the continuum of high- to low-context communication will contribute to officers' understanding of direct and indirect communication (or explicit and implicit communication). People or cultural groups who tend toward the high-context end of this communication continuum may exhibit the following characteristics, to varying degrees, in communication:

- Tendency to avoid saying no
- Tendency to avoid conflict
- Difficulty answering yes/no and either/or type questions; usually not "binary thinkers"—awareness of shades of gray and broad context or scope
- Concerned about saving face (theirs and others)
- Preference for harmonious communication; avoidance of disagreement
- Focus on "wide context" of interaction—past events, tone, nonverbal communication, relationship, and status of speakers; good readers of implicit communication
- Preference for getting to the point slowly and or indirectly
- Appearance of "beating around the bush" (i.e., this is a low-context communicator's perception and filter of the higher context style); beating around the bush in high-context communication is seen as a polite style of communication and the "right" way to communicate

Lower context communication tendencies include the following:

- "Yes" equals "yes" and "no" equals "no"
- Ease with direct communication and responding directly to conflict
- Saving face (theirs and others) not as important as saying the truth
- Focus more on words and what is verbalized than what is not communicated implicitly—less focus on tone, nonverbal, relationship, status, past events, implicit communication
- Preference for getting right to the point; "beating around the bush" seen as negative

As officers know, rapport-building with all citizens is essential in building trust, which is preliminary to their opening up. This is especially true when communicating with people who have higher context communication styles. Typically, these styles are more characteristic of cultural groups coming from Asian and Latin American cultures, and there are gender differences even in lower context cultures as well (i.e., women tend to have a higher context style than men). Law enforcement is basically a lower context communication style; police officers must adjust their context style when interacting with individuals who use higher context communication styles. Chapter 5 provides several examples of higher context communication in the law enforcement context and makes recommendations for responding effectively to this style. (See Law Enforcement Contact with Asian/Pacific Americans, section on "Verbal and Nonverbal Styles").

One of the key tools for building rapport in law enforcement is neurolinguistic programming (NLP), a communication model and a set of techniques for establishing rapport. Officers have successfully used this communication tool, for example, in building rapport in interviews with witnesses and victims of crimes. The basis for the use of the techniques involved have to do with a fundamental principle in interpersonal relationships, which is the need to create harmony with others in order to establish rapport. As such, the type of communication used with NLP is that of "matching" nonverbal and verbal behavior with a witness, victim, or interviewee (for example). Doing so may prove to be especially challenging, but useful, with people from different cultural backgrounds as a way to minimize the cultural gap between the officer's style and that of the citizen with whom he or she is interacting. It is beyond the scope of this chapter to detail the theory behind and steps involved in NLP. However, we have included in the Website Resources a link to an informative FBI publication entitled "Subtle Skills for Building Rapport."

CROSS-CULTURAL COMMUNICATION ATTEMPTS

It is sometimes less challenging to interact with people from one's own background than with those from a different group. Communication can be strained and unnatural when there is no apparent common ground. The "people are people everywhere" argument and "just treat everyone with respect" advice both fall short when we understand that there can be basic differences in the areas of behavior and communication across cultures. Some police officers feel that an understanding of cross-cultural communication is unnecessary if respect is shown to every person. Yet, if officers have had limited contact with people from diverse backgrounds, they may inadvertently communicate their lack of familiarity. In the next few sections, we exemplify typical ways people attempt to accommodate for or react to cultural or racial differences and how they may cover up their discomfort in communication across cultures.

Using Language or Language Style to Become Just Like One of "Them"

Black officer to a white officer: "Hey, what kind of arrest did you have?"

White officer: "Brotha-man was trying to front me. . . ."

Lieutenant Darryl McAllister from the Hayward, California, Police Department uses the preceding example to illustrate how obviously uncomfortable some non-African Americans are when communicating cross-racially. One of his pet peeves is hearing other officers trying to imitate him in speech and trying to act like a "brother." He explained that this type of imitative language is insincere and phony. The artificiality makes him feel as if people are going overboard to show just how comfortable they are (when, in fact, they may not be). He explained that he does not feel that this style of imitation is necessarily racist but that it conveys others' discomfort with his "blackness" (McAllister, 2003).

Similarly, officers attempting to establish rapport with citizens should not pretend to have too much familiarity with the language and culture or use words selectively to demonstrate how "cool" they are (e.g., using "señor" with Spanish-speaking people, calling an African American "my man," or referring to a Native American as "chief"). People of one cultural background may find themselves in situations in which an entire crowd or family is using a particular dialect or slang. If the officer lapses into the manner of speaking of the group, he or she will likely appear to be mocking that style. Ultimately, the officer should be sincere and natural. "Faking" another style of communication can have extremely negative results.

Walking on Eggshells

When in the presence of people from different cultural backgrounds, some people find that they have a tendency to work hard not to offend. Consequently, they are not able to be themselves or do what they would normally do. In a cultural diversity training workshop for employees of a city government, one white participant explained that he normally has no problem being direct when solicitors come to the door trying to sell something or ask for a donation to a cause. His normal response would be to say, "I'm not interested," and then he would promptly shut the door. He explained, however, that when a black solicitor comes to the door, he almost never rudely cuts him or her off, and most of the time he ends up making a donation to whatever cause is being promoted. His inability to be himself and communicate directly stems from his concern about appearing to be racist. It is not within the scope of this subsection to analyze this behavior in depth but simply to bring into awareness some typical patterns of reactions in cross-cultural and cross-racial encounters. A person must attempt to recognize his or her tendencies to reach the goal of communicating in a sincere and authentic manner with people of all backgrounds (Exhibit 4.3).

"Some of My Best Friends Are . . ."

In an attempt to show how tolerant and experienced they are with members of minority groups, many people often feel the need to demonstrate their tolerance strongly by saying things such as "I'm not prejudiced" or "I have friends who are members of your group" or "I know people . . . ," or, worse, "I once knew someone who was also [for example] Jewish/Asian/African American." Although the intention may be to break down barriers and establish rapport, these types of statements often sound patronizing. To a member of a culturally or racially different group, this type of comment comes across as extremely naïve. In fact, many people would understand such a comment as signifying that the speaker actually does have prejudices toward a particular group. Minority-group members would question a nonmember's need to make a reference to others of

---

- Self-awareness about one's early life experiences that helped to shape perceptions, filters, and assumptions about people
- Self-awareness about how one feels toward someone who is "different"
- Management of assumptions and discomfort in dealing with people who are different (e.g., do we try to deny that differences exist and laugh differences away, or imitate "them" in order to appear comfortable?)
- Ability to be authentic in communication with others while modifying communication style when necessary

Exhibit 4.3   Key areas for officers to consider: self-awareness.

the same background when there is no context for doing so. These types of remarks indicate that the speaker is probably isolated from members of the particular group. Yet the person making a statement such as "I know someone who is Asian" is trying to establish something in common with the other person and may even go into detail about the other person he or she knows. As one Jewish woman reported in a cross-cultural awareness session, "Just because a person I meet is uncomfortable meeting Jews or has very little experience with Jews doesn't mean that I want to hear about the one Jewish person he met 10 years ago while traveling on a plane to New York!"

"You People," or the We–They Distinction

Some may say "I'd like to get to know you people better" or "You people have made some amazing contributions." The use of "you people" may be another signal of prejudice or divisiveness in a person's mind. When someone decides that a particular group is unlike his or her own group (i.e., not part of "my people"), that person makes a simplistic division of all people into two groups: "we" and "they." Often, accompanying this division is the attribution of positive traits to "us" and negative traits to "them." Members of the "other group" (the out-group) are described in negative and stereotypical terms (e.g., "They are lazy," "They are criminals," "They are aggressive") rather than neutral terms that describe cultural or ethnic generalities (e.g., "They have a tradition of valuing education" or "Their communication style is more formal than that of most Americans"). The phenomenon of stereotyping makes it very difficult for people to communicate with each other effectively because they do not perceive others accurately. By attributing negative qualities to another group, a person creates myths about the superiority of his or her own group. Cultural and racial put-downs are often attempts to make people feel better about themselves.

"You Stopped Me Because I'm . . . ," or Accusations of Racial Profiling

There are three recurring situations in which an officer may hear the accusation: "You stopped me because I'm [black, Arab, etc.]." The first situation is when citizens from a neighborhood with people predominantly from one culture are suspicious of any person in their neighborhood from another background. Thus they may call 911 reporting a "suspicious character" and may even add such statements as "I think he has a gun" when there is no basis for such an accusation. In this situation, the police officer must understand the extreme humiliation and anger citizens feel when they are the object of racist perceptions. Once the officer determines that there is no reason to arrest the citizen, it is most appropriate for the officer to apologize for having made the stop and to explain that department policy requires that officers are obliged to investigate all calls.

Indeed, there are many incidents all over the country in which citizens call a police department to report a "suspicious character" just because he or she does not happen to fit the description of the majority of the residents in that area. Since there is a history of stopping minorities for reasons that are less than legitimate, the officer must go out of his or her way to show respect to the innocent citizen who does not know why he or she has been stopped and is caught totally off guard. Many people reported to be "suspicious" for merely being of a different race would appreciate an officer's making a final comment, such as "I hope this kind of racism ends soon within our community" or "It's too bad there are still people in our community who are so ignorant." Comments such as these, said with sincerity, may very well get back to the community and contribute to improved future interactions with members of the police department. Of course, some people who are stopped will not appreciate any attempt that the officer makes to explain why the stop was made. Nevertheless, many citizens will react favorably to an officer's understanding of their feelings.

A second situation in which an officer may hear, "You stopped me because I'm . . ." may occur not because of any racist intentions of the officer but rather as a "reflex response" of the citizen (in other words, it has no bearing on reality). Many people have been stopped without reason in the past or know people who have; they carry this baggage into each encounter with an officer. One police officer explained: "I don't consider myself prejudiced. I consider myself a fair person, but let me tell you what happens almost every time I stop a black in city X. The first words I hear from them are 'You stopped me because I'm black.' That's bugging the hell out of me because that's not why I stopped them. I stopped them because they violated the traffic code. It's really bothering me and I'm about to explode."

Officers accused of racially or ethnically motivated stops truly need to remain professional and not escalate a potential conflict or create a confrontation. Law enforcement officials should not only try to communicate their professionalism, both verbally and nonverbally, but also try to strengthen their self-control. The best way to deal with these types of remarks from citizens is to work on your own reactions and stress level. One could potentially receive such remarks on a daily basis. People react to officers as symbols and are using the officer to vent their frustration.

This response assumes no racial profiling has taken place.

Let's assume that the officer did not stop a person because of his or her ethnicity or race and that the officer is therefore not abusing his or her power. George Thompson, founder and president of the Verbal Judo Institute, believes that in these situations, people bring up race and ethnicity to throw the officer off guard. According to Thompson (who is white and a former English professor and police officer), the more professional an officer is, the less likely he or she is to let this type of statement become a problem. Newer officers, especially, can be thrown off by such allegations of racism when, in fact, they are simply upholding the law and keeping the peace as they have been trained to do. Thompson advocates using "verbal deflectors" when citizens make such remarks as "You stopped me because I'm . . ." He recommends responses such as "I appreciate that, but you were going 55 miles in a 25-mile zone," or "I hear what you're saying, but you just broke the law." Verbal deflectors (1) are readily available to the lips, (2) are nonjudgmental, and (3) can be said quickly. Thompson believes that statements from citizens should not be ignored because silence or no response can make people even more furious than they already are (because they were stopped).

Pay attention to what citizens say, but deflect their anger. You are not paid to argue with citizens. You are paid to keep the peace. If you use tactical language and focus every word you say so that it relates to your purpose, then you will sound more professional. The minute you start using words as defensive weapons, you lose power and endanger your safety. If you "springboard" over their arguments and remain calm, controlled, and nonjudgmental, you will gain voluntary compliance most of the time. The results of this professional communication are that (1) you feel good, (2) you disarm the citizen, and (3) you control them in the streets (and in courts and in the media). Never take anything personally. Always treat people with respect and explain the "why" in your communication with them. (Thompson, 2006)

The third and final situation in which an officer may hear "You stopped me because I'm . . ." is when the citizen is correct and, indeed, racial profiling is taking place. Police department personnel are not immune from the racism that still exists in our society. Reflecting biased attitudes outside the law enforcement agency, some officers use their positions of power to assert authority in ways that cannot be tolerated. We are referring not only to the white officer who subjugates citizens from different backgrounds but also, for example, to an African American officer who has internalized the racism of the dominant society and may actually treat fellow group members unjustly. Alternatively, this abuse of power could take place between, for example, a black or Latino officer and a white citizen. (See Chapter 14 for a detailed description of racial profiling.)

Officers must consider the reasons a citizen may say "You stopped me because I'm . . ." and respond accordingly. The situations described call for different responses* on the part of the officer (i.e., citizens call in because of racist perceptions and the "suspicious character" is innocent; the citizen stopped is simply "hassling" the officer, and may or may not have been unjustly stopped in the past; and the citizen making the accusation toward the officer is correct). The officer would do well, in all three situations, to remember the quote included in the final section of Chapter 1: "Remember the history of law enforcement with all groups and ask yourself the question, Am I part of the past, or a part of the future?" (Berry, 2006).

Communication Considerations—Post-9/11

Many Arab Americans, in particular, feel that they are automatic suspects when approached by law enforcement representatives. Since 9/11, there has been what Lobna Ismail, Arab American cross-cultural specialist, characterizes as collateral damage to the entire Arab American community. They may hesitate to call the police when they are victims of crimes, and they fear being treated as suspects rather than victims of a crime, (Ismail, 2003). For this reason, it is imperative to consider the importance of building trust, rapport, and relationships with Arab Americans and people from the Middle East. According to Dr. James Zogby (2003), president of the Arab American Institute Foundation in Washington, D.C., the more a community policing mindset has developed in a particular locale, the more easily do communication barriers come down between law enforcement and Arab Americans. Despite initiatives from the Department of Justice to call up several thousand Arab Americans (and, consequently,

---

*Brookline Police Department in Massachusetts uses an interactive simulation training exercise that creates a variety of scenarios, including those related to racial profiling. In responding to scenarios, officers have to focus on their own behavior and response in order to effectively control the situation ("Brookline," 2003).

widespread resentment and fear among Arab American community members), where police and community leaders held advisory meetings together, where police officers visited mosques and attended community events, effective communication, along with trust, ensued. "We have found that when FBI and police department leadership, for example, are willing to sit down and dialogue with community leaders, then it is much more likely that citizens will be willing to share information, provide tips because officers have gone out of their way to build trust" (Zogby, 2003).

Regarding communication with Arab Americans (and this applies to communication with other cultural groups as well), officers should not try too hard, and in an unnatural way, to demonstrate culturally sensitivity. An officer should understand differences in communication style where they exist but should not act stiff or uncomfortable in an attempt to get it right. With cultural groups that may appear very different from ones own, or where sensitivities may be high, as with members of the Arab American community, law enforcement representatives need to think about approaching others in a way that will increase their comfort level. This means being natural, not beginning with the assumption that they are foreign and strange, and avoiding such thoughts as "I can't communicate with them unless I know their ways" (Zogby, 2003). In the end, the spirit of respect toward fellow human beings, with some knowledge of cultural detail, will lead to effective communication.

INTERVIEWING AND DATA-GATHERING SKILLS

Interviewing and data-gathering skills form the basic techniques for communication and intervention work with multicultural populations. For the officer, the key issues in any interviewing and data-gathering situation are as follows:

- Establishing interpersonal relationships with the parties involved to gain trust and rapport for continual work
- Bringing structure and control to the immediate situation
- Gaining information about the problems and situations that require the presence of the law enforcement officer
- Giving information about the workings of the law enforcement guidelines, resources, and assistance available
- Providing action and interventions as needed
- Bolstering and supporting the different parties' abilities and skills to solve current and future problems on their own

Listed in Exhibit 4.4 are helpful guidelines for providing and receiving better information in a multicultural context.

In the area of data gathering and interviewing, the officer in a multicultural law enforcement and peacekeeping situation cannot assume that his or her key motivators and values are the same as those of the other parties involved. Recognizing such differences in motivation and values will result in greater effectiveness. For example, the values of saving face and preserving one's own honor as well as the honor of one's family are extremely strong motivators and values for many people from Asian, Latin

1. Be knowledgeable about who is likely to have information. Ask questions to identify the head of a family or respected community leaders.

2. Consider that some cultural groups have more of a need than others for rapport and trust building before they are willing to share information. Do not consider the time it takes to establish rapport a waste of time. For some, this may be a necessary step.

3. Provide background and context for your questions, information, and requests. Cultural minorities differ in their need for "contextual information" (i.e., background information) before getting down to the issues or business at hand. Remain patient with those who want to go into more detail than you think is necessary.

4. Expect answers to be formulated and expressed in culturally different ways. Some people tend to be linear in their answers (i.e., giving one point of information at a time in a chronological order), some present information in a zigzag fashion (i.e., they digress frequently), and others tend to present information in a circular style (i.e., they may appear to be talking in circles). And, of course, in addition to cultural differences, there are individual differences in ways of presenting information.

5. It is important to speak simply, but do not make the mistake of using simple or "pigeon" English. Remember, people's comprehension skills are usually better than their speaking skills.

6. "Yes" does not always mean "yes"; do not mistake a courteous answer for the facts or the truth.

7. Remember that maintaining a good rapport is just as important as coming to the point and getting work done quickly. Slow down!

8. Silence is a form of speech; do not interrupt it. Give people time to express themselves by respecting their silence.

Exhibit 4.4   Interviewing and data gathering in a multicultural context.

American, and Mediterranean cultures. An Asian gang expert from the Oakland, California, Police Department illustrated this value system with the case of a niece who had been chosen by the police to translate for her aunt, who had been raped. The values of honor and face-saving prevented the aunt from telling the police all the details of the crime of which she was the victim. Her initial story, told to the police through her niece's translation, contained very few of the facts or details of the crime. Later, through a second translator who was not a family member, the rape victim gave all the necessary information. Precious time had been lost, but the victim explained that she could not have revealed the true story in front of her niece because she would have shamed her family.

Exhibit 4.5 lists key values or motivators for police officers. In any given situation, these values may be at odds with what motivates the victim, suspect, or ordinary citizen of any background. However, when the officer and citizen are from totally different backgrounds, additional cultural or racial variables may also be in conflict.

Finally, when interviewing and data gathering in the area of hate incidents and crimes (as well as threats [phone calls, letters] targeted at individuals of particular backgrounds), the officer's need for control and structure may have to encompass hysterical or at least highly emotional reactions from other people of the same background. In the officer's attempt to control the situation, he or she must consider that there is also a community needing reassurance. For example, an officer must be willing to respond sensitively to heightened anxiety on the part of group members and not downplay their

1. Survival or injury avoidance	6. Avoiding conflict and tensions
2. Control and structure	7. Harmony and peacekeeping
3. Respect and authority	8. Conflict resolution and problem solving
4. Use of professional skills	9. Self-respect and self-esteem
5. Upholding laws and principles	

Exhibit 4.5   Key values or motivators in law enforcement.

fears. Interviewing and data gathering may therefore last much longer when the officer is required to deal with multiple community members and widespread fears.

NONVERBAL COMMUNICATION

Up until this point in the chapter, we have discussed verbal communication across cultures and its relevance to the law enforcement context. Nonverbal communication, including tone of voice, play a key role in the dynamics between any two people. Dr. Albert Mehrabian of the University of California at Los Angeles described in the classic and highly quoted book *Silent Messages* (1971) the general impact between two or three people when a person's verbal and nonverbal messages contradict each other. In this scenario, it is almost always tone of voice and body language, including facial expressions, that convey an individual's true feeling. Of course officers have to attend to citizens' words; however, tone of voice and body language can reveal much more. In addition, across cultures, there are other considerations that relate directly to the interpretation of meaning.

Consider the following examples of reactions to nonverbal differences across cultures and their implications for day-to-day police work:

> He didn't look at me once. I know he's guilty. Never trust a person who doesn't look you in the eye.
>
> —*American police officer*

> Americans seem cold. They seem to get upset when you stand close to them.
>
> —*Jordanian teacher*

In the first example, if an officer uses norms of eye contact as understood by most Americans, he or she could make an incorrect judgment about someone who avoids eye contact. In the second example, an officer's comfortable distance for safety might be violated because of a cultural standard defining acceptable conversational distance. The comments demonstrate how people can misinterpret nonverbal communication when it is culturally different from their own. Misinterpretation can happen with two people from the same background, but it is more likely when there are cultural differences. Universal emotions such as happiness, fear, and sadness are expressed in similar nonverbal ways throughout the world. However, nonverbal variations across cultures can cause confusion.

Take the example of the way people express sadness and grief. In many cultures, such as Arab and Iranian cultures, people express grief openly and out loud. In contrast, in other parts of the world (e.g., in China and Japan), people are generally more subdued or even silent in their expressions of grief. In Asian cultures, the general belief is that it is unacceptable to show emotion openly (whether sadness, happiness, or pain). Without this cultural knowledge, in observing a person who did not openly express grief, for example, one might conclude that he or she is not in emotional distress. This would be an incorrect and ethnocentric interpretation based on one's own culture.

The expression of friendship is another example of how cultural groups differ in their nonverbal behavior. Feelings of friendship exist everywhere, but their expression varies. It is acceptable for men to embrace and kiss each other (in Saudi Arabia and Russia, for example) and for women to hold hands (in China, Korea, Egypt, and other countries). Russian gymnasts of the same sex have been seen on television kissing each other on the lips; this is apparently an acceptable gesture in their culture and does not imply that they are gay or lesbian. What is considered "normal" behavior in one culture may be viewed as "abnormal" or unusual in another.

The following areas of nonverbal communication have variations across cultures; the degree to which a person displays the nonverbal differences depends on how Westernized the person has become. Note that some people who are very Westernized in their thinking may still display traditional forms of nonverbal communication simply because they are unaware that the differences exist.

1. *Gestures:* A few American gestures are offensive in other cultures. For example, the OK gesture is obscene in Latin America, the good luck gesture is offensive in parts of Vietnam, and the "come here" gesture (beckoning people to come with the palm up) is very insulting in most of Asia and Latin America (Levine and Adelman, 1992).

2. *Position of Feet:* A police sergeant relaxing at his desk with his feet up, baring the soles of his shoes, would most likely offend a Thai or Saudi Arabian (and other groups as well) coming into the office. To show one's foot in many cultures is insulting because the foot is considered the dirtiest part of the body. (Another example of this was the intended insult toward Saddam Hussein when Iraqis hit a statue of him with their shoes.) Officers need to be mindful of this taboo with respect to the foot, and should refrain, whenever possible, from making physical contact with the foot when, for example, someone is lying on the ground.

3. *Facial expressions:* Not all facial expressions mean the same thing across cultures. The smile is a great source of confusion for many people in law enforcement when they encounter people from Asian, especially Southeast Asian, cultures. A smile or giggle can cover up pain, humiliation, and embarrassment. Some women (e.g., Japanese, Vietnamese) cover up their mouths when they smile or giggle. Upon hearing something sad, a Vietnamese person may smile. Similarly, an officer may need to communicate something that causes a loss of face to a person, resulting in the person smiling. This smile does not mean that the person is trying to be a "smart aleck"; it is simply a culturally conditioned response.

4. ***Facial expressiveness:*** People in law enforcement have to be able to "read faces" in certain situations in order to assess situations correctly. The degree to which people show emotions on their faces depends, in large part, on their cultural background. Whereas Latin Americans, Mediterraneans, Arabs, Israelis, and African Americans tend to show emotions facially, other groups, such as many of the Asian cultural groups, tend to be less facially expressive and less emotive. An officer may thus incorrectly assume that a person is not being cooperative or would not make a good witness.

5. ***Eye contact:*** In many parts of the world, eye contact is avoided with authority figures. In parts of India, for example, a father would discipline his child by saying, "Don't look me in the eye when I'm speaking to you"; an American parent would say, "Look me in the eye when I'm speaking to you." To maintain direct eye contact with a police officer in some cultures would be disrespectful. Direct eye contact with some citizens can also be perceived as threatening to that citizen. A security officer in a large store in San Jose, California, offered the example of officers looking directly at Latino/Hispanic young people suspected of stealing items from the store. On a number of occasions, the officers' direct eye contact was met with a physical reaction (i.e., the young person attempting to punch the officer). He explained that the Latino/Hispanic individual mistook the eye contact as confrontation and a challenge for a fight.

6. ***Physical or conversational distance:*** All people unconsciously keep a comfortable distance around them when communicating with others, resulting in invisible walls that keep people far enough away. (This subcategory of nonverbal communication is called *proxemics.*) Police officers are perhaps more aware than others of the distance they keep from people in order to remain safe. When someone violates this space, a person often feels threatened and backs away or, in the case of an officer, begins to think about protective measures. Although personality and context also determine interpersonal distance, cultural background comes into play. In general, Latin Americans and Middle Easterners are more comfortable at closer distances than are northern Europeans, Asians, and the majority of Americans. An officer should not necessarily feel threatened, for example, if approached by an Iranian or a Greek in a manner that feels uncomfortably close. While maintaining a safe distance, the officer should also consider cultural background. Consider the example of a Middle Eastern suspect (for example) who ignores an officers' command to "step back." The social distance for interacting in the Middle East (as in other areas of the world) is much closer than it is in the United States. For officers, where safety is paramount, this could easily lead to misinterpretation. Generally, Americans are comfortable at a little more than an arm's distance from each other.

For the law enforcement professional, nonverbal communication constitutes a major role in all aspects of peacekeeping and enforcement. For multicultural populations, it is even more important that the officer be aware of the variety of nuances and differences that may exist from one group to another. Studies show that a large percentage of

1. Body language and nonverbal messages can override an officer's verbal content in high-stress and crisis situations. For example, the officer's statement that he or she is there to help may be contradicted by a body posture of discomfort and uncertainty in culturally unfamiliar households.

2. For people of different ethnic backgrounds, stress, confusion, and uncertainty can also communicate unintended messages. For example, an Asian may remain silent and look nervous and anxious at the scene of a crime. He or she may appear to be "uncooperative" when in fact this person may have every intention of helping the officer.

3. For people with limited English skills, the nonverbal aspects of communication become even more important. Correct gestures and nonverbal cues help the nonnative English speaker in understanding the verbal messages.

4. It is important for officers to learn about and avoid offensive gestures and cultural taboos. However, immigrants and international visitors are quick to forgive and to overlook gestures and actions made out of forgetfulness and ignorance. Officers should realize, too, that in time, newcomers usually learn many of the nonverbal mannerisms with which officers are more familiar. Nevertheless, learning about offensive gestures can help officers avoid interpersonal offenses.

Note: Each of the culture-specific chapters (Chapters 5 through 9) contains information about nonverbal characteristics of particular groups.

Exhibit 4.6   Nonverbal communication: key points for law enforcement.

interpersonal communication is understood because of the nonverbal body language aspects of the speaker. Moreover, in many cultures, as is true for many ethnic minorities in the United States, greater weight and belief are placed on the visual and nonverbal aspects of communication (Exhibits 4.6 and 4.7).

Officers must be authentic in their communication with people from various backgrounds. When learning about both verbal and nonverbal characteristics across cultures, officers do not need to feel that they must communicate differently each time they are in contact with someone of a different background. However, understanding that there are variations in communication style will help the officer interpret people's motives and attitudes more accurately and, overall, assess situations without a cultural bias.

- When is touch appropriate and inappropriate?
- What is the comfortable physical distance between people in interactions?
- What is considered proper eye contact? What do eye contact and lack of eye contact mean to the people involved?
- What cultural variety is there in facial expressions? For example, does nodding and smiling mean the same in all cultures? If someone appears to be expressionless, does that mean he or she is uncooperative?
- What are appropriate and inappropriate gestures for a particular cultural group?
- Is the person in transition from one culture to another and therefore lacking the knowledge of communication?

Exhibit 4.7   Key questions concerning nonverbal communication across cultures.

MALE–FEMALE COMMUNICATION IN LAW ENFORCEMENT

You have to go along with the kind of kidding and ribbing that the guys participate in; otherwise, you are not one of them. If you say that you are offended by their crass jokes and vulgar speech, then you are ostracized from the group. I have often felt that in the squad room men have purposely controlled themselves because of my presence, because I have spoken up. But what I've done to them is make them act one way because of my presence as a woman. Then they call me a prude or spread the word that I'm keeping track of all their remarks for the basis of a sexual harassment suit down the road. I have no interest in doing that. I simply want to be a competent police officer in a professional working environment. (Comments by a woman police officer [who wishes to remain anonymous] at a Women's Peace Officer Association [WPOA] Conference.

With the changing workforce, including increasing numbers of women in traditionally male professions, many new challenges in the area of male–female communication are presenting themselves. Within law enforcement, in particular, a strong camaraderie characterizes the relationships mainly among the male members of a police force, although, in some cases, women are part of this camaraderie. Women allowed into what has been termed the "brotherhood" have generally had to "become one of the guys" to gain acceptance into a historically male-dominated profession.

Camaraderie results when a group is united because of a common goal or purpose; the glue cementing the camaraderie is the easy communication among its members. The extracurricular interests of the members of the group, the topics selected for conversation, and the jokes that people tell all contribute to the cohesion or tightness of police department members. In some departments, women find that they or other women are the object of jokes about sexual topics or that there are simply numerous references to sex. Because certain departments within cities have consisted mostly of men, they have not had to consider the inclusion of women on an equal basis and have not had to examine their own communication with each other.

Young women who are new to a department feel that they must tolerate certain behaviors in order to be accepted. A female sheriff participating in a WPOA conference said that on a daily basis she confronts vulgar language and sexual references in the jail where she works. Her list was long: "I am extremely bothered about the communication of the men where I work. Without mincing words, I'll tell you—at the county jail, officers are very degrading to women. They sometimes make fun of rape victims, they are rude and lewd to female inmates, and they are constantly trying to get me to join into the 'fun.' A woman is referred to as a 'dyke,' a 'cunt,' a 'douche bag,' a 'whore,' a 'hooker,' a 'bitch,' and I'm sure I could come up with more. The guys don't call me those names, but they use them all the time referring to other women." This sheriff also noted that she did not experience the disrespectful verbal behavior in one-to-one situations with male deputies, only when they were in a group. She wondered out loud, "What happens to men when they group with each other? Why is there the change?"

It is not only the male grouping phenomenon that produces this type of rough, vulgar, and sexist language. One study of a large urban police department conducted for California Law Enforcement Command College documented inappropriate communications from patrol cars' two-way radios and computers. The language on the official system was often unprofessional—rough, vulgar, offensive, racist, and sexist. Obviously, both discipline and training were needed in this agency.

Certainly, not all men behave and talk in offensive ways, but the phenomenon is frequent enough that women in traditionally male work environments mention this issue repeatedly. Some women join in conversations that make them uneasy, but they do not let on that their working environment is uncomfortable and actually affecting their morale and productivity. Other women seem to be comfortable with the sexual comments of their male counterparts and may not object to the use of certain terms that other women find patronizing (e.g., "honey," "doll," "babe"). However, the percentage of women who fall into this category may very well be decreasing. Through sexual harassment policies, both women and men have learned that, for some, sexual innuendoes and patronizing terms can contribute to a hostile working environment.

In male-dominated institutions, vocations, and professions, women find that speaking out against this type of talk and joking creates discomfort for them and puts them in a double bind. A female police officer at a workshop on discrimination in the workplace said she felt that women's choices regarding communication with fellow male officers were limited. She explained that when a woman objects or speaks up, she risks earning a reputation or label that is hard to shed. If she remains quiet, she must tolerate a lot of verbal abuse and compromise her professionalism. This particular police officer decided to speak up in her own department, and, indeed, she earned a reputation as a troublemaker. In fact, she had no interest in going any further than complaining to her supervisor but nevertheless was accused of preparing for a lawsuit. She explained that a lawsuit was the farthest thing from her mind and that all she wanted was professional respect.

Some women who have objected to certain mannerisms of their male counterparts' communication say that when they come into a room or office, the men stop talking. The result is that the communication that normally functions to hold a group together is strained and tense. The ultimate result is that the workplace becomes segregated by gender. When shut out from a conversation, many women feel excluded and unempowered; in turn, many men feel resentful about having to modify their style of communication.

Women in traditionally male work environments such as police and fire departments find that they are sometimes put in a position of having to trade their professional identity for their personal one. A woman officer who proudly tells her sergeant about the arrest she made may be stunned when he, totally out of context, compliments the way she has been keeping in shape and tells her how good she looks in her uniform. This is not to say that compliments are never acceptable. But in this context, the woman is relating as a professional and desires reciprocal professional treatment. Men and women often ask, "Where do I draw the line? When does a comment become harassment?" In terms of the legal definition of sexual harassment, when the perpetrators are made aware that their comments are uninvited and unwelcome, then they must be reasonable enough to stop making them. It is not within the scope of this chapter to detail sexual harassment and all its legal implications; however, it should be noted that everyone has his or her own limits. What is harassment to one may be appreciated by another. When communicating across genders, each party must be sensitive to what the other party considers acceptable or insulting (see Exhibit 4.8). It is also the responsibil-

- Use terms that are inclusive rather than exclusive. Examples: "police officer," "chairperson," "commendations" (instead of the informal "atta boys")
- Avoid using terms or words that many women feel diminish their professional status. Examples: "chick," "babe"
- Avoid using terms or words that devalue groups of women or stereotype them. Example: Referring to women officers as "dykes"
- Avoid sexist jokes, even if you think they are not offensive. (Someone is bound to be offended; the same applies to racist jokes.)
- Avoid using terms that negatively spotlight or set women apart from men. Examples: "For a woman cop, she did a good job" (implying that this is the exception rather than the rule); also applies to references about other cultural groups: "He's Latino, but he works hard." "He's black, but he's really skilled."

Exhibit 4.8   Inclusive workplace communication.

ity of the individual who has been offended, whether male or female, to make it clear that certain types of remarks are offensive.

SUMMARY

In cross-cultural communication in law enforcement, officers' own filters and perceptions influence the assessment of each situation and the reactions the officers choose to exhibit. Each officer has unique "blind spots" and emotional "buttons" that may negatively affect the communication. To explore your own skills in this regard, you are urged to undertake a self-evaluation by filling out the Communications Inventory in Appendix D.

Officers must keep in mind that rapport building is related to trust for many persons of different backgrounds. The more trust officers earn with members of ethnic communities, the more helpful these group members will be when officers need cooperation and information. To improve communication across cultures, it is essential that people in law enforcement understand the overall style of communication of different groups, including the special challenges facing men and women in the profession, and utilize multicultural communication skills.

Finally, we reiterate two points made earlier in this chapter regarding police officer communication:

- Officers have traditionally used styles of communication and language that at one time were considered acceptable not only within the police agency but with citizens as well. Because of cultural diversity in the population and the accompanying need to respect all individuals, the unspoken rules about what is appropriate have changed dramatically.

- Through communication, officers have tremendous power to influence the behavior and responses of the citizens with whom they contact. This is true of all citizens, regardless of background. A lack of knowledge of the cross-cultural aspects of communication will diminish that power with people whose backgrounds differ from that of the officer.

DISCUSSION QUESTIONS AND ISSUES*

1. ***The Origins of Stereotypes.*** In this chapter, we argue that officers need to recognize how their early experiences in life and later adult experiences shape their perceptions and "filters" about people from groups different from their own. What do you remember learning about various ethnic and racial groups when you were young? Did you grow up in an environment of tolerance, or did you hear statements such as "That's the way they are," or "You've got to be careful with those people" or "They are lazy [or dishonest, etc.]"? Also discuss your experiences as an adult with different groups and how those experiences may be affecting your perceptions.

2. ***Police Officer Interaction with Speakers of Other Languages.*** The following dialogue illustrates a typical interaction between a police officer and a nonnative speaker of English, in this case a Vietnamese man. Judging from the English that the Vietnamese is speaking, how would you rate the officer's use of English? Analyze this interaction by being specific as to how the officer can improve.

    The following dialogue takes place when an officer pulls a car over, gets out of the car, and approaches the driver. The driver, who is Vietnamese, says, in poor English, "What happen? Why you stop me?"

    Officer: I pulled you over because you ran a red light.

    Citizen: (No response)

    Officer: This is a traffic violation. (Receives no feedback). Do you understand?

    Citizen: (Nodding) Yeah, I understand.

    Officer: I'm going to have to issue you a traffic citation.

    Citizen: (Stares at officer)

    Officer: Where's your driver's license?

    Citizen: License? Just a minute. (Leans over to open glove compartment, but finds nothing; gets out of car and goes to trunk)

    Officer (Irritated and slightly nervous): *Hey!* (In a loud voice) What's going on here? I asked to see your driver's license. Are you the registered owner of this car?

    Citizen: Yeah. I go get my license.

    Officer (Speaking much louder): Wait a minute. Don't you understand? Are you not the owner of this car? Do you even have a license?

    Citizen: Wait. (Finds license in trunk and produces it for officer)

    Officer: Okay. Would you mind getting back into the car now?

*See the Instructor's Manual accompanying this text for additional activities, role-play activities, questionnaires, and projects related to the content of this chapter.

Citizen: (Does nothing) Yeah, I understand.

Officer (Pointing to the front seat): Back into the car!

Citizen: (Does as told)

The officer could make improvements in at least four areas: (1) choice of words, (2) manner of asking questions, (3) use of idioms (there are at least two or three that could be changed to simple English), and (4) tone and attitude.

3. ***Police Officers' "Hot Buttons."*** Discuss how citizens (e.g., suspects, victims, complainants) affect your reactions in communication. Specifically, what words and attitudes do they use that break down your attempts to be professional? What emotionally laden language "sets you off"?

4. ***Professional Communication with Citizens.*** After you have discussed what affects your communication negatively (question 3), role-play with fellow officers situations in which you respond professionally to abuses you hear. (Refer back to the section on verbal judo if you need suggestions.)

5. ***Racially and Sexual Orientation Derogatory Remarks.*** Marge Schott (1928–2004) was the controversial primary owner, president, and CEO of the Cincinatti Reds for almost 15 years. She was the first female owner to buy a baseball team. Prior to being forced to sell her major interests to the team in 1999, she was suspended and fined for making racist remarks and negative comments regarding sexual orientation over a period of 7 years; she allegedly called two Reds outfielders her "million-dollar niggers" and admitted to keeping a swastika armband in her desk drawer. She also told *The New York Times* that Hitler was "good" but that he went too far. In addition, she said she did not want her players to wear earring because "only fruits wear earrings," and she did not see using the slur "Jap" as being offensive. Schott publicly told people she was not a racist. One of the issues related to her racially and culturally insensitive remarks was that her comments were made in front of other people, but no one said anything to her or objected. Some felt that she should have been confronted.

Answer the following questions as accurately as you can. If you were with friends in a social gathering and one friend made an off-color remark similar to those of Schott, what would you do? If you think that you would say something, what would it be? If you know that you would not say anything, does this mean that you condone the behavior? Would things change if the remarks were made in the law enforcement agency or you overheard officers on the streets making such remarks? Explain your answer and include what strategies you could use to correct the inappropriate behavior.

6. ***Cultural Observations.*** Make a list of your observations for each of the cultural groups with which you have had a substantial amount of contact. Then try to find someone from that culture with whom you can discuss your observations.

   a. Display of emotions and expressions of feelings

   b. Communication style: loud, soft, direct, indirect

   c. Expressions of appreciation; conventions of courtesy (i.e., forms of politeness)

   d. Need (or lack thereof) for privacy

    e. Gestures, facial expressions, and body movements

    f. Eye contact

    g. Touching

    h. Interpersonal space (conversational distance)

    i. Taboo topics in conversation

    j. Response to authority

7. ***Discomfort with Unfamiliar Groups.*** Try to recall a situation in which you found yourself in a culturally unfamiliar environment (e.g., responding to a call in an ethnically different household or being the only minority person of your background among a group of people from another cultural or ethnic group). How much discomfort, if any, did you experience? If the situation was uncomfortable, did it affect your communication effectiveness or professionalism?

8. ***Accusations of Racially or Ethnically Motivated Stops.*** Have you encountered, "You stopped me because I'm [any ethnic group]?" If so, how did you handle the situation? How effectively do you think you responded?

WEBSITE RESOURCES

Visit these websites for additional information about cross-cultural and general communication applicable to law enforcement.

Verbal Judo Institute: http://www.verbaljudo.com

This website centers around "verbal Judo," a tactical form of communication used to generate voluntary compliance from citizens under difficult situations. It lists various types of verbal Judo courses available as well as books and articles on the subject. There is a link to law enforcement explaining the applicability of verbal Judo to police officers.

United States Department of Justice Federal Bureau of Investigation:
http://www.fbi.gov/publications/leb/2001/aug01leb.htm

This FBI website makes available an excellent article on neurolinguistic programming entitled "Subtle Skills for Building Rapport" by Vincent A. Sandoval and Susan H. Adams.

Royal Canadian Mounted Police (RCMP):
http://www.rcmp-learning.org/vietnam/module_a.htm

This is the website for the Royal Canadian Mounted Police (RCMP) and their Cross Cultural Communications Series—"The Vietnamese" is the second in a new series of individualized instruction modules that have been developed to educate and sensitize employees of the RCMP.

International Association of Campus Law Enforcement Agencies (IACLEA):
http://www.iaclea.org/pubs/

This is the website for the IACLEA, which has many publications, and specifically, "If I Look Confused and Lost, It's Probably Because I Am." This is a video workshop on cross-cultural communications with a focus on foreign students. Created and conducted by Dr. Jennifer Lund, Director of International Student Services at Georgia State University, this 57-minute videotape is intended for use in training campus staff to deal positively with foreign students, and it comes with a discussion guide. The video covers mutual perceptions of foreign and U.S. students behavioral and attitudinal differences, and the twelve "shoulds" to improve communication.

REFERENCES

Berry, Ondra. (2003). Deputy Chief, Reno, Nevada, Police Department, personal communication. November, 2003.

DeGeneste, Henry I., and John D. Sullivan. (1997, July). "Policing a Multicultural Community." *Fresh Perspectives: A Police Executive Research Forum Publication,* p. 7.

Fernandez, Donya. (2000). Language Rights attorney for the Language Rights Project, Employment Law Center/Legal Aid Society, San Francisco, Calif., personal communication, December, 2000.

Gray, John. (2002). *Mars and Venus in the Workplace.* New York: Harper Collins.

Hall, Edward. (1959). *The Silent Language.* Garden City, N.Y.: Doubleday, 1959.

Hall Edward. (1966). *The Hidden Dimension.* Garden City, N.Y.: Doubleday, 1966.

"Helping People Who Lack English." (1999, September 19). *Contra Costa Times,* p. A32.

Ismail, Lobna. (2003, October). President of Connecting Cultures, a training and consulting organization specializing in Arab American culture; personal communication.

Levine, Deena, and Mara Adelman. (1992). *Beyond Language: Cross-Cultural Communication.* Englewood Cliffs, NJ: Prentice Hall.

McAllister, Daryl. (2003, December). Hayward, California, Police Department, Investigations Unit; personal communication.

Mehrabian, Albert. (1971). *Silent Messages.* Belmont, Calif.: Wadsworth Publishing.

Sandoval, V. A., and Susan H. Adams. (2001, August). "Subtle Skills for Building Rapport." *FBI Law Enforcement Bulletin, 70* (8), 1–9. Available: http://www.fbi.gov/publications/leb/2001/aug01leb.htm.

Thompson, George. (2006, July). President of Verbal Judo Institute, Yucca Valley, California; personal communication.

Thompson, George. (2004). *Verbal Judo: The Gentle Art of Persuasion.* Yucca Valley, Calif.: Verbal Judo Institute, Inc.

"The Troubled LA County Sheriff's Department." (1992, July 21). *Los Angeles Times,* p. A18.

Zogby, James. (2003, January & September). Director of the Arab American Institute Foundation; personal communication.

Part 2

CULTURAL SPECIFICS FOR LAW ENFORCEMENT

5 Law Enforcement Contact with Asian/Pacific Americans

6 Law Enforcement Contact with African Americans

7 Law Enforcement Contact with Latino/Hispanic Americans

8 Law Enforcement Contact with Arab Americans and Other Middle Eastern Groups

9 Law Enforcement Contact with Native Americans

Part Two presents information on Asian/Pacific, African American, Latino/Hispanic, Middle Eastern, and Native American cultural backgrounds with regard to the needs of law enforcement and criminal justice representatives. We have selected these groups, as opposed to other groups not described in this book, for one or more of the following reasons: (1) the group is a relatively large ethnic or racial group in the United States, (2) the traditional culture of the group differs widely from that of mainstream American culture, and/or (3) typically or historically there have been problems between the particular group and law enforcement officials.

In these culture-specific chapters, general information is presented on the following areas: historical background, demographics, and diversity within the cultural group. Following the introductory information, we present specific details relevant to law enforcement and criminal justice in the following areas: communication styles (both verbal and nonverbal), group identification terms, offensive labels, stereotypes, and family structure. Each chapter ends with key concerns for officers regarding the particular cultural group, a summary of recommendations for law enforcement officials, and resources for additional information about the cultural group.

Important note: In this section's presentation of specific cultural and racial groups, we reference the section "The Overlap of Race and Ethnicity" in Chapter 1 as a reminder that individuals in our multicultural population do not always easily fall into neat categories of only one race or culture. There can be an overlap of race and ethnicity, as in the example of a black Latino. Our categorization of different groups is a convenient way of presenting information; we do not wish to imply that there can be no overlap among the group categories.

Chapter 5

Law Enforcement Contact with Asian/Pacific Americans

OVERVIEW

This chapter provides specific ethnic and cultural information on Asian Americans and Pacific Islanders. The label Asian Americans/Pacific Islanders encompasses over 40 different ethnic and cultural groups. For ease of use, we use the shortened version Asian/Pacific Americans to refer to members of these ethnic groupings. We first define this very diverse group and then present a historical overview, focusing on the relationship between law enforcement and other criminal justice personnel and citizens. We present demographics and elements of diversity among Asian/Pacific Americans as well as issues related to ethnic and cultural identity. Aspects of the Asian/Pacific American family are discussed, including myths and stereotypes, assimilation and acculturation processes, the extended family and community, gender roles, generational differences, and adolescent and youth issues.

The section "Cultural Influences on Communication" discusses the subtle aspects of nonverbal and indirect communications that peace officers and others in emergency-related public safety roles often find troublesome. The closing section presents several key issues for law enforcement: underreporting of crimes, differential treatment, increasing Asian/Pacific American community police services, increasing the number of Asian/Pacific peace officers, and the rise in crimes within the Asian/Pacific community. Finally, we review recommendations for improved communication and relationships between law enforcement personnel and Asian/Pacific American communities.

COMMENTARY

For many Asian/Pacific American groups, especially those who have recently immigrated into the United States, the law enforcement system is somewhat of a mystery. As such, Asian/Pacific Americans may find it difficult to cooperate and to participate fully with law enforcement officers.

> To the Vietnamese immigrant, our law enforcement system doesn't seem to serve his community well. In Vietnam, if you are arrested, then the work of the attorney is to prove that you are innocent. You remain locked up in jail until your innocence is proven. In the United States, a suspect who is arrested is released upon posting bail, usually within 24 hours. To the Vietnamese

> immigrant, it would seem that if you have the money, you can buy your way out
> of jail! (Vietnamese community advocate's comments about a local merchant's
> reluctance to cooperate with the police)

Many law enforcement officers have difficulty understanding the diversity of customs, activities, behaviors, and values within the different Asian/Pacific American groups. They do not know where to go to get such cultural information without the fear of offending. Yet this cultural knowledge is vital to understanding and to effective peacekeeping in any Asian/Pacific American community.

> For some of the Asian groups, you just hear things that you're not sure about,
> but there's no one you can turn to ask sometimes. For example, in our work, we
> hear that Sikhs always carry a sword or knife on their person (which they carry
> as a religious object), so is it insensitive to confiscate it? We also hear that if it
> is drawn, they must also draw blood—true or false? Moreover, what is the thing
> to do with their turbans? Would it be an insult to pat-search a turban while it's
> on the person's head? (police officer's comments in a cultural awareness training session)

With the increased emphasis and attention on illegal immigration, human trafficking, and homeland security, law enforcement officers have heightened responsibilities and challenges in understanding and protecting emerging Asian/Pacific American communities.

INTRODUCTION

For the past four decades, the Asian/Pacific American population has experienced the largest proportional increases of any ethnic minority population in the United States (over 100 percent growth for the decades from 1960 to 1990 and 76 percent growth for the decade from 1990 to 2000). The population growth can be attributed to (1) higher immigration from the Pacific Rim countries, (2) greater longevity, (3) higher birth rates, (4) immigrants admitted for special skills and expertise for work in high-technology industries in the United States, and (5) existing ethnic groups added to this population category (including the Asian/Pacific Americans who consider themselves "multiracial"). Growth in major urban areas has been particularly striking, as is seen in New York City, Los Angeles, San Jose (CA), San Francisco, Honolulu, San Diego, Chicago, Houston, Seattle, Fremont (CA), Fairfax (VA), and Quincy (MA). Growth in the population as a whole is most dramatically reflected in terms of increased numbers of Asian/Pacific Americans in politics, community leadership, business, education, and public service areas. Law enforcement contact with Asian/Pacific people has increased because of their greater presence in communities. Asian/Pacific Americans have one of the highest citizenship rates among all foreign-born groups; in 2006, 52 percent of the immigrants from Asian/Pacific countries were naturalized citizens (U.S. Bureau of the Census, 2006).

ASIAN/PACIFIC AMERICAN DEFINED

The term Asian/Pacific Americans is actually a contraction of two terms, Asian Americans and Pacific Islander peoples. Although used throughout this chapter, Asian/Pacific Americans is, in fact, a convenient summary label for a very heterogeneous group.

There certainly is not universal acceptance of this labeling convention, but for practical purposes it has been adopted frequently, with occasional variations (e.g., Asian and Pacific Americans, Asian Americans/Pacific Islanders, Asians and Pacific Islanders). It represents the self-designation preferred by many Asian and Pacific people in the United States, particularly in preference to the more dated (and, to some, offensive) term Orientals. The U.S. government and other governmental jurisdictions usually use "Asian Americans/Pacific Islanders" to refer to members within any of the 40 or more groups comprising this category.

At least 40 distinct ethnic and cultural groups might meaningfully be listed under this designation:

1. Bangladeshi
2. Belauan (formerly Palauan)
3. Bhutanese
4. Bruneian
5. Cambodian
6. Chamorro (Guamanian)
7. Chinese
8. Fijian
9. Hawaiian (or Native Hawaiian)
10. Hmong
11. Indian (Asian, South Asian, or East Indian)
12. Indonesian
13. Japanese
14. Kiribati
15. Korean
16. Laotian
17. Malaysian
18. Maldivian
19. Marshallese (of the Marshall Islands, to include Majuro, Ebeye, and Kwajalein)
20. Micronesia (to include Kosrae, Ponape, Truk, and Yap)
21. Mongolian
22. Myanmarese (formerly Burmese)
23. Nauruan
24. Nepalese
25. Ni-Vanuatu
26. Okinawan
27. Pakistani
28. Pilipino (preferred spelling of Filipino)
29. Saipan Carolinian (or Carolinian, from the Commonwealth of the Northern Marianas)
30. Samoan
31. Singaporian
32. Solomon Islander
33. Sri Lankan (formerly Ceylonese)
34. Tahitian
35. Taiwanese
36. Tibetan
37. Tongan
38. Thai
39. Tuvaluan
40. Vietnamese

Although there are marked differences between the 40 groups listed, individuals within any of the 40 groups may also differ in a vast number of ways.

From the viewpoint of law enforcement, it is important to recognize some of the differences that may cut across or be common to all Asian/Pacific ethnic groups. For example:

1. Area of residence in the United States
2. Comfort with and competence in English
3. Generational status in the United States (first, second, third generation, and so forth)
4. Degree of acculturation and assimilation
5. Education (number of years outside and inside the United States)
6. Native and other languages spoken and/or written
7. Age (what is documented on paper and what may be the real age)
8. Degree of identification with the home country and/or region of self or parents' origin
9. Family composition and extent of family dispersion in the United States and globally
10. Extent of identification with local, national, and global Asian/Pacific sociopolitical issues
11. Participation and degree to which the individual is embedded in the ethnic community network
12. Religious beliefs and cultural value orientation
13. Economic status and financial standing
14. Sensitivity to ethnic and cultural experiences and perceptions as an Asian/Pacific person in the United States
15. Identification with issues, concerns, and problems shared by other ethnic-racial groups (e.g., racial profiling and other discrimination issues voiced by African American, Latino/Hispanic Americans, and Middle Eastern and Arab Americans)

It should be noted that the definition itself of the Asian/Pacific group points to and embodies an ever-emerging, ethnic mosaic of diverse constituencies. Groups are added and removed based on self-definition and needs for self-choice. In our definition, we have not added immigrants or refugees from the Central Asian nations of Kazakhstan, Kyrgyzstan, Tajikistan, Turkmenistan, and Uzbekistan (i.e., countries that were part of the former Soviet Union). We also do not include certain countries on the Asian continent even though they are specified in the "World Population Data Sheet" by the Population Reference Bureau (2005) because of the self-choice issue. As more immigrants from Central Asia settle in the United States, these groups may (or may not) be added to the definition of Asian/Pacific Americans. Clearly, the pooling of separate Asian and Pacific Islander groups under the label of Asian/Pacific Americans emerged, in part, out of the necessity to have a larger collective whole when a greater numerical count may make a difference (especially in political and community issue areas). Merging these 40 ethnic groups into a collective entity allowed for sufficiently large numbers for meaningful representation in communities and other arenas.

Although one may focus upon nationality or nation of origin as the basis of identifying Asian/Pacific American groupings (e.g., "Korean" for those whose ancestry is from Korea, "Vietnamese" for those whose ancestry is from Vietnam), there may be other demographic variables of greater importance than that of nationality. For example, whether one is from the Central Asian nation of Uzbekistan, the Southeast Asian nation of Vietnam, or the Pacific Island nation of Micronesia, the demographic variable of ethnicity, if one were Chinese, may be a more important identifier than that of national origin for some persons or groups. As another example, one's religion may be a more important group identifier than either ethnicity and/or nationality, as might be seen with Muslims (i.e., people who practice Islam). Given that the four largest countries with Muslim populations are in South Asia, that is, Indonesia, Pakistan, Bangladesh, and India (Glasse & Smith, 2003), Asian/Pacific American people who practice Islam might see religion as a more important identifier than ethnicity and nationality.

Other Key Definitions

Since a large proportion of Asian/Pacific Americans whom law enforcement officers may encounter are born outside the United States, it is important to understand some of the key differences that relate to immigration status. One key difference is that of Asian/Pacific Americans who are considered refugees and those who are considered immigrants at the time that they enter the United States. Some of the between-group hostilities (within the Asian/Pacific community and among other ethnic minority communities) have been a result of not understanding how refugee status differs from immigrant status in the United States.

Refugees are sponsored into the United States under the authority of the U.S. government. Although many ethnic groups have come in under the sponsorship of the federal government with refugee or émigré status, the largest numbers have come from Southeast Asia as a result of the past upheaval brought on by the Vietnam War. Refugees, since they are sponsored into the United States by the government, are expected to utilize public support services fully (welfare, English as a Second Language [ESL] programs, educational tuition, job training programs, and case management). Since it is part of being a "good refugee" to participate fully, case managers are often assigned refugee families to ensure that family members are fully utilizing all of the services provided. Such participation in public programs may also create dependency and learned helplessness that can result from having others help or interfere with what many could have done for themselves.

Immigrants enter into the United States under the direct sponsorship of individuals' families. The federal government establishes that immigrants are allowed to enter the United States only if their families can completely support or establish work for the individual. In fact, one criterion for being able to attain permanent residence status (a "green card") is that the immigrant will not become a burden to the government, which means that participation in any publicly funded program may jeopardize that individual's chances for attaining permanent residence status. (Thus, immigrants try very hard to avoid getting involved in public or community programs and services.) In contrast to the refugee, being a "good immigrant" means avoiding any participation in public service programs.

Type I	Asian/Pacific recently arrived immigrant or refugee (less than 5 years in the United States, with major life experiences in Asia or the Pacific Islands)
Type II	Asian/Pacific immigrant or refugee (5 or more years in the United States, with major life experiences in Asia or the Pacific Islands)
Type III	Asian/Pacific American (second generation; offspring of immigrant or refugee)
Type IV	Asian/Pacific Immigrant (major life experiences in the United States)
Type V	Asian/Pacific American (third or later generations in the United States)
Type VI	Asian/Pacific national (anticipates return to Asia or to the Pacific Islands, to include visitors and tourists)
Type VII	Asian/Pacific national (global workplace and residency)

Exhibit 5.1   Typology of Asian/Pacific Americans.

TYPOLOGY OF ASIAN/PACIFIC AMERICANS

As we look at Asian/Pacific American individuals, families, and communities, we have developed a seven-part typology that will be useful in understanding and in summarizing some of the differences between individuals within this group (see Exhibit 5.1).

Our typology suggests that as law enforcement and public safety organizations prepare and train their personnel to work with Asian/Pacific American communities, a focus on the key differences within each of the typological groups would be most effective. We will come back to this typology in a later section to discuss how the motivational components within each of the groupings can affect the way Asian/Pacific American persons may respond in law enforcement situations.

HISTORICAL INFORMATION

The first Asians to arrive in the United States in sizable numbers were the Chinese in the 1840s to work on the plantations in Hawaii. Then, in the 1850s, they immigrated to work in the gold mines in California and later on the transcontinental railroad. Of course, the native populations of the Pacific Island areas (e.g., Samoans, Hawaiians, Guamanians, Fijians) were there before the establishment of the 13 original colonies of the United States. The Chinese were followed in the late 1800s and early 1900s by the Japanese and the Pilipinos* (and in smaller numbers by the Koreans and South Asian Indians). Large numbers of Asian Indians (nearly 500,000) entered the United States as a result of Congressional action in 1946 for "persons of races indigenous to India" to have the right of naturalization. Most immigrants in these earlier years were men, and most worked as laborers and at other domestic and menial jobs. Until the change of the immigration laws in 1965, the number of Asian and Pacific Islander peoples immigrating into the United States was severely restricted (families often had to wait a decade or longer before members of a family could be reunited). With the change in the immigration laws, large numbers of immigrants from the Pacific Rim came to the United States from Hong Kong, Taiwan, China, Japan, Korea, South Asia (e.g., India, Ceylon,

*Preferred spelling for Filipino

Bangladesh), the Philippines, and Southeast Asia (e.g., Vietnam, Thailand, Singapore, Cambodia, Malaysia). After the Vietnam War, large numbers of Southeast Asian refugees were admitted in the late 1970s and early 1980s. The need for engineering and scientific expertise and skills by "high-tech" and Internet companies resulted in many Asian/Pacific immigrants (under special work visas) immigrating to the United States in the late 1990s and early 2000s.

Law Enforcement Interactions with Asian/Pacific Americans: Law Enforcement as Not User-Friendly

Asian/Pacific Americans have found the passage and enforcement of "anti-Asian" federal, state, and local laws to be more hostile and discriminatory than some of the racially motivated community incidents they have experienced. Early experiences of Asians and Pacific Islanders were characterized by the majority population's wanting to keep them out of the United States and putting tremendous barriers in the way of those who were already here. It was the role of law enforcement and criminal justice agencies and officers to be the vehicle to carry out these laws against Asian/Pacific American immigrants. From the beginning, the interactions of Asian/Pacific Americans with law enforcement officials were fraught with conflicts, difficulties, and mixed messages.

Anti-Asian Federal, State, and Local Laws

Almost all of our federal immigration laws were written such that their enforcement made Asian newcomers feel neither welcomed nor wanted. Following the large influx of Chinese in the 1850s to work in the gold mines and on the railroad, many Americans were resentful of the Chinese for their willingness to work long hours for low wages. With mounting public pressure, the Chinese Exclusion Act of 1882 banned the immigration of Chinese laborers for 10 years, and subsequent amendments extended this ban indefinitely. Because of this ban and because the Chinese population in the United States was primarily male, the Chinese population in the United States dropped from 105,465 in 1880 to 61,639 in 1920 (Takaki, 1989a). Since the Chinese Exclusion Act applied only to Chinese, Japanese immigration started around 1870 to Hawaii, with larger numbers to the mainland in the 1890s to work as laborers and in domestic jobs on farms on the West Coast. Similar to the Chinese, public pressure to restrict Japanese immigration ensued. In the case of the Japanese, the Japanese government did not want a "loss of face" or of international prestige through having its people "banned" from immigrating to the United States. Rather, the "Gentleman's Agreement" was negotiated with President Theodore Roosevelt in 1907, which resulted in the Japanese Government voluntarily restricting the immigration of Japanese laborers to the United States. Family members of Japanese already in the United States, however, were allowed to enter. Under the Gentleman's Agreement, large numbers of "picture brides" began entering into the United States, resulting in a large increase in Japanese American populations—25,000 in 1900 to 127,000 in 1940 (Daniels, 1988). Subsequent laws banned or prevented immigration from the Asiatic countries: The Immigration Act of 1917 banned immigration from all countries in the Pacific Rim except for the Philippines (a U.S. territory). The Immigration Act of 1924 restricted migration from all countries to 2 percent of the countries' national origin population living in the United States in 1890. This "2 percent" restriction was not changed until 1965. Moreover, it was not until 1952 that most Asian immigrants were eligible to become naturalized citizens of the United States and therefore have the right to vote (African Americans and American Indians were able to become citizens long before Asian/Pacific Americans were given the same rights).

While Pilipinos have been immigrating to the United States since the early 1900s (primarily for "practical training" as selected, sponsored, and funded by the United States government), large numbers of Pilipino laborers began entering in the 1920s because of the need for unskilled laborers (and due in part to the unavailability of Chinese and Japanese immigrants who were restricted entry by law). Similar to previous Asian groups, Pilipino immigration was soon to be limited to a quota of 50 immigrants per year with the passage of the Tydings-McDuffie Act of 1934. Moreover, Congressional resolutions in 1935 reflected clear anti-Pilipino sentiment by providing free, one-way passage for Pilipinos to return to the Philippines with the agreement that they not return to the United States.

Anti-Asian immigration laws were finally repealed starting with the removal of the Chinese Exclusion Act in 1943. Other laws were repealed to allow immigration of Asians and Pacific Islanders, but the process was slow. It was not until 1965 that amendments to the McCarran-Walter Act opened the way for Asian immigrants to enter in larger numbers (a fixed quota of 20,000 per country, as opposed to 2 percent of the country's national origin population living in the United States in 1890). The 1965 amendment also established the "fifth preference" category, which allowed highly skilled workers needed by the United States to enter this country. Because of the preference for highly skilled workers, a second major wave of immigrants from Hong Kong, Taiwan, India, Korea, the Philippines, Japan, Singapore, and other Asiatic countries entered in the mid-1960s. The earlier wave of South Asian immigrants (from India, Pakistan, and Sri Lanka) with expertise to help with America's space race against the Soviets resulted in large numbers of professional and highly educated South Asians immigrating into the United States under the "fifth preference" after 1965. For example, as part of this second wave of immigration, 83 percent of the Asian Indians who immigrated under the category of professional and technical workers between 1966 and 1977 were scientists with PhDs (about 20,000) and engineers (about 40,000) (Prashad, 2001).

With the upheaval in Southeast Asia and the Vietnam War, the third major wave of close to 1 million refugees and immigrants arrived in the United States from these affected Southeast Asian countries starting in the mid-1970s and lasting through the mid-1980s. The Refugee Act of 1980 (1) established the definition for "refugee," (2) reduced limits on the numbers of refugees entering the United States, (3) created the Office of Refugee Resettlement, and (4) permitted refugees to adjust their statuses after 1 year to become permanent residents, and after 4 more years, to become U.S. citizens (Povell, 2005). From the mid-1990s to the early 2000s, the need for personnel with high-tech, engineering, and Internet skills led to an additional influx of immigrants from India, Pakistan, Singapore, Korea, China (including Hong Kong), Taiwan, and other Asiatic countries.

Note that even today, in some state and local jurisdictions, anti-Asian laws need to be changed and removed, as shown by the following example:

> War and terrorism have hardened American attitudes toward immigration, but some legislators are pushing ahead with plans for a ballot measure asking voters to eliminate a little-known clause in the Florida Constitution that one lawmaker calls a "clearly racist Jim Crow provision." The provision allows the state to prohibit property ownership by "aliens ineligible for citizenship." It was added to the Constitution in 1926, aimed chiefly at Asians, who by federal decree were ineligible for U.S. citizenship at the time and were turning to farming in the United States. "It is an outdated, clearly racist Jim Crow provision," state Rep. Phillip Brutus, D-North Miami, told members of the Senate Committee on Home Defense, Public Security and Ports. "It's a stain on our Constitution." (Stockfisch, 2003, p. 1)

Although many immigrant groups (e.g., Italians, Jews, Poles) have been the target of discrimination, bigotry, and prejudice, Asian/Pacific Americans, like African Americans, have experienced extensive legal discrimination, hindering their ability to participate fully as Americans. This discrimination has gravely affected their well-being and quality of life. Some states had laws that prohibited intermarriage between Asians and whites. State and local laws imposed restrictive conditions and taxes specifically on Asian businesses and individuals. State courts were equally biased; for example, in the case of *People v. Hall,* heard in the California Supreme Court in 1854, Hall, a white defendant, had been convicted of murdering a Chinese man on the basis of testimony provided by one white and three Chinese witnesses. The California Supreme Court threw out Hall's conviction on the basis that state law prohibited blacks, mulattos, or Indians from testifying in favor of or against whites in court. The court's decision read:

> Indian as commonly used refers only to the North American Indian, yet in the days of Columbus all shores washed by Chinese waters were called the Indies. In the second place the word "white" necessarily excludes all other races than Caucasian; and in the third place, even if this were not so, I would decide against the testimony of Chinese on the grounds of public policy. (California Supreme Court: *People v. George W. Hall,* October 1854)

This section of anti–Asian/Pacific American laws and sentiments cannot close without noting that Japanese Americans are the only immigrant group of Americans in the history of the American people who have been routed out of their homes and interned without due process. President Roosevelt's Executive Order 9066 resulted in the evacuation and incarceration of 100,000 Japanese Americans in 1942. For Asian/Pacific Americans, the internment of Japanese Americans represents how quickly anti-Asian sentiments can result in victimization of innocent people in the forms of incarceration and punishment by law.

DEMOGRAPHICS: DIVERSITY AMONG ASIAN/PACIFIC AMERICANS

As we noted in the section defining Asian/Pacific Americans, this is an extremely heterogeneous population comprised of many different ethnic and cultural groups with generational differences within the United States, educational and socioeconomic diversity, and many other background and life experience differences. Asian/Pacific

Americans currently number about 12.8 million and represent approximately 4.5 percent of the U.S. population. As stated, the Asian/Pacific American population more than doubled with each census from 1970 to 1990 (1.5 million in 1970, 3.5 million in 1980, and 7.3 million in 1990) and increased by 76 percent from 1990 to 2000 (12.8 million in 2000). While greater longevity and higher birth rates contribute to this population increase, the major contributor to the growth of the Asian/Pacific American population is immigration from the Pacific Rim countries. Since the 1970s, Asian/Pacific American immigration has made up over 40 percent of all immigration to the United States (U.S. Bureau of the Census, 2002). As is evident in Exhibit 5.2, Chinese are the largest group, with 23.0 percent of the total Asian/Pacific American population. Pilipinos are close behind, with 19.9 percent of this population; in the next decade, Pilipinos will be the largest Asian/Pacific American group in the United States. Asian Indians are the fastest growing among the Asian and Pacific American population, with 16.0 percent. Vietnamese and Koreans each comprise approximately 10.3 percent of the Asian/Pacific American population. The Japanese American population was the third largest in 1990 and dropped to sixth place in 2000, with 9.7 percent, in part because of the lower immigration from Japan. All other Asian/Pacific American groups account for 10.8 percent of this population.

For law enforcement officers, the key Asian/Pacific American groups to understand are the six largest groups: Chinese, Pilipino, Asian Indian, Vietnamese, Korean, and Japanese (considering, in addition, local community trends and unique qualities of the community's populations). Knowledge of the growing trends among this Asian/Pacific American population are also important for officer recruitment and other human resource considerations. Current Asian/Pacific Americans involved in professional law enforcement and criminal justice careers are largely Japanese, Chinese, and Korean Americans. To plan for the changing Asian/Pacific American population base, it is critical to recruit and develop officers from the Pilipino, Vietnamese, and Asian In-

ASIAN/PACIFIC AMERICAN GROUPS	PERCENTAGE OF TOTAL
Chinese	23.0
Pilipino	19.9
Asian Indian	16.0
Vietnamese	10.3
Korean	10.3
Japanese	9.7
Cambodian	1.7
Pakistani	1.7
Laotian	1.7
Hmong	1.6
Thai	1.3
Taiwanese	1.2
All other groups	1.6
All Asian/Pacific Americans	100.0

Exhibit 5.2 Asian/Pacific American population by groups.
Source: Blake & Bennett (2002). The Asian Population: 2000. U.S. Bureau of the Census. Table 4.

dian communities. Moreover, given the anticipated growth of the world population in the coming decades, it would be wise to recruit and develop officers with cultural knowledge, languages, and skills pertaining to India, China, Indonesia, and Pakistan— nations with the largest world populations (Population Reference Bureau, 2005).

More than half of all Asian/Pacific Americans are foreign-born (7.2 million) and comprise 26 percent of the foreign-born population in the United States (Bennett, 2002). Five countries contributed the largest numbers of foreign-born Asian/Pacific Americans, as seen in Exhibit 5.3.

As noted earlier, foreign-born Asian/Pacific Americans constitute the second highest percentage of immigrants becoming naturalized citizens at 52 percent; only those born in Europe had a higher rate (U.S. Bureau of the Census, 2006). The vast majority of all Asian/Pacific Americans are not born in the United States. Most of the Japanese, Pilipinos, Cambodians, and Indonesians reside in the western states. Chinese, Koreans, Vietnamese, Laotians, and Thais are fairly widely distributed in the large urban areas of the United States. Most of the Asian Indians and Pakistanis live in the eastern states. The state of Minnesota and the city of Fresno, California, have the largest Hmong populations in the country. Proficiency in the English language varies within groups: groups that have immigrated most recently (Southeast Asians) have the largest percentage of those not able to speak English well.

Law enforcement and peace officers, depending on their jurisdictions, need to determine what additional languages and skills training might be appropriate in their work with Asian/Pacific American communities.

Asian/Pacific Americans' Key Motivating Perspectives

Earlier in this chapter, we provided a typology for viewing Asian/Pacific Americans. We provide in Exhibit 5.4 the same typology and have appended to it the key motivating perspectives for members in each group. By understanding some of these key motivating perspectives, law enforcement officers might be better able to understand the behaviors exhibited by citizens from these groups.

For example, the key to understanding the behavior of the most recent immigrants and refugee group (Asian/Pacific Refugee Type I; see Exhibit 5.1) is to recall that members are in a survival mode (see Exhibit 5.4). Many members from this category may remember that law enforcement and police officers in their country of origin were

COUNTRY OF BIRTH	NUMBER FOREIGN-BORN
China	1,391,000
Philippines	1,222,000
India	1,007,000
Vietnamese	863,000
Korean	701,000

Exhibit 5.3   Top Countries of Birth of Foreign-Born Asian/Pacific Americans.
Source: Bennett (2002). A Profile of the Nation's Foreign-Born Population from Asia (2000 Update), U.S. Bureau of the Census. P23-206.

Surviving	Asian/Pacific most recent immigrant or refugee (less than 5 years in the United States with major life experiences in Asia or the Pacific Islands)
Preserving	Asian/Pacific immigrant or refugee (5 or more years in the United States with major life experiences in Asia or the Pacific Islands)
Adjusting	Asian/Pacific American (second generation; offspring of immigrant or refugee)
Changing	Asian/Pacific immigrant (major life experiences in the United States)
Choosing	Asian/Pacific American (third or later generations in the United States)
Maintaining	Asian/Pacific national (anticipates return to Asia or to the Pacific Islands)
Expanding	Asian/Pacific national (global workplace and residency)

Exhibit 5.4   Key motivating perspectives in understanding Asian/Pacific American groups.

corrupt, aligned with a repressive government and the military, and subjected to bribes by those who were more affluent. All activities tend to be guided by this framework, which is to survive, to get through. This perspective also makes sense in terms of the traumatic ordeals faced by refugees in their journeys to the United States. Encounters with law enforcement personnel by these people usually involve saying and doing anything to discontinue the contact because of possible fears of personal harm (e.g., not speaking English, not having any identification, "Yes, I will cooperate!").

With regard to Asian/Pacific immigrants (Type II), understanding their behaviors should focus on preserving their home culture as the motivating perspective. Since the majority of their life experiences occurred in Asia or the Pacific Islands, members are trying to preserve much of the values and traditions of their culture as it was alive and operating. Many Asian businesspersons and investors in the United States are included in this category. Much intergenerational conflict between grandparents or parents and youths occurs within this group. Members are inclined to keep to their ethnic communities (e.g., Little Saigons, Chinatowns, Koreatowns, Japantowns, Manilatowns) and have as little to do with law enforcement as possible. Many remember that the police have not served them well in the past (e.g., immigration laws, Japanese internment).

For example, various South Asian community members have been targets of hate crimes because they stay within their ethnic community enclaves, preserve their ethnic customs and dress, and are stereotyped and/or misidentified. In the Detroit area, there is a sizeable South Asian community from Bangladesh (the people are called Bengalis). These citizens are Muslim and dark-skinned, and are often mistaken for Arabs.

Attacks on Asian-Americans, particularly Pakistani and Indian immigrants, increased greatly in the United States in the weeks after Sept. 11, a report by an advocacy group says. . . . Immigrants from South Asia appear to have been the subjects of attacks and other racially motivated incidents because they were perceived, often incorrectly, to be Arab or Muslim, . . . Sikhs, for example, a religious group with many members of South Asian descent, were victimized because the men wear turbans and long beards, the report said. About one out of five attacks was violent, mainly aggravated assault, the report said. But two people were killed. On Sept. 15, Balbir Singh Sodhi, 49, a Sikh from Mesa, Ariz., was fatally shot while working at a gasoline station. When the police arrested a man in the killing, the report said, he screamed, "I am a patriot." Waqar Hasan, 46, a Pakistani, was killed in September while working at a grocery store in Pleasant Grove, Tex. There was no indication of a robbery, the report said, and the Federal Bureau of Investigation is investigating the incident as a hate crime. ("A Nation Challenged," 2002, p. A12)

Asian/Pacific Americans (second generation, Type III) tend to be who we picture when we hear the term Asian American. Those of the second generation work very hard at being assimilated into the mainstream, adjusting and changing to be a part of mainstream America. Often, the expectations of second-generation parents are high; parents will sacrifice so that their offsprings will "make it" in their lifetime. Members may interact primarily with non-Asians and take on many of the values and norms of the mainstream society. This group may be considered "marginal" by some in that, try as each person may to become like the mainstream ("become white"), others may still consider them Asian. Many from this group try to minimize their contact with law enforcement personnel and agencies primarily because of the immigration and other experiences relayed to them by their parents' generation. Individuals of the second generation were born in the United States before the mid-1960s and may have had relatives (or parents) who entered the United States by using false papers. Fears of disclosure of such illegal entries have prevented many Asian/Pacific Americans from cooperating with peace officers and with other human and social service agencies and programs. With the emphasis on homeland security in the United States, many from this group have taken extra efforts to not be misidentified about their ethnicity (e.g., South Asians with darker skin tones being mistaken for Middle Easterners) or stereotyped because of their religion (e.g., Asian/Pacific Americans who are moderate Muslims, not fundamentalists).

The Asian/Pacific immigrant (Type IV), whose major life experience is in the United States, focuses much of the member's energies on changes (through assimilation or acculturation) that have to be made in order to succeed. Although these individuals have tended to continue to value the cultural and ethnic elements of their former homeland, most know that changes are necessary. Members of this group reflect the socioeconomic standings of the different waves on which each entered into the United States. For example, individuals who entered as part of the first wave of laborers and domestic workers (primarily Chinese and Japanese, with some Pilipinos, Koreans, and Asian Indians) represent one grouping. Others entered more as part of the second wave of immigration as foreign students and/or under the fifth preference as professional skilled workers. Asian/Pacific immigrants (Type IV) who are designated as entering the United States under fifth preference are those who checked the fifth category on the Immigration and Nationalization Service form. This category indicates that the reason for immigration into the United States was because the person has a professional skill in short supply in the United States and it would be in the best interest of the United States to allow that person to enter. This group consists of educated, professional individuals (e.g., the largest numbers of foreign-trained medical doctors and psychiatrists in the United States are from India, the Philippines, and Korea [President's Commission on Mental Health, 1978]). Since the fall of Saigon in 1975 and the beginning of the immigration of Southeast Asians into the United States, this third wave has included over 1 million Asian/Pacific immigrants who suffered great trauma in their escape; many are young adults today. For members of this group, reactions to law enforcement officials vary depending on their time of immigration and socioeconomic experiences. For law enforcement officers, it is critical to understand the differences among the immigrant groups (i.e., do not confuse the professional Asian/Pacific immigrant with one of the other groups).

The Asian/Pacific American (third or later generation, Type V) category includes individuals who are more able to choose which aspects of the old culture to keep and which of the new culture to accept. The focus is on choosing activities, values, norms, and lifestyles that blend the best of Asian/Pacific and American cultures. The importance of being bicultural is a unique aspect of this group. Many may no longer have as much skill with their native language and may rely on English as their primary or only language (thus an individual can be bicultural and not bilingual). Contact by members of this group with law enforcement personnel may not be any different than contact by any other Americans.

For the last two categories, Asian/Pacific nationals, we make a key distinction between those who plan to return to their own country following a work assignment in the United States (Type VI) and those whose work is truly global, in that individuals may have several residences in different parts of the world (Type VII). Those in the former category (Type VI, on a work assignment in the United States that may last 5 to 7 years) maintain their home-base cultural orientation and experiences knowing that when the work assignment is over, they will go back to their home country again. Because they mean to maintain their native cultures, some individuals of this group may be inadequately prepared to understand many of the laws and practices of the United States. For members of this group, being able to stay in the United States to complete their assignments is of key importance. Often, individuals may not be aware of the differences between "minor" violations (e.g., minor traffic violations, small claims) and "major" violations and crimes. Let's look at the following example:

> Mr. Sato is a manager assigned to oversee a technical department in a joint United States–Japan automobile plant in the Midwest. One evening, while driving home from a late night at the plant, Mr. Sato did not see a stop sign and went right through it on a nonbusy intersection. A police officer in a patrol car saw the violation and pulled Mr. Sato over. The interaction puzzled the police officer, since Mr. Sato seemed very cooperative but kept asking the officer "to forgive him and to please let him go!" After much discussion and explanation, it was discovered that Mr. Sato thought that the officer would have to confiscate his passport because of the stop-sign violation (something that is done in many Asiatic countries) and that he might be "kicked out" of the country and thus be unable to complete his work assignment. Upon clearing up this misconception, Mr. Sato accepted the traffic citation "with appreciation." (police officer's anecdote in a cultural awareness training session)

For the second group of Asian/Pacific nationals (Type VII), the key focus of these individuals is their ability to "expand" their actions and behaviors effectively into different global environments. These individuals see themselves as being able to adapt to life in a variety of global environments; many may speak three or more languages (including English). Individuals within this group pride themselves in knowing about the different laws, norms, values, and practices of the countries they encounter. Law enforcement personnel would find this group equally able to understand and to follow the laws and practices of a given community as well.

LABELS AND TERMS

As we noted earlier, the term Asian/Pacific Americans is a convenient summarizing label used to refer to a heterogeneous group of people. Which particular terms are used is based on the principle of self-designation and self-preference. Asian and Pacific Islander people are sensitive about the issue because up until the 1960 census the population was relegated to the "Other" category. With the ethnic pride movement and ethnic minority studies movement in the late 1960s, people of Asian and Pacific Islands descent began to designate self-preferred terms for group reference. The terms were chosen over the previous term Oriental, which many Asian/Pacific Americans consider to be offensive. Oriental is considered offensive because it symbolizes to many the past references, injustices, and stereotypes of Asian and Pacific people. It was also a term designated by those in the West (i.e., the Occident, the Western Hemisphere) for Asian people and reminds many Asian/Pacific Americans of the colonial mentality of foreign policies and its effects on the Pacific Rim countries.

In federal and other governmental designations (e.g., the Small Business Administration), the label used is "Asian American/Pacific Islanders." Although very few Asian/Pacific Americans refer to themselves as such, the governmental designation is used in laws and regulations and in most reports and publications. For individuals within any of the groups, often the more specific names for the groups are preferred (e.g., Chinese, Japanese, Vietnamese, Pakistani, Hawaiian). Some individuals may prefer that the term American be part of their designation (e.g., Korean American, Pilipino American). For law enforcement officers, the best term to refer to an individual is the term he or she prefers to be called. It is perfectly acceptable to ask an individual what ethnic or cultural group(s) he or she identifies with and what he or she prefers to be called.

The use of slurs such as "Jap," "Chink," "Gook," "Chinaman," "Flip," "Babas," and other derogatory ethnic slang terms is never acceptable in crime-fighting and peacekeeping, no matter how provoked an officer may be. The use of other stereotypic terms, including "Chinese fire drill," "DWO (Driving While Oriental)," "Fu Man Chu mustache," "Kamikaze kid," "yellow cur," "yellow peril," "Bruce Lee Kung Fu type," "slant-eyed," "Turban man," "Vietnamese bar girl," and "dragon lady," does not convey the professionalism and respect for community diversity important to law enforcement and peacekeeping and must be avoided in law enforcement work. Officers hearing these words used in their own departments (or with peers or citizens) should provide immediate helpful feedback about such terms to those who use them. Officers who may out of habit routinely use these terms may find themselves (or their superiors) in the embarrassing situation (on the evening news) of explaining to offended citizens and communities why these terms were used and that they had intended no prejudice.

MYTHS AND STEREOTYPES

Knowledge of and sensitivity to Asian/Pacific Americans' concerns, diversity, historical background, and life experiences will facilitate the crime-fighting and peacekeeping missions of peace officers. It is important to have an understanding about some of the myths, environmental messages, and stereotypes of Asian/Pacific Americans that contribute to the prejudice, discrimination, and bias they encounter. Many Americans do not have much experience with the diversity of Asian/Pacific American groups and learn about these groups only through stereotypes, often perpetuated by movies and the media. The effect of myths and stereotypes is to reduce Asian/Pacific Americans to simplistic, one-dimensional characters whom many people lump into one stereotypic group. Often, the complexities of the diverse Asian/Pacific American groups in terms of language, history, customs, cultures, religions, and life experiences become confusing and threatening, and it is easier to deal with stereotypes of these groups. Nonetheless, it is important for law enforcement officers to be aware of the different stereotypes of Asian/Pacific Americans. The key to effectiveness with any ethnic or racial group is not the complete elimination of myths and stereotypes about these groups, but rather, awareness of these stereotypes and management of our behaviors when the stereotypes are not true of the person with whom we are dealing.

Some of the stereotypes that have affected Asian/Pacific Americans in law enforcement include the following:

1. ***Viewing Asian/Pacific Americans as "all alike."*** That is, because there are many similarities in names, physical features, and behaviors, many law enforcement officers may make comments about their inability to tell people apart, or they may deal with them in stereotypic group fashion (e.g., they are all "inscrutable," involved in gangs). Cultural awareness training and sensitivity would allow the officer the skills and knowledge to avoid a mistake like the following:

   > The City Council of Des Moines avoided a lawsuit by agreeing to pay $7,500 to each of nine Asian-American men who were handcuffed and forced to kneel in the street outside a cafe in June. The men were handcuffed on June 24 as police searched for an armed assault suspect they believed to have gone to the cafe. The suspect was never identified and even the victim disappeared shortly after the incident, police said. Police have said the incident was mishandled and say they will change their policies. One of the nine men said he met with Police Chief William Moulder and one of the officers involved about a month ago. "We told the police chief how we felt about that day. We worked it out," said Cuong Nguyen. After hearing the police explanation of the incident, Nguyen said he does not feel it was a result of racial profiling. He also said $7,500 was fair compensation. ("Des Moines to Pay $7,500," 2001)

2. ***Viewing Asian/Pacific Americans as successful "model minorities" or as a "super minority."*** Some hold the stereotype that Asian/Pacific Americans are all successful, and this stereotype is further reinforced by the media (Kawai, 2005). Such stereotypes have resulted in intergroup hostilities and hate crimes directed toward Asian/Pacific Americans and have served to mask true differences and diversity among the various Asian and Pacific Islander groups. Some Asian/Pacific American groups have had to highlight the incorrect perceptions of the "model minority" stereotype:

   > Four outlaws gathered at a Decatur coffeehouse to talk over their crimes. One had married an African-American man. Another chose the wrong career. One is openly gay. The fourth, well, she just isn't submissive enough. The group looked like a caramel-colored version of the cast of

Friends: four attractive, well-educated Indian-Americans brimming with confidence and laughter. But each has become an outlaw of sorts in Atlanta's South Asian community—people from India, Pakistan, Sri Lanka, Bangladesh and Nepal—because they've broken the rules for being a good South Asian, sometimes considered a "model minority" in America. . . . More than 70,000 South Asians now live in the Atlanta metro area, with the Indian-American population alone having recorded a 230 percent increase in Georgia from 1990 to 2000. Indians are also estimated to own nearly half the roadside hotels and motels in the state. None of those numbers reflects the escalating divisions within the South Asian community, many of whose younger members say they're tired of being viewed as the "good minority": hardworking, submissive over-achievers. They say this image has become an ethnic straitjacket that stifles individuality—and is often used to demean African-Americans by comparison. (Blake, 2002, p. M1)

Clearly no groups of people are "all successful" or "all criminals." Nonetheless, the "success" and the "model minority" stereotypes have affected Asian/Pacific Americans negatively. For example, because of their implied success, law enforcement organizations may not spend the time to recruit Asian/Pacific American individuals for law enforcement careers (assuming that they are more interested in other areas such as education and business pursuits). This stereotype also hides the existence of real discrimination for those who are successful, as seen in glass ceilings in promotional and developmental opportunities, for example. The success stereotype has resulted in violence and crimes against Asian/Pacific persons. Two examples, one older but etched in the memories of many Asian/Pacific Americans, and the other more recent, are representative of issues very salient to Asian/Pacific Americans today:

The murder of Vincent Chin, and the subsequent inability of the court system to bring the murderers to justice, is now a well-known case among Asian/Pacific American communities. The perpetrators in this case, Ronald Ebens and Michael Nitz, were two white automobile factory workers who blamed Vincent Chin (a Chinese American) for the success of the Japanese automobile industry that was, in turn, blamed for taking away American jobs in the automobile factory. (Takaki, 1989b)

Hate-motivated killings have claimed eight Asian American lives in the past two years. In the latest incident, three Asian Americans, a Jewish American and an African American were killed in Pittsburgh on April 28. These hate-motivated killings have had a devastating effect on a broad cross-section of Asian Americans across the U.S., in part because the ethnic backgrounds of the victims have been so diverse, including South Asian, Filipino, Japanese, Korean, Vietnamese and Chinese. This horrible loss of life was for no other apparent reason than the color of the victims' skin and often their perceived immigrant status. It is an unprecedented number of hate killings of Asians since monitoring of such incidents began in the 1980s by the National Asian Pacific American Legal Consortium. (Kwoh, 2000)

3. ***Viewing some Asian/Pacific Americans as possible "foreign" terrorists because of their religious affiliation and cultural dress.*** Many Asian/Pacific

Americans immigrate from countries with very large populations that practice Islam (e.g., Indonesia, Pakistan, Bangladesh, India, and China), and the majority of these Muslims are from the more moderate wing of Sunni Islam (not from the more fundamentalist branch). However, it is highly possible for the unfamiliar to group Asian/Pacific Americans who are Muslims into a collective group associated with "fundamentalism" and "terrorism." Moreover, for many immigrants who may stay close to their cultural traditions and cultural dress (e.g., Sikhs who wear turbans and have beards), it is easy to misidentify cultural dress and nuances and come to stereotypic conclusions about who might be a "foreign" terrorist. Two examples: (1) One of the first suspects detained for questioning on September 11, 2001 (as seen on the national television news), was a Sikh who was wearing a turban and was misidentified as an Afghanistan Taliban (who also wear a head covering that is called a turban), and (2) South Asians (e.g., Bengalis) with darker skin tones in the Midwest were often misidentified as Arabs and were detained for questioning on homeland security issues.

> Asian Americans have long borne the stereotype of the perpetual foreigner—the unwelcome immigrant or the disloyal or distrusted foreign agent. Japanese Americans bore the brunt of this during World War II as 120,000 were interned. Filipino World War II veterans have never received proper recognition and benefits for fighting bravely under U.S. command. When the 1996 campaign finance scandal implicated a handful of Asian Americans, thousands were investigated or stigmatized without cause. The recent hate crime wave and treatment of scientists are reminders of this ugly past. (Kwoh, 2000, p. M8)

From a law enforcement perspective, many hate crimes against Asian/Pacific Americans are related to the stereotype of the group as foreigners and not as Americans.

4. ***Misunderstanding Asian/Pacific cultural differences and practices and viewing differences stereotypically as a threat to other Americans.*** The more than 40 Asian/Pacific American groups encompass great differences in life experiences, languages, backgrounds, and cultures. It is easy to make mistakes and draw incorrect conclusions because of such cultural differences. Certainly, when we lack information about any group, it is natural to draw conclusions based on our own filtering system, stereotypes, and assumptions. Most of the time, these incorrect assumptions and stereotypes are corrected by favorable contact and actual interpersonal relationships with Asian/Pacific American people. From a law enforcement perspective, the thrust of community policing, as well as cultural awareness training, is to provide the opportunities to modify stereotypes and to provide opportunities to learn about ethnic communities. Law enforcement agencies, however, have to intervene in situations in which individuals and/or groups view Asian/Pacific American cultural differences as perceived threats to themselves. For the Asian/Pacific American communities, violent incidents like that of Patrick Edward Purdy stand out in their minds and constantly remind them of their vulnerabilities to stereotypes. On January 17, 1989, Purdy entered the school yard at Cleveland Elementary

School in Stockton, California, firing an AK47 assault rifle. In the ensuing few minutes of fire, Purdy killed five Southeast Asian children and wounded 30 other children. He then turned the rifle on himself and killed himself. More than 60 percent of the children at this school were Southeast Asians. The California Attorney General's Report noted, "It appears highly probable that Purdy deliberately chose Cleveland Elementary School as the location for his murderous assault in substantial part because it was heavily populated by Southeast Asian children. His frequent resentful comments about Southeast Asians indicated a particular animosity against them" (Mathews & Lait, 1989). Stereotypic and racially biased views of Asian/Pacific Americans as threats require the ongoing attention of law enforcement agencies:

> In a case that invoked the Vietnam War, America's promise of freedom and the tragedy of Sept. 11, a 23-year-old Manitowoc man who helped burn a house down was sentenced Tuesday to nearly 19 years in prison. . . . Franz, a two-time burglar who has served prison time, had pleaded guilty in October to two hate crimes and a gun charge in the Hmong case. He said at the time that the 1998 arson, as well as an unfulfilled murder plot, were meant to "send a message" that Asians in the Manitowoc area should leave him and his friends alone. . . . Like other victims in the case, Lee and her family had resettled in the Manitowoc area from their native Laos after the war in Vietnam. Many Hmong fought with Americans and faced almost certain death had they remained in their homeland after the Communists took over. . . . One who saw combat with the CIA in Vietnam was Humphrey Chang, 57, who was wounded twice during the war. Three days before the Lee fire, Franz and two of his co-defendants, armed with shotguns, had gone to Two Rivers intending to shoot Asians. They ignited an explosive outside Chang's home, hoping it would flush people out, but no one fled and no shots were fired. "America is a country where freedom began," Chang said. Americans cannot allow such racial terrorism, "the act of killing innocent life for the only reason of hate," he said. (Kertscher, 2002, p. B1)

The misunderstanding of cultural differences that leads to erroneous conclusions about Asian/Pacific American behaviors has resulted in law enforcement involvement with the full range of the criminal justice system (e.g., courts, district attorneys, police, child protective services), as seen in the following case:

> Seng Chang and Kaying Lor were glad to learn Monday afternoon that their family's journey through the courts was over. Police took away the couple's four children on April 30 after employees at Sherman Elementary School noticed marks on the youngsters' bodies. The marks had been produced by a traditional Asian healing technique commonly called coining. The children were returned to their parents on May 3 but officially remained in state custody. Prosecutors Monday dropped the case against Chang and Lor after medical experts reviewed the case and determined that there was no evidence of child abuse. "We feel like everything can be like it was before," Lor said Monday. "We feel relieved." The family is Hmong, an ethnic group from the hills of Laos. Lor said he and his wife will continue using the coining remedy when their children

are sick. The technique involves rubbing ointment into the skin with a coin or a spoon. He said he hopes those who investigate abuse allegations have learned a lesson and will listen more carefully to what parents are saying before removing children from their homes. Six other children were taken from a Vietnamese couple in a separate but similar case. Prosecutors dismissed that case last week. (Morton, 2002, p. B1)

THE ASIAN/PACIFIC AMERICAN FAMILY

Obviously, with over 40 different cultural groups under the label of Asian/Pacific Americans, we find great differences in how families operate within the various subgroups. We would like to share some common characteristics to describe Asian/Pacific American families that might be of value in crime-fighting and community peacekeeping. Asian/Pacific American families generally exhibit very strong ties among extended family members. It is not unusual for three to four generations of the same family to live under one roof. Moreover, the extended family can even have an ongoing relationship network that spans great geographic distance. For example, family members (all of whom consider themselves as one family) can be engaged in extensive communications and activities with members in the same family in the United States, Canada, Hong Kong, and Vietnam, all simultaneously. It is not uncommon for an officer to come into contact with members of the extended Asian/Pacific American family in the course of servicing these communities. One key to the success of law enforcement officers in working with an extended family network is the knowledge of how best to contact an Asian/Pacific American family and which family member to speak to for information, help, and referral.

Culture Shock and the Asian/Pacific American Family

Because the traditional cultures of Asia and the Pacific Islands are so very different from that of the United States, many Asian/Pacific American families (whether refugees, immigrants, businesspersons, students, or tourists) experience some degree of culture shock when they enter and reside in the United States. Culture shock results not only from differences in values and traditions but also from differences in urbanization, industrialization, and modernization from technology that may be different from that in their homeland. Peace officers need to be aware that Asian/Pacific Americans may cope with their culture shock by becoming "clannish" (e.g., Chinatowns, Koreatowns). Other survival mechanisms include avoiding contact and interaction with those who are different (including police officers).

The Role of the Man and the Woman in an Asian/Pacific American Family

In most Asian/Pacific American families, relationship and communication patterns tend to be quite hierarchical, with the father as the identified head of the household. Although many decisions and activities may appear to be determined by the father, other individuals may influence his choices. Generally, if there are grandparents in the household, the father would still act as the spokesperson for the family, but he would consult the grandparents, his wife, and others regarding any major decision. As such, it may be important in any kind of law enforcement contact that requires a decision and/or choice to allow the parties time to discuss issues in, as much as feasible, a "private" manner. Self-control and keeping things within the family are key values for Asian/Pacific Americans. An officer thus may find that there is more control in a situation by allowing the Asian/Pacific American to come to the same conclusion as the officer with respect to a situation and to exercise his or her own self-choice (which may be the same as what the officer would want the parties to do anyway). For example, the officer can explain an arrest situation to the father of a family member, and instead of saying directly to the family member to be arrested that he or she has to leave with the officer, the officer can allow the father to suggest to the family member that he or she leave with the officer. What may appear to be a minor consideration in this case can result in a higher degree of persuasion, control, and cooperation by all parties concerned.

Although there are no clear-cut rules as to whether one goes to the male head of the household or to the female head to make a law enforcement inquiry, the general rule of thumb is that one would not go too wrong by starting with the father. It should be noted that for most Asian/Pacific American families, the role of the mother in discipline and decision making is very important. While the household may appear to be "ruled" by the father, the mother's role in finances, discipline, education, operations, and decision making is major.

Children, Adolescents, and Youths

Most Asian/Pacific American families involve at least two or more individuals within the same household working outside of the home. Thus, if young children are present, there is a high reliance on either family members or others to help care for them while the parents are at work. It is not uncommon for older children to care for younger children within a household. Moreover, latchkey children within an Asian/Pacific American home are common, especially for families that cannot afford external child care. In recent immigrant and refugee families, Asian/Pacific American children have a special role in being the intermediaries between parents and the external community because of the ability of the younger individuals to learn English and the American ways of doing things. Children often serve as translators and interpreters for peace officers in their communication and relations with Asian/Pacific American families involving recent immigrants and refugees. In such situations, it is suggested that the officer review the role expected of the youthful member of the family and determine how sensitive an area the translated content is to the different family members and the consequences if the content is incorrectly translated. (For example, asking a juvenile to translate to his or her parents who speak no English that the juvenile had been involved in a sexual abuse situation at the school may result in significant omission and/or changed content because of the embarrassment caused to the juvenile and possibly to the parents.) In all cases, when a child is acting as a translator, the officer should direct all verbal and non-verbal communication to the parents (as one would normally do without a translator). Otherwise, the parents may view the officer's lack of attention to them as an insult.

Asian/Pacific American Family Violence

Keeping family issues within the family and using self-help and personal effort strategies are part of Asian/Pacific cultural values and norms. Research studies on family violence (e.g., spousal physical abuse, child abuse, sexual abuse) by Asian/Pacific Americans show an increasing trend. It is only within the past two decades that researchers and community advocates have begun collecting such data. The few reported studies that exist seem to indicate significant and emerging problems with family violence within the Asian/Pacific American community. Tjaden and Thoennes (2000) conducted a telephone survey of a nationally representative sample of 8,000 men and 8,000 women of all ethnic backgrounds. Results showed that 12.8 percent of the Asian/Pacific American women reported having been physically assaulted by an intimate partner at least once during their lifetime (and 3.8 percent reported having been raped). Abraham (2000), in her survey of community-based women's service organizations, found that over 1,000 South Asian women sought help for abuse and family violence. The National Asian Women's Health Organization (2002) conducted telephone interviews with 336 Asian American women, aged 18 to 34 in the San Francisco and Los Angeles areas and found that 16 percent of the respondents reported having experienced "pressure to have sex without their consent by an intimate partner" and that 27 percent reported "emotional abuse" by an intimate partner. Tjaden and Thoennes (2000) also indicate that family violence within Asian/Pacific American communities has been underestimated and underreported. Song (1996) noted that most of the abused women used self-help efforts to keep the problem within the home (e.g., fought back physically and verbally, ignored the battering or did nothing, stared at the abusing person), and 70 percent of the battered women indicated that they did not know about community services that could have helped them.

The availability of bilingual outreach services is of key importance to the Asian/Pacific American community, as is illustrated in the following example:

> Shock rippled through Southern California's Asian-American community this month when three Korean-American fathers—including one in Fontana—killed their children. Financial strains may have pushed them over the edge, authorities said. As police continue to investigate the crimes, the community has been doing a bit of soul-searching. Was this just a bad string of coincidences? Or, as some community leaders have suggested, do these crimes highlight the need for more support services for the growing Asian immigrant population here? There are no service agencies serving the monolingual Asian-speaking population, said Janet Chang, a professor of social work at Cal State San Bernardino. "There's a huge service gap," Chang said. . . . Police say Bong Joo Lee shot and killed his 5-year-old daughter Iris Araa Lee on April 8 at his Fontana home with a 9 mm handgun and then killed himself. Police have said Lee had more than $200,000 in gambling debt. Court records show that Lee and his wife Gina split in 2004, the same year Lee pleaded no contest to battery on a spouse. Lee's ex-wife was awarded custody of their daughter, but Lee was granted visitation so long as he completed an anger management program. (Quan, 2006, p. B01)

The role of peace officers in detecting, assessing, and intervening in family violence situations within Asian/Pacific American communities is a critical one given this area of emerging needs and problems. The sensitivity of the peace officer to the cultural influences and patterns of communication (as noted in the next section) will be significant in the effective gathering of initial information and subsequent referral and interventions with Asian/Pacific American families involved in domestic violence and other issues of abuse.

CULTURAL INFLUENCES ON COMMUNICATION: VERBAL AND NONVERBAL STYLES OF ASIAN/PACIFIC AMERICANS

We do not wish to create any kind of stereotypes, but there are key features of Asian/Pacific American verbal and nonverbal communication styles that necessitate explanation. Misunderstanding resulting from style differences can result in perceptions of poor community services from police agencies, conflicts resulting from such misunderstandings, and safety and control issues for peace officers.

1. *It is important that officers take the time to get information from witnesses, victims, and suspects even if the individuals have limitations to their English speaking abilities.* The use of officers who may speak different Asian/Pacific dialects or languages, translators, and language bank resources would greatly enhance this process. Often Asian/Pacific Americans have not been helped in crime-fighting and peacekeeping situations because officers could not or did not take information from individuals who could not speak English well.

   > "We don't have a ton of stuff on Asian gangs," said Sgt. Bill Beall of the Fort Worth police gang unit. "Everything is really closemouthed. We can have a hard time getting information.". . . Several major clashes have come to police officers' attention in the past year, including the gang-related killing of a 21-year-old college student last year outside a Euless bowling alley. Police said two women held the student down while a man shot her in the head. . . . Language barriers discourage adults who are aware of gang problems from going to police, he said. That's why he thinks cities need more storefront programs like the one Haltom City had with Vietnamese-speaking officers about five years ago. Vietnamese-Americans could go to them with information and concerns, he said. "We need more police officers who understand the Vietnamese culture," Ha said. "People feel comfortable with them." (Branch, 2006)

2. *Asian/Pacific Americans tend to hold a more "family" and/or "group" orientation.* As such, the lack of the use of "I" statements and/or self-reference should not be evaluated as being evasive about oneself or one's relationships. The officer may be concerned because an Asian/Pacific American may wish to use the pronoun "we" when the situation may call for a personal observation involving an "I" statement. For example, in a traffic accident, the Asian/Pacific American may describe what he or she saw by saying "We saw. . . ." Using such group statements to convey what the individual saw is consistent with the family and group orientation of Asian/Pacific Americans.

3. *The officer must be aware that for many Asian/Pacific Americans, it is considered to be rude, impolite, and to involve a "loss of face" to directly say no to an authority figure such as a peace officer.* Peace officers must understand the following possibilities when an answer of yes is heard from an Asian/Pacific American. It can mean (1) "Yes, I heard what you said (but I

may or may not agree with you)"; (2) "Yes, I understand what you said (but I may or may not do what I understand)"; (3) "Yes, I can see this is important for you (but I may not agree with you on this)"; or (4) "Yes, I agree (and will do what you said)." Because the context of the communication and the nonverbal aspects of the message are equally meaningful, it is vital for law enforcement officers to be sure of the "yes" answers received, as well as of other language nuances from Asian/Pacific Americans. Two examples might be illustrative: (1) If an Asian/Pacific American says that he or she will "try his or her best to attend," this generally means that he or she will not be there, especially for more voluntary events and situations such as community neighborhood safety meetings. (2) If an Asian/Pacific national says in response to a question "It is possible," this generally means do not wait for the event to happen. Such communications, as noted previously, may be more applicable to some Asian/Pacific Americans than others, but sensitivity on the part of law enforcement officers to these language nuances will facilitate communication. Specific rules for interacting with each Asian/Pacific American group are not necessary, but officers should have a general understanding of language and cultural styles. In a communication situation in which the response of "yes" may be ambiguous, it is suggested that law enforcement officers rephrase the question so that the requested outcome in action and understanding are demonstrated in the verbal response.

Ambiguous Response
Officer: "I need you to show up in court on Tuesday. Do you understand?"
Asian witness: "Yes!"

Rephrasing of Questions to Show Understanding and Outcome
Officer: "What are you going to do on Tuesday?"
Asian witness: "I will be in court on Tuesday. I must go there."

4. ***Asian/Pacific Americans tend to be "high context" in communication style.*** This means that the officer must provide both interpersonal and situational contexts for effective communications. Context for Asian/Pacific Americans means that members of the community know the officers in the community. Community members may have had previous working relationships with the officer (e.g., crime prevention meetings, police athletic league). Moreover, other members of the community may help to provide information and context for police cooperation based on past relationships. Context also means providing explanations and education to members or groups within Asian/Pacific Americans about procedures and laws before asking them questions and/or requesting their participation in an activity. By providing background information and by establishing prior relationships with Asian/Pacific American communities, the Asian/Pacific American individual has a context for cooperating with law enforcement agencies and officers.

5. ***Be aware of nonverbal and other cultural nuances that may detract from the effective communication of the officer with a member of the Asian/Pacific American community.*** Many Asian/Pacific Americans find it uncomfortable and sometimes inappropriate to maintain eye contact with authority figures like police officers. It is considered in many Asian/Pacific American cultures

to be disrespectful if there is eye contact with someone who is of higher status, position, importance, or authority. As such, many Asian/Pacific Americans may look down on the ground and/or avert their eyes from gazing at a police officer. The officer should not automatically read this nonverbal behavior as indicating a lack of trust or respect, or as a dishonest response. Likewise, for the police officer, he or she should be aware of possible nonverbal gestures and actions that may detract from his or her professional roles (e.g., gesturing with the curled index finger for a person to come forward in a manner that might be used only for servants in that person's home culture).

6. ***Asian/Pacific Americans may not display their emotionality in the way that the officer expects.*** The central thesis guiding Asian/Pacific Americans is the Confucian notion of "walking the middle road." This means that extremes, too much or too little of anything, are not good. As such, Asian/Pacific Americans tend to moderate their display of positive and/or negative emotion. Often, in crisis situations, nonverbal displays of emotions are controlled to the point that the affect of the Asian/Pacific American appears "flat." Under such circumstances, the officer needs to correctly understand and interpret such displays of emotion appropriately. For example, just because the parent of a murder victim does not appear emotionally shaken by an officer's report does not mean that the person is not experiencing a severe emotional crisis.

KEY ISSUES IN LAW ENFORCEMENT

Underreporting of Crimes

Asian/Pacific Americans, because of their past experiences with some law enforcement agencies (e.g., anti-Asian immigration laws, health and sanitation code violations in restaurants, perceived unresponsiveness by police), are reluctant to report crimes and may not seek police assistance and help. Many Asian/Pacific Americans remember how police in their home countries have brutalized and violated them and others (e.g., in Southeast Asian and other Asian countries). Crimes that occur within a family's home (e.g., home invasion, family violence) or within the confines of a small family business (e.g., robbery of a Chinese restaurant) often go unreported unless these crimes are connected to larger criminal activities, as in the example that follows:

> A grand jury has indicted three Chinese nationals accused of traveling to Western New York last month to burglarize the Lancaster home of a man whose family owns a local Chinese restaurant. Law enforcement officials said Wednesday they were investigating allegations that the three are part of an organized-crime outfit that has been targeting the operators of Chinese restaurants. . . . Lin's family owns a local Chinese restaurant, and law enforcement officials said they believe the robbery may be tied to other recent robberies targeting the owners of Chinese restaurants. (Herbeck, 2000)

Many immigrants and refugees are simply not knowledgeable about the legal system of the United States and therefore avoid any contact with law enforcement personnel. Outreach and community policing perspectives will enhance the contact and relationship with Asian/Pacific American communities, helping to correct the underreporting of crimes.

Differential Treatment

Several areas have been highlighted for Asian/Pacific Americans who may have received different treatment in police services as a result of their culture or ethnic heritage. Incidents reported included police excessive force, misconduct, and harassment. The following two cases are examples:

> The family of a Vietnamese woman who was shot and killed in her kitchen by police as she brandished a vegetable peeler will receive $1.8 million in a settlement of its lawsuit against the city. The federal suit claimed that San Jose police officers were not properly trained or supervised and that the officer who shot Cau Bich Tran, 25, used excessive force. The settlement ends more than two years of litigation over the death of Tran, a Vietnamese mother of two who was shot while holding a vegetable peeler that police mistook for a cleaver. Tran, an immigrant who spoke little English, was killed July 13, 2003, after authorities were called to her home by a neighbor who reported hearing screaming and pounding. Officer Chad Marshall, 30, testified previously before a grand jury investigating criminal wrongdoing that he believed Tran was about to throw the item at him when he shot her. Marshall was ultimately cleared. The shooting outraged many in the Vietnamese American community, who pressed for an open inquiry into Tran's death. Critics wondered how Tran, who stood barely 5 feet tall and weighed less than 100 pounds, could be considered a credible threat. (Associated Press, 2005)

> A veteran Oakland police officer has been charged with making illegal traffic stops of immigrant Asian women and then trying to kiss or caress them, authorities said Friday. Officer Richard Valerga, 51, was charged Wednesday with seven misdemeanor counts, including two of false imprisonment and five of interference of civil rights, authorities said Friday. It was not yet clear when he would appear in court. The charges stem from traffic stops on five women made between January and April, police said. Police would not reveal the exact location or date of each stop. . . . "During the course of the investigation, it was determined that most of the women recently immigrated to the United States and were illegally detained by the officer," according to a police department statement released Friday by Officer Danielle Ashford, a spokeswoman. . . . Police said Valerga would pull over the victims, attractive Asian women ranging from teenagers to women in their 40s, on a pretext—and then come on to them. He is charged with one count of interference related to each woman. The two false-imprisonment charges stem from allegations by two women that when they asked Valerga to let them go, he refused, authorities said. (Zamora, 2005)

The second example of a rogue police officer acting on his own likely would be seen in very different lights by the Asian/Pacific American immigrant and refugee communities. Most of the victims did not voluntarily come forward, nor did they report the incident to police authorities. Most of the victims were discovered by police investigators on the basis of the names of Asian women that appeared as a result of a search of the officer's computer and later sought out for their testimony. Police investigators believed that there were probably more victims whom they were unable to find. For some in the Asian/Pacific American immigrant and refugee communities, this officer's actions would have been seen as their negative images of law enforcement and differential treatment received.

Positive Collaborative Asian/Pacific American Community and Law Enforcement Agencies

Increasingly, we see that when there are collaborative and cooperative efforts among the law enforcement, criminal justice, and community advocacy systems, the Asian and Pacific American communities will begin to gain greater trust and confidence resulting from effective multicultural and multidisciplinary law enforcement actions taken. The following case is a positive example of how police, prosecutors, courts, community advocates, and victims join together to ensure the conviction involving the rape cases for nine Asian women:

> Simply seeing the Mark Anthony Lewis rape case go to trial last week wasn't enough to satisfy Asian Americans in the Chicago area that police care about their fears. Just like it wasn't enough to see Lewis arrested almost two years ago in the Philippines, where he had traveled after the last of nine attacks against mostly Asian women that shocked the area from April to July 2000. . . . The rape on Chicago's North Side was the eighth of the nine assaults that prompted an unprecedented mobilization of police and community resources to catch the attacker. Police in Chicago, Mount Prospect, Arlington Heights, Skokie, Niles, Morton Grove and Cook County—where the attacks occurred— helped lead efforts. The guilty verdict in the first assault case to go to trial shows "it was worth it to bring out as many community advocates as we could at every step in this process," Dolar said. "It proves to the courts that Asians can step up and be active in stopping crime. It proves it to ourselves." Although prosecutors ultimately decided against trying Lewis on a hate crime charge, Asian community leaders say the prosecution has proved they understand the series of assaults two years ago had a racial maliciousness that struck the heart of their community. "Our focus was to get justice for the victim, so we understand if the state's attorney's office thought it was a stronger case to go on without it," said Jean M. Fujiu, executive director of the Japanese American Service Committee, of the hate crime charge. "We think the state's attorney's office has done a very good job acting on the evidence.". . . "I think this shows that there's not this need to have an assumed distrust of police or state's attorneys or the government or whoever that's outside the (Asian) community," Khan said of the guilty verdict. "I think they see that they're there to help us and help everyone in getting justice served." (Cliatt, 2002, p. 3)

Asian/Pacific American officers involved in community policing in their local neighborhoods have been seen as a viable model for cities with growing Asian/Pacific American populations:

> When Asian-Americans began moving into Quincy in the 1980s, there was not a single Asian-American police officer in the city. That lack of diversity, language barriers and a general fear of authority that developed in homelands thousands of miles away made many of the city's newest residents reluctant to turn to law enforcement for help. That reticence lingers today. To prove the point, Yee notes how several workers avert their eyes when the officers walk into Super 88 market under construction on Hancock Street. . . . But Yee and Mar—both Asian-American—say they are making progress. "Just being an Asian face to an Asian face seems to break some of those barriers down," Mar said. Both Yee and Mar speak Chinese dialects, enabling them to elicit information that might normally be difficult to get. Just recently, they helped with a

possible abduction investigation. Through a series of interviews, they learned that the man was picked up by federal immigration officers, something his family did not know. (Eschbacher, 2003, p. 8)

The Los Angeles Police Department Airport Police Bureau was one of the first police departments to establish storefront outreach efforts that resulted in improved police–community relationships and better service benefits to the Asian/Pacific American neighborhood in the Korean area of Los Angeles (Chin, 1987). Storefront outreach efforts are now utilized in most urban cities with large Asian/Pacific American communities like San Francisco, New York, Oakland, Chicago, Boston, and Seattle. (See Chapter 1 for further information on community policing.) Another outreach approach is the use of Asian/Pacific American bilingual community service officers (CSOs), nonsworn officers with badges and uniforms who serve the Southeast Asian communities in San Diego, California. The CSOs provide many of the supportive services available from the police department by using bilingual nonsworn personnel.

Increasing Asian/Pacific American Peace Officers

There is a noticeable underrepresentation of Asian/Pacific Americans in federal, state, and local law enforcement and criminal justice positions, although the number of Asian/Pacific Americans as peace officers and in law enforcement has increased in the past decade. According to a survey conducted by the Bureau of Justice Statistics in 2002, of the 93,000 full-time federal personnel authorized to make arrests and carry firearms in the 50 states and the District of Columbia, 2.5 percent are Asian/Pacific Americans. The federal agencies that employ the largest number of Asian/Pacific American peace officers are (1) Internal Revenue Service, (2) Postal Inspection Service, (3) Customs Service, and (4) the Bureau of Diplomatic Security (Reaves and Bauer, 2003). No specific local police and sheriff data were reported with respect to the percentages of Asian/Pacific American peace officers in the latest available Bureau of Justice Statistics Reports (Hickman and Reaves, 2006a, b).

The small number of Asian/Pacific American officers has hampered many departments in neighborhoods with large Asian/Pacific American populations in effectively serving those communities with appropriate role models and bicultural expertise. A variety of reasons exist for such underrepresentation, including (1) history of law enforcement relationships with Asian/Pacific American communities, (2) interest of Asian/Pacific Americans in law enforcement careers, (3) image of law enforcement personnel in Asian/Pacific American communities, (4) lack of knowledge about the different careers and pathways in law enforcement, (5) concern with and fear of background checks, physical requirements, and the application process, and (6) limited number of role models and advocates for law enforcement careers for Asian/Pacific Americans. With the growing Asian/Pacific American populations in areas throughout the United States, law enforcement has emphasized the importance of diversity in their recruitment efforts:

> Growing up in Minnesota's Twin Cities, Bob Yang never liked law enforcement. Routine traffic stops that turned into lengthy searches left the first-generation Hmong American suspicious and distrustful of the authorities. Yang's distrust was turned on its head, however, when a white officer treated him with respect during a traffic stop and urged him to use his Hmong language

skills on the force in St. Paul and Minneapolis. "It opened my eyes and got me thinking that it was something I'd like to try," said Yang, 26. "I felt the opportunity not only to show my family but to show the Hmong community that it's a good thing—law enforcement is a good thing." Now, Yang wants to change the minds of other young people about his profession when he hits the streets this month as one of the Sacramento Police Department's newest officers. Often underrepresented in the nation's police forces, ethnic minorities are helping change the face of law enforcement in the Sacramento region. Sacramento's most recent recruit classes boast more women and ethnic minorities than ever, with—for the first time—a near-even split between white men, women and ethnic minorities, said Police Chief Albert Najera. "It helps the organization to have various cultural perspectives when we're working on a crime series or problems in an area," Najera said. Among the new faces are rookies like Yang, the Police Department's second Hmong American man, and Nou Khang, its first Hmong American woman. Selina Lu, the department's first Chinese American woman, graduates in June. The department's first native Russian speaker, Yevgeniy "Eugene" Chernyavskiy, starts the six-month academy in July. The Sacramento County Sheriff's Department recently graduated its first Hmong American woman, Melissa Thao. (Jahn, 2006)

Crimes within Asian/Pacific American Communities

Many crimes committed in Asian/Pacific American communities are perpetrated by others within the same group, particularly among Asian/Pacific refugee and Asian/Pacific immigrant groups. Law enforcement officials have often found it difficult to get cooperation from refugee and immigrant victims of human trafficking, extortion, home robbery, burglary, theft, blackmail, and other crimes against persons. In part, the lack of cooperation stems from a fear of retaliation by the criminal, who is within the Asian/Pacific American community. Other concerns of Asian/Pacific American victims include (1) the perceived level of responsiveness of the peacekeeping officers and agencies, (2) lack of familiarity with and trust in police services, (3) perceived level of effectiveness of law enforcement agencies, and (4) prior stereotypes and images of law enforcement agencies as discriminatory (e.g., immigration laws) and unresponsive to crimes against Asian/Pacific Americans. Recent Asian/Pacific American refugees and immigrants are often prime targets, in part because of their distrust of most institutions (e.g., banks, police departments, hospitals). As a result, they are more inclined to hide and store cash and other valuables in the home. A key challenge for police agencies is to educate this group and to work cooperatively with Asian/Pacific Americans to reduce the crimes within these communities.

Human trafficking has been highlighted as one of the crimes by Asian/Pacific Americans perpetuated on other Asian/Pacific Americans (Cramer, 2006). Human trafficking refers to the transportation of persons for sexual exploitation, forced labor, or other illegal or criminal activities. Law enforcement agencies estimated that more than 1 million people worldwide (including 150,000 from South Asia and 225,000 from Southeast Asia) are trafficked annually around the world, while some researchers and experts say it could be more than twice that number (Asian Development Bank, 2003).

Human trafficking has become a global business with many victims from the Asian countries, and such illegal activities generate huge profits for traffickers and organized criminal groups (Office to Monitor and Combat Trafficking in Persons, 2006).

Because of its secret and hidden nature, human trafficking is likely to remain an increasingly underreported crime. As noted by the Asian Anti-Trafficking Collaborative (AATC), "Preying on the desperation and dreams of vulnerable immigrants around the world, human traffickers lure their victims to the U.S. with false promises and tales of living the American dream. Most victims are pulled to the U.S. by the hope of opportunity and pushed from their home country by the lack of the same chances of making a better life for themselves and their loved ones. But once in the U.S., the experiences of these individuals are strikingly similar: abuse, threats of violence and retaliation, elimination of personal liberty and free agency, and dehumanizing treatment that crushes the dignity, self esteem, and self worth of the victim" (API Legal Outreach, 2005). Law enforcement officers' involvement with Asian/Pacific American communities on human trafficking have emerged as one of the major areas of work as seen in the following example:

> Five Chinese citizens are in custody in the South Bay, charged with running an international smuggling ring that brought Asian women to residential neighborhoods to work as massage parlor prostitutes. The alleged half-million-dollar enterprise shuffled Taiwanese, mainland Chinese and Korean women among 10 massage parlors that men visited for sex in San Jose, Santa Clara, Sunnyvale and San Mateo, according to federal and state investigators who spent a year working undercover on the "Operation Bad Neighbor" case. The brothels operated out of homes and were called "10-day houses," because the women were moved every 10 days to avoid detection. Customers found the homes through word of mouth and Internet ads. After Wednesday's raid, officials took 31 women to safe houses, where they are being interviewed to determine if they came to California willingly or were trafficked—forced, defrauded or coerced into serving as sex slaves. The women range in age from 19 to 35. Victims of human trafficking can testify against their abusers in exchange for visas that will allow them to stay in the United States for three years plus receive monthly benefits, housing and job assistance. Those who refuse to testify or who say they came to the United States to work as prostitutes are deported. (May, 2005, p. B4)

Worldwide, police agencies in six countries (Cambodia, China, Laos, Burma, Thailand and Vietnam) have agreed to collaborate on the investigation and prosecution of human traffickers, as well as on working on the repatriation and help for victims (Reuters, 2005).

SUMMARY OF RECOMMENDATIONS FOR LAW ENFORCEMENT

As a result of the early immigration laws and other discriminatory treatment received by Asian/Pacific Americans in the United States, the experiences of Asian/Pacific Americans with law enforcement officials has been fraught with conflicts, difficulties, and mixed messages. Officers should realize that some Asian/Pacific Americans might still remember this history and carry with them stereotypes of police services as something to be feared and avoided. Law enforcement officials may need to go out of their way to establish trust and to win cooperation in order to effectively accomplish their goals to serve and protect Asian/Pacific Americans.

As noted earlier, the label Asian Americans/Pacific Islanders encompasses over 40 very diverse ethnic and cultural groups. Law enforcement officials must be aware that great differences exist between the 40 diverse ethnic groups (e.g., different cultural and language groups) and that the differences that may result from the individual life experiences of members within any one of the 40 groups (e.g., generational differences). Since a key stereotype of much concern to Asian/Pacific Americans is that they are regarded by mainstream Americans as very much alike, it is important that peace officers not make such errors in their interactions with Asian/Pacific Americans.

There is tremendous diversity among Asian/Pacific Americans, and one way to understand individuals within these communities is to look at some of the motivating forces that might affect decisions by Asian/Pacific American citizens. Earlier in this chapter, we provided a seven-part typology that will assist officers in viewing some of these motivational bases.

Although there are many ethnicities, cultures, and languages among the 40 or more groups within Asian/Pacific American communities, one way to understand the impact of their immigration and life experiences is by learning the motivational determinants of individuals within different generational and immigrant groups.

The self-preferred term for referring to Asian/Pacific Americans varies with contexts, groups, and experiences of the individual. Law enforcement officials need to be aware of terms that are unacceptable and derogatory and terms that are currently used. When in doubt, officers have to learn to become comfortable in asking Asian/Pacific Americans which terms they prefer. Officers are advised to provide helpful feedback to their peers when offensive terms, labels, and/or actions are used with Asian/Pacific Americans. Such feedback will help reduce the risk of misunderstanding and improve the working relationships between officers and Asian/Pacific American communities. Moreover, it will help enhance the professional image of the department for those communities.

Many Asian/Pacific Americans are concerned with their ability to communicate clearly, and this is of particular concern among Asian/Pacific Americans who are immigrants and refugees. Peace officers must recognize that bilingual individuals and nonnative English speakers want to communicate effectively with them, and officers must take the time to do so. Maintaining contact, providing extra time, using translators, and being patient with speakers will allow Asian/Pacific Americans to communicate their concerns.

Cultural differences in verbal and nonverbal communication often result in misinterpretation of the message and of behaviors. Officers need to be aware of nonverbal aspects of Asian/Pacific Americans in their communication styles, including eye contact, touch, gestures, and affect (show of emotions). Verbal aspects such as accent, limited vocabulary, and incorrect grammar may give officers the impression that an Asian/Pacific American individual does not understand what is communicated. It is important to remember that the English listening and comprehension skills of Asian/Pacific American immigrants and refugees are usually better than their speaking skills.

Asian/Pacific Americans, because of their past experiences with law enforcement agencies, along with their own concerns about privacy, self-help, and other factors, are reluctant to report crimes and may not seek police assistance and help. Law enforcement departments and officials need to build relationships and working partnerships with representative groups from the Asian/Pacific American communities. Relationship building is often helped by outreach efforts such as community storefront offices, bilingual officers, and participation of officers in community activities.

DISCUSSION QUESTIONS AND ISSUES*

1. *Law Enforcement as Not User-Friendly.* Many anti–Asian/Pacific American laws and events may leave Asian/Pacific Americans with the view that law enforcement agencies are not user-friendly. What are the implications of this view for law enforcement? What are ways to improve negative points of view?

2. *Diversity among Asian/Pacific Americans.* The Asian/Pacific American category comprises over 40 diverse ethnic and cultural groups. Which groups are you most likely to encounter in crime-fighting and peacekeeping in your work? Which groups do you anticipate encountering in your future work?

3. *How Asian/Pacific American Groups Differ.* A typology for understanding motives for some of the behaviors of Asian/Pacific American people (in terms of their generational and immigration status in the United States) was provided. How might you apply this typology to better understand an Asian/Pacific American refugee involved in a traffic moving violation? An Asian/Pacific American immigrant involved as a victim of a house robbery? An Asian/Pacific national involved as a victim of a burglary? Southeast Asian youths involved in possible gang activities?

4. *Choice of Terms.* The term Asian Americans and Pacific Islanders is used in many publications and by many people to refer to members of the more than 40 diverse groups included in this category. How might you find out which is the best term to use in reference to an individual if ethnic and cultural information of this kind is necessary?

5. *Offensive Terms and Labels.* We strongly urge that offensive terms such as Chinks, Gooks, and Flips not be used in law enforcement work at any time. Give three practical reasons for this perspective.

6. *Effects of Myths and Stereotypes.* Myths and stereotypes about Asian/Pacific Americans have greatly affected this group. What are some of the Asian/Pacific American stereotypes that you have heard of or encountered? What effects would these stereotypes have on Asian/Pacific Americans? What are ways to manage these stereotypes in law enforcement? How might your awareness of Asian/Pacific American stereotypes be helpful in an interview with an Asian/Pacific American about homeland security issues?

7. *Verbal and Nonverbal Variations among Cultures.* How do you think that the information in this chapter about verbal and nonverbal communication styles can help officers in their approach to Asian/Pacific American citizens? Does understanding the cultural components of the styles and behaviors help

*See the Instructor's Manual accompanying this text for additional activities, role-play activities, questionnaires, and projects related to the content of this chapter.

you to become more sensitive and objective about your reactions? Provide some examples of rephrasing questions in such a way that they elicit responses that show understanding and the intended actions on the part of Asian/Pacific Americans.

8. ***Self-Monitoring and Avoidance of Law Enforcement.*** Why do you think many Asian/Pacific Americans keep to their own communities and express the desire for self-monitoring and within-community resolution of their problems? When are such efforts desirable? When are they ineffective? How can police agencies be of greater service to Asian/Pacific American communities in this regard?

WEBSITE RESOURCES

Visit these websites for additional information about law enforcement contact with Asian/Pacific Americans, as well as for information about Asian/Pacific American community organizations.

Academy for Educational Development (AED): http://www.humantrafficking.org

This website brings government agencies in East Asia and the Pacific together to cooperate and learn from each other's experiences in anti-human trafficking efforts. The website has country-specific information such as national laws and action plans and contact information on useful governmental agencies.

American Immigration Law Foundation (AILF): http://www.ailf.org

This website provides information to increase public understanding of immigration law and policy and the value of immigration to American society; to promote public service and excellence in the practice of immigration law; and to advance fundamental fairness and due process under the law for immigrants.

Asian American Legal Defense and Education Fund (AALDEF):
http://www. aaldef.org

This website provides information about civil rights issues with Asian/Pacific Americans and highlights issues of immigration, family law, government benefits, anti-Asian violence and police misconduct, employment discrimination, labor rights, and workplace issues.

Asian American Network: http://www.asianamerican.net

This website provides a national listing of many of the networks of Asian/Pacific American community-based organizations in the United States (as well as some in Asia).

Asian and Pacific Islander Institute on Domestic Violence: http://www.apiahf.org

This website provides information on a national network of advocates and community members to serve as a forum for and a clearinghouse on information, research, resources, and critical issues about violence against women in Asian/Pacific American communities.

Asian and Pacific Islander Outreach: http://www.apilegaloutreach.org

This website provides information about Asian Pacific Islander Legal Outreach (API Legal Outreach), which has worked to tear down long-standing barriers that have denied Asians and Pacific Islanders equal justice and equal access to our legal system. The website's section on Asian human trafficking provides information on prevention, reporting, prosecution, and best practices.

National Asian Pacific American Legal Consortium: http://www.napalc.org

This website provides a national network of information about legal and civil rights issues affecting Asian/Pacific Americans in terms of litigation, advocacy, public education, and public policy.

National Asian Peace Officers Association: http://www.napoa.org/

This website provides information to promote the interests of Asian American peace officers on community issues, career development and opportunities, education and workshops, and awareness about the Asian culture.

National Council of Asian Pacific Americans: http://www.ncapaonline.org/

This website provides information on the coalition of twenty-one Asian/Pacific American organizations nation wide, founded in 1996 and based in Washington D.C, NCAPA serves to represent the interests of the greater APA community and to provide a national voice for Asian/Pacific American issues.

REFERENCES

Abraham, M. (2000). *Speaking the Unspeakable: Marital Violence against South Asian Immigrant Women in the United States.* New Brunswick, N.J.: Rutgers University Press.

Asian Development Bank. (2003). *Combating Trafficking of Women and Children in South Asia.* Washington, D.C.: Asian Development Bank.

Asian Pacific Islander (API) Outreach (2005). "Asian Anti-Trafficking Collaborative (AATC)." Available: http://www.apilegaloutreach.org/trafficking.html/

Associated Press. (2001, September 26). "Des Moines to Pay $7,500 to Men Who Were Handcuffed at Cafe."

Associated Press (2005, December 1). "Family of Vietnamese police shooting victim settles suit for $1.8M."

Barnes, J. S., and Bennett, C. E. (2002). *The Asian Population: 2000.* Washington, D.C.: U.S. Census Bureau.

Bennett, C. E. (2002). *A Profile of the Nation's Foreign-Born Population from Asia (2000 Update).* Washington, DC: U.S. Census Bureau.

Blake, J. (2002, February 3). "Ethnic Straitjacket: South Asians Confront Stereotype as 'Model Minority.'" *Atlanta Journal and Constitution,* p. M1.

Branch, A. (2006, January 20). "Asian Gangs Pose New Problems for Police." *Fort Worth Star-Telegram (Texas).*

Chin, J. (1987). "Crime and the Asian American Community: The Los Angeles Response to Koreatown." *Journal of California Law Enforcement, 19,* 52–60.

Cliatt, C. (2002, May 5). "Rape Case Rallies Asian Community: Fear of Police, Fierce Protection Gives Way to Doing What It Takes to Convict." *Chicago Daily Herald,* p. 3.

Cramer, M. (2006, January 28). "Police Seek to Stop Surge in Prostitution: Advocates Fearful for Women; Most Are Immigrants." *Boston Globe,* p. B12.

Daniels, R. (1988). *Asian America: Chinese and Japanese in the United States since 1850.* Seattle: University of Washington Press.

Eschbacher, K. (2003, August) "Two Asian-American Officers Make Inroads in Neighborhoods." *Patriot Ledger,* Special Report, p. 8.

Glasse, C., and Smith, H. (2003). *The New Encyclopedia of Islam* (Revised). Walnut Creek, CA: Alta Mira Press.

Herbeck, D. (2000, July 6). "Asian Organized-Crime Ties Eyed in Lancaster Robbery." *Buffalo News.*

Hickman, M. J. and Reaves, B. A. (2006a, May). "Local Police Department, 2003." Bureau of Justice Statistics: Law Enforcement Management and Administrative Statistics.

Hickman, M. J. and Reaves, B. A. (2006b, May). "Sheriffs' Offices, 2003." Bureau of Justice Statistics: Law Enforcement Management and Administrative Statistics.

Jahn, C. (2006, May 11). "New Officers Reflect Diverse Face of City: More Women, Ethnic Minorities Now Recruits," *Sacramento Bee,* p. B1

Kawai, Y. (2005). "Stereotyping Asian Americans: The Dialectic of the Model Minority and the Yellow Peril." *Howard Journal of Communications.* 16(2), 109–130.

Kempsky, N. (1989, October). "A Report to Attorney General John K. Van de Kamp on Patrick Edward Purdy and the Cleveland School Killings." Sacramento: State of California Attorney General's Office.

Kertscher, T. (2002, February 13). "Arsonist Sentenced for Hate Crimes; Hmong Family Tells of Fleeing Burning Home." *Milwaukee Journal Sentinel,* p. B1.

Kwoh, S. (2000, May 28). "Asians Battle Rights Abuses—in the U.S." *Los Angeles Times,* p. M8.

Mathews, J., and M. Lait. (1989, January 18). "Rifleman Slays Five at School: 19 Pupils, Teacher Shot in California; Assailant Kills Self." *Washington Post,* p. A1.

May, M. (2005, October 28). "5 Chinese Citizens Charged with Running Prostitution Ring: Police Move Women to Safe Houses to See If They Were Coerced," *San Francisco Chronicle,* p. B4.

Morton, J. (2002, May 14). "Second Coining Case is Dropped: Asian Dad Hopes Case Helps Others." *Omaha World Herald,* p. B1.

National Asian Women's Health Organization (2002). *Silence, Not an Option!* San Francisco, CA: Author.

Office to Monitor and Combat Trafficking in Persons (2006, June 5). *Trafficking in Persons Report.* Washington, DC: U.S. Department of State.

Population Reference Bureau (PRB). (2005). *World Population Data Sheet.* Washington, D.C.: Author.

Povell, M. (2005). *The History of Vietnamese Immigration.* Washington, D.C. The American Immigration Law Foundation. Available: http://www.ailf.org.

Prashad, V. (2001). *The Karma of Brown Folk.* Minneapolis: University of Minnesota Press.

President's Commission on Mental Health. (1978). *Report of the Special Population Subpanel on Mental Health of Asian/Pacific Americans, Vol. 3.* Washington, D.C.: U.S. Government Printing Office.

Quan, D. (2006, April 17). "Slayings Stun Asian Community; Soul-searching: Slayings of Their Children by Three Fathers Bring Calls for More Support Services," *The Press Enterprise (Riverside, CA)*, p. B01.

Reaves, B. A., and Bauer, L. M. (2003, April). "Federal Law Enforcement Officers, 2002." *Bureau of Justice Statistics Bulletin.*

Reuters. (2005, 31 March). "Six Asian Nations Act to Stop Human Trafficking."

Smith, S. (2000, May 20). "Grief after Girl's Death is Unspeakable." *Austin American-Statesman,* p. B1.

Song, Y. I. (1996). *Battered Women in Korean Immigrant Families.* New York: Garland.

Stockfisch, J. R. (2003, April 1). "Lawmakers Want End of 'Racist' Clause." *Tampa Tribune,* p. 1.

Takaki, R. (1989a). *Strangers from a Different Shore: A History of Asian Americans.* Boston: Little, Brown.

Takaki, R. (1989b). "Who Killed Vincent Chin?" in G. Yun (ed.), *A Look Beyond the Model Minority Image: Critical Issues in Asian America.* New York: Minority Rights Group, p. 23–29.

Tjaden, P., and Thoennes, N. (2005). *Extent, Nature, and Consequences of Intimate Partner Violence: Research Report.* Washington, DC: National Institute of Justice and the Centers for Disease Control and Prevention.

U.S. Bureau of the Census. (2006, March 27). *Facts for Features—Asian/Pacific Heritage Month: May 2006.* Washington, D.C.: U.S. Government Printing Office.

U.S. Bureau of the Census. (2002). *Census 2000 Brief Reports.* Washington, D.C.: U.S. Government Printing Office.

Zamora, J. H. (2005, August 27). "Officer Charged with Illegal Stops: Police Say He Pulled Over Asian Women, Came On to Them." *San Francisco Chronicle,* p. B3.

Chapter 6

Law Enforcement Contact with African Americans

OVERVIEW

This chapter provides specific cultural and historical information on African Americans that both directly and indirectly affects the relationship between law enforcement officials and citizens. It presents information about demographics and diversity among African Americans as well as issues related to cultural and racial identity. Following the background information is a section on group identification terms and a discussion of myths and stereotypes. Aspects of the family are discussed, including the extended family, the roles of men and women, single-mother families, and adolescents. A section on cultural influences on communication deals with Ebonics (also known as Black English Vernacular and African American Vernacular English); nonverbal and verbal communication, including emotionalism; and fighting words, threats, and aggressive behavior. The closing section presents several key concerns for law enforcement, including information on differential treatment, racial profiling, perceptions of and reactions to legal authority, excessive force and brutality, police interaction in poor urban communities, the needs of the inner city, and issues related to women. The summary of the chapter reviews recommendations for improved communication and relationships between law enforcement officials and African Americans.

COMMENTARY

The history of intimidation of African Americans by police continues to affect the dynamics of law enforcement in some black communities today.

> There is no point in telling blacks to observe the law. . . . It has almost always been used against them.
>
> —*Senator Robert Kennedy after visiting the scene of the Watts Riot, 1965*

> We must learn to live together as brothers or perish together as fools.
>
> —*Martin Luther King, 1964.*

If . . . inclusion of African Americans and other minorities in policing and in the broader society are continued, then community policing might finally realize a vision of police departments as organizations that protect the lives, property, and rights of all citizens in a fair and effective way. (Williams & Murphy, 1990)

Law enforcement should move away from thinking only about the inner city when "African American" comes to mind. African Americans are more sophisticated [than ten and twenty years ago]; they understand societal rules and community resources, including complaint procedures when it comes to law enforcement actions. Their expectations for law enforcement professionalism have risen significantly. (Berry, 2006)

African Americans today enjoy equal protection under the law and have higher expectations of law enforcement than they did in the past. Community leaders expect to become involved with law enforcement agencies in community-based policing formats. In Chapter 1, we presented an example of the San Diego Police Department whose leaders collaborated with African Americans and other community members (Latinos, Asians) to interpret racial profiling data and to deal jointly with the problem. While this example is not intended to gloss over the reality that law enforcement still has much progress to make with respect to relations with the African American community, it illustrates that a shift is beginning to take place between law enforcement and some segments of the African American population.

AFRICAN AMERICAN CULTURE

The overwhelming problems associated with the racial aspects of black–white relations sometimes overshadow the cultural differences between white and black Americans. The effects that slavery and discrimination have had on the black experience in America are not to be downplayed, but in addition, African American culture must also be considered. African American culture is in part influenced by African culture and is significantly different from white culture. Many police executives have come to recognize that when there is an influx of immigrants from a particular part of the world, their officers are better equipped to establish trust, good communication, and mutual cooperation if they have some basic understanding of the group's cultural background. However, history has shown when it comes to African Americans, cultural differences are seldom considered, even though they can cause serious communication problems between citizens and police officers. Failing to recognize the distinctiveness of black culture, language, and communication patterns can lead to misunderstandings, conflict, and even confrontation. In addition, understanding the history of African Americans (which is related to the culture) is especially important for law enforcement officials as they work toward improving relations and changing individual and community perceptions.

HISTORICAL INFORMATION

The majority of African Americans or blacks (we use the terms interchangeably) in the United States trace their roots to West Africa. They were torn from their cultures of origin between the 17th and 19th centuries when they were brought here as slaves. Blacks represent the only migrants to come to the Americas, North and South, against their will. Blacks from Africa were literally kidnap victims, kidnapped by Europeans, as well as purchased as captives by Yankee traders. This experience has made African Americans, as a group, very different from immigrants who chose to come to the United States to better their lives, and different from refugees who fled their homelands to escape religious or political persecution.

The very word *slave* carries the connotation of an "inferior" being; slaves were counted as three-fifths of a person during census-taking. Slave owners inwardly understood that treating people as animals to be owned, worked, and sold was immoral, but they wanted to think of themselves as good, religious, moral people. Hence they had to convince themselves that their slaves were not really human but a lower form of life. They focused on racial differences (skin color, hair texture, etc.) as "proof" that black people were not really people, after all. Racism began, then, as an airtight alibi for a horrifying injustice. The notion of the slave (and by extension, any African American) as less than human has created great psychological and social problems for succeeding generations of both black and white citizens. Slavery led to a system of inferior housing, schools, health care, and jobs for black people, which persists to this day.

The institution of slavery formally ended in 1863, but the racist ideas born of slavery have persisted. These ideas continue even now to leave deep scars on many African Americans. Today, particularly in the lower-socioeconomic classes, many blacks continue to suffer from the psychological heritage of slavery as well as from active, current discrimination that still prevents them from equal opportunity in many realms of life.

Until recently, the "public" history that many Americans learned presented a distorted, incomplete picture of black family life (emphasizing breakdown) during the slave era, which had crippling effects on families for generations to come. This version of history never examined the moral strength of the slaves or the community solidarity and family loyalty that arose after emancipation. There is no doubt that these strengths have positively affected the rebuilding of the African American community. Further, "it has long been hypothesized that one's racial identity attitudes relate to sense of self, comfort with one's own racial group, and comfort with persons of diverse racial group" (Ponterotto, Utsey, & Pedersen, 2006, p. 105).

> According to almost all witnesses, the roads of the South were clogged in 1865 [after emancipation] with Black men and women searching for long-lost wives, husbands, children, brothers and sisters. The in-gathering continued for several years and began in most communities with mass marriage ceremonies that legalized the slave vows. This was a voluntary process for husbands and wives who were free to renounce slave vows and search for new mates. Significantly, most freedmen, some of them 80 and 90 years old, decided to remain with their old mates, thereby giving irrefutable testimony on the meaning of their love. . . . (Bennett, 1989)

Despite slave owners' attempts to destroy black family life, slaves did manage to form lasting families headed by a mother and a father, and many slave couples enjoyed long marriages. Although white slave masters would often do everything possible to pull families apart (including the forced "breeding" and the selling of slaves), there is evidence that slaves maintained their family connections as best as they could and produced stable units with admirable values. According to U.S. historian Char Miller, "Despite the fact that slavery tore apart many families, blacks maintained links, loves, and relationships just as anyone else would under these circumstances" (2006). The more accurate version of history counters the impression that all slave families were so helpless that they were always torn apart and could never reestablish themselves, or that their social relationships were chaotic and amoral. The resolve of large numbers of blacks to rebuild their families and communities as soon as they were freed represents an impressive determination in a people who survived one of the most brutal forms of servitude that history has seen. African American survival, and consequently, African American contributions to American society, deserve a high level of respect and testify to a people's great strength. It is not within the scope of this chapter to discuss African American contributions to society, but suffice it to say that frequently the perceptions of some people in law enforcement are often conditioned by their exposure to the black underclass, for whom crime is a way of life.

Law Enforcement Interaction with African Americans: Historical Baggage

> Many of the police and African-American problems in our communities today go way back and stem from history. Some of the issues can be traced directly from the Civil War reconstruction era, in slavery days, when police and the military were required to return runaway slaves. (Patton, 2006)

In the United States during the late 17th and 18th centuries, following slave uprisings in a number of colonies, the colonists created strict laws to contain the slaves. Even minor offenses were punished harshly. This set the negative tone between law enforcement and blacks. American police were called on to form "slave patrols" and to enforce racially biased laws (Williams & Murphy, 1990). In many areas of the country, police were expected to continue enforcing deeply biased, discriminatory laws (including those setting curfews for blacks and barring blacks from many facilities and activities). Today, segments of the African American population continue to struggle with interaction with the police. "The fact that the legal order not only countenanced but sustained slavery, segregation and discrimination for most of our Nation's history—and the fact that the police were bound to uphold that order—set a pattern for police behavior and attitudes toward black communities that has persisted until the present day. That pattern includes the idea that blacks have fewer civil rights, that the task of the police is to keep them under control, and that the police have little responsibility for protecting them from crime within their communities" (Williams & Murphy, 1990).

Most police officers have had some exposure to the historical precedents of poor relationships between police and minority communities. The damages of the past give us no choice but to make a greater effort today with groups such as African Americans for whom contact with law enforcement has long been problematic.

DEMOGRAPHICS: DIVERSITY AMONG AFRICAN AMERICANS*

Currently, blacks comprise about 13 percent of the population of the United States, or approximately 35 million people (U.S. Bureau of the Census, 2003). Until the last few decades, the vast majority lived in the south. Between 1940 and 1970, over 1.5 million

---

*Refer back to Chapter 1, section, "The Overlap of Race, Culture, and Ethnicity," for information about individuals who do not "neatly" fit into one demographic category such as black.

blacks migrated initially to the north and then to the west coast, largely seeking better job opportunities. Historically, over 50 percent of the black population has lived in urban areas. Since 1980, that number has decreased slightly: 12.5 percent live in non-metropolitan areas and 36 percent live in suburban areas, up from 21.2 percent in 1980 (Frey, 1998). The rural black population has decreased, and the shifting flow has contributed to the increase in numbers in suburban areas (some rural blacks may migrate directly into the inner city while others may move to more suburban areas; the flow is not actually known). In any case, urban cores experience cycles of repopulation, mainly by blacks, Hispanics, and various new immigrant groups. The most vivid example is the city of Detroit, where approximately 85 percent of the population is black, while most whites and immigrant groups have settled in outlying areas. Similarly, other cities, such as Washington D.C., St. Louis, Chicago, and Cleveland, are populated mainly by blacks and new immigrants, creating layers of tension where diverse groups with conflicting values and customs suddenly find themselves crowded into the same urban neighborhoods.

These population shifts have created "two Americas." One America is the world of the suburbs, where schools, recreational facilities, and community resources are far better. The other is the inner city, where many African Americans (as well as Latinos and other ethnic groups) have much poorer access to educational and job opportunities and where living conditions are often closer to those of cities in the ravaged developing world than to those of America's comfortable suburban environment.

Although many African Americans belong to the lower socioeconomic classes, blacks are represented in all the classes, from the extremely poor to the extremely affluent, and have moved increasingly into the middle classes. As with all ethnic groups, there are significant class-related differences among blacks, affecting values and behavior. It is no more true to say that a poor black has a great deal in common with an affluent black than to say that poor and rich whites are the same. (Later in this chapter we discuss stereotyping of all blacks based on the black underclass.) However, color, more so than class, often determines how the larger society reacts to and treats blacks. Therefore, the racial (as opposed to cultural) experience of many African Americans in the United States is similar, regardless of an individual's level of prosperity or education.

The cultural diversity that exists among African Americans is related to a variety of factors. Over the last 400 years, black families have come from many different countries (e.g., Jamaica, Trinidad, Belize, Haiti, Puerto Rico). By far, the largest group's forefathers came directly to the United States from Africa. In addition, there are cultural differences among African Americans related to the region of the country from which they came. As with whites, there are "southern" and "northern" characteristics as well as urban and rural characteristics.

Religious backgrounds vary, but the majority of American-born blacks are Protestant, and many are specifically Baptist. The first black-run, black-controlled denomination in the country was the African Methodist Episcopal church (which was created because churches in the north and south either banned blacks or required them to sit apart from whites). In addition, a percentage of blacks belong to the Black Muslim religion, including the Nation of Islam and American Muslim Mission. (The term *Black Muslim* is often used but is rejected by some members of the religion.) There are also sizable and fast-growing black populations among members of the Seventh-Day Adventists, Jehovah's Witnesses, Pentecostals (especially among Spanish-speaking blacks), and especially among blacks of Caribbean origin, Santeria, Candomble, Voudun, and similar sects blending Catholic and West African (mainly Yoruba) beliefs and rituals. Rastafarianism has spread far beyond its native Jamaica to become an influential religious movement among immigrants from many other English-speaking Caribbean nations.

ISSUES OF IDENTITY

In the 1960s and 1970s, the civil rights and Black Pride movements marked a new direction in black identity. The civil rights movement opened many barriers to educational and employment opportunities and to active political involvement. Some adults marched in the civil rights movement knowing that they themselves might never benefit directly from civil rights' advances: they hoped that their efforts in the struggle would improve the lives of their children. The middle-class youths who attended community churches and black colleges became the leaders in the movement for equal rights (McAdoo, 1992).

Many blacks (both American-born and Caribbean-born), inspired by a growing sense of community identification and increased pride in racial identity, have determined to learn more about Africa. Despite the great differences in culture between African Americans and Africans, blacks throughout this hemisphere are discovering that they can take pride in the richness of their African heritage, including its high ethical values and community cohesiveness. Examples of African culture that have influenced American black culture or are held in high esteem by many African Americans are (Walker, 1982):

- Cooperative interdependence among and between people (contrasted with Western individualism)
- Partnership with nature and with the spirit world reflected in the approach to ecology and in communication with the spirit world (closer to Native American beliefs)
- Balance and harmony among all living things, reflected in the placing of human relations as a priority value (contrasted with the Western view of achievement and "doing" as taking priority over the nurturing of human relations)
- Joy and celebration in life itself
- Time as a spiral, focused on "now" (contrasted with the Western view of time as "money" and time running away from us)
- Focus on the group and not on the individual
- Giving of self to community
- Renewed interest in respecting elders

The combination of the Black Pride movement of the 1960s and 1970s and the more current focus on cultural roots has freed many African Americans from the "slave mentality" that continued to haunt the African American culture long after emancipation. A new pride in race and heritage has, for some, replaced the sense of inferiority fostered by white racial supremacist attitudes.

GROUP IDENTIFICATION TERMS

Several ethnic groups, including African Americans, in a positive evolution of their identity and pride, have initiated name changes for their group. This is not confusion (although it can be confusing) but rather represents, on the part of group members, growth and a desire to name themselves rather than be named by the dominant society. Until approximately the early 1990s, the most widely accepted term was *black,* this term having replaced *Negro* (which, in turn, replaced *colored people*). Negro has been out of use for at least two decades, although some older blacks still use the term (as do some younger African Americans among themselves). To many, the term Negro symbolizes what the African American became under slavery. The replacement of Negro with black came to symbolize racial pride. (The exception to the use of Negro and colored is in titles like United Negro College and National Association of Colored People [NAACP].) African American, a term preferred by many, focuses on positive historical and cultural roots rather than on race or skin color.

In the 1990s, the use of the term African American grew in popularity. (It is the equivalent of, for example, Italian American or Polish American.) Many feel that the word black is no more appropriate in describing skin color than is white. (Yet, some Americans who are black do not identify with African American because it does not fully represent their background, which may be Caribbean or Haitian; they may not identify with the African part at all.) Since the 1980s and early 1990s, the term *people of color* has sometimes been used, but this catchall phrase has limited use for police officers because it is used to describe anyone who is not white and can include Asian/ Pacific Americans, Latino/Hispanic Americans, as well as Native Americans. Indeed, there is much controversy and history associated with broad, collective terms that attempt to too quickly categorize people.

The use of the words *nigger, boy,* or *coon* is never acceptable at any time and especially in crime-fighting and peacekeeping, no matter how provoked an officer may be. (Although you may hear black youths using "nigger" to refer to each other, the word is absolutely taboo for outsiders—especially outsiders wearing badges.) Police who do not like to be called "pigs" can certainly relate to a person's feelings about being called "gorilla." Officers hearing these types of labels used in their own departments, even when they are not being used to address somebody directly, should remind their peers of the lack of professionalism and prejudice that those terms convey. Officers who fall into the habit of using these words in what they think are harmless situations may find that they are unable to control themselves during more volatile situations with citizens.

MYTHS AND STEREOTYPES

Many of the impressions that people in the society (and consequently, in law enforcement) form about African Americans come from their exposure to messages and images in the media about African Americans. Here the phenomenon of stereotyping is as much at work as it is when citizens see all police officers as repressive and capable of brutality. Police officers know that they will all take a beating nationwide when there is publicity about an instance of police brutality against blacks or reports of racial profiling.

The white majority's view of blacks reflects the same problem. Those who are bent toward prejudice may feel that their racism is justified whenever a crime involving an African American makes the evening news. A suburban African American mother addressing a community forum on racism pointed out: "Every time I hear that there has been a murder or a rape, I pray that it is not a black who committed the crime. The minute the media reports that a black person is responsible for a crime, all of us suffer. When something negative happens, I am no longer seen as an individual with the same values and hopes as my white neighbors. I become a symbol, and more so my husband and sons become feared. People treat us with caution and politeness, but inside we know that their stereotypes of the worst criminal element of blacks have become activated" (Personal communication, source wishes to remain anonymous).

Even the fact of a crime rate that is disproportionately high among young black males does not justify sweeping statements about all African Americans. Certainly, 36 million African Americans cannot be judged by a statistic about the criminal element. Unfortunately for the vast majority of the African American population, some whites do base their image of all blacks largely on the actions, including criminal behavior, of the black members of America's "underclass." It is well known that women clutch their purses harder when they see a black man approaching. Similarly, officers have been known to stop blacks and question them simply for not "looking like they belong to a certain neighborhood." (This is discussed and illustrated further in this chapter as well as in Chapter 14.) Many people, including whites and Asians, often harbor unreasonable fears about black people. Having never had a black friend or acquaintance, they feed such fears instead of reaching out to meet or get to know people who look different from themselves.

African Americans have to contend with many myths and stereotypes that are central to a prejudiced person's thinking. For example, one myth, related to "raw and uncontrolled sex," leads people to believe that blacks have no morals, easily surrender to their "instincts," and can't practice self-restraint (Bennett, 1989). This type of thinking gives some people a sense of moral superiority over blacks for what they perceive to be black sexual habits. In a nationwide survey on sex practices of married couples, including adultery, it was found that blacks are no more likely (or, expressed differently, precisely as likely) as whites to commit adultery. White sexuality never became a racial issue during the interlude of highly publicized "wife swapping" among middle- and upper-class suburbanites, nor did white sexuality become an issue during the 1960s and 1970s when many young people (e.g., white "hippies" in the 1960s and whites on the singles-bar scene a few years later) engaged in widespread sexual promiscuity. Although these practices were often criticized, the white racial element was ignored.

For African Americans, race has historically been connected to sexuality in ways that it would never occur to people to do with whites. This is another legacy of slavery and of the self-justifying racist thinking that arose from that institution. Many slave owners routinely and brutally raped their female slaves (often even before puberty), as well as forced their healthiest slaves to couple and breed regardless of the slaves' own attachments and preferences. (The fact that many African American's genetic background is part Caucasian is testimony to the slave owners' "tendencies" to violate slave girls and women.) While using slaves to indulge their desires, white slave owners convinced themselves that Africans had no morals and would couple indiscriminately like animals if left to do so. Like the myth of black inferiority, the white view of black sexuality was shaped by the need of slave owners to find an excuse for their cruel and unjust behavior.

CROSS-RACIAL PERCEPTIONS IN LAW ENFORCEMENT

Prejudice, lack of contact, and ignorance lend themselves to groups' developing perceptions about the other that are often based on biased beliefs. Unfortunately, perceptions are reality for the individuals and groups who hold them. Perceptions are seen as the truth, whether or not they are the truth. Exhibit 6.1 illustrates differing perceptions that some members of the dominant society have toward black and white males. In this case, the media and popular literature have contributed to the differing perceptions.

How about perceptions that African Americans have developed of police officers' actions? Because of a past history of prejudice and discrimination toward blacks, police officers have used techniques that indeed continue to create perceptions among many African Americans. In other words, while some officers no longer exhibit racist actions, the perceptions remain. The description of perceptions listed in Exhibit 6.2 were presented to northern California police officers in the early 1990s by then vice president of the Alameda, California, NAACP chapter (the late Al Dewitt). When Dewitt presented these perceptions to police officers, he explained that, over time, African Americans formed perceptions about police behavior that led to a lack of trust, riots, and race problems. According to Greg Patton (an African-American; former Washington State Patrol Trooper, district attorney investigator, and now a parole and probation supervisor and adjunct community college criminal justice cultural diversity instructor), the perceptions listed in Exhibit 6.2 are still entirely valid today. However, due to increased educational requirements and professional standards for police officers, the perceptions, fortunately, do not exist equally everywhere and vary by jurisdiction. Improving and preventing racial misperceptions will take time and effort on the part of

BLACK MALE	WHITE MALE
Arrogant	Confident
Chip on shoulder	Self assured
Aggressive	Assertive
Dominant personality	Natural leader
Violence prone	Wayward
Naturally gifted	Smart
Sexual prowess	Sexual experimentation

Exhibit 6.1   Are people viewed in equal terms?

POLICE ACTION	BLACK PERCEPTION
Being stopped or expelled from so-called "white neighborhoods."	Whites want blacks to "stay in their place."
Immediately suspecting and reacting to blacks without distinction between dope dealer and plainclothes police officer.	Police view black skin as itself as probable cause.
Using unreasonable force, beatings, adding charges.	When stopped, blacks must be submissive or else.
Negative attitudes, jokes, body language, talking down to people.	Officers are racists.
Quick trigger, take-downs, accidental shootings.	Bad attitudes will come out under stress.
Slow response, low priority, low apprehension rate.	Black-on-black crime not important.
Techniques of enforcing local restrictions and white political interests.	Police are the strong arm for the status quo.
Police stick together, right or wrong.	Us-against-them mentality; they stick together, so we have to stick together

Exhibit 6.2   Perceptions of police officers' actions by some blacks

the officer but will inevitably benefit him or her by way of increased cooperation and officer safety.

THE AFRICAN AMERICAN FAMILY

African American families generally enjoy very strong ties among extended family members, especially among women. Female relatives often substitute for each other in filling family roles; for example, a grandmother or aunt may raise a child if the mother is unable to do so. Sometimes several different family groups may share one house. When there is a problem (i.e., an incident that has brought an officer to the house), extended family members are likely to be present and to want to help. An officer may observe a number of uncles, aunts, brothers, sisters, sweethearts, and friends who are loosely attached to the black household. Enlisting the aid of any of these household members (no matter what the relationship) can be beneficial.

The Role of the Man and the Woman

A widespread myth holds that African American culture is a matriarchy, with one or more women heading the typical household. Historically, it is true that women did play a crucial role in the family, because of repeated attempts to break down "black manhood" (Bennett, 1989). However, in a true matriarchy (female-ruled society), women control property and economic activities. This is not generally true of black America, but outsiders often assume that African American women are always the heads of the household. In the 1960s and 1970s, for instance, the media stereotyped the black mother as loud and domineering, clearly the boss. In addition, African American women have, in a sense, been considered less of a threat to the status quo than the African American male and consequently have been able to be more assertive in public. Historically, in contacts with law enforcement, an African American man may feel that, unlike a woman, he risks arrest or at least mistreatment if he "talks back."

African American fathers, regardless of income, usually view themselves as heads of the household (Hines & Franklin, 2005), and thus any major decisions regarding the family should include the father's participation. It is insulting to the father when, with both parents present, officers automatically focus on the mother. An assertive mother does not mean that the father is passive or indifferent, and a father's silence does not necessarily indicate agreement. It is always worthwhile to get his view of the situation.

The Single Mother

Feeding the stereotype of the female-headed black household is the fact that in many urban African American homes, no father is present. In 1965, about 25 percent of African American families nationally were headed by women. Between 1970 and 1997, births to single African American women increased by 93 percent, resulting in 68.4 percent of black births being to single women in 2001 (National Center for Health Statistics, 2003). Police observed that in some urban core areas (particularly in housing projects) in 2000, it was not uncommon to find nearly 90 percent of African American women living alone with children.

The single mother, particularly in the inner city, does not always receive the respect that she is due; outsiders may be critical of the way she lives—or the way they think she lives. She is often stereotyped by officers who doubt their own effectiveness in the urban black community. For instance, an unmarried mother on welfare who has just had a fight with her boyfriend should receive the same professional courtesy that a married suburban mother is likely to receive from an officer of the same background. In practice, this is not always the case. Some officers may mistakenly speak to the single African American mother as if she were promiscuous, or treat her callously as though "she's seen it all and done it all; therefore, it does not matter how I [the officer] treat her." A complaint frequently heard in the African American community by women is that white men, in particular, treat African American women poorly. This means that they feel comfortable using profanity in the woman's presence and treat them with little respect.

Ondra Berry offers advice regarding relations between the peace officer and the single African American mother. He advises officers to go out of their way to establish rapport and trust. Following are his suggestions for assisting the single mother:

- Offer extra assistance to low-income mothers.
- Proactively engage youth and encourage them to participate in organized social activities.
- Show warmth to the children (e.g., touch them) as one would to any traumatized child.
- Offer the children something special, such as toy badges or other police souvenirs.
- Give your business card to the mother to show that you are available for further contact.

- Make follow-up visits when there are not problems so that the mother and the children can associate the officer with good times.

- Carefully explain to the mother her rights.

- Use the same discretion you might use with another minor's first petty offense (e.g., shoplifting), simply by bringing the child home and talking with the mother and child rather than sending the child immediately to juvenile hall.

All of these actions will build a perception on the part of the African American single mother (and her children) that you can be trusted and that you are there to help. "Since you are dealing with history, you have to knock down barriers and work harder with this group than with any other group" (Berry, 2006).

Children/Adolescents/Youth

Since there are so many homes, especially in the inner city, in which the father is absent, young boys in their middle childhood years (7 to 11) are at risk for serious behavior problems and school is often where these problems show up. According to Berry, many single mothers unwittingly place their young sons in the position of "father," giving them the message that they have to take care of the family. These young children can get the mistaken impression that they are the heads of the household, and in school situations, they may try to control the teacher—who is often female and often white. Berry observed that many young boys are placed in special education programs because they have been belligerent and domineering with the teacher. What these boys lack is an older male role model who can help them to grow into the appropriate behavior. An officer who refers these children to agencies that can provide such role models (even if only on a limited-time basis) will gain the family's and community's trust and respect. Eventually, he or she will win more cooperation from community members.

Among older African American male children, especially in inner cities, statistics indicate a disproportionately high crime rate, stemming from the difficult economic conditions of their lives. Officers have to remind themselves that the majority of African American teenagers, regardless of economic condition, are law-abiding citizens. Perfectly responsible African American teens and young adults report being stopped on a regular basis by officers when they are in predominantly "white neighborhoods" (including those where they happen to live). A 19-year-old African American male living in an upper-middle-class suburban neighborhood in Fremont, California, reported that he was stopped and questioned four times in two weeks by different officers. On one occasion, the conversation went this way:

Officer: What are you doing here?

Teen: I'm jogging, sir.

Officer: Why are you in this neighborhood?

Teen: I live here, sir.

Officer: Where?

Teen: Over there, in that big house on the hill.

Officer: Can you prove that? Show me your I.D.

On another occasion, when he was jogging, a different officer stopped him and asked (referring to the very expensive jogging shoes he was wearing), "Where did you get those shoes?" When the boy answered that he had bought them, the next question was, "Where do you live?" When the teen answered, "In that big house on the hill," the officer apologized and went on his way. (Racial profiling is discussed in depth in Chapter 14.)

LANGUAGE AND COMMUNICATION

Racial conflicts between African Americans and non–African American citizens can cover up cultural differences, which until recently had been largely ignored or minimized. Yet many would acknowledge that cultural differences between, for example, a white officer and a Vietnamese citizen could potentially affect their respective communication as well as their perceptions of each other. Similarly, culture comes into play when looking at patterns of language and communication among many African Americans.

"Ebonics," or African American Vernacular English

"The use of [what has been called] black language does not represent any pathology in blacks. . . . The beginning of racial understanding is the acceptance that difference is just what it is: different, not inferior. And equality does not mean sameness" (Weber, 1991). There are many varieties of English that are not "substandard," "deficient," or "impoverished" versions of the language. Instead, they often have a complete and consistent set of grammatical rules and may represent the rich cultures of the groups that use them. For example, Asian Indians speak a variety of English somewhat unfamiliar to Americans, while the British speak numerous dialects of British English, each of them containing distinctive grammatical structures and vocabulary not used by Americans. Similarly, some African Americans speak a variety of English that historically has been labeled as substandard because of a lack of understanding of its origins.

Many African Americans use [or have used at least some of the time] what has been called black English, African American Vernacular English (AAVE) or Ebonics. While some African Americans speak this variety of English, many enjoy the flexibility and expressiveness of speaking Ebonics among peers and switching to "standard English" when the situation calls for it (e.g., at work, in interviews, with white friends).

AAVE is recognized as a language and a dialect of English. It meets all of the requirements of a language; it possesses a coherent system of signs; it is a grammar of elements and rules; and it is used for communication and social purposes (Patrick, 2006). There are a number of other terms used for this variety of English: *African American English, Black English, Black Vernacular,* and *Black English Vernacular.* Colloquially, it is known as *Ebonics.*

To many white people, Ebonics merely sounds "southern." However, the fact that some of the same grammatical structures—spoken in a wholly different accent—are found throughout the English-speaking Caribbean (as far south as Trinidad, 8 miles north of Venezuela) points to an earlier, African origin for the grammar. Linguists have done years of research on the origins of Ebonics and now believe that it developed from the grammatical structures common to several West African tribal languages. For example:

Ebonics:	You lookin good.
Standard English:	You look good right now.
Ebonics:	You be looking good.
Standard English:	You usually look good.

That is, the presence of the word *be* indicates a general condition and not something related only to the present. Apparently, some West African languages have grammatical structures expressing these same concepts of time. Nonetheless, many people cling to an unscientific (and racist) view of language varieties of African Americans.

> One [view] says that there was African influence in the development of the language and the other that says there was not. Those who reject African influence believe that the African arrived in the United States and tried to speak English. And [according to this first view], because he lacked certain intellectual and physical attributes, he failed. This hypothesis makes no attempt to examine the . . . structures of West African languages to see if there are any similarities. . . . when the German said "zis" instead of "this," America understood. But, when the African said "dis" [instead of "this"], no one considered the fact that [the sound] *th* may not exist in African languages. (Weber, 1991)

Slaves developed Black English to overcome the differences in their tribal languages and communicate with one another and with their English-speaking slave masters. They also developed a type of "code language" so that they could speak and not be understood by their slave owners.

Many people still assume that Ebonics is "bad" English, and they display their contempt nonverbally, either facially or through an impatient tone of voice. They may interrupt and finish the speaker's sentences for him or her, as though that person were unable to speak for himself or herself. Acceptance of another person's variety of English can go a long way toward establishing rapport. People interacting with blacks who do not use standard English should realize that blacks are not making random "mistakes" when they speak and that they are not necessarily speaking badly. In fact, verbal skill is a highly prized value in most African-based cultures.

Finally, attempting to establish trust and rebuild relations with a people who historically have not been able to trust the police, white officers should not try to imitate black accents, dialects, and styles of speaking. Imitation can be very insulting and may give blacks the impression that they are being ridiculed—or that the officer is seriously uncomfortable with them. (This was elaborated on in Chapter 5.) Officers should not try to fake a style that is culturally different from their own. Being authentic and sincere when communicating with all citizens, while remaining aware and accepting of differences, is key to beginning to build better relationships with citizens.

Nonverbal Communication: Style and Stance

Black social scientists have been studying aspects of black nonverbal communication, which have been often misunderstood by people in positions of authority. Psychologist Richard Majors at the University of Wisconsin termed a certain stance and posturing as the "cool pose," which is demonstrated by many young black men from the inner city. "While the cool pose is often misread by teachers, principals and police officers as an attitude of defiance, psychologists who have studied it say it is a way for black youths to maintain a sense of integrity and suppress rage at being blocked from usual routes to esteem and success" (Goleman, 1992).

Majors explains that while the cool pose is not found among the majority of black men, it is commonly seen among inner city youth as a "tactic for . . . survival to cope with such rejections as storekeepers who refuse to buzz them into a locked shop." The goal of the pose is to give the appearance of being in control. However, a storekeeper, a passerby, or a police officer may perceive this stance as threatening, so a negative dynamic enters the interaction (e.g., the officer seeing the cool pose feels threatened, and then becomes more authoritarian in response). This form of nonverbal communication may include certain movements and postures designed to emphasize the youth's masculinity. The pose involves a certain way of walking, standing, talking, and remaining aloof facially. The pose, writes Majors, is a way of saying, "[I'm] strong and proud, despite [my] status in American society" (Goleman, 1992).

A Harvard Medical School psychiatrist, Dr. Alvin Poussaint, points out that because so many inner city male youths have no male role models in their families, they feel a need to display their manliness (Poussaint and Alexander, 2000). Problems occur when others read their nonverbal language as a sign of irresponsibility, apathy, defiance, and/or laziness. With the knowledge that for some black youths, the cool pose is not intended to be a personal threat, officers should be less on the defensive (and, consequently, less on the offensive) when observing this style.

In a *20/20* broadcast entitled "Presumed Guilty" (ABC News, 1992), the mother of an African American pre-med student referred to style and communication: "They don't have to be doing anything but being who they are, and that's young black men, with a rhythm in their walk and an attitude about who they are, and expressing their pride and culture by the clothes they choose to wear. . . ." This young man had been stopped on numerous occasions for no apparent reason. (This subject is discussed in the section "Differential Treatment" later in this chapter.)

Verbal Expressiveness and Emotionalism

The Ebonics vernacular style of speech emphasizes emotional response—being "real" is the term. This means it is okay to express one's indignation, to be emotional, and to express to someone how you feel. Many African Americans perceive that the mainstream culture is taught to be reserved and to temper their emotions. This is a cultural difference that can be misread by law enforcement. (Patton, 2006)

Linguist and sociologist Thomas Kochman has devoted his professional life to studying differences in black and white culture that contribute to misunderstandings and misperceptions. Of historical significance, Chicago's African American mayor Harold Washington passed out copies of Kochman's book *Black and White Styles in Conflict* (1981) to the city hall press corps because he believed that he was seriously misunderstood by the whites of the city. According to Kochman, "If a person doesn't know the difference in cultures, that's ignorance. But if a person knows the difference and still says that mainstream culture is best, that 'white is right,' then you've got racism."

Kochman explains in *Black and White Styles in Conflict* (which is still used widely) that blacks and whites have different perspectives and approaches to many issues, including conversation, public speaking, and power. This notion is supported in the following advice to police officers: "Don't get nuts when you encounter an African American who is louder and more emotional than you are. Watch the voice patterns and the tone. Blacks can sound militant [even when they are not]. Blacks have been taught (i.e., socialized) to be outwardly and openly emotional. Sometimes we are emotional first and then calm down and become more rationale" (Berry, 2006). Berry went on to say that often whites are rational at first but express more emotion as they lose control. This cultural difference has obvious implications for overall communication, including how to approach and react to angry citizens.

Kochman explains that many "whites [are] able practitioners of self-restraint [and that] this practice has an inhibiting effect on their ability to be spontaneously self-assertive." He continues that "the level of energy and spiritual intensity that blacks generate is one that they can manage comfortably but whites can only manage with effort." The problems in interaction come about because neither race understands that there is a cultural difference between them. Kochman states: "Blacks do not initially see this relative mismatch, because they believe that their normal animated style is not disabling to whites. . . . Whites are worried that blacks cannot sustain such intense levels of interaction without losing self-control [because that degree of 'letting go' of emotions for a white would signify a lack of control]." In other words, a white person or an Asian, for that matter, unaware of the acceptability in black culture of expressing intense emotion (including rage) may not be able to imagine that he himself could express such intense emotion without losing control. He may feel threatened, convinced that the ventilation of such hostility will surely lead to a physical confrontation.

While racism may also be a factor for some in communication breakdowns, differing conventions of speech do contribute in ways that are not always apparent. In several cultural awareness training sessions, police officers have reported that neighbors (non-African Americans), upon hearing highly emotional discussions (among African Americans), called to report fights. When the police arrived on the scene of the "fight," the so-called guilty ones responded that they were not fighting, just talking. While continuing to respond to all calls, officers can still be aware of different perceptions of what constitutes a fight. Although you can never make any automatic assumptions, an awareness of style can affect the way you approach the citizen.

Berry illustrated how a white police officer can let his or her own cultural interpretations of black anger and emotionalism influence judgment. He spoke of a fellow officer who made the statement: "Once they [i.e., blacks] took me on, I wanted to take control." This officer, working in a predominantly black area for a 3-month period, made 120 stops and 42 arrests (mainly petty offenses such as prowling and failure to identify). He then worked in a predominantly white area for the same period of time, made 122 stops and only six arrests. The officer went on to say, "One group will do what I ask; the other will ask questions and challenge me." His need to "take control" over people whom he perceived to be out of control was so extreme, it resulted in his being sued (Berry, 2006). His perception of the level of threat involved was much higher in the black community than in the white. One of the factors involved was, undoubtedly, this officer's inability to deal with being "taken on." If he had used communication skills to defuse citizens' anger rather than to escalate it, he might have been able to work situations around to his advantage rather than creating confrontations. Listening professionally, instead of engaging in shouting matches with citizens of other backgrounds, can require a great deal of self-control, but it will usually bring better results. (Once again, George Thompson of the Verbal Judo Institute reminds officers, "You are not paid to argue." See Chapter 4.)

Threats and Aggressive Behavior

Kochman, who has conducted cultural awareness training nationwide (for police departments as well as corporations) asks the question, "When does a fight begin?" Many whites, he notes, believe that "fighting" has already begun when it is "obvious" that there will be violence ("when violence is imminent"). Therefore, to whites, a fight begins as soon as the shouting starts. According to whites, then, the fight has begun whenever a certain intensity of anger is shown, along with an exchange of insults. If threats are also spoken, many whites would agree that violence is surely on its way.

Kochman explains that while the situation described (verbal confrontation, threats) may indeed be a prelude to a fight for blacks, many blacks have a clear boundary between their fighting words and their physical actions. Kochman includes a quote to show how fighting does not begin until one person does something physically provocative:

> "If two guys are talking loudly and then one or the other starts to reduce the distance between them, that's a sign, because it's important to get in the first blow. Or if a guy puts his hand in his pocket, and that's not a movement he usually makes, then you watch for that—he might be reaching for a knife. But if they're just talking—it doesn't matter how loud it gets—then you got nothing to worry about." (Allen Harris quoted in Kochman, 1981)

Of course, officers who are trained to think about officer safety might have a problem accepting this dismissal ("then you got nothing to worry about"). Similarly, a threat in today's society, where anyone may be carrying semiautomatic weapons, may be just that—a very real threat that will be carried out. A threat must always be taken seriously by officers. However, there can be instances when cultural differences are at work and extreme anger can be expressed without accompanying physical violence. When this is the case, an officer can actually escalate hostilities with an approach and communication style that demonstrates no understanding toward culturally/racially different modes of expression.

KEY ISSUES IN LAW ENFORCEMENT

Differential Treatment

The results of a national survey entitled Police Attitudes Toward Abuse of Authority showed race to be a divisive issue for American police. In particular, black and non-black officers had significantly different views about the effect of a citizen's race and socioeconomic status on the likelihood of police abuse of authority (Weisburd & Greenspan, May, 2000)

"I am not prejudiced. I treat all citizens fairly." This type of statement can be heard by police officers around the country. Inevitably, this statement holds true for some officers (although explicit utterance of this type of statement usually signals prejudice). In the wake of many publicized allegations of differential treatment towards African Americans (and other groups), officers who do hold prejudices have to face them and recognizing when the prejudices result in action:

> My partner and I several years ago went to an all-white night club. He found cocaine on this white couple. He poured it out and didn't make an arrest. Later we were at an all-black nightclub. He found marijuana on one individual and arrested him. I was shocked, but I didn't say anything at the time because I was fairly new to the department. He had told me on two occasions that he "enjoyed" working with black officers and "has no difficulty" with the black community. (African American police officer who wishes to remain anonymous)

In the ABC *20/20* television segment "Presumed Guilty," an undercover investigation set out to answer the question "Are black men being singled out by police, pulled over even when they're doing nothing wrong?" This program first aired in 1992 before the term *racial profiling* came into existence. Many officers will deny that they are doing this, and they register the counterpart complaint (heard repeatedly in cultural awareness training sessions), "They're always saying that I'm stopping them because they're black when, in fact, I've pulled them over because they have violated the law." African American parents continue to complain that their teenage and young adult children are pulled over or stopped as pedestrians and questioned when there has been no violation. How are these two viewpoints reconciled? How can perceptions be so far apart?

The truth most likely lies between the categorical denial of some police officers and the statement, "We're always being stopped only because we're black." Undoubtedly, there are police procedures of which citizens are unaware, and they do not see all the other people an officer stops in a typical day. However, the citizen is not getting paid to be professional, truthful, or even reasonable with the officer. We know that some officers feel that they are doing "good policing" when they stop citizens whom they feel will be guilty of a crime. However, this "feel" for who may be guilty can actually be a reflection of a bias or assumptions that substitutes for real "data." Observing and selecting "guilty-looking" motorists can be the result of unconscious biased thinking. (Refer to Chapter 14 for an explanation of the "Ladder of Inference" with respect to racial profiling.)

In a discussion of drug arrests among blacks, an African American high-ranking officer in a Southern California department made the following statement:

> When officers go out to make arrests, they'll go immediately into the inner city where they can find the "lowest hanging fruit." What I mean is, blacks are easy to identify, in the inner city they're standing out on the street and it's natural for officers to be suspicious and try to do their drug arrests there. But we all know that alcohol abuse is rampant among white kids and if we go to just about any campus, we'll find drugs. But that's not where officers first gravitate to. Whites don't stand on street corners, but they're still using drugs and alcohol pretty heavily. (African American police officer who wishes to remain anynomous)

Racial Profiling in the African American Community

> An ordinary commuter turns the key in the ignition, glances in the rear view mirror, and pulls away from the curb. Rounding the corner, his slightly worn tires slip on a fresh layer of light rain. He executes a perfect "California rolling stop" at an intersection and enters the freeway, accelerating to a comfortable 70 mph for the cruise into downtown. Our commuter just violated the traffic code at least four times, just as we all do each time we get behind the wheel. But if our commuter is a person of color, there's a good chance he won't make it to work without being pulled over for "driving while black or brown." (Opinion page, *San Diego Union,* October, 2000)*

Officers in cultural awareness training have said they have been surprised when suburban middle-class African Americans express as much anger and outrage about differential treatment, including racial profiling, as do poorer blacks in inner city areas. Many middle- and upper-class parents whose children have experienced the types of stops described here are likely to be even less forgiving: stops like these are painful indications, despite much hard-won social and economic success, that race prevails for some as the defining characteristic. (Once again, see Chapter 14 for an in-depth look at racial profiling.)

Reactions to and Perceptions of Authority

As a response to a series of racial events (in California) that received national and international attention in the 1990s, including the beating of black motorist Rodney King in 1991, riots in Los Angeles in 1992, and the trial of O. J. Simpson in 1995, the Public Policy Institute of California asked two social scientists to begin a study in which ethnic reactions to legal authority were studied.* (Huo & Tyler, 2000). Following are three of the major findings of the study:

- Compared to whites, African Americans (and Latinos) report lower levels of satisfaction with the interactions with legal authorities. They also report less willingness than whites to comply with the directives of the authorities they deal with. This pattern of difference between minorities and whites was especially apparent among those who reported interactions with the police compared to those who reported interactions with authorities in court.

- Much of the difference between minorities and whites in their reactions to legal authorities can be accounted for by differences in their perceptions of how fairly or unfairly they were treated. When asked whether the legal authorities involved in their encounters used fair procedures to make decisions, African Americans (and Latinos) reported experiencing less procedural fairness than did whites.

- The perception of fair treatment and positive outcomes was the most important factor in forming reactions to encounters with the police and courts. It

*From *Beyond the Mythology of Racial Profiling* by Linda Hills, Executive Director, ACLU of San Diego and Imperial Counties and Randa Trapp, President of NAACP of San Diego

*1,500 residents of Los Angeles and Oakland, California, were questioned.

was more important than the concerns about the outcomes people received from legal authorities. This pattern held up across different situations and ethnic groups.

African Americans (and Latinos) are still reporting more negative treatment from legal authorities than are whites. These perceptions, on the part of minorities, are significant in that they directly relate to compliance rates with authority among members of minority groups (Huo & Tyler, 2000). The study indicated that all groups were equally satisfied with their experiences in the court and that, as a result, there was compliance with court directives. However, African Americans (and Latinos) were less willing to comply with directives from police. The findings in this study were similar to results found from the Milwaukee Domestic Violence Experiment conducted in 1997. In that study, African Americans (and Latinos) perceived that "legal authorities treated them with less procedural fairness than they do whites" (Paternoster, Bachman, Brame, & Sherman, 1997). The results of both studies suggest that "group differences in perceived procedural fairness may lead to group differences in compliance with legal directives" (Huo & Tyler, 2000).

> Even as opinion polls across the country reflect the perception among both blacks and whites that race relations are improving, according to a 2003 ABC/Washington Post poll, only 28% of blacks think that they "receive equal treatment as whites from police," as opposed to 66% of whites, who believe that both groups are treated equally. The poll found that within the black population, 65% of the men surveyed reported being stopped "just because of your race," as opposed to 22% of black women; from that, 61% of the women and 79% of the men said that blacks don't get the same treatment as whites from the police in their communities. (ABC News, 2003)

Excessive Force and Brutality

A controversial and complex issue is the use of excessive force. The International Association of Chiefs of Police defines excessive force as "the application of an amount and/or frequency of force greater than that required to complete compliance from a willing or unwilling subject" (IACP, 2001). When excessive force is used by a police officer, the conduct of the police often comes under public scrutiny and will receive attention from the media, the community, and legislators. A police officer's use of excessive force usually results in lawsuits by members of the public who feel they have been treated with unnecessary physical or deadly force (surviving family if deadly force). When the use of excessive force is aberrant behavior by the actions of an invidual officer or is a common practice of the culture of the law enforcement agency, public opinion will erode the police department's credibility.

> Patrolling the mean streets can be a dangerous and dehumanizing task for police officers. Drawing the line between necessary force and deliberate brutality is perhaps the toughest part of the job. . . . A career of confronting the vicious, conscienceless criminal-enemy frays the nerves. (Morrow, 1991)

The case of Rodney King in 1992, brought public attention to the fact that excessive force and brutality were serious problems in America. The existence of brutality has been a problem that blacks and other racial and ethnic groups have asserted, but until the early 1990s (i.e., with several highly publicized cases), many whites either did not believe or closed their eyes to this reality. Nearly a decade after the Rodney King event, in 1999, Americans and citizens worldwide witnessed another incident of brutality against a black American, Abner Louima, a Haitian immigrant. Then again in 2002, the nation saw on television, an Inglewood, California, city police officer, Jeremy Morse, caught on videotape slamming 15-year-old Donovan Jackson's face onto the trunk of a police patrol vehicle. It was later revealed that the teenager suffered from a mental impairment that left him unable to respond rapidly to verbal commands (Schmalleger, 2005). The majority of police officers around the nation do not use excessive force. Nevertheless, we know that police brutality is not yet a thing of the past.

Controlling racist behavior based on biases and prejudices must be a priority training issue in all departments across the country (Chapter 1 deals with prejudices and biases). Police departments need to recognize that reducing an officer's buildup of stress has to be addressed as frequently and seriously as, for example, self-defense. Finally, the individual officer must remember that even though abusive behavior from citizens constitutes one of the worst aspects of the job, it is not the citizens who have to behave like professionals.

Law Enforcement Interaction with Poor, Urban, African American Communities

Many police officers feel that they are putting their lives in danger when going into certain communities, particularly those in urban areas where poverty and crime go hand in hand. As a result, some segments of the African American community feel police are not protecting them, and they are extremely fearful of "black-on-black" crime. The increase in citizens' weapons in urban areas, including increased self-protective weaponry, contributes to defensive reactions among both the police and the citizens. There is a vicious cycle that escalates and reinforces hostilities. Police are often expected to solve the social ills of society but have neither the resources nor the training to deal with problems that are rooted in historical, social, political, and economic factors. African Americans and police officers are often frustrated with each other, and barriers seem insurmountable. While the following quote comes from a source in the early 1970s, the dynamic described is still operative:

> Many policemen find themselves on the alert for the slightest sign of disrespect. One author [McNamara] has shown that the police [officer] is often prepared to coerce respect and will use force if he feels his position is being challenged. Likewise, the attitudes and emotions of the black citizen may be similar when confronted with a police [officer]. Intervention by police is often seen as an infringement on the blacks' rights and as oppression by the white population. Consequently many blacks are on the alert for the slightest sign of disrespect that might be displayed by the police [officer]. (Cross & Renner, 1974; personal communication with African American criminal justice college student who wishes to remain anonymous, cultural diversity classroom session, 2006)

Cross and Renner explain that fear of belittlement and fear of danger operate for both the African American citizen and the officer, and these fears cause both sides to misinterpret what might otherwise be nonthreatening behavior. The problem often arises not from the reality of the situation but from the results of mutual fears. In some parts of the country, this is as true now as it was in the mid-1970s when the article cited previously was written.

Social scientists have been studying the problems of inner city young men, in particular, since this group is most endangered. Consider the following statistics:.

> Authors of the National Urban League's report, the "State of Black America 2003," found that although "blacks make up about 12% of the nation's population, they account for nearly half of the people in prison." The authors said that the "incarceration disparities have been fueled by drug enforcement policies that have harsher effects on blacks . . . [who] account for 13% of the nation's drug users, but 35% of drug arrests and 53% of drug convictions." (National Urban League, 2003)

Victimization: Offenders and Incarceration

The following data is from the Bureau of Justice Statistics' 2006 report:

- Based on the data from 1976 to 2004, blacks are disproportionately represented as both homicide victims and offenders. The victimization rates for blacks were six times higher than those for whites. The offending rates for blacks were seven times higher the rates for whites.

- On June 30, 2005, there were 2,186,230 prisoners held in federal, state, or local jails. This is an increase of 2.6 percent from midyear 2004. There were an estimated 488 prison inmates per 100,000 U.S. residents, up from 411 compared to 1995. The number of women under the jurisdiction of state or federal prison authorities increased 3.4 percent from midyear 2004, reaching 106,174, and the number of men rose 1.3 percent, totaling 1,406,649. At year end 2004, there were 3,218 black male sentenced prison inmates per 100,000 black males in the United States, compared to 1,220 Hispanic male inmates per 100,000 Hispanic males and 463 white male inmates per 100,000 white males.

Of interest, Clinton's Council of Economic Advisors found that "Discriminatory behavior on the part of police and elsewhere in the criminal justice system may contribute to blacks' high representation in arrests, convictions, and prison admissions. . . ." (Council of Economic Advisors, 1998). Clinton was the last U.S. president to conduct a study on the disproportionate representation of African Americans in the criminal justice system.

African American Women and Police

It is beyond the scope of this book to delve in depth into the specific issues and attitudes of African American women toward police and authority. However, one area is particularly worthy of attention. There is a perception and (in some cases) the reality, that the rape of an African American woman has not always been considered as serious by law enforcement as the rape of a white woman either legally or psychologically (Wriggins, 1983; Wyatt, 1992). Some African American women perceive that their assailants are less likely to be tried and convicted. Perceptions by African American women are indeed supported by research.

Research shows white women indicated a greater likelihood to report rape or sexual assault to law enforcement than did women of other races. Although these data do not report actual rates of reporting behavior among women of different ethnic groups, they do suggest that white women are more likely to report a sexual assault to law enforcement agencies than are women of other races. Race—because of commonplace stereotypes and myths about blacks and rape—is likely to affect attitudes, perceptions, judgments, and reactions concerning rape. (Wheeler & George, 2005).

Law enforcement officials alone cannot solve social ills but should realize that African Americans in disadvantaged communities desperately need excellent police protection. The perception that whites in middle-class communities are better served by the police forces naturally reinforces existing antipolice attitudes among the lower class.

Addressing the Needs of the Inner City

"Black-on-black crime seems to be tolerated and even accepted as inevitable" (*USA Today,* 1991). This statement, made by an African American chief of police in 1991, is as true today as it was then. African Americans and other racial and ethnic groups have criticized law enforcement for underpolicing in the inner city; however, progress has been made to improve relations between police and community members. There are increasing numbers of African American officers and police executives who are influencing and changing policy that directly affects police–black relations. Many departments (although by no means all) have put into writing strict rules regarding the use of excessive force, discourtesy, racial slurs, racial profiling, and aggressive patrol techniques. Police management in some locales is beginning to understand why many people in urban black communities believe they receive unequal police services.

Efforts Toward a Positive Relationship Between Police and the Community

Communities and police departments differ widely in the way they build positive relationships with each other. On the one hand, "consent decrees" have forced a change of inappropriate (prejudicial, or unjust) behavior or actions. A consent decree is an out-of-court settlement whereby the accused party (i.e., accused of inappropriate behavior or actions) agrees to modify or change behavior rather than plead guilty or go through a hearing on charges brought to court (CSIS, 2003). It is beyond the scope of this chapter to explore the controversy surrounding consent decrees; however, many inappropriate police actions within African American communities have resulted in the implementation of consent decrees. Some police leaders believe that a consent decree is not a symbol of a positive relationship; at the same time, many community leaders have supported them.

> One leader mentioned that the . . . decree had given the community greater confidence in the police. Another leader commented that the consent decree "gave people an opportunity to feel as though they had a voice." One community leader felt that some white and black officers were working better together and that they were responding more quickly to calls for service from the African-American community. "It seems they are trying to ask more questions and there is more respect for the community," she said. (Davis, 2002)

While there is controversy around consent decrees, and some officers complain that they add too much paperwork and bureaucracy to their already demanding jobs, they serve a purpose. They are an attempt, on the part of the federal government, local and state police departments, and communities, to try to improve community–police interaction in a quick and dramatic manner. Some outcomes can be influenced informally and others by consent decrees. The key to improved relationships deeply rests on all of the following:

- Leadership
- Vision
- Respect
- Goals
- Strategies
- Mutual benefits for police and community
- Effective communication and practices of both law enforcement agencies and the community

Added to all of the above, community members, leaders, and police officers need to rely upon private means—one-on-one and face-to-face interaction—as well as goodwill, to improve relations. The following words are those of Detroit-based Pastor Ronald Griffin, a prominent leader in the African American community:

> Face-to-face contact opens up dialogue. We as human beings really say we listen, but we often don't, and instead we come prepared to respond. So sometimes we put up our defenses and get into attack mode. We're already predisposed and most of us, then, are willing and ready for battle. This leads to a lot of pointless negative action even if both sides have a lot in common. We have had executive officers come to church activities to encourage the members and to help the members see officers in another light. So we're building on this and learning to trust each other. There's nothing I can't ask of the precinct, and the same from them for me. (Griffin, 2003)

SUMMARY OF RECOMMENDATIONS FOR LAW ENFORCEMENT

1. The experiences of slavery and racism as well as cultural differences have shaped African American culture.
   - Patterns of culture and communication among black Americans differ from those among white Americans. In face-to-face communication, officers should not ignore or downplay these differences.
2. For many African Americans, particularly those in the lower-socioeconomic rungs of society, the history of slavery and later discrimination continues to leave its psychological scars.
   - Law enforcement officials, in particular, represent a system that has oppressed African Americans and other minorities. To protect and serve in many

African American communities across the nation necessarily means that officers will need to go out of their way to establish trust and win cooperation.

3. The changing terms that African Americans have used to refer to themselves reflect stages of racial and cultural growth as well as empowerment.

   • Respect the terms that African Americans prefer to use. *Negro* and *colored* are no longer used and have been replaced by *black* for the purposes of many police communications. However, in speech, many people prefer the term *African American.* Officers can learn to become comfortable asking a citizen which term he or she prefers if there is a need to refer to ethnicity in the conversation.

   • Officers are advised to stop each other when they hear offensive terms being used. Not only does this contribute to the first step of making a department free of overt prejudices, it also helps the individual officer to practice control when he or she is faced with volatile citizens. An officer in the habit of using offensive terms may not be able to restrain himself or herself in public situations. Therefore, officers monitoring each other will ultimately be of benefit to the department.

4. African Americans react as negatively to stereotypes that they hear about themselves as officers do when they hear such statements as "Police officers are biased against blacks" or "All police officers are capable of brutality."

   • Many of the stereotypes about African Americans stem from ignorance as well as an impression people receive from the criminal element. Law enforcement officers must be particularly sensitive to how their own perceptions of African Americans are formed. The disproportionately high crime rate among African American males does not justify sweeping statements about the majority of African Americans, who are law-abiding citizens.

5. The predominance of households headed by women, particularly in the inner city, coupled with the myth of woman as the head of the household, has created situations in which officers have dismissed the importance of the father.

   • Despite common myths and stereotypes regarding the woman, officers should always approach the father to get his version of the story and to consider his opinions in decision making. If the father is ignored or not given much attention, he is certain to be offended.

6. Young African American males, in particular, and their parents (of all socioeconomic levels) feel a sense of outrage and injustice when officers stop them for no apparent reason.

   • You will destroy any possibility of establishing trust (and later winning cooperation) for stopping people because it "looks like they don't belong in a given neighborhood." Every time an instance of this nature occurs, police–community and police–youth relations suffer.

7. The use of African American varieties of English does not represent any pathology or deficiency and is not a combination of random errors but rather reflects patterns of grammar from some West African languages.

- Many people have strong biases against this variety of spoken English. Do not convey a lack of acceptance through disapproving facial expressions, a negative tone of voice, or a tendency to interrupt or finish the sentences for the other person.

- When it comes to "black English" or an accent, do not fake it in order to be accepted by the group. People will immediately pick up on your lack of sincerity; this, in and of itself, can create hostility.

8. People in positions of authority have often misunderstood aspects of black nonverbal communication, including what has been termed the *cool pose.*

  - Police officers may interpret certain ways of standing, walking, and dressing as defiant. Such interpretations can create defensive reactions on the part of the police officer. In many cases, the police officer need not take this behavior personally or feel threatened.

9. Cultural differences in verbal communication can result in complete misinterpretation.

  - Do not necessarily equate an African American's expression of rage and verbal threats with a loss of control that leads automatically to violence. Within the cultural norms, it can be acceptable to be very expressive and emotional in speech. This is in contrast to an unspoken white mainstream norm that discourages the open and free expression of emotion, especially anger.

10. The existence of racial profiling, excessive force, and brutality is still a reality in policing in the United States. When acts of bias, brutality, and injustice occur, everyone suffers, including officers and entire police departments.

  - Every officer should be on the lookout for unchecked biases within themselves and others that could result in inappropriate language or force with citizens of all backgrounds. This also involves awareness of one's own level of stress and frustration and having the means and support to release tension before it breaks loose in the streets.

11. A dynamic exists between some officers and African Americans, particularly in poor urban areas, whereby both the officer and the citizen are on the "alert" for the slightest sign of disrespect.

  - The fear that both the citizen and the officer experience can interfere with what may actually be a nonthreatening situation.

  - The police officer can be the one to break the cycle of fear by softening his or her verbal and nonverbal approach.

12. In areas populated by African Americans and other racial and immigrant groups all over the United States, there is a need for increased and more effective police protection.

  - Bridging the gap that has separated police from African Americans involves radical changes in attitudes toward police–community relations. Together with changes in management, even the individual officer can help by making greater efforts to have positive contact with African Americans.

• The task of establishing rapport with African Americans at all levels of society is challenging because of what the officer represents in terms of past discrimination. Turning this image around involves a commitment on the part of the officer to break with deeply embedded stereotypes and to have as a goal respect and professionalism in every encounter.

DISCUSSION QUESTIONS AND ISSUES*

1. ***Racism: Effects on Blacks and Whites.*** Under "Historical Information" in this chapter, the authors state that the fact of African Americans having been slaves in this country has created great psychological and social problems for blacks and whites for generations to come. How is this true for both races? What are the implications for law enforcement?

2. ***Offensive Terms.*** The authors advise refraining from using such offensive terms as "nigger" at all times, even where there are no African Americans present. Give two practical reasons for this.

3. ***"Cool Pose" and the Use of Threats.*** How do you think the information in this chapter about threats, emotional expression (including rage), and the cool pose can help officers in their approach to citizens? Describe or role-play how an officer would communicate if he or she did not feel threatened by such behavior. Describe or role-play how an officer might approach and interact with the citizen if he or she was threatened by the behavior.

4. ***Inner Cities: Officers and Citizens' Reactions.*** Toward the end of the chapter, the authors mention the vicious cycle that is created in urban areas, especially where citizens have become increasingly armed (with highly sophisticated weapons) and officers, consequently, have to take more self-protective measures. Each views the other with fear and animosity and approaches the other with extreme defensiveness. Obviously, there is no simple answer to this widely occurring phenomenon, and police alone cannot solve the ills of society. Discuss your observations of the way officers cope with the stresses of these potentially life-threatening situations and how the coping or lack thereof affects relations with African Americans and other minorities. What type of support do police officers need to handle this aspect of their job? Do you think police departments are doing their job in providing the support needed?

5. ***When Officers Try to Make a Difference.*** Many young African American children, especially in housing projects in inner cities, live without a father in the household. This means that they do not have a second authority figure as a role model and are consequently deprived of an important source of adult support. No one can take the place of a missing parent, but there are small and

---

*See Instructor's Manual accompanying this text for additional activities, role-plays, questionnaires and projects related to the content of this chapter.

large things a police officer can do to at least make an impression in the life of a child. Compile a list of actions officers can take to demonstrate their caring for children in these environments. Include in your first list every gesture, no matter how small; your second list can include a realistic list of what action can be taken given resources available. Select someone to compile both sets of suggestions (i.e., the realistic and ideal suggestions). Post these lists as reminders of how officers can attempt to make a difference in their communities not only with African American children but with other children as well.

6. ***Racial Profiling.*** Every criminal justice and police academy student and law enforcement representative needs to look closely at instances of racial profiling and learn from previous officers' mistakes. Discuss the following incident of racial profiling, using the questions that follow as guidelines for your discussion.

> A student from Liberia attending college in North Carolina was driving along I-95 in Maryland when he was pulled over by state police who said he wasn't wearing a seatbelt. The officers detained him and his two passengers for two hours as they searched the car for illegal drugs, weapons, or other contraband. Finding nothing, they proceeded to dismantle the car and removed part of the door panel, a seat panel and part of the sunroof. Again finding nothing, the officers in the end handed the man a screwdriver as they left the scene saying, "You're going to need this." (Rice, 1999)

Describe in detail all the potential negative consequences from this police incident.

What else do we need to know about this incident to determine whether the stop was legitimate or related to racial profiling? For example, would we want to know the following?

- Time of day (could the trooper have seen that the driver wasn't wearing a seat belt)?

- Does the state police administration encourage stops on I-95 of individuals and vehicles that fit the profile of drug runners?

- What other information would you want to know?

Officers usually ask for permission or consent to search a vehicle they stop when probable cause does not exist for a search. Do you think the officer(s) requested a voluntary consent to search this vehicle?

Was the length of the detention reasonable? Was it disrespectful and unwarranted to leave the student to replace his vehicle parts? If you are a police officer, could you justify this sort of traffic stop to your supervisor, department, or community or in your own conscience?

WEBSITE RESOURCES

American Civil Liberties Union (ACLU): http://www.aclu.org

This website contains multiple locations for information about many issues, including racial profiling.

National Organization of Black Law Enforcement (NOBLE):
http://www.noblenatl.org

> This website provides information on the public-service organization itself and its involvement in issues of interest and concern to law enforcement and the black community. It is the source of information on many subjects, including recommended policy and procedure. It provides information on NOBLE activities such as community outreach and professional development. The goal of NOBLE is to be recognized as a highly competent, public-service organization at the forefront of providing solutions to law enforcement issues and concerns as well as to the changing needs of communities.

Police Executive Research Forum (PERF): http://www.policeforum.org/racial.html

> This website has an abundance of information about racial profiling and model programs. PERF produced a free video and guide to facilitate police–citizen discussions on racially biased policing. They also produced a helpful guide titled *Racially Biased Policing: A Principled Response.*

National Association of Black Criminal Justice (NABCJ): http://www.nabcj.org

> This website provides information on the organization itself (e.g., member chapters and events) as well as on issues toward improving law enforcement. NABCJ seeks to focus attention on relevant legislation, law enforcement, prosecution, and defense-related needs and practices, with emphasis on the courts, corrections, and the prevention of crime. Among its chief concerns is the general welfare and increasing influence of African Americans and people of color as they relate to the administration of justice.

VERA Institue of Justice: http://www.vera.org

> This website provides information on the research projects and activities of the VERA Institute of Justice. This organization works closely with leaders in government and civil society to improve the services people rely on for safety and justice. VERA develops innovative, affordable programs that often grow into self-sustaining organizations, studies social problems and current responses, and provides practical advice and assistance to government officials in New York and around the world.

African American Web Connection: http://www.aawc.com/aawc.html

> This website is devoted to providing the African American community with valuable resources on the Web. It includes such topics as arts and poetry, businesses, churches, organizations, and topics of concern, to name a few.

REFERENCES

ABC News. (1992, November 6). *20/20* ABC News Report, "Presumed Guilty," Transcript 1247.

ABC NEWS/*Washington Post.* (2003). Race Relations—1/20/03: "Despite a Chasm in Perceptions of Racism, Public Views of Race Relations Improve."

Bennett, Lerone Jr. (1989, November). "The 10 Biggest Myths about the Black Family." *Ebony.* pp. 1, 2.

Berry, Ondra. (2000). Deputy Chief, Reno, Nevada Police Department. Interview, December 8, 2003.

Bradley, Yvette. (1999). Statement of Yvette Bradley, Victim of Racial Profiling at Newark Airport, ACLU Freedom Network News. Available: http://www.moncriefassociates .com/programs.html

Council of Economic Advisors. (1998, Sept.). *Changing America: Indicators of Social and Economic Well-Being by Race and Hispanic Origin.* Chapter 7, Crime and Criminal Justice. President's Initiative on Race (National Center for Health Statistics, Bureau of Justice Statistics).

Cross, Stan, and Edward Renner. (1974). "An Interaction Analysis of Police–Black Relations." *Journal of Police Science Administration, 2* (1).

CSIS. (2003). Consumer Services Information Systems Project—Glossary. Available: http://csisweb.aers.psu.edu

Davis, Robert C., et al. (2002). "Turning Necessity Into Virtue: Pittsburgh's Experience with a Federal Consent Decree," Vera Institute of Justice. Available: http://www .cops.usdoj.gov/Default.asp?Item=565.

Frey, William H. (1998). "New Demographic Divide in the US: Immigrant and Domestic 'Migrant Magnets.'" *The Public Perspective, 9* (4).

Goleman, Daniel. (1992, April 21). "Black Scientists Study the 'Pose' of the Inner City." *New York Times.*

Griffin, Ronald Pastor. (2003). Detroit-based Pastor and Community Leader, personal communication, October, 2003).

Hines, Paulette Moore, and Nancy-Boyd Franklin. (1982). "Black families," *in Ethnicity and Family Therapy,* M. McGoldrick et al. (Eds.). New York: Guilford Press.

Huo, Yuen J., and Tom R. Tyler. (2000). *How Different Ethnic Groups React to Legal Authority.* Public Policy Institute of California. San Francisco, California.

International Association of Chiefs of Police. (2001). Police Use of Force in America 2001. Alexandria, Va.: IACP.

Kochman, T. (1981). *Black and White Styles in Conflict.* Univ. of Chicago Press, 121.

McAdoo, Harriet Pipes. (1992). "Upward Mobility and Parenting in Middle Income Families," in *African American Psychology.* Newbury Park, Calif.: Sage.

Miller, Char (2003). U.S. Historian and Professor Trinity College, San Antonio, Texas, Personal Communication, December 2000.

Morrow, Lance. (1991, April 1). "Rough Justice." *Time,* pp. 16, 17.

National Center for Health Statistics, Series 21, Number 53, 1995, report of Final Natality Statistics, 1996, Monthly Vital Statistics Report, Vol. 46, No. 11, National Center for Health Statistics, 1998 and National Vital Statistics Report, June 25, 2003 (http://www.childtrendsdatabank.org/figures/75-Figure-1.gif)

Paternoster, R., R. Bachman, R. Brame, and L. W. Sherman. (1997). "Do Fair Procedures Matter? The Effect of Procedural Justice on Spouse Assault." *Law and Society Review.* pp. 163–204.

Patrick, Peter L. (2006). Answers to Questions about Ebonics. Univeristy of Essex, UK. Retreived on July 8, 2006, from http://privatewww.essex.ac.uk/~patrickp/ aavesem/EbonicsQ&A.html.

Patton, Greg. (2006, July). Supervisor, Parole and Probation, Clackamas County Community Corrections, Clackamas, Oregon; Adjunct Criminal Justice Cultural Diversity Instructor at Portland Community College, personal communication.

Ponterotto, Joseph G., Shawn O. Utsey, and Paul B. Pederson. (2006). *Preventing Prejudice: A Guide for Counselors, Educators, and Parents,* 2nd ed. Thousand Oaks, Calif.: Sage.

Poussaint, Alvin and Amy Alexander. (2000). *Lay My Burden Down: Unraveline Suicide and the Mental Health Crisis Among African-Americans.* Boston, MA: Beacon Press.

Rice, George. (1999). *People and Possibilities, Racial Profiling: Prejudice or Protocol?* Enterprise Foundation Horizon.

Schmalleger, Frank. (2005). *Criminal Justice Today,* 8th ed. Upper Saddle River, N.J.: Pearson Prentice Hall.

Shusta, Robert. (2006, July). Retired captain, personal communication.

Thompson, George. (2003). President of Verbal Judo Institute, Yucca Valley, California. Personal communication, November, 2003.

Thompson, George. (2004). *Verbal Judo: The Gentle Art of Persuasion.* Yucca Valley, Calif., Verbal Judo Institute, Inc.

U.S. Census Bureau, Current Population Reports. (2003, April). "The Black Population in the United States: March 2002."

U.S. Department of Justice: Bureau of Justice Statistics: Homicide trends in the U.S. http://www.ojp.usdoj.gov/bjs/homicide/race.htm.

U.S. Department of Justice Bureau of Justice Statistics. (2006, May). Prison Statistics in the U.S. Retrieved on July 8, 2006, from http://www.ojp.usdoj.gov/bjs/prisons.htm.

USA Today, "Black on Black Crime," April 24, 1991.

Walker, Samuel. (1992). *The Police in America.* New York: McGraw-Hill.

Weber, Shirley N. (1991). "The Need to Be: The Socio-Cultural Significance of Black Language," in *Intercultural Communication: A Reader.* 6th ed., Larry Samovar and Richard Porter (Eds.). Belmont, Calif.: Wadsworth Press.

Weisburd, David, and Rosann Greenspan. (2000, May). "Police Attitudes toward Abuse of Authority: Findings from a National Study." National Institute of Justice Research in Brief.

Wheeler, Jennifer, and William H. George. (2005). "Race and Sexual Offending," in *Race, Culture, Psychology, & Law* K. Holt and W. George (Eds.). Thousand Oaks, Calif.: Sage.

Williams, H., and P. V. Murphy. (1990). *The Evolving Strategy of Police: A Minority View.* Washington D.C.: The National Institute of Justice, U.S. Department of Justice.

Wriggens, J. (1983). "Rape, Racism, and the Law." *Harvard Women's Law Journal,* 6, 103–141.

Wyatt, G. E. (1992). "The Sociocultural Context of African American and White Women's Rape." *Journal of Social Issues, 48,* 77–91.

Chapter 7

Law Enforcement Contact
with Latino/Hispanic Americans

OVERVIEW

This chapter provides specific ethnic and cultural information on Latino/Hispanic Americans. The label Latino/Hispanic Americans encompasses over 25 different ethnic and cultural groups from Central and South America and the Caribbean. For ease of use, we use the term Latino/Hispanic Americans to refer to members of these ethnic groupings. We first define this highly diverse group and then provide a historical overview as a basis for understanding of the relationship between law enforcement personnel and citizens. We present demographics and elements of diversity among Latino/Hispanic Americans, as well as issues related to ethnic and cultural identity: myths and stereotypes, the extended family and community, gender roles, generational differences, and adolescent and youth issues. The section "Cultural Influences on Communication" introduces the subtle aspects of nonverbal and indirect communications that law enforcement and other related personnel (e.g., 911 dispatchers, emergency medical technicians, criminal justice staff) often find challenging in their interactions with Latino/Hispanic Americans. We present, in the closing section, several key issues for law enforcement: undocumented immigrants, underreporting of crimes, victimization, differential treatment, racial profiling of Latino/Hispanic Americans, exposure to environmental risks and job hazards, and increasing police services to the Latino/Hispanic American community. Finally, we review recommendations for improved communication and relationships between law enforcement personnel and members of Latino/Hispanic American communities.

COMMENTARY

In this chapter, we refer to Latino/Hispanic Americans more in terms of the similarities shared across groups rather than the differences. Certainly, there are great differences with respect to culture, values, and behaviors among the various groups that comprise the broad categorization "Latino/Hispanic Americans." Labeling groups, especially when describing a high level of diversity, is a challenge; ethnic and minority group members themselves can be sensitive to the way others refer to them. Accordingly, a first concern by many law enforcement officers is how to refer to the different groups comprising Latino/Hispanic Americans.

The term Hispanic means so many different things to so many different people. To the typical American, stereotypes of poverty, illegal aliens, laborers, and the uneducated come to mind. For those who are part of the so-called Hispanic group, there is really no agreement as to what we want to be called: Is it Latino, Hispanic, or the people from the specific countries of origin like Mexican, Puerto Rican, Cuban, Salvadorian, Colombian, Dominican, Nicaraguan, Chilean, Argentinean, Brazilian, and other South and Central Americans? (Latino/Hispanic American community organizer)

The Latino/Hispanic American community reflects the full range of economic, educational, and cultural diversity. Nevertheless, law enforcement officers, in response to community members' concerns and complaints, may see only one side of a diverse group of people. Law enforcement officers are called to respond to community members' concerns or complaints against Latino/Hispanic Americans. At the same time, law enforcement officers are asked to serve and protect the Latino/Hispanic community. Often, such complaints are made by individuals who do not understand the Latino/Hispanic American community. This dichotomy is illustrated by the following descriptions, one by a police office and the other a business owner:

Every day, we get complaints from parents, merchants, and commuters wanting the police to do something about the "Mexicans" and other "Latino/Hispanic" types waiting to be picked up for a job around the freeway on-ramps. They stand there for hours waiting for a patron, a boss, to drive up and employ them for a day, a week, or a few hours. It's a community issue, yet the police are expected to solve it. We can ask them to disband and move on, but all that would do is to have them move around the corner. (Police officer's anecdote told at a cultural awareness training session)

It is unfortunate that for the average American, the stereotypes of Latino/Hispanic Americans include the characteristics of poor, uneducated immigrants, and perhaps those of illegal status. What's missing from the picture are the vast numbers of us who are successful in business, university-educated, community leaders, and active in shaping the political future of our country. (Business owner's comment at a Hispanic Chamber of Commerce Conference in Denver, Colorado)

INTRODUCTION

Latino/Hispanic Americans are the fastest growing cultural group in the United States in terms of overall numbers of people. Between the 1990 and 2000 censuses, the population increased by more than 50 percent, from 22.4 million in 1990 to 32.8 million in 2000. The Hispanic population reached 41.3 million as of July 1, 2004, according to national estimates by the U.S. Census Bureau (Bernstein, 2005). Growth in all urban and rural areas of the United States has been striking, with the Hispanic population having a sizeable presence in virtually all geographic areas within the United States. The population growth can be attributed primarily to higher birthrates (Cohn, 2005) and secondarily to the following three factors: (1) higher immigration from Mexico, Central and South America, and the Caribbean; (2) greater longevity, since this is a relatively young population; and (3) larger numbers of subgroups being incorporated into the Latino/Hispanic American grouping (Korzenny & Korzenny, 2005). Moreover, the

U.S. Census estimates for 2004 did not include the number of undocumented immigrants or unauthorized migrants. The Pew Hispanic Institute estimated that the total number of unauthorized migrants in the United States in 2004 was 10.3 million, with 5.9 million from Mexico and another 2.5 million from the rest of Latin America (Passel, 2005). In Chapter 1, we discussed general issues related to the undocumented immigrant. Various other labels have been applied to this group of unauthorized migrants, including *illegals, illegal aliens,* and *illegal immigrants.* For the Latino/Hispanic American community, we use the specific term *unauthorized migrant* to mean "a person who *resides* in the United States, but who is *not* a U.S. citizen, has *not* been admitted for permanent residence, and is *not* included within a set of specific authorized temporary statuses permitting longer-term residence and work" (Passel, Van Hook, & Bean, 2004).

The total number of unauthorized migrants from Mexico and the rest of Latin American is estimated to be 8.3 million, and if these numbers were added to the Census estimates for the documented Hispanic population in the United States, the total Hispanic presence would be 49.6 million people. At 49.6 million total Latino/Hispanic people in the United States, that would make the United States the second-largest nation in the world for Latino/Hispanic presence, second only to Mexico, and with a population greater than the third-largest Hispanic nation, Spain, with 40 million people (Central Intelligence Agency, 2006). Although Brazil, with 188 million people, is in South America, the vast majority of the people are of Portuguese decent, and only a minority would be considered to be Latino/Hispanic (Korzenny & Korzenny, 2005). Given the current and anticipated growth of this population, all federal, regional, state, and local law enforcement agencies need to prepare to serve this growing presence in our communities.

LATINO/HISPANIC AMERICANS DEFINED

Hispanic is not a racial group; for example, a person can be white, black, or Asian and still be considered Hispanic. Hispanic is a generic term referring to all Spanish-surname and Spanish-speaking people who reside within the United States and Puerto Rico (a commonwealth). Latino is generally the preferred label on the West Coast, parts of the East Coast, and the Southeast. The term Latino is a Spanish word indicating a person of Latin American origin, and it reflects the gender-specific nature of its Spanish language derivation: Latino, for men, and Latina, for women. Hispanic is generally preferred on the East Coast, specifically within the Puerto Rican, Dominican, and Cuban communities (although individual members within each of these communities may prefer the specific term referring to their country of heritage). Objections to the use of the term Hispanic include the following: (1) Hispanic is not derived from any culture or place (i.e., there is no such place as "Hispania"), and (2) the term was primarily invented for use by the U.S. Census Bureau. In the most recent decade, many Latino/Hispanic Americans, inspired by (1) a growing sense of community identification, (2) high-profile and successful role models, and (3) increased pride in ethnic and cultural identity, have embraced the use of Hispanic and Latino/Latina for self- and group reference. A new and dynamic pride, confidence, and self-esteem in the Latino/Hispanic culture and heritage have emerged for many (especially among the younger Latino/Hispanic Americans) and have replaced some of the past negative associations with the term Latino and Hispanic, often fostered in the past by negative stereotypes, government designations, undocumented immigration statuses, migrant work roles, educational underachievement, and impoverished communities.

Sometimes, the term *Spanish-speaking* or *Spanish-surnamed* may be used to recognize that one may have a Spanish surname but may not speak Spanish (which is the case for a large number of Latino/Hispanic Americans). *La Raza* is another term used, primarily on the West Coast and in the Southwest, to refer to all peoples of the Western Hemisphere who share a cultural, historical, political, and social legacy of the Spanish and Portuguese colonists and the Native Indian and African people; it has its origins within the political struggles of this region and the mixing of the races, *el mestizaje*.

Like La Raza, *Chicano* is another term that grew out of the ethnic pride and ethnic studies movement in the late 1960s. Chicano refers specifically to Mexican Americans, and it is used primarily on the West Coast, in the Southwest, and in the Midwest. It is also commonly used in college communities across the United States that provide an ethnic studies curriculum.

In 1976, Congress passed Public Law 94-311, called the Roybal Resolution, which required the inclusion of a self-identification question on Spanish origin or descent in government surveys and censuses. As such, Hispanic is the official term used in federal, state, and local governmental writings and for demographic references. Federal standards implemented in 2003 allow the terms Latino and Hispanic to be used interchangeably (Office of Management and Budget, 1997).

As noted earlier, the terms Hispanic and Latino/Latina have been more readily accepted and embraced in the past decade, especially by the younger generation. The definition of Latino/Hispanic is still considered by many (especially among those who have fought to be identified by the different specific Hispanic nationalities and cultures) to be associated with stereotypical perceptions caused by a "mega-label" that does not represent well all members within this group. This point of view is illustrated in the following example:

> One version of this objection argues against all existing ethnic names, and particularly "Hispanic" or "Latinos/Latinas," because these labels have had connotations among the general population. They create a negative perception of those named and tend to perpetuate their disadvantageous situation in society. To call someone Hispanic or Latino/Latina, like calling someone negro or colored, carries with it all sorts of negative baggage, demeaning the person and harming him or her in diverse ways. (Gracia, 2000)

As the Latino/Hispanic American communities grow and develop in the United States, the preferred and specific terms to be used will evolve and change according to the preferences of these community members.

HISTORICAL INFORMATION

The historical background of Latino/Hispanic Americans contains key factors that affect their interactions with and understanding of law enforcement and peacekeeping personnel. Clearly, this brief historical and sociopolitical overview can only highlight some of the commonalities and diverse cultural experiences of Latino/Hispanic Americans. Our historical review focuses primarily on the larger Latino/Hispanic communities in the United States (those with Mexican, Puerto Rican, and Cuban ethnic and historical roots).

In the 1800s, under the declaration of Manifest Destiny, the United States began the expansionist policy of annexing vast territories to the south, north, and west. As Lopez y Rivas (1973) noted, the United States viewed itself as a people chosen by "Providence" to form a larger union through conquest, purchase, and annexation. With the purchase (or annexation) of the Louisiana Territories in 1803, Florida in 1819, Texas in 1845, and the Northwest Territories (Oregon, Washington, Idaho, Wyoming, and Montana) in 1846, it seemed nearly inevitable that conflict would occur with Mexico. The resulting Mexican-American War ended in 1848 with the signing of the Treaty of Guadalupe Hidalgo, in which Mexico received $15 million from the United States for the land that is now Texas, New Mexico, Arizona, and California, with more than 100,000 Mexican people living in those areas. As is obvious from this portion of history, it makes little sense for many Mexican Americans to be stereotyped as "illegal aliens," especially since more than a million Mexican Americans (some of whom are U.S. citizens and some of whom are not) can trace their ancestry back to families living in the southwestern United States in the mid-1800s (Fernandex, 1970). Moreover, for Latino/Hispanic Americans (especially Mexican Americans), the boundaries between the United States and Mexico are seen as artificial. "The geographic, ecological, and cultural blending of the Southwest with Mexico is perceived as a continuing unity of people whose claim to the Southwest is rooted in the land itself. (Montiel, 1978)

While one third of Mexican Americans can trace their ancestry to families living in the United States in the mid-1800s, the majority of this group migrated into the United States after 1910 because of the economic and political changes that occurred as a result of the Mexican Revolution.

Puerto Rico, on the other hand, was under the domination of Spain until 1897, at which time it was allowed the establishment of a local government. The United States invaded Puerto Rico and annexed it as part of the Spanish-American War (along with Cuba, the Philippines, and Guam) in 1898. Although Cuba (in 1902) and the Philippines (in 1949) were given their independence, Puerto Rico remained a territory of the United States. In 1900, the U.S. Congress passed the Foraker Act, which allowed the president to appoint a governor; to provide an Executive Council consisting of 11 presidential appointees (of which only five had to be Puerto Rican); and to elect locally a 35-member Chamber of Delegates. In reality, the territory was run by the president-appointed governor and the Executive Council. The Jones Act of 1917 made Puerto Ricans citizens of the United States. It was not until 1948 that Puerto Rico elected its first governor, Luis Munoz Marin. In 1952 Puerto Rico was given Commonwealth status, and Spanish was allowed to be the language of instruction in the schools again (with English taught as the second language).

Following World War II, large numbers of Puerto Ricans began migrating into the United States. With citizenship status, Puerto Ricans could travel easily, and they settled in areas on the East Coast, primarily New York City (in part because of the availability of jobs and affordable apartments). The estimated number of Puerto Ricans in the United States is 2 million on the mainland and 3.8 million on the island (Therrien & Ramirez, 2000).

Cubans immigrated into the United States in three waves. The first wave occurred between 1959 and 1965 and consisted of primarily white, middle-class, or upper-class Cubans who were relatively well educated and had business and financial resources. The federal government's Cuban Refugee Program, Cuban Student Loan Program, and Cuban Small Business Administration Loan Program were established to help this first wave of Cuban immigrants achieve a successful settlement (Bernal & Estrada, 1985). The second wave of Cuban immigrants occurred between 1965 and 1973. This wave resulted from the opening of the Port of Camarioca, allowing all who wished to leave Cuba to exit. Those who left as part of the second wave were more often of the working class and lower middle class, primarily white adult men and women. The third wave of immigrants leaving Cuba from Mariel occurred from the summer of 1980 to early 1982. This third wave was the largest (about 125,000 were boat-lifted to the United States) and consisted primarily of working-class persons, more reflective of the Cuban population as a whole than were previous waves. Most immigrated into the United States with hopes for better economic opportunities. Within this group of *Marielito* were many antisocial, criminal, and mentally ill persons released by Fidel Castro and included in the boat lift (Gavzer, 1993).

In addition to the three major groups that have immigrated to the United States from Mexico, Puerto Rico, and Cuba are immigrants from 21 countries of South and Central America, as well as the Caribbean. Arrival of these immigrants for political, economic, and social reasons began in the early 1980s and has added to the diversity of Latino/Hispanic American communities in the United States. The total numbers of some groups, such as the Dominicans (a rapidly growing group on the East Coast), are difficult to determine because of their undocumented entry status within the United States.

DEMOGRAPHICS: DIVERSITY AMONG LATINO/HISPANIC AMERICANS

The historical background illustrates the heterogeneity of Latino/Hispanic Americans. Composed of many different cultural groups, this broad label encompasses significant generational, educational, and socioeconomic differences; varying relocation experiences; and many other varieties of life experience. Although the Spanish language may provide a common thread among most Latino/Hispanic Americans, there are cultural and national differences in terms and expressions used, including nonverbal nuances. Moreover, the language of Brazil is Portuguese, not Spanish, and thus the language connection for Brazilian Latino/Hispanic Americans is unique. As noted earlier, the U.S. Census indicates that the Latino/Hispanic American population numbers about 41.3 million and represents 14 percent of the U.S. population, not including the 3.9 million people who live in Puerto Rico. About 85 percent of Latino/Hispanic Americans trace their roots to Mexico, Puerto Rico, and Cuba, while the remaining 15 percent are from other countries of Central and South America, the Caribbean, and Spain. The numerical growth of the Latino/Hispanic American population is the fastest of all American ethnic groups, with more than 10 million people added to the U.S. population between the 1990 and 2000 censuses (Therrien & Ramirez, 2002).

Latino/Hispanic Americans are concentrated in five states: California (31.1 percent), Texas (18.9 percent), New York (8.1 percent), Florida (7.6 percent), and Illinois (4.3 percent). Some of the key demographics information about this population includes the following from the 2000 U.S. Census (the implications of the following demographic information are presented in the "Key Issues in Law Enforcement" section):

1. *Age:* The Latino/Hispanic American population tends to be younger than the general U.S. population. The median age is 25.9 years, in contrast to 35.3 for the rest of America.

2. *Size of household:* The average Latino/Hispanic household consists of 3.5 people, nearly one person more for every Latino/Hispanic household than for other U.S. households, which average 2.6 persons per household.

3. *Birthrate:* Latino/Hispanic Americans have a higher birthrate than the general U.S. population. The Latino/Hispanic American birthrate per 1,000 is 104.8, in comparison to 65.4 for the rest of America.

4. *Purchasing power:* The estimated purchasing power of Latino/Hispanic Americans in the United States in 2003 was $653 billion and will be over a trillion dollars by the year 2008 (Humphreys, (2003).

5. *Urban households:* About 88 percent of all Latino/Hispanic Americans live in metropolitan areas, making this group the most highly urbanized population in the United States. For example, Latino/Hispanic Americans constitute notable percentages of the population for the following large cities: El Paso (74 percent), Corpus Christi (57 percent), San Antonio (52 percent), Fresno (41 percent), Seattle-Tacoma (40 percent), Los Angeles (38 percent), Albuquerque (38 percent), Miami-Ft. Lauderdale (37 percent), Tucson (27 percent), San Diego (25 percent), Austin (24 percent), and San Francisco-Oakland (19 percent).

6. *Language:* Latino/Hispanic American self-identification is most strongly demonstrated in the knowledge and use of Spanish. The Spanish language is often the single most important cultural aspect retained by Latino/Hispanic Americans. The 2000 U.S. Census indicated that 80 percent of the Latino/Hispanic Americans reported that they spoke Spanish at home. However, the same Census data indicated that over 70 percent of those who spoke Spanish in the home also spoke English "well" or "very well." Latino/Hispanic Americans continue to grow and emerge as a bilingual community capable of communicating in both Spanish and English. The 2003 Yankelovich Monitor Multicultural Study reported that for Latino/Hispanic Americans who learned Spanish as their first language, 44 percent stated that they understood English "very well" and 18 percent stated "somewhat." Over 60 percent of the Latino/Hispanic Americans whose first language is Spanish indicated that they were also proficient in English. The bilingual preferences of Latino/Hispanic Americans were illustrated by the following examples (Yankelovich Monitor, 2003):

   • 62 percent of the respondents indicated that "the Spanish language is more important to me now than it was five years ago."

   • 70 percent stated that Spanish was one of the elements of the culture and traditions that was most important to preserve.

   • 84 percent agreed that "all immigrants should learn English if they plan to stay in this country."

In the same 2003 Yankelovich Monitor Multicultural Study, when Latino/Hispanic Americans were asked, "What language would you prefer to use if you could only use one?" 51 percent of the respondents indicated English and another 15 percent did not have a preference for one language over the other. As might be expected, with the large number of Latino/Hispanic Americans born in the United States, English may soon be the dominant language as this population moves into successive future generations.

LABELS AND TERMS

As noted earlier, the term Latino/Hispanic American is a convenient summarizing label to achieve some degree of agreement in referring to a very heterogeneous group of people. Similar to the case of Asian/Pacific Americans, the key to understanding which terms to use is based on the principle of self-preference. Sensitivity is warranted in use of the term Hispanic with the Latino/Hispanic American community. For those who have origins in the Caribbean (e.g., Puerto Rican, Cuban, Dominican), the term Latino may be equally problematic for self-designation and self-identification.

Until 2003, federal and other governmental designations used only Hispanic; Latino and Hispanic are now used interchangeably. The governmental designations are used in laws, programs, and regulations and in most reports and publications. For individuals within any of the groups, often the more specific names for the groups are preferred (e.g., Mexican, Puerto Rican, Cuban, Dominican, Argentinean, Salvadorian). Some individuals may prefer that the term American be part of their designation (e.g., Mexican American). For law enforcement officers, the best term to use in referring to individuals is the term that they prefer to be called. It is perfectly acceptable to ask individuals what nationality they are.

The use of slurs like "wetback," "Mex," "Spic," "Greaser," or other derogatory ethnic slang terms is never acceptable by law enforcement officers, no matter how provoked an officer may be. Other stereotypic terms like "Illegal," "New York Rican," "Macho man," "Latin lover," "Lupe the Virgin," and "Low Rider" do not convey the kinds of professionalism and respect for community diversity important to law enforcement and peacekeeping and must be avoided in law enforcement work. Officers hearing these or similar words used in their own departments (or with peers or citizens) should provide immediate feedback about the inappropriateness of the use. Officers who may, out of habit, routinely use these terms may find themselves or their superiors in the embarrassing situation of explaining to offended citizens and communities why they used the term and how they intended no bias, stereotype, or prejudice.

TYPOLOGY OF LATINO/HISPANIC AMERICANS

Similar to our typology for Asian/Pacific American individuals, families, and communities, we have developed a seven-part typology that may be useful in understanding and summarizing some of the differences between individuals within this Latino/Hispanic American group (see Exhibit 7.1).

Our typology suggests that as law enforcement, criminal justice, and public safety organizations prepare and train their personnel to work with Latino/Hispanic American communities, a focus on the key differences within each of the typological groups

Type I	Latino/Hispanic recently arrived immigrant or refugee (less than 3 years in the United States with major life experiences in Mexico, the Caribbean, or South and Central America)
Type II	Latino/Hispanic immigrant and refugee (3 or more years in the United States with major life experiences in Mexico, the Caribbean, or South and Central America)
Type III	Latino/Hispanic American (second-generation offspring of immigrant or refugee)
Type IV	Latino/Hispanic immigrant (major life experiences in the United States)
Type V	Latino/Hispanic American (third-generation or longer in the United States)
Type VI	Latino/Hispanic national (anticipates return to Mexico, the Caribbean, or South and Central America, to include visitors and tourists)
Type VII	Latino/Hispanic multinational (global workplace and residency)

Exhibit 7.1   Typology of Latino/Hispanic Americans.

would be most effective. Please refer to Chapter 5 for examples with Asian and Pacific Americans on the use of this typology. It is a convenient framework for discussing how the motivational components within each of the group may affect the way people respond in a law enforcement situation (in the case for those of Latino/Hispanic descent).

MYTHS AND STEREOTYPES

Knowledge of and sensitivity to Latino/Hispanic Americans' concerns, diversity, historical background, and life experiences will facilitate the crime-fighting and peace-keeping mission of law enforcement officers. It is important to have an understanding about some of the myths and stereotypes of Latino/Hispanic Americans that contribute to the prejudice, discrimination, and bias this population encounters. Many law enforcement officers do not have much experience with the diversity of Latino/Hispanic American groups and learn about these groups only through stereotypes (often perpetuated by movies) and through the very limited contact involved in their law enforcement duties. Stereotypic views of Latino/Hispanic Americans reduce individuals within this group to simplistic, one-dimensional characters and have led many Americans to lump members of these diverse groups into one stereotypic group, "Mexicans." It is important for law enforcement officers to be aware of the different stereotypes of Latino/Hispanic Americans. The key to effectiveness with any ethnic or racial group is not that we completely eliminate myths and stereotypes about these groups but that we are aware of these stereotypes and can monitor our thinking and our behaviors when the stereotypes are not true of those persons with whom we are interacting.

Some of the stereotypes that have affected Latino/Hispanic Americans in law enforcement include the following:

1. ***Viewing all Latino/Hispanic Americans as illegal aliens.*** Although many may argue over the number of illegal and undocumented Latino/Hispanic people in the United States, most Latino/Hispanic Americans do not fall into this stereotype; the vast majority are U.S. citizens or legal residents (U.S. Census, 2002). The issues of illegal aliens and undocumented immigrants are complex (see Chapter 1 and previous discussion), but cultural awareness and sensitivity will

allow officers the knowledge to avoid an offensive situation by acting on the stereotype of Latino/Hispanic Americans as illegal immigrants. The following illustrates this point:

> Juan Vasquez worked in the maintenance department of one of the larger downtown hotels in southern California. While at work on his day shift, all "immigrant members" of his maintenance department were asked to go to personnel. When he arrived, he found himself (and others) questioned by several Immigration Enforcement Officers, asking for identification and "papers." Juan was asked if he was an illegal and undocumented alien. He explained that he was a fourth-generation Mexican American, that he was born and grew up in Arizona, and that his family had lived for several generations in Arizona and Colorado. When Juan was asked for proof of citizenship and/or permanent residency, he told the officers that he had a driver's license and car insurance papers. He further explained that he had grown children in college and one was even pursuing a master's degree. While the officers were finally satisfied with his explanations, Juan felt very insulted and offended by the assumption made that he was an illegal alien and not a United States citizen. (anonymous)

2. ***Viewing Latino/Hispanic Americans as lazy and as poor workers.*** This is a stereotype that has been perpetuated in the workplace. Moreover, this stereotype of Latino/Hispanic Americans is often extended to include being a "party people." A workplace law enforcement example illustrates this stereotype:

> A flyer was sent out through interdepartmental mail announcing the retirement party for Sergeant Juan Gomez. The flyer showed a man (with sergeant's stripes) dressed in traditional Mexican garb (sombrero, serape, sandals) sleeping under a large shade tree. While Sergeant Gomez did not appear offended by the stereotype, a Latina nonsworn departmental employee was deeply offended by this flyer and requested that it not be used to announce a party by the organization. The people planning the event said that she was being "overly sensitive" and ignored her request. (police officer's anecdote told at a cultural awareness training session)

It is difficult to understand why some people continue to hold this stereotype or what factors continue to perpetuate it given what we know about the Latino/Hispanic American workforce in the United States and globally. Latino/Hispanic American community advocates make the argument that it is difficult to imagine anyone being labeled as "lazy" or "poor workers" if they are willing to work as laborers from dawn to dusk in the migrant farm fields, day in and day out, year after year.

3. ***Perceiving Latino/Hispanic Americans as uneducated and uninterested in educational pursuits.*** Prior to 1948, many Latino/Hispanic American children were denied access to the educational system available to others and instead were relegated to "Mexican" schools. A challenge in the U.S. courts on segregated schools allowed Latino/Hispanic children access to the "regular" school system (see *Mendez v. Westminster School District,* 1946, and *Delgado v. Bastrop Independent School District,* 1948). This stereotype of "uneducated" relates to how Latino/Hispanic officers may be inappropriately stereotyped and

seen in terms of their ability to learn and to achieve in law enforcement and other professional peacekeeping training.

Regardless of your race, ethnicity, religion or culture, if you are wondering if the American dream is still alive, I have proof for you. All you have to do is find a 2005 dollar bill and read the signature of Anna Escobedo Cabral, who last year was sworn in as the 42nd treasurer of the United States, becoming the highest-ranking woman in the U.S. Treasury Department. . . . It began with her great-grandparents, who brought their families from Mexico to settle in California's Santa Clara Valley, where they built a life in the fields, picking cherries, apricots, prunes, grapes and oranges. Neither of her parents graduated from high school, and when Anna's father suffered a serious back injury, the opportunities for work were pretty much limited to garbage collecting and scrap-metal recycling. As the oldest of five children, Anna was expected to pitch in. Many a day, she searched for recyclable metals just so the family could eat. They moved often, and she attended more than 20 elementary schools. Even so, she managed to be a good student. By the time she was 16, she had accumulated enough credits to graduate. It's easy to understand why she had no dreams beyond the valley. Her goals had to do with ways to help her family. But when her algebra teacher, Phil Lamm, heard about her decision, he took her aside and convinced Anna that she could do much more for her family with an education, and that she should go away to college. He even offered to talk to her father about this new world of opportunity. Somehow, Anna's father trusted the man whose idea meant that his daughter would be going away, the man who talked about a world of opportunity that was greater than any they could have imagined. Lamm helped Anna fill out the college application and get fees waived. Soon she was on her way to the University of California Santa Cruz on a scholarship. From there she went on to Harvard's John F. Kennedy School of Government and eventually became the treasurer of the United States. (Irvin, 2006)

Most Latino/Hispanic immigrants from Mexico and Central America are uneducated and come from poor and/or lower income backgrounds. However, young people, with their access to mass media, are wiser than the older generation about how things work in the United States. On the other hand, most of the South Americans in the United States have been fairly well educated within formal schools because they are often from affluent and educated backgrounds. Because of the great geographic distance, they are usually the only ones who can afford to come to the United States, while their poorer counterparts cannot afford to make the long journey. The estimated Latino/Hispanic American population with origins from South America in 2004 in the United States is only about 5 percent (Synovate, 2004).

4. ***Seeing Latino/Hispanic American young males as gang members and drug dealers.*** Some hold the stereotype, especially among young males in inner cities, that Latino/Hispanic Americans are commonly involved in gangs and the illegal drug trade. Latino/Hispanic cultures are group oriented, and people from young to old tend to congregate as groups rather than as individuals or couples. "Hanging out" as a group tends to be the preferred mode of socializa-

tion. However, given the stereotype of Latino/Hispanic American young males as being gang members, it is easy to perceive five young Latino/Hispanic males walking together as constituting a "gang." Such stereotypes have resulted in suspicion, hostility, and prejudice toward Latino/Hispanic Americans and have served to justify improper treatment (e.g., routine traffic stops) and poor services (e.g., in restaurants and stores). Such stereotypes can be perpetuated by the television media (as illustrated in the following account) and can lead law enforcement officers to associate Latino/Hispanic Americans with criminal activity.

> A *Law & Order* episode about violence during New York's Puerto Rican Day parade provoked angry complaints from Hispanic groups and a promise from NBC never to air the hour again. The episode that aired depicted a parade day rampage by Puerto Rican youths in which women are molested and one is killed. A Brazilian youth is shown convicted in the death. NBC made the decision after a meeting in New York with Hispanic representatives, including Manuel Mirabal, head of the National Puerto Rican Coalition, and Maria Roman, parade president. . . . Mirabal said the drama distorted a real occurrence on parade day last year in which groups of men sexually assaulted women in Central Park. The attacks occurred after, not during, the parade and the majority of those arrested were not Latino, Mirabal said. "Every Puerto Rican shown in that show was portrayed negatively as a criminal, as a delinquent, as someone who abuses women," he said in a telephone interview from New York. Such depictions reflect negatively on all Hispanics because many viewers fail to distinguish between different groups, he said. (Elber, 2001)

5. ***Assuming that all Latino/Hispanic Americans speak Spanish.*** As noted earlier in the chapter, the 2000 U.S. Census data indicated that over 70 percent of those who spoke Spanish in the home also spoke English "well" or "very well." Many Latino/Hispanic Americans have been in the United States for six generations or more and English is the only language that they speak and write. George Perez is a Latino/Hispanic American cultural awareness trainer for many law enforcement, emergency service, and other public service organizations. As one of the outstanding trainers in his field, he is not surprised by the frequently heard stereotypic comment, "You speak English so well, without an accent. How did you do it?" His reply is, "It's the only language I know! I'm a fifth-generation Latino/Hispanic American. I grew up in northern California and received my bachelor's and master's degree in the field that I teach."

THE LATINO/HISPANIC AMERICAN FAMILY

Understanding the importance of family for Latino/Hispanic Americans might be of significant value in community peacekeeping and crime-fighting. Obviously, with over 25 different cultural groups that make up the Latino/Hispanic American category, many differences exist among the groups in this collective in their family experiences. We would like to address some family characteristics that many of the different cultural groups share. *La familia* is perhaps one of the most significant considerations in working and communicating with Latino/Hispanic Americans. (In places where we use the

Spanish term, we have done so to indicate the additional cultural meanings encompassed in a term such as *La familia* that are not captured in the English term *family.*) The Latino/Hispanic American family is most clearly characterized by bonds of interdependence, unity, and loyalty and includes nuclear and extended family members as well as networks of neighbors, friends, and community members. Primary importance is given to the history of the family, which is firmly rooted in the set of obligations tied to both the past and the future. In considering the different loyalty bonds, the parent–child relationship emerges as primary, with all children owing *respecto* to parents (*respecto* connotes cultural meanings beyond those in the English term *respect*). Traditionally, the role of the father has been that of the disciplinarian, decision-maker, and head of the household. The father's word is the law, and he is not to be questioned. The father tends to focus his attention on the economic and well-being issues of the family and less on the social and emotional issues. The mother, on the other hand, is seen as balancing the father's role by providing for the emotional and expressive issues of the family. Extended family members such as grandmothers, aunts and uncles, and godparents (*compadrazgo*) may supplement the mother's emotional support. In the Latino/Hispanic American family, the oldest son is traditionally the secondary decision-maker to the father and the principal inheritor (*primogenito*) of the family. Because of the central nature of the Latino/Hispanic American family, it is common for police officers to come into contact with members of nuclear and extended families in the course of working with the Latino/Hispanic American community. One key to the success of law enforcement officers in working with the Latino/Hispanic American extended network is the knowledge of how best to communicate within the family context and an understanding of with whom to speak for information, observations, and questions.

The Role of the Man and the Woman in a Latino/Hispanic American Family

In many Latino/Hispanic American families, the relationship and communication patterns are hierarchical with the father as the identified head of the household who is held in high respect. When it comes to family well-being, economic issues, and discipline, the father may appear to be the decision-maker; however, many other individuals may come into the picture. Generally, if there are grandparents in the household, the father may consult them, as well as his wife, on major decisions. In the case of law enforcement matters, it may be of great importance for officers to provide the father and the family with some privacy, as much as possible, to discuss key issues and situations. With central values like *respecto* and *machismo* in the Latino/Hispanic American culture, it is critical for the father and other family members to demonstrate control in family situations. In this way, law enforcement officers may find that there is more control in a situation by allowing the citizen to think through a decision, come to the same conclusion as that of the officer, and exercise self-control in behaving in the best interests of all parties concerned.

Within the Latino/Hispanic American family, the sex roles are clearly defined; boys and girls are taught from childhood two different codes of behavior (Comas-Diaz & Griffith, 1988). Traditional sex roles can be discussed in the context of the two codes of gender-related behaviors: *machismo* and *marianismo. Machismo* literally means maleness, manliness, and virility. Within the Latino/Hispanic American cultural context, *machismo* means that the male is responsible for the well-being and honor of the family and is in the provider role. *Machismo* is also associated with having power over women, as well as responsibility for guarding and protecting them. Boys are seen as strong by nature and do not need the protection that is required by girls, who are seen as weak by nature.

Women are socialized into the role of *marianismo,* based on the beliefs about the Virgin Mary, in which women are considered spiritually superior to men and therefore able to endure all suffering inflicted by men (Stevens, 1973). Women are expected to be self-sacrificing in favor of their husbands and children. Within the context of the Latino/Hispanic American family, the role of the woman is as homemaker and caretaker of the children. In the current U.S. context, the traditional gender roles of women and men in the Latino/Hispanic American community have undergone much change, which has resulted in key conflicts. Since women have begun to work, earn money, and have some of the financial independence men have (e.g., they can go out and socialize with others outside of the family), they have pursued many experiences inconsistent with the traditional Latino/Hispanic female role. Although there are no clear-cut rules as to whether officers should go to the male head of the household or to the female family member, law enforcement officers would probably be more correct to address the father first in law enforcement inquiries. Consistent with the cultural values of *machismo* and *marianismo,* the Latino/Hispanic American household appears to be run by the father; however, in actual practice, the mother's role in discipline, education, finance, and decision making is also central.

Children, Adolescents, and Youth

Within the Latino/Hispanic American family, the ideal child is obedient and respectful of his or her parents and other elders. Adults may at times talk in front of the children as if they are not present and as if the children cannot understand the adults' conversations. Children are taught *respecto,* which dictates the appropriate behavior toward all authority figures, older people, parents, relatives, and others. If children are disrespectful, they are punished and scolded. In many traditional families, it is considered appropriate for parents (and for relatives) to physically discipline a disrespectful and misbehaving child.

In Latino/Hispanic American households, there is a high reliance on family members (older children and other adults) to help care for younger children. Both parents within a Latino/Hispanic American family often work. As such, it is not uncommon for Latino/Hispanic American families to have latchkey children or have children cared for by older children in the neighborhood. As in other communities in which English is the second language, Latino/Hispanic American children have a special role in being the intermediaries for their parents on external community matters because of the ability of the younger individuals to learn English and the American ways of doing things. Children often serve as translators and interpreters for peace officers in their communication and relations with Latino/Hispanic American families involved in legal matters, immigration concerns, and community resources. Although the use of children and family members as translators is viewed as professionally and culturally inappropriate, often it is the only means available to the law enforcement officer. In such situations, it is suggested that the officer review what role is expected of the youthful member of the family. The officer needs to see how sensitive a topic might be for different family members. Moreover, the consequence of an incorrect translation must be evaluated (e.g., asking a juvenile to translate to his or her parents who speak no English that the juvenile has been involved in drinking and riding in a stolen vehicle may result in significantly changed content). Because of the embarrassment and fear of punishment by the juvenile and possibly a sense of shame or embarrassment to the parents, the message may be altered to avoid negative ramifications by the child. In all cases, when a child is acting as a translator for parents, the officer should direct all verbal and nonverbal communication to the parents. Otherwise, the parents may view the officer's lack of attention to them as an insult. Such sensitivity by the peace officer is particularly important for Latino/Hispanic Americans because of the cultural value of *personalismo,* which emphasizes the importance of the personal quality of any interaction. This cultural concept implies that relationships occur between particular individuals as persons, not as representatives of institutions (e.g., law enforcement) or merely as individuals performing a role (e.g., as a person who enforces the law).

Cross-National Family Issues

In Exhibit 7.1, we provide a typology of the Latino/Hispanic American to identify the different immigration and migration patterns within Latino/Hispanic American communities. This typology can also be used to understand the family, personal, and political issues involved in the interactions of Latino/Hispanic Americans crossing several types. For example, the Latino/Hispanic American (third generation or later; Type V) category consists of individuals who desire to choose which aspects of the old culture to keep and which of the new culture to accept. The focus is on choosing activities, values, norms, and lifestyles that blend the best of that which is Latino/Hispanic and the best of that which is American. The importance of being bicultural is a unique aspect of this group. However, much conflict may occur when there are family conflicts that involve cross-national value differences between being American and being bicultural, as was illustrated in the custody case of 9-year-old Elian Gonzalez (Lewis, 2000). In this particular case, Elian Gonzalez had escaped from Cuba with his mother, and during the hazardous trip, the mother died at sea. Elian's relatives in Miami took the boy into their home; however, Elian's father, a Cuban national, fought to regain legal custody of his son and to return him to Cuba. Local law enforcement agencies were working with the Cuban American community in Miami to maintain order while the family was trying to negotiate a workable settlement with Elian Gonzalez's father. While local law enforcement officials were working to maintain the peace, U.S. Attorney General Janet Reno ordered armed U.S. immigration agents to seize the boy in a surprise predawn raid. The boy was returned to his father in Cuba, and the Cuban American community protested and clashed with the Miami police, resulting in more than 260 arrests (Bragg, 2000). As illustrated by the case, today's law enforcement personnel may often have to intervene in such family and domestic disputes as well as in cross-national political situations involved in community peacekeeping assignments.

CULTURAL INFLUENCES ON COMMUNICATION: VERBAL AND NONVERBAL STYLES OF LATINO/HISPANIC AMERICANS

Although we do not wish to create stereotypes of any kind, key features of Latino/ Hispanic American verbal and nonverbal communication styles necessitate explanation. Misunderstanding resulting from style differences can result in perceptions of poor community services from police agencies, conflicts resulting from such misunderstandings, and safety and control issues for the peace officer.

1. Latino/Hispanic Americans' high cultural value for *la familia* results in a very strong family and group orientation. As such, officers should not view the frequently seen behavior of "eye checking" with other family members before answering and the lack of the use of "I" statements and/or self-reference as Latino/Hispanic Americans not being straightforward about themselves or their relationships. The officer may be concerned because a Latino/Hispanic American witness may wish to use the pronoun *we* when the situation may call for a personal observation involving an "I" statement. For example, a Latino/Hispanic American family member who witnessed a store robbery may first nonverbally check with other family members before describing what he or she saw. Such verbal and nonverbal behavior is consistent with the family and group orientation of Latino/Hispanic Americans.

2. Speaking Spanish to others in the presence of a law enforcement officer, even though the officer requested responses in English, should not automatically be interpreted as an insult or as attempts to hide information from the officer. In times of stress, those who speak English as a second language automatically revert to their first and native language. In a law enforcement situation, many individuals may find themselves under stress and may speak Spanish, which is the more accessible and comfortable language for them. Moreover, speaking Spanish gives the individual a greater range of expression (to discuss and clarify complex issues with other speakers and family members), thus yielding clearer, more useful information to law enforcement personnel about critical events.

3. It is important for officers to take the time to get information from witnesses, victims and suspects even if the individuals have limited skills in speaking English (the use of officers who speak Spanish, translators, and language bank resources will help). Often Latino/Hispanic Americans have not been helped in crime-fighting and peacekeeping situations because officers could not or did not take information from nonnative English speakers.

> One incident involving officer Luis Franco shows why it helps to have officers who can communicate with non-English speakers. Franco recalled a domestic dispute where he found a middle-aged Hispanic man wouldn't cooperate with other officers. The man spoke no English and aggressively resisted the investigation of the dispute between him and his wife. Franco immediately told him to calm down and asked—in Spanish—what the problem was. The man turned toward Franco and answered quickly. The man said he expected the police to beat him up, then

take him downtown. We don't do that here, Franco explained. Sit down and tell us your side of the story and we'll work it out. The man calmed and agreed. Afterward, he went downtown anyway, but the arrest stayed peaceful as Franco explained each step. (Associated Press, 2001)

4. Although Latino/Hispanic Americans may show respect to law enforcement officers because of police authority, they do not necessarily trust the officers or the organization. *Respecto* is extended to elders and those who are in authority. This respect is denoted in the Spanish language by the use of *usted* (the formal you) rather than *tu* (the informal you). Showing respect, however, does not ensure trust. The cultural value of *confianza* (or trust) takes some time to develop. Like many from ethnic minority communities, Latino/Hispanic Americans have experienced some degree of prejudice and discrimination from the majority community, and citizens with such experiences need time to develop trust with law enforcement officers, who are identified as being a part of the majority community.

5. The cultural value of *personalismo* emphasizes the importance of the person involved in any interaction. Latino/Hispanic Americans take into strong consideration not only the content of any communication but also the context and relationship of the communicator. This means it is important for the officer to provide information about why questions are asked, who is the person asking the question (i.e., information about the officer), and how the information will be used in the context for effective communications. Additionally, context for Latino/Hispanic Americans means taking some time to find out, as well as to self-disclose, some background information (e.g., living in the same neighborhood, having similar concerns about crime). Additional contextual elements, such as providing explanations and information to Latino/Hispanic Americans about procedures, laws, and so forth before asking them questions or requesting their help will ease the work of the officer. By providing background information and establishing prior relationships with community members, law enforcement agencies and officers build a context for cooperation with Latino/Hispanic American individuals.

6. Officers should recognize nonverbal and other cultural nuances that may detract from effective communication. Many Latino/Hispanic Americans, especially younger individuals, find it uncomfortable and sometimes inappropriate to maintain eye contact with authority figures such as police officers. Strong eye contact with someone who is of higher position, importance, or authority is considered a lack of *respecto* in Latin/Hispanic American cultures. As such, many citizens from this background may deflect their eyes from police officers. It is important that officers not automatically read this nonverbal behavior as indicative of a lack of trust or as a dishonest response.

7. Latino/Hispanic Americans may exhibit behaviors that appear to be evasive, such as claiming not to have any identification or by saying that they do not speak English. In some of the native countries from which many Latino/Hispanic Americans have emigrated, the police and law enforcement agencies are aligned with a politically repressive government. The work of the police

and of law enforcement in those countries is not one of public service. Therefore, many Latino/Hispanic Americans may have similar "fear" reactions to law enforcement officers in the United States. It is suggested that officers take the time to explain the need for identification and cooperation and that they acknowledge the importance of comprehension on the part of the Latino/Hispanic American individual(s) involved.

> Carlos and his family had escaped from one of the South American countries where he saw the police serving as part of the politically repressive force upon his community. He was aware of the role of some of the police as members of the "death squad." He and his family were admitted to the United States and given political asylum and lived in southern California. Although he speaks fluent English and Spanish and has been in the United States for over 5 years, he relates how on one occasion when he was pulled over by the police (for a broken taillight) he automatically had this fear reaction and had the thought of saying to the officer, "No habla English," in the hope of avoiding any further contact. (Latino/Hispanic American trainer's anecdote told in a police cultural awareness training course)

KEY ISSUES IN LAW ENFORCEMENT

Underreporting of Crimes

Latino/Hispanic Americans, because of their past experiences with some of the law enforcement agencies within their countries of origin (e.g., repressive military force in their native country as well as perceived "unresponsiveness" by police), are reluctant to report crimes and may not seek police assistance or help. Many people bring with them memories of how police within their home countries have brutalized and violated them and others (e.g., as members of the death squad). In addition, many immigrants and refugees are just not knowledgeable about the legal system of the United States and may try to avoid any contact with law enforcement personnel. Outreach and community policing perspectives will enhance the contacts and relationships with Latino/Hispanic American communities and may help alleviate the underreporting of crimes.

> Police are concerned that some Hispanic residents aren't reporting when they are victims of crime. Since January, 10 aggravated robberies have been reported to the Rogers Police Department, Cpl. Kelley Cradduck said. In each case, victims reported being robbed by two or more Hispanic men who stole wallets, money or personal items. In all but one of the cases, the victims have also been Hispanic. But Cradduck said the number of Hispanic victims is expected to be much higher, but they are not reporting crimes out of fear. He said it's possible that because Hispanics don't report crimes, it makes them a target. "[Hispanics] don't always report because they don't trust cops," Cradduck said Friday. "It's sad because they may have information that will solve the case." According to a recent victimization study by the U.S. Department of Justice, Hispanics are less likely to report crimes to police than non-Hispanics by at least 8 percent. (Crawford, 2005)

Victimization

The Bureau of Justice Statistics' National Crime Victimization Survey (Catalano, 2005), "Criminal Victimization 2004," indicated that Hispanics were victims of overall violence and simple assault at rates lower than were non-Hispanics in 2004. Hispanics and non-Hispanics were equally likely to experience rape/sexual assault, robbery, aggravated assault, and theft. Although the Bureau of Justice Statistics' report indicated lower rates of overall violence and simple assault victimization by Latino/Hispanic Americans, Latino/Hispanic American community advocates are concerned that such crimes may be underreported, as noted in the following two examples:

> Hispanic day laborers in Forest Park are the latest metro Atlanta Latinos to become victims of armed robberies. . . . Some Latinos simply don't trust banking institutions, preferring to leave their money at home where they can see it, observers say. . . . The problem is not isolated to Forest Park, where police estimate 75 percent of robberies involve this type of Hispanic victim. Observers say it is a common offense in counties where there's a concentration of immigrants. Over a nine-month period ending in 1999, there were 34 robberies of Hispanic victims in one Atlanta apartment complex alone. In 1998, DeKalb County detectives charged two men with more than 50 home invasion robberies stretching from Buford Highway to Marietta. Their victims were all Hispanic families. At the time, police said it was the longest string of robbery cases in DeKalb County history. In Cobb County, Marietta police say about 95 percent of person-to-person robberies in the last two years in the southeastern part of the city, where there's a concentration of Latinos, have been against Hispanic immigrants. Smyrna police say the majority of person-to-person robberies and home invasion robberies in the last three years have involved Hispanic victims. (Bruner, 2001, p. B1)

> You've heard the explanations of why Hispanics are targeted for robbery: They're less likely to have bank accounts and are more likely to carry cash. And they're less likely to run to the cops since the police, as well as the banks, in their homelands tend to be untrustworthy. Because of that, "they're the perfect victim," said Richmond police Lt. Michael A. Zohab, who covers a section of South Richmond with a high percentage of Hispanics. Citywide, Hispanics represent 8 percent to 10 percent of the population, based on estimates from Richmond's Hispanic Liaison Office. The 2000 census indicated that Hispanics made up about 3 percent of Richmond's population. Zohab said robbery victims "weren't even calling the police because they were scared we were going to do something to them." Police and community activists have been working hard to combat that perception, and it's working. Hispanics are now much more likely to report crimes than they were three years ago. In 2004, they represented 11 percent of the city's 1,300 robbery victims. In 2005, they made up 16 percent of the victims. Now, it's 25 percent. "It's going to go even higher," Zohab predicted. (Holmberg, 2006, p. B1)

As noted by Rennison (2002) in the Bureau of Justice Statistics Special Report "Hispanic Victims of Violent Crime, 1990–2000," Hispanics most vulnerable to violent crimes were males (54 victimizations per 1,000 annually), juveniles age 12 to 17 (90 per 1,000), those with household incomes under $7,500 (64 per 1,000), and those who had never married (72 per 1,000). Violence against Hispanics, as with other victims, most often took the form of simple assault (59 percent). About equal percentages of Hispanics were robbed (20 percent) or were victims of aggravated assault (19 percent). Two percent of Hispanic victims of violence sustained a rape or sexual assault in 2000 (Rennison, 2002). The following case example illustrates the specifics of the report:

> A teenager covered with 18 tattoos, including swastikas and white supremacist symbols, has confessed that he left his Queens home before 5 on a Sunday morning and traveled 50 miles to a Long Island town to attack two day laborers because they were Mexican, the police said today. The teenager, Ryan Wagner, a 19-year-old construction worker who lives with his parents in Maspeth, was arraigned today in Islip on two counts of attempted murder and two counts of aggravated harassment in the Sept. 17 attack, in which the police say he used a knife. He was held without bail at the Suffolk County jail in Riverhead. The two laborers said that two white men, posing as contractors promising work, had picked them up in a car in Farmingville and driven them to an abandoned factory in Shirley, where they were attacked but managed to escape. . . . In a confession on Tuesday, the police said, Mr. Wagner said he was simply doing what the other suspect wanted him to do. "What we gather from his confession was, the motive was in fact to go out and attack Mexicans," said Detective Sgt. Robert Reecks, commanding officer of the bias crimes unit. "We cannot say they are tied to any organization, or they were hired by anybody, or they were prompted to do this by any particular group." (Kelley, 2000, p. B5)

Differential Treatment

Many of the crimes within Latino/Hispanic American communities are perpetrated by others of the same ethnic group. Additionally, for this community, as noted in the Bureau of Justice Statistics' report, more than half of the violent crimes are committed by strangers (Rennison, 2002). Law enforcement officials have often found it difficult to get cooperation from Latino/Hispanic American crime victims. To some degree, this lack of cooperation relates to the fear of retaliation within the Latino/Hispanic community. Other concerns of the Latino/Hispanic American victim include (1) the perceived nonresponsiveness of the peacekeeping officers and agencies, (2) lack of familiarity with and trust in police services, (3) perceived lack of effectiveness of the law enforcement agencies, and (4) stereotypes and images of law enforcement agencies as discriminatory. A key challenge for police agencies is to educate this group and to work cooperatively with the communities to reduce crime.

Racial Profiling of Latino/Hispanic Americans

Racial profiling, as discussed in Chapter 14, is a major problem and concern for people within minority groups. This is particularly so for African Americans and Arab Americans, but also for Latino/Hispanic Americans. They believe that the determining factor in whether peace officers exercise their discretion in stopping a vehicle driven by a Latino/Hispanic American is the driver's race and ethnicity. To many Latino/Hispanic

Americans, racial profiling may even be "encouraged," as noted in the following example:

> Jose Pineda says he wasn't breaking any traffic law in January 1999 when a Mount Prospect police officer pulled him over and ticketed him for driving without insurance. Hiram Romero claims he was pulled over in Mount Prospect in May 1999 and ticketed for a defective front license plate—even though the officer could not see the front of Romero's car when he signaled him to stop. And Silvia Meyers, stopped by an officer in July 1999 while driving a Mercedes-Benz, says she was asked if she really owned the car. The three people—all Hispanic—filed a class-action lawsuit against the village contending police singled them out because of their race. On Wednesday, a federal judge set the stage for them to be awarded $3,000 each. As many as 3,200 other Hispanic drivers ticketed in Mount Prospect between Feb. 11, 1998, and Feb. 11, 2000, will each be eligible for $75 to $225 under a legal settlement recently agreed to by village officials. . . . In March 2000, Mount Prospect paid $900,000 to settle three lawsuits from three of its police officers who claimed they were encouraged to pull over Hispanic drivers. Mount Prospect admitted no wrongdoing in those settlements, a position it also took in the class-action case. (Fusco, 2002, p. 5)

According to Hill and Trapp (2000), "Every study of racial profiling shows that, contrary to popular belief, people of color are not more likely to carry drugs or other contraband in their vehicles than whites. In Maryland, the percentage of black and white drivers carrying contraband was statistically identical. The U.S. Customs Service's own figures show that while over 43 percent of those searched were minorities, the 'hit rates' for these searches were actually lower for people of color than for whites." In a study by the San Diego Police Department (Hill & Trapp, 2000), African Americans and Latino/Hispanic Americans were stopped more often than would be expected given their numbers in the local population; that is, 40 percent of those stopped and 60 percent of those searched were African Americans and Latino/Hispanic Americans, whereas both groups together represent only 28 percent of the driving population. The Associated Press (2005) study conducted in Illinois illustrates the racial profiling issues for Latino/ Hispanic Americans (and other minorities):

> Black and Hispanic drivers in large downstate cities are pulled over by police at a rate that far exceeds their share of the local population, according to an analysis of data from more than 2 million traffic stops last year. Springfield had the biggest gap: 42 percent of its traffic stops involved minorities even though its population is only 16 percent minority. It was followed by cities such as Peoria, Rockford and Joliet. An Associated Press analysis of the traffic study also found that after being pulled over, minorities were more likely to be ticketed than white drivers. And minority drivers were more likely to have their cars searched and to be found with drugs and weapons, the numbers show. Some police departments contend the data is flawed and doesn't paint an accurate picture of their work. But minority leaders say the results show police sometimes target minorities. "I really don't need statistics to tell me racial profiling is an issue or that it exists," said Sen. Kwame Raoul, D-Chicago. "I think the statistics serve more than the purpose of identifying whether a problem exists. It helps hopefully to target the problem." The study was approved in 2003 at the

urging of minority groups and lawmakers who complained that too many people were being pulled over simply for "driving while black" or Hispanic. (Associated Press, 2005)

Law Enforcement Issues Involving Immigration and Custom Enforcement (ICE)

One of the key situations for a law enforcement agency involves decision making whereby the local public safety agencies and departments become involved in enforcing and working with the Immigration and Custom Enforcement (ICE) section, now a part of the Department of Homeland Security, as noted in Chapter 1. The ramifications for Latino/Hispanic American community relationships and network-building are significant. The decision making and strategic responses to the enforcement of ICE efforts are not clear cut, nor "givens," for any law enforcement agency. However, the general argument in support of leaving illegal immigrants alone (unless they have committed a criminal act or are creating a disturbance) is based on the perspective that tracking down and deporting illegal workers is technically the job of the ICE and not the police. Central to the clarity of roles required by the officer in the field is the delineation by police agencies of specific policies related to determining, reporting, and turning in illegal immigrants to ICE. Sometimes the trust of the entire community (illegal and legal immigrants) is at stake with the Latino/Hispanic American community. As noted in Chapter 1, Donya Fernandez, a language rights attorney in San Francisco, California, suggests that police departments make it clearly known to the people within Latino/Hispanic American immigrant communities the circumstances under which the decision is made not to turn in illegal immigrants to ICE. When this is known, there will be less fear of the police when it comes to reporting crimes and seeking help and assistance (Fernandez, 2000).

Latino/Hispanic Americans must be able to trust that they will be treated fairly and protected as part of their involvement and association with local law enforcement and public safety. This is of particular importance when there might be some perceptions, assumptions, and/or stereotypes among community residents as to who might end up being reported to ICE and who might be questioned by ICE (with the possibility of deportation and detention because of real or suspected immigration status). The following recommendations are made for local law enforcement agencies in working with the Latino/Hispanic American community, concerning legal and undocumented immigration status:

1. ***Develop agency and departmental policies with regard to reporting and working with ICE:*** Law enforcement agencies must have clear policies and procedures to address the circumstances in reporting to ICE. The policy must include (1) under what circumstances a person will be reported to ICE; and (2) no person will be reported or referred to ICE where no laws have been violated.

2. ***Maintain contact with the Latino/Hispanic American community leaders:*** Law enforcement officers need to work closely with community leaders to establish a cooperative plan to inform them of the agency's policies and their implementation. Often, announcements made by Latino/Hispanic American

community leaders, to inform their respective communities of any fears associated with reporting crimes and/or assistance to the police department, have been very helpful. Community leaders could, for example, work with law enforcement agencies' community relations offices to develop a communication plan for the effective dissemination of information about their policies in working with ICE.

3. ***Utilize a communication plan:*** It is essential to have a well-developed and pilot-tested communication plan to ensure that the proper messages are provided to the community when it involves a person who may or may not be reported or referred to ICE. This is particularly important when language translations and interpreting are necessary. A carefully pretested "core message" regarding the department's procedures will usually work better than on-the-spot messages subject to the momentary interpretation of those who first hear such information.

4. ***Clearly define the implications for any contact with the law enforcement agency and possible reporting to ICE:*** When it comes to the possibility that a contact with the local police department may result in a person being questioned by ICE and/or being involved in deportation procedures, members from Latino/Hispanic American communities tend to be quite cautious. The fear that they might be stereotyped as "illegal" (or have experienced prejudice by others in this regard) would naturally make any contact with law enforcement agencies and officers tenuous. It is essential to provide clearly defined procedures and information as to how any contact would normally be reported or not be reported to ICE. Additionally, if there are possible consequences of such reporting, these elements should be clearly stated to ensure an ongoing relationship of trust with members of the Latino/Hispanic American community involved.

5. ***Train all sworn and nonsworn personnel with respect to the agency or departmental policy for working with ICE:*** Law enforcement agencies need to provide training and education to enable officers to effectively utilize legal enforcement tools so that they can perform their work professionally and effectively within today's multicultural communities. Clearly, most law enforcement officers know not to act on the prejudices and stereotypes that they might hold. However, the nature of prejudice is such that some people are not aware of their prejudices or biases. Therefore, they make inferences and take actions toward certain groups based upon these biased perceptions, such as who might or might not be an unauthorized migrant and/or an illegal immigrant. Establishing training that provides accurate information concerning groups for which officers might have prejudices and stereotypes is one of the approaches police departments should use to ensure implementation of the department's policy in working with ICE.

6. ***Utilize Latino/Hispanic American law enforcement personnel and translators/interpreters from the same or similar communities:*** To the extent that it is possible, the use of law enforcement personnel from the same or similar Latino/Hispanic American communities would add to the sustaining of relationships and trust necessary in law enforcement within these communities.

7. ***Ensure Latino/Hispanic community outreach services:*** Every police and community interaction requires a strong, ongoing link to community groups and advocacy organizations. A link is established when community task forces are assembled to address issues, especially issues involving possible police interactions with undocumented immigrants and/or unauthorized migrants. These steps demonstrate respect for the Latino/Hispanic American community and create shared responsibility for whatever action is taken. The police hold primary responsibility for community outreach on every level, but the community is also responsible for becoming involved in activities that form positive relationships with the police. Policing within the community can function only in an environment of mutual engagement and respect.

8. ***Provide real-time linkage and referral to Latino/Hispanic community-based advocacy services:*** Police departments may want to provide real-time linkage and referral to the resources and community-based advocacy services available to facilitate knowledge regarding any police interactions that might involve people with undocumented immigration issues. In this way, Latino/Hispanic American citizens would have a third-party opinion and support for their actions. Law enforcement's referral of Latino/Hispanic citizens to these services would facilitate and support the trust-building and relationships necessary to effective work in the Latino/Hispanic American community.

ICE cooperation by local law enforcement agencies is of particular concern for the Latino/Hispanic American community where there has been a history of legal as well as illegal immigration. Indeed, some Latino/Hispanic American community members will be prosecuted and deported. However, where no wrong has been committed, then law enforcement must keep a check on potential stereotyping and the prejudicial act of singling out individuals based on those stereotypes.

Exposure to Environmental Risk and Job Hazards

The Environmental Protection Agency (2001) confirms in its Toxic Release Inventory (TRI) emissions research studies what Morales and Bonilla (1993) documented in the state of California: that Latino/Hispanic Americans live in some of the most polluted neighborhoods and work in many of the most hazardous jobs. For example, in Oakland, California, 24 percent of whites and 69 percent of Latino/Hispanic Americans live in communities with hazardous waste sites; in Los Angeles, the percentages are 35 percent for whites and 60 percent for Latino/Hispanic Americans. In addition to Latino/Hispanic American community members' concerns regarding crime and violence are the concerns for the environmental safety of their homes and fears over their exposures to environmental hazards and risks. Such concerns add to the role of law enforcement and peace officers within Latino/Hispanic American communities.

Additionally, some job risks are related to stereotypic and oppressive actions of co-workers in creating a hostile work environment:

Twelve Hispanic workers at a Grand Junction aerospace plant won a $1.25 million settlement after dropping a discrimination suit alleging they were subjected to racial slurs and taunting by white co-workers. Hamilton Sundstrand, a prime contractor for NASA, Boeing and Lockheed Martin, agreed to the pay-out this week to resolve a 2003 discrimination lawsuit brought by the Equal Employment Opportunity Commission. Documents filed in Denver federal court state the money is solely for "emotional distress damages." . . . Denver EEOC attorney Anjuli Kelotra said racial harassment at the Mesa County plant was tolerated by supervisors since at least 1997. "It was a day-after-day bar-rage," said Kelotra, referring to the ethnic name-calling. "It hurts the ears to hear it." Lead plaintiff Raymond Arellano, 45, alleged he was choked by one of the taunting workers in January 2000 and then labeled a "problem child" after reporting the attack to managers. At times, even managers used ethnic slurs when referring to Hispanic employees, said the suit. Bill Martinez, a former EEOC attorney representing Arellano, said of the roughly 250 workers at the nonunion plant, no more than 20 were Hispanic. Some of the racial hostility di-rected toward Hispanics seemed related to the relatively high wages the plant paid to all workers, regardless of their education and race, he said. "There is a real mentality in that town that Hispanics should be out in the fields or washing dishes in restaurants, but not taking $25 an hour machinist jobs from whites," Martinez said. (Accola, 2005)

Law enforcement professionals need to be alert to environmental risks, including workplace exploitation of Latino/Hispanic Americans, and to be particularly sensitive to the fear that many immigrants have in reporting crimes to the police.

Increasing Police Services to the Latino/Hispanic American Community

The Police Neighborhood Resource Center model, started in 1991 in the largely His-panic community of Rolling Meadows, Illinois, has shown the positive cooperative re-sults of the police department, the Latino/Hispanic American community, and the local and regional businesses:

In 1991, police opened a substation called the Police Neighborhood Resource Center on the south side, nestled among a troubled cluster of apartment com-plexes. . . . "I believe that because we faced up to a high problem area and looked for ways to resolve that, we became problem solvers as compared to just trying to push a problem away," Menzel said. Other communities might have tried to push a troubled immigrant population out of town, but Rolling Mead-ows set a national standard for finding a way to assimilate its Hispanic resi-dents. Police departments in West Chicago, Mundelein and Riverdale soon followed Rolling Meadows' example. More recently, resource centers opened in Hoffman Estates, Palatine, Des Plaines and even Cleveland, Ohio. (Cliatt, 2001, p. 1)

The outreach approach of using bilingual community service officers (CSOs) who are nonsworn officers (i.e., they hold badges and wear uniforms) to serve the ethnic communities in San Diego, California, provides yet another viable model for the Latino/Hispanic American community as a whole. The CSOs provide many of the in-formational, referral, educational, and crime-reporting services available through the police department. The use of bilingual CSOs increases the effectiveness of law enforcement in Spanish-speaking communities. The use of Latino/Hispanic American police outreach coordinators is similar to the CSO approach:

> The police department has hired its first Latino outreach coordinator to combat many Latinos' distrust of police officers and overcome the language barrier. . . . As a civilian member of the police department, Sanchiz will oversee the dozen part-time translators for the department, serve as a translator himself and organize outreach efforts in Burlington's Latino neighborhoods. He has already reached an agreement with Burlington's lone Catholic parish, Blessed Sacrament, to speak to its Latino parishioners at Saturday's Mass. Sanchiz will immediately help the police, Lt. Steve Smith said. "In the past, we've sometimes had trouble getting cooperation from Latino witnesses because of distrust or language barriers," Smith said. "I can see Juan going out to a crime scene with our detectives and helping overcome those difficulties." "Latino people come from countries where police are often abusive," Sanchiz said. "They come here and think, 'It's going to be the same.' " (Frago, 2001, p. B1)

To bridge the service gap and to reinforce the Latino/Hispanic American community with local and statewide law enforcement and public safety agencies, cities like Durham, North Carolina, have experimented with the Spanish Police Academy (Associated Press, 2003). The classes meet twice each week and mirror the regular Citizens' Police Academy, with the major difference being the use of translators. Another way to bridge the gap is to have officers learn Spanish, and some officers will attest that even "survival" Spanish-language training and "crash courses" in minority community relations (Taylor, 2000) have some degree of effectiveness.

The willingness of law enforcement officers to use Spanish phrases in their interactions with Latino/Hispanic Americans is very useful even if the officers have not attained Spanish-language fluency. The use of everyday greetings and courteous phrases in Spanish indicates officers' respect and positive attitude and is seen favorably by members of the Latino/Hispanic American community. (See Chapter 4 for a discussion of language training in police departments.)

Increasing the Number of Latino/Hispanic American Police Officers

In the past decade, Latino/Hispanic Americans have significantly increased their numbers in federal, state, and local law enforcement positions. In 2002, of the 93,000 full-time, federal law enforcement officers with arrest and firearm authority, Latino/Hispanic Americans comprised 16.8 percent of that total (Reaves & Bauer, 2003). For police departments, from 2000 to 2003, the number of Latino/Hispanic American officers increased by 4,700, which brings Latino/Hispanic American officers to 9.6 percent of the total full-time sworn and nonsworn personnel in local police departments (Hickman & Reaves, 2006a). For sheriffs' offices, from 2000 to 2003, the number of Latino/Hispanic American officers increased by 1,960, which brings Latino/Hispanic American officers to 7.4 percent of the total full-time sworn and nonsworn personnel in sheriffs' offices (Hickman & Reaves, 2006b).

Latino/Hispanic Americans are still underrepresented in local police departments and sheriffs' offices. Local law enforcement attempts to effectively serve states, cities, and community neighborhoods with large Latino/Hispanic American populations are still hampered by the proportionately small number of Latino/Hispanic American officers (given the dispersion of the Latino/Hispanic American population within the United States). A variety of reasons exist for such underrepresentation in local police departments and sheriffs' offices, including (1) history of law enforcement stereotypes and relationships with Latino/Hispanic American communities; (2) interests of Latino/Hispanic Americans with respect to law enforcement careers; (3) image of law enforcement personnel in Latino/Hispanic American communities; (4) lack of knowledge about the different careers and pathways in law enforcement; (5) concern with and fear of background checks and immigration status, physical requirements, and the application process; (6) ineffective and misdirected law enforcement recruitment and outreach efforts within the Latino/Hispanic American community; and (7) lack of role models and advocates for law enforcement careers for Latino/Hispanic Americans.

Clearly, role models are needed to help clarify to the community what is required for a career in law enforcement. Law enforcement agencies have clearly seen the need for increasing their ability to serve the Latino/Hispanic American community with more bilingual/bicultural personnel. The following examples have been used in a variety of agencies to increase understanding of the law enforcement and criminal justice agencies, to create more favorable recruitment possibilities, and to increase understanding between law enforcement and public safety agencies and the Latino/Hispanic American community:

1. ***Red carpet mystery:*** Latino/Hispanic American families are invited to solve "crime scene" mysteries staged by the police agency and other local organizations:

   > Waukesha—A 37-year-old man is found dead on an apartment floor. Evidence of excessive drug and alcohol use is in plain view. Clearly, the death is due to an overdose. Or is it? Other clues indicate a possible violent end. In a first-of-its-kind program, the mock mystery will be solved not by police but by 30 Hispanic families who have recently immigrated to Waukesha. . . . Avila said the effort is important, because about 100 Hispanic immigrant families move to Waukesha annually and need to feel safe while adjusting to the community. "They need to learn that here police can be friends," she said. UW Extension staff, along with police and the medical examiner's office, have created a five-part series called "The Red Carpet Mystery," financed with a $191,000 federal grant aimed at stemming domestic violence. (Enriquez, 2003, p. B4)

2. ***Establishing recruitment opportunities at community festivals and events:*** The Jacksonville Sheriff's Department and other local and regional law enforcement agencies have used large-size community events as a venue for passing out recruitment brochures and scanning the crowd for potential candidates (Andino, 2002). Events like the World of Nations Festival, which represents more than 40 countries and attracts about 70,000 people across cultural, racial, and ethnic lines, provide opportunities for recruitment. "It's such a wide, diverse group that you might not otherwise get all together in one place," said Wendy Raymond Hacker, a spokeswoman for the city's special events office. Law enforcement agencies see events like this as excellent opportunities

for meeting possible candidates to serve the growing Latino/Hispanic American communities.

SUMMARY OF RECOMMENDATIONS FOR LAW ENFORCEMENT

The experience of Latino/Hispanic Americans with law enforcement officers in the United States has been complicated by the perceptions of Latino/Hispanic Americans regarding the enforcement of immigration laws against undocumented immigrants and/or unauthorized migrants; by the discriminatory treatment received by Latino/Hispanic Americans in the United States; and by community conflicts as well as perceptions of police ineffectiveness and unresponsiveness. Officers should realize that some citizens may still remember this history and carry with them stereotypes of police services as something to be feared and avoided. Law enforcement officials need to go out of their way to establish trust, to provide outreach efforts, and to win cooperation in order to effectively accomplish their goals to serve and protect Latino/Hispanic Americans. Building partnerships focused on community collaboration in the fight against crime is important.

The label Latino/Hispanic American encompasses over 25 very diverse ethnic, cultural, and regional groups from North, Central, and South America. Law enforcement officials must be aware of the differences between the diverse groups (e.g., nationality, native cultural and regional differences and perceptions, and language dialects), as well as the within-group differences that may result from individual life experiences (e.g., sociopolitical turmoil). Since key stereotypes of Latino/Hispanic Americans by mainstream Americans are regarded as more negative than positive, it is important that peace officers make a special effort to extend respect and dignity to this community of very proud people with a culturally rich heritage.

The preferred term for referring to Latino/Hispanic Americans varies with the contexts, groups, and experiences of Latino/Hispanic American individuals. Law enforcement officials must be aware of terms that are unacceptable and derogatory and terms that are currently used. When in doubt, officers have to learn to become comfortable in asking citizens which terms they prefer. Officers are advised to provide helpful feedback to their peers whenever offensive terms, slurs, labels, and/or actions are used with Latino/Hispanic Americans. Such feedback will help reduce the risk of misunderstanding and improve the working relationships of officers within the Latino/Hispanic American communities. Additionally, it will help enhance the professional image of the department for those communities.

Many Latino/Hispanic Americans are concerned with their ability to communicate clearly and about possible reprisal from the police, as associated with the role of law enforcement in more politically repressive countries. Peace officers must take the time needed to understand communications. They must be aware that bilingual and nonnative English speakers want to communicate effectively with them. Maintaining contact, providing extra time, using translators, and being patient with speakers encourage citizens to communicate their concerns. Cultural differences in verbal and nonverbal communication often result in misinterpretation of messages and of behaviors. Officers must recognize the nonverbal aspects of some Latino/Hispanic Americans' communication styles, such as eye contact, touch, gestures, and emotionality. Verbal aspects such as accent, mixing English with Spanish, limited vocabulary, and incorrect grammar may give the officer the impression that the individual does not understand what is communicated. As in all cases when English is the second language, it is important to remember that listening and comprehension skills with English are usually better than speaking skills.

Latino/Hispanic Americans, because of their past experiences with law enforcement agencies, along with their own concerns about privacy, self-help, and other factors, are reluctant to report crimes and may not seek police assistance and help. It is important for law enforcement departments and officials to build relationships and working partnerships with Latino/Hispanic American communities. This effort is helped by outreach efforts such as community offices, bilingual officers, and participation of officers in community activities.

Latino/Hispanic Americans tend to hold a severe, punishment-oriented perception of law enforcement and corrections. That is, citizens have strong authoritarian views and an equally strong sense of "rightness" and of punishing the criminal. Because of this perspective, law enforcement personnel must be aware that members from this community may view law enforcement as more severe than it really is.

DISCUSSION QUESTIONS AND ISSUES*

1. *Latino/Hispanic Americans Viewing Law Enforcement as Not Sensitive.* In the historical information section of this chapter, we noted many associations made about immigration law enforcement and events that may leave Latino/Hispanic Americans with the view that law enforcement agencies are not sensitive, effective, and responsive. What are ways to improve such possible negative points of view?

2. *Diversity among Latino/Hispanic Americans.* Latino/Hispanic Americans consist of over 25 diverse regional, national, ethnic, and cultural groups. Which groups are you most likely to encounter in crime-fighting and peace-keeping in your work? Which groups do you anticipate encountering in your future work?

3. *Choice of Terms.* Use of the terms Latino, Hispanic, Chicano, Mexican, La Raza, Puerto Rican, and so forth is confusing for many people. How might you find out which term to use when referring to an individual if ethnic and cultural information of this kind is necessary? What would you do if the term you use seems to engender a negative reaction?

4. *Offensive Terms and Labels.* Offensive terms such as "Wetbacks," "Illegals," and "Spics" should not be used in law enforcement work at any time. Give three practical reasons for this perspective. How would you go about helping other officers who use these terms in the course of their work to become aware of their offensiveness?

5. *Effects of Myths and Stereotypes.* Myths and stereotypes about Latino/Hispanic Americans have affected this group greatly. What are some of the

*See the Instructor's Manual accompanying this text for additional activities, role-play activities, questionnaires, and projects related to the content of this chapter.

Latino/Hispanic American stereotypes that you have heard of or encountered? What effect might these stereotypes have on Latino/Hispanic Americans? What are ways to manage these stereotypes in law enforcement? In what ways can you help an officer who uses stereotypes about Latino/Hispanic Americans to become aware of the effects of these stereotypes?

6. ***Verbal and Nonverbal Variations among Cultures.*** How do you think the information in this chapter about verbal and nonverbal communication styles can help officers in their approach to Latino/Hispanic American citizens? Does understanding the cultural components of the style and behaviors help you to become more sensitive and objective about your reactions? In what ways might you use your understanding about Latino/Hispanic American family dynamics in law enforcement?

7. ***Avoidance of Law Enforcement and Underreporting of Crimes.*** Why do you think that many Latino/Hispanic Americans keep to their own communities and underreport crimes of violence? When are such efforts desirable? When are they ineffective? How can police agencies be of greater service to Latino/Hispanic American communities in this regard?

8. ***The Future of Latino/Hispanic Americans and Law Enforcement.*** The Latino/Hispanic American population is the fastest growing segment in the U.S. population. What implications do you see for law enforcement in terms of services, language, recruitment, and training?

WEBSITE RESOURCES

Visit these websites for additional information about law enforcement contact with Latino/Hispanic Americans and related community organizations:

National Council of La Raza (NCLR): http://www.latino.sscnet.ucla.edu/community/nclr.html

This website provides information about capacity-building assistance to support and strengthen Hispanic community-based programs and information regarding applied research, policy analysis, and advocacy for Latino/Hispanic Americans.

League of United Latin American Citizens (LULAC): http://www.lulac.org

This website provides information on education, training, scholarships, and services to underprivileged and unrepresented Latino/Hispanic Americans. LULAC is the largest and oldest Latino/Hispanic organization in the United States, with over 115,000 members.

Hispanic American Police Command Officers Association (HAPCOA): http://www.hapcoa.com/

This website provides information to promote the interests of Hispanic American peace officers for recruitment, career development, promotion, and retention of qualified Hispanic police command officers.

Latin American Law Enforcement Association (LALEY): http://www.laley.org/

This website provides law enforcement links important to the Latino/Hispanic American community in the areas of advocacy, education, and leadership, and it identifies key organizations.

Pew Hispanic Center: http://pewhispanic.org/

This website provides law enforcement links important to the Pew Hispanic Center, which is a nonpartisan research organization supported by the Pew Charitable Trusts. Its mission is to improve understanding of the U.S. Hispanic population and to chronicle Latinos' growing impact on the entire nation. The Center does not advocate for or take positions on policy issues.

REFERENCES

Accola, J. (2005, May 21). "Aerospace Firm OKs Discrimination Pact: Hispanics at Plant in Mesa Co. Sued over Racial Slurs." *Rocky Mountain News* (Denver, CO), p. C3.

Andino, A. T. (2002, April 26). "Police to Scan Ethnic Fest for Potential New Recruits." *Florida Times-Union* (Jacksonville, FL), p. B1.

Associated Press. (2001, October 8). "Wanted in Wichita: Bilingual Police Officers."

Associated Press. (2003, June 9). "Durham Civilian Police Academy Caters to Hispanics."

Associated Press. (2005, July 15). "New Study Shows Minorities Face More Stops on Some Illinois Roads."

Barnhardt, L. (2003, July 31). "Latino Activists in County Urge Police Training Aids in Spanish: Fatal Shooting of Honduran Highlights Need, They Say." *Baltimore Sun,* p. B3.

Bernal, G., and A. Estrada. (1985). "Cuban Refugee and Minority Experiences: A Book Review." *Hispanic Journal of Behavioral Sciences, 7,* 105–128.

Bernstein, R. (2005, June 9). "Hispanic Population Passes 40 Million, Census Bureau Reports." Washington, DC: U.S. Census Bureau News.

Bragg, R. (2000, April 23). "The Elian Gonzalez Case: The Overview: Cuban Boy Seized by U.S. Agents and Reunited with His Father," *New York Times,* p. 1.

Bruner, T. K. (2001, October 15). "International Atlanta: Cash in Hand Makes Latinos Robbery Targets: Police, Banks Try to Build Trust." *Atlanta Journal and Constitution,* Metro News, p. B1.

Catalano, S. M. (2005). *Criminal Victimization, 2004.* Washington, D. C.: Bureau of Justice Statistics National Crime Victimization Survey.

Central Intelligence Agency. (2006). *World Fact Book.* Washington, D.C.: Central Intelligence Agency.

Cliatt, C. (2001, September 6). "How Small Steps Healed Town: Innovative Police Outpost Plays Key to Cutting Crime." *Chicago Daily Herald,* p. 1.

Cohn, D. (2005, June 9). "Hispanic Growth Surge Fueled by Births in U.S." *Washington Post,* p. A1.

Comas-Diaz, L., and E. E. H. Griffith (Eds.). (1988). *Cross-Cultural Mental Health.* New York: Wiley.

Crawford, S. (2005, October 3). "Police Say Hispanics Not Reporting Crimes: Fear of Reprisal, Distrust of Cops Cited." *Arkansas Democrat-Gazette* (Little Rock).

Delgado v. *Bastrop Independent School District,* 388 W. D. Texas (1948).

Elber, L. (2001, January 25). "NBC Apologizes for 'Law & Order' Episode That Offended Some Hispanics." Associated Press.

Enriquez, D. (2003, April 10). "Mystery Program Offers Clue About Culture: Waukesha Hispanic Families Get Lessons on Criminal Justice System." *Milwaukee Journal Sentinel,* p. B4.

Environmental Protection Agency. (2001). "Comprehensive Environmental Response, Compensation, and Liability Act Overview." Washington, DC: Author. Available: http://www.epa.gov/superfund/action/law/cercla.htm.

Fernandex, L. F. (1970). *A Forgotten American.* New York: B'nai B'rith.

Fernandez, Donya. (2000, December 20). Language Rights Attorney for the Language Rights Project, Employment Law Center/Legal Aid Society, San Francisco, California, personal communication.

Frago, C. (2001, September 24). "Police Bridge Gap with Latinos: New Outreach Coordinator Juan Sanchiz Will Help Build Trust Between the Burlington Department and Spanish-Speaking Residents." *News & Record* (Greensboro, NC), p. B1.

Fusco, C. (2002, November 14). "Suburb Settles in Profiling Suit: Up to 3,200 Hispanic Motorists May Get as Much as $225 Each." *Chicago Sun-Times,* p. 5.

Gavzer, G. (1993, March 21). "Held without Hope." *Parade.*

Hickman, M. J., and B. A. Reaves. (2006a, May). "Local Police Department, 2003." Bureau of Justice Statistics: Law Enforcement Management and Administrative Statistics.

Hickman, M. J., and B. A. Reaves. (2006b, May). "Sheriffs' Offices, 2003." Bureau of Justice Statistics: Law Enforcement Management and Administrative Statistics.

Hill, L., and R. Trapp. (2000, October 29). "African Americans and Latinos in a San Diego Study." *San Diego Union-Tribune,* p. B11.

Holmberg, M. (2006, April 5). "Robbers Preying on Hispanics," *Richmond Times Dispatch,* p. B1.

Humphreys, J. M. (2003). *The Multicultural Economy 2003: America's Minority Buying Power,* Vol. 63, No. 2. Athens, Ga.: Selig Center for Economic Growth, University Georgia.

Irvin, N. (2006, February 12). "A Story of Success You Can Take to the Bank." *Winston-Salem Journal,* p. 21.

Kelley, T. (2000, October 12). "Suspect Admits Attacking Immigrant." *New York Times,* p. B5.

Korzenny, F., and B. A. Korzenny. (2005). *Hispanic Marketing: A Cultural Perspective.* Burlington, Mass.: Elsevier Butterworth Heinemann.

Lewis, A. (2000, April 29). "Abroad at Home: Elian and the Law." *New York Times,* p. A13.

Lopez y Rivas, G. (1973). *The Chicanos.* New York: Monthly Review Press.

Mendez v. *Westminster,* 64 F. Supp. 544 (D. C. Cal. 1946), aff. d, 161 F. 2d 774 (9th Cir. 1947).

Montiel, M. (1978). *Hispanic Families: Critical Issues for Policy and Programs in Human Services.* Washington, D.C.: Coalition of Spanish-Speaking Mental Health Organizations.

Morales, R., and F. Bonilla (Eds.). (1993). *Latinos in a Changing U.S. Economy.* Newbury Park, Calif.: Sage.

Office of Management and Budget. (1997, October 30). "Revisions to the Standards for the Classification of Federal Data on Race and Ethnicity." *Federal Register,* *62*(280), 58,782–85,790.

Passel, J. S. (2005). *Unauthorized Migrants: Numbers and Characteristics.* Washington, D.C.: Pew Hispanic Center.

Passel, J. S., J., Van Hook, and F. D. Bean. (2004). *Estimates of Legal and Unauthorized Foreign Born Population for the United States and Selected States, Based on Census 2000.* Washington, D.C.: Report to the Census Bureau, Urban Institute.

Reaves, B. A., and L. M. Bauer. (2003, April). "Federal Law Enforcement Officers, 2002." *Bureau of Justice Statistics Bulletin.*

Rennison, C. M. (2002). *Hispanic Victims of Violent Crime, 1990–2000.* Washington, D.C.: Bureau of Justice Statistics Special Report.

Stevens, E. (1973). "Machismo and Marianismo." *Transaction-Society, 10*(6), 57–63.

Synovate (2004). *2004 Hispanic Market Report.* Miami, Fla.: Synovate.

Taylor, L. G. (2000, March 1). "Police Get Crash Course in Minority Relations." *Pittsburgh Post-Gazette,* p. B4.

Therrien, M., and R. R. Ramirez. (2000). "The Hispanic Population in the United States." (Current Population Reports, P20-535). Washington, D.C.: U.S. Census Bureau.

U.S. Bureau of the Census. (2002). *Census 2000 Brief Reports.* Washington, D.C.: U.S. Government Printing Office.

Yankelovich Monitor. (2003). *2003 Yankelovich Monitor Multicultural Marketing Study.* Chapel Hill, N.C.: Yankelovich Monitor.

Chapter 8

Law Enforcement Contact with Arab Americans and Other Middle Eastern Groups

OVERVIEW

This chapter provides specific cultural information on the largest group of Middle Easterners to settle in the United States, Arab Americans. We begin with an explanation of the scope of the term Middle Easterner as it is used in this chapter and provide information briefly on non-Arab Middle Eastern groups. This is followed by a summary of the two major waves of Arab immigration to the United States. The chapter presents demographics and the diversity among Arab Americans as well as information on traditional Arab values and beliefs. The background information leads into a discussion of commonly held stereotypes of Arabs as well as how those stereotypes contributed to anti-Arab incidents and ongoing repercussions since September 11, 2001. Specifically, we share findings from the Vera Institute of Justice research regarding Arab American continuing fears of racial profiling and hate crime victimization. A brief presentation of some aspects of the Islamic religion is included in the chapter, as well as a summary of the commonalities between Islam, Christianity, and Judaism. Elements of family life are presented, including a discussion of the role of the head of the household and issues related to children and "Americanization."

The next section presents various cultural practices and characteristics, including greetings, approach, touching, hospitality, verbal and nonverbal communication, gestures, emotional expressiveness, and general points about English language usage. The final section describes several key concerns for law enforcement, with information on perceptions of police, women and modesty, Arab store-owners in urban areas, and hate crimes against Arab Americans. The chapter summary provides recommendations for improved communication and relationships between law enforcement personnel and Arab American communities.

COMMENTARY

Middle Easterners come to the United States for numerous reasons: to gain an education and begin a career, to escape an unstable political situation in their country of origin, and to invest in commercial enterprises with the goal of gaining legal entry into the country. People in law enforcement continue to have contact with Middle Easterners from a number of different countries. Officers would benefit from having a rudimentary knowledge about past and present world events related to Middle Easterners and should be aware of stereotypes that others hold of them. Attitudes toward Middle Easterners in this country as well as geopolitical events in the Middle East can have implications for law enforcement.

Established Americans of Arab origin are sometimes treated as if they had just come from the Middle East and may be potential terrorists. This perception increased significantly after the terrorist attacks of September 11, 2001, and continues into the present. Stereotypes, which have long been imprinted in people's minds, can and do significantly affect people's perceptions of Arab Americans, whether they are second or third generation or recent refugees.

MIDDLE EASTERNERS AND RELATED TERMINOLOGY DEFINED

Among the general population there is considerable confusion as to who Middle Easterners are and, specifically, who Arabs are. Although commonly thought of as Arabs, Iranians and Turks are not Arabs. Many people assume that all Muslims are Arabs, and vice versa. In fact, many Arabs are also Christians, and the world's Muslim population is actually comprised of dozens of ethnic groups. The largest Muslim population is in Asia, not the Middle East. Nevertheless, the predominant religion among Arabs is Islam, and its followers are called Muslims. They are also sometimes called Moslems, but Muslim is the preferred term because it is closer to the Arabic pronunciation.

The following excerpt is from *100 Questions You Have Always Wanted to Ask about Arab Americans* (Detroit Free Press, 2001); it clears up common confusion around terminology related to Arab Americans.

Should I say Arab, Arabic, or Arabian?

Arab is a noun for a person and is used as an adjective as in "Arab country." Arabic is the name of the language and generally is not used as an adjective. Arabian is an adjective that refers to Saudia Arabia, the Arabian Peninsula, or the "Arabian horse." When ethnicity or nationality are relevant, it is more precise and accurate to specify the country by using Lebanese, Yemeni, or whatever is appropriate.

What all Arabs have in common is the Arabic language, even though spoken Arabic differs among countries (e.g., Algerian Arabic is different from Jordanian Arabic). The following countries constitute the Middle East and are all Arab countries with the exception of three:

• Aden	• Oman
• Bahrain	• Palestinian Authority
• Egypt	• Qatar
• Iran (non-Arab country)	• Saudi Arabia
• Iraq	• Syria
• Israel (non-Arab country)	• Turkey (non-Arab country)
• Jordan	• United Arab Emirates
• Kuwait	• Yemen
• Lebanon	

There are other Arab countries that are not in the Middle East (e.g., Algeria, Tunisia, Morocco, Libya) in which the majority population shares the Arabic language (though a different variety of Arabic) and the religion, Islam, with people in the Arab countries of the Middle East. In this chapter, we cover primarily information on refugees and immigrants from Arab countries in the Middle East. These constitute the majority of Middle Eastern newcomers who bring cultural differences and special issues requiring clarification for law enforcement. We briefly mention issues related to the established Arab American community (i.e., the people who began arriving in the United States in the late 19th century). We begin with a brief description of the population from the three non-Arab countries.

Iranians and Turks

Iranians use the Arabic script in their writing but for the most part speak mainly Farsi (Persian), not Arabic. Turks speak Turkish, although there are minority groups in Turkey who speak Kurdish, Arabic, Greek, and Armenian. More than 99.8 percent of Iranians and Turks are Muslim; Islam is the most common religion among people in many other Middle Eastern countries (Central Intelligence Agency, 2003). Armenians, who are largely Christian, were a persecuted minority in Turkey. The Armenian genocide, between 1915 and 1923, claimed the lives of between 1 and 1.5 million people. Animosity still exists between some Armenians and Turks. As of the writing of this book's fourth edition, Turkey continues to deny that the Armenians were the victims of a genocide during World War I (Armenian National Institute, 2006).

Many Iranians in the United States are Jewish and Bahai, both of which groups are minorities in Iran. Of the Muslim population in Iran, most belong to the Shi'a sect of Islam, the Shi'a version of Islam being the state religion. Persians are the largest ethnic group in Iran, making up about 50 percent of the population (Central Intelligence Agency, 2003), but there are other ethnic populations, including Kurds, Arabs, Turkmen, Armenians, and Assyrians, most of whom can be found in the United States. During the Iranian hostage crisis in 1979, many Iranians in the United States were targets of hate crimes and anti-Iranian sentiment: the same attitudes prevailed against other Middle Easterners (Arabs) and South Asians (Indians from India) who were mistakenly labeled as Iranian. Iranians and Turks are not Arabs, but some of the cultural values related to the extended family with respect to pride, dignity, and honor are similar to those in the traditional Arab world. Many Iranian Americans and Turkish Americans came to the United States in the 1970s and were from upper-class, professional groups such as doctors, lawyers, and engineers. Many of the Jewish Iranians in the United States left Iran after the fall of the Shah. In the United States, there are large Iranian Jewish populations in the San Francisco Bay Area, Los Angeles, and New York. Also, populations of Muslim Iranians are found in major U.S. cities, such as New York, Chicago, and Los Angeles.

Israelis

Israel is the only country in the Middle East in which the majority of the population is not Muslim. Approximately 20 percent of the population in Israel is made up of Arabs, both Christian and Muslim. Approximately three quarters of the Israeli population is

Jewish (Central Intelligence Agency, 2006), with the Jewish population divided into two main groups: Ashkenazim and Sephardim. The Ashkenazim are descended from members of the Jewish communities of Central and Eastern Europe. The majority of American Jews are Ashkenazi, while currently the minority of Israeli Jews (by an increasingly small margin) are Sephardim, having come originally from Spain, other Mediterranean countries, and the Arab countries of the Middle East. Israeli immigrants in the United States may be either Ashkenazi or Sephardic; their physical appearance will not indicate to an officer what their ethnicity is. An Israeli may look like an American Jew, a Christian, or a Muslim Arab—or none of these.

Most of the Israeli Arabs who live within the borders of Israel are Palestinians whose families stayed in Israel after the Arab–Israeli war in 1948, following the birth of Israel as a nation. The Six-Day War in 1967 resulted in the occupation of lands that formerly belonged to Egypt, Syria, and Jordan, but where the majority of the population was Palestinian. Thus, until the signing of the Oslo 1993 peace accords between Israel and the Palestine Liberation Organization (PLO), Israel occupied territories with a population of approximately 1 million Palestinians. The Palestinian–Israeli situation in the Middle East has created a great deal of hostility on both sides. In the fall of 2000, failure to reach a negotiated settlement agreement required by the Oslo peace accords of 1993 resulted in a period of increased hostilities. The tension continued and intensified during what is referred to as the second *intifada* or Palestinian "uprising," which took place between 2001 and 2004. Hostilities continued in 2006 with the outbreak of war involving Israel and Lebanon, associated with the rocket attacks of Hezbollah and Hamas into Israel proper. These political tensions have definite implications for law enforcement officials in the United States, especially in communities where there are large populations of Jews and Arabs, or where Israelis and Palestinians reside in large numbers (e.g., Los Angeles, New York, Chicago). All law enforcement agencies should become knowledgeable of individuals and groups with extremist views who operate in their jurisdiction and region

Public events such as Israeli Independence Day celebrations and Israeli or Palestinian political rallies have the potential for confrontation, although the majority of these events have been peaceful. Police presence is required at such events, but as with other situations, excessive police presence can escalate hostilities. Law enforcement officials need to be well informed about current events in the Middle East as conflicts there often have a ripple effect across the world. The monitoring of world events and community trends will help police officers take a preventive posture that can ultimately help to avoid confrontation among various Middle Eastern ethnic groups in this country.

HISTORICAL INFORMATION

Although many recent Middle Eastern immigrants and refugees in the United States have come for political reasons, not all Arab Americans left their country of origin because of these. There have been two major waves of Arab immigrants to the United States. The first wave came between 1880 and World War I and were largely from Syria and what is known today as Lebanon (at the time these areas were part of the Turkish Ottoman Empire). Of the immigrants who settled during this wave, approximately 90 percent were Christian. Many people came to further themselves economically (thus these were immigrants and not refugees forced to leave their countries), but in addition, many of the young men wanted to avoid the military in the Ottoman Empire (Samhan, 2006). A substantial percentage of these immigrants were farmers and artisans and became involved in the business of peddling their goods to farmers and moved from town to town. In the way of crime statistics, not much is reported, partly because in the Arab immigrant community, people took care of their own. (Samhan, 2006)

In sharp contrast to the characteristics and motivation of the first wave of immigrants, the second wave of Arab immigrants to the United States, beginning after World War II, came in large part as students and professionals because of economic instability and political unrest. As a result, these groups brought a "political consciousness unknown to earlier immigrants." (John Zogby, 2006) The largest group of second-wave immigrants is made up of Palestinians, many of whom came around 1948, the time of the partition of Palestine, which resulted in Israel's independence. In the 1970s, after the Six-Day War between Israel and Egypt, Syria, and Jordan, another large influx of Palestinians came to the United States. In the 1980s, a large group of Lebanese came as a result of the civil war in Lebanon. Yemenis (from Yemen) have continued to come throughout the century; Syrians and Iraqis have made the United States their home since the 1950s and 1960s because of political instability in their countries (John Zogby, 2006). Thus these second-wave immigrants came largely because of political turmoil and have been instrumental in changing the nature of the Arab American community in the United States.

The most dramatic example of how Arab immigration has affected a U.S. city is the Detroit area in Michigan. There Arabs began to arrive in the late 19th century, but the first huge influx was between 1900 and 1924, when the auto industry attracted immigrants from all over the world (Woodruff, 1991). The Detroit–Dearborn area has the largest Arab community in the United States, with Arab Americans constituting about 30 percent of the population in Dearborn. A large percentage of the Detroit area's Middle Eastern population is Chaldean, Christian Iraqis who speak the Chaldean language. While they are from the heart of the Middle East, most do not identify themselves to be Iraqi, and some are deeply offended if referred to as Arab (Haddad, 2006). This is particularly true in the Detroit area, as well as in other large urban concentrations, but may be less applicable to Chaldeans in other areas (Samhan, 2006).

DEMOGRAPHICS

Immigrants from all over the Arab world continue to settle in the United States. For example, in 2000, approximately 12,000 visas (combined total) were issued to immigrants coming to the United States from Bahrain, Egypt, Iraq, Jordan, Kuwait, Lebanon, Qatar, Saudi Arabia, Syria, the United Arab Emirates, and Yemen (Samhan, 2006).

There are approximately 3.5 to 4 million Americans of Arab ancestry in the United States, and the number of people who identified Arab ancestry in the 2000 census is about 1.3 million (Samhan, 2006). The communities with the largest Arab American populations are in Los Angeles/Orange County, Detroit, the greater New York area, Chicago, and Washington, D.C. California has the largest "cluster" of Arab American communities (Samhan, 2006).

After the September 11 attacks, immigration to the United States declined significantly because of the increased security and background checks given to people wishing to come to America ("Immigration Down," 2003, p. A3).

DIFFERENCES AND SIMILARITIES

There is great diversity among Arab American groups. Understanding this diversity will assist officers in not categorizing Arabs as homogeneous and will encourage people to move away from stereotypical thinking. Arabs from the Middle East come from at least 13 different countries, many of which are vastly different from each other. The governments of the Arab countries also differ, ranging from monarchies to theocracies to military governments to socialist republics (Central Intelligence Agency, 2006). Arab visitors such as foreign students, tourists, businesspeople, and diplomats to the United States from the Gulf states (e.g., Saudi Arabia, Qatar, Oman, Bahrain, United Arab Emirates) are typically wealthy, but their Jordanian, Lebanese, and Palestinian brethren do not generally bring wealth to the United States, and in fact, many are extremely poor. Another area of difference is in clothing. In a number of countries in the Middle East, many older men wear headdresses, but it is less common among men who are younger and who have more education. Similarly, younger women in the Middle East may choose not to wear the head covering and long dress that covers them from head to toe.

The younger generation of Arabs, much to the disappointment of the parents and grandparents, may display entirely different behavior from what is expected of them (as is typical in most immigrant and refugee groups). In addition, as with other immigrant groups, there are Arab Americans who have been in the United States for generations who have completely assimilated into the American culture. Consequently, they may not identify in any way with their roots. Others, although they have also been in the United States for generations, consciously try to keep their Arab traditions alive and pass them on to their children. Officers should not treat established Arab Americans as if they were newcomers.

There are broad differences among Arab American groups associated with social class and economic status. Although many Arab Americans who come to the United States are educated professionals, there is a percentage who come from rural areas (e.g., peasants from southern Lebanon, West Bank Palestinians, Yemenis) and who differ in outlook and receptiveness to modernization. On the other hand, despite traditional values, many newcomers are modern in outlook. Many people have a stereotypical image of the Arab woman, yet many women of Arab descent do not adhere to this image. John Zogby, president of Zogby International, describes many modern Arab women who defy the stereotype: "Among the upper-class, educated Palestinian population, for example, you can find many women who are vocal and outspoken. You might see the young husbands wheeling the babies around in strollers while the women are discussing world events" (John Zogby, 2006).

On the other hand, certain Arab governments (e.g., Saudi Arabia) place restrictions on women, mandating that they do not mix with men, that a woman must always be veiled, and that she not travel alone or drive a car. Women from less restrictive Arab countries (e.g., Egypt and Jordan) might exhibit very different behavior from those whose governments grant them fewer freedoms. Nevertheless, women in traditional Muslim families from any country typically have limited contact with men outside their family and wear traditional dress. Some implications of these traditions, as they relate to Arab women and male police officers in the United States, are discussed further in this chapter.

It is important to look at people's motivation for coming to the United States to help avoid stereotypical thinking. Arab American police Corporal Mohamed Berro of the Dearborn, Michigan, Police Department makes a distinction between immigrants (who have "few problems adjusting to the United States") and refugees. He explains that refugees, having been forced to leave their country of origin, believe that they are here temporarily because they are waiting for a conflict to end. As a result, they may be more hesitant to change and relationship building may take more time (Berro, 2006).

Similarities

Despite most differences, whether apparent in socioeconomic status, levels of traditionalism, or motivation for coming to the United States, there are values and beliefs associated with Arab culture that law enforcement officials should understand in order to establish rapport and trust. Officers will recognize that some of the information listed below does not only apply to Arab culture. At the same time, the following will help officers understand deeply held beliefs that many Arab Americans would agree are key to understanding traditional Arab culture.

Basic Arab Values

1. Traditional Arab society upholds honor; the degree to which an Arab can lose face and be shamed publicly is foreign to the average Westerner. Officers recognize that dignity and respect should be shown to all individuals, but citizens from cultures emphasizing shame, loss of face, and honor (e.g., Middle Eastern, Asian, Latin American) may react even more severely to loss of dignity and respect than do other individuals. People will go so far to avoid shame that they will not report crimes. "It is often difficult to get members of Arab communities to be full-fledged complainants, because they either don't complain in the first place, or do not follow through. Therefore, because of their primary concern to save face, avoid shame, and maintain harmony, it becomes more difficult to gain successful prosecution" (Haddad, 2006). Keep in mind that "shame" cultures have sanctioned extreme punishments for loss of face and honor (e.g., death if a woman loses her virginity before marriage).

2. Loyalty to one's family takes precedence over other personal needs. A person is completely intertwined with his or her family; protection and privacy in a traditional Arab family often overrides relationships with other people. Members of Arab families tend to avoid disagreements and disputes in front of others, many preferring to resolve issues themselves (Haddad, 2006).

3. Communication should be courteous and hospitable, and harmony between individuals is emphasized. Too much directness and candor can be interpreted as extremely impolite. From a traditional Arab view, it may not be appropriate for a person to give totally honest responses if they result in a loss of face, especially for self or family members (this may not apply to many established Arab Americans). From this perspective, the higher goals of honor and face-saving are operative. This aspect of cross-cultural communication is not easily understood by most Westerners and is often criticized. Certainly, officers will not accept anything but the whole truth, despite arguments rationalized by cultural

ideals having to do with face and shame. However, it may not lead an officer to draw attention explicitly to a face-saving style. The officer would be well advised to work around the issue of the indirect communication rather than insinuating that the citizen may not be honest.

STEREOTYPES

The Arab world has been perceived in the West in terms of negative stereotypes, and these have been transferred to Americans of Arab descent. Prejudice against Arabs based on stereotypes has been constant for decades. As with all distorted information about ethnic groups, it is important that police officers understand how stereotypes interfere with a true understanding of a people. For some people, the word *Arab* brings several images to mind: (1) wealthy sheik despite the class distinctions in the Middle East between, for example, a wealthy Gulf Arab sheik and a poor Palestinian or Lebanese; (2) violent terrorist (the majority of Arabs worldwide want peace and do not see terrorism as an acceptable means for achieving peace); (3) sensuous harem owner; man with many wives (harems are rare and for the most part, polygamy, or having more than one wife, has been abolished in the Arab world); and (4) ignorant, illiterate, and backward. Arab contributions to civilization have been significant in numerous areas, including mathematics, astronomy, medicine, architecture, geography, and language, but the West is largely unfamiliar with those contributions. Despite these stereotypes, there are high-profile Arab Americans in all sectors of the professional world. Since the first edition of this book in 1995, sizeable percentages of Arab Americans have moved out of marginal urban areas and into the suburbs (James Zogby, 2006). Organizations like the National Arab American Medical Association and the Michigan Arab American Legal Society have highly respected and substantial memberships (Haddad, 2006).

Movies and Television

Perhaps the most offensive type of Arab stereotypes comes from the media; programs and movies routinely portray Arabs as evil womanizers, wealthy oil sheiks who wear turbans, thieves, and terrorists. Even films and programs aimed at children propagate this stereotype of the Arab as a villain. The original lyrics of the opening song of Disney's *Aladdin,* "Arabian Nights," are sung by an Arab who has been portrayed as a stereotype: "Oh I come from a land, from a faraway place / Where the caravan camels roam / Where they cut off your ear if they don't like your face / It's barbaric, but hey, it's home" (Shaheen, 2001, p. 51).

Because many Americans do not know Arabs personally, media images become embedded in people's minds. Jack Shaheen, author of *Reel Bad Arabs: How Hollywood Vilifies a People* (2001), writes, "By depicting Arabs solely as slimy, shifty, violent creeps, Hollywood has been not only misrepresenting the Arab world, but also creating a climate for hate" (Shaheen, 2001).

Shaheen argues that the atmosphere created by Hollywood contributed to the recorded 326 hate crimes against Arab Americans in the first month alone following the terrorist attacks. Though military retaliations after the attacks were labeled "antiter-rorist" rather than "anti-Islamic," the movie industry has continued the negative stereo-typing of Arabs and Muslims. In Shaheen's view, "There certainly should be movies based on what happened, but if [images of Arabs as terrorists] are the only images we see from now on, if we continue to vilify all Muslims and all Arabs as terrorists instead of making clear this is a lunatic fringe, what are we accomplishing?" (Shaheen, 2001). He adds that the more a people is defamed, the easier it is to "deny them civil rights and no one will say anything. Look at all the hate crimes since [9/11]. Could it be that stereotypes in part played a role?" (Shaheen, 2001).

While some filmmakers and studios have become more sensitive to the potential they have in terms of perpetrating stereotypes, a number of Muslim and Arab American organizations feel that there is room for improvement.

The "Terrorist" Stereotype and Post-9/11 Backlash

Images of those responsible for the attacks of September 11, 2001, were eerily similar to the terrorist image described previously. The backlash that ensued against Arab Americans, Muslim Americans, and those thought to be of Middle Eastern origin was predicted by many organizations and individuals, including critics of the media's stereotyped image of a Middle Easterner as a terrorist. Even prior to the attacks, Arabs were labeled as terrorists. A most convincing example of the persistence of discrimina-tion against Arabs occurred after the Oklahoma City bombing in April 1995. Immedi-ately following the bombing, many journalists and political leaders said that the tragedy appeared to be the work of Muslim terrorists. This was the initial conclusion without any supporting evidence; the arrest and conviction of Timothy J. McVeigh proved them wrong. The paranoia that led to the conclusion of Arab involvement in the bombing gave way to Arab-bashing, including many hate calls to Arabs. The scape-goating against Arabs spread pervasively across the country.

The justifiable rage that ensued after September 11, 2001, turned into general Arab- and Muslim-bashing; thus predictions made by representatives of Arab Amer-ican and Muslim American organizations became a reality. Within the first 9 weeks following the attacks, there were more than 700 reported violent crimes against Arab Americans and Muslim Americans, or those who were perceived to be. Even Sikhs, who may be dark-skinned and wear turbans but are neither Muslim nor of Middle Eastern descent, were targets and victims of hate crimes in the aftermath of the attacks.

After September 11, the government instituted new emergency legislation aimed at avenging the terrorist attacks and also at preventing future ones. Such measures al-lowed law enforcement officials to search homes without a warrant and to detain sus-pects without due cause. Other measures included a more stringent tracking of international students in the United States, registration of foreign nationals (non-U.S. citizens), and Operation TIPS (Terrorist Information and Prevention System), which many viewed as encouragement of low-level espionage. The Attorney General also requested "voluntary" interviews with thousands of young Arab men (discussed fur-ther in Chapter 11). From the Arab American community's perspective, these were acts of organized racial profiling by government officials who appeared to define young Arab men as inherently dangerous. This was a very controversial program and was discontinued.

In addition to feeling targeted by the government, a November/December 2001 poll by Zogby International found that 57 percent of American Muslims felt that the attitude of Americans toward Muslims or Arabs after September 11 was somewhat or very unfavorable, compared to 37 percent who felt somewhat or very favorable attitudes from Americans. Zogby International reports that the majority of reported discrimination was against young immigrants, with a large proportion of incidents against young women. Indeed, a CNN/USA Today/Gallup poll conducted immediately following the attacks found that 60 percent of Americans believed there should be more intensive security checks for Arab Americans wishing to fly on American planes, and 50 percent of Americans believed that *all* Arab Americans should be required to carry a special form of identification ("Who are Arab Americans?," 2001). The terrorist stereotype seemed to overpower the words denouncing the attacks by Muslim American and Arab American leaders. In fact, the Zogby International Poll also found that Muslim Americans gave President George W. Bush a 58 percent approval rating for handling the attacks and 41 percent of those interviewed felt more patriotic after the attacks (compared to 5 percent who felt less patriotic and 56 percent who felt the same). "I know I speak for millions of Muslims in this country," writes freelance writer Mona Elahawy, "when I say I feel a disconnect between what our beliefs and lives are actually like and what we hear they are like in government statements and news reports" ("All Muslims," 2003, p. 9).

ISLAMIC RELIGION

Misunderstanding between Americans and Arabs or Arab Americans can often be traced, in part, to religious differences and to a lack of tolerance of these differences. Islam is practiced by most Middle Eastern newcomers to the United States as well as by many African Americans. Many Arab Americans (especially those from the first wave of Arab immigration) are Christian, however, and prefer that others do not assume they are Muslim simply because they are Arabs.

Muslims refers to the people who practice the religion, which is called Islam. By and large, most Americans do not understand what Islam is and, because of stereotyping, wrongly associate Muslims with terrorists or fanatics. Many, but by no means all, Arab Muslims in the United States are religious and have held on to traditional aspects of their religion, which are also intertwined with their way of life. However, some Muslims only attend a mosque on holy days. Islam means submission to the will of God and for traditional, religious Muslims, the will of God (or fate) is a central concept. The religion has been called Mohammedanism, which is an incorrect name for the religion because it suggests that Muslims worship Mohammed* rather than God (Allah). It is believed that God's final message to man was revealed to the prophet Mohammed. *Allah* is the shortened Arabic word for the God of Abraham, and it is used by both Arab Muslims and Arab Christians.

*An alternate spelling is Muhammad, which is closer to the Arabic pronunciation of the name.

The Qur'an (Koran) and the Pillars of Islam

The Qur'an is the holy text for Muslims, and is regarded as the word of God (Allah). There are five Pillars of Islam, or central guidelines, that form the framework of the religion:

1. Profession of faith in Allah (God)
2. Prayer five times daily
3. Alms giving (concern for the needy)
4. Fasting during the month of Ramadan (sunrise to sunset)
5. Pilgrimage to Mecca (in Saudi Arabia) at least once in each person's lifetime

There are several points where law enforcement officials can show respect for a Muslim's need to practice his or her religion. The need to express one's faith in God and to be respected for it is one area. Usually, people pray together as congregations in mosques, the Islamic equivalent of a church or synagogue. People, however, can pray individually if a congregation is not present. Religious Muslims in jails, for example, will continue to pray five times a day and should not be ridiculed or prevented from doing so. Remember that prayer, five times a day, is a "pillar" of Islam and that strict Muslims will want to uphold this "command" no matter where they are. Call to prayer takes place at the following times:

- One hour before sunrise
- At noon
- Midafternoon
- Sunset
- Ninety minutes after sunset

Taboos in the Mosque

A police officer conveys respect to a Muslim community if he or she can avoid, where possible, entering a mosque and interrupting prayers (emergencies may occasionally make this impossible). Religion is vital in Arab life; one of the quickest ways to build rapport with the Muslim community is to show respect for Islamic customs and beliefs. Thus, other than in emergency situations, officers are advised to:

- Avoid entering a mosque, or certainly the prayer room of a mosque, during prayers.
- Never step on a prayer mat or rug with shoes on.
- Never place the Qur'an on the floor or put anything on top of it.
- Avoid walking in front of people who are praying.
- Speak softly while people are praying.
- Dress conservatively (both men and women are required to dress conservatively; shorts are not appropriate).
- Invite people out of a prayer area to talk to them.

Proper protocol in a mosque (also referred to as a *masjid*) requires that people remove their shoes before entering, but this must be left to the officer's discretion. Officer safety, of course, comes before consideration of differences.

Ramadan: The Holy Month

One of the holiest periods in the Islamic religion is the celebration of Ramadan, which lasts for one month. There is no fixed date because, like the Jewish and Chinese calendars, the Islamic calendar is based on the lunar cycle (related to the phases of the moon) and dates vary from year to year. During the month of Ramadan, Muslims do not eat, drink, or smoke from sunrise to sunset. Muslims fast during Ramadan in order to practice self-discipline and to experience and demonstrate unity with Muslims all over the world who identify with their religion. On the 29th night of Ramadan, when there is a new moon, the holiday is officially over. The final fast is broken and for up to 3 days, people celebrate with a feast and other activities. Throughout the month of Ramadan, Muslim families tend to pray more often in the mosque than during other parts of the year.

For Muslims, Ramadan is as important and holy as Christmas; this fact is appreciated when others, who are not Muslim, recognize the holiday's importance. One city with a sizable Arab American population puts up festive lights in its business district during Ramadan as a gesture of acceptance and appreciation of the diversity that the Arab Americans bring to the city. The Arab American community reacted favorably to this symbolic gesture. Meanwhile, in the same city, at the end of Ramadan, while many families were in the mosque, police ticketed hundreds of cars that were parked in store parking lots across from the mosque, even though, according to some Arab American citizens, the stores were closed. When people came out of the mosque and saw all the tickets, the mood of the holiday naturally was spoiled. The perception from the Arab American citizens was that "They don't want to understand us . . . they don't know how we feel . . . they don't know what's important to us." (Readers can analyze this situation from an enforcement and community relations' point of view and discuss whether the situation could have been prevented. See question 1 in the discussion section at the end of the chapter.)

Knowledge of Religious Practices

Knowledge of religious practices, including what is considered holy, will help officers avoid creating problems and conflicts. A belief in the Islamic religion that may occasionally arise in the course of police work will illustrate this point. In a suburb of San Francisco, California, a group of police officers and Muslims (from Tunisia, an Arab country in North Africa) were close to violence when, in a morgue, police entered to try to get a hair sample from a person who had just been killed in a car accident. Apparently, the body had already been blessed by an *Imam* (a religious leader) and, according to the religion, any further contact would have been a defilement of the body since the body had already been sanctified and was ready for burial. The police officers were merely doing what they needed to do to complete their investigation and were unaware of this taboo. This, together with a language barrier, created an extremely confusing and confrontational situation in which officers lost necessary control. In this case they needed to explain what had to be done and communicate their needs in the form of a request for permission to handle a body that had already been sanctified. If the citizens had not granted permission, the police would then have had to decide how to proceed. Most members of the Arab American community would comply with the wishes of police officers. As in many other situations involving police–citizen communication, the initial approach sets the tone for the entire interaction.

Similarities between Christianity, Judaism, and Islam

In reading the above tenets of the Muslim faith, notice that there are certain practices and aspects of Islam also found in Christianity and Judaism. All three religions are monotheistic, that is, each has a belief in one God. Followers of the religions believe that God is the origin of all, and is all-knowing as well as all-powerful. Because God is merciful, it is possible for believers to be absolved of their sins, though the practices for obtaining absolution vary in the different ideologies. All three religions have a Holy Book central to the faith: Judaism has the Torah (the first five books of the Old Testament), Christianity the Bible, and Islam the Qur'an (Koran). All three religions regard their texts to be either the direct word of God, or inspired by the word of God. There are similarities between the three books. For example, the concept of the Ten Commandments is present in each. All three contain stories about many of the same people, such as Adam, Noah, Abraham, Moses, David, and Solomon. The Bible and Qur'an also both contain stories about Mary, Jesus, and John the Baptist. The oral reading or recitation of each book constitutes part of regular worship. Prophets exist in each tradition and are revered as those who transmit the word of God to the people. Chronologically, Judaism became a religion first, followed by Christianity and then Islam. Islam builds upon the foundations of the previous ones and believes in the authenticity of the prophets of earlier books. For example, Islamic belief sees both Moses and Jesus as rightful prophets and as precursors to Mohammed, who is believed to be the final prophet of God. As there are different interpretations of Christianity and Judaism, so too do followers of Islam interpret the religion in different ways. Differing readings of the Qur'an can lead to more or less tolerance within the religion. Lastly, both the Islamic and Judeo-Christian traditions are said to stem from the same lineage; Abraham was father to both Isaac, whose progeny became the people of Israel, and Ishmael, who started the Arab lineage.

FAMILY STRUCTURE

Arab Americans typically have close-knit families in which family members have a strong sense of loyalty and fulfill obligations to all members, including extended family (aunts, uncles, cousins, grandparents). Traditionally minded families also believe strongly in the family's honor, and members try to avoid any behavior that will bring shame or disgrace to the family. The operating unit for Arab Americans (and this may be less true for people who have been in the United States for generations) is not the individual but the family. Thus if a person behaves inappropriately, the entire family is disgraced. Similarly, if a family member is assaulted (in the Arab world), there would be some type of retribution. For the police officer, three characteristics of the Arab family will affect his or her interaction with family members:

- Extended family members are often as close as the "nuclear family" (mother, father, children) and are not seen as secondary family members. If there is a police issue, officers can expect that many members of the family will become involved in the matter. Although officers might perceive this as interference, from an Arab cultural perspective, it is merely involvement and concern. The numbers of people involved are not meant to overwhelm an officer.

- Family loyalty and protection is seen as one of the highest values of family life. Therefore, shaming, ridiculing, insulting, or criticizing family members, especially in public, can have serious consequences.

- Newer Arab American refugees or immigrants may be reluctant to accept police assistance. Because families are tightly knit, they can also be closed "units" whereby members prefer to keep private matters or conflicts to themselves. As a result, officers will have to work harder at establishing rapport if they want to gain cooperation.

There is an important point of contact between all three of these characteristics and law enforcement interaction with members of Arab American families. Berro explains: "When we respond to a call at a home, the police car is like a magnet. Every family member comes out of the house and everyone wants to talk at once. It can be an overwhelming sensation for an officer who doesn't understand this background" (Berro, 2006).

A police officer who is not trained in understanding and responding appropriately and professionally to cultural differences could alienate the family by (1) not respecting the interest and involvement of the family members, and (2) attempting to gain control of the communication in an authoritarian and offensive manner. The consequences may be that he or she would have difficulty establishing the rapport needed to gain information about the conflict at hand and would then not be trusted or respected. To do the job effectively, law enforcement officials must respect Arab family values, along with communication style differences (the latter is discussed shortly).

Head of the Household

As in most cultures with a traditional family structure, the man in the Arab home is overtly the head of the household and his role and influence are strong. The wife has a great deal of influence, too, but it can often be more "behind the scenes." An Arab woman does not always defer to her husband in private as she would in public. However, as mentioned earlier in the chapter, there are many women who have broken out of the traditional mold and tend to be more vocal, outspoken, and assertive than their mothers or grandmothers. Traditionally, in many Arab countries, some fathers maintain their status by being strict disciplinarians and demanding absolute respect, thus creating some degree of fear among children and even among wives. Once again, Arab Americans born and raised in this country have, for the most part, adopted middle-class "American" styles of child-raising whereby children participate in some of the decision making and are treated in an egalitarian manner just as an adult would be. In addition, as with changing roles among all kinds of families in the United States, the father as traditional head of the household and the mother as having "second-class" status is not prevalent among established Arab Americans in the United States. Wife abuse and child abuse are not considered respectable practices by educated Arab Americans, but the practice still occurs, just as it does in mainstream American society (particularly, but not exclusively, among people on the lower socioeconomic levels).

In traditional Arab society, displays of power and influence are common male behavioral characteristics. While this can be viewed in a negative light, from certain Western perspectives, this trait can be helpful in securing the compliance of the family in important matters. The husband or father can be a natural ally of authorities. Officers would be well advised to work with both the father and the mother, for example, in matters where children are involved. On family matters the woman frequently is the authority, even if she seems to defer to her husband. Communicating with the woman, even if indirectly, while still respecting the father's need to maintain his public status, will win respect from both the man and the woman.

Children and Americanization

Americanization, the process of becoming "American" in behavior, attitudes, and beliefs, has always been an issue with refugees/immigrants and their children. Typically, children are better able than their parents to learn a language and pick up the nuances of a culture. In addition, peer influence and pressure in American society begin to overshadow parental control, especially beginning in the pre-teen years. Arab children, who are cherished by their parents, face an extremely difficult cultural gap with their parents if they reach a stage where they are more "American" than "Arab." Children in Arab families are taught to be respectful in front of parents and to be conscious of family honor. Parents do not consider certain aspects of Americanized behavior, in general, to be respectful or worthy of pride. When children exhibit certain behaviors that bring shame to the family, discipline can indeed be harsh.

In extreme and infrequent cases, shame to the family can result in crimes against the children, involving violence. A police officer in a Midwest police department described a case in which a father shot his daughter because she had a boyfriend (Arab women are not allowed to associate freely with men before marriage and are expected to remain virgins). This case does not suggest that violent crime, in the Arab cultural context, is an appropriate response. Mental problems or drugs and alcohol accompany most violent acts. However, when a child's (and especially a girl's) behavior involves what is seen as sexual misconduct, the family's "face" is ruined. When this happens, *all* members of the family suffer. Culturally, when a crime is committed by a family member, there is great shame that colors the reputation of the entire family (Ismail, 2006).

There is very little an officer can do to change the attitudes of parents who oppose their children's behavior. However, if an officer responds to calls during which he or she notices that the family has become dysfunctional because of children's behavior, it would be a service to the family to initiate some sort of social service intervention or make a referral. If a family is already at the point of needing police assistance in problems involving children and their parents, then more likely than not, they need other types of assistance as well. At the same time, newer immigrants and refugees will not necessarily be open to social service interventions, especially if the social workers do not speak Arabic. On the other hand, according to Lobna Ismail, President of Connecting Cultures, a training and consulting company, some individuals may end up revealing more information to people outside the community even if it means having to speak in English. This is because the refugee or immigrant may be concerned about a loss of face or shame on the family if something were revealed to fellow community members (Ismail, 2006).

CULTURAL PRACTICES

As with all other immigrant groups, the degree to which people preserve their cultural practices varies. The following descriptions of everyday behavior will not apply equally to all Arab Americans, but they do not necessarily apply only to newcomers. Immigrants may preserve traditions and practices long after they come to a new country by conscious choice or sometimes because they are unaware of their cultural behavior (i.e., it is not in their conscious awareness).

Greetings, Approach, Touching

Most Arab American newcomers expect to be addressed with a title and their last name (e.g., Mr. or Miss followed by the last name) although in many Arab countries, people are addressed formally by a title and their first name. Most Arab women do not change their names after they are married or divorced. They therefore may not understand the distinction between a maiden name and a married name. The usual practice is to keep their father's last name for life (Boller, 1992).

Many Arab Americans who have retained their traditional customs shake hands and then place their right hand on their chest near the heart. In the Middle East, Americans are advised to do the same if they observe this gesture. This gesture signifies warmth and sincerity. Officers can decide whether they are comfortable using this gesture—most people would not expect it from an officer, but some might appreciate the gesture as long as the officer was able to convey sincerity. Generally, when Arabs from the Middle East shake hands, they do not shake hands briefly and firmly. (The expression "He shakes hands like a dead fish" does not apply to other cultural groups!) Traditional Arab style is to hold hands longer than other Americans and shake hands more lightly. Older children are taught to shake hands with adults as a sign of respect. Many Arabs would appreciate an officer shaking hands with their older children. With a recent immigrant or refugee Arab woman, it is generally not appropriate to shake hands unless she extends her hand first. This would definitely apply to women who wear head coverings.

Many Arabs of the same sex greet each other by kissing on the cheek. Two Saudi Arabian men, for example, may greet each other by kissing on both cheeks a number of times. This is a completely common form of greeting. Public touching of the opposite sex is forbidden in the traditional Arab world and officers should make every effort not to touch Arab women, even casually (discussed further under "Key Issues in Law Enforcement").

Police officers should be aware that some Arab American citizens (e.g., Lebanese) who are new to the United States may react to a police officer's approach in an unexpected way. For example, an officer who has just asked a person to give his driver's license may find that this person will then get out of his car in order to be able to talk to the officer. From the person's perspective, he or she is simply trying to be courteous (since this is done in the home country). An officer, always conscious of safety issues, may simply have to explain that in the United States, officers require citizens to remain in their cars.

Hospitality

Hospitality is a byword among Arabs, whatever their station in life. As a guest in their homes, you will be treated to the kindest and most lavish consideration. Hospitality in the Arab culture is not an option; it is more an obligation or duty. In some parts of the Arab world, if you thank someone for their hospitality, they may answer with a common expression meaning, "Don't thank me. It's my duty." (Here the word *duty* has a more positive than negative connotation.) To be anything but hospitable goes against the grain of Arab culture. Officers need to understand how deeply ingrained the need to be hospitable is and not to misinterpret this behavior for something that it is not. Whether entering a home or a business owner's shop or office, an Arab American may very well offer coffee and something to eat. This is not to be mistaken for a bribe and, from the Arab perspective, carries no negative connotations. According to Berro (2006), most people would be offended if you did not accept their offers of hospitality. However, given police regulations, you may have to decline. If this is the case, Berro advises that officers decline graciously. On the other hand, if the decision to accept the Arab American's hospitality depends on the officer's discretion, accepting can also be good for police–citizen relations. The period of time spent socializing and extending one's hospitality gives the person a chance to get to know and see if he or she can trust the other person. Business is not usually conducted among strangers. Obviously, on an emergency call, there is no time for such hospitality. However, with the move toward increasing community-based police organizations, officers may find that they are involved in more situations in which they may decide to accept small gestures of hospitality, if within departmental policy.

Verbal and Nonverbal Communication

Arabs in general are very warm and expressive people, both verbally and nonverbally, and appreciate it when others extend warmth to them. There are some areas in the realm of nonverbal communication in which Americans, without cultural knowledge, have misinterpreted the behavior of Arab Americans simply because of their own ethnocentrism (i.e., the tendency to judge others by one's own cultural standards and norms).

Conversational distance. Acceptable conversational distance between two people is often related to cultural influences. Officers are very aware of safety issues and keep a certain distance from people when communicating with them. Generally, officers like to stand about an arm's length or farther from citizens to avoid possible assaults on their person. This distance is similar to how far apart "mainstream Americans" stand when in conversation. Cultures subtly influence the permissible distance between two people. When the distance is "violated," a person can feel threatened (either consciously or unconsciously). Many but not all Arabs, especially if they are new to the country, tend to have a closer acceptable conversational distance with each other than do other Americans. In Arab culture, it is not considered offensive to "feel a person's breath." Yet many Americans, unfamiliar with this intimacy in regular conversation, have misinterpreted the closeness. While still conscious of safety, the law enforcement officer can keep in mind that the closer than "normal" behavior (i.e., "normal" for the officer) does not necessarily constitute a threat.

When Americans travel to the Middle East, they will notice the tendency for people to stand quite close to each other as compared to mainstream U.S. cultural norms. This is relevant to police officers in the United States, especially in conjunction with communication with recent immigrants and refugees. (It is recommended that you not back away when an Arab stands very close while speaking to you in order to maintain rapport.) Some Arabs may stare into other people's eyes, watching the pupils for an indication of the other person's response (i.e., dilated pupils mean a positive response). Police officers, however, should avoid staring directly into a woman's eyes.

Gestures. Many gestures used by Arabs from some countries are distinctly different from those familiar to non-Arab Americans. In a section entitled "Customs and Manners in the Arab World," Devine and Braganti (1991, p. 13) describe some commonly used gestures among Arabs:

- *What does it mean?* or *What are you saying?* Hold up the right hand and twist it as if you were screwing in a light bulb one turn.
- *Wait a minute.* Hold all fingers and thumb touching with the palm up.
- *No.* This can be signaled in one of three ways: moving the head back slightly and raising the eyebrows, moving the head back and raising the chin, or moving the head back and clicking with the tongue.
- *Go away.* Hold the right hand out with the palm down and move it as if pushing something away from you.
- *Never.* A forceful never is signaled by holding the right forefinger up and moving it from left to right quickly and repeatedly.

As with many other cultural groups, pointing a finger directly at someone is considered rude.

Emotional Expressiveness

When I came to my brother's house to see what the problem was [i.e., with the police], I asked, "What the hell is going on?" I held my hands out and talked with my hands as I always do. I repeated myself and continued to gesture with my hands. Later (i.e., at a trial) the police officer said that the Arab woman was yelling and screaming and acting wild, waving her arms and inciting observers to riot by her actions.*

The Arab American involved in the above situation explained that Arab women, in particular, are very emotional and that police sometimes see this emotionalism as a threat. She explained that upon seeing a family member in trouble, it would be most usual and

---

*The names of individuals and departments have been omitted even though permission has been granted to quote. The purpose of including these incidents is not to put undue attention on any one department or individual but rather to provide education on police professionalism in interethnic relations.

natural for a woman to put her hands to her face and say something like, "Oh, my God" frequently and in a loud voice. While other Americans can react this same way, it is worth pointing out that in mainstream American culture, there is a tendency to subdue one's emotions and not to go "out of control." What some Americans consider to be "out of control," Arabs (like Mexicans, Greeks, Israelis, and Iranians, among other groups) consider to be perfectly "normal" behavior. In fact, the lack of emotionalism that Arabs observe among mainstream Americans can be misinterpreted as lack of interest or involvement.

Although a communication-style characteristic never applies to all people in one cultural group (and we have seen that there is a great deal of diversity among Arab Americans), there are group traits that apply to many people. Arabs, especially the first generation of relatively recent newcomers, tend to display emotions when talking. Unlike many people in Asian cultures (e.g., Japanese and Korean), Arabs have not been "taught" that the expression of emotion is a sign of immaturity or a lack of control. Arabs, as other Mediterranean groups, such as Israelis or Greeks, tend to shout when they are excited or angry and are very animated in their communication. They may repeatedly insert expressions into their speech such as, "I swear by God." This is simply a cultural mannerism.

Westerners, however, tend to judge this "style" negatively. To a Westerner, the emotionalism, repetition, and emphasis on certain statements can give the impression that the person is not telling the truth or is exaggerating for effect. An officer unfamiliar with these cultural mannerisms may feel overwhelmed, especially when involved with an entire group of people. It would be well worth it for the officer to determine the spokesperson for the group, but to refrain from showing impatience or irritation at this culturally different style. The following comment was made by an Arab American community member (who prefers not to be identified) about police reactions to Arab Americans:

> Police see Arab emotionalism as a threat. They see the involvement of our large families in police incidents as a threat. They don't need to feel overwhelmed by us and try to contain our reactions. We will cooperate with them, but they need to show us that they don't view us as backward and ignorant people who are inferior just because we are different and because we express ourselves in a more emotional way than they do. . . . (Arab American community member)

Swearing, obscenities, and insults. Officers working in Arab American communities should know that for Arabs, words are extremely powerful. If an officer displays a lack of professionalism by swearing at an Arab (even words like "damn"), it will be nearly impossible to repair the damage.

In one case of documented police harassment of several Arab Americans (names have been omitted in order not to single out this department), witnesses attest to officers' saying, "Mother-f_____ Arabs, we're going to teach you. Go back home!" One of the Arab American citizens involved in the case reported that officers treated him like an animal and were very insulting by asking in a demeaning tone questions such as, "Do you speak English? Do you read English?" (The man was a highly educated professional who had been in the United States for several years.) In asking him about his place of employment (he worked at an Arab American organization), the man reported that they referred to his place of employment as "the Arab Islamic shit or crap? What is that?"

Officers who understand professionalism are aware that this type of language and interaction is insulting to all persons. The choice to use obscenities and insults, especially in conjunction with one's ethnic background, however, means that officers risk never being able to establish trust within the ethnic community. This can translate into not being able to secure cooperation when needed. Even a few officers exhibiting this type of behavior can damage the reputation of an entire department for a long period of time.

English language problems. If time allows, before asking the question, "Do you speak English?" officers should try to assess whether the Arab American is a recent arrival or an established citizen who might react negatively to the question. A heavy accent does not necessarily mean that a person is unable to speak English (although that can be the case). There are specific communication skills that can be used with limited-English-speaking persons (see Chapter 4) that should be applied with Arab Americans. Officers should proceed slowly and nonaggressively with questioning and wherever possible, ask open-ended questions. An officer's patience and willingness to take extra time will be beneficial in the long run.

KEY ISSUES IN LAW ENFORCEMENT

Perceptions of and Relationships and Interactions with Police

It is not possible to generalize Arab Americans' perception of the police. As mentioned earlier, the Arab immigrants who came in the late 19th century through World War II had the Turkish military police with whom to compare the American police. Their experiences, then, in the United States were largely positive and they were cooperative with police. Since the majority of Arab Americans today are from that wave of immigrants, it is fair to say that a large part of the Arab American community does respect the police. On the other hand, some of the immigrants, such as Jordanians and Palestinians, do not understand the American system and have an ingrained fear of police because of political problems in their own region of the world (James Zogby, 2006). Since they distrust government, they are more likely to reject help from the police and this puts them at a decided disadvantage in that they can more easily become victims. Their fear, in combination with the interdependence and helpfulness that characterizes the extended family, results in families not wanting assistance from the police. Thus police will encounter some families who would prefer to handle conflict themselves even though police intervention is clearly needed. Some of the newer immigrants and refugees feel that it is dishonorable to have to go outside the family (e.g., to police and social service providers) to get help, and if given a choice, they would choose not to embarrass themselves and their families in this manner.

In the Arab world of the Middle East, there are major differences in the institution of policing and the manner in which citizens are required to behave with police. In 2000, a new wave of violence, known as the *intifada,* broke out in the occupied territories. Palestinians developed a deep distrust and fear of the law enforcement institution because of the way that they (the Palestinians) were treated by their occupiers. Law enforcement officials in the United States, then, must assure Palestinian immigrants that "they are not an occupier and not against them" (James Zogby, 2006). Immigrants from Iraq, for example, have complained that "Saddam's enforcers robbed them of their jewelry, even if it meant cutting off their fingers to get it" (Haddad, 2006). Similarly, in Saudi Arabia there is more of a fear of police than in some other countries because the punishments are stricter. For example, if a person is caught stealing, he or she will have a hand removed if a repeat offender. A Saudi Arabian woman caught shoplifting in a San Francisco Bay Area 7-11 store begged a police officer on her knees not to make the arrest because she feared being sent back to Saudi Arabia and did not know what would happen to her there. As it turned out, the officer did let her go since it was her first offense. He felt that he had some discretion in this case and decided to consider the woman's cultural background and circumstances. When it comes to interpreting cultural influences on police incidents and crimes, especially those of a lesser nature, each officer has to decide for himself or herself. (This aspect of law enforcement is discussed in Chapter 1.)

Modesty, Women's Dress, and Diversity Among Women

In many parts of traditional Arab society, women do not socialize freely with men and tend to dress modestly. However, the everyday practices in the various Arab countries differ greatly. In countries, such as Lebanon, Jordan, and Egypt, women sometimes dress in a contemporary and modern manner and may, at the same time, cover their hair with a headscarf.

In Saudi Arabia, strict rules are maintained about public dress (e.g., the "morals police" may tap women on the ankles with a stick if their dresses are too short). How some Arab women perceive the norms around their attire can differ greatly from how that same attire is perceived in the United States. For example, one of this text's co-authors (D. L.) spoke with several women in Algeria who appreciated the anonymity they could achieve with the *sefsari* (i.e., their clothing that completely covered them). The contrasts in women's attire in the Middle East are striking. Lobna Ismail, President of Connecting Cultures (a Washington, D.C. firm specializing in Arab American cross-cultural understanding) described the cover of a 2003 publication of a book entitled *Teen Life in the Middle East:*

> Two young women are talking to each other. One is wearing a black cloak or "abaya" and her hair is covered with a black scarf. The other is also wearing a black cloak, but it is open and you can see that the young woman is wearing ripped jeans and her knee cap is exposed, she has a tight shirt, and she is smoking a cigarette." (Ismail, 2006)

Ismail points out the tremendous diversity among women in the various Arab countries, and the need to stay away from stereotypes based on an image of a woman in traditional Arab dress. She adds that it is not possible to draw conclusions about a woman's degree of religiosity, political affiliation, and education level just based on how she dresses (Ismail, 2006).

Similarly, according to Ismail, there is a great deal of diversity in the United States as to how people interpret the religious preference for dressing modestly (Ismail, 2006). What a woman chooses to do differs among families. Some traditional families, even in the United States, may encourage their daughters and wives to dress modestly. In some cases, young women themselves choose to dress more modestly than their parents expect. For example, in the United States, some young women cover their hair even if their mothers do not (Ismail, 2006). In the Middle East, women may or may not wear head coverings; the choice depends on multiple factors such as their family, their age, personal preference, and background.

Modesty for a traditional Arab Muslim woman may include the need to cover her head so that men will not see her hair. In some traditional Islamic societies, a man must not see a woman's hair, and officers should understand that asking a woman to remove a head covering (e.g., for the purpose of searching her or getting a photo identification) is analogous to asking her to expose a private part of her body. Corporal Berro, an Arab American at the Dearborn, Michigan, Police Department, advises officers to approach this matter sensitively: "Don't overpower the woman, intimidate her, or grab her head cover. Ask her to go into a private room and have her remove it or get a female officer to help with the procedure" (Berro, 2006).

American officers may have difficulty understanding the violation that a traditional Arab woman feels when her head covering is taken away forcibly. Even if a woman is arrested for something like disorderly conduct, she will be offended by any aggressive move on the part of the officer to remove her head cover or touch her in any way. When police procedures require that a head cover be removed, the officers should explain the procedure and offer some kind of an apology to show respect. Having dealt with this same issue, Immigration and Customs Enforcement (ICE), formerly the Immigration and Naturalization Service (INS), modified its regulations in the following way: "Every applicant . . . shall clearly show a three-quarter profile view of the features of the applicant with the head bare (unless the applicant is wearing a head scarf as required by a religious order of which he or she is a member)" (formerly INS Regulation 8 C.F.R. 331.1(a), 1992). Thus, ICE officials photograph Muslim women with their head coverings on. Because police departments deal with safety issues (such as concealed weapons), they may not have the liberty to accommodate this particular cultural difference in the same way as the ICE does. The matter of women and head coverings must be handled with extreme sensitivity. Similar to the advice that Berro gives, Lobna Ismail advises that if a woman has to remove her head covering (whether for a photo or a search), first ask her to remove it herself in a private area and away from the view of a male (Ismail, 2006). The authors of this book also recommend that law enforcement officers and corrections personnel use good judgment in this matter and not compromise their individual safety in the performance of their duties.

A final note regarding the perception of women who cover their hair—Ismail has observed that people often assume that an American Muslim woman covering her hair is a newcomer to the United States and cannot speak English well. This can be quite contrary to the reality (Ismail, 2006).

Arab Small Business Owners

Racial and ethnic tensions exist between Arab grocers and liquor-store-owners in low-income areas (such as Detroit and Cleveland) and members of other minority groups. The dynamics between Arab store-owners and African Americans are similar to those between Koreans and African Americans in inner cities. The non-Arab often views the Arab as having money and exploiting the local residents for economic gain. Dr. James Zogby explains that this perception is reinforced because, in some locales, one rarely sees a non-Arab working in an Arab-owned store. The local resident, according to

Zogby, does not understand that the Arabs, for the most part, are political refugees (e.g., Palestinians) and have come to the United States for a better life. Despite stereotypes that these store-owners have connections to "Arab money" (i.e., oil money), when they first arrive, the only work that they can do is operate small "marginal" businesses. Most of the small Arab-run grocery stores, liquor stores, and gas stations are family-operated businesses where two brothers or a father and two sons, for example, are managing the operation. It would not be economically possible for them to hire outside their family (the situation is similar to Korean family-run businesses) (James Zogby, 2006). Police officers, in the midst of the conflicts between the store-owners and the residents, can attempt to explain the position of the refugees, but of course, the explanation by itself cannot take care of the problem. Many poor American-born citizens harbor a great deal of animosity toward immigrants and refugees because of scarce resources.

Alcohol is forbidden in the Muslim religion, yet Arab liquor-store-owners sell it to their customers. There has been a debate in the Arab American community as to whether Muslim immigrants and refugees should go into this type of business. For the majority of newcomers, however, the choices are very limited. Members of other ethnic groups have also owned many of the mom-and-pop stores throughout the years.

Finally, there is another dimension to the problem of Arab store-owners in inner cities. Many inner-city residents (Arab Americans and African Americans included) do not feel that law enforcement officials take the needs of the inner city as seriously as they do elsewhere. A pattern in the Arab American community has emerged whereby Arab American store owners feel that they themselves have to take on problems of crime in their stores (John Zogby, 2006). If an Arab store-owner is robbed and is treated in a nonsupportive or harsh way by the police, he feels that he has to defend himself and his store alone. In some cases, Arab store-owners have assaulted shoplifters in their stores, potentially risking becoming the victims themselves. Like other minority-group members, some Arab shop owners in the inner city have given up on the police. Police officers cannot solve the social ills that plague the inner city but at a minimum need to instill the confidence that they will be as supportive as possible when dealing with the crimes that immigrant/refugee store-owners experience. Additionally, Arab shop or gas station owners will assist their more recently arrived relatives in opening a similar business. Many of these recent immigrants do not know the system or all the regulations for running a business. There have been instances of store-owners being chastised for running "illegal" businesses, when in fact they were not familiar with the complete process required for proper licensing (Haddad, 2006).

Hate Crimes against Arab Americans

Hate crimes are discussed fully in Chapter 12. The following explanation deals mainly with the stereotyping and scapegoating of Arabs that often takes place when a crisis in the Arab world involves Americans, or when significant events in America are linked to Arabs. Arab Americans also have a special need for protection during times of political tensions in the Middle East. As discussed in the section "Terrorist Stereotype and Post-9/11 Backlash," the weeks and months following the attacks were accompanied by a huge spike in hate crimes directed at Arab Americans, Muslim Americans, and those thought to be of the same background. There were more than 700 violent crimes against Arab Americans reported within the first 9 weeks after the tragedy of September 11, and

165 reported hate crimes from January 1, 2002, through October 11, 2002, a figure higher than most years in the previous 10 years (ADC Report, 2002). However, the American-Arab Anti-Discrimination Committe (ADC) emphasized that this did not represent the actual total number of hate crimes; victims feared additional violence against them; thus many cases were not made public. Senior Deputy Chief Ronald Haddad points out that fear is a universally human emotion when one is victimized, and this fear factor plays an important role in why many hate crimes go unreported. However, in explaining the lack of reporting incidents to police, it is also important to recognize the Arab value of saving face and maintaining harmony whenever possible. (Haddad 2006)

Prior to the terrorist attacks of 9/11, "single-bias" hate crimes (with a single motivation) against people from one ethnic or national group were the second *least* reported hate crimes. According to the FBI's recorded hate crimes of 2000, of 8,144 single-bias incidents against people (as opposed to property or society), 11.3 percent of those were based on an ethnic or national origin bias, whereas more hate crimes were motivated by racial bias, religious bias, or a prejudice against sexual orientation. In 2001, the total number of single-bias hate crimes rose to 9,730, representing a 19 percent increase (see Exhibit 8.1). Of those, 21.6 percent were the results of a bias against an ethnicity or national origin. In 2000, there were 36 victims of anti-Islamic hate crimes. In 2001, that number rose to 554 victims, more than a 1,500 percent increase (see Exhibit 8.2). Referencing the Hate Crime Statistics of 2001, the FBI states, "Hate crimes touch not only the individual victim, but they also affect the entire group associated with the particular bias motivation. Unfair and inaccurate stereotyping can make victims of all who share the same race, religion, ethnicity or national origin, sexual orientation, or disability."

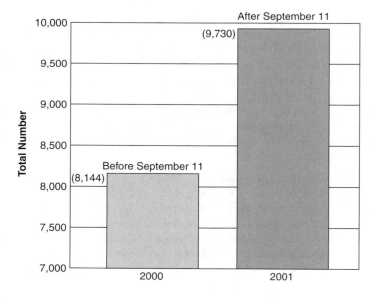

Exhibit 8.1   Total single-bias hate crimes before and after September 11, 2001. *Source:* FBI Hate Crime Statistics

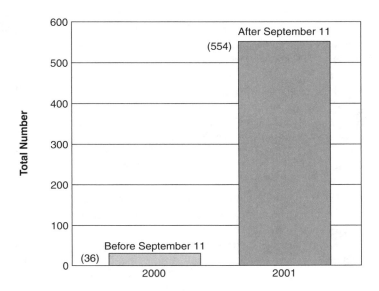

Exhibit 8.2   Anti-Islamic hate crimes, before and after September 11, 2001. *Source:* FBI Hate Crime Statistics

The initial spike in post-9/11 hate crimes declined significantly as community members and law enforcement officers worked together to curb the number of incidents. Just weeks before the war with Iraq, however, the FBI warned of a potentially similar surge in hate crimes. Top FBI officials met with Arab and Muslim leaders in the United States to assure them of the FBI's priority to prevent and investigate hate crimes. This was a step that they had *not* initially taken in the aftermath of September 11. The targeted interviews of thousands of Iraqis living in the United States were also organized in part to reassure the Iraqi community that law enforcement officials would not tolerate any ethnic backlash in the case of a war (FBI, 2003). Many Arab American agencies reported an increase in discriminatory incidents after the 2003 American intervention in Iraq, though this increase was less dramatic than that which followed the terrorist attacks. Continual positive work of government and local leaders to eliminate ethnic backlash is evidenced by the May 2003 Senate resolution written by Senator Dick Durbin (D-IL) and unanimously approved, condemning violence and bigotry against Arab Americans, Muslim Americans, South Asian Americans, and Sikh Americans.

Sensitivity to Homeland Security Legislation

Homeland security measures require that many local and federal law enforcement officers be in constant and close contact with Arab American or Muslim American communities. It is necessary to proceed with caution in enforcing required alien registration or "voluntary" interviews by integrating sensitivity and techniques to avoid implicitly labeling people as threats to the nation. Following are both positive and negative examples of different communities and techniques, as well as recommendations from the ADC as to how to overcome this new challenge in law enforcement.

Following the attacks, the Attorney General demanded that FBI agents interview over 5,000 Arab and Muslim men. A representative from the ADC said these plans, along with later plans to interview 3,000 more, "smacks of racial profiling" (ADC Fact Sheet, 2002). Some law enforcement experts and officials, including police chiefs, also deemed these interviews to be an "unacceptable form of racial profiling and unwise use of time" that led increasingly to more distrust. Many agencies did not participate in these interviews (ADC Report, 2002). When approached regarding how to enforce this legislation in his precinct, Senior Deputy Chief Haddad of Detroit suggested involving community leaders and members, such as Imams of the local mosques. Personal communication in such instances is of utmost importance for fostering and maintaining trust and cooperation. However, in some cases, police officers arrived unannounced at businesses or private homes to request that the residents or employees sign up for these interviews. Patterns of this could lead to deteriorating relationships between communities and law enforcement officials. Dr. Zogby stressed the importance of increasing the comfort level of those approached for interviewing. Law enforcement officials must remember that they are not interacting with hardened criminals in this instance, but with immigrants, many of whom are recent arrivals to the United States. For many of them, an unannounced visit from police officers is inherently humiliating, because of baggage from the "old country." Police officers must win the trust of the people they wish to interview before they can expect cooperation (James Zogby, 2006).

One month following the attacks of September 11, in attempts to strengthen security in their communities, police officers felt unable to target potential suspects because the FBI had "cut them [officers] out of almost every aspect of the probe and refused to share vital intelligence about possible terrorist suspects in their communities ("They're not Sharing Anything," 2001, p. 6). Local police reported lists are too general to suspect someone, and police could only chance upon a suspect during a routine check. A November 2001 *Boston Globe* article reported that while interrogating a Sikh man (Sikhs are of Indian descent and are not Muslim), officers strip-searched the man while deriding him with such comments as "How is Osama bin Laden?" (ADC Report, 2002). While this example does not represent the vast majority of police actions, it is essential to avoid emotional reactivity in situations such as this one. Heightened cultural awareness can also contribute to necessary sensitivity.

Relations between Law Enforcement and Arab Americans Post–September 11

According to a study released by the Vera Institute of Justice in 2006, "In the aftermath of September 11, Arab Americans have a greater fear of racial profiling and immigration enforcement than of falling victim to hate crimes." Nearly 100 Arab Americans and over 100 law enforcement personnel (FBI agents and police officers) participated in the study, which was conducted from 2003 to 2005. Interviewees in the study, both from the Arab American community as well as law enforcement representatives felt that cooperation and trust post-9/11 had deteriorated. Arab Americans reported an "increasing sense of victimization, suspicion of law enforcement, and concerns about protecting their civil liberties" (Vera Institute of Justice, 2006).

Interview inquiries confirmed that:

> September 11 had a substantial impact on Arab American communities. In every site, Arab Americans described heightened levels of public suspicion exacerbated by increased media attention and targeted governmental policies (such as special registration requirements, voluntary interviews, and the detention and deportation of community members). Although community members also reported increases in hate victimization, they expressed greater concern about being victimized by federal policies and practices than by individual acts of harassment or violence. Among law enforcement, the most notable change was a new pressure to incorporate counterterrorism into their work. Local police and FBI participants alike reported that this pressure had frequently resulted in policies that were poorly defined or inconsistently applied. . . . (Vera Institute of Justice, 2006)

In addition to looking at the continued repercussions of September 11, both within the Arab American and the law enforcement communities, the study also examined relations between these two communities post–September 11 and through 2005. While most of the FBI field offices in the study had made attempts to "reach out" to Arab American communities, many of the Arab American interviewees feared federal efforts and remained suspicious of them. In contrast, there was less fear and animosity when it came to local police departments. Furthermore, where local departments had made efforts to "cultivate goodwill," there appeared to be reduced tensions between community members and local police. (Vera Institute of Justice, 2006)

The findings of the Vera Institute Study support the recommendations of the ADC that were published soon after September 11. To build trust, the ADC recommends that law enforcement agencies and Arab Americans work closely with one another especially to foster a safe environment where citizens feel comfortable reporting hate crimes. The ADC recommends that law enforcement officials avoid stereotyping as suspects those involved in lawful political and religious activities, with the reminder that racial profiling is neither effective nor acceptable (ADC Report, 2002).

SUMMARY OF RECOMMENDATIONS FOR LAW ENFORCEMENT

1. There are several basic Arab cultural values that officers should keep in mind when interacting with Arab American citizens:
   - The cultural values of "face" and "saving face," which relate to dignity, reputation, and honor, are of paramount importance. Every effort should be made to protect one's face or honor.
   - Family loyalty often takes precedence over other needs.
   - Communication should be courteous and hospitable; honor and face-saving govern interpersonal interactions and relationships.

2. Arab Americans have been wrongly characterized and stereotyped by the media, and as with all stereotypes, inaccurate perceptions have affected people's thinking on Arab Americans. Officers should be aware of stereotypes that may influence their judgments. Common stereotypes of Arabs include:

   - Illiterate and backward
   - Passive, uneducated women
   - Thief
   - Terrorist

3. Officers can demonstrate to Muslim Arabs a respect for their culture and religion by:

   - Respecting the times when people pray (five times a day)
   - Maintaining courteous behavior in mosques, such as not stepping on prayer mats, not walking in front of people praying, and speaking softly
   - Working out solutions with community members regarding religious celebrations (e.g., parking problems, noise)

4. The basic unit for Arab Americans, especially recent arrivals and traditional families, is not the individual but the family (including the extended family).

   - If a family member is involved in a police incident, officers should expect that other family members will become actively involved.
   - Officers should not automatically assume that this involvement is an attempt to interfere with police affairs.
   - The traditional Arab family is used to working out their conflicts themselves; this is further reason for all members to become involved.

5. Traditionally and outwardly, the father is the head of the household and much of the conversation should be directed toward him. Officers should, however, keep in mind the following:

   - Many Arab women are outspoken and vocal. Do not dismiss their input because men may appear to be, at least publicly, the ones with the power.
   - Traditional Arab women who do not freely communicate with men may have difficulty expressing themselves to a male police officer. In their own families, however, they are often the real decision-makers. Consider various ways of getting information (e.g., the use of a female translator, female police officer, and indirect and open-ended questions).

6. There are a number of specific cultural practices and taboos that officers should consider when communicating with Arab Americans who have preserved a traditional lifestyle (i.e., this does not apply to the majority of Arab Americans who have been in the United States for generations).

   - Avoid even the casual touching of women. Be respectful of the need that some Arab women have to be modest.
   - Never point the sole of one's shoes or feet at a person.

- Expect people to extend hospitality by offering coffee or food (this is not a bribe, from their cultural perspective).

- Arab Americans may stand closer to each other than other Americans do when talking. This is not meant to be threatening; it is largely unconscious and reflects a cultural preference for closer interpersonal interaction.

7. There are cultural differences in communication style that can affect officers' judgments and reactions:

   - Becoming highly emotional (verbally and nonverbally) and speaking loudly is not looked down upon in the Arab world. Officers who may have a different manner of communication should not express irritation at this culturally different style. Nor should they necessarily determine that the people involved are being disrespectful. Developing patience with culturally different styles of communication is a key cross-cultural skill.

   - When a person speaks with an accent, it does not necessarily mean that he or she is not fluent in English or is illiterate. Many highly educated Arab Americans speak English fluently but with an accent, and would be insulted if they were treated as if they were not educated.

8. In areas where there are Arab American grocery, liquor store, and gas station owners as well as poor residents, there is great potential for conflict.

   - Arab American grocery, liquor store, and gas station owners need to be able to depend on local police services. Many do not feel that they have the protection they need.

   - Police officers may be in positions to explain to other residents why Arab American store-owners are usually not in positions to hire people from the community. This will not solve the conflicts, but at least officers can attempt to make some people understand the economic realities of life for refugees and immigrants.

9. During times of crises in the Middle East, Arab Americans become targets of prejudice and racism.

   - Police departments need to monitor communities and keep informed of world events so that Arab American communities have more protection during times when they may be vulnerable to hate crimes.

10. As community members desire to be involved in decision-making processes that affect their lives, law enforcement officials are strongly urged to communicate personally with Arab American leaders. If police chiefs reach out to communities, showing their desire to foster good relations, they are more likely to have positive interactions with the community, while at the same time increasing the willingness of the community to provide tips crucial to keeping the peace. Police chiefs are also encouraged to develop a community policing model to help enforce new federal mandates in a more culturally sensitive manner.

DISCUSSION QUESTIONS AND ISSUES*

1. ***Police–Ethnic Community Relations.*** In the section entitled "Islamic Religion," the authors mention an incident that took place at the end of the holy month of Ramadan: officers ticketed many cars parked across the street from a mosque. According to community people, the stores adjacent to the parking lots were closed, and although parking was technically for customers only, the Arab Americans did not anticipate that there would be a problem utilizing the parking lot after hours. From a community relations point of view, the mass ticketing created some very negative feelings and a collective perception that "They (meaning the police) don't respect us; they don't want to understand us." What is your opinion regarding the way things were handled? Do you have any suggestions as to how this situation could have been prevented? Comment on both what the community and the police could have done to prevent the problem.

2. ***Who Is the Head of the Household?*** The stated head of the household in most traditional Arab families is the father, although the mother actually has a great deal of power within the family. Although in public many Arab women will defer decision making to their husbands, a police officer should not totally discount what the woman might have to offer in various police-related situations. How can the police officer, while respecting the status of the father, still acknowledge the mother as well as get input from her?

3. ***Nonverbal Variations across Cultures.*** When Arab Americans greet each other, they sometimes shake hands and then place their right hand on their chest near their heart. This is a sign of sincerity. In your opinion, should officers greet Arab Americans using this gesture if a person greets them in this way? What would be the pros and cons of doing this?

4. ***Hospitality toward Officers: A Cultural Gesture.*** Hospitality is a virtue in Arab culture and also functions to help people get to know (and see if they can trust) others with whom they are interacting. Given this cultural emphasis on being hospitable, what should an officer do if offered a cup of coffee and something to eat? If an officer has to decline the hospitality, how should it be done politely? Should department policy regarding the acceptance of hospitality be reexamined in light of this cultural tendency? Would your answer be different for departments that have adopted a community-based policing philosophy?

5. ***"But It's the Custom in My Country."*** In January 1991, the Associated Press reported that a Stockton, California, man originally from Jordan was arrested for investigation of "selling his daughter into slavery" because he allegedly accepted $25,000 for her arranged marriage. After police officers had taken the girl to a shelter, a police lieutenant reported that the father protested that "he was within his rights to arrange his daughter's marriage for a price." The father contacted police and explained it was the custom in his country and was

---

*See Instructor's Manual accompanying this text for additional activities, role-plays, questionnaires, and projects related to the content of this chapter.

perfectly acceptable. The police explained that you can't do that in this country: "It is slavery. . . ." The father then went to the shelter where the daughter was and was arrested after creating a disturbance. If you were investigating this case, how would you proceed? How might you assess the validity of what the father was saying? If you found out that the act was indeed "perfectly acceptable in his country," how would you explain practices in the United States? Comment on the statement that the police made ("It is slavery"). From the perspective of needing cooperation from this man, what type of approach should be taken?

6. ***Officer Discretion: To Let Her Go?*** In the section on the perceptions of police, the authors mention an incident involving a Saudi Arabian woman who was caught shoplifting in a 7–11. She begged the officer to let her go because she feared being sent home, and there she would receive a harsh punishment (typically, in Saudi Arabia, a person's hand is cut off if he or she steals). The officer decided that since this was her first offense, he would let her go. What is your reaction to the officer's decision? What would you have done?

WEBSITE RESOURCES

Visit these websites for additional information about law enforcement contact with Arab Americans and Middle Easterners in the United States.

American-Arab Anti-Discrimination Committee (ADC): http://www.adc.org

This website provides information about the ADC's civil rights efforts and useful summary data about cases and complaints regarding discrimination and hate crimes involving Arab Americans.

Arab American Institute Foundation (AAI): http://www.aaiusa.org

This website is dedicated to the civic and political empowerment of Americans of Arab descent. AAI provides policy, research, and public affairs services to support a broad range of community activities. In addition, the AAI also is a census information center on demographics of Arab Americans. On the website, you can access a PDF file entitled *Healing the Nation: The Arab-American Experience After September 11.*

Connecting Cultures: http://www.connecting-cultures.net

This website introduces Connecting Cultures, a consulting organization that designs and implements workshops and seminars on diversity, religion, and cross-cultural communication. It provides resources for understanding how culture and religion impact the way we communicate and work with one another. Connecting Cultures' specialty is Arab and Muslim Americans, as well as Arab culture, the Middle East, and the Muslim world.

FBI website: http://www.fbi.gov

This website provides hate crime statistics as a key feature.

Vera Institute of Justice: http://www.vera.org

The Vera Institute of Justice works closely with leaders in government and civil society to improve the services people rely on for safety and justice. Vera develops innovative, affordable programs that often grow into self-sustaining organizations, studies social problems and current responses, and provides practical advice and assistance to government officials around the world. They have publications on many law enforcement subjects, including a June 2006 study looking at law enforcement and Arab American community relations after September 11.

Zogby International: http://www.zogby.com

This website provides statistics from the latest international public opinion polls covering a variety of issues, including those related to attitudes toward Arab Americans post-9/11. On the website, go to http://www.zogby.com/news/ReadNews .dbm?ID=629, *What Arabs Think: Values, Beliefs and Concerns Landmark Study of Arab Values and Political Concerns,* which contains the views of 3,800 Arab adults polled by Zogby International.

REFERENCES

"All Muslims Not In on Terrorist Plot." (2003, March 2). *Contra Costa Times,* p. 9.

American-Arab Anti-Discrimination Committee. (1992). *1991 Report on Anti-Arab Hate Crimes: Political and Hate Violence Against Arab-Americans.* Washington, D.C.: ADC Research Institute.

American-Arab Anti-Discrimination Committee. (2002). *Arab Stereotypes and American Educators* (by Wingfield and Karaman, 1995). Available: http://www.adc.org.

American-Arab Anti-Discrimination Committee. (2002). *Report on Hate Crimes and Discrimination against Arab Americans: The Post-September 11 Backlash, tracking crimes from September 11, 2001 through October 11, 2002.* Available: http://www.adc.org.

American-Arab Anti-Discrimination Committee. (2002). *ADC Fact Sheet, Condition of Arab Americans post-9/11.* Washington, D.C.: ADC Research Institute.

Arab American Institute. (2000). *Arab-Americans: Issues, Attitudes, Views,* Zogby International/Arab American Institute study.

Armenian National Institute (ANI). (2006). *Frequently Asked Questions about the Armenian Genocide.* Washington, D.C.

Berro, Mohammed. (2006 June). Corporal-Dearborn, Michigan, Police Department, personal communication.

Boller, Philip J., Jr. (1992, March). "A Name Is Just a Name—Or Is It?" *FBI Law Enforcement Bulletin,* p. 6.

Central Intelligence Agency, *World Fact Book,* 2006.

Detroit Free Press. (2001). *100 Questions and Answers about Arab Americans: A Journalist's Guide.* Detroit, Mich.: Author.

"FBI: War Could Trigger Hate Crimes." (2003, March 12). Online at http://www .cbsnews.com.

"Immigration Down in U.S. after 9/11." (2003, May 5). *Contra Costa Times,* p. A3.

Haddad, Ronald. (2006, July). Senior Deputy Chief, Detroit Police Department, Detroit, Michigan, personal communication.

Ismail, Lobna. (2006, June 6). President of Connecting Cultures, Washington, D.C., Personal Communication.

Jabara, Abdeen. (n.d.). "Time for a Change." In *The Arab Image in American Film and Television. Cineaste, 17*(1; Suppl.).

Mahdi, Ali Akbar (Ed.). (2003). *Teen Life in the Middle East.* Westport, Conn.: Greenwood Press.

Samhan, Helen. (2006, August). Executive Director, Arab American Institute, Foundation, Washington, D.C., personal communication.

Shaheen, Jack G. (2001). *Reel Bad Arabs: How Hollywoood Villifies A People.* New York: Olive Branch Press.

Smith, Houston. (1991). *The World's Greatest Religions.* San Francisco: HarperCollins.

San Jose Mercury News. (2003, July 15). "Hate Crimes Hit Low in 2003."

Suleiman, Michael W. (Ed.). (2000). *Arabs in America: Building a New Future.* Philadelphia: Temple University Press.

"They're Not Sharing Anything." (2001, October 15). *Newsweek,* p. 6.

Vera Institute of Justice. (2006). *Law Enforcement and Arab American Community Relations After September 11, 2001: Engagement in a Time of Uncertainty.* (By Nicole Henderson, Christopher W, Ortiz, Naomi F. Sugie, and Joel Miller).

"Who are Arab Americans? Doug Flutie, Paula Abdul, Ralph Nader." (2001, October 18). Online at http://www.diversityinc.com.

Woodruff, David. (1991, February 4). "Letter from Detroit: Where the Mideast meets the Midwest——Uneasily." *Business Week,* p. 30A.

Zogby International Study. (2000). *Arab Americans: Protecting Rights at Home and Promoting a Just Peace Abroad.*

Zogby, James, PhD. (2006, August). Director, Arab American Institute Foundation, Washington, D.C., personal communication.

Zogby, John, PhD. (2006, August). President, Zogby International, New York, personal communication.

Chapter 9

Law Enforcement Contact with Native Americans

OVERVIEW

This chapter provides specific cultural information on Native Americans, including aspects of their history that both directly and indirectly can affect the relationship with law enforcement officials. It presents information about Native American identity and group identification terms as well as explains briefly the tribal system, reservations, Native American mobility, and family structure. Chapter 9 addresses the diversity that exists among Native American groups and includes a description of cultural differences and similarities found among various Indian groups. We include labels, terms, and stereotypical statements that are offensive to Native Americans. The final section outlines several key concerns for law enforcement, including information on perception of police, Native American victimization rates, police jurisdiction problems, peyote, medicine bags, trespassing, violation of Indian sacred places, Indian casinos and gaming, and problems related to fishing rights. In the summary of the chapter, we provide recommendations for improved communication and relationships between law enforcement personnel and members of Native American communities.

COMMENTARY

"It's just a bunch of Indians—let them go!"

Retired Chief Jim Cox, a Comanche Indian formerly with the Midwest City Police Department in Oklahoma, heard a police officer utter these words in the context of a traumatic moment he experienced as a youth in Oklahoma (1992). He was riding with other Native American teenagers in an old Nash automobile. Police officers stopped the car and discovered that the teens had been drinking. Instead of taking the appropriate action, which would have been to arrest the young people or at least to call the parents to pick the kids up, the officers let them go. Cox recalls to this day having heard one of the officers tell the other that Indians were not worth the time or bother: Cox interpreted this statement to mean that if the young people had killed themselves, it did not matter because they were "just Indians." The impression of biased and prejudicial treatment of Indians remained with him even after he had become a police officer. Dr. Peggy Bowen, Native American and Assistant Professor of Criminal Justice, expressed the sentiment that "as distasteful as the remark was then, it is absolutely still the reality today" (2006).

Jose Rivera, Native American California State Peace Officer (retired)

When an officer contacts an Indian person, there is often 500 years of frustration built up. . . . Officers should be aware of the "baggage" that they bring to the encounter. (Rivera, 2006)

Sitting Bull [Lakota], in **The Spirit of Crazy Horse**

What treaty that the whites have kept has the red man broken? Not one. What treaty that the white man ever made with us have they kept? Not one. When I was a boy the Sioux owned the world; the sun rose and set on their land; they sent ten thousand men to battle. Who slew [the warriors]? Where are our lands? Who owns them? What white man can say I ever stole his land . . . ? Yet, they say I am a thief. What white woman, however lonely, was ever captive or insulted by me? Yet they say I am a bad Indian. What white man has ever seen me drunk? Who has ever seen me . . . abuse my children? What law have I broken? Is it wicked for me because my skin is red? (Matthiessen, 1992)

In this chapter, the authors use the terms *Native American, American Indian,* and *Indian* interchangeably. Native American is often preferred as the generic name; however, government agencies often break down this overly broad category into American Indian and Alaska native. In modern usage, the term Native Americans can also include Native Hawaiian, Chamorros (native peoples of Guam), and American Samoans. This chapter does not include information about these cultural groups.

HISTORICAL INFORMATION AND BACKGROUND

Recorded history disputes the origins of the first "Indians" in America. Some researchers claim that they arrived from Asia more than 40,000 years ago; others claim that they did not arrive from anywhere else. In either case, despite their long history in North America and the fact that they were the first "Americans," traditional U.S. history books did not recognize their existence until the European conquests, beginning with Christopher Columbus in 1492. The subject of native peoples as either nonexistent or insignificant reflects an ethnocentric and Eurocentric view of history. Even the word *Indian* is not a term that Native Americans originally used to designate their tribes or communities. Because Columbus did not know that North and South America existed, he thought he had reached the Indies, which then included India, China, the East Indies, and Japan. In fact, he arrived in what is now called the West Indies (in the Caribbean), and he called the people he met Indians (*Los Indios*). Eventually, this became the name for all the indigenous peoples in the Americas. However, before the white settlers came to North and South America, almost every "Indian" tribe had its own name, and despite some shared cultural values, Native Americans did not see themselves as one collective group or call themselves Indians. Most tribes refer to themselves in their own languages as "The People," "The Allies," or "The Friends." Some of the terms that whites use for various tribes are not even authentic names for that tribe. For example, the label Sioux, which means enemy or snake, was originally a term given to that group by an enemy tribe and then adopted by French traders. In many cases, a tribe's real name is not necessarily the name commonly used.

Today in public schools across the country, some educators are only beginning to discuss the nature of much of the contact with Native Americans in early American history. Traditionally, rather than being presented as part of the American people's common legacy, Native American cultural heritage is often presented as bits of colorful "exotica." Genocide, or the killing of entire tribes, is not a chapter in U.S. history on which people have wanted to focus. The reality is that Euro-American and Indian relations have been characterized by hostility, contempt, and brutality. The native peoples have generally been treated by Euro-Americans as less than human or as "savages," and the rich Native American cultures have been ignored or crushed. For this reason, many culturally identifying American Indians do not share in the celebrations of Thanksgiving or Christopher Columbus Day parades. To say that Columbus discovered America implies that Native Americans were not considered "human enough" to be of significance. Ignoring the existence of the Native Americans before 1492 constitutes only one aspect of ethnocentrism. American Indians' experience with the "white man" has largely been one of exploitation, violence, and forced relocation. This historical background has shaped many Native American views of Euro-Americans and their culture. While most people in the United States have a sense that Native Americans were not treated with dignity in U.S. history, many are not aware of the extent of the current abuse toward them, perhaps because this group is a small and traditionally "forgotten minority" in the United States, constituting approximately 1.5 percent of the overall population.*

It would not be accurate to say that no progress at all has been made in the United States with respect to the awareness and rights of our nation's first Americans. On November 6, 2000, President Clinton renewed his commitment to Tribal Sovereignty by issuing an Executive Order on consultation with tribal governments. The purpose of the Order is "to establish meaningful consultation and collaboration with tribal officials in the development of federal policies having tribal implications, to strengthen the administration's government-to-government relationship to tribes, and to reduce the imposition of unfounded mandates by ensuring that all executive departments and agencies consult with tribes and respect tribal sovereignty as they develop policies on issues that impact Indian communities." (Legix, 2000)

President Bush, in 2002, announced the following in A Proclamation in Honor of National American Indian Heritage Month:

> My administration is working to increase employment and expand economic opportunity for all Native Americans. Several federal agencies recently participated in the National Summit on Emerging Tribal Economies to accomplish this goal. In order to build upon this effort, my Administration will work to promote cooperation and coordination among Federal agencies for the purpose of fostering greater economic development of tribal communities. By working together on important economic initiatives, we will strengthen America . . . with hope and promise for all Native Americans. (White House, 2002)

Despite progress that has been made on the record in Washington D.C., many Native Americans do not see that the spirit behind the foregoing sentiments have actually

*This includes Alaska Natives. *Source:* Census 2000.

changed their lives. Indians have among the highest school dropout rates and unemployment rates of all the ethnic and racial groups. As for protection from the federal government, American Indians continue to fight legal battles over the retention of Indian lands and other rights previously guaranteed by U.S. treaties. They still feel abused by a system of government that has committed many treaty violations against tribes and individuals. The U.S. government has often not acted in good faith toward its Native American citizens by seriously and repeatedly disregarding Indian rights that have been guaranteed in the form of binding treaties.

Consequently, individuals and tribes are reluctant to trust the words of the government or people representing "the system" because of the breach of many treaties. Whether they are aware of it or not, law enforcement agents are perceived this way and carry this "baggage" into encounters with Native Americans. Historically, the police officer from outside the reservation has been a symbol of rigid and authoritarian governmental control that has affected nearly every aspect of Indian life, especially on reservations. Officers, like most citizens, have only a limited understanding of how the government, including the criminal justice system, caused massive suffering by not allowing Indians to preserve their cultures, identities, languages, sacred sites, rituals, and lands. Because of this history, officers have a responsibility to educate themselves about the history of the treatment of Indian peoples in order to deal with them effectively and fairly today. Law enforcement officers must understand Indian communities and put forth extra efforts to establish rapport. Doing so will increase the possibility of success at winning cooperation and respect from people who never before had any reason to trust any representative of government.

Military Service

For some American Indians, an additional phenomenon aggravates the repeated breach of trust by the federal government. There is a very proud tradition of American Indians serving in the military. For more than 200 years, they have participated with distinction in United States military actions. American military leaders, beginning with George Washington in 1778, recognized American Indians to be courageous, determined, and as having a "fighting spirit" (CEHIP, 1996). American Indians contributed to the military in the 1800s and contributed on an even larger scale beginning in the 1900s. In World War I, it is estimated that 12,000 American Indians served in the military.

> More than 44,000 American Indians, out of a total Native American population of less than 350,000, served with distinction between 1941 and 1945 in both European and Pacific theaters of war. Native American men and women on the home front also showed an intense desire to serve their country and were an integral part of the war effort. More than 40,000 Indian people left their reservations to work in ordnance depots, factories, and other war industries. American Indians also invested more than $50 million in war bonds and contributed generously to the Red Cross and the Army and Navy Relief societies. . . . The Native American's strong sense of patriotism and courage emerged once again during the Vietnam era. More than 42,000 Native Americans, more than 90 percent of them volunteers, fought in Vietnam. (CEHIP, 1996)

In Desert Storm, Bosnia, and the war in Afghanistan and Iraq, Native Americans continue to serve with honor in the United States Armed Forces with an estimated number exceeding 12,000 American Indians (*Indian Country Today,* 2003).

In being the first woman soldier to die in the Iraqi War and the first Native American woman to die in combat, Private First Class Lori Piestewa of the United States Army and from the Hoppi tribe served with devotion to duty. The U.S. Army reported that PFC Piestewa died fighting the enemy when her convoy was ambushed on March 23, 2003, near Nasiriyah, Iraq. PFC Piestewa died in battle along with eight other soldiers as PFC Jessica Lynch was taken prisoner and later rescued by U.S. troops on April 1, 2003. PFC Piestewa was 23 years old, a single mother of a four-year-old son and a three-year-old daughter. She carried on the tradition of her father, a Vietnam veteran, and her grandfather, a World War II veteran. Her determination shone through in a local television interview before being sent to Iraq from her hometown of Tuba, Arizona: "I am ready to go," she said, looking straight at the camera. "I learned to work with people. It's very important to me to know that my family is going to be taken care of." After her death, thanks to donations from the public, a scholarship fund was set up for Piestewa's children. Two Phoenix landmarks, Squaw Peak and Squaw Peak Freeway, have been renamed Piestewa Peak and Piestewa Freeway—a decision hailed by American Indian groups who consider the word "squaw" offensive. (Legon, 2005)

THE QUESTION OF NATIVE AMERICAN IDENTITY

Law enforcement officials may find themselves confused about who is an American Indian. Individuals may claim to have "Indian blood," but tribes have their own criteria for determining tribal membership. Because the determination of tribal membership is a fundamental attribute of tribal sovereignty, the federal government generally defers to tribes' own determinations when establishing eligibility criteria under special Indian entitlement programs. However, there are a number of Indian tribes that, for historical and political reasons, are not currently "federally recognized" tribes. Members of such tribes, although Indian, are not necessarily eligible for special benefits under federal Indian programs. On the other hand, fraud in this area is quite rampant, whereby people falsely claim Indian ancestry to take unfair advantage of governmental benefits and other perceived opportunities.

Officers may find themselves in situations in which an individual claims to be Indian when he or she is not. If officers have any doubt, they should ask to what tribe the person belongs and then contact the tribal headquarters to verify that person's identity. Every tribe has its own administration and authority, the members of which will be able to answer questions of this nature. By verifying information with tribal authorities rather than making personal determinations of "Indianness," officers will help create a good rapport between tribal members and law enforcement officials (Rivera, 2006).

In January 2006, the U.S. Department of Health and Human Services reported there were 3.3 million (or 0.9 percent of the entire U.S. population) who identified themselves as American Indian or Alaska Native (Indian Health Services, 2006). However, there is a great deal of numerical misinformation because of the lack of a method for verifying the accuracy of people's claims to be Native American. The term Native

American came into popularity in the 1960s and referred to groups served by the Bureau of Indian Affairs (BIA), including American Indians and natives of Alaska. Later, the term under certain federal legislation began to include natives from Hawaii. Native American, however, has rarely been accepted by all Indian groups and is seldom used on reservations. Alaska Natives, such as Eskimos and Aleuts, are separate groups and prefer the term Alaska Native. To know by what terms individuals or tribes prefer to be called, officers should listen to the names they use for themselves rather than try to guess which one is "correct."

In the area of mislabeling, some Native Americans have Spanish first or last names (because of intermarriage) and may "look" Hispanic or Latino (e.g., the Hopis). Identification can be difficult for the officers, so they should not assume that the person is Latino just because of the name or appearance. Many Native Americans do not want to be grouped with Latinos because (1) they are not Latinos; (2) they may resent that some Latinos deny their Indian ancestry and instead identify only with the Spanish part of their heritage; and (3) many tribes have a history of warfare with the "mestizo" populations of Mexico. As an aside, the majority population in Mexico, Central America, and South America is of "Indian" ancestry. However, they adopted or were given Spanish names by the Conquistadores (conquerors). Many Hispanics in U.S. border communities are really of Indian, not Spanish, heritage, or they may be a mixture of the two.

NATIVE AMERICAN POPULATIONS, RESERVATIONS, AND TRIBES AND RELATED HISTORY

Census 2000 revealed that of all cities in the United States with a population of 100,000 or more, New York and Los Angeles had the largest American Indian populations. In general, the West has the largest population (43 percent of the Native American population), the South has 31 percent, the Midwest has 17 percent, and the Northeast has 9 percent (U.S. Bureau of the Census, Census 2000). Cherokee, Navajo, and Latin American Indian comprised the most populated tribal groupings. See Exhibit 9.1 for a historical listing of Native American tribes and the corresponding regions in which they lived in North America. As of July 1, 2003, California with nearly 700,000 people had the highest number of American Indian and Alaska Native residents of any state. Oklahoma had the next highest with nearly 400,000, followed by Arizona with nearly 330,000 (U.S. Department of State, 2005).

According to BIA figures, there were over 561 federally recognized tribal governments in the United States (the words *tribe* and *nation* may also be used), and these include native groups of Alaskans such as Aleuts (BIA, 2006). The federally recognized tribes each have a distinct history and culture and often a separate language. Federal recognition means that a legal relationship exists between the tribe and the federal government. There are still many tribes that do not benefit from federally recognized status. Some may be state recognized or in the process of seeking federal recognition, while others may not seek recognition at all. The issue of the increasing rivalry among some Indian groups seeking recognition is reflected in the sentiment that some Indian tribes are pitted against each other over government benefits and resources.

An Indian reservation is land that a tribe has reserved for its exclusive use through the course of treaty-making, statutes, or executive order. It may be on ancestral lands or

Northeast

Abenaki, Algonkin, Beothuk, Delaware, Erie, Fox, Huron, Illinois, Iroquois, Kickapoo, Mahican, Mascouten, Massachuset, Mattabesic, Menominee, Metoac, Miami, Micmac, Mohegan, Montagnais, Narragansett, Nauset, Neutrals, Niantic, Nipissing, Nipmuc, Ojibwe, Ottawa, Pennacook, Pequot, Pocumtuck, Potawatomi, Sauk, Shawnee, Susquehannock, Tionontati, Wampanoag, Wappinger, Wenro, Winnebago.

Southeast

Acolapissa, Asis, Alibamu, Apalachee, Atakapa, Bayougoula, Biloxi, Calusa, Catawba, Chakchiuma, Cherokee, Chesapeake Algonquin, Chickasaw, Chitamacha, Choctaw, Coushatta, Creek, Cusabo, Gaucata, Guale, Hitchiti, Houma, Jeags, Karankawa, Lumbee, Miccosukee, Mobile, Napochi, Nappissa, Natchez, Ofo, Powhatan, Quapaw, Seminole, Southeastern Siouan, Tekesta, Tidewater Algonquin, Timucua, Tunica, Tuscarora, Yamasee, Yuchi.

Plains

Arapaho, Arikara, Assiniboine, Bidai, Blackfoot, Caddo, Cheyenne, Comanche, Cree, Crow, Dakota (Sioux), Gros Ventre, Hidatsa, Iowa, Kansa, Kiowa, Kiowa-Apache, Kitsai, Lakota (Sioux), Mandan, Metis, Missouri, Nakota (Sioux), Omaha, Osage, Otoe, Pawnee, Ponca, Sarsi, Sutai, Tonkawa, Wichita.

Great Basin

Bannock, Paiute (Northern), Paiute (Southern), Sheepeater, Shoshone (Northern), Shoshone (Western), Ute, Washo.

Plateau

Carrier, Cayuse, Coeur D'Alene, Colville, Dock-Spus, Eneeshur, Flathead, Kalispel, Kawachkin, Kittitas, Klamath, Klickitat, Kosith, Kutenai, Lakes, Lillooet, Methow, Modac, Nez Perce, Okanogan, Palouse, Sanpoil, Shushwap, Sinkiuse, Spokane, Tenino, Thompson, Tyigh, Umatilla, Wallawalla, Wasco, Wauyukma, Wenatchee, Wishram, Wyampum, Yakima.

Southwest

Apache (Eastern), Apache (Western), Chemehuevi, Coahuiltec, Hopi, Jano, Manso, Maricopa, Mohave, Navaho, Pai, Papago, Pima, Pueblo, Yaqui, Yavapai, Yuman, Zuni. Pueblo could potentially be defined further: Acoma, Cochiti, Isleta, Jemez, Laguna, Nambe, Picuris, Pojoaque, Sandia, San Felipe, San Ildefonso, San Juan, Santa Ana, Santa Clara, Santo Domingo, Taos, Tesuque, Zia.

Northwest

Calapuya, Cathlamet, Chehalis, Chemakum, Chetco, Chilluckkittequaw, Chinook, Clackamas, Clatskani, Clatsop, Cowich, Cowlitz, Haida, Hoh, Klallam, Kwalhioqua, Lushootseed, Makah, Molala, Multomah, Oynut, Ozette, Queets, Quileute, Quinault, Rogue River, Siletz, Taidhapam, Tillamook, Tutuni, Yakonan.

California

Achomawi, Atsugewi, Cahuilla, Chimariko, Chumash, Costanoan, Esselen, Hupa, Karuk, Kawaiisu, Maidu, Mission Indians, Miwok, Mono, Patwin, Pomo, Serrano, Shasta, Tolowa, Tubatulabal, Wailaki, Wintu, Wiyot, Yaha, Yokuts, Yuki, Yuman (California).

Exhibit 9.1 Historical Tribal Groupings and Corresponding Regions in North America (*Source:* Saltzman, 2003)

on the only land available when tribes were forced to give up their own territories through federal treaties. A reservation is also land that the federal government holds in trust for the use of an Indian tribe. The BIA administers and manages 55.7 million acres of land that, as of 2006, was held in trust for American Indians, Indian tribes, and Alaska natives. In its Fiscal Year 2005 Performance and Accountability Report, the BIA estimated there were 1.5 million Indians living on reservations.

The BIA uses the term *Indian Country* interchangeably in its report with the word *reservation*. At the federal level, Indian Country means all land within the limits of any Indian reservation under the jurisdiction of the United States government, including all dependent allotments as described in federal law 18 USC 1151. The largest of the reservations is the Navajo reservation and trust lands, which extends into three states. Since reservations are self-governing, most have tribal police; the resulting issues of jurisdiction are discussed later in this chapter. Indians are not forced to stay on reservations, but many who leave have a strong desire to remain in touch with and be nourished by their culture on the reservations. For this reason and because of culture shock experienced in urban life, many return to reservations.

In general, the Indian population is characterized by constant movement between the reservation and the city, and sometimes relocation from city to city. In urban areas, when officers contact an Indian, they will not necessarily know how acculturated to city life that individual is. In rural areas it is easier for officers to get to know the culture of a particular tribe. In the city, the tribal background may be less important than the fact that the person is an American Indian.

Since the early 1980s, more than half of the Native American population has been living outside of reservation communities; many have left to pursue educational and employment opportunities, as life on some of the reservations can be very bleak. Although a large number return home to the reservations to participate in family activities and tribal ceremonies, many attempt to remake their lives in urban areas. A percentage of Indians do make adjustments to mainstream educational and occupational life, but the numbers are still disproportionately low. As with other culturally or ethnically defined categories of people (e.g., Asian, African American), it would be a mistake to lump all Native Americans together and to assume that they are homogeneous. For example, in Arizona alone, one finds a number of different tribes with varying traditions: there are Hopis in the northeast, Pimas and Papagos in the south, Apache in the north-central region, and Yuman groups in the west. All of these descend from people who came to what is now called Arizona. The relative "newcomers" are the Navajos and Apaches, who arrived about 1,000 years ago. These six tribes represent differences in culture, with each group having its own history and life experiences.

Broadly speaking, in the United States there are distinct cultural groups among Native Americans in Alaska, Arizona, California, the Central Plains (Kansas and Nebraska), the Dakotas, the Eastern Seaboard, the Great Lakes area, the Gulf coast states (Florida, Alabama, Mississippi, Louisiana, Texas), the Lower Plateau (Nevada, Utah, Colorado), Montana, Wyoming, New Mexico, North Carolina, Oklahoma, and the Northwest (Washington, Oregon, and Idaho). Every tribe has evolved its own sets of traditions and beliefs, and each sees itself as distinct from other tribes despite some significant broad similarities. It is beyond the scope of this book to delve deeply into differences among tribes. Again, Exhibit 9.1 lists many of the tribes in North America from a historical perspective (Saltzman, 2003). The list illustrates the variety and number of historical tribes there were, each sharing similarities and differences with other tribes. However, since the governmental removal of entire tribes from their homelands, tribes ended up spread out across the country as forced migrants from their homes. For example, as a result of the Indian Removal Act of 1830, five tribes—Cherokee, Choctaw, Chickasaw, Creek, and Seminole—were forced to relocate to Oklahoma in an area designated as Indian territory. Some of these tribes were traditional enemies, though in current times, they have learned to co-exist peacefully. Some readers may have heard of the Trail of Tears, the Cherokee nation's description of their forced migration in 1838 and 1839 from Georgia, Tennessee, and North Carolina to an area in present-day Oklahoma. They called this journey the Trail of Tears because of the tragic effects of hunger, disease, and exhaustion on the forced march during which several thousand Cherokee men, women, and children died. The bitterness remains today among some descendents of the original people of the Trail of Tears. While no records were kept, there are also many stories of people who refused to go on the forced march and were killed by federal authorities (Bowen, 2006).

Similarities among Native Americans

It is possible to talk about general characteristics of Native American groups without negating their diversity. The cultural characteristics described in the following section do not apply to all such Americans but rather to many who are traditionally "Indian" in their orientation to life. While being aware of tribal differences, the law enforcement officer should also understand that there is a strong cultural link between the many worlds and tribes of Native Americans and their Indian counterparts throughout the American continent.

Philosophy toward the Earth and the Universe

"The most striking difference between . . . Indian and Western man is the manner in which each views his role in the universe. The prevailing non-Indian view is that man is superior to all other forms of life and that the universe is his to be used as he sees fit . . . an attitude justified as the mastery of nature for the benefit of man [characterizes Western man's philosophy]" (Bahti, 1982). Through this contrast with Western philosophy (i.e., that people have the capacity to alter nature), we can gain insight into the values and philosophies common to virtually all *identifying* Native Americans. While acknowledging the character of each Indian tribe or nation, there is a common set of values and beliefs involving the earth and the universe, resulting in a deep respect for nature and "mother earth." According to American Indian philosophy, the earth is sacred and is a living entity. By spiritual involvement with the earth, nature, and the universe, individuals bind themselves to their environment. Indians do not see themselves as superior to all else (e.g., animals, plants, etc.) but rather as part of all of creation. Through religious ceremonies and rituals, the Indian is able to transcend himself such that he is in harmony with the universe and connected to nature.

The inclination of some people who do not understand this philosophy would be to dismiss it as primitive and even backward. The costumes, the rituals, the ceremonies, the dances, are often thought of as colorful but strange. Yet from an Indian perspective: "It is a tragedy indeed that Western man in his headlong quest for Holy Progress could not have paused long enough to learn this basic truth—one which he is now being forced to recognize (with the spoilage of the earth), much to his surprise and dismay. Ever anxious to teach 'backward' people, he is ever reluctant to learn from them" (Bahti, 1982). Many non-Indians now embrace certain Native American beliefs regarding the environment; what people once thought of as primitive, they now see as essential in the preservation of our environment.

An Indian prayer:
Oh our Mother the earth, Oh our Father the sky,
Your children are we, and with tired backs
We bring you the gifts you love.
Then weave for us a garment of brightness . . .
May the fringes be the falling rain.
May the border be the standing rainbow.
That we may walk fittingly where birds sing . . . and where grass is
green, Oh our mother earth, Oh our father sky. (Author unknown)

When law enforcement officers make contact with people who are in the midst of celebrating or praying, whether on reservations or in communities, it is vitally important to be as respectful as possible. They must refrain from conveying an air of superiority and ethnocentrism, conveying an attitude that "those rituals" are primitive. Native American prayers, rituals, and ceremonies represent ancient beliefs and philosophies, many of which have to do with the preservation of and harmony with the earth. An officer should, at all costs, try to avoid interrupting prayers and sacred ceremonies, just as one would want to avoid interrupting church services. (As an aside, officers should also be aware that taking photographs during ceremonies would constitute an interruption and is forbidden. In general, officers should seek permission before taking photos of Indians; this is true for many of the Indian tribes. Visitors to some reservations may be told that their cameras will be confiscated if they take pictures.)

Acculturation to Mainstream Society

Significant differences exist among the cultures, languages, history, and socioeconomic status of Native American tribes, communities, and individuals. Nevertheless, in studies on suicide and ethnicity in the United States, much has been written about patterns of what can be described as self-destructive behavior that has been generalized to many Indian groups. According to the Friends Committee on National Legislation (FCNL), the suicide rate for American Indians and Alaska Natives is 72 percent greater than the rate for all other races in the United States. The suicide rate for males between the ages of 15 and 34 is double that of the national average (FCNL, 2001).

Mortality rates attributed to alcohol consumption are nearly seven times as high for American Indians and Alaska Natives as for other races (FCNL, 2001). Alcoholism is the leading health and social problem of American Indians. According to a study conducted by the Indian Health Service (IHS), Native Americans have an alcoholism rate that is over 600 percent higher than average (IHS, 2003). The use of crystal methamphetamine on reservations is also creating tremendous problems whereby families experience domestic violence and neglect of children (Bowen, 2006). However, it cannot be stressed enough that the origins of the psychosocial problems that some Indians experience in mainstream society are not a result of their own weaknesses or deficiencies. The cause of the problems dates back to the way government has handled and regulated Indian life. The dominant society in no way affirmed the cultural identity of Indians; thus many Indians have internalized the oppression that they experienced from the outside world. Furthermore, many young people feel the stresses of living between two cultural worlds. They are not fully part of the traditional Indian world as celebrated on the reservation or in a community that honors traditions; they are not fully adapted to the dominant American culture. Many younger people feel alienated when it comes to their native identity. Following is a quote from a Native American law enforcement officer in a Southern California police department (officer wishes to remain anonymous): "I know very little about my roots. My mother and grandmother were denied the opportunity to learn about their culture [forced assimilation] and nothing was passed on. I feel empty and have intense anger toward those who held the power to decide that certain traditions were not worth preserving. Forced denial of our ethnicity has resulted in extremely high alcohol and suicide rates as a collective response."

People who are caught between two cultures and are successful in neither run the risk of contributing to family breakdown, often becoming depressed, alcoholic, and suicidal. Comparing the suicide rate of white youths and Native American, the most recent statistics from the Pan American Health Organization indicate that, again, for Indian males 15 to 24 years old, it was one-third higher. Indian group members who have remained tightly identified with their culture and religion and who have close-knit extended families tend not to exhibit the type of behavior described here. With cultural and family support, their isolation from mainstream culture is not as pronounced (Bowen, 2006).

Despite the persistence of many social problems, progress has been made with respect to education and political participation. Law enforcement officials must not hold on to the stereotype of American Indians as being uneducated. There is a growing population attending colleges and rising to high positions in education, entertainment, sports, and industry. In some parts of the country, people are revitalizing Native American culture rather than letting it die. For some tribes and individuals, the result is a sense of "pan-Indianism" in which there is a growing pride around ethnic Indian identity. In some cases, members of tribes or communities with very different traditions identify as a group by following certain practices that are associated with Indians. Examples include males wearing long hair, a symbol of strength and power: if you shame yourself, you cannot have long hair (Bowen, 2006); the use of the sacred pipe (i.e., the pipestone pipe, sometimes called the peace pipe); and participation in sweat lodges, purification rituals, and the sacred sun dance for purification. Many tribes have these elements in their traditions, and tribes practice them to varying degrees, gravitating more toward one tradition over another (Rivera, 2006).

These rituals are not practiced by every tribe but are, for some, symbols of a growing movement reflecting American Indian pride. In "A Short History of Pan-Indianism," a brief synopsis of the movement is provided:

> Pan-Indianism involves the process of synthesizing the collective spiritual reality and traditional wisdom of more than one Native American Nation. [It] is a non-violent liberation philosophy with roots in Native American [philosophies]. The Pan-Indian movement serves to stabilize Indian youth . . . and to provide a way of practicing Native American spirituality [in order to] . . . stimulate the next generation to remain Indian. . . . [It] is open to all peoples. . . . (Flattery, 1997).

It should be noted that the pan-Indian movement is not necessarily viewed positively by all Indians; some believe that there is a strong possibility of misusing a tradition or diluting the meaning of a ritual. According to some experts on Native American culture, there is a growing emphasis on individual tribal identity. Many tribes are reviving their own identities by emphasizing their unique customs and strengths rather than identifying with a pan-Indian movement.

LANGUAGE AND COMMUNICATION

It is possible to make some generalizations about the way a group of people communicate, even when there is great diversity within the group. The following contains information about nonverbal and verbal aspects of communication as well as tips for the law enforcement officer interacting with Native Americans. The paragraphs that follow describe patterns of communication and behavior as exhibited by some American Indians who are traditional in their outlook. No description of communication traits, however, would ever apply to everyone within a group, especially one that is so diverse.

Openness and Self-Disclosure

Many Native Americans, in early encounters, will approach people and respond with caution. Too much openness is to be avoided, as is disclosing personal and family problems. This often means that the officer has to work harder at establishing rapport and gaining trust. In the American mainstream culture, appearing friendly and open is highly valued, especially in certain regions, such as the west coast and the south. Because different modes of behavior are expected and accepted, the non-Indian may view the Indian as aloof and reserved. The Indian perception can be that the Euro-American person, because of excessive openness, is superficial and thus untrustworthy. Mainstream American culture encourages open expression of opinions, while American Indian culture does not.

Silence and Interruptions

The ability to remain quiet, to be still, and to observe is highly valued in Native American culture; consequently, silence is truly a virtue. (In mainstream American culture, it is said that "silence is golden," but this is probably more of an expression of an ideal than a description of a fact.) Indians are taught to study and assess situations and only act or participate when one is properly prepared. Indians tend not to act impulsively for fear of appearing foolish or bringing shame to themselves or to their family (Bowen, 2006). When law enforcement officials contact Native Americans, they may mistake this reticence to talk as sullenness or lack of cooperation. The behavior must not be misinterpreted or taken personally. A cultural trait must be understood as just that: a behavior, action, or attitude that is not intended to be a personal insult. The officer must also consider that interrupting an Indian when he or she speaks is seen as very aggressive and should be avoided whenever possible. As a survival skill on the reservation, Dr. Peggy Bowen, as a child, learned to remain silent and especially to avoid speaking directly to a male. Direct communication was perceived as a challenge to male authority. While this has changed to a certain extent because of the influence of the media, a reticence to talk directly to authority is prevalent (Bowen, 2006).

Talking and Questions

Talking just to fill the silence is not seen as important. The small-talk that one observes in mainstream society ("Hi. How are you? How was your weekend?" and so on) is traditionally not required by Native Americans. Words are considered powerful and are therefore chosen carefully. This cultural trait may result in a situation in which Native Americans retreat and appear to be withdrawn if someone is dominating the conversation. When law enforcement officials question Native Americans who exhibit these tendencies (i.e., not being prone to talkativeness), the officer should not press aggressively for answers. Aggressive behavior, both verbal and physical, is traditionally looked down upon. Questions should be open-ended, with the officer being willing to respect the silence and time it may take to find out the needed information.

Nonverbal Communication: Eye Contact, Touching

With respect to American Indian cultures, people often make the statement that Indians avoid making direct eye contact. Although this is true for some tribes, it does not hold true for all. An officer can simply watch for this signal (i.e., avoidance of eye contact) and follow the lead of the citizen. In this section, we explain the phenomenon of avoidance of eye contact from the perspective of groups who do adhere to this behavior. Some Indian tribes believe that looking directly into another person's eyes for a prolonged period of time is disrespectful, just as pointing at someone is considered impolite. Lakota tribe members, for example, generally believe that direct eye contact is an affront or an invasion of privacy (Mehl, 1990). Navajo tribe members tend to stare at each other when they want to direct their anger at someone. An Indian who adheres to the unspoken rules about eye contact may appear to be shifty and evasive. Officers and other law enforcement officials must not automatically judge a person as guilty or suspicious simply because that person is not maintaining direct eye contact. To put a person at ease, the officer can decrease eye contact if it appears to be inhibiting the Native American citizen. Avoidance of eye contact with the officer can also convey the message that the officer is using an approach that is too forceful and demanding. Where such norms about eye-contact avoidance apply, and if an officer has to look at a person's eyes, it would help to forewarn the person (e.g., "I'm going to have to check your eyes").

With regard to their sense of space, most Native Americans are not comfortable being touched by strangers, whether a pat on the back or the arm around the shoulder. Either no touching is appropriate or it should be limited to a brief handshake. Married couples do not tend to show affection in public. Additionally, people should avoid crowding or standing too close. Keep in mind that many Indian relations with strangers are more formal than those of the mainstream culture; therefore, an officer might be viewed as overly aggressive if he or she does not maintain a proper distance. Officers, therefore, who are going to pat down or search a Native American should first explain the process.

Officers may experience particular difficulty when trying to communicate with female Native Americans. Bowen recalls that until she left the reservation, she was unable to maintain direct eye contact with authority because it was never a behavior that was reinforced. As with speaking directly to males, girls and women could get into trouble if they attempted direct eye contact with men. This is still the case, to a certain extent, particularly on reservations that are more isolated than others (Bowen, 2006).

Language

Some Native Americans speak one or more Indian languages. English, for many, is a second language. Those who do not speak English well may be inhibited from speaking for fear of "losing face" because of their lack of language ability. In addition, because many Native Americans tend to speak quietly and nonforcefully, law enforcement agents must demonstrate patience and allow extra time; interaction must not be rushed. The Native American who is not strong in English needs to spend more time translating from his or her own language to English when formulating a response (this is true of all second-language speakers who are not yet fluent). As with all other languages, English words or concepts do not always translate exactly into the various Indian languages. Indian languages are rich and express concepts reflecting views of the world. It is mandatory that the utmost respect be shown when Native Americans speak their own language. Remember that the Indians have a long history of forced assimilation into the Anglo society, in which, among other things, many were denied the right to speak their native languages.

Offensive Terms, Labels, and Stereotypes

In the interview mentioned in the opening of this chapter, retired chief of police Jim Cox, a Comanche Indian, described situations in which insensitive police officers told Indian jokes or used derogatory terms in his presence. He stated that he is proud of his heritage and is offended by commonly held stereotypes. The use of racial slurs toward any group is never acceptable in crime-fighting and peacekeeping, no matter how provoked an officer may be. Officers hearing disrespectful terms and stereotypes about Native Americans should educate fellow officers about the lack of professionalism and respect for community diversity that such terms convey.

There are a number of words that are offensive to Native Americans: *chief* (a leader who has reached this rank is highly honored), *squaw* (extremely offensive), *buck, redskin,* Indian *brave,* and *skins* (some young Indians may refer to themselves using "skins" but would be offended by others using the term). In addition, the use of Indian tribal names or references as mascots for sports' teams has been highly objectionable.

Other terms used to refer to Native Americans are "apple" (a slightly dated term referring to a highly assimilated Indian: "red" on the outside, "white" on the inside) and "the people" (more commonly used by some groups of Indians to refer to themselves). In some regions of the country, a reservation is called a "rez" by Indians, but this word would not be appreciated when uttered by those who are not Native Americans (Bowen, 2006). It is also patronizing when non-Indians use certain kinship terms, such as "grandfather" when talking to an older man, even though other Indians may use that term themselves. However, as a rule of thumb, it is advisable to ask others how *they* would like to be addressed, and then respect their preference. The key is not to make assumptions about the name you use to directly call or indirectly refer to an individual (Bowen, 2006).

Other offensive and commonly used terms include "sitting Indian style" to refer to sitting in a cross-legged position on the floor; "Indian giver" to characterize someone who takes back a present or an offer; "wild Indians" to describe misbehaving children; "pow wow" to mean a discussion; or "bottom of the totem pole" to mean lowest ranking. In addition, it is worth noting that some American Indians deliberately choose not to reveal their ethnic identity in the workplace because of concerns about stereotypes about Indians. Coworkers may make comments about Indians or use offensive expressions because they do not "see one in the room." People can be deeply offended and hurt by "unintentional" references to American Indians.

Many people growing up in the United States can remember the stereotypical picture of an Indian as a wild, savage, and primitive person. In older textbooks, including history books recounting Native American history, Indians were said to "massacre" whites, whereas whites simply "fought" or "battled" the Indians (Harris, Moran, & Moran, 2004). Other common stereotypes or stereotypical statements that are highly resented are "All Indians are drunks" (despite the large percentage of alcohol-related arrests, not all Indians have a problem with liquor; furthermore, the argument has been put forth that the white man introduced "fire water" or alcohol to the Indian as a means of weakening him); "You can't trust an Indian"; "Those damn Indians" (as if they are simply a nuisance); and "The only good Indian is a dead one"—a remark that can be traced back to a statement made by a U.S. general in 1869 (Harris, Moran, & Moran, 2004).

Indians find it offensive when non-Indians make claims that may or may not be true about their Indian ancestry, such as "I'm part Indian—my great-grandfather was Cherokee." Although this may be an attempt to establish rapport, it rings of "Some of my best friends are Indians" (i.e., to "prove" that one does not have any prejudice). People should not assume affinity with American Indians based on novels, movies, a vacation trip, or an interest in silver jewelry. These are among the most offensive, commonly made errors when non-Indians first encounter an American Indian person or family. Another is a confidential revelation that there is an Indian "princess" in the family tree—tribe unknown, identity unclear, but a bit of glamour in the family myths. The intent may be to show positive bonding, but to the Indian they reveal stereotypical thinking.

FAMILY-RELATED ISSUES

Respect for Elders

"Nothing will anger an Indian more than them seeing [his or her] grandmother or grandfather being spoken to belligerently or being ordered around with disrespect. [If that happens], that's a firecracker situation right there" (Rivera, 2003). Unlike mainstream American culture, Indians value aging because of the respect they have for wisdom and experience. People do not feel that they have to cover up signs of aging because this phase of life is highly revered. The elders of a tribe or the older people in Native American communities must be shown the utmost respect by people in law enforcement. This includes acknowledging their presence in a home visit, even if they are not directly involved in the police matter at hand. In some tribes (e.g., the Cherokee) the grandmother often has the most power in the household and is the primary decision-maker. It is advisable for people in law enforcement to include the elders in discussions so they can give their advice or perspective on a situation. The elders are generally respected for their ability to enforce good behavior within the family and tribe.

It should also be noted, however, that because of assimilation or personal preference among some Native Americans, the elders in any given household may tend to avoid interfering with a married couple's problems. And although the elders are respected to a higher degree than in mainstream culture, they may withdraw in some situations in which there is police contact, letting the younger family members deal with the problem. If in doubt, it is advisable to begin the contact more formally, deferring to the elders initially. Then officers can observe how the elders participate and if the younger family members include them.

Extended Family and Kinship Ties

In mainstream society, people usually think of and see themselves first as individuals, and after that, they may or may not identify with their families or various communities and groups with which they are affiliated. In traditional Native American culture, a person's primary identity is related to his or her family and tribe. Some law enforcement agents may be in positions to make referrals when there is a problem with an individual (e.g., an adolescent) in a family. A referral for counseling for that person only may be culturally alienating. Individual Western-style counseling or therapy is a foreign way to treat problems. Additionally, Native American culture is highly group oriented.

Today, some family and tribal cohesiveness has lessened because of forced assimilation, extreme levels of poverty, and lack of education and employment. However, many Native Americans still have large networks of relatives who are in close proximity to each other. It is not uncommon for children to be raised by someone other than their father or mother (e.g., grandmother, aunts). When law enforcement officials enter an Indian's home and, for example, ask to speak to the parents of a child, they may actually end up talking to someone who is not the biological mother or father. Officers must understand that various other relatives can function exactly as a mother or father would in mainstream culture. This does not mean that Indian "natural" parents are necessarily being lazy about their child-rearing duties, even when the child is physically living with another relative (and may be raised by several relatives throughout childhood). The intensely close family and tribal bonds allow for this type of child raising. The officer must not assume that something is abnormal with this type of arrangement or that the parents are neglecting their children.

Children and Separation from Parents

It is crucial that police officers understand the importance of not separating children from family members if at all possible. Many families in urban areas and on reservations have memories of or have heard stories from elder family members that involved the federal government's routine and systematic removal of Indian children from their homes; in many cases, children were placed in boarding schools operated by the BIA that were often hundreds of miles away. This phenomenon, including education for the children that stripped them of their language and culture, began in the late 19th century. The belief was that Indians were savages and did not know how to treat children. Children were punished for speaking their own language and for saying prayers from their own religious traditions. They were basically uprooted and placed in an alien environment in an attempt by the government to eliminate the Indian population (Bowen, 2006).

Although for many families, the severe trauma of children being forcibly separated from parents took place years ago, the aftereffects still linger (Rivera, 2006). In the early 20th century, there was a famous case in which Hopi Indian fathers were sentenced to years in high-security prisons and were subject to the fullest persecution. Their crime was hiding their children from BIA officials because they did not want the children to be taken by the BIA boarding schools. By hiding the children, the Hopi fathers violated federal law. This case is still talked about today (Rivera, 2006). The memory of a "uniform coming to take away a child" is an image that can be conjured up easily by some Indians. It is this "baggage" that the law enforcement officer today encounters when interacting with Native Americans. He or she may be totally unaware of the power of Native Americans' memories of these deplorable actions.

Since Native American parents can be very protective of their children, an officer is well advised to let the parents know about any action that needs to be taken with regard to the child. Law enforcement officers must become knowledgable about the Indian Child Welfare Act (ICWA), passed by Congress in 1978. Prior to the passage of this Act, Indian children removed from their homes were placed with white foster parents. There were no Indian foster homes, and the tribes did not have any way to deal with cases involving children. With the passage of ICWA, the mandate exists to find viable homes in which to place the children, first with a tribal member, and if not possible, then in an Indian home. When officers go out on calls to pick up children, there can be serious consequences if officers are not aware of this act. (Further information about the ICWA is available from the American Bar Association; its web address is listed in Website Resources.) Law enforcement officials are more likely to establish a good rapport with Indian families if they treat the children well, which includes understanding the legal rights of Indian children (Bowen, 2006).

KEY ISSUES IN LAW ENFORCEMENT

Perception of Police

The general distrust of police by Native Americans stems from a history of negative relations with "the system," which can refer to federal, state, and local governments. In their view, officers represent a system that has not supported Indian rights and their tribes or communities. Most of their contact with the police has been negative contact. Thus many Native Americans often have not had a chance to build a relationship of trust and cooperation with people in law enforcement.

Victimization Rates/Comparisons with Other Groups

According to the Bureau of Justice Statistics on American Indians and Crime, the rate of violent victimization of Native Americans far exceeds that of other racial or ethnic groups in the United States and is more than double that of the national average (BJS, 2004). These rates affect American Indians of all age groups, geographies, economic

	POPULATION (%)	VIOLENCE VICTIMS (%)
Whites	84%	82.2%
Blacks	12.1%	14.7%
American Indians	0.5%	1.3%
Asian/Pacific Islander	3.3%	1.8%

Exhibit 9.2   Percent of Population: Violent Victimizations
Source: Bureau of Justice Statistics; National Crime Victimization Survey, 1992 to 2000.

status levels, and (both) genders. According to the National Crime Victimization Survey, between 1992 to 2001, American Indians experienced violence at rates more than twice that of blacks, two and a half times that of whites, and four and a half times that of Asians (BJS, 2004). American Indians comprised 0.5 percent of the survey for the U.S. population but 1.3 percent of all violent crime victims (see Exhibit 9.2).

When asked the race of their offender, American Indian victims of violent crime primarily said the offender was white (57 percent) followed by other race (34 percent) and black (9 percent). Nearly four in five American Indian victims of rape/sexual assault indicated the offender was white. About three in five American Indian victims of robbery (57 percent), aggravated assault (58 percent), and simple assault (55 percent) described the offender as white (BJS, 2004). The less serious the offense, the higher was the percentage of American Indian victims describing the offender's race as other than black or white.

Jurisdiction

In 1885, the Major Crimes Act was passed in the United States. This gave exclusive jurisdiction to the federal government on major crimes committed on reservations. The 1994 Crime Act expanded federal criminal jurisdiction in Indian Country because of the sovereign status of federally recognized Indian tribes, which precludes most states from exercising criminal jurisdiction in Indian Country over Indian persons. Jurisdiction resides with the tribes themselves on a limited basis or with the federal government. Federal criminal jurisdiction in Indian Country is derived from the Federal Criminal Code, Title 18, USC 1152 (Indian Country Crimes Act and Title 18, USC 1153, Major Crimes Act).

FBI responsibility and jurisdiction for the investigation of federal violations in Indian Country under the Indian Country Crimes Act or Major Crimes Act is statutorily derived from Title 28 USC Section 533, pursuant to which the FBI was given investigative responsibility by the Attorney General. The resources allocated by the FBI to various locations throughout the country are based on a number of factors, including identified crime problems; jurisdictional responsibilities; and the availability of non-FBI investigative resources. Also, by virtue of the Indian Gaming Regulatory Act (IGRA) enacted in 1988, the FBI has federal criminal jurisdiction over acts directly related to casino gaming in Indian Country gaming establishments, including those locations on reservations under state criminal jurisdiction.

The FBI has established the following priorities in Indian Country in an effort to ensure that the most egregious and violent criminal acts receive priority attention by investigative personnel:

1. Homicide/Death
2. Child Sexual/Physical Abuse
3. Violent Felony Assault
4. Drugs and Gangs
5. Corruption/Fraud Against the Government/Theft of Tribal Funds
6. Gaming Violations
7. Property Crimes

Thirty-two FBI divisions have active Indian Country programs, with fourteen divisions accounting for the majority of Indian Country investigations by the FBI. The top four Indian Country Field Divisions (Albuqerque, Minneapolis, Phoenix, and Salt Lake City) accounted for 77 percent of all Indian Country case initiations for the FBI in 2005. The FBI currently has 114 special agents assigned to Indian Country matters full time and funds twelve Safe Trails Task Forces (STTF) in Indian Country to address violent crime or identified crime problems that would normally go unaddressed if not for the existence of the STTF (FBI, 2006).

Since 1997, the Indian Country unit has conducted integrated training with FBI agents; BIA law enforcement officers; and tribal, state, county, and local police officers. In December 2003, FBI and BIA law enforcement officers fully integrated all regional training efforts (personnel and resources) and moved to standardize all Indian Country training curricula. In fiscal year 2005, over 1,000 Indian Country law enforcement officers, support personnel, and community leaders were training in FBI- and BIA-sponsored regional training (FBI, 2006).

Tribal and BIA Police

Historically, Native American reservations have been policed by federal officers employed with the BIA or by their own tribal police. The BIA's preference in filling police officer vacancies is given to qualified Indian candidates in accordance with the Indian Preference Act of 1934 (Title 25, USC, Section 472). Many tribal governments have their own tribal police departments consisting of 171 law enforcement agencies; they hire their own police officers numbering over 2,000 full-time sworn personnel and over 1,000 full-time nonsworn employees. They do not primarily rely upon the BIA's 37 law enforcement agencies, which are staffed by over 300 full-time sworn officers (BJS, 2003). In those geographic areas where there is a smaller Indian population, more reservations are hiring a substantial number of non–Native American police officers (Barlow & Barlow, 2000).

Not all non–Native American tribal police officers are well received or respected by the Indian community. A European American police officer (wishing to remain anonymous) said at a 2005 cultural diversity workshop, "As a white tribal police officer, I have been spit upon, and racial epithets have been directed against me on several occasions by Native Americans."

Tribal and Civilian Police

Policing on tribal lands can cause a great deal of friction between tribal and civilian law enforcement, particularly on reservations where the lines of jurisdiction are not clear. Jurisdiction of the tribal police may be limited, but the non-Indian is not always subject to Indian tribal law. Some tribes have decriminalized their codes and taken on civil codes of law (for example, for basic misdemeanors, civil fines may go to the tribal court), yet still conduct a trial of the non-Indian in a tribal court. Who has authority and who has responsibility can be an ambiguous area in tribal and civilian law enforcement (Setter, 2000). Police officers are put into an unusual situation when it comes to enforcing the law among Indians. They may make an arrest in an area that is considered to be "Indian land" (on which tribal police have jurisdiction). The land may be adjacent to non-Indian land, sometimes forming "checkerboard" patterns of jurisdiction. In the case of an Indian reservation (on which tribal police usually have authority), civilian law enforcement agencies are challenged to know where their jurisdiction begins and ends. With the multijurisdictional agreements that many tribes have signed with local and state officials, nontribal police officers may have the right to enter reservations to continue business. It is not uncommon for a person suspected of a crime to be apprehended by a nontribal police officer on a reservation.

It is expected and desired (because it does not always happen) that civilian law enforcement agents inform tribal police or tribal authorities when entering a reservation. Going onto reservation land without prior notice and contacting a suspect or witness directly is an insult to the authority of the tribal police (Bowen, 2006). In other words, civilian police should see themselves as partners with tribal police. Obviously, in dangerous or emergency situations, time may prevent civilian authorities from conferring with the tribal police. Where possible, it is essential that the authority of the reservation be respected. As we mentioned, on some reservations, it may not be clear who has jurisdiction, and it becomes all the more necessary to establish trusting relations. When on the reservation, the police officer must refrain from using abusive language or mannerisms. Officers need to know when and how federal laws apply to reservations.

Levels of cooperation and attitudes toward civil and tribal law enforcement partnerships differ from area to area. The Sac and Fox Nation, headquartered in Oklahoma, is an example of a tribe that initiated a relationship with civilian law enforcement resulting in a cooperative approach to law enforcement. The cross-deputization that resulted from the Sac and Fox Nation's efforts enabled both sets of officers (from the tribal and civilian police) to make arrests in each other's jurisdiction without being sued. Similarly, certain police departments, such as in Albuquerque, New Mexico, worked hard to form relationships with local Indian tribes. On a statewide scale, tribal police officers in Oregon are federally commissioned and state-certified police officers with full law enforcement authority. In Oregon, if a tribal police officer arrests a non-Indian, the non-Indian will be lodged in the county jail and arraigned in the county circuit court. If the same tribal police officer arrests an Indian, the Indian will be lodged in the tribal jail (usually housed in the county jail) and arraigned in tribal court. If there is a will to work cooperatively, police departments and Indian tribal departments can be of tremendous benefit to each other. Initiating this type of effort for both Indians and non-Indians means putting aside history and transcending stereotypes. Furthermore, individual officers should be sensitive to their own potentially condescending attitudes toward tribal police and tribal law.

> American Indians have struggled to retain as much of their own culture and tradition within tribal police operations as possible. Within the very limited jurisdiction in which tribal police have been allowed to exercise their tribal police powers, American Indians have struggled to incorporate tribal laws and procedures. Dominant white authorities are reluctant to allow Indian police agencies to have power over their own when whites do not control the law and procedures of that agency. (Barlow, 2000)

According to Deloria and Lytle, *American Indians, American Justice* (quoted in Barlow, 2000):

> The tribal police continue to play an important role in resolving criminal cases on reservations. They are usually the ones who discover the crime, conduct initial interviews, know the personalities and circumstances involved, and provide continued assistance throughout the case. Their recommendations are well respected by the federal government.

Police Stops

Just as other groups such as Latinos and African Americans have routinely been victims of profiling, so too have Native Americans. If a group of Native Americans is driving a large, poorly maintained car, there is the potential that they will be stopped simply because they are perceived as suspicious and because negative stereotypes are operating. Negative biases against Native Americans are strong and have persisted for generations. A group of Indians in an old, run-down car should not signal anything but what it really is (i.e., a group of friends driving around together). When there is not a legitimate reason to stop a car, the next step is for officers to check their own stereotypes of who they think is a criminal. Like members of other groups, Indians have repeatedly reported being stopped for no reason, which obviously adds to their distrust of police.

Peyote

Many states have specific laws exempting the traditional, religious use of peyote by American Indians from those states' drug enforcement laws. Following is a definition of peyote:

> Peyote is a small turnip-shaped, spineless cactus [containing] nine alkaloid substances, part of which, mainly mescaline, are hallucinogenic in nature; that is, they induce dreams or visions. Reactions to peyote seem to vary with the social situation in which it is used. In some it may merely cause nausea; believers may experience optic, olfactory and auditory sensations. Under ideal conditions color visions may be experienced and peyote may be "heard" singing or speaking. The effects wear off within twenty-four hours and leave no ill aftereffects. Peyote is non-habit forming. (Bahti, 1982)

There have been a variety of uses associated with peyote: (1) as a charm for hunting, (2) as medicine, (3) as an aid to predict weather, (4) as an object to help find things that are lost (the belief being that peyote can reveal the location of the lost object through peyote-induced visions; peyote was even used to help locate the enemy in warfare), and (5) as an object to be carried for protection. People have faith in peyote as a powerful symbol and revere its presence.

Peyote is carried in small bags or pouches and these can be "ruined" if touched.* Police officers may need to confiscate peyote but should do it in a way that is appropriate and respectful. It is far better to ask the Native American politely to remove the bag containing the peyote rather than forcibly take it away.

In a 1990 freedom of religion case, the Supreme Court dealt a severe blow to traditional American Indians when the Court ruled that state governments could have greater leeway in outlawing certain religious practices. The ruling involved the ritual use of peyote by some American Indians who follow the practices of the Native American Church (NAC), which has a membership of 250,000 people (Miller, 2004). Until that time, the U.S. government allowed for the religious use of peyote among Native Americans based on the Bill of Rights' Free Exercise of Religion guarantee; in other words, peyote use was generally illegal except in connection with bona fide American Indian religious rituals.

From a law enforcement perspective, if drugs are illegal, no group should be exempt, and indeed, officers have to uphold the law. From a civil rights perspective, religious freedom applies to all groups and no group should be singled out for disproportionately burdensome treatment. The historical legal and illegal status of peyote is complex. There have been many attempts to prohibit the use of peyote on the federal level, and many states passed laws outlawing its use. However, several states modified such prohibitions to allow traditional American Indians to continue using peyote as a sacrament. Moreover, in some states, such as Arizona, anti-peyote laws have been declared unconstitutional by state courts insofar as they burden the religious practice of American Indians. The following is an example of how one state, Arizona, revised its statutes with respect to the use of peyote (see B):

Arizona Revised Statutes State Law 13-3402(B). Possession and sale of peyote; classification

A. A person who knowingly possesses, sells, transfers or offers to sell or transfer peyote is guilty of a class 6 felony.

B. In a prosecution for violation of this section, it is a defense that the peyote is being used or is intended for use: 1. In connection with the bona fide practice of a religious belief, and 2. As an integral part of a religious exercise, and 3. In a manner not dangerous to public health, safety or morals.

---

*Native Americans from many tribes across the country wear small bags called medicine bags; these are considered to be extremely sacred. The medicine bags do not carry drugs or peyote but hold symbols from nature (e.g., corn pollen, cedar, sage, tree bark), and they are believed to have certain powers. Law enforcement officers should handle these (if it becomes necessary) as they would handle any sacred symbol from their own religion. Ripping into the bags would be an act of desecration. The powerful medicine contained in the bags is often blessed and therefore must be treated in a respectful manner.

This historic ambiguity on the state level, together with the 1990 ruling on the federal level, causes confusion and resentment on the part of many Native Americans. In recognizing that the existing Act of August 11, 1978 (42 USC 1996), commonly called the American Indian Religious Freedom Act, was no longer adequate in protecting Native Americans' civil rights in their traditional and cultural religious use of peyote, Congress passed and President Bill Clinton signed into law the American Indian Religious Freedom Act Amendments of 1994. To provide clarity to police officers about the legal rights of Native Americans in the use of peyote and the public safety issues associated, we present portions of the amended section of this federal law which is under Public Law 103-344 of the 103rd U.S. Congress, October 6, 1994:

Section 3. (a) The Congress finds and declares that—

(1) for many Indian people, the traditional ceremonial use of the peyote cactus as religious sacrament has for centuries been integral to a way of life, and significant in perpetuating Indian tribes and cultures;

(2) since 1965, this ceremonial use of peyote by Indians has been protected by Federal regulation;

(3) while at least 28 States have enacted laws which are similar to, or are in conformance with, the Federal regulation which protects the ceremonial use of peyote by Indian religious practitioners, 22 States have not done so, and this lack of uniformity has created hardship for Indian people who participate in such religious ceremonies;

(4) the Supreme Court of the United States, in the case of Employment Division v. Smith, 494 U.S. 872 (1990), held that the First Amendment does not protect Indian practitioners who use peyote in Indian religious ceremonies, and also raised the uncertainty whether this religious practice would be protected under the compelling State interest standard; and

(5) the lack of adequate and clear legal protection for the religious use of peyote by Indians may serve to stigmatize and marginalize Indian tribes and cultures, and increase the risk that they will be exposed to discriminatory treatment.

(b) (1) Notwithstanding any other provision of law, the use, possession, or transportation of peyote by an Indian for bona fide traditional ceremonial purposes in connection with the practice of a traditional Indian religion is lawful, and shall not be prohibited by the United States or any State. No Indian shall be penalized or discriminated against on the basis of such use, possession or transportation including, but not limited to, denial of otherwise applicable benefits under public assistance programs.

(2) This section does not prohibit such reasonable regulation and registration by the Drug Enforcement Administration of those persons who cultivate, harvest, or distribute peyote as may be consistent with the purpose of this Act.

(3) This section does not prohibit application of the provisions of section 481.111(a) of Vernon's Texas Health and Safety Code Annotated, in effect on the date of enactment of this section, insofar as those provisions pertain to the cultivation, harvest, and distribution of peyote.

(4) Nothing in this section shall prohibit any Federal department or agency, in carrying out its statutory responsibilities and functions, from promulgating regulations establishing reasonable limitations on the use or ingestion of peyote prior to or during the performance of duties by sworn law enforcement officers or personnel directly involved in public transportation or any other safety-sensitive positions where the performance of such duties may be adversely affected by such use or ingestion. Such regulations shall be

adopted after consultation with representatives of traditional Indian religions for which the sacramental use of peyote is integral to their practice. Any regulation promulgated pursuant to this section shall be subject to the balancing test set forth in section 3 of the Religious Freedom Restoration Act (Public Law 103-141; 42 U.S.C. 2000bb-1).

(5) This section shall not be construed as requiring prison authorities to permit, nor shall it be construed to prohibit prison authorities from permitting, access to peyote by Indians while incarcerated within Federal or State prison facilities.

(6) Subject to the provisions of the Religious Freedom Restoration Act (Public Law 103-141; 42 U.S.C. 2000bb-1), this section shall not be construed to prohibit States from enacting or enforcing reasonable traffic safety laws or regulations.

(7) Subject to the provisions of the Religious Freedom Restoration Act (Public Law 103-141; 42 U.S.C. 2000bb-1), this section does not prohibit the Secretary of Defense from promulgating regulations establishing reasonable limitations on the use, possession, transportation, or distribution of peyote to promote military readiness, safety, or compliance with international law or laws of other countries. Such regulations shall be adopted only after consultation with representatives of traditional Indian religions for which the sacramental use of peyote is integral to their practice.

The use of peyote outside the NAC (established in 1918) is forbidden and regarded by church members as sacrilegious. If individuals use peyote under the guise of religion, they are breaking the law. Within the NAC, there are very specific rules and rituals pertaining to its sacramental use. Establishing respectful communication with the leaders of the NAC will assist officers in determining whether peyote was being abused in certain circumstances.

Law enforcement officials should understand the importance and place of peyote in the culture from a Native American point of view. It is not the intent of the authors to recommend a particular course of action with regard to enforcement or lack thereof. If the use of peyote is understood from an Indian perspective, officers will communicate an attitude that shows respect for an ancient ritual that some researchers say dates back 10,000 years. When police officers come in suddenly to a meeting or ceremony where peyote is being used (often along with prayers and drumming) and they aggressively make arrests, it will be very difficult to establish trust and rapport with the community. When peyote is an issue, officers must recognize their own ethnocentrism (i.e., unconsciously viewing other cultures or cultural practices as primitive, abnormal, or inferior). Appreciating that cultures are acquired (i.e., they are not passed on through the genes) includes the realization that "If I had been born in any other culture, I would be doing things similar to those being done by the majority of other people in the culture." With this attitude in mind, it is easier to remain respectful of differences. Law enforcement personnel working in communities where peyote use is an issue should anticipate the problems that will occur and should discuss it with members of the Indian community. Historically, the federal government actively tried to suppress and change Native American cultures. The banning of peyote was and has been viewed by Native American groups as a failure of the Bill of Rights to truly guarantee the freedom to practice one's own religion. Officers must also understand the law and their agencies' policies on enforcement of the law.

Trespassing and Sacred Lands

In a number of states, traditional Indian harvest areas or sacred burial and religious sites are now on federal, state, and especially private lands. Indians continue to visit these areas just as their ancestors did to collect resources or to pray. The point of concern for law enforcement involves conflicts occurring between the ranchers, farmers, and homeowners on what Indians consider their holy ground. How the officer reacts to Indians' allegations of trespassing determines whether there will be an escalated confrontation (Rivera, 2006). When there is a dispute, the officer will alienate Indians by choosing an authoritarian and aggressive method of handling the problem (for example, "You're going to get off this land right now"). Alternatively, he or she could show some empathy and the Native American may very well be more supportive of the officer's efforts to resolve the immediate conflict. If there is no immediate resolution, the officer can, at a minimum, prevent an escalation of hostilities.

Since police officers cannot solve this complex and very old problem, the only tool available is the ability to communicate sensitively and listen well. "The officer is put between a rock and a hard place. If the officer is sensitive, he could try to speak to the landowner and describe the situation, although often the landowners don't care about the history (claiming, 'It's my land now'). However, there have been some people who have been sensitive to the needs of the Native Americans and who have worked out agreements" (Rivera, 2006).

Native American Sites—Use of, Desecration, and Looting

The Native American Free Exercise of Religion Act of 1993 (Senate Bill 1021, introduced to the 103rd Congress), Title I—Protection of Sacred Sites, gives tribal authority over Native American religious sites on Indian lands:

   a. ***Right of Tribe***—All Federal or federally assisted undertakings on Indian lands which may result in changes in the character or use of a Native American religious site or which may have an impact on access to a Native American religious site shall, unless requested otherwise by the Indian tribe on whose lands the undertakings will take place, be conducted in conformance with the laws or customs of the tribe.
   b. ***Protection by Tribes***—Indian tribes may regulate and protect Native American religious sites located on Indian lands.

Beyond use or undertaking of religious sites by the federal government or any governmental agency is the history of desecration and looting of sacred sites and objects. Most often, the looting has been done to make a profit on Native American articles and artifacts. Native Americans witness vandalism on their archeological sites, often without any criminal prosecution. In 1996, President Clinton signed an Executive Order (13007) protecting Indian sacred lands from anything affecting their physical integrity and preserving Indian religious practices on those sites. At the time of the writing of this edition of this book, U.S. Representative Nick Rahall made the following statement:

> Across the country, sites of religious importance are in danger of becoming casualties of the current Administration's push to open federal lands to development. Despite several laws in place aiming to protect the religious freedom of

Native Americans, and the historic and cultural value of their lands, there is no comprehensive or approachable law to protect sacred lands from energy development and other potentially harmful activities. (Rahall, 2003)

Even more degrading to Native Americans than the violation of sacred lands is the taking of human remains (skulls and bones) from Indian reservations and public lands. Officers in certain parts of the country may enter non-Indian homes and see such remains "displayed" as souvenirs of a trip into Indian country. The Native American Grave Protection and Repatriation Act (NAGPRA) passed by Congress and signed by President George H. W. Bush resulted as a response to such criminal acts. If an officer sees any human remains, he or she must investigate whether foul play might have been involved. Officers should contact state agencies established to enforce laws that protect Indian relics to determine how to proceed in such situations.

Indian Casinos and Gaming

Native American reservations in the United States are considered to be sovereign nations, and as such, leaders are responsible for providing and securing financing in order to pay for basic infrastructure and services (as in any city). To date, the most successful industry on the reservations has been casinos and other types of gaming for profit. The legal wording on most documents referring to this industry uses the term *Indian gaming*. In addition, there is the National Indian Gaming Association, thus *Indian gaming* is the most common term used in publications on the subject.

Legalized gambling on reservations dates back to a landmark case in 1976 in which the Supreme Court ruled that states no longer could have regulatory jurisdiction over Indian tribes. Because of lawsuits that followed, it was later ruled that states did not have the right to prohibit Native American tribes from organizing and participating in for-profit legalized gambling. The Indian Gaming Regulatory Act became law in 1988. For the first time, Native Americans were given the right to regulate all gaming activities on their sovereign lands.

According to the National Bureau of Economic Research (NBER), there are over 310 gaming operations of various types in more than 200 of the 550 plus tribes in the United States (NBER, 2002). About 220 are casinos in the style of Las Vegas, and they include slot machines, table games, or both. There is great controversy around the Indian gaming industry. On the one hand, according to NBER, "four years after tribes open casinos, employment . . . increase[s] by 26 percent, and tribal population . . . increase[s] by about 12 percent [i.e., Native Americans return to the reservation because of the promise of work]. . . . The increase in economic activity appears to have some health benefits in that four or more years after a casino opens, mortality has fallen by 2 percent." On the other hand, according to the same 2002 NBER study, "bankruptcy rates, violent crime, auto thefts and larceny are up 10 percent in counties with a casino."

Fishing

"If you ever want to get into a fight, go into a local bar [e.g., in parts of Washington State] and start talking about fishing rights. The fishing issue is a totally hot issue" (Rivera, 2006).

The wording of the treaties with regard to the fishing rights of Native Americans is clear and unequivocal in English as well as in the language of the specific tribes concerned. For example, the treaty with Indians of the Northwest regarding fishing rights on the rivers gives these rights to the Indians "for as long as the rivers shall flow." The rivers in the Northwest are still flowing, and the Indians are still struggling with the state of Washington about the state's violations of the treaty's terms, even on Indian property.

Indians in the year 2003 continue to say, "We have treaties with the government allowing us to fish here." Commercial and sports fishermen, on the forefront of trying to prevent Native Americans from exercising their treaty rights, claim that Indians are destroying the industry. From the Native Americans' perspective, they are providing sustenance to their families and earning extra money for themselves or their tribes to make it throughout the year. (For 150 years, there has been no industry on many, if not most, of the reservations.) Once again, the officer on the front line will be unable to solve a problem that has been raging for generations. The front-line officer's actions, in part, depend on the sensitivity of his or her department's chief executive. Admittedly, the commander is in a difficult position. He or she is between the state fish and game industry and the people trying to enforce federal treaties. Nevertheless, he or she can communicate to officers the need for cultural sensitivity in their way of approaching and communicating with Native Americans. The alternative could be deadly, as illustrated by at least one situation when, in northern California, peace officers with flack jackets and automatic weapons resorted to pursuing Native Americans with shotguns up and down the river (Rivera, 2006).

There are many complex dimensions to cases involving Native Americans "breaking the law" when, in parallel, the federal government is not honoring its treaties with them. Native Americans are frustrated by what they see as blatant violations of their rights. The history of the government's lack of loyalty to its American Indian citizens has caused great pain for this cultural group. Clearly, sensitivity and understanding on the part of the officer are required. The officer has to have patience and tact, remembering that history has defined many aspects of the current relationships between law enforcement and American Indians. Being forceful and displaying anger will alienate Native Americans and will not result in the cooperation needed to solve issues that arise.

SUMMARY OF RECOMMENDATIONS FOR LAW ENFORCEMENT

1. Those who are entrusted with keeping the peace in rural areas, in cities, or on Native American reservations should exhibit respect and professionalism when interacting with peoples who have traditionally been disrespected by governmental authority. It is important to remember that the U.S. government has violated many treaties with Americans Indians and that their basic rights as Americans have repeatedly been denied.

   • Understand the initial resistance to your efforts to establish rapport and goodwill and do not take it personally.

   • Make an effort to get to know the community in your particular area. Make positive contact with American Indian organizations and individuals. This behavior on your part will be unexpected and will result in more cooperation.

2. The younger, more environmentally conscious generation of Americans has adopted much valuable ideology from the culture of America's original peoples.

   • Convey a respect for Native American values. They are not alienating or "un-American," and many believe that those very values of preservation are necessary for our environmental survival.

3. Indians have been victims of forced assimilation whereby their languages, religions, and cultures have been suppressed. The negative effects have stayed with generations of Indians.

   • The point of contact between a law enforcement professional and an American Indian can often involve issues related to poor adjustment to urban life. While the law must be upheld, consider the conditions that led some Native Americans toward, for example, alcoholism and unemployment. Having empathy for the conditions that lead to a person's circumstance need not make one any less effective in his or her line of duty.

4. Preferred mainstream American ways of communication often run counter to American Indian styles of communication. Keep the following in mind when trying to build rapport with citizens who are Indians:

   • Do not take advantage of the American Indian just because he or she may be silent, appear passive, or not be fluent in English.

   • Do not interrupt Indian people when they are speaking; it is seen as aggressive and rude.

5. Many American Indians who favor traditional styles of communication tend toward:

   • Closed behavior and slow rapport-building with strangers. (This does not mean that the person is aloof or hostile; rather, this can be a cultural trait.)

   • Silent and highly observant behavior. (This is not necessarily an indication that an individual does not want to cooperate.)

   • Withdrawal if the method of questioning is too aggressive. (Remember to use time, patience, and silence, which will assist you in getting the response you need.)

   • Indirect eye contact for members of some tribes, but not all. (Your penetrating or intense eye contact may result in intimidating the person and, consequently, in his or her withdrawal.)

6. The terms *chief, redskin, buck, squaw, braves,* and *skins* are offensive when used by a non-Indian (sometimes younger Indians may use some of the terms themselves, but this does not make it acceptable for others to use the terms).

   • If you need to refer to the cultural group, ask the person with whom you are in contact whether he or she prefers the term Indian, Native American, or another tribal name. Your sensitivity to these labels can contribute to establishing a good rapport. If asking seems inappropriate, listen carefully to how the individuals refer to each other.

7. The extended family is close-knit and interdependent among Native American peoples. Keep in mind the following:

   - Be respectful and deferential to elders.
   - The elders should be asked for their opinion or advice, where applicable, because they are often major decision-makers in the family.
   - If there are problems with a child, consider other adults, besides the mother and father, who may also be responsible for child-raising.
   - Whenever possible, do not separate children from parents. This can bring back memories of times when children were forcibly taken from their parents and sent to Christian mission schools or government boarding schools far from their homes.

8. With regard to key issues of law enforcement and contact with American Indians, particularly sensitive areas include:

   - Use of peyote
   - Allegations of trespassing
   - Sacred sites violations
   - Fishing
   - Indian gaming and casinos
   - Victimization rates
   - Jurisdiction

   These all involve matters in which Native Americans feel they have been deprived of their rights: in the case of peyote, the right to religious expression; in the case of trespassing, the right to honor their ancestors (e.g., when visiting burial grounds); and in the case of fishing, the ability to exercise their rights as guaranteed by treaties made with the U.S. government.

9. From a Native American perspective, many people feel that they are abused by a system of government that is neither honest nor respectful of their culture. They believe that the government degrades the land upon which all people depend. To a large extent, Indian rights are still ignored because members of the dominant society do not always uphold the laws that were made to protect Indians. This background makes it especially difficult for people in law enforcement vis-à-vis their relationships and interactions with Indians. For this reason, law enforcement officials need to go out of their way to demonstrate that they are fair, given the complexities of history and current law. In addition, chief executives and command staff of police departments have a special responsibility to provide officers an accurate education on American Indian cultural groups, with an emphasis on government–tribal relations, and to address the special needs and concerns of the Indian peoples.

10. Finally, treat Native Americans in the same respectful way as you would want to be treated. Don't look down on them; they are not stupid or different even if their culture and customs are very unfamiliar to you. A little kindness can go a long way in defusing situations that could otherwise become very hostile (Bowen, 2006).

DISCUSSION QUESTIONS AND ISSUES*

1. ***Popular Stereotypes.*** What are some commonly held stereotypes of Native Americans? What is your personal experience with Native Americans that might counter these stereotypes? How have people in law enforcement been influenced by popular stereotypes of Native Americans?

2. ***Recommendations for Effective Contact.*** If you have had contact with Native Americans, what recommendations would you give others regarding effective communication, rapport building, and cultural knowledge that would be beneficial for officers?

3. ***The Government's Broken Promises to American Indians.*** The famous Lakota chief, Sitting Bull, spoke on behalf of many Indians when he said of white Americans: "They made us many promises . . . but they never kept but one: They promised to take our land, and they took it." There was a time when many acres of land in what we now call the United States were sacred to Native American tribes. Therefore, today many of us are living on, building on, and in some cases destroying the remains of Indian lands where people's roots run deep. How would you deal with the problem of an Indian "trespassing" on someone's land when he or she claims to be visiting an ancestral burial ground, for example? What could you say or do so as not to totally alienate the Native American and thereby risk losing trust and cooperation?

4. ***Jurisdiction.***
   a. What should law enforcement agents do when the state law is in conflict with a federal law that has been based on treaties with Native Americans signed by the federal government? How can officers who are on the front lines win the respect and cooperation of Native Americans when they are asked to enforce something that goes against the treaty rights of the Indians?
   b. A special unit in the early 1990s was established by the San Diego Sheriff's department to patrol Native American reservations, which were overrun from the outside by drugs and violence. Federal Public Law 280 transferred criminal jurisdiction and enforcement on reservations to some states. Research law enforcement jurisdiction issues and tribal lands in your region or state (if applicable); note where there are still unresolved areas or areas of dispute.

WEBSITE RESOURCES

American Bar Association: http://www.abanet.org/genpractice/compleat/f95child.html

This website describes the Indian Child Welfare Act (ICWA) in an article entitled, "The Indian Child Welfare Act: The Need for a Separate Law." The ICWA, which was adopted by Congress in 1978, applies to child custody proceedings in state courts involving "Indian" children—children of Native American ancestry.

---

*See Instructor's Manual that accompanies this text for additional activities, role-plays, questionnaires, and projects related to the content of this chapter.

The Bureau of Indian Affairs (BIA): http://www.doi.gov/bureau-indian-affairs.html

This website has been temporarily shut down as part of the Cobell Litigation accusing the U.S. government of improperly managing Indian assets entrusted to it (see http://www.washingtonpost.com/ac2/wp-dyn/A25625-2002Apr21?); the page still references a wide variety of links to governmental and nongovernmental organizations related to Native Americans.

National Congress of American Indians (NCAI): http://www.ncai.org

This website contains information on issues and events relevant to the organization and to Native Americans.

The National Museum of the American Indian (Washington D.C.):
http://www.nmai.si.edu/

This website provides links to the resources of The National Museum of the American Indian, including information on education and outreach.

Native American Support Group of New York City: http://graywolf94.tripod.com/

This website provides a wide variety of information on and for Native Americans in the New York City area as well as information of general interest to those interested in Native American issues locally, regionally, and nationally.

Office of Tribal Justice (OTJ): http://www.usdoj.gov/otj/

The information contained in this website pertains to the Department of Justice's involvement with Native American tribes and organizations. The office is the single point of contact within the department for meeting responsibilities to the tribes.

Public Community Listing of Bay Area Native American Cultural Events:
http://groups.msn.com/bayareaindiancalendar

Focused on Native Americans in the San Francisco Bay Area, this website offers chat rooms, articles, calendars, and other features for the community to stay connected locally, regionally, and nationally.

REFERENCES

American Indian Religious Freedom Act Amendment of 1994, Public Law 103-344 [H.R. 4230]; October 6, 1994, 103rd Congress.

Bahti, Tom (1982). *Southwestern Indian Ceremonials.* Las Vegas, Nev.: KC Publications.

Barlow, David, & Melissa Barlow. (2000). *Police in a Multicultural Society.* Long Grove, IL: Waveland Press.

Barlow, David. (2000). *Criminal Justice in America.* Upper Saddle River, N.J.: Prentice-Hall.

Bowen, Peggy. (2006). Assistant Professor of Criminal Justice, Alvernia College, Reading, Pennsylvania, personal communication (August 10, 2006).

Bureau of Indian Affairs (BIA). (2005). "Bureau of Indian Affairs: Performance and Accountability Report for Fiscal Year 2005." Available: http://www.doi.gov/bia/BIA_PAR_2005_FINAL_02242006_web.pdf.

Bureau of Indian Affairs (BIA). (2006). "Bureau of Indian Affairs." Available: http://www.doi.gov/bureau-indian-affairs.html.

Bureau of Justice Statistics (BJS). (2004). *A BJS Statistical Profile, 1992–2002: American Indians and Crime.* Washington D.C.: Department of Justice.

Bureau of Justice Statistics (BJS). (2003, August). *Federal Law Enforcement Officers, 2002.* Washington D.C: Department of Justice.

CEHIP. (1996). "20th Century Warriors: Native American Participation in the United States Military." (Prepared for the United States Department of Defense by CEHIP Incorporated, Washington, D.C., in partnership with Native American advisors Rodger Bucholz, William Fields, Ursula P. Roach. Department of Defense, 1996.) Available: http://www.history.navy.mil/faqs/faq61-1.htm.

Federal Bureau of Investigation (FBI, 2006). "Indian Country Crime." Retrieved August 3, 2006, from http://www.fbi.gov/hq/cid/indian/background.htm.

Federal Register. (2002, July 12). BIA Publication: Indian Entities Recognized and Eligible to Receive Services from the U.S. Bureau of Indian Affairs. Vol. 6, #134.

Cox, Jim. (1992). Retired Police Chief, Midwest City, Oklahoma, personal communication, December 18, 1992.

Flattery, Elaine. (1997). "A Short History of Pan-Indianism." Available: http://www.nativenet.uthsca.edu.

Friends Committee on National Legislation (FCNL). (2001). Available: http://www.fcnl.org/issues/nat/sup/indians_healthfacts_41701.htm.

Harris, Philip R., Robert T. Moran., and Sarah V. Moran. (2004). *Managing Cultural Differences: Global Leadership Strategies for the 21st Century,* 6th ed. Oxford, UK: Butterworth-Heineman.

Indian Country Today Staff Reports. (2003). "First American Female and Native Soldier Killed in Iraq War Is Remembered." Available: http://www.indiancountry.com/content.cfm?id=1050072510.

Indian Health Services (IHS). (2006). "Indian Population Trends." Retrieved July 26, 2006, from http://www.ihs.gov/publicinfo/publicaffairs/ihsbrochure/people/1_indianpoptrends-jan2006.doc.

Indian Health Services (IHS). (2003). Quoted in Democratic Policy Committee (DPC) Reports. September 27, 2004. Available: http://democrats.senate.gov/dpc/dpc-new.cfm?doc_name=sr-108-2-257.

Legon, Jeordan. (2005). "War in Iraq: Heroes of War." Available: http://edition.cnn.com/SPECIALS/2003/iraq/heroes/piestewa.html.

Legix. (2000). Social and General Update: A Native American lobbying firm specializing in issues involving housing, tribal justice, sovereignty, education, economic development, and gaming. Available: http://www.legix.com.

Matthiessen, Peter. (1992). *The Spirit of Crazy Horse.* New York: Penguin Books.

Mehl, Lewis. (1990). "Creativity and Madness." Presentation held in Santa Fe, New Mexico, sponsored by the American Institute of Medical Education.

Native American Free Exercise of Religion Act of 1993, Senate Bill 1021, introduced to 103rd Congress.

Miller, Timothy. (2004). "Native American Church." Retrieved July 26, 2006, from http://religiousmovements.lib.virginia.edu/nrms/nachurch.htm.

National Bureau of Economic Research (NBER). (2002, February). "The Social and Economic Impact of Native American Casinos." NBER Working Paper No. w9198.

Rahall, Nick J. (2003, June 11). House Resources Committee, Native American Sacred Lands Act.

Rivera, Jose. (2006, November). Retired California State Peace Officer, Manager of Audience Development and Community Partnerships of Bay Area Discovery Museum, personal communication.

Saltzman, Lee. (2003). Compact History Geographic Overview. Available: http://www .dickshovel.com/up/html.

Setter, Drew. (2000 December). Legix Company, personal communication.

U.S. Bureau of the Census. (2000). http://www.census.gov/population/wwwsocdemo/ race/censr-28.pdf

U.S. Bureau of the Census. (2002). Available: http://www.census.gov/prod/2002pubs/ c2kbr11o1-15.pdf.

U.S. Department of State. (2005, January 28). International Information Programs, Washington D.C.

White House Government News Release. (2002). Available: http://www.whitehouse .gov/news/releases/2002/11/20021101-7-html.

Part 3

MULTICULTURAL LAW ENFORCEMENT ELEMENTS IN TERRORISM AND HOMELAND SECURITY

10 Multicultural Law Enforcement and Terrorism: Overview, Response Strategies, and Multicultural Communities

11 Multicultural Law Enforcement in Homeland Security and Disaster Preparedness

Part Three provides information on working with multicultural communities in the areas of domestic and international terrorism. Peacekeeping efforts of homeland security and disaster preparedness within our local, state, regional, national, and global multicultural communities are addressed. Research and documented findings indicate that acts of terrorism and efforts toward homeland security start with key elements that are "local" in prevention, response, and implementation (Howard & Sawyer, 2004; IACP, 2001; Nance, 2003). Generally speaking, acts of terrorism in the United States usually involve local law enforcement agencies and other public safety personnel as first responders. Thus, specific strategies and practices regarding the role of law enforcement personnel as first responders are provided as critical background information. Part Three highlights law enforcement prevention and response strategies related to the war on terrorism, homeland security, and disaster preparedness within multicultural communities. The chapters that follow contain (1) overviews, background, and historical information with respect to law enforcement's emerging and changing roles in terrorism, in homeland security, and in disaster preparedness; (2) multicultural considerations important to law enforcement personnel as first responders to terrorist attacks and incidents; (3) policies, procedures, and practices relevant to multicultural law enforcement in dealing with crimes of terrorism and homeland security; (4) key multicultural law enforcement communication issues in dealing with terrorism, homeland security, and natural disasters; and (5) relationships and processes inherent in multijurisdictional efforts and responses related to terrorism, homeland security, and natural disaster work. Each chapter ends with key concerns relevant to officers and specific challenges involved in emerging roles and practices in dealing with terrorism, homeland security, and disaster preparedness within multicultural communities.

Chapter 10

Multicultural Law Enforcement and Terrorism: Overview, Response Strategies, and Multicultural Communities

OVERVIEW

This chapter provides specific information on the vital role that law enforcement holds in dealing with domestic and international terrorism within multicultural communities and other venues. Although crimes involving terrorism affect our nation as a whole (and thus are seen as national in scope), the immediate targets, outcomes, and results are local in effect. Local law enforcement personnel and agencies are called upon to respond, provide assistance, establish order, and protect the immediate and larger community from any additional harm and danger. Multicultural knowledge and the skill that is required to work within diverse communities provide key resources in preventing and dealing with the aftermath of terrorism, investigation of crimes, and required intelligence gathering. We first provide an overview of the importance of multicultural law enforcement knowledge and skills for handling terrorism. We then define the scope of the problem in dealing with terrorism involving multicultural populations and communities. The section "Local Community Issues/National and Regional Issues" highlights the complexities in responding to and solving crimes involving terrorism. We provide specific "Response Strategies" and "Key Issues for Law Enforcement" in terms of collaborative and partnership work in the war on terrorism with the variety of public safety agencies across diverse departmental levels of government. We close the chapter with specific recommendations for law enforcement officers and other emergency services personnel in actively responding to terrorism within multicultural communities.

COMMENTARY

In the entire history of crime-fighting and public safety, law enforcement has never before had a challenge of the scope and complexity that it faces today with terrorism. Today's terrorists respect neither law nor community-established practices; they honor neither law enforcement personnel nor humanitarian-serving professionals. Their sole goal and mission is to inflict maximum casualty, mass destruction, and public fear, as is highlighted by the following excerpt from an al-Qaida terrorist manual found in a police raid of a cell member's home in Manchester, England:

Pledge, O Sister:
   . . . to make their women widows and their children orphans.
   . . . to make them desire death and hate appointments and prestige.
   . . . to slaughter them like lambs and let the Nile, al-Asi, and Euphrates flow with their blood.
   . . . to be a pick of destruction for every godless and apostate regime.
   . . . to retaliate for you against every dog who touches you with even a bad word.

Moreover, terrorists may not come to the attention of local law enforcement officers and agencies until they have committed their terrorist acts:

Terrorism poses a fundamental challenge to the legal system. Terrorists often do nothing indictable until they commit the act. Ninety percent of the time sleepers are absolutely legal, so you can't do anything about them even if you know who they are. Terrorism challenges our categories of what is legal and what is illegal. (Ford, 2002, p. 1)

Although terrorists commit crimes to bring national and international attention to their causes and purposes, the response to terrorist attacks and the actions that might prevent them are, nevertheless, usually accomplished in local cities, neighborhoods, and communities.

In panel after panel, the same hard truths were expressed repeatedly: With the events of 9/11, the nation entered a new and sobering era. 9/11 shocked the nation with the chilling realization that foreign enemies from both within and without are bent on destroying our institutions, our lives, our very civilization. Terrorist crime, though national in scope, is usually local in execution. In the war on terror, community police will therefore have to shoulder an increasingly heavy burden. (Bankson, 2003)

Law enforcement's knowledge of and responsiveness to local and regional issues is central to the success in the war on terrorism. Relationships with multicultural local and regional community leaders will be an essential resource in dealing with and preventing terrorism. Law enforcement personnel have the dual role of protecting: the public from acts of terrorism by those terrorists who may be hiding in multicultural communities in the United States and protecting the members of multicultural communities who may have no ties to terrorists or criminals but are stereotyped, harassed, or discriminated against because of the biases and prejudices of others.

DEFINITIONS

For the purposes of this chapter, we use the general definitions of terrorism developed by the U.S. Department of Justice (1997):

Terrorism: A violent act or an act dangerous to human life, in violation of the criminal laws of the United States or any segment to intimidate or coerce a government, the civilian population, or any segment thereof, in furtherance of political or social objectives.

The FBI (1996) further defines two types of terrorism that occur in the United States:

Domestic terrorism involves groups or individuals whose terrorist activities are directed at elements of our government, organizations, or population without foreign direction.

International terrorism involves groups or individuals whose terrorist activities are foreign-based and/or directed by countries or groups outside the United States or whose activities transcend national boundaries.

Both the U.S. Department of State and the Department of Defense have their respective definitions of terrorism, which we provide for comparison and reference purposes as follows:

Premeditated, politically motivated violence perpetrated against non-combatant targets by subnational groups or clandestine agents, usually intended to influence an audience. (U.S. Department of State, 1997)

The calculated use of violence or threat of violence to inculcate fear, intended to coerce or to intimidate governments or societies in the pursuit of goals that are generally political, religious or ideological. (U.S. Departments of the Army and the Air Force, 1990)

Weapons of Mass Destruction (WMD): Three types of weapons are most commonly categorized as weapons of mass destruction" (WMD): (1) nuclear weapons, (2) biological weapons, and (3) chemical weapons. The subcategories of WMD include activities that may be labeled as "agro terrorism," which is to harm our food supply chain, and "cyber terrorism," which is to harm our telecommunications, Internet, and computerized processes and transactions.

B-NICE Incident: An acronym for any terrorist incident involving biological, nuclear, incendiary, chemical and/or explosive weapons of mass destruction.

The Department of Justice's (1997) definition of terrorism tends to be more specifically and narrowly defined for use by law enforcement and with respect to other criminal justice objectives. For the purposes of this textbook, our definition of terrorism is broadened in scope to include all crimes involving terrorism, bombings, and weapons of mass destruction, whether domestic or international. It is clear that criminals who resort to terrorism and weapons of mass destruction, regardless of their motives, are usually not restricted by any definition and/or categories. Since the primary goal of law enforcement is to ensure public safety and security, terrorist threats alone are a public safety issue and can send a community into confusion and even chaos. Law enforcement is called upon to respond to threats of terrorism as well as to actual incidents and acts of terrorism. Law enforcement's knowledge, skills, resources, and sensitivity to multicultural community issues and concerns will facilitate the effectiveness of its response in the three stages of a terrorism incident: before, during, and after an act of terrorism.

HISTORICAL INFORMATION AND BACKGROUND

Terrorism has always been a part of organized society (Hoffman, 1998; Ahmad & Barsamian, 2001). From the earliest history of establishing order through the enforcement of laws and government, extremist groups and individuals have used property damage and violence against people to generate fear and compel "change" in society and organizations. The Department of Justice (1997), in its training manual *Emergency Response to Terrorism: Basic Concepts,* highlights some of the following historical examples of terrorism over the past 300 years, and current events provide additional contemporary examples:

18th Century

- Infected corpses were used by the Russians in areas held by Sweden.
- Organized violence against government taxation included Shays's Rebellion in 1786 and the Whiskey Rebellion in 1791.
- British officials provided blankets from smallpox patients to Native Americans.

19th Century

- Ku Klux Klan began acts of violence against African Americans.
- An unknown person threw a bomb into a peaceful labor rally at Haymarket Square in Chicago, killing seven and injuring many others.
- Catholic churches were burned in Boston, Philadelphia, and other cities.
- Labor activists used 3,000 pounds of dynamite to blow up the Hill and Sullivan Company mine in Idaho, along with other housing units.

20th Century to Current Times

- In 1954, Puerto Rican nationalists wounded five members of Congress by gunfire.
- In 1975, a bombing at New York City's LaGuardia Airport by Croatian nationalists killed 11 and injured 75.
- In 1983, two left-wing radicals detonated a bomb in the cloak room of the U.S. Senate in the Capitol Building.
- Numerous airline hijackings and bomb threats occurred in the latter half of the 20th century.
- The 1993 World Trade Center bombing in New York City killed 6 people.
- The 1995 Alfred P. Murrah Federal Building bombing in Oklahoma City killed 168 people.
- In 1996 and 1997, multiple bombing incidents occurred in Atlanta, including one at the 1996 Summer Olympic Games.
- On September 11, 2001, 3,047 died and many more injuries occurred with the attacks on the World Trade Center buildings, the Pentagon, and a hijacked plane in Pennsylvania.
- On March 11, 2004, ten explosions resulting from improvised explosive devices (IEDs) occurred at the height of the rush hour aboard commuter trains in Madrid, Spain, killing 190 people and injuring over 2,000.
- On July 7, 2005, a series of coordinated bombings occurred on London's public transportation system during the morning rush hour, killing 52 commuters and 4 suicide bombers.

The targets and tactics of terrorists have changed over time (Hoffman, 1998). In the past, targets of terrorists were often more individually directed. The death of a unique, single individual like a head of state, president, or prime minister would produce the major disruption that the terrorist desired. In modern times, governments and organizations have become far more bureaucratic and decentralized. The targets of terrorists have included unique individuals, their surrounding networks, affiliated organizations and institutions, and any functions or processes associated with any targeted individual or groups. Today, terrorists attack not only prominent individuals and their organizations but also a wider range of targets that have been considered immune historically. For example, prior to modern times, terrorists have granted certain categories of people immunity from attack (e.g., women, children, elderly, disabled, and doctors). By not recognizing any category of people as excluded from attack, terrorists today have an unlimited number of targets for attack. The apparent randomness and unpredictability of terrorist attacks make the work of law enforcement and other public safety officers extremely challenging, and solutions require a high level of sophistication (see Oliver [2007] for a timeline and history of terrorist attacks in the United States).

As a result of the greater range of potential victims and the demographic background of terrorists, multicultural knowledge, skills, and resources constitute critical elements in the (1) preparation of local communities for safety and security with regard to terrorism, (2) prevention of possible terrorists' crimes and incidents, (3) participation in emergency response to terrorism, (4) investigation and information gathering involving terrorists, and (5) follow-up actions and prosecution of crimes involving and/or resulting from terrorism. The following case illustrates the broad range of multicultural people, communities, organizations, agencies, and countries involved in the prevention and criminal prosecution of one terrorism threat:

> Revealing the fruits of an elaborate, 18-month-long sting operated with agents of the Russian secret police, federal authorities on Wednesday unveiled criminal charges against three men who they say conspired to sell a shoulder-mounted missile and sought to acquire as many as 50 more. A government affidavit in the case, filed in U.S. District Court here, spins an eerie tale of the ready availability of the deadly weapons on world markets and of the shadowy cast of characters standing ready to supply arms to terrorists. . . . The smuggling plot never came close to being executed. Court documents made public Wednesday showed that U.S. and Russian authorities constructed a complex ruse to lure a British arms dealer into the transaction, including a "cooperating" federal witness who posed as the buyer of the Russian-made SA-18. The disarmed weapon had been shipped into the United States—under the control of Russian and U.S. authorities—as "medical equipment," according to the affidavit. . . . In addition to Lakhani, who was charged with attempting to provide material support to terrorists and attempting to sell arms without a license, the government filed charges against two men who they said had conspired to help transfer money to pay for the Russian missile and as many as 50 more. They were identified as Yehuda Abraham, 76, a New York City gem dealer and money remitter, and Moinuddeen Ahmed Hameed, 38, a Malaysian who arrived in Newark on Tuesday, expecting to negotiate more missile sales, the government said. (Schmitt, Goldman, & Silverstein, 2003, p. MN1)

MYTHS AND STEREOTYPES ABOUT TERRORISTS

Knowledge of the concerns, diversity, and historical backgrounds of various multicultural communities will facilitate the public safety and peacekeeping mission of law enforcement officers in dealing with terrorism. It is important to have an understanding about some of the myths and stereotypes that are held of groups associated with terrorism and how these stereotypes might contribute to prejudice, discrimination, and biased encounters with members of these populations. Stereotypic views of multicultural groups who might be potential terrorists reduce individuals within this group to simplistic, one-dimensional caricatures as either "incompetent cowards" who can't fight face to face or "suicidal bogey persons" who can't be stopped. It is important for law enforcement officers to be aware of the different stereotypes of potential terrorists. The key to effectiveness in multicultural law enforcement with any group is to intelligently discern the myths and stereotypes about these groups. Further, we need to be aware of these stereotypes and be able to monitor our thinking and our behaviors when the stereotypes do not apply to those persons with whom we are interacting.

Some of the current stereotypes that might affect law enforcement officers' perceptions of terrorists include the following:

1. ***Arab and middle eastern nationality or muslim religious background:*** As a result of high-profile attention to terrorists incidents such as the September 11, 2001, attacks by al-Qaida and the foiled terrorist plot to down 10 or more trans-Atlantic flights using components of bombs assembled on board during summer 2006, it is easy to stereotype terrorists as having Arab and Middle Eastern nationality or Muslim religious backgrounds. Terrorists can be foreign or domestic, and clearly, the majority of the domestic terrorist incidents and attacks in the United States have not come from groups or individuals of Arab and Middle Eastern nationality or Muslim religious backgrounds. For example, a review of the FBI Bomb Incidents Report with the most current data available (FBI, 1999) shows that the vast majority of the terrorist incidents in the United States are conducted by Americans against other Americans. Corley, Smith, and Damphousse (2005), in their research on the Changing Face of American Terrorism, reviewed the files of the American Terrorism Study (ATS), a project that included demographic data on persons indicted under the FBIs Counterterrorism Program since the 1980s. In the 1980s, of the 215 terrorists indicted, 79 percent were Americans (48 percent in the right-wing category and 31 percent in the left-wing or environmental categories) and only 21 percent were international terrorists. Similar findings were noted for their 1990s findings: of the 231 terrorists indicted, 70 percent were Americans (45 percent in the right-wing groups and 25 percent in the left-wing or environmental groups) and 30 percent were in the international terrorist groups.

   Foreign terrorist groups include (examples from Howard & Sawyer, 2004):
   - Abu Nidal Organization (Libya)
   - Aum Shinrikyo, Aleph (Japan)
   - Harakat ul-Mujahidin (Pakistan)
   - Sinn Fein (Ireland)
   - Euzkadi Ta Askatasuna (Spain)
   - Red Army Faction (Germany)
   - Red Brigade (Italy)
   - Popular Front for the Liberation of Palestine (PLO)
   - Sendero Luminoso (Peru)
   - Black Tigers (Sri Lanka)
   - November-17 (Greece)
   - Interahamwe (Africa)

- Abu Sayyaf (Philippines)
- AUC (Colombia)
- People's War (Nepal)
- Free Aceh (Indonesia)
- Corsican Army (France)

Any of the current terrorist organizations around the world could combine forces or utilize operatives from other organizations to "look different" than expected or stereotyped.

2. ***Insane and/or behave like automatons:*** Unlike the movie industry's portrayal of terrorists, these individuals are usually not insane, although their actions may appear insane or irrational (Dershowitz, 2002). According to Malcolm W. Nance, a 20-year veteran of the U.S. intelligence community's Combating Terrorism Program and author of *The Terrorist Recognition Handbook,* most terrorists are generally intelligent, rational, decisive, and clear-thinking. In the heat of an attack, terrorists may focus on and harness their energies to accomplish their mission with dedication, motivation, ruthlessness, and commitment that may appear to outsiders as "insane."

3. ***Not as skillful or professional as U.S. law enforcement officers and personnel:*** As would be obvious, terrorists are not all similar in skills, training, and background. They vary in terrorist-training background from foreign-government-trained professionals who make up the foreign intelligence agencies of countries like Libya, Cuba, Iran, and North Korea to the novice, untrained civilian militia, vigilante, and criminals. The training and experience of *some* of the terrorists render them as skillful in their craft as any law enforcement professional in the United States. On the other hand, others have skill levels similar to petty criminals on the street. The use of intelligence information (i.e., not assumptions or stereotypes) to assess the skill and ability levels of terrorists or terrorist groups is central to homeland security.

Throughout this text, the authors have emphasized attitudes and skills required of law enforcement officials in a multicultural society to include (1) respecting cultural behaviors that may be different from one's own, (2) observing and understanding behaviors important to diverse communities, and (3) analyzing and interpreting diverse behaviors for application within multicultural communities. Similarly, multicultural skills and knowledge are also elements that can contribute to detecting and predicting terrorist actions and activities for homeland security when coupled with an intelligence-based approach. Just as it is important to understand one's own biases and stereotypes about multicultural communities in order to effectively serve those communities, law enforcement officers need to change their perceptions of who the terrorists are before they can effectively detect terrorist activities.

1. ***Anyone could be a terrorist:*** Law enforcement officers who start to look at specific groups may be blinded and overlook a group or individuals who may actually be the real terrorists sought. For example, if one were going by Arab descent or nationality, one would have missed Richard C. Reid, the Shoe Bomber (i.e., who was of British citizenship), and Jose Padilla, the alleged plotter for releasing a "dirty bomb" in the United States (born in Chicago of

U.S. citizenship and Puerto Rican descent). If one thought that terrorists were inferior and not intelligent, one would have missed apprehending Theodore Kaczynski, the Unabomber, who was a professor at several major universities.

2. ***Learn to acknowledge the terrorist's motivation, skills, and capabilities:*** Because of the actions of terrorists, law enforcement officers may view terrorists with contempt along with other negative stereotypic descriptors like "crazies," "camel jockeys," "suicidal," "scum of the earth," and "rag heads." Such contempt and disdain for terrorists may indeed be the perspective that blinds law enforcement officers and others to seeing the lethal actions and goals of terrorists. Law enforcement officers must, with clear insight and perceptions, acknowledge terrorists for what they are: motivated, ruthless human beings who use destruction, death, and deceit to meet their lethal goals. For example, prior to the bombing of the Alfred P. Murrah Federal Building in Oklahoma City, one law enforcement and intelligence stereotype held that U.S. domestic terrorists were not capable of mass destruction but were merely a criminal nuisance element of society (Heymann, 2001).

3. ***Observe and interpret street-level behaviors:*** Law enforcement officers are trained to observe and interpret street-level criminal behaviors, and such skills are applicable to recognizing some of the behaviors of terrorists. Terrorists are not invisible "ghosts" (i.e., terrorists' behaviors and actions are usually visible to the trained observer); however, stereotypes based on race, ethnicity, gender, age, nationality, and other demographic dimensions may blind a law enforcement officer from observing and correctly interpreting the actions and behaviors of possible terrorists. Racial profiling would be one of the actions that could blind law enforcement efforts in detecting a terrorist's intent. The only time that one could appropriately use racial profiling alone to detect a terrorist is when one has already had specific intelligence on a specific person as the terrorist (Howard & Sawyer, 2004).

Without proper intelligence, it is almost impossible to effectively interpret behaviors that one observes. For example, three of the September 11, 2001, terrorists were involved in traffic stops by the police for speeding on three separate occasions prior to the terrorists' attacks:

- Mohammed Atta, the al-Qaida 9/11 skyjacker who piloted the American Airlines Flight 77 into the North Tower of the World Trade Center, was stopped in July 2001 by the Florida State Police for driving with an invalid license. A bench warrant was issued for his arrest because he ignored the issued ticket. Atta was stopped a few weeks later in Delray Beach, Florida, for speeding, but the officer was unaware of the bench warrant and let him go with a warning (Kleinberg & Davies, 2001, p. A1).

- Zaid al-Jarrah, the al-Qaida 9/11 skyjacker who investigators believe was a pilot on United Airlines Flight 93, which crashed in Pennsylvania, was stopped and cited by the Maryland State Police on September 9, 2001, for driving 90 miles per hour in a 65-mph zone near the Delaware state line (a $270 fine). Trooper Catalano, who made the stop, reported that he looked over the car several times, videotaped the entire transaction, and said that the stop was a "regular, routine traffic stop" ("A Nation Challenged," 2002, p. A12).

- Hani Hanjour, one of the al-Qaida 9/11 skyjackers aboard the plane that crashed into the Pentagon, was stopped for speeding within a few miles of the military headquarters 6 weeks before the attack and was ticketed by the Arlington, Virginia, police for going 50 miles per hour in a 35-mph zone. Hanjour surrendered his Florida driver's license to the police officer who stopped him but was allowed to go on his way (Roig-Franzia & Davis, 2002, p. A13).

In the case of Timothy McVeigh, the Oklahoma City bomber, law enforcement officials properly interpreted information, which led to his arrest at a traffic stop. McVeigh was stopped by Trooper Charles Hanger of the Oklahoma Highway Patrol about 90 minutes after the bombing of the Alfred P. Murrah Federal Building. Trooper Hanger was looking for suspicious vehicles headed his way given the approximate travel distance to his location and time of the bombing.

> Oklahoma Highway Patrol Trooper Charles Hanger pulled over McVeigh's yellow Mercury Marquis on I-35 about 63 miles north of Oklahoma City because his car was missing a rear license plate. Hanger told the jury he took shelter behind the door of his cruiser as McVeigh got out of the car and walked toward him. As McVeigh reached for his camouflage wallet, Hanger said he noticed a bulge under his light windbreaker. "I told him to take both hands and slowly pull back his jacket," Hanger said. "He said, 'I have a gun.' I pulled my weapon and stuck it to the back of his head." As Hanger searched and cuffed him, McVeigh told the trooper he was also carrying a knife and a spare clip of ammunition. In the chamber of the pistol, Hanger found a round of Black Talon ammunition, bullets designed to inflict maximum damage on a shooting victim. Hanger then arrested McVeigh for carrying a concealed pistol in a shoulder holster. Three days later, McVeigh was tied to the blast as he waited for a court hearing on the gun charge ("Trooper Describes Arrest," 1997, p. A2).

4. *Analyze and utilize intelligence and other source information:* Law enforcement officers are trained to gather and use sources of information in a criminal investigation. For homeland security, key sources of information include not only local, state, and federal intelligence sources, but also knowledge, relationships, and networks developed within the local multicultural communities. As noted by Nance (2003), "Terrorism against America can only be defeated through careful intelligence collection, surveillance, cooperative efforts among law enforcement and intelligence agencies, and resolving the root complaints of the terrorist-supporting population."

LOCAL COMMUNITY ISSUES AND GLOBAL, NATIONAL, AND REGIONAL ISSUES

The targets and methods of terrorists have become more diverse and more difficult to predict. The terrorist attacks on September 11, 2001, clearly demonstrate that the global issues involving the Unites States in other parts of the world can result in terrorism within our own borders and affect victims in our local cities and towns. As highlighted by the Department of Justice,

Terrorists in the United States continued a general trend in which fewer attacks are occurring in the United States, but individual attacks are becoming more deadly. Extremists in the United States continued a chilling trend by demonstrating interest in—and experimenting with—unconventional weapons. Over the past ten years, a pattern of interest in biological agents by criminals and extremists has developed. America and Americans have also been a favorite choice of target for terrorists. Reprisals for U.S. legal actions against domestic and international terrorists increase the likelihood that America will be the target of terrorist attacks either in the United States or overseas. (Terrorist Research and Analytical Center, 1995)

Often, clues surrounding the terrorist incident and/or attack will reveal whether domestic or international terrorism was involved and will point toward possible motives and the perpetrators behind the incident. Clues that might be helpful surrounding a terrorist event include the following:

Timing of the event may be signifant to the terrorist group or individual. For many years to come, September 11 will be a day for which all United States facilities around the world will operate at a heightened state of security and awareness because of the al-Qaida simultaneous terrorist attacks. Within the United States, April 19 will continue for some time to be a day of heightened alert because it is the anniversary of both the bombing of the Alfred P. Murrah Federal Building in Oklahoma City and the fire at the Branch Dividian compound in Waco, Texas. The more that law enforcement works with a community-policing model to understand the makeup of a multicultural community, the greater the likelihood that officers will have the knowledge to predict potential terrorist targets within communities.

Occupancy, location, and/or purpose related to the target include the following types of elements:

- *Controversial businesses* are those that have a history of inviting the protest and dislike of recognized groups, which include one or more components of extremist elements. For example, controversial businesses include abortion clinics, logging mills, nuclear facilities, and tuna fishing companies.

- *Public buildings and venues with large numbers of people* are seen by terrorist as opportunities for attention-getting with mass casualties and victims. For some terrorists, causing massive destruction and casualties in targeted public buildings or in venues containing large numbers of people is linked to the identity of the operator/owner of the building or venue. Examples of these targets are the World Trade Center, World Bank, entertainment venues, athletic events, tourist destinations, shopping malls, airports, and convention centers.

- *Symbolic and historical targets* are links that the terrorists make regarding the relationship of the target and the organization, event, and/or services that specifically offend extremists. Examples of symbolic and historical targets include the offices of the Internal Revenue Service (IRS) for tax resisters, the offices of the Bureau of Alcohol, Tobacco and Firearms (ATF) for those who oppose any form of gun control, and African American churches and Jewish synagogues for those who are members of white supremacist groups.

- *Infrastructure systems and services* include those structures and operations that are vital for the continued functioning of our country. Throughout the United

States, these targets include communication companies, power grids, water treatment facilities, mass transit, telecommunication towers, and transportation hubs. Terrorists' attacks on any of these targets have the potential for disabling and disrupting massive areas and regions, resulting in chaos, especially with respect to huge numbers of injuries and fatalities across large geographical areas. Law enforcement officers' and agencies' knowledge of possible targets linked to occupancy, location, and/or purpose of an organization within the local, multicultural communities will enhance the ability to prevent and to prepare for a terrorist incident. For any of the noted indicators of a terrorist incident or attack, law enforcement officers would nearly always be among the first responders to the scene (IACP, 2001).

THE FIRST-RESPONSE CHALLENGE FOR LAW ENFORCEMENT

Law enforcement officers as first responders to a terrorism attack confront tremendous challenge, risk, and responsibility. The terrorist attack or crime scene is complicated by the confusion, panic, and casualty of the attack as well as any residual effects in the event that weapons of mass destruction were used. Moreover, it has been quite typical for terrorists to deliberately target responders and rescue personnel at the crime scene. Terrorists have utilized "secondary devices" to target law enforcement and other public safety personnel responding to a terrorist's attack. For example, in the 1997 bomb attack at an Atlanta abortion clinic, a second bomb went off approximately one hour after the initial explosion and was very close to the command post established for the first bomb attack.

As in all hazardous law enforcement situations, *officer safety* and *self-protection* are top priorities. However, in some terrorist attacks, as in the September 11, 2001, multiple-site scenario, no amount of self-protection at the scene would have prevented the deaths of the 69 police, fire, and port officers from New York and New Jersey who were killed in the attack. Neither could the U.S. Secret Service agent, FBI agent, and the U.S. Fish and Wildlife Service agent aboard Flight 93 that crashed in rural Pennsylvania have protected themselves from becoming victims (Oliver, 2007).

Law enforcement personnel, as first responders to terrorists' crimes, need to know that the forms of self-protection can be defined in terms of the principals of time, distance, and shielding. Law enforcement personnel must have sufficient cross-cultural language skills to communicate the importance of these principles for effective action and response within multicultural communities during a terrorist incident:

1. ***Time*** is used as a tool in a terrorist crime scene. Spend the shortest amount of time possible in the affected area or exposed to the hazard. The less time one spends in the hazard area, the less likely one will become injured. Minimizing time spent in the hazard area will also reduce the chances of contaminating the crime scene.

2. ***Distance*** from the affected terrorist area or hazardous situation should be maximized. The greater the distance from the affected area while performing one's functions, the less the exposure to the hazard. Maintaining distance from the hazard areas will also ease the evacuation of the injured, allow for other emergency personnel requiring immediate access, and facilitate crowd control by law enforcement officers.

3. ***Shielding*** can be used to address specific types of hazards. Shielding can be achieved through buildings, walls, vehicles, body armor, and personnel protective equipment including chemical protective clothing, fire protective clothing, and self-contained breathing apparatuses.

Law enforcement officers must understand the various types of danger and harm that may result from a terrorist situation not only for their own self-protection but in order to understand the reactions of affected victims and to be able to provide effective assistance to those affected by terrorist activities. Law enforcement personnel need to be aware that the many people who form multicultural communities may have had prior experiences (or have heard of prior experiences) with WMD incidents within their home countries (e.g., Vietnamese Americans' experience with thermal harm during the napalm bombing of their villages; Iraqi Americans' experience with chemical harm from mustard gas attacks within their communities).

RESPONSE STRATEGIES

Detecting and Preventing Attacks of Terrorism

Law enforcement officers spend years studying criminal behaviors in order to prevent crimes and to capture and prosecute criminals. Public safety roles for law enforcement agencies now require the use of some of these same skills in identifying the criminal behaviors of potential terrorists. As noted by Hoffman (1998) and others, the most difficult and critical component of homeland security is to recognize and prevent a terrorist attack. As such, criminal justice officers need to be competent in recognizing the Terrorist Attack Pre-incident Indicators (TAPIs), a term used by the intelligence community to describe actions and behaviors taken by terrorists before they carry out an attack (Nance, 2003). We discuss in Chapter 14 one source of TAPIs, which include the tools of "profiling" used in law enforcement today. For example, Secret Service officers are trained to watch for individual behaviors, compiled as a profile, which may serve as indicators for possible actions toward those whom the officers are protecting. El Al, the Israeli airline, has used very successfully a behavior-recognition profile to detect individuals who might be potential skyjackers of its airliners (Howard & Sawyer, 2004).

Law enforcement officers, with training in observing and working with cultural differences and diverse communities would benefit by applying their skills and training to recognizing terrorist's behaviors. As noted in Chapter 14, public safety officers must avoid a stereotype-based approach to detecting criminals; this holds equally true in detecting terrorists. Stereotypes alone do not help in the detection and prevention of terrorism regardless of whether they are based on race or on the notion of what constitutes a "terrorist." Stereotyping will obscure law enforcement officers' perceptions of the real dangers and issues in providing for our homeland security. For example, several of the September 11, 2001, terrorists behaved in ways that threw off any surveillance based on cultural and religious stereotypes: more than one skyjacker was seen in nightclubs and strip bars. Such behaviors would be contrary to the American stereotype of devout Muslim fundamentalists who would be adverse to alcoholic beverages, nightclub exotic dancers, and overt sexual behaviors of men and women at bars. Although it is beyond the scope of this chapter to detail the development of law enforcement skills for recognizing terrorist's behaviors, it is critical to emphasize that the application of stereotyping, racial profiling, and biased perceptions will not lead to the detection and capturing of terrorists (see Nance, 2003 for additional information on developing skills and tools with TAPIs).

Law Enforcement Response to Terrorism

Responding to a terrorist event presents unique law enforcement and public safety challenges. Four key activities need to be simultaneously implemented and coordinated: (1) initial considerations and assessment, (2) perimeter control, (3) public protection and safety considerations, and (4) crime scene security considerations.

Initial considerations and assessment. Law enforcement and other emergency first responders must accurately and efficiently evaluate the incident area and determine the severity of the danger. Upon establishing the magnitude of the terrorist incident, efforts to control and isolate the danger can begin.

Knowledge of the multicultural communities, customs, and practices of people affected in an incident would facilitate establishing control zones to enhance public safety, security, and care for the casualties and victims. For example, many multicultural communities have members who live in very large, extended families within several households of the same community. Law enforcement officers who do not recognize this may wonder why an order to evacuate and to leave the area resulted in limited and very delayed movement. It is important for them to understand that some members of the extended family might be separated or missing and that family members may be involved in efforts to locate them. Prior multicultural knowledge of and community policing relationships with the affected communities and people would enhance the control and rescue efforts. For example, information about the most effective ways to communicate and to rapidly disseminate warnings based upon the multicultural communities involved might be obtained through community leaders who could assist in interpreting and leading an evacuation (i.e., by keeping the community intact and by assisting in establishing perimeter control), as well as in the identification of sacred and religious structures for safeguarding.

Clearly, law enforcement first responders, given the severity of the situation, must use any and all available resources in an efficient, effective, and humane manner to prepare the scene for ongoing operations and public safety. However, knowledge and sensitivity to some of the prior experiences as victims of terrorism among multicultural people within the community may help to enhance action and safety.

Perimeter control. Law enforcement officers need to use their standard operating procedures for establishing and maintaining perimeter control for "stand-off" distances and for work zones. The magnitude and complexity of the terrorist incident will determine the need for having outer and inner perimeters. The *outer perimeter* is the most distant control boundary for the incident and is used to restrict all public access to the incident. Outer perimeters can be quite large and restrictive; for example, the outer perimeter established after the bombing of the Alfred P. Murrah Federal Building in Oklahoma City included 20 square city blocks. Following any establishment of perimeters, law enforcement officers may need to communicate to the multicultural community the reasons for their exclusion from the area. This is especially important if an *outer perimeter* resulted in community members being excluded or prohibited from their key meeting structures for religious, family, group, and other supports. For example, in their prior home country, people may have been able to return to their homes and community shortly after a terrorist incident (without consideration for the crime-scene investigative elements). If such exclusion is necessary for investigative work or for the protection of the community, effective communication with community members in this regard would be critical.

Public safety and protection considerations. The extent that law enforcement and other first responders are able to act quickly and accurately in conducting a hazard and risk assessment of the affected population of a terrorist incident will determine the approach to public safety and protection. The following three options are available:

1. Evacuation of all threatened and affected population

2. Protection-in-place for all

3. Combination of evacuation and protection-in-place by evacuating some population and protecting other in-place

Effective communication of information and explanation of public safety and protection procedures to members of multicultural communities may be key challenges for many law enforcement agencies. During a terrorist incident, there is no time to locate bilingual personnel or interpreters for assistance in communicating with speakers of other languages, and the customary resources like the AT&T language bank would be ineffective or unavailable. Explaining why multicultural community residents have to evacuate their homes and familiar surroundings, even in the event of a terrorist incident, will require personnel with language skills.

Evacuating the public from the affected area is based upon a decision that indicates the public is at greater risk by remaining in or near the terrorists' incident area. The decision to evacuate is determined in part by the following elements:

1. ***Degree or severity*** of public dangers, harm, and threats as estimated by the hazards and risk assessment.

2. ***Number of individuals*** or the magnitude of the population area affected by the danger or threat.

3. ***Resources*** available to evacuate the affected population to include law enforcement, fire, emergency and other personnel, school buses, privately owned vehicles, and/or public mass transit.

4. ***Notification and instructional resources*** to provide information to the public before and during the evacuation. For multicultural communities, these may include the use of local community leaders as well as ethnic-group media such as radio/television, mobile public address systems, and door-to-door contact. For communities with residents who are primarily speakers of other languages, the need for interpreters and translators is very important in ensuring timely communication and notification.

5. ***Route security*** is a key factor that law enforcement officers and agencies need to ascertain and to maintain so that evacuees are not subjected to further terrorist attacks.

6. ***Opportunity*** to implement the evacuation requires assessing ongoing risks and hazards such as airborne chemical contamination, unexploded bombs, and other unexpected terrorist activities.

7. ***Special needs*** of the evacuees are taken care of to include accurate information regarding the terrorist event and updated summaries of the recovery effort.

Protection-in-place allows the affected populations to remain within the confines of their own dwelling. Like evacuations, the decision for protection-in-place depends on the risk and hazard assessment of the terrorist incident. Basically, if the anticipated dangers and the presenting hazards to the public are made less by having the affected population remain in place, the protection-in-place option is the better solution. Consideration needs to be made for multicultural communities in which there are large, multifamily residents within one household involving family members who are frail, elderly, or very young children. For some within multicultural communities, the preference for the entire extended family to be together may be paramount. In their home countries, if family members became separated or moved, it often meant having members "disappear" and never be seen again. Protection-in-place, if safe and possible, may be much more easily implemented than attempts to evacuate such families, especially in multicultural communities where there may be some language issues involved in receiving and providing specific instructions for an evacuation.

Crime scene security considerations. The *incident commander* has responsibility for the overall entry and exit routes from the incident area. The police are usually the first responders to most catastrophes, including a terrorist attack. However, depending on the nature, severity, and circumstances of the terrorist attack, the on-scene *incident commander* who will oversee the incident command system may or may not be from the police force. Clear communication within the command structure is central to the effective work of the on-scene incident management system, which may consist of personnel from many local public safety departments, as well as state, regional, and federal agencies and personnel. Effective language skills supported by prior multicultural communications training would be a positive benefit in these multijurisdictional, diverse-leadership-style crisis command systems. For example, law enforcement officers and managers who are experienced in knowing that different multicultural groups have different norms, values, communication styles, languages, and practices could transfer those experiences to understanding and working with the differences found within multijurisdictional and multiagency personnel involved in a terrorist incident. The key role of the incident commander is to ensure coordination and collaboration of the responders to the terrorist incident.

Conventional law enforcement procedures and methods should be used for (1) controlling the access points, (2) organizing evacuation or stay-in-place efforts, (3) isolating unstable conditions, (4) preserving crime scene evidence, (5) establishing contamination reduction corridors and areas, and (6) maintaining security and site control. Generally, the agency assigned or designated with site security responsibilities may vary depending on the hazards encountered and the nature of the first responders on scene (usually police or fire in the early stages of a terrorist incident). Clearly, any time there is ongoing criminal activity potential or presence, law enforcement officials need to determine and direct the security measures for crime scene control. In time, control of the perimeter will be the responsibility of law enforcement unless the terrorist incident is of the magnitude that response activities may continue for several weeks. In such prolonged periods for perimeter security and control, the use of military units may be advised on the basis of the decisions of the incident commander and the incident command system that is established for the incident.

Incident Command System for Coordination of Multiple Response Agencies

The responsibilities for responding to a terrorist incident or attack involving nuclear, biological, and chemical WMD materials are outlined in Presidential Decision Directive-39 (PDD-39)—details provided in FEMA (1997). PDD-39 identifies the FBI as the lead agency for crisis management during terrorist attacks and incidents involving nuclear, biological, and chemical materials. PDD-39 also identifies the Federal Emergency Management Agency (FEMA) as the lead agency for the consequence and recovery management during terrorist attacks and incidents involving nuclear, biological, and chemical materials. The Federal Response Plan (FRP) is used as the outline and vehicle for coordinating consequence management efforts under PDD-39. FRP directs *other* federal agencies to support the FBI and FEMA as needed.

Crisis Management

PDD-39 and the FRP designate the FBI with the federal lead responsibility for crisis management in response to threats or acts of terrorism that take place within the United States territory or in international waters and that do not involve the flag vessel of a foreign country. During crisis management, the FBI coordinates closely with local law enforcement authorities to provide a successful law enforcement resolution to the terrorist incident. The FBI also coordinates with other federal agencies and authorities, including FEMA. The FBI field office responsible for the incident site modifies the Field Office Command Post to function as the Joint Operations Center (JOC). The JOC, in turn, has responsibility for coordinating the crisis management effort with the local incident commander and the local incident command system established for the terrorist incident.

Multijurisdictional Action

As noted, in the command structure for crisis management, a variety of diverse federal, state, and local agencies and organizations are involved in multijurisdictional actions that are involved in a terrorist incident or attack. Some of the key elements ensuring success for law enforcement agencies and officers in such incidents include the following:

1. ***Preparation and planning*** provide some of the best avenues for successful crisis management and subsequent recovery from a terrorist incident. The following planned steps are critical:

    *   Develop pertinent plans and policies for terrorist incidents and attacks

- Establish multijurisdictional plans/protocols and mutual-aid agreements
- Ensure availability of multicultural law enforcement personnel with language expertise
- Implement, as much as possible, preventive procedures and plans
- Train law enforcement personnel as first responders and as members of multi-jurisdictional teams involved in a terrorist incident
- Provide background information about the makeup of the different multicultural communities and their prior experiences as victims of terrorism
- Rehearse possible events and incidents
- Acquire the necessary protective and communication equipment
- Establish multidiscipline community service teams (and, again, where possible, provide for the range of language expertise required by the community)
- Establish a network of multicultural leaders and communities for communication, intelligence, and response implementation

2. ***Cost and deployment*** of resources have been highlighted by most local governments with respect to the degree of burden and expenditure needed by local law enforcement and by other public safety agencies involved in possible terrorism incidents.

> Government resources increasingly have been thrown into the fight against terrorism, and that endangers community policing, Los Angeles Police Chief William J. Bratton declared at a public forum yesterday. Community policing caused a downward trend in crime nationally in the 1990s, but crime is beginning to rebound because less money and attention is being devoted to community policing in this decade, he said. Many of those resources have been siphoned to prevent terrorism, and there has been a general disinvestment in policing, he said. In the previous decade, 100,000 additional police were hired and $3 billion was spent on research, including the application of DNA evidence, and on the equipping of police forces. Bratton called for a balancing of the expenditures so that both policing and terrorism are addressed. (Smith, 2006)

Since local tax-based funds are insufficient to address the enormity of costs involved in the planning, prevention, and deployment of resources to address terrorism concerns and issues, one of the key concerns within multicultural communities is the diversion of funds from community-policing activities to the war on terrorism.

3. ***Access to intelligence and informational databases*** provides the information necessary for the prevention of and response to terrorist threats. The best prevention against terrorist incidents and acts at the local community level is to ensure coordination with federal and state intelligence sources and access to ongoing intelligence-gathering capacity from the federal level. On the local level, it is important that law enforcement officers and agencies develop critical relationships and networks with the local multicultural communities. Developing such relationships requires both ongoing efforts and constant renewal of the relationships through clear communication and trust between law enforcement and community members. For example, in the foiled terrorist plot to

down trans-Atlantic British airlines with explosives, the tip to the local police department came from a person in the Muslim community who had been concerned about the activities of an acquaintance after the July 7, 2005, terror attacks in London (Arena, 2006).

As noted in the IACP publication *Leading From the Front* (2001), "A very practical tool to ensure that this [developing informational database] is done is to keep a running log, 24 hours a day, of all unusual events. This way, even if the immediate staff handling the incident does not perceive its intelligence value, senior staffs' later review of the log may pick up the opportunity and justify further investigation."

4. *Multijurisdictional training and rehearsal* have been identified as critical elements in the successful implementation of terrorist incident management and recovery. Clearly, in multijurisdictional efforts, there would have been very few prior opportunities to develop the relationships, awareness, communication, and other processes necessary for a coordinated effort. As illustrated in the following example, the involvement of these multijurisdictional agencies and their personnel provides valuable lessons learned for any possible terrorist incidence.

> A massive cloud of lethal gas, dozens of agonizing deaths by asphyxiation, an unknown number of hidden nuclear devices, executions, a ship full of hostages, and an enemy mine bobbing in the harbor: If any of it had been real, it would have been an absolutely horrible couple of days at the Port of Hueneme. Fortunately, the series of catastrophes was part of an anti-terrorism exercise, an elaborate two-day drama staged Tuesday and Wednesday with the help of the Navy, the Coast Guard, some 140 FBI agents, 81 officers from the Ventura County Sheriff's Department—in all, representatives from 18 military and law-enforcement agencies. . . . Along the way, the participating agencies picked up lessons they will use to streamline some of their procedures. "There won't be wholesale changes," said Banks, of the warfare center. "But even an hour saved could be a crucial hour." The Ventura County sheriff's SWAT team learned that storming a ship is a lengthier process than taking over a home, said department spokesman Eric Nishimoto. With the FBI taking the lead in the antiterrorist operations, officers also realized that dealing with a hierarchy of agents from all over the U.S. was not equivalent to dealing with operatives from the local office. "It's a totally different dynamic," Nishimoto said. Simply communicating with other agencies was sometimes difficult. "Everyone's enmeshed in their own acronyms," said Tom Netzer, who coordinated the exercise for the Center for Asymmetric Warfare. "It helped when we got everyone to just speak English." (Chawkins, 2003, p. M1)

Training for terrorist incidents that are multijurisdictional in nature would allow for the rehearsal and practices necessary for effective overall terrorism response efforts. As in any simulated practice exercise, not all components of a terrorist incident can be anticipated or incorporated. Nonetheless, such training and rehearsal would allow for a timelier implementation of the response strategies important to a terrorist incident, as noted in the next section. Training in response to terrorism, to date, has included limited scenarios related to multicultural community elements. In time, emphases upon language expertise, bilingual communications, and interpreter participation need to be added to training exercises.

Building Community Networks and Resources

In order to detect and deter terrorist incidents and attacks, the development of strong community networks, relationships, and resources is critical. As noted earlier, the ability to obtain critical information from a community assessment depends on ongoing, positive, and trusted relationships within the multicultural communities.

> In Boston police's new antiterror strategy, some of the frontline recruits will be neighborhood watch groups. Police Commissioner Kathleen M. O'Toole is planning to spend federal homeland security money to help watch groups spot possible terrorists an initiative designed at the same time to rebuild the city's once nationally recognized community policing program. "There's no bright line between terrorism and ordinary inner-city crime," O'Toole told the *Globe*. "The federal government has made it very clear that if we launch homeland security initiatives that also have some benefit via ripple effect on other aspects of policing, then that's OK." The Department of Homeland Security advises the US Justice Department on a program called Citizen Corps, which includes a national neighborhood watch program incorporating terrorism awareness education with crime prevention. "It serves as a way to bring residents together to focus on emergency preparedness and emergency response training," said Steven Llanes, a Homeland Security spokesman. (Smalley, 2005)

It is equally important to develop the internal networks and relationships within the different agencies and departments of the local and statewide public safety community, as illustrated by this example involving several agencies from New Jersey:

> About 2,000 police officers statewide have already been trained by a consortium of federal and state experts to assist the anti-terror effort. One of those most involved with the effort to share intelligence with the myriad of local, county, state, and federal agencies is Sidney J. Caspersen, the director of the state Office of Counter-Terrorism. Armed with an $8.6 million budget, the former FBI agent is directing the installation of a terrorism database that will be linked to computer terminals in every police station in the state. Caspersen also sends out intelligence bulletins to several hundred private industrial concerns ranging from the state's largest corporations to more modest businesses. His office also sends similar bulletins to local officials, alerting them to potential terrorist threats, suspicious incidents, and vulnerabilities in the state's infrastructure. "I believe we are the intelligence-gathering organization for the state," Caspersen said, adding that he has been hiring analysts who understand the culture that fosters terrorism and investigators who can develop a network of informants. "My goal is to detect and deter," he said. "I'm not really looking at taking people to court." (Maddux, 2003, p. A1)

Part Two, "Cultural Specifics for Law Enforcement," includes discussion of group-specific strategies that may be used to enhance communications, develop relationships, and widen the community network within the different multicultural communities to develop strategies for effective detection and deterrence within those communities.

Using Ethnic and Multicultural Media as a Resource

For any terrorist incident, law enforcement agencies must help to provide a constant flow of credible information to the local community. Clearly, if positive relationships have been formed with the diversity of residents and the multicultural community leaders, the law enforcement agency's credibility would not be suspect and/or in question. Media sources used for the release of information should include the ones used by most populations, as well as those used by specific multicultural groups, especially that broadcast or print in the language of the key multicultural groups of the community. Some public safety agencies may be concerned about not having their information already prepared and translated into the language of the diverse ethnic and cultural groups; however, given the nature and importance of the information, most ethnic media will do the translation in order to provide critical information to their audiences.

Policies, procedures, and mechanisms need to be in place for releasing information to enable the safety and security of all community residents. This means that the involvement of ethnic and multicultural media is critical; the readiness of translations and interpretations are key in ensuring appropriate responses, alleviating any unnecessary fears or concerns, and providing assurances that public safety agencies and officers are in control of the situation. The media has been shown to be the most efficient and reliable means to disseminate information rapidly to the community regarding a terrorist incident and to notify community residents of the subsequent response by the public safety agencies. Strategic media events should be held to continuously inform the public that the incident is well under control, the personnel are well prepared and trained to handle the incident, and the community's recovery is fully expected.

Whether dealing with a terrorist incident or an everyday event, the basis for effective communications with the community through the media is a strong partnership and established positive relationships with the media. Law enforcement agencies need to understand that whether in crisis management or in daily peacekeeping, the media has a dual role: to obtain information, stories, and perspectives on the incident for news-reporting objectives and to inform the community efficiently of impending dangers and threats stemming from the incident. Good media relations allow for the strategic communication of critical incident information to the communities served by the law enforcement agencies. To reach multicultural communities, police officers must go beyond the conventional and mainstream media sources and become familiar with all media, in English and in other languages, that will reach the broadest populations in the shortest amount of time.

KEY ISSUES IN LAW ENFORCEMENT

1. *False Tips from Informants:* As with any information-gathering and intelligence operations, there will always be the need to determine the validity, reliability, and trustworthiness of information received. Law enforcement agencies have always depended on informants for sources of critical information as part of any investigative process. In a terrorism incident, some of these informants would be very connected with the criminal and often most notorious elements within the community. Moreover, some of these informants may be keenly

aware of what is "on the street" but may have ulterior or personal motives for providing information. Both standard interviewing and incident interview skills and tools need to be used to sort out false information and to confirm the credible sources important to the facts of a terrorist incident.

2. ***Training to Heighten Awareness:*** Until recently, issues of terrorism and weapons of mass destruction were primarily the domain of the federal law enforcement agencies, with minor involvement of local law enforcement personnel. The awareness of terrorism cues, situations, and warnings of possible acts are not part of the everyday experience of local law enforcement personnel and their agencies. Terrorist-related awareness training has been used as an approach to heighten the awareness and skill levels of local law enforcement officers:

> Charles Anderson, a five-year detective with the Baltimore Police Department, said he's seen a lot more training—nearly all of it terrorist-related. Anderson teaches a class on informant training, he said. "It kind of makes you more aware of what's going on," said the 34-year-old, dressed in a navy-blue shirt with his department's name on it. "You are not as laid-back. More cautious, I should say." The feeling is shared by officers in less urban areas, who also see their communities as vulnerable. An example is St. Charles Parish, in southeast Louisiana. Detective Othello Carter, with the parish's Sheriff's Office, said he views as targets the nuclear power plant, chemical plants and oil refineries in his jurisdiction, about 25 miles west of New Orleans. "You used to give it a little glance," the 40-year-old Carter said, about checks of the facilities. "Now, you're vigilant about looking around more." He continued: "You can always say something like that wouldn't happen here. But you just look at places now, and imagine how easily you could get into them." (Lewis, 2003).

3. ***Extension of Community Policing Approaches:*** Community-based policing has been proven to be a valuable approach to working with multicultural community groups and to learning about their needs, concerns, and problems (Oliver, 2004). Chapter 1 discusses some of the key concepts, principals, and practices for community-oriented policing within multicultural communities. In this chapter, we highlight the importance of using these same community-policing concepts, tools, and practices for information gathering as well as for information disseminating following a terrorism incident. As noted in the next example, the process of community policing could provide the "eyes and ears" for our country in the war on terrorism:

> To stop terrorists before they strike, the Department of Homeland Security should implement some of the preventative policing initiatives that were used to combat crime in the 1990s, Flynn said. "What did we learn in the 1990s, when we got federal assistance to deal with crime? We learned about community policing, problem solving, prevention, partnerships with the community. . . . And doing all those things helped us produce the greatest crime decreases in American history. All those attributes apply to terrorism. . . . It's a false dichotomy to separate homeland security from criminal justice. It's the same fabric." (Deleo, 2005)

SUMMARY

Law enforcement agencies today have an emerging and vital role in the war on terrorism that involves the critical step of building key relationships and networks with multicultural communities, including ethnic and multicultural media sources. Multicultural knowledge and skills of local law enforcement can contribute to uncovering key information, resources, and tools in dealing with the prevention and criminal investigation of terrorism, including intelligence-gathering needs. The chapter covered problems in dealing with terrorism involving multicultural communities and the actions of law enforcement officers' possible bias, prejudice, and stereotyping of certain multicultural groups. The chapter closed with specific recommendations important to the emerging roles of law enforcement officers and other emergency services personnel in dealing with terrorism within multicultural communities.

DISCUSSION QUESTIONS AND ISSUES

1. ***Stereotyping and Biased Perceptions:*** Law enforcement officers and agencies must guard themselves from using a stereotype-based or racial profiling approach for detecting terrorism and in providing homeland security. Which groups or individuals in your community might be stereotyped as possible terrorists? What characteristics of these groups and individuals make them susceptible to stereotyping and biased perceptions? What are ways for professional peace officers to guard themselves against such ineffective practices?

2. Select an area in your city or town that would have the greatest diversity of population (e.g., race, ethnicity, age, income, and other dimensions of diversity) for this discussion question. How would you implement and coordinate the four key activities (i.e., initial considerations and assessment, perimeter control, public protection and safety considerations, and crime scene security considerations) in responding to a possible chemical terrorist incident in the area that you have selected?

3. The authors identified media resources as an effective way to communicate and disseminate information to community residents. What media resources might you use for communicating a terrorist incident involving B-NICE materials in your city or town? Provide some examples of multicultural media resources that might be used in your area. What approaches might you use to develop positive and effective relationships between these media resources and your local law enforcement agency?

4. Select an area in your city or town that would have the greatest diversity of languages spoken. How would you plan for and ensure adequate bilingual personnel or other language resources to assist these community residents in the case of a terrorist incident?

WEBSITE RESOURCES

Visit these websites for additional information about multicultural law enforcement issues in dealing with terrorism:

Federal Bureau of Investigation, Explosive Unit:
http://www.fbi.gov/hq/lab/org/eu.htm

> This website provides the latest information about bombing incidents in the United States as well as international incidents affecting U.S. citizens.

Federal Bureau of Investigation Disaster Squad:
http://www.fbi.gov/hq/lab/disaster/disaster.htm

> This website provides information about the FBI Disaster Squad, which is currently made up of approximately 40 people—four agents and the rest latent fingerprint specialists—all from the Forensic Analysis Branch in the FBI Laboratory.

Federal Emergency Management Agency: http://www.fema.gov/

> This website provides a range of useful information related to the management of community, state, and national emergencies.

U.S. Army Medical Research Institute of Chemical Defense:
http://ccc.apgea.army.mil/

> This website provides both general as well as research-oriented information and findings on chemical weapons of mass destruction.

U.S. Department of Defense Chemical and Biological Defense Information Analysis Center (CBIAC): http://www.cbiac.apgea.army.mil/

> The website provides background and technical information on biological and chemical weapons that might be encountered in a terrorist attack.

REFERENCES

"A Nation Challenged: The Terrorists; Hijacker Got a Speeding Ticket." (2002, January 9). *New York Times,* p. A12.

Ahmad, E., and Barsamian, D. (2001). *Terrorism: Theirs and Ours.* New York: Seven Stories Press.

Arena, K. (2006, August 11). "Officials: Plot Suspects Met Alleged al Qaeda Bomber." CNN.com, posted August 11, 2006, 12:36 PM, at http://www.cnn.com/2006/ WORLD/ europe/08/11/terror.plot/index.html.

Bankson, R. (2003). *Terrorism: National in Scope, Local in Execution.* Community Links. Washington, D.C.: Community Policing Consortium.

"Burdens of Security: Omaha-Area Agencies Are Cooperating Well in Guarding against Attacks by Terrorists." (2003, June 16). *Omaha World Herald,* p. B6.

Chawkins, S. (2003, November 6). "Agencies Get a Taste of Terrorism in Action: Simulated Attacks at the Port of Hueneme Help Build Teamwork among Emergency Groups." *Los Angeles Times.*

Corley, S. H., B. L., Smith, and K. R. Damphousse. (2005). "The Changing Face of American Terrorism." In L. L. Snowden and B. C. Whitsel (Eds.), *Terrorism: Research, Readings, and Realities.* Upper Saddle River, NJ: Pearson/Prentice Hall.

Deleo, D. (2005, August 5). "Call for Broader Anti-Terror Effort," *Patriot Ledger,* p. 11.

Department of Justice Office of Justice Programs. (1997). *Emergency Response to Terrorism: Basic Concepts.* Washington, D.C.: U.S. Department of Justice.

Dershowitz, A. M. (2002). *Why Terrorism Works: Understanding the Threat, Responding to the Challenge.* New Haven Conn.: Yale University Press.

Federal Bureau of Investigation. (1996). *Terrorism in the United States 1995.* Washington, D.C.: Terrorist Research and Analytical Center, National Security Division.

FBI Bomb Data Center. (1999). *1999 Bombing Incidents.* General Information Bulletin 99-1. Washington, D.C.

Federal Emergency Management Agency (FEMA). (1992). *The Federal Response Plan for Public Law 93-288, as amended.* Washington, DC: Author.

Federal Emergency Management Agency (FEMA). (1997). *The Federal Response Plan Notice of Change: Terrorism Incident Annex.* Washington, DC: Author.

Ford, P. (2002, March 27). "Legal War on Terror Lacks Weapons." *Christian Science Monitor,* Section 4, p. 1.

Heymann, P. B. (2001). *Terrorism and America: A Commonsense Strategy for a Democratic Society.* Cambridge, MA: MIT Press.

Hoffman, B. (1998). *Inside Terrorism.* New York: Columbia University Press.

Howard, D. R., and R. L. Sawyer. (Eds.). (2004). *Terrorism and Counterterrorism: Understanding the New Security Environment.* Guilford, Conn.: McGraw-Hill/Dushkin.

International Association of Chiefs of Police (IACP). (2001). *Leading from the Front: Project Response: Terrorism.* Alexandria, VA: Author.

International Association of Chiefs of Police (IACP). (2002). *Project Response: The Oklahoma City Tragedy.* Alexandria, VA: Author.

Kleinberg, E., and D. Davies. (2001, October 19). "Delray Police Stopped Speeding Terror Suspect." *Palm Beach Post* (Florida), p. A1.

Lewis, R. C. (2003, August 4). "FBI Director Speaks of 'New Era' of Cooperation Since Attacks." *Associated Press.*

Litchblau, E. (2003, June 18). "Threats and Responses: Law Enforcement; Bush Issues Racial Profiling Ban But Exempts Security Inquiries." *New York Times,* p. A1.

Maddux, M. (2003, September 8). "Guarding Against Future Acts of Terror." *Bergen Record* (NJ), p. A1.

Nance, M. W. (2003). *The Terrorist Recognition Handbook.* Guilford, Conn.: Lyons Press.

Oliver, W. M. (2007), *Homeland Security for Policing.* Upper Saddle River, NJ: Prentice Hall.

Oliver, W. M. (2004). *Community-Oriented Policing: A Systemic Approach to Policing* (3rd ed.). Upper Saddle River, NJ: Prentice-Hall.

Roig-Franzia, M., and P. Davis. (2002, January 9). "For Want of a Crystal Ball; Police Stopped Two Hijackers in Days Before Attacks." *Washington Post,* p. A13.

Schmitt, R. B., Goldman, J. J., and Silverstein, K. (2003, August 14). "Details of Sting Tell of Wider Threat." *Los Angeles Times,* p. MN1.

Smalley, S. (2005, May 30), "Terror plan relies on watch groups," *The Boston Globe,* p. B1.

Smith, G. (2006, March 2), "Community policing guru issues warning," *The Providence Journal* (Rhode Island), p. C01.

Snowden, L. L. and B. C. Whitsel. (Eds.). (2005). *Terrorism: Research, Readings, and Realities.* Upper Saddle River, NJ: Pearson/Prentice Hall.

Terrorist Research and Analytical Center. (1995). *Terrorism in the United States.* Washington, D.C.: U.S. Department of Justice.

"Trooper Describes Arrest 90 Minutes after Bombing." (1997, April 28). *Deseret News* (Salt Lake City), p. A2.

U.S. Departments of the Army and the Air Force. (1990). *Military Operations in Low Intensity Conflict.* Washington, D.C.: Author.

U.S. Department of State. (1995). *Patterns of Global Terrorism.* Washington, D.C.: U.S. Department of State, Publication No. 10239.

U.S. Department of State. (1997). *Patterns of Global Terrorism. 1996.* Washington, D.C.: Office of the Coordinator for Counterterrorism, U.S. Department of State, Publication No. 10433.

Chapter 11

Multicultural Law Enforcement in Homeland Security and Disaster Preparedness

OVERVIEW

The President of the United States created the Department of Homeland Security (DHS) as a cabinet-level department on November 25, 2002, with the main objective of protecting the United States from terrorism. With the development of the DHS, law enforcement officers and agencies face many new and changing roles and responsibilities. These include detecting threats of terrorism, developing and analyzing information regarding threats and vulnerabilities, using information and intelligence provided, and coordinating the security efforts against terrorism. Law enforcement officers' changing roles also include assisting in the security of the transportation system, cooperating in the enforcement of the immigration laws, ensuring for the security of our borders, and preparing for emergencies, disasters, and community assistance in coordination with the DHS. The major goals of the DHS focus on:

1. Preventing attacks of terrorism
2. Reducing vulnerabilities for terrorist attacks
3. Analyzing threats of terrorism and issuing warnings accordingly
4. Providing security for our transportation systems and for U.S. borders.
5. Preparing for emergency readiness and response
6. Minimizing the damage from terrorism and facilitating recovery from terrorist attacks

This chapter highlights the roles and functions of law enforcement officers and agencies in their work in addressing the six goals of homeland security in multicultural communities. Clearly, criminal justice practices and public safety procedures already define much of the homeland security and disaster preparedness work and activities within law enforcement agencies. The emphasis in this chapter is on the specific aspects of multicultural law enforcement applicable to homeland security and disaster preparedness issues in the context of our diverse communities.

COMMENTARY

Americans' sense of security with respect to terrorism was "shattered" following the September 11, 2001, attacks on American soil. In one concerted and orchestrated set of terrorist attacks it was clear to all Americans that the security of our homeland was vulnerable.

> . . . with the grace of Allah, the battle has moved inside America. We will strive to keep it going—with Allah's permission—until victory is attained, or until we meet Allah through martyrdom. (Osama bin Laden interview, October 21, 2001, quoted in Robbins, 2002)

The United States rallied quickly to institute measures for overcoming the fear and shock of the terrorists' attacks. As noted by Donohue (2002), more than 97 percent of the business conducted by Congress between September 11, 2001, and January 11, 2002, was related to terrorism and more than 450 bills, amendments, and resolutions relating to counterterrorism were proposed. Since national security was at stake, our reaction to the fear and vulnerability generated by terrorism was to move forward.

> As we are the first responders in any natural disaster or terrorist attack that takes place in our communities, we know quite well that the role of law enforcement is key to the nation's homeland security. This is what we have been trained to do. We take steps to improve our community's safety. We handle crises. We deal with emergencies. We reduce vulnerability to known threats and hazards. We provide oversight of police training to deal with unusual circumstances. And we coordinate with other emergency management and law enforcement agencies. This is the core of our profession. (Chief R. Gil Kerlikowske, Seattle Chief of Police, remarks given at the Washington Association of Sheriff and Police Chiefs Conference, Spokane, Wash., May 21, 2003)

The nation advanced and created the DHS, which incorporated the roles and functions of 22 federal agencies with 170,000 employees (the largest reorganization of the federal government since the creation of the Department of Defense in 1947). The DHS, in turn, extended, created, and developed new roles and functions for law enforcement in the war against terrorism and in providing homeland security, which were never before within the central realm of work for the public safety and legal systems. In 2004, DHS presented its Strategic Plan that further articulated the major strategic goals to be achieved by DHS (Office of Homeland Security, 2004; Office of Domestic Preparedness, 2003):

1. *Awareness:* Identify and understand threats, assess vulnerabilities, determine potential impacts, and disseminate timely information to our homeland security partners and the American public

2. *Prevention:* Detect, deter, and mitigate threats to our homeland

3. *Protection:* Safeguard our people and their freedoms, critical infrastructure, property and the economy of our Nation from acts of terrorism, natural disasters, or other emergencies

4. *Response:* Lead, manage, and coordinate the national response to acts of terrorism, natural disasters, or other emergencies

5. ***Recovery:*** Lead national, state, local, and private sector efforts to restore services and rebuild communities after acts of terrorism, natural disasters, or other emergencies

6. ***Service:*** Serve the public effectively by facilitating lawful trade, travel, and immigration

7. ***Organizational Excellence:*** Value our most important resource, our people. Create a culture that promotes a common identity, innovation, mutual respect, accountability, and teamwork to achieve efficiency, effectiveness, and operational synergies.

According to the DHS, these new and changing roles for law enforcement present additional challenges for the day-to-day work within the criminal justice system and to the collaborative, cooperative, and interagency efforts required in dealing with terrorism, homeland security, and disaster preparedness. Obviously, the changing work and new initiatives within law enforcement have stretched the resources and knowledge base necessary for implementation, especially within multicultural communities. Chapter 10 presented the unique issues of multicultural law enforcement in responding to acts of terrorism and the follow-up actions necessary to address such attacks and incidents. This chapter focuses on the challenges of multicultural law enforcement agencies and officers in detecting and preventing terrorism and the actions necessary to address the goals of homeland security within our diverse communities.

HISTORICAL INFORMATION AND BACKGROUND

Homeland security, through the gathering, processing, and application of intelligence, provides our nation with a blanket of protection against attacks. As a result of the geographic isolation of the United States, most Americans in the past have felt secure about their homeland and did not perceive that attacks could be launched on U.S. shores. Both Mexico and Canada were seen as friendly neighbors, and not as sources of threat or danger to Americans' sense of homeland security.

Prior to September 11, 2001, many Americans, from the person on the street to governmental leaders, perceived that enemies would need to surmount the tremendous burden of first having to cross vast expanses of ocean just to get their troops in our country for an attack. Pearl Harbor was seen as an exception, and no troops had actually landed on American soil. Moreover, extensive logistics were thought to be necessary to sustain any kind of attack effort for replenishing supplies and troops, even if enemy troops could land on our shores. As a result of the perceived advantage of the intervening ocean to the United States, much of the efforts and activities for homeland security in the past were located within the functions of the federal government (e.g., FBI, CIA, military, Department of State) to be implemented outside of the United States.

Local and state criminal justice agencies like the police, sheriff, probation, and prison departments had limited roles in homeland security. The lesser involvement of local law enforcement in homeland security was unlike most countries around the world in which local and regional law enforcement agencies work closely with national departments on issues of homeland security. The roles of local and regional law enforcement agencies in the United States, with respect to homeland security, have increased greatly in recent times, and will most likely begin to resemble many of their global counterparts in cities and states around the world.

Throughout the Cold War era with Russia and the communist bloc countries, and in the Vietnam War era, there were many indications that homeland security encompassed much more than merely keeping enemy troops from marching on U.S. soil. Some examples of the need for greater homeland security efforts during this period were (1) spies infiltrating into agencies of the United States government, (2) Soviet missiles based in Cuba that would lead to the Missile Crisis and the Bay of Pigs invasion of Cuba, (3) assassinations of President John F. Kennedy and Rev. Martin Luther King, Jr., and (4) violent riots and demonstrations against the Vietnam War. However, the notion of the security of our country continued to be viewed as less the work of local law enforcement and more the work of the national agencies (e.g., CIA, National Security Agency [NSA], FBI, Defense Intelligence Agency [DIA]). Even for many of the college student demonstrations and riots related to the protest of the war in Vietnam, security efforts were conducted via the mobilization of national troops into the local regions (e.g., the use of the National Guard at Kent State University and at the University of California, Berkeley). In part because of the student riots on campus and surrounding areas, law enforcement agencies began to develop procedures and acquire specialized tools for gathering intelligence and for securing local areas (e.g., Special Weapons and Tactics [SWAT] teams). The lines of operation continued to be clearly drawn: (1) Issues affecting the security of our nation (even though local in nature) continued to be handled by federal agencies like the FBI and Federal Emergency Management Agency (FEMA), and (2) issues related to the enforcement of local laws and regulations remained the jurisdiction of the public safety agencies of the respective areas.

Until the attacks of September 11, 2001, almost all of the homeland security efforts were seen as national in direction, leadership, and scope. Our policies for counterterrorism were still centered on dealing with enemies and events primarily outside of the United States. For example, the U.S. policy regarding terrorism included:

1. Make no concessions and strike no deals.

2. Bring terrorists to justice for their crimes.

3. Isolate and bring pressure on countries that sponsor terrorism to force them to change their behaviors.

4. Develop the counterterrorism capabilities of those countries that work with the United States and that request assistance (Pillar, 2001; FEMA, 1997).

Starting around the mid-1990s, national policies and procedures for dealing with terrorism and homeland security were enacted; however, the focus was still very much on leadership and direction on a national level with implementation by federal agencies (FEMA, 1997). Involvement of local and regional law enforcement agencies was minimal in the planning, policy development, and implementation of the federal response to terrorism and homeland security.

Subsequent inquiries following the terrorist attacks on September 11, 2001, made it very clear that the detection and prevention of terrorism and the response to both international or domestic terrorists, would require the coordinated and collaborative efforts of local public safety agencies and officers with federal departments and organizations. The role of the DHS is one of facilitating and developing the avenues of communication between these entities to ensure viable and effective leadership, policies, and procedures for homeland security in the United States.

A truly successful national strategy must recognize, embrace, and value the vast diversity that exists among state, tribal, and local law enforcement and public safety agencies. These agencies serve communities that have vastly different needs and expectations. Consequently their public safety agencies have developed capabilities that are tailored to their unique needs. As a result of this vibrant diversity, it is clear that a one-size-fits-all approach to homeland security planning is neither appropriate, nor will it be successful. It is also vital, as we strive to establish the necessary infrastructure, all public safety agencies at all levels of government, work together in a noncompetitive, collaborative fashion. Public safety agencies must work together to determine what is the most effective and efficient means to meet their shared responsibilities of protecting the public. Only by remaining unified and speaking with one voice can first responders hope to ensure limited resources are allocated in a fashion that will ensure maximum benefit for the communities they serve (International Association of Chiefs of Police, 2005).

ENSURING MULTICULTURAL CONSIDERATIONS IN HOMELAND SECURITY AND DISASTER PREPAREDEDNESS STRATEGIES

Oliver (2007) summarized the process and major steps taken to develop a national strategy for homeland security by the police which include some of the following key research studies and reports:

1. *National Strategy for Homeland Security* (Office of Homeland Security, 2002), which details the broad array of strategies and issues for the United States

2. *From Hometown Security to Homeland Security* (IACP, 2005), which highlights the role of local police in homeland security and the "best practices" for achieving a national strategy for homeland security and disaster preparedness

3. *Homeland Security: Best Practices for Local Government* (Kemp, 2003), which identifies best practices from local law enforcement for homeland security

4. *Protecting Your Community from Terrorism: Strategies for Local Law Enforcement* (Murphy and Plotkin, 2003), a joint effort by the Police Executive Research Forum (PERF) and the office of COPS, which provides the insights of national, state, and local law enforcement leaders on homeland security strategies.

Chief Kerlikowske (2003) of the Seattle Police Department highlighted the critical areas that local law enforcement officials and departments need to address as part of the national strategy for homeland security and disaster preparedness:

1. Intelligence and Warning

2. Border and Transportation Security

3. Domestic Counterterrorism

4. Protecting Critical Infrastructure and Key Assets

5. Defending Against Catastrophic Threats

6. Emergency Preparedness and Response

In the following sections, we address each of the six critical areas noted above and the key factors important to multicultural communities within each area for multicultural law enforcement.

Intelligence and Warning

As emphasized in the IACP (2005) report "Hometown Security is Homeland Security," with over 700,000 offices involved in daily law enforcement and public safety efforts, police departments and their officers have close knowledge of their constituencies and have developed valuable relationships within their multicultural and diverse communities. The strengths of such day-to-day law enforcement efforts in local communities enable state, local, and tribal law enforcement officials to develop unique relationships within their communities to: (1) assess and gather intelligence and information; (2) identify, investigate, and apprehend suspected terrorists; and (3) provide and disseminate information and warnings to the local communities (IACP, 2005).

Since the establishment of the DHS, law enforcement agencies have been receiving a variety of intelligence information, advisories, warnings, and other pertinent communications regarding the efforts and activities to be implemented in local communities. As noted earlier, local law enforcement agencies and officers, because of their knowledge of the existing multicultural communities and networks, have been called upon to aid in the data gathering and development of useful intelligence regarding possible terrorists. Such efforts have often sparked a mixed reception by law enforcement agencies. Some have regarded requests for cooperative efforts as putting a strain on the established relationships of community policing within multicultural communities. As noted in Chapter 10, public confidence and trust in law enforcement agencies are essential for the effective prevention of and response to terrorism and for homeland security. Residents in diverse communities representing different races, ethnic backgrounds, religions, and other aspects of diversity must be able to trust that they will be treated fairly and protected as part of homeland security. This is of particular importance when there might be some perceptions, assumptions, and/or stereotypes among community residents as to who might be a "terrorist amongst us." When local law enforcement agencies and officers are called upon to provide assistance, the tasks of information gathering and interviewing possible terrorist suspects within multicultural communities involve the following critical steps:

1. ***Contact with Community Leaders:*** Law enforcement officers need to work closely with community leaders to establish a cooperative plan for gathering the needed information. Often, announcements made by the community leaders to inform the multicultural communities of the reasons for information gathering and the processes involved can be very effective. Community leaders could, for example, work with law enforcement agencies' community relations offices to develop a communication plan for the effective dissemination of information.

2. ***Utilize a Communication Plan:*** It is essential to have a well-developed and pilot-tested communication plan to ensure that the proper messages are provided

to the multicultural communities involved. This is particularly important when language translations and interpreting are necessary. A carefully pretested core message regarding data-gathering procedures and interviews will usually work better than on-the-spot messages subject to the momentary interpretation of those who first hear such information.

3. ***Clearly Define and Spell out the Implications for Participation in the Data-Gathering Process:*** When it comes to accusations of terrorism and/or fears related to homeland security, members from multicultural communities who might be stereotyped as "terrorists," or have experienced prejudice by others in this regard, would naturally be quite cautious of any contact with law enforcement agencies and officers. Providing clearly defined procedures and information regarding how the data gathering and interviews are to be used would be most important. Additionally, if there are federal-agency consequences (e.g., being reported to the ICE for a visa violation), these elements should be clearly stated to ensure an ongoing relationship of trust with members of the multicultural communities involved.

4. ***Utilize Law Enforcement Personnel and Translators/Interpreters from the Same or Similar Multicultural Communities:*** To the extent it is possible, use of law enforcement personnel who are from the same or similar ethnic/cultural communities would add to sustaining the building of relationship and trust necessary in such information-gathering processes. Clearly, the availability of bilingual personnel will make a significant difference to speakers of other languages.

Using Information and Intelligence Provided

Law enforcement agencies are provided many intelligence and information sources for their work related to homeland security. Such information generally is packaged from the different U.S. intelligence agencies and distributed by the FBI. The FBI's Strategic Information Operations Center (SIOC) is one of the key centers for homeland security and the war on terrorism. Agents from the FBI, CIA, Defense Department, Customs, ATF, Secret Service, and NSA work side-by-side to consolidate the interagency intelligence work.

The Terrorist Threat Integration Center (TTIC), which opened in January 2003 functioning under the CIA's direction, will incorporate the intelligence from both foreign and domestic sources regarding terrorists identified by the DHS, the FBI's Counterterrorism Division, the CIA's Counterterrorism Center, and the Department of Defense.

Law enforcement agencies' and officers' use of intelligence to deter and prosecute terrorists may be more troublesome in practice than in concept. Most terrorists commit no crime until their act of terrorism. The extent to which law enforcement agencies are able to take action prior to a terrorist act or incident presents legal and jurisdictional dilemmas. As noted by Norwitz (2002), because "the objective of a criminal investigation is successful prosecution, all law enforcement effort must withstand judicial scrutiny at trial. Provision of Articles IV, V, and VI of the U.S. Constitution, as well as the Bill of Rights, offer powerful protections against law enforcement excess, which, by extension, applies to international terrorists operating on our soil."

Moreover, law enforcement must continue to maintain positive police–community relationships in order to properly serve the diverse society and multicultural communities within its jurisdiction. Such services include protecting those who might be wrongly accused and/or incorrectly stereotyped as terrorists. Clearly, the sentiment of members from multicultural communities, as well as those from the mainstream majority community, is one of protecting the civil rights of citizens.

> The federal government wants to take the war on terrorism to the grass-roots level by encouraging truckers, bus drivers, railroad conductors, mail carriers and local utility workers to call in tips about suspicious activity. . . . As the program gears up to begin as soon as August with up to 1 million volunteers recruited in 10 cities. Muslims and civil liberties groups say they fear that the war on terrorism is about to take a decidedly ominous turn. "The American Civil Liberties Union of Wisconsin is concerned that the TIPS proposal may not make us safer, but will turn millions of Americans into government informants," Wisconsin ACLU director Chris Ahmuty said last week. He fears tipsters might phone in false reports about a disliked neighbor, or fall prey to racial profiling or bias. Syed Ahsani, chairman of the Southwest region of the American Muslim Alliance and a resident of Arlington, Texas, said he envisions amateur sleuths spying on innocent Americans—particularly those of Middle Eastern descent—in truck stop breakrooms, along isolated rail lines and in their own neighborhoods. . . . The Justice Department would act as a clearinghouse for the tips. Postal Service won't do it. Workers across the nation, and in Madison, offered mixed reactions to Operation TIPS last week. ("Tipline or a Spy Force?," 2002, p. B1)

For now and certainly for the near future, the work of law enforcement agencies in homeland security and in dealing with terrorism will continue to be a work in progress. This will be especially true in the collection and application of intelligence information related to homeland security. Ford (2002) has noted the need for a new paradigm for law enforcement's efforts on homeland security that does not exist at this time. It is clear that law enforcement agencies have roles in the DHS' fight against terrorism; however, what exists now in terms of coordination and collaboration remains untested and is often beset with many limitations for law enforcement agencies.

Border and Transportation Security

As noted by DHS "The United States shares a 5,525 mile border with Canada and a 1,989 mile border with Mexico. Our maritime border includes 95,000 miles of shoreline and navigable waterways as well as a 3.4 million square mile exclusive economic zone. All people and goods legally entering into the United States must be processed through an air, land, or sea port of entry. Many international airports are dispersed throughout the United States. Each year, more than 500 million people legally enter our country. Some 330 million are noncitizens; more than 85 percent enter via land borders, often as daily commuters" (Office of Homeland Security, 2002). Police and local law enforcement agencies are central to the border and transportation security operations. Two key multicultural law enforcement issues in border and transportation security are: (1) racial profiling within the context of homeland security, and (2) collaborative and enforcement efforts with ICE.

Racial Profiling within the Context of Homeland Security

The issue of racial profiling, as noted in Chapter 14, is a major problem and concern for African Americans, Arab Americans, Latino/Hispanic Americans, and members of other groups, as well. Citizens from different cultural and racial backgrounds believe the determining factor in whether peace officers exercise their discretion in stopping a vehicle has to do with the driver's race and ethnicity. In the area of homeland security, current federal policy prohibits the use of racial profiling except under narrow circumstances to deal with terrorism and homeland security efforts:

> The new policy, representing the first time that the federal government has imposed across the board guidelines on racial profiling, governs the conduct of 70 federal law enforcement agencies. A narcotics agent, for instance, cannot focus on a specific neighborhood simply because of its racial makeup, the policy states. In national security operations, however, the policy allows agents to use race and ethnicity in "narrow" circumstances to help "identify terrorist threats and stop potential catastrophic attacks," officials said. (Litchblau, 2003, p. A1)

The use of race and ethnicity is allowed under federal policy and guidelines for the identification of terrorist threats and to stop possible terrorist attacks. Law enforcement officers should be cautious in the use of racial profiling for detecting terrorists and in homeland security matters. Hoffman (1998) has documented that terrorists will "do whatever it will take" to avoid detection and accomplish a mission. Even though the use of racial profiling in circumstances involving terrorism is legal and justifiable, its use may result in actually not detecting the terrorist because the terrorist is knowledgeable about the racial profiling used.

Working with Immigration and Custom Enforcement (ICE)

One of the key situations for a law enforcement agency involves decision-making where the local public safety agencies and departments become involved in enforcing and working with ICE section, a part of the DHS. The ramifications for multicultural community relationships and network-building are significant. The decision-making and strategic responses to terrorism within these collaborative and possible joint efforts are not clear-cut, nor "given," for any law enforcement agency, as exemplified by the following law enforcement departmental stance:

> According to Homeland Security figures, 7 million immigrants are in the country illegally. About 87,000 illegal immigrants are in Massachusetts. More than 25,000 foreign-born people live in Worcester, according to the 2000 Census. Detective Lt. Robert F. Rich, Worcester Police liaison to anti-terrorism agencies, said that his department does not enforce immigration laws and does not foresee doing so. "We always cooperate with all law enforcement agencies," he said. "We work with ICE and federal agencies, and immigration law is strictly their purview." Lt. Rich said that there are times when police are trying to identify a suspect who has several aliases. They look for assistance from immigration agencies. "We look to identify who the individual is," he said. "Again, we don't get involved whether the person is legally here or not. We don't enforce that. We are enforcing criminal statutes in Massachusetts." (Echegaray, 2003, p. A2)

However, the general argument supporting leaving illegal immigrants alone (unless they have committed a criminal act or are creating a disturbance) is based on the perspective that tracking down and deporting illegal workers is technically the job of ICE, not the police as we have noted in Chapter 1. Central to the clarity of roles required by the officer in the field is that police agencies have to create policies related to determining, reporting, and turning in illegal immigrants to ICE. Sometimes the trust of the entire community (unauthorized migrants and legal immigrants) is at stake with multicultural communities.

The following recommendation are made for local law enforcement agencies working with multicultural communities concerning legal and undocumented immigration status (a more detailed version with specific examples is provided in Chapter 7 for the Latino/Hispanic American community):

1. ***Develop Agency and Departmental Policies with Regard to Reporting and Working with ICE:*** Law enforcement agencies must have clear policies and procedures to address the circumstances in reporting to ICE. The policy must include: (1) under what circumstances will a person be reported to ICE; and (2) no person will be reported or referred to ICE where no laws have been violated.

2. ***Contact with the Multicultural Community Leaders:*** Law enforcement officers need to work closely with community leaders to establish a cooperative plan to inform them of the agency's policies and their implementation. Community leaders could, for example, work with law enforcement agencies' community relations offices to develop a communication plan for the effective dissemination of information about its policy in working with ICE.

3. ***Utilize a Communication Plan:*** It is essential to have a well-developed communication plan to ensure that the proper messages are provided to the specific multicultural communities involving when a person may or may not be reported or referred to ICE. This is particularly important when language translations and interpreting are necessary.

4. ***Clearly Define and Spell out the Implications for Any Contact with the Law Enforcement Agency and Possible Reporting to ICE:*** When it comes to the possibility that contact with the local police department may result in a person being questioned by ICE and/or being involved in deportation procedures, members from multicultural communities tend to be quite cautious. The fear they might be stereotyped as illegal (or have experienced prejudice by others in this regard) would naturally make any contact with law enforcement agencies and officers tenuous.

5. ***Train All Sworn and Nonsworn Personnel on the Agency or Departmental Policy with Regard to Working with ICE:*** Law enforcement agencies need to provide training and education to enable officers to utilize legal enforcement tools effectively so they can perform their work professionally within today's multicultural communities. Training that provides accurate information concerning groups about which officers might have stereotypes is one approach that will help to ensure implementation of a department's policy in working with ICE.

6. ***Utilize Law Enforcement Personnel and Translators/Interpreters from the Same or Similar Communities:*** To the extent that it is possible, the use of law

enforcement personnel who are from the same or similar multicultural communities would add to developing and sustaining the trust that is needed between law enforcement and those communities.

7. **Ensure Community Outreach Services:** Every police and community interaction requires a strong, ongoing link to community groups and advocacy organizations. A link is established when community task forces are assembled to address issues, and especially those involving possible police interactions with undocumented immigrants and/or unauthorized migrants.

8. **Provide Real-Time Information and Referral to Community-Based Advocacy Services:** Police departments may want to provide real-time information and referral to the resources and services available from specific multicultural community-based advocacy services related to undocumented immigration issues.

Immigration and Custom Enforcement cooperation with local law enforcement agencies is of particular concern for multicultural communities where there has been a history of legal as well as illegal immigration (e.g., Latino/Hispanic American, Asian/Pacific American, Arab and Middle Eastern American). Indeed, some multicultural community members will be prosecuted and deported. However, where no wrong has been committed, law enforcement must keep a check on potential stereotyping and the prejudicial act of singling out individuals based on those stereotypes.

To assist local law enforcement agencies and their leadership in developing policies and procedures in working with ICE, the Major Cities Chiefs (MCC, 2006) developed the following nine point position and guidance statement:

1. **Securing the borders:** Illegal immigration is a national issue and the federal government should first act to secure the national borders to prevent illegal entry into the United States.

2. **Enforcing laws that prohibit the hiring of illegal immigrants:** The federal government and its agencies should vigorously enforce existing immigration laws prohibiting employers from hiring illegal immigrants. Enforcement and prosecution of employers who illegally seek out and hire undocumented immigrants or turn a blind eye to the undocumented status of their employees, will help to eliminate one of the major incentives for illegal immigration.

3. **Consulting and involving local police agencies in decision making:** MCC and other representatives of the local law enforcement community such as the International Association of Chiefs of Police and local district attorneys and prosecutors should be consulted and brought in at the beginning of any process to develop a national initiative to involve local police agencies in the enforcement of federal immigration laws.

4. **Ensuring completely voluntary participation of agencies:** Any initiative to involve local police agencies in the enforcement of immigration laws should be completely voluntary. The decisions related to how local law enforcement agencies allocate their resources, direct their workforce, and define the duties of their employees to best serve and protect their communities should be left in the control of state and local governments.

5. ***Creating incentive-based approaches with full federal funding:*** Any initiative to involve local police agencies in the enforcement of immigration laws should be an incentive-based approach with full federal funding to provide the necessary resources to local agencies who choose to enforce immigration laws.

6. ***Maintaining current assistance funding without reductions and/or shifting of funds:*** The funding of any initiative to involve local police agencies in the enforcement of immigration laws should not be at the detriment of current funding or consist of a reduction either directly or indirectly in any current federal funded program focused on assisting police agencies with local policing or homeland security activities.

7. ***Clarifying the authority and limitation of liability:*** The authority of local police agencies and their officers to become involved in the enforcement of immigration laws should be clearly stated and defined. The statement of authority should also establish liability protection and an immunity shield for police officers and police agencies that take part in immigration enforcement as authorized by clear federal legislation.

8. ***Ensuring of the removal of civil immigration detainers from the NCIC [National Crime Information Center] System:*** Until the borders are secured and vigorous enforcement against employers who hire illegal immigrants has taken place, federal agencies should cease placing civil immigration detainers in N.C.I.C. and remove any existing civil detainers currently within the system. Moreover, local law enforcement agencies have concerns regarding the lack of authority and the uncertainty over the authority of local agencies to enforce immigration laws. The inclusion of civil detainers within the system has created confusion for local police agencies and subjected them to possible liability for exceeding their authority by arresting a person upon the basis of a mere civil detainer.

9. ***Continuing enforcement against criminal violators regardless of immigration status:*** Immigrants, documented and/or unauthorized, who commit criminal acts will find no safe harbor or sanctuary from their criminal violations within any major city, but will instead face the full force of criminal prosecution.

Domestic Counterterrorism

DHS (2002) defined its law enforcement mission to focus on the prevention of all terrorist acts within the United States, whether international or domestic in origin, using all legal means—both traditional and nontraditional—to identify, halt, and, where appropriate, prosecute terrorists in the United States. ICE, as a key component of DHS, will prosecute or bring immigration or other civil charges against such individuals where appropriate. DHS will utilize the full range of its legal authorities to pursue, not only the individuals directly engaged in terrorist activity, but also their sources of support (to include the people and organizations that knowingly fund the terrorists) and those that provide them with logistical assistance. In order to achieve these aims, DHS's domestic counterterrorism operation had to strengthen the federal law enforcement community and augment the scope and quality of information available to all law enforcement agencies. In that regard, DHS had to build and continually update a fully integrated, fully accessible terrorist watch list in order to identify any suspected terrorist activities by using all the tools in our nation's legal arsenal, including investigative, criminal, civil, immigration, and regulatory powers to stop those who wish to do harm to the United States.

A key component of this legal arsenal is the USA PATRIOT Act signed into law by the president on October 26, 2001, to improve government coordination in law enforcement, intelligence-gathering, and information-sharing. The official title for this act was the U.S.A. P.A.T.R.I.O.T. Act, in which the acronym stands for, "Uniting and Strengthening America by Providing Appropriate Tools Required to Intercept and Obstruct Terrorism" (Doyle, 2002). In this text, we refer to this act by its common reference, the Patriot Act, which has ten Titles that provide for additional powers for government to use against terrorists. Key parts of the Patriot Act have raised concern with multicultural communities, including the power of law enforcement officers to: (1) question, detain, and remove foreign terrorists within our borders; (2) enhance surveillance methods to track and intercept communications without customary court orders; and (3) increase information-sharing for key infrastructure protection by allowing for cooperation between federal, state, and local law enforcement agencies through the expansion of the Regional Information Sharing System (RISS). The Patriot Act expired in 2005 (Doyle, 2005), but most of its components and titles have been renewed in 2006.

The key component of the Patriot Act that has caused the most concern in multicultural communities, especially within Arab and Middle Eastern communities, is the power of law enforcement officials to question, detain, and remove possible terrorists from the country. The FBI and DHS have requested the assistance of state and local law enforcement and public safety agencies in data-gathering and interviewing efforts for homeland security purposes under the provisions of the Patriot Act.

Law enforcement agencies must be concerned about how they participate in homeland security data-gathering efforts in order to avoid possible negative effects on their relationships with multicultural communities. For example, the effort to hunt down potential terrorists shortly after September 11, 2001, resulted in much concern by law enforcement agencies regarding their relationships with the Arab American and Muslim communities. The FBI's request to local law enforcement agencies for locating and interviewing terrorist suspects received a variety of responses. Law enforcement agencies in cities such as Dearborn and Detroit, Michigan, assisted by helping to locate interviewees and by observing interviews conducted by the FBI (although they did not participate in conducting any of the interviews). Law enforcement agencies in Madison, Wisconsin, decided not to have local law enforcement officers involved in any aspect of locating and interviewing terrorist suspects. Law enforcement agencies in Cleveland, Ohio, participated fully and even had assigned a police detective to the interview process (Smith & Reed, 2001, p. A18). According to most commentators on the subject, the entire DHS effort to register over 85,000 men resulted in very few gains in homeland security as is noted in the following news article:

> The Department of Homeland Security has decided to discontinue a controversial program that required thousands of Arab and Muslim men to register with immigration authorities in the aftermath of the Sept. 11 attacks, officials said on Friday. Hoping to hunt down terrorists, immigration officials fingerprinted, photographed and interviewed about 85,000 Muslim and Arab noncitizens be-

tween November 2002 and May 2003 under the program. The effort—the largest to register immigrants in decades—required annual registration. Men from Iran, Iraq, Syria, Libya, and Sudan have already begun reporting to immigration offices for a second round of registrations this month. Officials have acknowledged that most of the Arab and Muslim immigrants who have complied with the registration requirements had no ties to terrorist groups. Of the 85,000 men who showed up at immigration offices earlier this year, and the tens of thousands more screened at airports and border crossings during that time period, 11 had links to terrorism, officials said. ("U.S. Halts Arab Registry Effort," 2003, p. A8)

Clearly, as a nation built on the rule of law, DHS must utilize federal laws to win the war on terrorism while always protecting the civil liberties of those individuals within multicultural communities and within the larger national communities as a whole. DHS uses our federal immigration laws and customs regulations to protect our borders and ensure uninterrupted commerce, and encourages states and local governments to strengthen their codes and regulations to protect our public welfare, to prosecute terrorists, and to be partners in countering the domestic and global threat of terrorism.

Protecting Critical Infrastructure and Key Assets

As noted by DHS (2002), terrorists are opportunistic, and they exploit vulnerabilities we leave exposed, choosing the time, place, and method to attack weaknesses they observe or perceive. Increasing the security of a particular type of target, such as aircraft or buildings, makes it more likely that terrorists will seek a different target. Increasing the countermeasures to a particular terrorist tactic, such as hijacking, makes it more likely that terrorists will favor a different tactic. Protecting America's critical infrastructure and key assets is thus a formidable challenge. As a result of America's open and technologically complex society, an almost infinite array of potential targets are possible. It is impossible to completely protect all targets at all times. On the other hand, we can help deter or deflect attacks, or mitigate their effects, by making strategic improvements in protection and security. While we cannot assume we will prevent all terrorist attacks, we can substantially reduce America's vulnerability, particularly to the most damaging attacks on our critical infrastructure in the following sectors:

- Agriculture
- Food
- Water
- Public Health
- Emergency Services
- Government
- Defense Industrial Base
- Information and Telecommunications
- Energy
- Transportation

- Banking and Finance
- Chemical Industry
- Postal and Shipping Services

Community Assessment

Preventing, limiting, and reducing a community's vulnerability to attack requires a careful and ongoing community assessment to locate and measure the risks involved in the particular community. Such assessments would involve reviewing and analyzing all the localities that are likely targets for terrorism and working to improve the security of these locations. Some law enforcement agencies have developed a rating system and have cataloged their possible problem areas into different priority levels. The following four priority level assessment categories could be used in a community assessment or to a particular law enforcement department or agency (U.S. Department of Justice, 1997):

1. ***First Priority Level—Fatal:*** These are processes and functions that if they fail would result in death, severe financial loss, massive legal liabilities, or catastrophic consequences. Such processes and functions would include all essential mission-critical elements such as electrical power, communications, information systems, and command and leadership functions.

2. ***Second Priority Level—Critical:*** These would be processes and functional units of the agency, department, or organization that are critical to its operations and would be difficult to do without for any long period of time. Some examples of "critical" functional units might include computer terminals, elevators, perimeter security lights, and heat/air conditioning in the building. Examples of critical processes might include building entry and exit security and two-way communication radio network.

3. ***Third Priority Level—Important:*** These would include those processes and functional units that are not critical to the department, agency, or organization such as facsimile, copier, videotape player, video camera, and tape recorders. Some examples of important processes would include files and record access, administrative training, and new-hire orientation.

4. ***Fourth Priority Level—Routine:*** These would include processes and functional units that are not strategically mission-important (although they may cause some inconvenience) to the agency, department, or organization, such as coffeemakers, microwave ovens, and room thermostats. Nonessential and routine processes might include providing parking lot stickers and duty lists for staff personnel and providing information at the reception area.

Community assessments of functional units and processes should be ongoing and scheduled routinely so that information of possible terrorist targets could be updated on a regular basis.

The ultimate goal of the DHS is for the United States to create an unprecedented level of cooperation and integrated collaboration throughout all levels of government, with private industry and institutions, and with the American people to protect our critical infrastructure and key assets from terrorist attack.

Defending Against Catastrophic Threats

As noted by DHS (2002), the expertise, technology, and material needed for building the most deadly weapons known to mankind—including chemical, biological, radiological, and nuclear weapons—are proliferating. If our enemies acquire these weapons, they are likely to try to use them, and the consequences of such an attack could be far more devastating than those we suffered on September 11, 2001. Attacks using weapons of mass destruction, or WMD (which include chemical, biological, radiological, or nuclear weapons) in the United States, could cause large numbers of casualties, mass psychological disruption, and contamination, and could overwhelm local medical capabilities. Of greatest vulnerability would be many of the multicultural communities in our nation. Such multicultural community vulnerabilities were evident in recent natural disasters such as Hurricanes Katrina and Rita. Currently, the DHS has highlighted that chemical, biological, radiological, and nuclear detection capabilities are modest and response capabilities are dispersed throughout the country at differing levels of government. In the near future, the DHS will need to unify much of the federal government's efforts to develop and implement scientific and technological countermeasures against human, animal, and plant diseases that could be used as terrorist weapons. Responsibility for chemical, biological, radiological, and nuclear surveillance, as well as for initial response efforts, often rests with state and local hospitals and public health agencies.

Emergency Preparedness and Response

Regional and local law enforcement and public safety agencies must prepare to minimize the damage and to recover from any future terrorist attacks that may occur despite our best efforts at prevention. Past experience has shown that preparedness efforts are key in providing an effective response to major terrorist incidents and natural disasters. As such, we need a comprehensive national system to bring together and command all necessary response assets quickly and effectively. We must equip, train, and exercise many different response units to mobilize for any emergency without warning. DHS has been building on the strong foundation already laid by FEMA, and plans to lead our national efforts to create and employ a system that will improve our response to all disasters, manmade and natural. Many pieces of this national emergency response system are already in place. As noted by most of the research studies to date, America's first line of defense in the aftermath of any terrorist attack is its first responder community—police officers, firefighters, emergency medical providers, public works personnel, and emergency management officials. These individuals include specially trained hazardous materials teams, search and rescue units, bomb squads, and tactical units. The ultimate goal of the DHS is to create a fully-integrated national emergency response system that is adaptable enough to deal with any terrorist attack (no matter how unlikely or catastrophic) as well as to handle all manners of natural disasters.

WORKING WITH MULTICULTURAL COMMUNITIES ON PREVENTION AND RESPONSE

In an earlier section we quoted Nance (2003), who highlighted a key element for homeland security and for winning the fight against terrorism that must include "cooperative efforts among law enforcement and intelligence agencies, and resolving the root complaints of the terrorist-supporting population." Clearly, law enforcement agencies are not in a position to resolve the root complaints involved with any terrorist-supporting nation or community. Law enforcement agencies are, however, in an excellent position to prevent the erosion of positive community–policing relationships with the multicultural communities that might include community members who hold concerns of root complaints and other issues of unfairness, bias, and discrimination.

Training Law Enforcement Agencies in Multicultural Community Homeland Security Issues

Law enforcement professionals have recognized that prejudices acted upon, yet left unchecked, can result in not only humiliation and citizen complaints, but also missed opportunities for building long-term police–community relationships important for homeland security. Social scientists have noted that stereotypes and prejudices become more pronounced when fear, danger, and personal threat enters the picture, as may happen in possible terrorism incidents. Training in understanding multicultural communities and in Terrorist Attack Pre-incident Indicators (TAPIs) might have prevented the following situation:

> Pavel Lachko, a Russian student at the University of Texas at Arlington, was in America for about a month when he received a rude cultural lesson he won't soon forget: In these post-September 11 times, young foreign men aren't allowed innocent mistakes. On September 6, Lachko and his roommate, fellow Russian student Boris Avdeev, wandered on their bicycles into the employee parking lot of the Arlington police station looking for someone to give them directions. Rather than giving them answers, police locked them in handcuffs, held them for questioning by an agent from the Department of Homeland Security and charged them with criminal trespassing. . . . "I heard the male officer say into his radio that we are Pakistanis," Lachko says. "We said, 'No, no, no. We are not Pakistanis. We're Russians.'" After about 20 minutes of standing with the police, he says, the officers took out their handcuffs and placed the men under arrest. . . . Johnson said he did not know whether the two young men were initially taken to be Middle Easterners, and he insisted the arrests had nothing to do with their nationality. "They were arrested because they violated the traffic control device. There is no access except through a traffic control device," he says. "Nationality played no role in the decision." The two Russians' American friends say that is difficult to believe. "The police were either paranoid, which I doubt, or they were simply harassing foreigners," says Michael Dailey, a retiree taking graduate classes in German at the school. He says foreign students, who number about 3,000 at UTA, should be treated with more understanding. (Korosec, 2003)

Cultural awareness and understanding of the different multicultural populations of the community would have helped to prevent misidentifying the nationalities of the students. Moreover, training in terrorist's behavioral cues would have allowed the law enforcement officers in the preceding example to correctly recognize and identify some of the specific behaviors and cues of possible terrorists and discern behaviors of likely nonterrorists.

Educating Multicultural Communities on Homeland Security

Most cities and states currently have websites and online information on homeland security for their communities. However, information and education regarding homeland security–specific actions for the prevention of terrorism are not available for most communities in the United States. This lack of information is even more pronounced for some of the multicultural communities with recent immigrants and refugees (including those from South and Central America, Asia, Eastern Europe, and the Middle East). The role of law enforcement officers in providing such information offers another viable avenue for developing positive relationships with multicultural communities and for community-policing efforts. Clearly, all communities are interested in acquiring specific information regarding activities of homeland security, as the following example illustrates:

> The East Side college has entered into a partnership with the American Institute of Homeland Defense to offer both continuing education courses and college-credit courses in homeland security and anti-terrorism preparation. Also, AIHD has designated St. Philip's as their Homeland Security Regional Center of Excellence for the San Antonio area. . . . "There's a great need for homeland security training for first responders," said John Carnes, dean of applied sciences and technology at St. Philip's. "That might mean that the first person on the scene could be someone from the fire department or the police department or a hotel employee." "Our (program) will be focused on first responders," added Ray Boryczka, director of continuing education for St. Philip's. "We're actually going to be training the people who will be the first ones on the scene." Boryczka said that since passing the word along about this new program, the college has received requests from organizations and individuals interested in what the program will offer. "Our phones have been ringing off the hook," he said. "It's a much bigger response than what we first expected, and these weren't fire departments, police departments or EMTs (emergency medical technicians). These were calls from the general public and from school districts and from businesses. This is a hot issue. The sensitivity is still there." (Conchas, 2003, p. H1)

Law enforcement agencies may also want to include into their Citizen's Police Academies information regarding homeland security and ways that the multicultural communities could participate and provide assistance to the public safety departments. Additionally, law enforcement agencies might utilize the nonsworn and CSO personnel to provide such information in a bilingual mode to ensure proper information to communities with large populations of immigrants and refugees. Community-based presentations at familiar neighborhood centers, associations, churches, mosques, and temples may facilitate greater multicultural population attendance and participation. Likewise, collaborative programs of law enforcement agencies and community-based organizations have resulted in positive dissemination of information and an ongoing building of trust with multicultural communities (for example, see IRCO and Dial-911 in Chapter 6 and Spanish Police Academy in Chapter 7).

KEY ISSUES IN LAW ENFORCEMENT

Reluctance to Report and Participate in Homeland Security Efforts

Multicultural groups that have been stereotyped as possible terrorists (e.g., Arab and Middle Eastern Americans, Muslims, South Asians, Central Asians) may be reluctant to report crimes related to these stereotypes and may not seek police assistance and help for violations of their civil rights. Moreover, many may avoid contact with law enforcement agencies entirely with respect to homeland security efforts. Many of the multicultural groups may come from countries with extensive terrorism problems and may remember how police in their home countries have brutalized and violated them and others (in quelling terrorism). Sensitivity to the experiences of these multicultural groups and a knowledge of their history of being victimized by terrorists will be of positive value in gaining participation and cooperation in homeland security efforts. Another key challenge to effective cooperation with multicultural communities on homeland security issues is to help allay the fears and concerns expressed by community members with regard to their multiple interactions with law enforcement officers. Inquiries relating to homeland security, for example, may coexist with the investigation into other crimes and code enforcements like immigration, health, sanitation, housing, and welfare.

Victimization

Law enforcement agencies protect the safety and security of citizens in multicultural communities where harassment and discrimination resulting from being stereotyped as a terrorist may lead to victimization. Documentation of such crimes against Arab and Middle Eastern Americans and Asian/Pacific Americans are provided in Chapters 5 and 9 and in Chapter 14 in this text. Some victims are harassed and attacked because of their attire or their appearance. For example, men from the Sikh religion wear turbans, and this is often stereotyped to be indicative of foreign terrorists:

> After 26 years of living in the United States, Thakar Basati of Palatine was rudely reminded that he is a foreigner here. Despite his American passport, Basati has had to endure interrogation at airports whenever he travels. On a routine traffic stop, he had to wait an hour for the police officer to write a citation. "Suddenly, I became a criminal," Basati said. "I've been a citizen for over 20 years." . . . Professor Sukhchain Singh, dean and administrator of the Sikh Religious Society, shared how post-Sept. 11 profiling had hurt his community. His group manages the largest Sikh religious center in the Midwest out of Palatine. "There are more than 250 recorded hate crimes against Sikhs in the United States so far," he said attributing it to his group's unique religious attire. (Krishnamurthy, 2003, p. N1)

Victimization also includes unfair accusations of being a terrorist. Those accused, or so identified, must have the trust that the police and other public safety personnel are not against them. Furthermore, they must believe that their well-being and safety are just as important as those of others who are not subject to these perceptions, assumptions, or stereotypes. Moreover, residents who are discriminated against or stereotyped as terrorists must be able to trust that prosecutors, judges, parole, and probation will utilize their full armamentarium to deter and jail terrorists, as well as those who unjustly terrorize, discriminate, and/or harass those who are unfairly stereotyped as terrorists, as seen in the next example:

> At an F.B.I academy meeting last year, in which strategies for gathering intelligence were discussed, one participant warned that officials were overlooking the effect that pursuing suspects has had on Muslim and other targeted groups. . . . Some early tips fell apart in highly public ways, as when a security guard named Ronald Ferry claimed to have found a ground-to-air radio in a certain room in a hotel across from the World Trade Center. The guest who was occupying that room, Abdallah Higazy, was jailed for nearly a month on suspicion that he had helped guide the hijackers who crashed airplanes into the twin towers. Mr. Ferry's falsehood was uncovered when an airplane pilot, who has not been publicly identified, came forward to claim the radio. A lawsuit Mr. Higazy has brought against Mr. Ferry and the F.B.I. says the agents who took the tip failed to press Mr. Ferry for a sworn statement, to subject him to a lie detector, or to interview a second guard who helped search the room, said Robert S. Dunn, a lawyer for Mr. Higazy. "They just took his word and ran with it," said Mr. Dunn. F.B.I. officials in New York declined to comment, citing the pending litigation. (Litchblau, 2003, p. A1)

As this example illustrates, it would be difficult for others from similar ethnic, religious, or cultural backgrounds as the accused to perceive the criminal justice system would treat them fairly if the facts, as started in the case above, were found to be true.

Differential Treatment

In this chapter, as well as in the culture-specific chapters, we have provided examples of how members of multicultural communities have been treated unfairly because of law enforcement officers' perceptions that they are threats to homeland security or possible terrorists. Especially if a target is a possible terrorist, expressions of bias and prejudice in law enforcement agencies may go unchallenged because of the tremendous fear of the potential terrorist threat, as well as the need to rally around the issues of homeland security. Often such bias and prejudice are expressed via inappropriate language and disrespectful terms such as, "rags," "suicidal rag-heads," "A-rabs," "Arab-bombers," "Muslim fanatics."

Under such circumstances, both law enforcement executive leadership and officers' professionalism will determine whether such bias and prejudices go unchecked or whether the treatment of a possible terrorist suspect will be fair and justifiable. Clearly, should the suspect not be a terrorist, then an injustice had occurred because of differential treatment. Moreover, the multicultural community of which the suspect is a member will begin to question their trust and reliance on the police agency that shows such bias and prejudice. Should the suspect indeed have been correctly identified as a possible terrorist, then any stereotypic and differential treatment may jeopardize the prosecution of the case as well.

Sustaining Police Services to the Multicultural Communities in Light of Homeland Security

One of the key challenges in developing and implementing law enforcement efforts in homeland security includes sustaining the community-policing and law enforcement services within multicultural neighborhoods. In times of scarce funding resources, on-the-street community-policing efforts might take a back seat to homeland security and the fight on terrorism issues, as is shown by the following example:

> At Hartsfield, cutbacks by the federal government have trimmed six to eight officers per shift 24 hours a day, Peter Andresen said just before he was promoted from airport commander to deputy chief in August. Funding was cut in June. "We had to release people," Andresen said. "We still have people on every checkpoint, we just don't have the number that we had." . . . Councilman Ceasar Mitchell, chairman of the City Council's Public Safety Committee, says Atlanta should get help. "We're committed to safety, but at the same time those unfunded mandates are taking officers and dollars away from our streets," he said. "I hope the federal government will say we're going to bring funding to the table so you can spend your allocated budget on tackling crime in your neighborhoods." (Bruner, 2003, p. JD1)

Since contact with multicultural communities will increase because of the emerging roles for law enforcement in homeland security, the need for additional bilingual officers and personnel will be paramount for the communities. As part of emergency preparation, the need to provide clear communications and to ensure understanding of emergency instructions will require bilingual personnel and translators in these diverse communities.

Increasing Multicultural Peace Officers for Homeland Security Functions

There is a significant underrepresentation of multicultural and bilingual personnel in federal, state, and local law enforcement and criminal justice positions. On all governmental levels, there have been extensive efforts at recruiting and filling law enforcement positions important for homeland security with multicultural and language-expert personnel. The small number of multicultural and language-expert officers has already hampered many departments in neighborhoods with multicultural populations in effectively serving those communities. When appropriate, multicultural police services and bilingual expertise are not provided, the added roles and functions for homeland security further exacerbate the problems in serving multicultural communities.

A variety of reasons exist for such underrepresentation, including:

1. History of law enforcement relationships with multicultural communities
2. Image of law enforcement personnel in multicultural communities
3. Lack of interest by multicultural community members in law enforcement careers
4. Lack of knowledge about the different careers and pathways in law enforcement
5. Concern with and fear of background checks, physical requirements, and the application process

6. Concerns with roles assigned in these communities, especially in the areas of homeland security

7. Lack of advocates for law enforcement careers

With the growing need for multicultural and language-expert law enforcement personnel for homeland security roles and functions throughout the United States, law enforcement agencies need to emphasize and be committed to the importance of diversity in their recruitment efforts.

SUMMARY

The experience of law enforcement agencies involved in homeland security and the war on terrorism within multicultural communities is evolving. Likewise, the new and changing roles and functions for law enforcement in homeland security and disaster preparedness present many challenges for the day-to-day work within the criminal justice system and the Federal Response Plan (FRP) against terrorism. Homeland security challenges for law enforcement agencies include the following: (1) detecting and preventing attacks of terrorism; these can be made more complex within multicultural communities because of the past histories of those communities with law enforcement in the United States, as well as in their native homelands; (2) avoiding stereotypes and possible biased perceptions based on ethnicity, culture, race, and religion that may be evoked within multicultural communities; and (3) working with multicultural community leaders regarding their perceptions of police actions and efforts in homeland security. Officers should realize that some citizens may have been both victimized by terrorism as well as harmed by the antiterrorism efforts within their native homeland (while innocent of any involvement with terrorism). These citizens carry with them stereotypes of police services as something to be feared and avoided. Law enforcement officials need to go out of their way to work with multicultural communities to establish trust, to provide outreach efforts, and to win cooperation in order to effectively accomplish their goals for homeland security efforts. Building partnerships focused on community collaboration in the fight against terrorism is important locally and nationally.

Attitudes and skills that enhance multicultural law enforcement include: (1) respecting multicultural communities and cultural behaviors that may be different from one's own, (2) observing and understanding behaviors important to diverse communities, and (3) analyzing and interpreting diverse behaviors for services application within multicultural communities. These same multicultural attitudes and skills form the core elements, when coupled with an intelligence-based approach, in detecting and predicting terrorist actions and activities for homeland security.

The DHS has been providing law enforcement agencies a variety of intelligence information, advisories, warnings, and other pertinent communications regarding the efforts and activities to be implemented within local communities. Local law enforcement agencies and officers, because of their knowledge of the existing multicultural communities and networks, have been called upon to aid in the data gathering and development of useful intelligence regarding possible terrorists. Such efforts have often produced a mixed reception by law enforcement agencies. When local law enforcement agencies and officers are requested to provide assistance for homeland security information-gathering and the interviewing of possible terrorist suspects, some of the following steps are recommended with the multicultural communities involved:

1. ***Contact with community leaders:*** Law enforcement officers need to work closely with community leaders to establish a cooperative plan for gathering the necessary information. Community leaders could work with the law enforcement agencies' community relations office to develop a communication plan for the effective dissemination of information.

2. ***Utilize a communication plan:*** It is critical to have a well-developed communication plan to ensure proper messages are provided to the multicultural communities involved. This is particularly important when language translations and interpreting are necessary.

3. ***Define explicitly and spell out the implications for participation in the data-gathering process:*** Providing clearly defined procedures and information regarding how the data gathering and interviews would be used is most important. Additionally, if there are possible consequences (e.g., with the INS), these elements should be delineated to ensure an ongoing relationship of trust with members of the multicultural communities involved.

4. ***Utilize law enforcement personnel and translators/interpreters from the same or similar multicultural communities:*** Use of law enforcement personnel from the same or similar ethnic or cultural communities would contribute to maintaining relationships, building the trust necessary in such information-gathering processes.

Some multicultural community members, because of their past experiences with law enforcement, may be reluctant to participate in homeland security efforts. It is important for law enforcement departments and officials to build relationships and working partnerships with multicultural communities to ensure effective participation in combating terrorism and implementing homeland security.

A key challenge for law enforcement efforts in homeland security includes sustaining the community-policing and law enforcement services within multicultural neighborhoods. In times of scarce funding resources, on-the-street, community-policing efforts might take a back seat to homeland security and the fight on terrorism. Moreover, since contact with multicultural communities will increase because of the emerging roles for law enforcement in homeland security, the need for additional bilingual officers and personnel will be paramount for these communities. As part of emergency preparation, the need to provide clear communications and to ensure understanding of emergency instructions will require additional bilingual personnel and translators for these diverse communities.

DISCUSSION QUESTIONS AND ISSUES

1. ***Homeland Security Roles for Law Enforcement in Your Community:*** The chapter provided the six major goals of the DHS. Review the homeland security roles of law enforcement in your community using the six major DHS goals. List the special challenges and opportunities involved in implementing

the top two or three DHS goals for law enforcement agencies in your community. What are some of the unique law enforcement challenges related to implementation of these six goals within multicultural communities?

2. ***Terrorist Targets in Your Local Community:*** The chapter provided a four-priority-level approach to implementing a community assessment of possible terrorist targets. Review the possible terrorist targets in your community using the four priority-level categorization. List the special challenges involved in protecting the top two priority levels of possible terrorist targets in your community. List some of the unique challenges in working with multicultural communities in this regard (either within your community or in a nearby community with multicultural neighborhoods).

3. ***Working with Multicultural Groups in Your Community on Homeland Security and Disaster Preparedness:*** The authors recommended some guidelines and approaches for collaborative efforts in information gathering and in implementing homeland security efforts within multicultural communities. Select one or more multicultural groups that are part of your community (or a part of a nearby community). How would you apply the suggested guidelines and approaches to working with these multicultural groups?

4. ***Recruiting and Using Multicultural and Language-Expert Law Enforcement Personnel:*** The authors noted the importance of having multicultural and language-expert personnel in working with multicultural communities. How would you go about recruiting and using such personnel in your local community? Do you see roles for the use of volunteers who have such backgrounds and language expertise in homeland security efforts? What are the advantages and disadvantages in using community volunteers in homeland security activities?

5. ***Victimization includes being unfairly accused or identified as a possible terrorist:*** What are ways to prevent and to help multicultural communities so members would not be the recipients of unjust accusation and victimization? What approach would you suggest for your local law enforcement agencies to prevent such victimization? What would you suggest that your multicultural community agencies do to prevent discrimination and harassment for those who are unfairly stereotyped?

WEBSITE RESOURCES

Visit these websites for additional information about multicultural law enforcement issues in responding to homeland security efforts.

Association of Former Intelligence Officers (AFIO): http://www.afio.com

This website provides the *Weekly Intelligence News,* which summarizes some of the homeland security issues from the perspectives of the AFIO.

Central Intelligence Agency—Factbook:
https://www.cia.gov/cia/publications/factbook/index.html

This website provides background and current information about groups and countries affecting the homeland security of the United States.

Department of Homeland Security (DHS): http://www.dhs.gov/dhspublic/

This website provides extensive information regarding the DHS, as well as the threat level for the United States at any point in time. Suggestions and tips are provided for local communities in their preparation for homeland security.

Department of State—Travel Warnings and Consular Information: http://travel.state.gov/travel/cis_pa_tw/tw/tw_1764.html

This website highlights countries and areas around the world that might be of a terrorist threat to citizens of the United States and its homeland security.

Federal Bureau of Investigation: http://www.fbi.gov/

This website provides the latest annual report of terrorism incidents in the United States.

Federal Emergency Management Agency: http://www.fema.gov/

This website provides a range of useful information related to the management of community, state, and national emergencies and homeland security issues.

Homeland Security Information Center (HSIC): http://www.ntis.gov/hs/

This website provides a range of useful information related to resources for national emergencies, homeland security, and natural disasters.

Transportation Security Administration (TSA): http://www.tsa.gov/

This website provides information on the Transportation Security Administration (TSA), which oversees security for the highways, railroads, buses, mass transit systems, ports, and the 450 U.S. airports.

U.S. Coast Guard (USCG): http://www.uscg.mil/USCG.shtm

The U.S. Coast Guard is responsible for the protection of all our ports and waterways within the DHS. The website highlights many of the specific aspects of homeland security for a law enforcement agency.

REFERENCES

Bruner, T. K. (2003, September 11). "Homeland Security: Police get help but not at Hartsfield." *Atlanta Journal and Constitution,* p. JD1.

Conchas, E. (2003, October 22). "College gets homeland security nod; St. Philip's to offer anti-terrorism preparation classes." *San Antonio Express-News,* p. H1.

Dershowitz, A. M. (2002). *Why Terrorism Works: Understanding the Threat, Responding to the Challenge.* New Haven Conn.: Yale University Press.

Donohue, L. K. (2002). "Fear Itself: Counterterrorism, Individual Rights, and U.S. Foreign Relations Post-9-11." Paper presented at the International Studies Association Convention, New Orleans, LA, March, 2002 (and parts published in "Bias, National Security, and Military Tribunals." *Criminology and Public Policy* July, 2002).

Doyle, C. (2005). "The USA PATRIOT Act Sunset: Provisions that Expire on December 31, 2005." *CRS Report for Congress,* June 29, 2005.

Doyle, C. (2002). "The USA PATRIOT Act: A Sketch." *CRS Report for Congress,* April 18, 2002.

Echegaray, C. (2003, November 26). "More Work Awaits Police if Criminal Alien Bill Passes." *Worcester Telegram and Gazette* (MA), p. A2.

Federal Bureau of Investigation. (1996). *Terrorism in the United States 1995.* Washington, D.C.: Terrorist Research and Analytical Center, National Security Division.

FBI Bomb Data Center. (1999). *1999 Bombing Incidents.* General Information Bulletin 99-1. Washington, D.C.: Federal Bureau of Investigation.

Federal Emergency Management Agency (FEMA). (1997). *The Federal Response Plan Notice of Change: Terrorism Incident Annex.* Washington, D.C.: Author.

Ford, P. (2002, March 27). "Legal War on Terror Lacks Weapons." *Christian Science Monitor,* Section 4, p. 1.

Hoffman, B. (1998). *Inside Terrorism.* New York: Columbia University Press.

Howard, D. R., and R. L. Sawyer, (Eds.). (2004). *Terrorism and Counterterrorism: Understanding the New Security Environment.* Guilford, CT: McGraw-Hill/Dushkin.

International Association of Chiefs of Police. (2005). *From Hometown Security to Homeland Security: IACP's Principles for a Locally Designed and Nationally Coordinated Homeland Security Strategy.* Alexandria, VA: IACP.

Kemp, R. L. (2003). *Homeland Security: Best Practices for Local Government.* Washington, D.C.: International City/County Management Association (ICCM).

Kerlikowske, R. G. (2003, May 21). "Remarks Given at the Washington Association of Sheriff and Police Chiefs Conference," Spokane WA, Seattle Chief of Police.

Korosec, T. (2003, September 25). "A Texas Welcome: Two UTA Students Make a Wrong Turn, End Up Jailed in Arlington." *Dallas Observer.*

Krishnamurthy, M. (2003, August 12). "160 Turn Out for Forum in Libertyville on Immigration Issues." *Chicago Daily Herald,* p. N1.

Litchblau, E. (2003, June 18). "Threats and Responses: Law Enforcement; Bush Issues Racial Profiling Ban But Exempts Security Inquiries." *New York Times,* p. A1.

Major City Chiefs. (2006, June). "M.C.C. Immigration Committee Recommendations for Enforcement of Immigration Laws by Local Police Agencies." Adopted by the Major Cities Chiefs, June 2006.

Murphy, G. R., and M. R. Plotkin. (2003). *Protecting Your Community from Terrorism: Strategies for Local Law Enforcement.* In The Strategies for Local Enforcement Series, Volume 1: Improving Local-Federal Partnerships. Washington, D.C.: PERF and COPS.

Nance, M W. (2003). *The Terrorist Recognition Handbook.* Guilford, CT: Lyons Press.

National Commission on Terrorism. (1999). *Countering the Changing Threat of International Terrorism.* Washington, D.C.: Author. Available: www.fas.org/irp/threat/commission.html

Norwitz, J. H. (2002, August). "Combating Terrorism: With a Helmet or a Badge?" *Journal of Homeland Security.* Available: http://www.homelandsecurity.org/journal/articles/displayarticle.asp?article=72.

Office of Domestic Preparedness. (2003, June). *The Office of Domestic Preparedness Guidelines for Homeland Security, June 2003: Prevention and Deterrence.* Washington, D.C.: DHS.

Office of Homeland Security. (2004). *Securing Our Homeland: U.S. Department of Homeland Security Strategic Plan.* Washington, D.C.: GPO.

Office of Homeland Security. (2002). *National Strategy for Homeland Security.* Washington, D.C.: GPO.

Oliver, W. M. (2007). *Homeland Security for Policing.* Upper Saddle River, NJ: Pearson/Prentice Hall.

Pillar, P. R. (2001). "The Dimensions of Terrorism and Counterterrorism." In *Terrorism and U.S. Foreign Policy.* Washington, D.C.: The Brookings Institution Press.

Robbins, J. S. (2002). "Bin Laden's War." In D. R. Howard and R. L. Sawyer (Eds.), *Terrorism and Counterterrorism: Understanding the New Security Environment.* Guilford, CT: McGraw-Hill/Dushkin.

Smith, R. L., and E. Reed. (2001, November 29). "Local Police to Begin Questioning Visitors from Mideast." *Plain Dealer* (Cleveland, Ohio), p. A18.

"Tipline or a Spy Force? Bush Proposal for a Hotline to Report Suspicious Activity Has Met with Skepticism in Madison and around the Country." (2002, July 21). *Wisconsin State Journal* (Madison, WI), p. B1.

U.S. Department of Justice Office of Justice Programs. (1997). *Emergency Response to Terrorism: Basic Concepts.* Washington, D.C.: U.S. Department of Justice.

"U.S. Halts Arab Registry Effort." (2003, November 22). *St. Petersburg Times* FL, p. A8.

Part 4

RESPONSE STRATEGIES FOR CRIMES MOTIVATED BY HATE/BIAS AND RACIAL PROFILING

12 Hate/Bias Crimes: Victims, Laws, Investigations, and Prosecutions

13 Hate/Bias Crimes: Reporting, Monitoring, and Response Strategies

14 Racial Profiling

Part Four provides a detailed explanation of strategies for preventing, controlling, reporting, monitoring, and investigating crimes that are based on hate or bias because of the victim's race, ethnicity, national origin, religion, or sexual orientation. Criminal cases of these types have come to be known as bias or hate crimes; noncriminal cases are referred to as incidents. Some agencies refer to these acts as civil rights violations. The chapters that follow contain policies, practices, and procedures for responding to these types of crimes or incidents. We recognize that other groups, such as women, the elderly, the homeless, and the disabled, are sometimes victimized. However, in this book we focus primarily on hate crimes and incidents wherein the motivation was related to the victim's race, ethnicity, national origin, religion, or sexual orientation. The reasons for collecting data on crimes and incidents motivated by hate/bias committed by individuals or organized groups are included in Chapter 13. The end of that chapter provides examples to help students, members of the criminal justice system, and the community to develop sensitive and workable programs for handling these crimes and incidents. The recommended policies, training, practices, and procedures outlined in this text are currently in operation in most law enforcement agencies across the nation and are based on studies and recommendations by the U.S. Department of Justice's

Community Relations Service. The Commission on Peace Officer Standards and Training, found in all states of the nation, is another major source of materials. The final chapter provides information about racial profiling for members of the criminal justice system. The type of policing reviewed in this unit is a civilizing process that will contribute to multicultural coexistence and cooperation. All law enforcement professionals should have a good working knowledge of the guidelines that follow.

Chapter 12

Hate/Bias Crimes: Victims, Laws, Investigations, and Prosecutions

OVERVIEW

This chapter focuses on hate/bias crimes and how they are investigated and prosecuted. The chapter first discusses the scope of the problem, providing historical perspectives and examples. We stress that the law enforcement professional must be aware of discrimination and hate crimes directed toward immigrants and people from different ethnic, national origin, racial, sexual orientation, and religious backgrounds. We present some aspects of urban dynamics as they relate to the economy, hate violence, move-in violence, and hate/bias crimes and incidents. In this chapter, while we devote some attention to crimes against new immigrants, the primary focus is on hate crimes against Jews, gays, and lesbians. We discuss the importance of hate crime investigations and treatment of the victims because of the unique impact on them as well as on the community. The chapter highlights the need for law enforcement officials to treat hate violence with the same degree of concern as heinous crimes such as rape and sexual assault. It presents information on special statutes that provide not only for the investigations of hate/bias crimes but also for increased penalties for the perpetrators.

COMMENTARY

Violence motivated by racial, religious, ethnic/national origin, or sexual orientation hatred has existed for generations in the United States and throughout the world. The criminal justice system as well as every community must address this problem. Consider the following:

> In a recent Center [Southern Poverty Law Center (SPLC)] survey, a startling majority of respondents reported witnessing some form of bias or bigotry within the last 12 months. One of the survey's most dramatic results came when respondents were questioned about their personal experience with prejudice. An overwhelming majority, 70 percent, reported having personally witnessed an incident of everyday bigotry such as racial stereotyping or the use of derisive names for people of a given color, gender, or sexual identity over the last year. Finally, nearly all who responded to the survey believe that race continues to divide the country. (SPLC Report, 2006, p. 8)

Our estimates [of ethnoviolence] derive from rigorous case studies of cities, neighborhoods, campuses, and work organizations. The preponderance of evidence does indicate a rate of 20 to 25 percent. This means that one out of every four or five adult Americans is harassed, intimidated, insulted, or assaulted for reasons of prejudice during the course of a year. ("Facts Sheet on Ethnoviolence," 2004, p. 1)

Reports of hate crimes and harassment against Muslims in California tripled last year from the year before, the highest number recorded outside the immediate aftermath of Sept. 11, according to a report to be released today by the national American Muslim organization. Nationally, the council [Council on American-Islamic Relations] reported 1,019 anti-Muslim incidents, representing a 69 percent increase. The report attributed the increased incidents to several factors, including a "lingering atmosphere of fear" stemming from the Sept. 11 attacks, fallout from the Iraq war, anti-Islam rhetoric from some conservative religious leaders, increased reporting of incidents by communities to the council, and U.S. anti-terrorism policies, which Muslims allege adversely affect them. ("Anti-Muslim Hate Crimes Triple," 2004, p. A12)

THE HATE/BIAS CRIME PROBLEM

Introduction

Crimes motivated by hate in the United States have occurred for generations. Most of the immigrant groups that have come to America, including the Irish, Italian, Chinese, Polish, and Puerto Rican, to name a few, have been victimized. Although they are indigenous peoples, Native Americans have not been immune to hate crimes. The descendents of African slaves continue to be victims of bias, discrimination, and crimes motivated by hate. This chapter, however, addresses only crimes motivated by hate in which the victims are Jewish or gay, lesbian, bisexual, or transgender individuals. We include earlier in this chapter information about Arab and Middle Eastern victims of hate/bias crimes following 9/11. Additional examples of specific racial, ethnic, and religious groups hate/bias crimes are discussed in the culture-specific chapters (Chapters 5 through 9).

An unprecedented upward spiral of crimes motivated by hate began in the 1990s. Whether there was an actual increase or simply new documentation procedures is not known. In either case, the figures were disturbing. History has shown that increasing diversity has led to intergroup conflict in countries throughout the world. This fact requires police to consider seriously their role in moderating complex intergroup relationships in the communities they serve. Consider the perspective offered by *Los Angeles Times* journalist Robin Wright (1993) when she wrote, "The world's now dizzying array of ethnic hot spots—at least four dozen at last count—starkly illustrate how, of all the features of the post–Cold War world, the most consistently troubling are turning out to be the tribal hatreds that divide humankind by race, faith, and nationality (p. A1). Wright indicates that fewer than 10 percent of the world's 191 nations are still ethnically or racially homogeneous; fueled by widespread migration and cultural intermixing, "there are now between 7,000 and 8,000 linguistic, ethnic or religious minorities in the world. This mass migration is focused on cities. Its sheer magnitude in an increasingly complex and crowded world makes clashes and conflict a virtually unavoidable consequence of modern urban life" (p. A13). Wright identified four key factors that contribute to intergroup conflict: migration, power quest, insecurity, and limited resources. According to Wright:

> In the aftermath of migration, individuals or groups seeking power often exploit ethnic, religious and cultural differences. This drive for personal power and individual gain is characterized as a "power quest." Similarly, the transition that accompanies migration contributes to uncertainty, which can fuel ethnic and religious passions or rivalry. Coping with change, many people seek refuge within "their" group. When combined with limited resources, this heightened sense of group consciousness can exacerbate ethnic/cultural tensions. This economic dimension is critical and must be recognized by community police. (p. A13)

Minorities, already frustrated with their poor economic situation, are particularly prone to resentment and intolerance of actual or perceived racism and discrimination, especially when the police are suspect. The combination is often the triggering event for a riot.

Victims of hate/bias crimes are particularly sensitive and unsettled because they feel powerless to alter the situation, since they cannot change their racial, ethnic, or religious background. Furthermore, the individual involved is not the sole victim, because often fear of similar crimes can affect an entire group of citizens. A physical attack on a person because of race, religion, ethnic background, or sexual orientation is a particularly insidious form of violent behavior. Verbal assaults on persons because of others' perceptions of their "differences" are equally distressing to both the victim and society. And, unfortunately, these kinds of incidents can also occur in the law enforcement workplace among coworkers. When law enforcement treats such occurrences seriously it sends a message to community members that the local police agency will protect them. Doing the same within the law enforcement organization sends a vitally important message to all employees.

The criminal justice system, and especially local law enforcement agencies, will become the focus of criticism if attacks are not investigated, resolved, and prosecuted promptly and effectively. A hate/bias crime can send shock waves through the ethnic or racial community in which the act was aimed. These acts create danger, frustration, concern, and anxiety in our communities. Law enforcement personnel must have some perspective on both the global and local situation when it comes to hatred and bias within the population they serve. Criminal justice system practitioners must be trained to counteract hate crimes and violence, as well as to address their inhumane impact. The importance of local law enforcement officials' monitoring of such world events is discussed in Chapter 13. This is a major undertaking as we begin the 21st century because the United Nations is currently actively involved in peacekeeping efforts in many different countries.

Many studies over the years have determined that a large number of hate crime perpetrators are youthful thrill-seekers, and the same research statistics indicate that as many as 60 percent of offenders committed crimes for the thrill associated with the victimization. The second most common group responsible for hate crimes is reactive offenders who feel that they are answering an attack by their victims. The least common perpetrators, according to the report, are hard-core fanatics who are driven by racial or religious ideology or ethnic bigotry. These individuals are often members of or potential recruits for extremist organizations. Some perpetrators of hate crimes live on the U.S. borders and are petrified by what they consider to be "brown hordes" of Mexicans, Cubans, and Haitians who enter the United States both legally and illegally. They feel that if they cease their militant rhetoric and violence toward these immigrants, the country will be inundated with them. It is a fact that Mexicans are the largest immigrant group in the country. Their visibility makes them a magnet for anti-immigrant sentiment including discrimination and hate crimes. There are also many racists living near Native American reservations; their aim is to challenge, through violence, the few remaining treaty rights granted to native people.

Community awareness of hate violence grew rapidly in the United States during the late 1980s and the 1990s. Many states commissioned special task forces to recommend ways to control such violence, and new legislation was passed. Despite the abundance of rhetoric deploring acts of bigotry and hate violence, however, few communities have utilized a holistic approach to the problem. Typically, efforts to prevent and respond to such crimes by local agencies have not been coordinated. Indeed, there are many effective programs that deal with a particular aspect of bigotry or hate in a specific setting; however, few models weave efforts to prevent hate violence into the fabric of the community.

In 2006, a series of deadly racial attacks in jails and prisons, especially in California, cast a spotlight on long-simmering but little discussed tensions between blacks and Latinos. According to interviews with teachers, students, politicians, researchers, government officials, civil rights lawyers, police officers, and businesspeople:

> [I]n almost every arena of public life—schools, politics, hospitals, housing, and the workplace—blacks and Latinos are engaged in an edgy competition. The racial attacks and competition highlight a nationwide issue, or trend between the two groups. Unlike in the past when whites were involved in the lion's share of hate crimes, 73 percent of the identified suspects in anti-black hate crimes are Latino. And in anti-Latino crimes, 80 percent of the suspects are black, according to a report by the county's [Los Angeles] Commission on Human Relations. ("Jail brawls," 2006, p. A8)

Hate crimes are the most extreme and dangerous manifestations of racism. Law enforcement professionals, including neighborhood police officers (the best sources of intelligence information), must be aware of the scope of the hate/bias crime problem from both historical and contemporary perspectives.

A U.S. Commission on Civil Rights, Intimidation, and Violence (1990) report identified several factors that contribute to racial intimidation and violence, including the following:

- Racial integration of neighborhoods, leading to "move-in violence" (explained later in the chapter)
- Deep-seated racial hatred played on by organized hate groups
- Economic competition among racial and ethnic groups
- Poor police response to hate crimes

The unprecedented numbers of Latin American and Asian immigrants moving into neighborhoods that were unprepared for the social, economic, political, and criminal justice system consequences of multicultural living has also been a factor in some communities.

The Scope of Hate Crimes Nationally

Tracking hate crimes, which are typically underreported, did not begin in earnest until 1992. The federal Hate Crime Statistics Act of 1990 encourages states to collect and report hate crime data to the Federal Bureau of Investigation (FBI). The FBI, in partnership with local law enforcement agencies, began collecting data on hate/bias incidents, offenses (see later in this chapter for definitions of hate/bias incidents and offenses), victims, offenders, and motivations. The FBI publishes an annual report as part of the Uniform Crime Reporting (UCR) Program. The UCR Program collects data for crimes motivated by biases against race, religion, sexual orientation, ethnicity/ national origin, or disability. Each bias type is then broken down into more specific bias. For example, when a law enforcement agency determines that a hate crime was committed because of bias against an individual's race, the agency may then classify the bias as anti-white, anti-black, anti-American Indian/Alaskan Native, anti-Asian/Pacific Islander, or anti-multiple races group, which describes a group of victims in which more than one race is represented (UCR Hate Crimes Statistics, 2003). Most hate/bias crime statistics are, by definition, "single-bias incidents" (i.e., those that involve one type of bias). Multiple-bias incidents are those that involve two or more offense types motivated by two or more biases.

The UCR Program is a nationwide cooperative statistical effort of more than 17,000 city, county, state, federal, tribal, university, and college law enforcement agencies. The collection of hate crime information, reported in the UCR, is voluntary, however, and not all law enforcement agencies gather or submit data to the FBI. During 2004 (the most recent year available), law enforcement agencies active in the UCR Program represented 94.2 percent of the total population, a vast improvement from when the program first began.

The FBI annual hate crime report is an essential tool for understanding our nation's hate crime problem; however, it alone does not provide a clear picture of the extent and nature of hate/bias crime. The data provide little information about the characteristics of crimes, victims, offenders, or arrests. Recognizing these deficiencies, the FBI created the National Incident-Based Reporting System (NIBRS). NIBRS staff interview persons about their experience with crime, both reported and not reported, which results in more details on more categories of crime, including concurrent offenses, weapons, injury, location, property loss, and characteristics of the victims, offenders, and arrestees, including their gender, race, and age. The information is analyzed and becomes a report known as the National Crime Victimization Survey (NCVS). The information is combined with the statistics collected by the FBI as part of the UCR Program and results in a more thorough report and analysis of the data. To make the data comparable between the UCR Program and NCVS data, only those crimes in which an individual was the victim are utilized for this report. A comparison of UCR and NCVS data provides some striking similarities but also some major differences between the two.

NCVS and UCR demonstrate similar motivations for hate crimes. Motivations reported for hate crimes in 2004 were similar for the NCVS's victimizations reported to police and UCR statistics collected. In both, race is identified as the primary motivation for a hate crime (56 percent for NCVS and 51 percent for UCR). Ethnicity is similarly ranked for the NCVS (29 percent) and for UCR (17 percent). Both NCVS and

UCR numbers indicate about one in six hate crimes were motivated by bias against a sexual orientation and one in nine by bias against a religion. Motivations perceived by NCVS victims of crimes not reported to police are similar to those for NCVS crimes reported to police. Race is still thought to be the primary reason for the commission of hate crimes (56 percent for crimes reported to police and 55 percent for those not reported). Ethnicity provides the basis for about 29 percent of crimes reported to police and 27 percent for those not reported. About 21 percent of NCVS crimes reported to police and 16 percent not reported were thought to be motivated by sexual orientation. The data collected by NCVS indicates that only about 44 percent of hate crimes are reported to the police (Bureau of Justice Statistics, 2005).

The authors used UCR reports covering the period 2000 through 2004, the most recent time period available, to examine trends occurring in reported hate crime incidents and offenses in the United States. These data are shown in Exhibit 12.1. The data for the 5-year period selected reveals that, except for 2001, there was a decrease (1 percent) in the number of hate/bias incidents and offenses reported. The data illustrate the tremendous increase in bias-motivated crimes involving ethnicity or national origin following September 11, 2001. Many Muslims, or those who appeared to be Arab, became the targets of hate/bias crimes because of their perceived or actual ethnicity or national place of origin. See Chapter 7 for further details.

HATE CRIMES	*2000*	*2001*	*2002*	*2003*	*2004*
1. Incidents	8,053	9,730	7,459	7,485	7,642
Offenders Bias:					
Racial	54%	45%	49%	51%	53%
Religious	18%	19%	19%	18%	18%
Sexual Orientation	16%	14%	17%	17%	16%
Ethnic/National Origin	11%	22%	14%	14%	13%
2. Incidents by Category					
Against Persons	62%	65%	68%	63%	59%
Against Property	40%	35%	32%	36%	44%
3. Offenses	9,430	11,430	8,825	8,706	9,021
Offenders Bias:					
Racial	55%	46%	50%	52%	54%
Religious	17%	18%	18%	16%	16%
Sexual Orientation	16%	14%	17%	16%	16%
Ethnic/National Origin	12%	22%	15%	14%	13%
4. Offenses by Category					
Against Persons	65%	68%	65%	61%	62%
Against Property	34%	32%	35%	39%	37%

Exhibit 12.1   Hate Crime: Single-Bias Incidents and Offenses, 2000–2004.
(*Source:* Bureau of Justice Statistics Reports: Hate Crimes: 2000, 2001, 2002, 2003, 2004)
Notes:
1. Columns might not total 100% due to rounding off.
2. Disability bias and crimes against society are not included because they are less than 1 percent of the total in each category.

	2000	*2001*	*2002*	*2003*	*2004*
Racial Bias	5,171	5,290	4,393	4,574	4,863
Antiblack	66%	67%	68%	66%	68%
Antiwhite	20%	20%	20%	21%	21%
Anti-Asian/Pacific Islander	6%	7%	6%	6%	5%
Anti-American Indian	1%	2%	2%	2%	2%
Anti-Multiple Racial Groups	6%	5%	5%	5%	5%
Religious Bias	1,556	2,004	1,576	1,426	1,480
Anti-Jewish/Semitic	75%	56%	66%	69%	68%
Anti-Islamic	2%	27%	11%	11%	13%
Anti-Other	12%	11%	14%	8%	12%
Anti-Catholic	4%	2%	4%	6%	4%
Anti-Protestant	4%	2%	4%	4%	3%
Sexual Orientation	1,486	1,592	1,464	1,430	1,406
Anti–Male Homosexual	69%	69%	65%	62%	61%
Anti-Homosexual	14%	13%	18%	21%	21%
Anti–Female Homosexual	14%	15%	14%	15%	14%
Anti-Heterosexual/Bisexual	3%	3%	2%	1%	4%
Ethnicity/National Origin	1,164	2,544	1,345	1,236	1,201
Anti-Hispanic	63%	30%	48%	43%	51%
Anti-Other	37%	70%	55%	57%	49%

Exhibit 12.2   Hate Crime: Single-Bias Offenses, Specific Bias Motivation, 2000–2004.
(*Source:* Bureau of Justice Statistics Reports: Hate Crimes, 2000, 2001, 2002, 2003, 2004)
Notes:
1. The term victim may refer to a person, business, institution, or society as a whole.
2. Anti-Jewish/Semitic as a percentage of total religious bias.
3. Columns might not total 100% due to rounding off.

Exhibits 12.1 and 12.2 show that each year, most of the reported single-bias hate crimes were motivated by racial bias. The percentages of bias-motivated hate crimes due to religious intolerance and sexual orientation were similar, followed closely in percentages by biases against ethnicity or national origin. The statistics for hate/bias crimes motivated by disability and those against society (government buildings, for example) are not shown because they each amount to less than 1 percent of the total.

The reports show that African Americans were by far the largest group of victims of bias hate crime (anti-black), as they have been since the FBI began gathering hate crime statistics. Hate crimes against African Americans averaged 67 percent of the total of crimes motivated by racial bias over the 5 years studied. Typically, among racially motivated incidents, six in 10 targeted blacks, three in 10 targeted whites, and the remainder targeted Asians or American Indians. After African Americans, the most victimized groups included Jews, gay men, and whites. The reports for the period studied also showed that 63 to 68 percent of hate crimes were committed against people and 32 to 37 percent against property. Not shown in the exhibits but highlighted in the UCR reports is that white people were the most common offenders in hate crimes. The Bureau of Justice Statistics released a report indicating that American Indians experience the highest level of hate crimes per capita, according to data from the NCVS. The

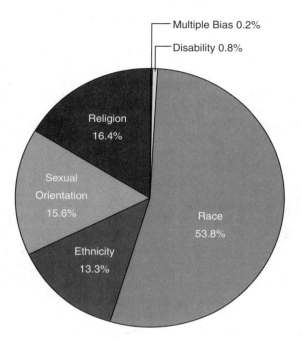

Exhibit 12.3   Hate Crime: Bias-Motivated Offenses, Percent Distribution 2004.
Note: Due to rounding, the percentages may not add to 100%.

NCVS study discovered that the overall rate of violent victimization (excluding homicide) for American Indians is 118.8 per 1,000, which is at least two times the rate of any other racial group (Rennison, 2001, p. 10).

Using the 2005 UCR report analyzing hate/bias offenses for 2004, it becomes apparent that the percent distribution of bias motivation is typical of other years, except in 2001 for reasons already mentioned; see Exhibit 12.3 and compare to the data listed in Exhibits 12.1 and 12.2. Exhibit 12.4 shows the number and bias motivation for murders for the same 5-year period.

DEFINITION OF HATE CRIME AND HATE INCIDENT

Hate Crime

The federal definition of hate crime addresses civil rights violations under Title 18 U.S.C. Section 45. Although state definitions vary, in general a hate crime is considered to be:

- a criminal act or attempted act,
- against a person, institution, or property,
- that is motivated in whole or in part by the offender's bias against a
  - race,
  - color,

MURDERS	2000	2001	2002	2003	2004
Number:	19	10	11	14	5
Motivation:					
Racial	10	4	4	5	5
Sexual Orientation	2	1	4	6	3
Ethnic/National Origin	6	5	2	2	0
Religion	1	0	0	0	1
Disability	0	0	1	1	0

Exhibit 12.4   Hate Crime: Bias-Motivated Murders, 2000–2004.
(*Source:* Bureau of Justice Statistics Reports: Hate Crimes, 2000, 2001, 2002, 2003, 2004)

- religion,
- gender,
- ethnic/national origin group,
- disability status, or
- sexual orientation group.

Definitions of hate crime often incorporate not only violence against individuals or groups but also crimes against property such as arson or vandalism, in particular those directed against community centers or houses of worship.

Hate Incident

Hate incidents involve behaviors that, though motivated by bias against a victim's race, religion, ethnic/national origin, gender, age, disability, or sexual orientation, are not criminal acts. Hostile or hateful speech, or other disrespectful or discriminatory behavior, may be motivated by bias but is not illegal. Such incidents become crimes only when they directly incite perpetrators to commit violence against persons or property or if they place a potential victim in reasonable fear of physical injury (IACP, 1999).

Ethnoviolence. The Prejudice Institute uses the term *ethnoviolence* instead of hate crime to describe an act or an attempted act that is motivated by group prejudice and intended to cause physical or psychological injury. The organization indicates that these violent acts include intimidation, harassment, group insults, property defacement or destruction, and physical attacks. "The targets of these acts involve persons identified because of their race or skin color, gender, nationality or national origin, religion, or other physical or social characteristic of groups such as sexual orientation" ("Facts Sheet on Ethnoviolence," 2004).

The Prejudice Institute maintains that the term hate crime was developed for legislative and political reasons. It refers to legislatively defined crimes such as murder, robbery, assault, burglary, arson, and property damage, as well as some forms of intimidation. This definition is much narrower than that of ethnoviolence. Also, it implies that all crimes that are motivated by prejudice involve "hate." In fact, hate has a strong, negative emotional connotation that is not necessarily involved. Many ethnoviolent incidents are committed impulsively, or as acts of conformity, or as deliberate acts of intimidation designed to achieve specific ends of the perpetrator ("Facts Sheet on Ethnoviolence," 2004).

According to the Prejudice Institute, counting ethnoviolent acts is a difficult task. Its estimates derive from rigorous case studies of cities, neighborhoods, campuses, and work organizations. According to the Prejudice Institute's studies, the preponderance of evidence indicates a rate of 20 to 25 percent, which means that one out of every four or five adult Americans is harassed, intimidated, insulted, or assaulted for reasons of prejudice during the course of a year. The research reveals that there appears to be variation by group (black, white, Jewish, gay, etc.) and by the site of an incident (residence, neighborhood, school, workplace, etc.). For example, the majority of all ethnoviolent incidents seem to be motivated by racial prejudice, while the majority of incidents involving violent physical assaults seem to be motivated by prejudice based on sexual orientation ("Facts Sheet on Ethnoviolence," 2004). This text uses the words *hate crime* or *hate incident* because the terms are commonly known and accepted.

HATE CRIME SOURCE THEORIES

Urban Dynamics Theories

The relationships among the clustering of new immigrant groups, the economy, move-in violence, and hate/bias incidents and crimes in cities are well documented. It is important to understand that hate incidents and crimes often do not occur in a vacuum but are part of a larger social and economic interchange.

Clustering and target zone theory. Studies have shown that initially new immigrants tend to locate or cluster where people of their own ethnic and racial background are already established. They tend to congregate in the same areas of the country or within a city to be near relatives or friends; to have assistance in finding housing and jobs and in coping with language barriers; and to find the security of a familiar religion and social institutions. One study on new immigrant grouping by Steven Wallace for the University of California, San Francisco, which is still valid today, noted that

> for the first generation or two, ethnic communities are helpful because they provide a sense of continuity for immigrants while easing subsequent generations into American values and society. . . . The existence of an ethnic or immigrant community is obvious evidence that a group has not assimilated. A community represents a place where immigrants are able to associate with others like themselves. An immigrant community provides a safe place to engage in those activities that deviate from dominant norms such as speaking a language other than English, honoring "foreign" symbols of pride, and exhibiting other non-Anglo behavior. Commonly located in low-rent districts, ethnic communities are functionally found where members can afford to live while they work at low wage jobs. (Wallace, 1987, pp. 88–89)

These core areas are typically where low-socioeconomic-class whites, blacks, Hispanics, and established immigrants have settled because housing is cheap (or government subsidized), employment or welfare services are available, and there is a great deal of comfort derived from living with people of one's own race or culture. These areas are often impoverished ghettos, with substandard, older housing, and they are frequently overcrowded, with a high incidence of social conflict and crime, including drug and gang activity. As new immigrants and members of varied racial and cultural groups move into the core area, they come into conflict with existing members of that community—a phenomenon that has been going on for generations. The newcomers and the established community members compete for housing, jobs, financial resources (e.g., welfare, food stamps), and education. When there is a collapse of affordable health services, lack of affordable housing, and reductions in benefits (cuts in social programs by federal and state authorities), as occurred in the 1990s and again in 2003, conflicts escalate between racial and ethnic groups. As these circumstances intensify, incidents of discrimination, bias, and hate violence increase. Those who are more established want to move out, not just to improve their lot but also to escape the conflict.

Wallace indicates that the rewards of better education and jobs tend to come with assimilation into mainstream society. Some groups of immigrants can be seen as "temporary inhabitants" of the inner city; they work toward and achieve their goal of moving into the suburbs as they improve their economic situation. As they gain wealth and education, they acquire the same economic and educational advantages as long-time Americans (Wallace, 1992).

The economy and hate violence. Poor economic times contribute greatly to hate violence. In many areas of the country, when major industries such as steel and auto manufacturing have downturns, go out of business, or relocate, the likelihood of economic distress among low-skilled and unskilled workers increases. Scapegoating often results when blue-collar jobs are unavailable. The distress that accompanies unemployment and rising prices is often directed toward immigrants and minorities and manifests itself as harassment and violence.

Sociologists indicate that hate frequently stems from being deprived or having one's needs unsatisfied, so the poor despise the rich, the uneducated ridicule the intellectual, and the established ghetto inhabitant hates the new immigrant or refugee who moves into the area. Social scientists argue that the government definition of poverty does not measure the experience of being poor or the changes taking place in inner cities: not only has the number of ghetto poor increased but also the severity of economic deprivation among them. Ghetto poverty and concentrations of diverse populations in one area often lead to conflict in these neighborhoods. The stresses of urban life, especially in inner cities, give rise to increased incidents of violence, especially in depressed economic conditions and reduced space.

Move-in violence. Move-in violence can occur when people of one ethnicity or race move into a residence or open a business in a neighborhood composed of people from a different race or ethnicity. It can also take place when the new resident is of the same ethnicity or race—for example, a Cuban moving into a Mexican neighborhood or a Caribbean black moving into an African American community. Changing diversity and demographics can have a significant impact on a community because of hostility based on both perceived and real group differences. However, the presence of new migrants or immigrants in a racially or ethnically different neighborhood does not automatically result in intergroup conflict or violence.

Historically, most cases of move-in violence have involved black, Hispanic, or Asian victims who locate housing or businesses in previously all-white suburbs or neighborhoods. Whites have not been the sole perpetrators, however, and they have also been victims. For example, in Worcester, Massachusetts (in 1999), and in Sacramento,

California (in 2000), Russian immigrants moved into nonwhite neighborhoods and community conflict occurred. New residents or business owners have moved into areas that are primarily black, Hispanic, or Asian and experienced friction with the original residents. According to the U.S. Department of Justice's Community Relations Service, there have been cases of Hispanic migration or immigration into communities that had been presided over for many years by black leaders. In some of these new mixed communities, such as the Los Angeles–area neighborhoods of Lakewood, Watts, and Pomona, Hispanic/Latino community members have sometimes perceived that their concerns are being ignored. Other cases of conflict have involved communities with new immigrants from the Middle East and South Asia. For the past three decades, Middle Easterners have made up one of the fastest-growing immigrant groups in the country, their numbers increasing sevenfold since 1970 compared to a tripling of the overall immigrant population during that period. Nationwide, the largest newcomer groups from the Middle East consist of Iranians and Israelis, but there has also been a large number of Pakistanis from south Asia.

Targets of Hate Crimes

The psychocultural origin of hate crimes stems from human nature itself. To hate means to dislike passionately or intensely—to have an extreme aversion to or hostility toward another person, idea, or object. Hate can have a benign manifestation, such as when one hates evil, or bad weather, or certain foods, or it can have an abnormal expression when it becomes obsessive or is wrongly directed at someone who has done no harm. People can be culturally conditioned to hate those who are different from them because of their places of origin, looks, beliefs, or preferences. As the song in the musical *South Pacific* reminds us, "We have to be taught to hate and fear / We have to be taught from year to year." Crimes and acts of hate serve as frightening reminders to vulnerable citizens that they may not take safety for granted. Collectively, they begin to develop a mentality that hate crimes can take place anywhere—in streets, in neighborhoods, at workplaces, and even in their homes. Not all crimes motivated by prejudice or bias involve hate. Many nonviolent incidents are committed impulsively, or as acts of conformity, or as deliberate acts of intimidation designed to achieve specific ends of the perpetrator that do not necessarily involve hate.

There are innumerable examples of hate/bias crimes that have victimized blacks, Asians, and Hispanics. Clearly, such hate goes back for many generations. These are discussed in Part Two, "Cultural Specifics for Law Enforcement." The following sections address Jews and lesbian, gay, bisexual, and transgender people as victims of hate or bias crimes.

JEWS AND ANTI-SEMITISM

Jews

Jews belong to a religious and cultural group, although they have sometimes been incorrectly labeled as constituting a separate racial group. Jews have experienced discrimination, persecution, and violence throughout history because their religious beliefs and practices often set them apart from the majority. Even when they were totally assimilated (i.e., integrated into society), as was true in Germany early in the 20th century, they were still not accepted as full citizens and eventually experienced the ultimate hate crime—genocide. The term anti-Semitism means "against Semites," which literally includes Jews and Arabs. Popular use of this term, however, refers to anti-Jewish sentiment.

European anti-Semitism had religious origins: Jews did not accept Jesus Christ as the son of God and were portrayed as betrayers and even killers of Christ. This accusation gave rise to religious anti-Semitism and what Christians saw as justification for anti-Jewish acts. In the past three decades, there have been great strides made by religious leaders to eliminate centuries of prejudice. For example, a 1965 Roman Catholic decree (the Nostra Aetate) stated that the church did not hold Jews responsible for the death of Christ. The decree, written by the Second Vatican Council under the leadership of the pope, encouraged people to abandon blaming Jews and instead work for stronger links and increased understanding between the religions. But despite some progress in ecumenical relations, there are still individuals who, 2,000 years after the birth of Christ, believe that Jews today are responsible for Christ's death. Abraham Foxman, National Director of the Anti-Defamation League (ADL), said in 2005:

> of great concern is the persistence of two of the most insidious manifestations of anti-Semitism: The beliefs that Jews are more loyal to Israel than to America, and that Jews were responsible for the death of Jesus. Since so much of the history of anti-Semitism relates to the charges that Jews are always aliens in the societies in which they live and are Christ-killers, these realities should not be taken lightly. In our recent survey, 33 percent of those polled said American Jews were more loyal to Israel than America, a remarkably consistent finding that goes back four decades. Thirty percent of Americans said Jews were responsible for the death of Jesus. (Foxman, 2005)

According to Foxman, anti-Semitism also increased because of the United States' war in Iraq. In the same article he said,

> What happened in our country shortly before the start of fighting in Iraq was a reminder. The old canard espoused by Charles Lindbergh before WWII—that Jews, because of their narrow self-interest, were bringing the country to war— was now *being updated* to blame neo-conservative Jews. Unlike when Pat Buchanan accused Jews of causing the first Gulf War, this time the accusations took on a life of their own.

A 2005 survey by the ADL found that 14 percent of Americans had anti-Semitic attitudes, which was a dramatic decline since their initial survey in 1964 when 29 percent of Americans were deemed to possess anti-Semitic attitudes. The 2005 survey report indicates that their findings are generally consistent with what they found over the last decade, with some variation: in 1998, the number was 12 percent; in 2002 it was 17 percent (Foxman, 2005). Another type of anti-Semitism falls under what some would label as anti-Zionism (i.e., against the establishment of the state of Israel as a homeland for Jews). Although politically oriented, this type of anti-Semitism still makes references to "the Jews" and equates "Jews" with the suppression of the Palestinian people.

The 2006 terrorist attacks by Hezbollah operating from Lebanon resulted in extreme unrest in the Middle East and severe criticism of Israel. From the Israeli perspective, the

Hezbollah as well as Hamas (responsible for rocket attacks from the Gaza strip) had never formally accepted Israel's right to exist as a nation. Israel was directly threatened by Hezbollah's widespread presence, especially in South Lebanon where attacks directly into Israel could occur. The Arab world and some of the non-Arab world criticized Israel for what they believed to be extreme military actions in Lebanon in which infrastructure was destroyed and attacks lasted longer than was expected. This 2006 Middle East conflict resulted in demonstrations in the United States by both pro-Palestinian and pro-Israeli contingents. Police officers must be aware of the potential fallout in the United States when such conflicts arise in the Middle East. Anti-Israel attitudes are sometimes expressed as anti-Zionist and anti-Jewish sentiments around the world, including in the United States, despite that Jewish political identification with Israel varies greatly. Thus reaction to Middle Eastern politics can be tied to anti-Semitism. One unfortunate example of violence occurred in Seattle in July, 2006, where a man who, according to authorities, was angered by the war in Iraq and the apparent U.S. cooperation with Israel in Lebanon, entered a Jewish Federation office and randomly shot six women, killing one. He was quoted as saying, "These are Jews, and I'm tired of getting pushed around and our people [he is a Muslim] getting pushed around by the situation in the Middle East." "He repeatedly blamed the Jewish people for all of these problems," Seattle Police Chief Gil Kerlikowske said at a news conference. A Seattle Islamic Center issued a statement, which read in part, "we disassociate this act from our Islamic teachings and beliefs" ("Seattle Shooting," 2006).

Finally, racially based anti-Semitism originated in 19th-century pre-Nazi ideology, which claimed that Jews were an inferior race. In their attempts to eliminate the Jewish "race," the Nazis considered people "impure" if one grandparent or even great-grandparent in their family was Jewish.

Prevalence of Anti-Semitic Crimes

The ADL annually collects data on the prevalence of anti-Semitic incidents. The audit identifies both criminal and noncriminal incidents of harassment and intimidation, including distribution of hate literature, threats, and slurs. The audit includes incidents such as physical and verbal assaults, harassment, property defacement, vandalism, and other expressions of anti-Jewish sentiment.

A 2005 ADL audit of anti-Semitic incidents in the United States determined that despite a slight reduction in the number from 2004 (3 percent), they remained at disturbing levels. The number of anti-Semitic incidents was at a 9-year high in 2004, according to the ADL. Public activity by organized neo-Nazi and other hate groups, harassment and intimidation in schools, and anti-Semitic activity on college campuses all contributed to the higher numbers.

In 2005, 42 states and the District of Columbia reported 1,757 anti-Semitic incidents, according to the ADL, a 3 percent decrease over 2004, as is shown in Exhibit 12.5. Anti-Semitic activity reported in 2005 comprised 1,140 acts of harassment (intimidation, threats, and assaults) and 617 acts of vandalism (property damage as well as arson and cemetery desecration). Exhibit 12.5 is a national audit of anti-Semitic incidents year by year, with totals from 1984 to 2005. Five states continued the trend of reporting the most anti-Semitic incidents. They are those with the largest Jewish populations and thus the most targets—New York, California, New Jersey, Massachusetts, and Florida.

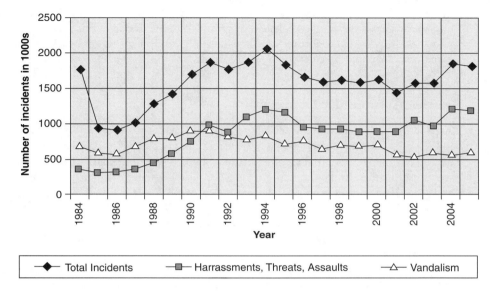

Exhibit 12.5   Hate Crime: Audit of Anti-Semitic Incidents, Year-by-Year National Totals, 1984–2005.
(*Source:* "Annual ADL Audit: Anti-Semitic Incidents Decline in 2005 but Levels of Concern in U.S." (2006). Anti-Defamation League.)

Anti-Semitic Groups and Individuals

Several types of groups in the United States have exhibited anti-Semitic attitudes, and some of the most extreme groups have committed hate crimes against Jews. The most glaringly anti-Semitic organizations are white supremacist groups, such as the Ku Klux Klan (KKK), the Aryan Nation, White Aryan Resistance (WAR), the Order, the Posse Comitatus, the Covenant and the Sword, the Arm of the Lord, and neo-Nazi skinheads (discussed further in Chapter 13). These groups tend to hate all who are different from them but focus a great deal of attention on blacks and Jews. Some messianic individuals who believe that Armageddon (the end of the world) is imminent have been known to threaten Jews by phone or mail, but rarely have these threats been carried out. These people believe that Jews need to repent and see themselves as instruments of God, connected to the coming of the end of the world. Those who argued that it was this country's support of Israel that led to the September 11, 2001, attacks have demonstrated another aspect of anti-Semitism. Some hate groups used this argument to stir up anti-Jewish feelings and to erode sympathy and support for Jews and for Israel at their organization's rallies and within the general public. In addition, those who are vehemently pro-Arab and anti-Israel may exhibit strong anti-Jewish attitudes. While it is not as common for anti-Zionist attitudes to result in acts of violence against Jews in the United States as it is in Europe, Jewish Americans, like Arab Americans, can nevertheless become targets during Middle Eastern crises. Finally, in times of recession, Jews are often blamed for the economic decline, and the notion of Jewish "influence" (i.e., the baseless charge that Jews control the media, the banks, and even the world economy) provides a convenient scapegoat. It is not within the scope of this section to delve into these myths, but we point out that there is widespread harmful misinformation about Jews that anti-Semites continue to spread.

Jewish Community Concerns

Around the holiest days of the Jewish year (Rosh Hashanah and Yom Kippur, occurring in the early fall), there can also be heightened anxiety among some community members regarding security. Indeed, many synagogues hire extra security during times of worship over this 10-day holiday period. Acts of defilement can occur in synagogues and other Jewish institutions at random times as well. These acts and manifestations of prejudice bring back painful memories for Jews who experienced violent expressions of anti-Semitism in other countries, especially those who lived through the Holocaust; some of the memories and fears have been passed on to subsequent generations. At the same time, some people may overreact to an insensitive remark that stems from ignorance on the part of the speaker rather than from malicious anti-Semitism. Some people may not understand that a swastika painted by teenagers on a building does not necessarily precede any acts of anti-Jewish violence. Yet a swastika almost always evokes a fearful reaction among many Jewish community members because of the historical significance of the symbol.

Police officers must understand that different segments of the Jewish community feel vulnerable to anti-Semitism, and therefore officers are advised to listen to and take seriously Jews' expressions of concern and fear. At the same time, they need to explain that sometimes acts of vandalism are isolated and are not targeting any group in particular (e.g., many skinheads or "thugs" are unhappy with their lot in life and tend to hate everyone). Finally, officers who take reports from citizens should reassure those citizens that their local law enforcement agency views hate crimes and incidents seriously and that extra protection will be provided if the need arises.

What Law Enforcement Can Do

By discussing the concerns and fears of some Jewish community members, we do not imply that all Jewish citizens are overly concerned for their safety. In fact, a large percentage of American Jews do not even identify as Jews and do not share a collective or community consciousness with other Jews. At the other extreme are people who interpret events or remarks as anti-Semitic rather than as ignorance or insensitivity. Whatever the case, police officers should be aware that anti-Semitism has a long and active history, and even if some fears appear to be exaggerated, they have a basis in reality.

Officers can take some steps to establish rapport and provide protection in Jewish communities when the need arises:

1. When an officer hears of an act that can be classified as a hate crime toward Jews, it should be investigated, tracked, and dealt with as such. Dismissing acts of anti-Semitism as petty crime will result in a lack of trust on the part of the community.

2. When hate crimes and incidents are perpetrated against other groups in the community (e.g., gay, African American, Asian American groups), officers should alert Jewish community leaders immediately. Their institutions may be the next targets.

3. Officers should be aware of groups and individuals who distribute hate literature on people's doorsteps. Publications such as *Racial Loyalty,* for example, target Jews and "people of color" and accuse Jews of poisoning the population. A book published by the same organization, *On the Brink of a Bloody Racial War,* has been left on many Jews' doorsteps. Even if no violence occurs, the recipients of such hate literature become very fearful.

4. In cooperation with local organizations (e.g., Jewish community relations councils, ADL), officers can provide information through joint meetings on ways that individuals can heighten the security of Jewish institutions (e.g., information on nonbreakable glass, lighting of facilities in evenings).

5. Law enforcement officials should be familiar with the important dates of the Jewish calendar, especially when the High Holidays (Rosh Hashanah and Yom Kippur) occur. Some people are concerned about safety and protection during events at which large groups of Jews congregate.

6. Finally, officers may contact a Jewish umbrella organization in the community to assist them in sending necessary messages to local Jewish institutions and places of worship. Two organizations in particular are worth noting: the national JCRC (Jewish Community Relations Council) and the ADL. The JCRC has representative organizations in almost every major city in the United States. This organization, the regional ADL organizations, and the Jewish Federations can be of great assistance to law enforcement in disseminating information to members of the Jewish community.

Because of their history, some Jews expect anti-Semitic incidents, and the reality is that there are still anti-Semites in our society. According to Riva Gambert (2003), former associate director of the JCRC of the Greater East Bay, whether an act is simply insensitive or whether it is indeed a hate crime, an officer still has to be responsive to generated fears and community concerns. An officer's ability to calm fears as well as to investigate threats thoroughly will result in strong relations between law enforcement officials and Jewish community members.

LESBIAN, GAY, BISEXUAL, AND TRANSGENDER VICTIMIZATION

Introduction

The terms homosexual, lesbian, gay, bisexual, and transgender are defined in the glossary of this textbook. A related term that is important to understand is *phobia,* which is defined in Webster's Dictionary as an irrational, excessive and persistent fear of some particular thing or situation. Gays and Lesbians Initiating Dialogue for Equality (GLIDE) defines homophobia as "an irrational fear, hatred, ignorance, or general discomfort with gay, lesbian, bisexual, or transgender persons, topics, or issues." Sometimes, homophobia results in homophobic acts, which can run the full spectrum from antigay jokes to physical battery resulting in injury or death. In this text, as in government reporting systems, homophobic acts are referred to as antisexual orientation bias incidents and offenses. The acronym LGBT is used throughout this section and refers to lesbian, gay, bisexual, and transgender.

Hate crimes targeting LGBT individuals are distinct from other bias crimes because they target a group made up of every other category discussed within this textbook. In the United States today, there are organizations whose membership includes gay Jews, Catholics, Mormons, Buddhists, Armenians, Latinos/as, African Americans, Asians and Pacific Islanders, and virtually every other ethnic, racial, and religious group. Every year in the United States, thousands of LGBT persons are harassed, beaten, or murdered solely because of their sexual orientation or gender identity.

Hate Crime Laws Specific to LGBT Persons as Victims

As of 2006, 47 states and the District of Columbia have hate crime laws, and of those, 29 states and the District of Columbia include sexual orientation. Seven of the 29 states and the District of Columbia include protections for persons based on gender identity. There are no federal laws either protecting victims of crimes based on sexual orientation or gender identity or providing for an additional penalty enhancement for such crimes. The Hate Crimes Sentencing Act, which applies only to federal offenses, allows judges to consider homophobia as a motive only during sentencing. In 2004, the U.S. Senate passed the Local Law Enforcement Act, which allows the federal government to provide assistance for the investigation and prosecution of hate crimes based on sexual orientation ("U.S. Senate Passes Hate Crimes Act," 2004, p. 12).

LGBT Persons as Victims of Hate Bias Incidents and Offenses

The scope of LGBT victimization. The authors used 5 years of UCR reports covering the period 2000 through 2004 to study the trends in reported hate crime incidents and offenses and their respective motivation in the United States. The data is shown in Exhibits 12.1 and 12.2. An analysis of the data for the period seems to indicate that of the total of hate crime incidents and offenses reported each year, the average related to sexual orientation bias was 16 percent. A look at Exhibit 12.2, showing the specific motivation for sexual orientation bias offenses, shows that antimale homosexual bias had the highest percentage for each year of the study period, ranging from 61 to 69 percent; antihomosexual (in general) averaged from 13 to 14 percent; and antifemale homosexual averaged over the 5-year period was 14 percent. Extreme increases in the percentage of incidents and offenses that were classified as motivated by antihomosexual bias 2002 through 2004 were noted, and these increases are discussed later.

The National Coalition of Anti-Violence Programs (NCAVP) is a consortium of over 20 antiviolence organizations that monitor and respond to incidents and offenses of bias, hate, and domestic violence targeting the LGBT and HIV communities. A study involving a coalition of 13 NCAVP member agencies completed in 2006 mirrored the statistics presented in the FBI's UCR reports for 2005 in regard to anti-LBGT violence. Both reports indicated there was a 13 percent decrease in anti-LGBT violence between 2004 and 2005. Researchers and gay rights groups, however, question these studies, both the findings and the implications. As already mentioned in this chapter, because law enforcement compliance with the Hate Crime Statistics Act of 1990 is voluntary, many agencies in the United States do not report hate bias incidents and offenses to the FBI for use in the UCR Program report. UCR reports, therefore, are viewed by some as being inaccurate and not a true measure of the numbers of hate/bias crimes. For example, in the entire state of California, only 235 of 727 agencies that participate in the UCR program reported any hate crimes in 2003 and listed only 337 such hate-motivated incidents based on sexual orientation. Yet the Community United Against Violence organization in San Francisco (just one agency in California participating in NCAVP's report) submitted data on 340 incidents. In Colorado, only 35 of 185 participating law enforcement agencies reported any hate crimes during all of 2003, and these agencies reported only 10 hate-motivated incidents based on sexual orientation. Yet the Colorado Anti-Violence Program, based in Denver, submitted data on 155 incidents. Other states studied had similar findings (NCAVP, 2006).

The FBI's 2004 UCR program report indicated there were 1,406 single-bias offenses based on antisexual orientation bias. According to the report, the data collected represented 92.4 percent of the nation's population. The NCAVP, relying on data representing areas covering only 27.2 percent of the population, captured 1,792 incidents, a difference that can be explained only by law enforcement agencies' not submitting reports or not documenting them properly and/or victims not reporting crimes to their local police department. Despite the shortcomings of even the NCAVP's Anti-Lesbian, Gay, Bisexual and Transgender Violence 2005 report, however, it is still considered to be the most definitive on the subject of anti-LBGT violence.

The increases noted in sexual orientation, antihomosexual bias crimes from 2002 through 2004, occurred during years when gays and lesbians were trying to legally marry and gain adoption rights, which resulted in movements in some states as well as on the national level to block these efforts (i.e., the controversial issues of "same-sex marriage" and adoption of children). In short, LGBT persons and communities had garnered more visibility, both positive and negative, during the years in question. Both statistical and anecdotal evidence clearly demonstrates that when LGBT issues are in the limelight, LGBT communities and individuals are targeted for violence. Many of the driving political and cultural forces behind the era of violence described in 2004 were not nearly as prominent during 2005. In short, events both specific and ancillary to LGBT communities help create an environment that fosters increased violence against LGBT persons (NCAVP, 2006).

LGBT Victim Profiles. The distribution of LGBT victims across various demographics remains fairly constant: victims of African descent comprised 17 percent of all victims whose race or ethnicity was known. Latinos and Latinas were 25 percent, and whites were 48 percent of the victims. Arab/Middle Eastern persons as victims rose 37 percent, and Indigenous/Native American increased by 18 percent between 2004 and 2005 (NCAVP, 2006, p. 7). The majority of LGBT victims reporting to the NCAVP in 2005 were gay men (59 percent) or lesbians (18 percent) and the largest age group was between 30 and 49 (40 percent) (NCAVP, 2006, p. 36).

Anti-LGBT murders are often easily distinguished from other murders by the level of brutality involved. LGBT murder victims are often dismembered, stabbed multiple times, or severely bludgeoned. A study conducted by the NCAVP determined that almost 60 percent of anti-LGBT murders involve "extraordinary violence." Clarence Patton, executive director of the nation's largest anti-violence project, in New York, makes reference to the "extraordinary levels of violence involved" in such anti-LGBT crimes, saying that "many bias-motivated physical assaults against gay, bisexual, HIV-positive, and transgender persons are extremely violent and brutal" ("Gay and Lesbian Anti-Violence Project," 2006). The following are just a few examples of this phenomenon:

- Following an attack in a Santa Fe motel parking lot, where five men beat two gay men while yelling antigay epithets, one New Mexico victim spent eight days in a coma and had to learn to walk and talk again ("Two Defendants in Gay Bashing Case Avoid Prison," 2006, p. 36).

- In 2003, the Alabama Supreme Court set an execution date for a death row inmate who helped two other men rob and kill a 60-year-old gay man, stabbing him 78 times before slashing his throat repeatedly, nearly decapitating him ("Alabama Supreme Court," 2003, p. 30).

- A gay Latino man was murdered in the Bronx in August 2002. Reports indicate he had been stabbed 46 times and asphyxiated ("Stonewalled," 2005, p. 76).

- In July 2004, three suspects beat, stabbed, and strangled an 18-year-old gay man, then burned his body in the woods near his mobile home in Bay Minette, Alabama ("New Call for Hate Crime Change," 2005, p. 35).

- A Fulton County jury convicted an Atlanta man of murder and other crimes for fatally stabbing a coworker in the restaurant's restroom. The defendant stated he was defending himself from the victim's sexual advance when he stabbed the man 40 times. ("DA Lashes Out," 2004, p. 30).

In the Fulton County trial, the District Attorney issued a statement condemning the use of the "gay panic" defense used by the defendant's attorneys to justify the actions of perpetrators of anti-LGBT crimes. The use of gay panic defense is currently at the forefront of much debate among members of the criminal justice system, as well as among politicians who have been seeking to bar this defense.

The Phenomenon of Underreporting Antisexual Orientation Incidents and Offenses

Various reasons have been postulated for the phenomenon of LGBT hate crimes being seriously underreported to law enforcement, including the following:

1. *Law enforcement is not required to collect and report LGBT hate/bias crimes.* Under the Hate Crimes Statistics Act, local law enforcement agencies are not required to report hate crimes to the FBI, and some do not. An additional criticism is that of the agencies that do submit data, many do not include hate crime statistics, either denying these sorts of crimes occur in their community or not classifying them as such.

2. *LGBT individuals do not report being victimized.* Unwillingness to "come out" (be identified as LGBT) by reporting these crimes to authorities is thought to be the most common reason that some victims do not report a crime. If this were the only factor, however, then the phenomenon would not remain constant within metropolitan areas with large, open LGBT populations

and organizations that provide outreach on such issues. In fact, data from the Los Angeles Gay and Lesbian Center, the primary agency that provides victim services and documentation of homophobic hate violence for L.A. County (including the independent city of West Hollywood, whose population comprises approximately 35 percent LGBT residents), clearly demonstrates that the underreporting of hate crimes is continuing into the new century. The truth is that many members of the LGBT community remain mistrustful of the police or suspect that their reporting of such incidents will not result in any significant action by law enforcement ("Stonewalled," 2005).

The NCAVP 2005 report listed the following reasons victims of anti-LGBT bias hesitate to report their experiences, either to police or to organizations within their own community. The victim:

a. fears reprisal from the offender(s).

b. fears embarrassment or abuse from police.

c. would be ostracized from family, friends, or coworkers and would possibly lose employment, custody of children, or housing.

d. at the urging of family members, friends, and coworkers does not to report the incident.

e. is so emotionally impacted by the experience that he or she wishes to "forget" it and "move on" and not deal with reporting the occurrence.

f. blames himself or herself for being in the "wrong" place, saying the "wrong" thing, or acting in the "wrong" way.

g. either does not believe anything can be done about the situation or believes the police will not do anything about the situation.

h. dismisses hate incidents (versus hate offenses/crimes) such as eggs or lit cigarettes being thrown at him/her as not being serious enough to report.

i. is not aware of national or local antiviolence programs or other alternatives to the police (or the victim believes the organizations will not help if he or she does not make an official police report).

Differences in culture and language, along with gender, age, and class, often lead to perceptions that advocacy organizations may not be sensitive to the victim's own background. The NCAVP strongly believes that the incidence of anti-LGBT bias crime affecting younger and older people, immigrants, people of color, people in the military, and those within other marginalized populations is *grossly* underreported (NCAVP, 2006, p. 35).

3. ***Other reasons for antisexual orientation crimes being underreported:***

    a. ***Mixed motive or pick-up crimes.*** According to Sgt. Mitchel Grobeson, retired LAPD, though victims' advocates believe that a crime in which bias was a *primary* motivation should be classified as a hate crime, law enforcement officers are often unwilling to do so if there is any other motive in addition to bias (Grobeson, 2006). These advocates point out that law enforcement personnel have a practice of looking for "pick-up crimes." That is, some law enforcement personnel tend to drop the hate bias motivation of any incident or offense in which an element of *any* other crime is involved (e.g., assault with a deadly weapon or robbery).

Amnesty International confirms this practice in a study that revealed that in some instances, any indication of "mixed motives" for a crime, (e.g., although homophobic slurs were used, the victim was also robbed) means that the case is discounted as a hate crime (e.g., and classified as a robbery) ("Stonewalled," 2005, p. 38).

b. ***Conflicting police training policies and practices.*** Another facet of the issue of underreporting is that law enforcement personnel who receive training in the handling of hate crimes are often instructed *not* to ask about a person's sexual orientation, so assaults and batteries motivated by homophobia are often not classified as hate crimes. The reluctance of some LGBT victims to reveal the homophobic component of a crime to police, for reasons already discussed, leads to low criminal justice figures on homophobic hate crime (Grobeson, 2006). Law enforcement is a key component in combating violence against lesbian, gay, bisexual, and transgender people, and victims expect appropriate action and professionalism when reporting an assault.

Transgender Persons as Victims of Sexual Orientation Hate Crimes. Statistically, transgender people, per capita, are 16 times more likely to be murdered than the general population and three times more likely than African American males, which is the next closest category ("Literary Stereotyping," 2003, p. 88). Of transgender murder victims in the United States, nonwhite youths are disproportionately represented (Manley, 2006). The Los Angeles Commission on Human Relations released a report that showed that hate crimes against transgender people had the greatest likelihood of violence of any victim group: 88 percent involved violence compared to 58 percent for hate crimes against gay and lesbian people (Felsenthal, 2004).

Though there have been numerous hate crimes against transgender individuals throughout the United States, few have garnered the national media attention of the murders of two transgender teenagers:

> In June of 2001, Fred Martinez, a 16-year-old "two-spirited" Navajo youth who was well known and liked within his small community, was chased down, brutally beaten and left to die of blood loss and exposure in Cortez, Colorado. The murderer was caught because he bragged to friends that he had "beat up a fag." ("The News," 2003, p. 17)

> Three Bay Area men were convicted of killing transgender teenager Gwen Araujo. The 17-year-old Araujo, who was biologically male, was slapped, punched, kicked and hit with a soup can and a frying pan, bound with rope and strangled. The body was buried in a remote location near South Lake Tahoe ("Killers Get Maximum," 2006, p. A1 & A6).

Tools for law enforcement (transgender protocol). Most law enforcement personnel are unlikely to have had any significant contact with members of the transgender community prior to or even during their careers, depending upon where they work. Most problems for police officers in their encounters with transgender individuals involve a lack of experience, education, training, department policy and procedure, or protocol. Consider the following:

- Washington, D.C.: A transgender woman, arrested in a domestic dispute, was placed in a male cell-block at the D.C. Superior Court after authorities determined that they had no procedure for changing her gender from male to female in the court's criminal record system even though she had identification that had been legally corrected to reflect her gender ("Stonewalled," 2005, p. 61).

- An African-American transgender woman told Amnesty International that she was dressed in "drag" when they detained her in "the tank" with males at the Bexar County Jail, San Antonio (p. 60).

A protocol for law enforcement or corrections should include the following:

1. Officers should refer to the transgender person either by the name on the identification, the person's adopted name, or in the gender pronoun for which he or she is dressed or seeking to be perceived. (For example, refer to a transgender man in woman's attire as "miss" or "ma'am.").

2. In investigative circumstances, an officer may respectfully ask gender- and name-related questions. Once those questions have been answered, an officer should refer to that person by the name the individual regularly uses.

3. If a frisk or search is necessary, under governing legal standards and barring exigent circumstances, two officers of the gender requested by the transgender individual should search the person. The frisk or search should be consistent with maintenance of physical integrity and human dignity of the person, but also officer safety. If a transgender individual does not specify a preference, then officers of the same gender presentation should conduct the search (for example, a transgender female who expresses no preference should be searched by female officers).

4. Officers should avoid any behavior that harasses transgender persons.

5. If incarcerated, transgender persons should be housed in the appropriate location according to his or her gender identification.

6. A narrative report should indicate the gender the individual is living as in the first paragraph and state that he or she is transgender. The person should thereafter be referred to throughout the report by the adopted name or appropriate pronoun based upon gender presentation.

7. Statistical or booking pages are based upon the legal name and gender (genitalia) of the individual.

   Sources: San Francisco Police Department Protocol; Amnesty International; Grobeson, 2006.

It is important that hate crime reports document the perspective of the perpetrator as well as the victim in attacks on transgender individuals. Most homophobic incidents targeting transgender individuals include epithets such as "You fucking queer." It is important for reporting, investigating, and collecting accurate statistical data that these incidents be documented as targeting persons because they are gay, transgender, or both (Manley, 2006).

It is suggested that large police agencies have personnel specifically assigned to investigate hate crimes against LGBT individuals. Most agencies assign hate crimes to investigators, often to those assigned to handle "crimes against persons," as a corollary duty. "If you assign a robbery detective to investigate hate crimes, you will wind up with a robbery filing," says Grobeson. At the very least, agencies should ensure that those who investigate such crimes receive appropriate training.

MINI CASE STUDY

Officers respond to a call at a motel and are met by a nude, intoxicated individual who has breasts but also male genitalia. The individual is arrested for public intoxication. All indications are that the individual is living as a woman, but because of the male genitalia, the individual is placed in the all-male jail. Officers learn that she is a "pre-op" transsexual, a person who is in the process of becoming, in this case, a woman. How should this situation have been handled by the police department?

Perpetrators of Crime Related to Sexual Orientation

Grobeson suggests that many gay-bashing suspects fit specific profiles, such as being a gang member or member of a white supremacist group. Sometimes gangs incorporate gay-bashing into their new-member initiation. White supremacists (including neo-Nazi, skinheads, and the like) advocate violence against LGBT persons. It is important to note that those who engage in homophobic acts almost always engage in actions that discriminate against other groups as well. One example of such a crime, gay-bashing, occurred in July 2006 when "three white gang members were arrested in San Diego in connection with a series of unprovoked attacks on men who were leaving a gay pride festival. One of the victims remains hospitalized with a fractured skull. One victim was stabbed" ("Teen Arrested on Suspicion of Hate Crime," 2006).

Another view of offender profiles is found in a research paper submitted to the American Psychological Association. The report found that 32 percent of young college students had engaged in verbal anti-LGBT harassment, and 18 percent had made threats or committed actual physical violence ("Stonewalled," 2005). While this one study showed that the perpetrators were fairly ordinary young adults, not prone to joining gangs or hate groups, the most commonly cited anti-LGBT offenders have been classified into categories of "thrill seekers," "moral ideologues," or "turf defenders." In 2005, the offenders were predominately male (82 percent). Of the offenders whose age was known, they were almost equally divided among ages 17 and under, 18 to 29, and 30 to 49. In comparison with prior years, the most significant growth (+67 percent) was among older offenders, aged 50 to 59. Of those offenders whose race/ethnicity was known in 2005, most were Caucasian (39 percent), followed by African descent (27 percent), and Latino/a (24 percent). The largest group of offenders (63 percent) had no prior relationship to their victims. When categorized by those of-fenses *for which relationship information was available,* the percentage of offenders unknown or stranger to the victim was 37 percent in 2005; an equal number of offenders were known by the victim (37 percent). The proportion of offenders who had some type of prior contact with the victim has shown a trend that has been increasing in recent years (NCAVP, 2006).

Sexual Orientation Hate/Bias Crimes and the Military

The military does not recruit or retain persons known to be homosexual. The military, however, has a "don't ask, don't tell" policy put into place under former President Bill Clinton, which means that if a homosexual is recruited or already in the military and the fact has not come to the attention of authorities (who are not to ask), then there is no action taken. There are, however, a large number of gay and lesbian individuals who are discharged each year from all branches of the armed forces. There have been horrific homophobic hate crimes committed by military personnel against fellow service members. One example is discussed in a 2004 publication of the Servicemembers Legal Defense Network (SLDN) that describes the brutal murder of Private First Class Barry Winchell at Fort Campbell, Kentucky:

> Winchell was bludgeoned to death with a baseball bat by fellow soldiers while asleep in his bed in the barracks. Winchell had been harassed mercilessly by fellow soldiers for months prior to his murder, which occurred after an army sergeant violated the "Don't Ask, Don't Tell" policy and inquired about Winchell's sexual orientation. The SLDN report covers the six years of harassment and violence against gay service members left unchecked by military leaders. ("Executive Summary," 2004)

For the same year as the murder of PFC Winchell, the SLDN documented a 120 percent increase in reports of antigay harassment, including death threats, within the armed forces. The military's stated policy was eventually expanded to "don't ask, don't tell, don't pursue, and *don't harass.*"

It is important that FBI agents, military police, and law enforcement agencies that have adjacent military installations become familiar with organizations such as SLDN as well as the updated policies issued by the Department of Defense (DOD). Military police officers should be aware that in response to the public outcry over the handling of the Winchell case, the DOD issued an action plan for each of the military services to address relevant (anti-LGBT) issues, including eliminating mistreatment, harassment, and inappropriate comments or gestures; training; reporting of harassment; enforcement of policies prohibiting harassment; and measurement of antiharassment program effectiveness.

Sexual Orientation Hate/Bias Crimes and School Campuses

Campus police need to be aware that many states have enacted "Safe Schools" laws mandating environments that are free of harassment and discrimination, where no student is subjected to abuse or a hostile learning environment. There are many cases nationwide wherein students who were not protected by administrators or were subjected to unequal restrictions have sued their schools. Most of the court decisions found school administrators liable for failing to provide an environment free of hostility and resulted in expensive verdicts. Consider the following examples:

- In 2002, Washoe County School District in Reno, Nevada, paid over $450,000 for failing to protect a gay student. Two students strung a lasso around his neck and threatened to drag him from their pick-up truck (as was done to African American hate crime victim James Byrd in Texas). His school principal repeatedly demanded that he hide his sexual orientation, stating, "I won't have you acting like a fag." Two school police officers witnessed the student being punched in the face six times by another student and then tried to discourage him from reporting the incident. ("Coming Down Hard on Hate," 2002, p. 46)

- In 2002, the Titusville Area School District in Pennsylvania paid $312,000 for failing to protect a gay student who suffered for five years from pervasive anti-gay abuse. ("Youth to Get Landmark Settlement," 2002)

- As an openly lesbian high school student had classmates call her names, threaten violence, and throw things at her in hallways, so the 16-year-old dropped out. Such treatment inspired a 1999 California law requiring schools to protect students from discrimination based on sexual orientation or perceived gender. ("Gay Teens' Tales of Torment," 2004)

As of 2005, only nine states and the District of Columbia have comprehensive antibullying laws that specifically address bullying and harassment based on sexual orientation, and only three of these have laws that mention gender identity. Nine other states have "generic" antibullying laws that do not provide specific definitions or define protected classes. On a federal level, it has been ruled that the effects of "bullying" students perceived to be gay cannot be dismissed, and that school districts can be held liable should they deny the impact of "bullying" on students ("Alito's Landmark Ruling," 2005).

Studies by the National Mental Health Association (NMHA) in 2002, and by the Gay, Lesbian and Straight Education Network (GLSEN) in 2005, determined that antigay bullying and physical harassment is widespread in America's schools. The studies found that antigay bullying occurs in many forms and is directed not only at students who are gay but also at students who are perceived to be gay. The research indicates that the harassment also increases the risk of other problems for the target, such as skipping school, running away, and even suicide. The NMHA study found that 85 percent of those polled said overweight kids are picked on the most, followed by gay students or those thought to be gay (78 percent), and kids who dress differently (76 percent) ("Anti-Gay Bullying Prevalent," 2002). The GLSEN study revealed:

> Over a third (37.8 percent) of students experienced physical harassment at school on the basis of sexual orientation and more than a quarter (26.1 percent) on the basis of their gender expression. Nearly one-fifth (17.6 percent) of students had been physically assaulted because of their sexual orientation and over a tenth (11.8 percent) because of their gender expression. Continuing the trend from previous years, the survey revealed that LGBT students were five times more likely to report having skipped school in the last month because of safety concerns than the general population of students. The survey also revealed that the presence of supportive school staff and schools with a Gay Straight Alliance (GSA) club provided a range of positive indicators including greater sense of safety and fewer reports of missing days of school. The report also determined that a school policy that includes protection for LGBT students resulted in

lower incidence of homophobic remarks and higher rates of intervention by school staff when remarks were made. ("Teasing to Torment," 2006)

LBGT teens, according to the U.S. Department of Health and Human Services, account for 30 percent of all teen suicides, 28 percent of all dropouts, and 40 percent of homeless teens ("Gay Miami Teen Gets Accolades," 2005).

It is important to note that law enforcement, particularly campus police, are becoming more involved in campus situations such as sexual orientation bias crimes. They are expected to complete official documentation regarding alleged violations and physical assaults based on a student's perceived or actual sexual orientation or gender identity. It is particularly important for campus police to be vigilant because most LGBT teens do not report that they are victims of bias incidents or crimes at school because they fear that school officials will tell their parents about their real or perceived sexual orientation and/or that school officials will not do anything to stop the abusers. Also, all police agencies that have educational facilities within their jurisdiction need to be cognizant of the increasing trend of high schools to create safe environments for LGBT students. The creation of GSA clubs on campus not only presents a quagmire of hotly contentious protests and debates that require peacekeeping but also are often a prelude to incidents of juvenile hate crimes.

Police Relations with Gay and Lesbian Communities

Historically, in most cities and counties in the United States, relations between the police and the gay and lesbian communities have been strained. The strained relationships are sometimes caused by how the community members, as individuals or as a group, have been mistreated or abused by law enforcement officers. Many LGBT persons believe that the police regard them as deviants, criminals, and second-class citizens who are unworthy of protection or equal rights. Because of this perception, many gay and lesbian victims do not report the crimes to the police or cooperate with investigations. Even though negative attitudes and stereotypes will probably continue, progressive police departments have found that communication and mutual respect between the department and gay and lesbian communities are in the best interests of all concerned.

Examples of police departments in which outreach and communication have resulted in cooperation between the agencies and the gay community include San Francisco, Boston, New York, and Baltimore. These departments have observed a noticeable difference in reporting by lesbian and gay crime victims, fewer complaints of police abuse, and a general improvement in relations between law enforcement and gay and lesbian communities. It is also important that community-based policing principles and protocol be utilized in LGBT communities. Officers should recognize issues and concerns not only about sexual-oriented bias crimes but also about domestic violence within the LGBT community. Domestic violence, although virtually invisible in LGBT communities, is commonplace and should be investigated following the same guidelines and policies as those used for heterosexual relationships.

Researcher Kevin Berrill observed that there are numerous ways to improve relationships between the justice system and gay and lesbian groups. One of the keys to good relations, according to Berrill, is regular, institutionalized communication at the department, in committees and councils, and in public forums. In addition, he mentions the following:

1. The creation of task forces and councils to establish ongoing dialogue and networking on important issues.

2. Public forums that allow police officials to meet the LGBT community and help officials to recognize that they are a constituency with legitimate needs and concerns.

3. The appointment of a police official to be a liaison with the LGBT community to respond to complaints and requests.

4. The involvement of prosecutors in the development of policies, procedures, communications, and awareness training to improve relations between the criminal justice system and LGBT groups and individuals (Berrill, 2006).

Almost every community has extremist and even militant segments, and the LGBT community is no exception. Some activists or activist groups may require additional attention and special interaction with local law enforcement. The goal of the agency liaison and its management should be to avoid costly litigation and to communicate effectively with persons representing such groups. Departments should have an assigned liaison officer meet with these groups in an attempt to agree on acceptable behavior before any public demonstration occurs. Some groups obtain press coverage by orchestrating arrests by the police; in such cases, liaison and close monitoring by field supervisors, a press relations officer, a police video unit, and a department manager would be an absolute necessity. This methodology has been successful with agencies in the San Francisco Bay Area, resulting in no physical confrontation with groups, no negative press or photos, and no legal action. However, even the best police outreach efforts may prove ineffective. For example, some activist groups have refused to communicate with police during their "actions." Nevertheless, police officers should not permit negative publicity from previous incidents with any group to stop them from attempting to make positive contact prior to scheduled public events. The willingness of the police to work with any community group, particularly LGBT activist groups, always results in positive publicity for the law enforcement agencies and the cities or counties they serve (Grobeson, 2006).

Conclusion

The handling and investigation of hate crimes require specialized and unique expertise. The epidemic of hate crimes will continue unabated as long as law enforcement management does not address it proactively. It is important for law enforcement administrators to realize that they can be subjected to litigation and even punitive damages for the actions of their subordinates if they fail to provide proactive policies or take affirmative stances in regard to officer training or discipline (vicarious liability). It is equally important that military and campus police officers know the laws and establish protocol for preventing and investigating crimes motivated by hate for LGBT individuals. U.S. Senator Gordon Smith from Oregon said:

Hate crimes tear at the very fabric of our nation. These kinds of crimes do more than harm the victims. They terrorize our entire society and send a message of hate and intolerance to millions of Americans. ("U.S. Senate Passes Hate Crimes Act," 2004, p. 12).

HATE CRIME LAWS

Federal Laws

Federal laws provide criminal and civil causes of action for victims of hate crimes in the United States, regardless of whether they are citizens. Federal law does not prohibit all acts of hate violence, however. Federal statutes forbid violence by private parties only when there is intent to interfere with a federally protected right—that is, one specifically guaranteed by a federal statute or by the U.S. Constitution. Federal authorities can intervene only when a crime is motivated by race, religion, or national origin and, when at the time the crime is committed, the victim is engaged in a "federally protected activity." Such activity includes voting, serving on a jury, going to work, or enrolling in or attending public school. Nevertheless, these rights are broadly interpreted when a perpetrator's motive is tainted by racial hatred. Similar protection is provided to victims of crimes motivated by sexual orientation, gender, or disability.

A victim of a hate/bias crime that violates a federal law can initiate criminal prosecution by reporting the crime to a local office of the FBI. That office then assigns an investigator to the case. A victim may also contact the local U.S. attorney's office or the criminal section of the Civil Rights Division at the U.S. Department of Justice in Washington, D.C. In addition to criminal prosecution, a victim can pursue a civil suit if the facts support a civil action under the federal statutes. The victim can seek both damages and injunctive relief in civil action against the perpetrator of violence that is motivated by racial, sexual orientation, gender, or disability hatred.

In general, the federal criminal statutes are intended to supplement state and local criminal laws. Procedurally, the U.S. Department of Justice (DOJ) will not become actively involved in prosecuting a particular action until local authorities have concluded their case. After a person is convicted or acquitted in state courts, the DOJ evaluates the result before determining whether to prosecute under federal statutes. There is no set time within which the Justice Department makes its decision.

State Laws

Almost every state and the District of Columbia have enacted laws that can be invoked to redress bias-motivated crimes. Many states have also enacted "penalty-enhancements" statutes, which were upheld unanimously by the U.S. Supreme Court in June 1993 in its decision in a Wisconsin case (*Wisconsin v. Mitchell,* 508 U.S. 476, 1993). Penalty enhancements are legal when the defendant intentionally selects his or her victim based on the victim's race, religion, national origin, sexual orientation, gender, or disability. Many states have also enhanced criminal penalties for vandalism aimed at houses of worship, cemeteries, schools, and community centers.

Why Special Laws?

There are those, including some law enforcement leaders, who argue that there is no need for special laws dealing with hate/bias crimes because there are already statutes covering specific crimes. For example, an assault by one person on another is prosecutable in all jurisdictions. Therefore, the argument runs, why would such an assault be prosecuted differently even if it was motivated by a person's hate or bias toward victims because of their color, ethnic background, religion, sexual orientation, gender, or disability? Localities and states headed by leaders with this perspective have no system for identifying, reporting, investigating, and prosecuting hate/bias crimes. Thus, there are deficiencies in the way some law enforcement agencies and prosecutors process hate crimes.

First, incidents are not classified by racial, ethnic, sexual orientation, or religious motivation, making it virtually impossible to tabulate acts of hate violence, spot trends, perform analyses, or develop response strategies. Second, an inaccurate characterization of certain types of hate violence crimes occurs. For example, cross burnings are variously classified as malicious mischief, vandalism, or burning without a permit. Swastika paintings are often classified as graffiti incidents or malicious mischief. The reason for special hate/bias crime laws and penalty enhancement is that they send a clear message to the perpetrator and the public that these crimes will not be tolerated and will be treated as serious offenses.

There are some key differences that make hate/bias crimes more serious than standard offenses. Crimes of this sort deny the free exercise of civil rights, sometimes frightening the victim out of exercising freedom of speech, association, and assembly. Furthermore, these crimes tend to be more violent than other crimes. Often, the attacks are acts of terrorism intended to punish the victim for being visible (i.e., a person who looks or acts different is easy for a bigoted person to single out). Finally, these acts against individuals are also often meant to terrorize entire communities.

HATE/BIAS CRIME AND INCIDENT INVESTIGATIONS

Hate Crime and Incident Investigations

Criminal justice agencies must make hate/bias crimes a priority for response, from the initial report through prosecution. To ensure that all personnel treat such crimes seriously, each agency must have written policies and procedures that establish protocol for a quick and effective response. Only when policies and procedures as well as feasible community programs, are in place, will society begin to control and reduce hate crimes.

Law enforcement agencies must provide investigators with training that includes such critical elements as understanding the role of the investigator, identifying a hate/bias crime, classifying an offender, interviewing a victim, relating to a community, and prosecuting an offender. When hate/bias crimes occur, they require investigators' timely response, understanding, and vigilance to ensure a careful and successful investigation. Investigators must have a comprehensive knowledge of the general elements and motivations behind hate/bias crimes and must recognize the potential of these crimes to affect not only the primary victim, but also the victim's family, other members of the victim's group, and the larger community.

There are general and specific procedures and protocols that should be used in response to crimes and incidents motivated by the victim's race, religion, ethnic background, or sexual orientation (RRES). These include actions to be taken by each of the following categories of personnel:

- Assigned officer/first responder
- Patrol field supervisor

- Watch commander
- Assigned investigator or specialized unit
- Crime prevention, community relations, or specialized unit
- Training unit

The actual guidelines may vary among jurisdictions, but the basics are the same. Specific guidelines are available from federal and state organizations or police and sheriffs' departments. Some law enforcement agencies have model protocols that could be secured and used in the classroom or by departments who have not developed their own procedures.

Models for Investigating Hate/Bias Crimes

The following are suggested guidelines for law enforcement agencies without standardized protocol for follow-up of hate/bias crimes and incidents. The suggested formats are based on the size of the department.

Small department (agencies of 1 to 100 sworn). A small department may not have the staffing depth to have a specialized unit or investigator who can deal solely with hate crimes. Officers in small departments are usually generalists, meaning that they carry any type of case from the initial report through the investigation and submission to the district attorney. Therefore, all personnel should receive awareness training on cultural and racial issues and learn the requirements of handling crimes and incidents motivated by hate. The officer who takes the crime or incident report must have it approved by his or her supervisor. Some small departments have allowed patrol officers to specialize in the investigation of certain crimes; they might be involved in either providing advice and direction or actually taking the case and handling it to its conclusion. These officers are usually the ones allowed to attend training and conferences that will teach and update them on the investigations of these crimes and incidents. Some departments have a patrol supervisor perform the follow-up investigation and submit the case to the prosecutor's office. It is important that the officer and his or her supervisor keep command officers informed of major cases. Small agencies with a detective follow-up investigations unit must be sure that unit members are trained in aspects of dealing with crimes motivated by hate.

Medium-sized department (agencies of 100 to 500 sworn). The following is a model suggested for a medium-sized department with a crimes-against-persons investigations unit and an administration unit responsible for community relations or affairs. The format follows this protocol: The responding patrol officer takes the initial report, decides if what occurred was indeed a crime or incident motivated by hate or bias, and then completes a preliminary investigation. Then the officer documents the findings on the department offense report form and follows the policy and procedure as established by the agency. The officer's supervisor and watch commander approve the report (which may or may not already be classified as a hate/bias or civil rights violation, depending on department policy). Then it is forwarded to the investigations unit that follows up on such cases (usually the crimes persons unit). Then the investigations unit supervisor reviews the report and again evaluates whether a crime or incident took place. If it is decided that it is a hate/bias crime, the report is assigned to a crimes persons investigator *who specializes in this type of investigation.*

A copy of the report is also forwarded (through the appropriate chain of command) to the administration or community relations unit for follow-up. The staff of the latter unit is also trained to handle hate/bias and civil rights violations investigations and to provide victim assistance. The administrative follow-up would include:

- Investigations required
- Referrals and support for the victim
- Conducting of public meetings to resolve neighborhood problems
- Conflict resolution
- Liaison with the diverse organizations in the community and victim advocates

Some cases may require that the criminal investigator and administrative officer work jointly to resolve the crime or incident under investigation.

Large departments (agencies of 500-plus sworn). Most large departments have enough staff that they can have a specialized unit. There are many advantages to having a specialized unit that focuses on crimes motivated by hate/bias or civil rights violations. The investigators become familiar and experienced with the law and special procedures required and can handle more complex, sensitive cases. Investigators who are allowed to specialize can form networks with victim advocate organizations, other police agencies, and community-based agencies. They work closely with the district attorney's office (probably with a special bias unit within that agency), establishing the working relationships and rapport important to successful prosecutions. The investigators develop a sense of pride in their efforts and a commitment to provide a competent investigative and victim assistance response. Since the primary function of the unit is hate/bias crime investigations, officers can sometimes develop knowledge of individuals and groups that commit such offenses and become more aware of where the incidents occur.

Detectives who handle a multitude of cases do not have the time to track and monitor these crimes and therefore may not spot trends. Specialized units can evaluate the field performance of the patrol officers who have handled such crimes and can provide suggestions for improvement or commendations when the response has been effective or innovative.

There are also disadvantages to specialized units. Often, when there is a specialized unit, patrol officers believe that what is happening in the neighborhood in which they work is not their problem—it is the problem of the specialized unit. The officer takes reports and then transfers responsibility for resolution of problems. Patrol officers may be unaware of a problem or its magnitude or even what resources are being marshaled to resolve it unless there is good communication between them and the members of the specialized unit. These disadvantages are surmountable, however, especially if the department uses community-oriented policing strategies, which usually involve a higher degree of communication among agency units and with the community.

Hate crimes that fit certain criteria, to be discussed later, are investigated at the federal level by the FBI's Bias Crimes Unit and the Bureau of Alcohol, Tobacco and Firearms (BATF) church arson and explosives experts. BATF investigators also focus on regulating the illegal sale to and possession of firearms by potential perpetrators of hate crimes.

HATE/BIAS CRIME PROSECUTION

District Attorneys' or Prosecutors' Office

Many district attorneys' offices in the United States now have attorneys and/or units that specialize in hate crime prosecution. These agencies have established policies and procedures designed to prosecute such crimes effectively and efficiently. There are compelling reasons for district attorneys to devote special attention and resources to these crimes. A prosecutor has discretion to influence, if not determine, what might be called the public safety climate that citizens in the communities he or she serves will experience. To establish a public safety climate that fosters the full enjoyment of civil and political rights by the minority members of our communities requires a focused political will directed to that end, as well as resources and capacity. The most effective and successful approaches to building a climate of public safety have been those that:

- Established specialized hate crimes or civil rights violations units.
- Standardized procedures to prosecute hate crime cases (this standardization should include vertical prosecution of cases).
- Appointed attorneys to be liaisons with various ethnic, racial, religious, and sexual orientation groups in the community.
- Provided all attorneys on staff with cultural awareness or sensitivity training.
- Provided alternative sentencing programs aimed at rehabilitating individuals who commit hate-motivated crimes. (One example is the ADL's "The Juvenile Diversion Program: Learning about Differences," a 9-week series for students and sometimes parents on civil rights law, racism, anti-Semitism, the Holocaust, and the legacy of discrimination against minorities in America.)

District attorneys can play a major role in educating judges on the nature, prevalence, and severity of hate crime and in encouraging effective sentences for this offense. They can also be very effective in their working relationships with and encouragement of police officers investigating these crimes. The effort involves each member of the criminal justice system, but the prosecutor has one of the most important roles.

Special Problems in Prosecuting Hate/Bias Crimes

Prosecutors confront an array of issues when considering a potential hate crime. Ascertaining the real motivation for someone's behavior is difficult, and actually proving a person took an action because of hate can be an arduous task. Hate crime charges are the only ones for which proving motive becomes as important as proving modus operandi. Juries can often find it impossible to conclude with certainty what was going on in a suspect's mind during the crime. Attorneys who handle hate/bias crimes indicate that there are four potential obstacles to successful prosecutions:

1. Proving the crime was motivated by bias
2. Uncooperative, complaining witnesses
3. Special defenses
4. Lenient sentences

Prosecutors, given these obstacles, sometimes have difficulty deciding whether to file hate crime charges. Consider the following examples:

- A man got into an argument over napkins at a restaurant. He screamed his hatred for the Arab proprietors and later came back and bashed a clerk with a baseball bat. But there was no hate crime charge. The prosecutor said the argument over the napkins was more of a motive than anti-Arab prejudice.

- Prosecutors declined to file a hate crime allegation against a Hindu man who allegedly raped a Muslim coworker at a drugstore. Police booked the Hindu man on hate and rape charges based on the victim's saying he had tormented her about her religion for months and called her a "stupid Muslim" right after the assault. But an assistant district attorney, who wrote a primer on hate crime prosecutions, said his office did not feel they could prove to a jury that his alleged hatred of Muslims was a substantial motivation in the charged crime.

As indicated, it is often difficult to accurately identify hate-motivated crimes or incidents. Usually, no single factor is sufficient to make the determination, and sometimes the perpetrator disguises the incident so that it does not appear to be a hate/bias crime. Even cases that have been well investigated may lack sufficient evidence to prove that the crime was motivated, beyond a reasonable doubt, by hate or bias. Generally, prosecutors follow established guidelines for determining whether a crime was bias related. Their criteria include:

- Plain common sense
- Perceptions of the victim(s) and witnesses about the crime
- Language used by the perpetrator
- Background of the perpetrator
- Severity of the attack
- Lack of provocation
- History of similar incidents in the same area
- Absence of any apparent motive

The National District Attorneys Association developed a comprehensive desk manual for prosecutors for identifying, responding to, and preventing hate violence. The desk manual, titled *Hate Crime: A Local Prosecutor's Guide for Responding to Hate Crime,* contains information about working with outside agencies and organizations, case screening and investigation, case assignment and preparation, victim and witness impact and support, trial preparation, sentencing alternatives, and prevention efforts. The manual could be useful in the development of a training curriculum specifically designed for prosecutors. The association's website, which is listed at the end of this chapter, provides information on how to order the desk manual.

Objective Evidence: Bias Motivation

It is important that first responders and investigators properly identify and classify bias-motivated crimes. Officers unsure about identifying a potential hate/bias crime should consult with a supervisor or an expert (even outside the agency) on the topic. To help investigators determine whether an incident has sufficient objectively determined criteria to classify it as a hate/bias crime, the U.S. Department of Justice developed a document, "Summary Reporting System: Hate Crime Data Collection Guidelines," which contains a series of examples related to the reporting of hate crime incidents. These examples are intended to ensure uniformity in reporting data to the state and the FBI's UCR Section. The following are a few examples of guidelines:

- The offender and the victim were of different racial, religious, ethnic/national origin, or sexual orientation groups. For example, the victim was black and the offenders were white.

- Bias-related oral comments, written statements, or gestures were made by the offender that indicated his or her bias. For example, the offender shouted a racial epithet at the victim.

- Bias-related drawings, markings, symbols, or graffiti were left at the crime scene. For example, a swastika was painted on the door of a synagogue.

- The victim was visiting a neighborhood where previous hate crimes had been committed against other members of his or her racial, religious, ethnic/national origin, or sexual orientation group and where tensions remain high against his or her group.

- Several incidents have occurred in the same locality, at or about the same time, and the victims are all of the same racial, religious, ethnic/national origin, or sexual orientation group.

- A substantial portion of the community where the crime occurred perceives that the incident was motivated by bias.

For a complete list of guidelines recommended by the Department of Justice, the website where "Summary Reporting System: Hate Crime Data Collection Guidelines" can be ordered is listed at the end of this chapter.

Because of the difficulty of knowing with certainty that a crime was motivated by bias, the Hate Crimes Statistics Act stipulates that bias is to be reported only if the investigation reveals sufficient objective facts that would lead a reasonable and prudent person to conclude that the offender's actions were motivated, in whole or in part, by bias. The specific types of bias to be reported are as follows (U.S. Department of Justice, 1990, p. 15):

Racial Bias

Antiwhite

Antiblack

Anti-American Indian or Alaskan Native

Anti-Asian/Pacific Islander

Anti-multiracial group

Religious Bias

Anti-Jewish

Anti-Catholic

Anti-Protestant

Anti-Islamic (Moslem)

Anti–other religion (Buddhism, Hinduism, Shintoism, etc.)

Anti-multireligious group

Anti-atheist or anti-agnostic

Ethnicity/National Origin Bias

Anti-Arab

Anti-Hispanic

Anti–other ethnicity/national origin

Sexual Orientation Bias

Anti–male homosexual (gay)

Anti–female homosexual (lesbian)

Antihomosexual (gays and lesbian)

Antiheterosexual

Antibisexual

Antitransgender

Training is available to help criminal justice agency personnel make decisions regarding hate/bias crimes. A few of those sources are:

- Office for Victims of Crime (OVC)
- Bureau of Justice Assistance (BJA)
- Office of Juvenile Justice and Delinquency Prevention (OJJDP)

All three sponsor grants to agencies to fund the development of programs and to provide training seminars and technical assistance to individuals and local agencies regarding hate crimes. OVC is working to improve the justice system's response to victims of hate crimes and OJJDP funds agencies to develop training for professionals and to address hate crimes through preventive measures and community resources. BJA has a training initiative for law enforcement agencies designed to generate awareness and to help in identifying, investigating, and taking appropriate action for bias crimes, as well as arming agencies with tools for responding effectively to incidents. Websites for all three agencies are listed at the end of this chapter.

In 2002, the Southern Poverty Law Center and Auburn University at Montgomery initiated an innovative online hate crime–training program. The two organizations teamed up to develop the course Introduction to Hate and Bias Crimes, which is offered to law enforcement officers from the United States and Canada. Such training has been offered for years through a variety of agencies, both public and private, but constraints such as the expense of travel, time away from work, and the low priority given the matter by many police agencies have hampered officers' efforts to pursue it. The online course is a way to reach law enforcement officers in small towns and rural areas.

Using material from the Federal Law Enforcement Training Center (FLETC), it introduces officers to the basics of hate crime, terminology, and categories of offenders. The course uses video clips, discussion boards, and online chats with veteran hate crime experts. Completion of the course earns students either one semester hour of college credit or 10 continuing education units. Information about the course schedule, future courses, and scholarship opportunities is available online at a website listed at the conclusion of this chapter.

MINI CASE STUDY

Discuss in class: What evidence would be required to prove the vandalism was bias motivated? What steps should the city, police, church, and community take to resolve this situation?

In October 2003 in the city of Pleasant Hill, California, vandals crushed two American Indian sweat lodges. The lodges—low, dome-shaped structures made of willows and covered with tarpaulins—contained fire pits and a few benches. The lodges were where local Indians from a variety of tribes had gathered several times a week for 10 years for ceremonies. The lodges are located behind a Lutheran Church in a residential neighborhood. In 1996, the Lutheran Church got a permit from the Pleasant Hill Planning Commission to build the lodges. The ceremonies have been the focus of a neighborhood controversy for at least seven years and, in 1997, neighbors worked with Indians and the church to mitigate some of the smoke and noise. Run-ins with neighbors, who complain about the ceremonies going on too late, about the singing being too loud, and about the smoke from the fires, continued. One nearby resident has accumulated a folder thick with papers documenting the neighborhood's fight against the sweat lodges.

After the vandalism, a few neighbors expressed to newspaper reporters their delight that the damage had been inflicted on the lodges. Leaders of the sweat ceremonies believe the vandalism was a hate crime. The police said that the incident could not be ruled a hate crime because there was no proof it was bias motivated.

HATE/BIAS CRIME AND INCIDENT VICTIMOLOGY

Introduction

Meaningful assistance to victims of major crimes became a priority only in the 1980s. The growth of a body of "victimology" literature (President's Task Force on Victims of Crime created by President Reagan in 1982; the 1982 the Omnibus Victim and Witness Protection Act of 1982; and the 1984 the Comprehensive Crime Control Act, to name a few) and the emergence of numerous victim advocate and rights organizations began at about that time, reflecting a growing concern about crime, the victims of crime, and their treatment by the criminal justice system. The public mood or perception had become (and may still be) that the criminal justice system cares only about the defendant. The perception was that the defendant's rights were a priority of the system, while the victim was neglected in the process. As a result of the task force recommendations, state and federal legislation, and research by public and private organizations (most notably the National Institute of Justice), improvements were made in victim services and treatment as well as in the criminal justice system.

Law Enforcement and the Victim

For the most part, perpetrators of hate crimes commit them to intimidate a victim and members of the victim's community so that the victims feel isolated, vulnerable, and unprotected by the law. Many victims do not report their attacks to police out of fear and believe their best defense is to remain quiet. Other reasons, in addition to those outlined earlier in this chapter, include:

- fear of revictimization or retaliation
- fear of having privacy compromised
- for gays, lesbians, bisexual, or transgender individuals, fear of repercussions from being "outed" to family, friends, and employers
- fear of law enforcement and uncertainty about the criminal justice system responses
- for aliens, fear of jeopardizing immigration status, being reported to INS, or deportation
- humiliation or shame about being victimized
- lack of support systems within the community
- cultural and language barriers

In the law enforcement field, courses in recruit academies and in-service advanced officer programs typically include training about victimization that covers such topics as sociopsychological effects of victimization, officer sensitivity to the victim, victim assistance and advocacy programs, and victim compensation and restitution criteria as well as procedures for applying. Classes normally stress the importance of keeping victims informed of their case status and of the criminal justice process. How patrol officers and investigators of such crimes interact with victims affects the victims' immediate and long-term physical and emotional recovery. Proper treatment of victims also increases their willingness to cooperate in the total criminal justice process. Because of such training programs, the victims of hate crimes began receiving special attention and assistance in progressive cities and counties all over the country.

Victims of hate/bias violence generally express three needs: (1) to feel safe, (2) to feel that people care, and (3) to get assistance. To address the first two needs, law enforcement agencies and all personnel involved in contacts with victims must place special emphasis on victim assistance to reduce trauma and fear. Such investigations sometimes involve working with people from diverse ethnic backgrounds, races, and/or sexual orientation. Many victims may be recent immigrants with limited English who are unfamiliar with the American legal system or have fears of the police, courts, or government rooted in negative experiences from their countries of origin. In many

Asian countries, for example, there is a history of police corruption. Often, immigrants who are victims of crimes in the United States think that reporting of a crime may not only be futile but could invite unwanted and costly attention because of experiences in their own countries.

Therefore, the officer or investigator must be not only a skilled interviewer and listener but also must be sensitive to and knowledgeable about cultural and racial differences and ethnicity. He or she must have the ability to show compassion and sensitivity toward the victim and his or her plight while gathering the evidence required for prosecution. As when dealing with other crime victims, officers involved in the investigation must

- approach victims in an empathic and supportive manner and demonstrate concern and sensitivity;

- attempt to calm the victim and reduce the victim's alienation;

- reassure the victim that every available investigative and enforcement tool will be utilized by the police to find and prosecute the person or persons responsible for the crime;

- consider the safety of the victim by recommending and providing extra patrol and/or providing prevention and precautionary advice;

- provide referral information to entities such as counseling and other appropriate public support and assistance agencies;

- advise the victim of criminal and civil options.

The stress experienced by victims of hate/bias crime or incidents may be heightened by a perceived level of threat or personal violation. Just like the victims of rape or abuse, many become traumatized when they have to recall the details of what occurred. Sometimes the victim, because of what happened to him or her, transfers his or her anger or hostility to the officer—a psychological reaction called transference. The officer must be prepared for this reaction and must be able to defuse the situation professionally without resorting to anger. It is imperative that investigators and officers make every effort to treat hate crime victims with dignity and respect so that they feel a sense that they will receive justice. Insensitive, brash, or unaware officers or investigators may not only alienate victims, witnesses, or potential witnesses but also create additional distrust or hostility and cause others in the community to distrust the entire police department.

Addressing the victim's need to get assistance requires that the community have established resources that can assist the victim and the victim group (e.g., gays, Hispanics). Few communities have the resources necessary to offer comprehensive victim services. Even where resources are available, victims are often unaware of them because of poor public awareness programs or the failure of the criminal justice system to make appropriate referrals because of a lack of training or motivation. A key resource is the availability of interpreters for non-English-speaking victims and witnesses. Ideally, jurisdictions with large populations of non-English-speaking minorities should recruit and train an appropriate number of bilingual employees. If the jurisdiction does not have an investigator who speaks the same language, an interpreter system should be in place for immediate callout. Victims of hate-motivated incidents are encouraged to report the circumstances to the National Hate Crimes Hotline (1-800-347-HATE).

Readers wishing additional information about victims can refer to *Victims of Crime,* by Robert A. Jerin and Loura J. Moriarty (1997). It is a well-developed textbook for the field of victimology that has many criminal justice applications. Another resource for first responders, *Bringing Victims into Community Policing,* was developed by the National Center for Victims of Crime and the Police Foundation. The publication, available on the NCVC website, provides guidelines for dealing with specific types of crime victims.

SUMMARY

Racism and crimes motivated by hate are two of the most challenging issues confronting the United States today. Our nation includes people from around the world who are guaranteed the rights to be free of discrimination, bias, and violence. Yet we continue to witness incidents of hatred manifested in violence toward people perceived as "different." Racism and the resulting hate violence, biased treatment, and discrimination cause divisions between people and deny them their dignity. Racism is a disease that devastates society. Police officers should be at the forefront in the battle to combat such criminal behavior within society. Law enforcement must lead in the protection of human and civil rights of all citizens.

The prevalence of hate/bias crimes and incidents is often attributed to changing national and international conditions, immigration, and ethnic demographic change translated to a local environment. As immigrants, persons of color, or persons of different religious beliefs or sexual orientation move into previously unintegrated areas, increased threat of hate/bias crimes can be expected. It is not just a problem for the criminal justice system, but rather it must be addressed by the whole community, including families, schools, business, labor, and social services. In taking the lead, law enforcement agencies can motivate other groups to join with them in their efforts to reduce hate violence.

Progress toward tolerance among peoples, mutual respect, and unity has been painfully slow in our country and marked with repeated setbacks. Criminal statutes and civil remedies to curb the problem in various jurisdictions across the nation have also been enacted slowly. Divisive racial attitudes, anti-immigrant sentiment, the increased number of hate/bias incidents, and the deepening despair of minorities and the poor make the need for solutions even more pressing.

DISCUSSION QUESTIONS AND ISSUES

1. ***Hate/Bias Crimes and Incident Reduction.*** Make a list of important elements in the design of a community-based program to reduce the number of hate/bias crimes and incidents in your area.

2. ***Move-in Violence.*** Discuss, in a group setting, what strategies might be used by a community to reduce the impact of move-in violence on a new immigrant.

3. ***Victims of Hate/Bias Crimes or Incidents.*** Have you been the victim of a hate/bias crime or incident? Share the experience with others in a group setting: the circumstances, the feelings you experienced, how you responded, and what action was taken by any community-based agency or organization.

4. Find out what resources exist in your community to assist victims of hate/bias crimes.

   a. Which groups provide victim assistance?

   b. Which coalition groups exist, and what types of community outreach programs are offered?

   c. What types of pamphlets or other written materials are available?

   d. Which groups have speakers' bureaus?

   e. Which groups are working with local law enforcement agencies with regard to response programs or cultural awareness training?

   f. Which groups are working with the district attorney's office?

   g. What types of legislative lobbying efforts are taking place, and who is championing the work?

WEBSITE RESOURCES

Visit these websites for additional information about hate crimes and victim assistance:

American-Arab Anti-Discrimination Committee (ADC): http://www.adc.org

This website offers information about the ADC's civil rights efforts and useful summary data about cases and complaints regarding hate crimes and discrimination involving Arab Americans.

Anti-Defamation League (ADL): http://www.adl.org

The ADL provides a source of model policies and procedures for the investigation and tracking of crimes motivated by hate.

Bureau of Justice Statistics (BJS): http://www.ojp.usdoj.gov/bjs

This website contains data about crimes reported by law enforcement agencies across the nation to the FBI. BJS is also a resource center for justice topics such as training, technical assistance, publications, and grants.

Community Relations Service (CRS): http://www.usdoj.gov/crs/

The Community Relations Service is the Department of Justice's "peacemaker" for community conflicts and tensions arising from differences of race, color, and national origin. CRS assists communities in developing local mechanisms, conducting training, and instituting other proactive measures to prevent or reduce racial/ethnic tension.

National District Attorneys Association: http://www.ndaa.org

This website is a resource for information on many subjects. The association produced a guide titled *Hate Crime: A Local Prosecutor's Guide for Responding to Hate Crime,* which covers several issues that arise during hate crime prosecutions. By highlighting model protocols and procedures from offices around the nation, the resource guide will help prosecutors' offices develop policies and procedures on handling hate crime investigations and prosecutions. It also will provide a comprehensive roadmap to individual prosecutors who handle hate crime cases. Both prosecutors who are working on their first hate crime case and more experienced prosecutors of bias crimes will find the resource guide helpful.

National Gay and Lesbian Task Force (NGLTF): http://www.ngltf.org

NGLTF gathers and studies information about lesbian, gay, bisexual, and transgender individuals as victims of crimes motivated by hate.

Office for Victims of Crime (OVC): http://www.ojp.us.doj.gov/ovc

The site provides information about victims of crime and models for providing victim services. It also provides resources for training, publications, research, statistics, program funding, and grants pertaining to victims of crime.

International Association of Chiefs of Police: http://www.theiacp.org

This website provides an online resource for law enforcement issues publications including *Recruitment/Retention of Qualified Police Personnel: A Best Practices Guide,* December 7, 2001.

National Conference for Community and Justice (NCCJ): http://www.ncjj.org

NCCJ's programming facilitates community and interfaith dialogues and provides workplace consultations, youth leadership development, and seminarian and educator training. Its nationally recognized research provides data and analysis to the evolving study of intergroup relations, and its public policy arm works with government leaders and advocates policies that reflect understanding and respect.

National Congress of American Indians (NCAI): http://www.ncai.org

NCAI addresses a broad range of policy matters in its efforts to advocate on behalf of American Indian and Alaska Native tribal governments.

National Council of La Raza (NCLR): http://www.nclr.org

NCLR is the largest national Hispanic civil rights and advocacy organization in the United States. The private, nonprofit, nonpartisan organization works to improve opportunities for Hispanic Americans. NCLR conducts research, policy analysis, and advocacy, providing a Latino perspective in five key areas: assets/ investments, civil rights/immigration, education, employment and economic status, and health.

National Office of Victim Assistance (NOVA): http://www.nova.org

NOVA is a good resource for victim assistance networks. The organization is based in Washington, D.C., and can be reached at (202) 393-6682.

Office of Juvenile Justice and Delinquency Prevention (OJJDP):
http://www.ojjdp.ncjrs.org

OJJDP is a resource center for programs, publications, training, and grants regarding juvenile justice and delinquency prevention.

The Prejudice Institute: http://www.prejudiceinstitute.org

A resource for activists, lawyers, and social scientists, the Prejudice Institute is devoted to policy research and education on all dimensions of prejudice, discrimination, and ethnoviolence.

Simon Wiesenthal Center: http://www.wiesenthal.com

The Simon Wiesenthal Center is an international Jewish human rights organization dedicated to preserving the memory of the Holocaust by fostering tolerance and understanding through community involvement, educational outreach, and social action. The Center confronts important contemporary issues including racism, anti-Semitism, terrorism, and genocide.

Southern Poverty Law Center (SPLC): http://www.splcencter.org

SPLC is an excellent resource for information about and statistics concerning hate organizations. As mentioned in this chapter, SPLC offers an online training course, "Introduction to Hate and Bias Crimes," for law enforcement officers from the United States and Canada. Information about the course is available at http://www.intelligenceproject.org.

U.S. Department of Justice (DOJ): http://www.doj.gov

The U.S. Department of Justice developed a document, "Summary Reporting System: Hate Crime Data Collection Guidelines," which contains a series of examples related to the reporting of hate crime incidents. These examples are intended to ensure uniformity in reporting data to the state and the FBI's UCR section. The guidelines can be ordered via the website. The FBI offers training for law enforcement officers and administrators on developing data-collection procedures. For more information, contact the FBI at 1-888-UCR-NIBR. See also *Hate/Bias Crimes Train-the-Trainer Program,* conducted by the National Center for State, Local and International Law Enforcement Training, Federal Law Enforcement Training Center (FLETC), U.S. Treasury Department. Also available from the DOJ is "Twenty Plus Things Law Enforcement Agencies Can Do to Prevent or Respond to Hate Incidents Against Arab-Americans, Muslims, and Sikhs." The document lists a number of ways law enforcement agencies can prevent or respond to hate incidents against these persons. These include community assessments, patrol practices, community outreach, conduct training, and departmental policies and procedures review. The website for this particular document is http://www.usdoj.gov/crs/twentyplus.htm

Vera Institute of Justice: http://www.vera.org

The Vera Institute of Justice works closely with leaders in government and civil society to improve the services people rely on for safety and justice. Vera develops innovative, affordable programs that often grow into self-sustaining organizations, studies social problems and current responses, and provides practical advice and assistance to government officials around the world. It has publications on many law enforcement subjects.

REFERENCES

"Alabama Supreme Court Sets Execution Date for Gay Man's Killer." (2003, March 27). *Gay & Lesbian Times,* p. 30.

"Alito's landmark ruling supports bullied gay students." (2005, November 11). *Gay & Lesbian Times,* p. 38.

Anti-Defamation League. (2004). "ADL Audit Finds Anti-Semitic Incidents Remain Constant; More than 1,500 Incidents Reported Across U.S. in 2003." New York; Anti-Defamation League Online: http://www.adl.org.

Anti-Defamation League. (2006). "Annual ADL Audit: Anti-Semitic Incidents Decline in 2005 but Levels of Concern in U.S." Anti-Defamation League Online: http:www.adl.org.

"Anti-Gay Bullying Prevalent, Study Says." (2002, December 13). *Contra Costa Times,* p. A20.

"Anti-Muslim Hate Crimes Triple in '03." (2004, May 3). *Contra Costa Times.* p. A12.

Berrill, Kevin. (1986, October 9). Testimony before the House Judiciary Committee on Criminal Justice: Second Session on Anti-Gay Violence, Serial no. 132. (Personal communications, 2006).

Bureau of Justice Statistics—Special Report. (2005, November). "Hate Crime Reported by Victims and Police," U.S. Department of Justice, Office of Justice Programs, Washington D.C.

Bureau of Justice Statistics Report. (2004, November). Hate Crime Statistics, 2003. U.S. Department of Justice, Office of Justice Programs, Washington D.C.

"Coming Down Hard on Hate." (2002, September 27). *Frontiers,* p. 46.

"DA Lashes Out at Use of Gay Panic Defense." (2004, August 12). *Gay & Lesbian Times,* p. 30.

"Executive Summary: 10th Annual Report on 'Don't Ask, Don't Tell.'" (2004). Servicemembers Legal Defense Network.

"Facts Sheet on Ethnoviolence." (2004). The Prejudice Institute, Number 1, Baltimore, MD.

Felsenthal, Alan. (2004, June 14). "Hate Crimes Bill Passes Senate." *IN Magazine* p. 13.

Foxman, Abraham. (2005, April 22). "After 350 Years, Still a Lot to Do" *Haaretz.*

Gambert, Riva. (2003, December). Former Associate Director of the Jewish Community Relations Council (JCRC) of the Greater (SF) East Bay, personal communication.

"Gay and Lesbian Anti-Violence Project Releases Data on 2005 Hate Incidents." (2006, May 22). AVP Media Release, on-line: Anti-Violence Project, El Paso, Tex. Available: www.lambda.org.

"Gay Miami Teen Gets Accolades for Inspiring Peers." (2005, January 6). *Gay & Lesbian Times,* p. 28.

"Gay Teens' Tales of Torment Led to State Anti-Discrimination Law." (2004, April 18). *Contra Costa Times,* p. A4.

Grobeson, Mitchell. (2006). Sergeant (Ret.), Los Angeles Police Department, personal communication.

International Association of Chiefs of Police (IACP). (1999). "Responding to Hate Crimes: A Police Officer's Guide to Investigation and Prevention." Publications online: www.theiacp.org

"Jail brawls reflect larger race-relations problems." (2006, February 21). *Washington Post,* p. A8.

Jerin, Robert A., and Loura J. Moriarty. (1997). *Victims of Crime.* Chicago, Ill.: Nelson-Hall.

"Killers Get Maximum Prison Time." (2006, January 28). *Contra Costa Times,* p. A1 & A6.

"Literary Stereotyping." (2003, January). *The Blade—Transitions: Transgender News & Commentary,* p. 88.

Manley, Roslyn. (2003, March). Columnist, Transgender Activist (National Transgender Action Coalition). Personal communications with Mitchell Grobeson, 2006.

Meyer, Kate. (2005, June 10). "Gay Bash Victim In Coma." *Daily News.*

National Coalition of Anti-Violence Programs. (2006). "Anti-Lesbian, Gay, Bisexual and Transgender Violence in 2005."

"New Call for Hate Crime Change in Alabama." (2005, December 15). *Gay & Lesbian Times,* p. 35.

"The News Affecting Our Community in 2002." (2003, January 3). *Frontiers,* p. 17.

Rennison, Callie. (2001). "Violent Victimization and Race, 1993–98." Washington, D.C.: National Institute of Justice.

"Seattle Shooting Details Emerge." (2006, July 30). *Contra Costa Times,* p. A18.

SPLC Report. (2006, March). Volume 36, Number 1. Montgomery, Ala.: Southern Poverty Law Center. p. 8.

"Stonewalled: Police Abuse and Misconduct against Lesbian, Gay, Bisexual, and Transgender People in the U.S." (2005). New York: Amnesty International USA.

"Teen Arrested on Suspicion of Hate Crime." (2006, August 3). *Contra Costa Times,* p. A8.

"Teasing to Torment: A Profile of School Climate in Arizona." (2006, June 15). *GLSEN,* by Riley Snorton.

"Two Defendants in Gay Bashing Case Avoid Prison." (2006, June 22). *Gay & Lesbian Times,* p. 36.

U.S. Department of Justice. (1990). Summary Reporting System: Hate Crime Data Collection Guide Lines. Washington, D.C.: U.S. Government Printing Office.

U.S. Commission on Civil Rights, Intimadation, and Violence. (1990, September). Racial and Religious Bigotry in America (Clearing House Publications No. 96). Washington, D.C.: U.S. Government Printing Office.

"U.S. Senate Passes Hate Crimes Act." (2004, August). *Lesbian News,* p. 12.

Wallace, Steven. (1987). "Elderly Nicaraguans and Immigrant Community Formation in San Francisco." Unpublished doctoral dissertation, University of California, San Francisco.

Wallace, Steven. (1992, November 9). Personal communication.

Wright, Robin. (1993, June 8). "Ethnic Strife Owes More to Present Than to History." *Los Angeles Times,* pp. A1, A13.

"Youth to Get Landmark Settlement on Anti-Gay Harassment Case." (2002, January 17). *Erie Times News,* p. 2.

Chapter 13

Hate/Bias Crimes: Reporting, Monitoring, and Response Strategies

OVERVIEW

In this chapter, we discuss the nationwide reporting system and clearinghouse for hate crimes data collected from state and local police. Criminal justice leaders in every sector of the United States must utilize standardized and comprehensive statistics as one tool to analyze hate crime/bias trends. Using this data will aid in directing their resources more effectively against crimes of hate or bias and civil rights violations. In the first section of the chapter, we define the problem and establish why data collection is important. The second section continues with a discussion of the various organizations that monitor hate crimes and hate groups. The third section contains information about organized hate groups. In the fourth section, we explore conditions within communities that require monitoring and subsequent deployment of law enforcement and community resources (community-oriented policing) that will prevent or reduce hate/bias crimes and incidents. The final section presents community response strategies to reduce hate crimes and incidents. The chapter considers the need for the community (religious institutions, schools, public agencies, private organizations, and neighborhood residents) to deal with the problem cooperatively because the challenge of hate crimes is not solely one for law enforcement agencies.

COMMENTARY

The need for quick and effective investigation and prosecution of hate/bias crimes combined with comprehensive reporting and monitoring is exemplified in the following quotations:

> Racial prejudice was a factor in more than half the 7,649 hate crimes reported to the FBI in 2004. Hate crimes against African Americans were most prevalent. The number of race-based incidents rose by 5 percent last year, from 3,844 to 4,042. Authorities identified prejudice against blacks in 2,732 of those crimes. The data also showed that crimes against Muslims have leveled off since a spike following the Sept. 11, 2001, attacks. "We tend to see the number of incidents go in cycles in large part tied to international events," said Ibrahim Hooper, spokesman for the Council on American-Islamic Relations. ("Report Says Race Factors into Most Hate Crimes," 2005, p. A15)

The American Psychological Association says of hate crime, ". . . not only is it an attack on one's physical self, but it is also an attack on one's very identity." Attacks on individuals because of their appearance, their manner of prayer, or their behavior have long been a part of human history. It is only recently, however, that our society has given this phenomenon a name and decided to study and monitor it as well as legislate against it. As a result, law enforcement has been given the task of identifying and responding to bias-motivated crime. In order to discharge this duty, the criminal justice community must have adequate information about the nature and prevalence of hate crime. (Bureau of Justice Statistics Report, 2005)

A crowd that gathered to protest a white supremacists' march turned violent, throwing baseball sized rocks at police, vandalizing vehicles and stores, and setting fire to a neighborhood bar, authorities said [in Toledo, Ohio]. At least two dozen members of the National Socialist Movement, which calls itself "America's Nazi Party," had gathered at a city park to march under police protection. Mayor Jack Ford blamed the rioting on [black] gangs taking advantage of a volatile situation. "It's exactly what they wanted," Ford said of the group that planned the march, which was cancelled because of the rioting. ("Riots Break Out in Ohio," 2005, p. A16)

INTRODUCTION

Changing demographics in almost every part of the United States requires that all localities deal with issues of intergroup relations. The ideal of harmony in diversity is offset by increased stress on the social fabric of a community, stress that often leads to bigoted or violent acts. Newspaper headlines across the country provide convincing examples of disharmony on a daily basis. Hate/bias crimes are not a new phenomenon; they have been present for generations. It is crucial for law enforcement to maintain accurate and thorough documentation of such crimes.

Data must be collected at local levels and sent in a standardized fashion to state and national clearinghouses so that proper resources may be allocated to hate/bias crime investigations, prosecutions, and victim assistance. Such a system provides information necessary not only to the criminal justice system but also to public policy-makers, civil rights activists, legislators, victim advocates, and the general public. The data, if comprehensive and accurate, provide a reliable statistical picture of the problem. Agencies collecting data have also been able to use the statistics to strengthen their arguments and rationale for new hate crime penalty enhancements. In addition, the information is used in criminal justice training courses and in educating communities on the impact of the problem. Another, and possibly the most important, rationale for expending energy on tracking, analyzing, investigating, and prosecuting these crimes is that a single incident can be the tragedy of a lifetime to its victim and may also be the spark that disrupts an entire community.

Increased public awareness of and response to such crimes has largely been the result of efforts by community-based organizations and victim advocate groups. By documenting and drawing public attention to acts of bigotry and violence, these organizations laid the groundwork for the official action that followed. It is extremely important that hate groups across the United States be monitored by criminal justice agencies. Documenting and publicizing a problem does not guarantee it will be solved, but is a critical part of any strategy to create change. It also raises consciousness within the community and the criminal justice system. It is a simple but effective first step toward mobilizing a response.

HATE CRIMES REPORTING

Purpose of Hate/Bias Crime Data Collection

Establishing a good reporting system within public organizations (e.g., human relations commissions) and the justice system is essential in every area of the country. Hate/bias crime data are collected to help police:

- Identify current and potential problems (i.e., trends)
- Respond to the needs of diverse communities
- Recruit a diverse force
- Train criminal justice personnel on the degree of the problem and the reasons for priority response

When police have information about crime patterns, they are better able to direct resources to prevent, investigate, and resolve problems pertaining to them. Tracking hate/bias incidents and crimes allows criminal justice managers to deploy their resources appropriately when fluctuations occur. Aggressive response, investigation, and prosecution of these crimes demonstrate that police are genuinely concerned and that they see such crimes as a priority. As departments show their commitment to addressing hate/bias crime, the diverse communities they serve will be more likely to see police as responsive to their concerns. A secondary benefit for a responsive agency is that blacks, Asians, Hispanics, lesbians, gays, and women would be more apt to consider law enforcement as a good career opportunity.

The Boston Police Department began recording and tracking civil rights violations in 1978, when it created its Civil Disorders Unit. Boston was probably the first law enforcement agency in the United States to record and track such crimes. The Maryland State Police Department was also a forerunner when it began to record incidents on a statewide, systematic basis as part of a pioneering government-wide effort to monitor and combat hate violence in 1981. Agencies that implemented policies and procedures to deal with hate/bias crimes during the 1980s proved to be leaders in the field; in addition to Boston and Maryland, New York, San Francisco, and Los Angeles had forward-looking programs. The policies and procedures of these agencies have been adopted as models by other organizations.

Congressional Directive: Federal Hate Crime Legislation

In response to a growing concern and in an attempt to understand the scope of the hate crime problem, the U.S. Congress enacted the federal Hate Crimes Statistics Act (HCSA) of 1990 and subsequent acts that amended the directive. The Act requires the attorney general to establish guidelines, and to collect and publish data on the prevalence of crimes motivated by bias or hate. The U.S. attorney general delegated his agency's responsibilities under the Act to the FBI. The Uniform Crime Report (UCR) section of the FBI was assigned the task of developing the procedures for and managing the implementation of the collection of hate crime data. The national clearinghouse for hate/bias crime data enables the criminal justice system to monitor and respond to trends in those localities that voluntarily submit the information.

Uniform Crime Report System

The approach adopted by the U.S. Department of Justice incorporated a means of capturing hate crime data received from law enforcement jurisdictions into the already established nationwide UCR program. As part of the UCR Program, the FBI publishes statistics annually in *Hate Crime Statistics*. The U.S. Department of Justice encouraged law enforcement agencies to follow the spirit of the federal legislation and to collect data voluntarily. The first UCR data was published in 1992 with participation from 6,200 law enforcement agencies. A total of 12,711 law enforcement agencies, representing 49 states and the District of Columbia (Hate Crime Statistics, 2004), took part in the UCR program in 2004, the most recent report available. Only the state of Hawaii has never participated in the program. Although there was not 100 percent participation, the statistics represented over 94 percent of the nation's population. As part of the attorney general's Hate Crime Initiative, the Bureau of Justice Statistics has examined ways to improve participation by law enforcement agencies in collecting and reporting hate crime statistics to the FBI and in profiling local responses to hate crime. The findings will assist the federal government in improving the accuracy of hate crime statistics and reporting practices and in developing a model for hate crime reporting. FBI hate crime statistics can be found on a website, which is cited at the end of Chapter 12.

Almost all states lack a central repository for police intelligence on hate crimes. That means an investigator working in one city might not even know about a critical piece of information gathered in another location within the same state during a different incident. In 2000, California unveiled what it called the first high-tech database in the country aimed at combating hate crimes. The state implemented a computer system allowing police departments statewide to call up names, mug shots, and even the types of tattoos that identify particular individuals or groups linked to hate crimes.

HATE/BIAS CRIMES MONITORING

Monitoring Hate Groups

Monitoring extremist groups is an important obligation of law enforcement. A nationwide criminal justice reporting system tracks these groups, and their activities are also monitored through nongovernmental organizations such as:

> ***SPLC Report (formerly Klanwatch) and SPLC Intelligence Project:*** The SPLC Report and Intelligence Project are two products of the Southern Poverty Law Center located in Montgomery, Alabama. SPLC considers the monitoring of white supremacist groups on a national scale and the tracking of hate crimes among its primary responsibilities. The group disseminates this information to law enforcement agencies through a bimonthly publication, the Intelligence Report. The organization also publishes e-mail newsletters: "Hatewatch," "Mix It Up Monthly," "Tolerance.org," "Teaching Tolerance," and, in 2006, added "Immigration Watch"

to report on and monitor hate and extremism in the anti-immigration movement. The center, which began as a small civil rights law firm in 1971, is now internationally known for its hate/bias publications, tolerance education programs, legal victories against white supremacist groups, and tracking of hate groups.

Anti-Defamation League: The Anti-Defamation League (ADL) was founded in 1913 "to stop the defamation of Jewish people and to secure justice and fair treatment to all citizens alike." The ADL has been a leader of national and state efforts in the development of legislation, policies, and procedures to deter, investigate, and counteract hate-motivated crimes. The organization is also respected for its research publications and articles dealing with such crimes. The ADL developed a recording system that has served as a model of data collection nationwide since its launch in 1979.

National Gay and Lesbian Task Force (NGLTF) and NGLTF Policy Institute: The NGLTF works to eradicate discrimination and violence based on sexual orientation and Human Immunodeficiency Virus (HIV) status. The NGLTF was founded in 1973, to serve its members in a manner that reflects the diversity of the lesbian and gay community. In 1991, the task force was restructured into two organizations—the NGLTF and the NGLTF Policy Institute—to improve its lobbying efforts and expand its organization and educational programs.

Center for Democratic Renewal: The Center for Democratic Renewal (CDR; formerly the National Anti-Klan Network) has tracked bias activity since 1982. CDR's strategy to end bigoted violence focuses on tracking bias activity, educating society through publications, and assisting victims through various programs.

Simon Wiesenthal Center: The Simon Wiesenthal Center, based in Los Angeles, is a human rights group named for the famed Nazi hunter. It monitors the Internet worldwide for tactics, language, and symbols of the high-tech hate culture. The center shares its information with affected law enforcement agencies. The organization, in some states, also operates Holocaust exhibits that are used as shocking examples of atrocities committed against Jewish people during World War II. Police academies and in-service, advanced officer training courses often use the exhibits for training on hate violence.

ORGANIZED HATE GROUPS

Knowledge of hate groups is essential when policing in a multicultural society. It is imperative for the criminal justice system to investigate (using methods including informants, surveillance, and infiltration), monitor, and control organized hate groups. Aggressive prosecution and litigation against these groups is also critical. The Southern Poverty Law Center (SPLC) documented a 5 percent increase in hate groups in 2005 over 2004, and a 30 percent rise over the past five years.

There's no doubt that the white supremacist movement is growing—"We have seen a substantial jump in the number of hate groups in just the last five years," said Mark Potok, director of the Intelligence Project [Southern Poverty Law Center]. "And unfortunately, much of that growth has been in the most violent sectors of the movement, skinheads and Christian Identity adherents." (SPLC Report, March 2006)

The possible reasons for these increases, suggested by the ADL, are discussed in the section "Racist Skinheads."

The white supremacist movement. "The white supremacist movement is composed of dozens of organizations and groups, each working to create a society totally dominated by white Christians, where the human rights of lesbians and gay men and other minorities are denied. Some groups seek to create an all 'Aryan' territory; others seek to re-institutionalize Jim Crow segregation" (Center for Democratic Renewal, 1992). While most of these organizations share a common bigotry based on religion, race, ethnicity, and sexual orientation, they differ in many ways. They range from seemingly innocuous religious sects or tax protesters to openly militant, even violent, neo-Nazi skinheads and Ku Kluxers. No single organization or person dominates this movement. Frequently individuals are members of several different groups at the same time. The increase in hate group membership, especially since September 11, 2001, leads many sources to confirm that numbers of white supremacists are on the rise.

Numbers of hate groups in the United States. The SPLC, as previously mentioned, tracks active hate groups in the United States. They identify hate groups by gathering information from their publications, citizens' reports, law enforcement agencies, field sources, and news reports. The number of groups known to be active is determined by surveying marches, rallies, speeches, meetings, leafleting, published literature, and criminal acts. Some white supremacist groups consist of only a few members, while others have tens of thousands. In 2005, SPLC documented 803 active hate groups (see Exhibit 13.1), up 5 percent from 2004, and up 30 percent from 2000 (SPLC Report, March 2006, p.1). The rise in numbers reflected a pattern of growth dating back to the mid-1990s.

Hate groups are categorized by the Center as Ku Klux Klan, Neo-Nazi, Racist Skinhead, Christian Identity, Black Separatist, Neo-Confederate, and Other. The Other

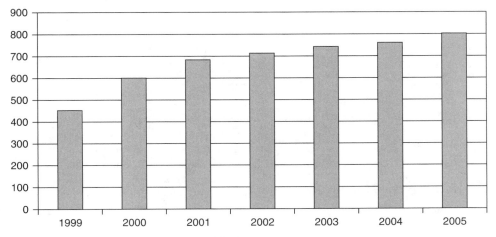

Exhibit 13.1 Hate Groups in the United States Since 1999
(*Source:* SPLC Report, March 2006.)

category includes groups, vendors, and publishing houses endorsing a hodgepodge of racist doctrines. Although the numbers of white supremacists in the United States are small in comparison with the total population, Loretta Ross, program research director of the CDR, explains why they should be taken seriously:

> Because the percentage of whites who actually belong to white supremacist groups is small, there is a general tendency to underestimate their influence. What is really significant is not the number of people actually belonging to hate groups, but the number who endorse their messages. Once known primarily for their criminal activities, racists have demonstrated a catalytic effect by tapping into the prejudices of the white majority. (Ross, 1995, p. 7)

The following groups are described only briefly because there is constant change within them.

Neo-Nazis and Klans

The reason for concern about the activities of neo-Nazis and Klans are obvious from their history of criminal activities and plots to launch race wars and kill officials who oppose them.

The largest of the neo-Nazi and Klan groups include the following:

Neo-Nazi-Type Groups	**Klan-Type Groups**
Aryan Nations	Alabama White Knights of the KKK
Knights of Freedom	America's Invisible Empire Knights of the KKK
National Alliance	
Nationalist Socialist Movement	American Knights of the KKK
World Church of the Creator (Creative Movement)	Imperial Klans of America
	Invincible Empire Knights of the KKK
	Knights of the White Kamellia
	New Order Knights of the KKK
	White Shield Knights of the KKK

The ideology of Klan members, neo-Nazis, and other white supremacists has been clear since the formation of these groups. They commonly advocate white supremacy, anti-Semitism, homophobia, and racism.

The most violent groups are the neo-Nazis, and their movements are growing in the United States and in countries such as Germany and Austria. Young people ages 13 to 25 who wish to join these organizations are required to commit a hate crime as part of the induction process. They openly idealize Hitler, and have committed murders and hundreds of assaults as well as other violent crimes; most of their victims are African Americans, Latinos, Asian Americans, gays, lesbians, bisexuals, transgender individuals, and even the homeless.

World Church of the Creator or Creative Movement. The World Church of the Creator (WCOTC), classified as a neo-Nazi-type group, was founded in 1973 by Ben

Klassen, who wrote the organization's manifesto, *The White Man's Bible.* The organization's existence ended in mid-1990 following the suicide of Klassen and the imprisonment of other leaders. In 1996, however, the WCOTC was reborn and, according to authorities, has again become America's most dangerous white supremacist group. The group's rallying cry is "Rahowa," which stands for Racial Holy War. The group is also violently anti-Christian. A judge of the U.S. District Court in Chicago, ruled in December 2002 that the WCTOC, founded in Illinois, would have to surrender the name because an Oregon-based religious group already had a trademark on it. The group now calls itself the Creative Movement and has moved its headquarters to Riverton, Wyoming. The organization has not only a large membership that is active in many states but also has one of the largest white prison gang memberships. It has been tough to control because of its religious facade, which allows its members to gather for meetings in prison.

Aryan Nations. The group Aryan Nations was formed in the early 1970s and operates out of northern Idaho. It is considered primarily an identity group but also embraces neo-Nazi philosophy. The organization preaches that God's creation of Adam marked "the placing of the White Race upon this earth," that all nonwhites are inferior, and that Jews are the "natural enemy of our Aryan (white) race" (Berkowitz, 1999).

The National Alliance. The neo-Nazi group, National Alliance, believes it is part of nature and subject to nature's laws only; therefore, members are able to determine their own destiny regardless of laws imposed by the government. They profess that those who believe in a divine control over mankind absolve themselves of responsibility for their fate. They also believe they are members of the Aryan (or European) race and are superior to other races.

Racist Skinheads

Membership of young adults in Racist Skinhead groups has grown considerably since the group's inception in 1986. According to a 2006 report by the ADL, the United States has seen a "significant and troubling" resurgence of racist skinhead activity, with a rise in the number of organized racist skinhead groups as well as a rise in the number of unaffiliated racist skinheads. The report indicates that the increase in number of racist skinhead groups, in all parts of the country, has been accompanied by a rise in violent hate crimes carried out by them against Jews, African-Americans, Hispanics, gays and lesbians, and immigrants ("ADL Reports Resurgence of Racist Skinheads," 2006). ADL's report identifies 110 racist skinhead groups, the majority of which did not exist five years ago. Also, not all groups are equal; one may have five members, while another may have hundreds. Racist skinheads have been behind several attempted acts of terrorism; for example, in 2005, a racist skinhead was convicted for plotting to firebomb an Oklahoma City synagogue.

The ADL report cites several factors for the resurgence in racist skinhead activity:

- Alienated white youth have found a welcome reception on the Internet from white supremacists hungry for new recruits. The Internet has made it very easy for young people to be exposed to online message forums and social networking Web sites prevalent in the racist skinhead subculture;

- The white power music industry, around which the racist skinhead subculture revolves, has experienced a substantial growth in online promotion and sales;
- Racist skinhead groups such as Hammerskin Nation and Blood & Honor have expanded globally using the Internet to create a network of international white supremacist sites and giving haters in different parts of the country—indeed, the world—the ability to connect online;
- Less competition exists from the major established white supremacist groups, whose activity has diminished because of the arrests or deaths of leaders and serious factional infighting.

Skinheads should also be considered dangerous because of a history of bombings, such as the 1993 bombings at the offices of the National Association for the Advancement of Colored People (NAACP) in Washington and California, and other hate crime violence by members. One of the largest such groups, the Keystone State Skinheads, have two leaders up on charges of attempted murder for attacks on minorities and nonracist skinheads (SPLC, 2006, p. 1). Racist Skinheads, easily recognized by their closely shaven heads, are transient and sometimes do not join with Skinhead groups.

SPLC indicates their numbers are hard to assess because of this fact. The influence of adult white supremacist groups on Racist Skinheads and neo-Nazi skinheads has been substantial. The youth participate in adult hate group rallies and show a great deal of solidarity with them. Skinhead groups have developed their own leadership and appeal distinct from adult Klan and neo-Nazi groups. The adult hate groups seek to replenish their membership ranks from the Racist Skinhead groups. Prominent skinheads established several new hate music vendors in 2005, which allow these groups to capture profits from the white power music trade (SPLC, 2006).

Identity

Identity describes a religion that is fundamentally racist, anti-Semitic, and antihomosexual. According to SPLC, the active Identity groups across the United States are organized under different names but with similar ideologies. The goal of Identity groups is to broaden the influence of the white supremacist movement under the guise of Christianity. They form their views of diverse people based on a particular interpretation of the Bible. For example, "[Identity] teaches that people of color are pre-Adamic, that is not fully human and are without souls; that Jews are children of Satan and that white people of northern Europe are the Lost Tribes of the House of Israel" ("World Church," 1992, pp. 42–44). The movement takes the position that white Anglo-Saxons—not Jews—are the real biblical "chosen people," and that blacks and other nonwhites are "mud people" on the same level as animals and therefore are without souls (Berkowitz, 1999). Identity followers believe that the Bible commands racial segregation; interpreting racial equality as a violation of God's law.

Christian Identity. Followers of this sect, founded in California by Wesley Swift after World War II, use the Bible as the source of their ideology. It is a quasi-theological movement of small churches, tape and book distribution businesses, and radio ministries.

Posse Comitatus. Another Identity group is Posse Comitatus, which means "power of the country" in Latin. The group is antitax and anti–federal government. The Posse believes that all government power is rested in the county, rather than the federal, level.

Christian Patriots. The followers of this Identity group belong to many different organizations, all of which espouse white supremacy. The core beliefs are as follows:

- White people and people of color are fundamentally two different kinds of citizens, with different rights and responsibilities.
- The United States is not properly a democracy, but a republic in which only people with property should vote.
- Democracy is the same as "mobocracy," or mob rule.
- The United States is a Christian republic, with a special relationship between Christianity and the rule of law.
- Internationalists (usually identified as Jews) and aliens (sometimes identified as Jews, sometimes as immigrants or people of color) are attempting to subvert the U.S. Constitution and establish one-world socialism or, alternatively, the New World Order.
- The Federal Reserve banking system is unconstitutional and a tool of the "International Jewish Banking Conspiracy" (CDR, 1992).

Black Separatists

The SPLC has identified black separatist groups active in the United States under two different names: the House of David and the Nation of Islam. Black separatist groups are organizations whose ideologies include tenets of racially based hatred. Black separatist followers share the same agenda as white supremacists: racial separatism and racial supremacy. The two movements also share a common goal of racial purity and a hatred of Jews. One example of a black separatist, militant organization espousing hatred of Jews is the Black African Holocaust Council (BAHC). BAHC, based in Brooklyn, New York, was established in 1991. Membership is restricted to African Americans and Native Americans. The organization publishes a monthly magazine, the *Holocaust Journal,* which is replete with anti-Semitic and anti-white rhetoric. BAHC holds monthly meetings and conducts weekly lectures and study groups on anti-white or anti-Semitic issues.

Despite the differences between black extremists and white supremacists groups and their mutual contempt, these groups are able to join rhetorical forces to demean and slander Jews.

RESPONSE ALTERNATIVES TO ORGANIZED HATE GROUPS

Law enforcement agencies must actively work to fight and control organized hate groups, tracking their activities, establishing when they are responsible for crimes, and assisting in their prosecution. Intelligence gathering is crucial to efforts to reduce and prevent hate/bias crimes. Equally important is networking and sharing hate group information with other criminal justice agencies. Many have called this approach a cross-disciplinary coalition against racism. It involves statewide and regional commitments by criminal justice agencies to work with other public and private entities, including the Internal Revenue Service. All the institutions jointly develop and implement components of multitiered intervention strategies targeting enforcement, education, training, victim assistance, media relations, political activism and advocacy, and ongoing self-evaluation.

The fight begins with an assessment of the size and scope of the various supremacist groups, their movements, their leaders, and their publications. When hate crimes are perpetrated against one group in the community, law enforcement must immediately alert any other organizations that are potential targets. For example, if a synagogue is the object of an arsonist, not only should other synagogues be notified by law enforcement, but also the NAACP, National Council of La Raza, and other minority organizations in the region, state, and adjoining states. The investigating agency should notify other law enforcement agencies (i.e., city, county, state, and federal) in their county and region of the incident as well.

MINI CASE STUDY: LEWISTON, MAINE, 2003

An excellent example of how a community and the police can organize around diversity and counter the actions of hate groups occurred in Lewiston, Maine, in early 2003. The WCOTC and the National Alliance planned a rally at a local college in connection with a controversy regarding a growing Somali immigrant community in the town. More than 1,000 Somalis had moved into Lewiston, and by the fall of 2002, tensions had risen. Somali leaders and others thought racism was surfacing in the community. WCOTC and the National Alliance saw this as an opportunity to come to the town to organize the community against the Somalis.

The city of Lewiston and its police department created a steering committee for a new group, the Many and One Coalition, with 200 members. Utilizing advice from the SPLC (especially its publication *Ten Ways to Fight Hate: A Community Response Guide*) and other local and national human rights groups, they planned the community's response to the pending rally. An outreach coordinator for the SPLC Tolerance Project arrived in Lewiston days prior to the rally to help the town organize its efforts. The day before the rally, the college hosted a forum on issues of tolerance and diversity. The following day, about 5,000 townspeople showed up for a separate rally in support of diversity and the Somali community. Only 30 people turned out for the hate rally (SPLC, 2003).

TRENDS AND PREDICTIONS FOR ORGANIZED HATE GROUPS

Some experts predict that white supremacists will continue to commit traditional crimes (e.g., cross burnings, vandalism) but will also venture into high-tech activities such as computer system infiltration and sabotage. Their political activism will include "white rights" rallies, protests, and demonstrations; election campaigns by racist candidates; and legislative lobbying. These activities are expected to incite countermovements and will create very labor-intensive situations for law enforcement to handle.

Observers of hate groups have also noted the shift in tactics by white supremacists in the United States. Discovering that supremacists could no longer effectively recruit members using the ideology of open racism with the focus on persons of color, Jews, immigrants, and the like, they are now targeting lesbians and gays. According to those who study hate groups, they find that while many whites may share their racial, religious, and ethnic prejudices, most are no longer willing to act on them openly. Thus a new strategy is being employed that combines old hatreds with new rhetoric. This new approach does not imply that supremacists no longer hate people of color, Jews, and so on. Rather, it means they are refocusing their energies; they are exploiting white fear of change; and they have adopted not only homophobia as a prominent part of their new agenda but also anti-abortion, anti-immigration, and so-called pro-family and pro-American values, in addition to their traditional racist and anti-Semitic beliefs. Ross (1995) says the broadening of issues and the use of conservative buzzwords have attracted the attention of whites who may not consider themselves racist but do consider themselves patriotic Americans concerned about the moral decay of "their" country.

One disturbing trend is the age and gender of new members of supremacist groups. They are younger than in the past (including teenagers) and many are young women. Organized hate is no longer the exclusive domain of white men over 30 years of age. To recruit new membership, radical rights groups around the country are staging "European" festivals. It is an attempt to draw ethnic whites into their racist movement. Many attendees at festivals have been shocked to learn the coordinators are members of racist organizations. One such festival, held in Sacramento, California, in February, was advertised as "Euro-Fest 2003." The literature about the event described Celtic music, ethnic food, and activities. According to SPLC, however, organizers:

> had Mein Kampf and little baby blankets in blue and white with little swastikas all over them. Women in knee-length skirts and Bavarian bustiers sold copies of *ABC: Arian Beginnings for Children,* along with *Talk Back,* a publication of the White Student Alliance. At a nearby table, photos were on sale of two beautiful young blonde girls giving the Nazi salute. A fellow with a black T-shirt bearing a swastika strolled by; near him, another man's shirt urged "David Duke for Senate." Over at the table of the neo-Nazi National Alliance, women's thongs with the Alliance symbol embroidered on the front, available in green, pink, yellow, white and red, were moving briskly. (SPLC Report, Summer 2003)

Organizations and officials tracking hate groups have offered other predictions on the evolution and future of hate groups. These experts believe groups that have traditionally shunned or actively opposed each other for ideological reasons will join forces against their "common enemies." For one example among many, although neo-Nazis have long despised Arabs and Muslims, they have increasingly allied with Arab and Muslim extremists against common enemies, most often Jews. American neo-Nazis have also been increasingly working with their counterparts in Europe.

The Internet and Hate Groups

As noted above, the Internet has become the medium of choice for recruiting young members to hate groups and for disseminating hate dogma and racist ideology. The Internet enables people to spread hate around the world instantaneously, in a cheap, easy, and anonymous manner. The medium provides hate groups the ability to send unsolicited mass e-mailings simultaneously into millions of homes, some of them seeking to recruit today's affluent and educated youth to their cause. Their hundreds and possibly thousands of websites entice viewers with online games, comic strips, and music, or simply a friendly pitch from another kid. College and university sites are being bombarded with messages and lures from hate groups. In some areas the Internet is also being used to provide tips on how to target groups' opponents with violence. SPLC tracks hate sites and has developed its own website with a special online campaign, "Hate Hurts," about the impact of hate. Internet companies must work with the police, within the realm of freedom of speech requirements, to enforce their own standards and to block hate dogma websites or hate e-mail within their system.

HATE/BIAS CRIME AND INCIDENT CONTROL

Hate/bias crimes and incidents can be controlled only through the combined efforts of the community (schools, private organizations, government agencies, churches, service organizations, and families), federal and state legislatures, and the criminal justice system—a holistic approach. It is important to profile communities to determine if they are at risk of strife or conflict caused by the social, economic, and environmental conditions that can result in hate crimes and incidents.

Identifying Communities at Risk

Community profiling. Law enforcement agencies experiencing demographic changes in their communities are well advised to perform an analysis of what is taking place: community profiling. Community profiling involves a demographic analysis of the community with regard to the ethnicity/national origin, race, religion, and sexual orientation of groups whose members work or reside there. Such a profile must include a sense of timing: what can the community and law enforcement personnel expect from profiled groups with regard to the observance of holidays and religious or cultural ceremonies?

Progressive agencies send their patrol officers lists of religious and cultural holidays and world crisis events that could affect the area they serve. If officers wait to identify at-risk communities until after hate crimes are committed, they are not fulfilling their professional responsibilities. Knowing how to identify at-risk communities and then committing resources to resolve problems before they escalate is proactive police work, which is crucial to preventing conflict. While this involves more departmental time and personnel initially, the ultimate savings through the prevention of community disruption is well worth the effort.

Neighborhood and police partnership. Neighborhoods (citizens and all those local institutions encompassed by the term) working together with the police provide the best means of identifying communities at risk. The term *at risk* refers to communities having a high level of criminal activity or disorder and usually a higher number of incidents of civil rights violations—hate/bias crimes, discrimination, racism, and bigotry. How does a city determine if a neighborhood is at risk? Who is responsible for the assessment?

What strategies can be utilized to reduce the at-risk status? The best approach is community policing, described in Chapter 1, whereby police help the community protect itself and enhance the quality of life of its members. Officers and citizens meet to discuss the neighborhoods' most serious problems and work together to resolve them.

Community policing encourages officers to delve into observations and feelings to determine not only what is happening but also who is involved, what their motivation is, and where they are from. Officers should consider themselves as first-line intelligence assets for their community. For example, they should watch for graffiti and/or other materials posted on walls, fences, telephone poles, and buildings. These markings could signal a racist operation in progress or a locally active hate group. In addition, to be effective, officers who patrol highly diverse areas must have some degree of cultural awareness and ability to engage in cross-cultural communication. It has been said that if officers are scrambling to understand communities only after a crime is committed, it is a terrible indictment of their lack of professionalism.

Additionally, officers must know neighborhood leaders and ways to locate them quickly if they are needed to provide general assistance or to help control rumors or people. Neighborhood leaders can also provide invaluable help when it comes to dealing with victims who distrust police. A problem-focused approach provides officers with a solid understanding of social, economic, and environmental problems in the community. There are limits to what the police can do without community help. In many communities, however, police first have to overcome their traditional role identification as crime fighters independent of the community before they can become an integral part of a team that works together to solve local problems. However, when officers patrol neighborhoods daily, they can interact with citizens to engender trust and can be the best resources to monitor activities. Herman Goldstein, University of Wisconsin law professor and the architect of the problem-oriented policing (POP) concept, said that "the police department, more than any other agency of government, must have a bird's eye view of the dynamics within its community, including the demographics, agendas of various groups, and an in-depth understanding of the hopes, aspirations and frustration of various groups. This will give the police a feel for the mood and tensions that exist within a community" (Parker, 1991, p. 13).

Role of human relations commissions (HRCs). Many cities and counties nationwide have established community HCRs. Created as independent agencies, they are responsible for fostering equal opportunity and eliminating all forms of discrimination. These objectives are accomplished by means of investigating, mediating, and holding public hearings on problems that arise from discrimination prohibited by federal, state, and local laws. Most HRCs will not investigate incidents of discrimination where such a function is preempted or prohibited by state or federal legislation. In cases where there is a violation of state or federal law, the HRC refers the complainant to the appropriate agency. It then monitors the progress of the complaint. Each HRC has established procedures that govern how it receives, investigates, holds hearings on, and mediates and resolves complaints. Confidentiality is a protected right of the complainant in discrimination cases reported to HRCs. As established by state or federal law, the names of the parties may not be made public, with few exceptions, without the written consent of both. Human relations commissions should also be part of the community–police partnership in which they all take responsibility for educating their community about its diversity. This includes serious and sustained efforts to bring people together for dialogue.

Community Relations Service (CRS). The CRS, an arm of the U.S. Department of Justice, is a specialized federal conciliation service available to state and local officials to help prevent and resolve racial and ethnic conflict, violence, and civil disorder. When governors, mayors, police chiefs, and school superintendents need help to defuse racial or ethnic crises, they turn to CRS. This service helps local officials and residents tailor locally defined resolutions when conflict and violence threaten community stability and well-being. Created by the Civil Rights Act of 1964, CRS is the only federal agency dedicated to preventing and resolving racial and ethnic tensions, incidents, and civil disorders. CRS gathers data in seven areas: demographic balance, administration of justice (particularly police–community relations), employment, education, housing, health and welfare, and community relationships. The statistical data is then used to assess six critical factors:

1. Relationship of minorities to the administration of justice system
2. Impact of the economy
3. Level of minorities' inclusion in and/or exclusion from the system and the number of minorities serving as elected officials
4. Quality of intergroup relationships
5. Level of violence currently in the community/neighborhood and/or city
6. Basic demographic influences

It is time-consuming to perform this type of analysis and to develop a program based on the findings. Police departments have access to the same kind of data and they possess a great deal of the experience and expertise necessary to complete the same type of analysis within neighborhoods, if they choose to do so.

TRENDS TO MONITOR: STEEP TYPOLOGY

Trend Monitoring in Multicultural Communities

Monitoring conditions in a community provides useful information for forecasting potential negative events and preparing accordingly. The framework for evaluating any predictions should include an analysis of economic circumstances, social and cultural conditions, as well as the political environment within the community.

The acronym STEEP stands for social, technological, environmental, economic, and political. There is often a connection between the economy, social conditions, and politics and the numbers of hate/bias crimes that occur. This relationship is explained in Chapter 12. It is important for agency personnel and officers involved in community-oriented policing to understand the basic economic, social, and political issues contributing to social unrest.

Economic Circumstances

Crime, social unrest, riots, and disturbances have often occurred during depressed economic times. Waves of immigrants (both legal and illegal) also affect the scramble for available jobs and services. Internationally, poverty, overcrowding, and wars have been pressuring more people to migrate than ever before, laying the conditions for what the United Nations called "the human crisis of our age." In Florida, for example, refugees from Cuba and Haiti flooded the state in the 1980s and 1990s. Many areas experienced real conflict as established residents who were already struggling now had masses of people competing with them for services and jobs. California continually experiences legal and illegal immigration from Mexico and Central and South America. The new immigrants (the weakest group) become the target for people's frustrations as their own sense of well-being decreases. The established ethnically and racially mixed groups in neighborhoods see what they perceive as preferential treatment for the newcomers and react accordingly.

Federal decisions that lead to settlement of immigrants into economically depressed communities have frequently been made without regard to the capacity of local resources to handle the influx. Polls reflect a subsequent increase in anti-immigrant attitudes. Eventually, police and community problems evolve as a consequence of these well-meaning national policies that have not been thoroughly worked through. Tracking influxes of immigrants into communities, plus an awareness of political decisions, should keep law enforcement executives and officers alert to relocation and acculturation problems of newcomers in their communities. Tracking also provides an opportunity to work with the community to develop transition management plans as well as preventive programs for keeping the peace. National immigration policies and politics have a tremendous impact on cities and counties, and therefore criminal justice agencies must monitor them and plan accordingly.

Henry DeGeneste and John Sullivan wrote the following in *Fresh Perspectives,* a Police Executive Research Forum publication in 1997, and clearly it is still true today:

> Urban tensions are fueled by a combination of . . . wealth disparity and the pressures of large scale migration, which are present not only in American cities, but in cities worldwide . . . . [Robin] Wright [a journalist for the Los Angeles Times] notes, "[T]ensions in cities are often complicated by another dimension—racial or ethnic diversity." . . . [M]inorities are increasingly left stranded in urban outskirts—slums or squatter camps—excluded politically and financially. Their ensuing frustrations contribute to the volatility of urban life. Conflict (such as riots) resulting from urban decay, overcrowding, poor social services and ethnic tension has occurred in cities world-wide and can be expected to continue, particularly as swelling migrant populations flock to cities. (DeGeneste, 1997, p. 2)

Political Environment

Executives of criminal justice agencies must monitor legislation, sensitive court trials, and political events that affect not only the jurisdictions they serve, but also the nation and the world. Often what goes on outside of the United States has an impact on local populations. Law enforcement must be aware of foreign political struggles and their potential to polarize ethnic and racial groups in their community, leading to conflict. Police must have the ability to recognize potential problems and strive to prevent or mitigate intergroup conflict. Only by acknowledging their primary role in preventing and mediating conflict in the community can peace officers begin to remediate long-standing and emerging tensions. The criminal justice system cannot operate in a vacuum.

Social and Cultural Conditions

Typically, poverty and frustration with the system, the perception of racism, and unequal treatment are conditions for social unrest. Diverse peoples living in close proximity can also create potentially unstable social conditions. Furthermore, on familial level, a decline in the cohesiveness of the nuclear family (including divorce) adds to stresses within micro units in the society. Unemployment, especially among youth, is another social condition with potentially dangerous consequences.

Finally, gangs and the heavy use of illegal drugs and their impact on neighborhoods lead to social and cultural conditions ripe for explosive events. None of these elements alone, however, account for community violence. But all these factors, in combination with political and economic conditions, contribute to discontent. Officers frequently are frustrated because they cannot undo decades of societal precursors that set the stage for upheavals.

LAW ENFORCEMENT RESPONSE STRATEGIES

Public confidence and trust in the criminal justice system and law enforcement in particular are essential for effective response to hate/bias crimes. Residents in communities where people of a different race, ethnic background, religion, or sexual preference reside must be able to trust that they will be protected. They must believe that the police are not against them, that the prosecutors are vigorously prosecuting, that the judges are invoking proper penalties, and that parole, probation, and corrections are doing their share to combat crimes motivated by hate or bias. If people believe they have to protect themselves, tensions build, communication breaks down, and people try to take the law into their own hands.

Community Programs to Reduce and Control Hate Crimes

Some solutions to reduce hate/bias crimes involve going back to basics, involving grassroots institutions such as families, schools, workplaces, and religious organizations. Partnerships between the criminal justice system and these institutions are often more successful in instituting crime reduction programs than is the criminal justice system alone. However, some institutions that once built positive values or exercised some control over people are no longer working or have diminishing influence. The broken or dysfunctional family, for example, contributes significantly to society's problems, including the increase in criminal activity.

An effort must be made to reinstitute values that reinforce noncriminal behavior; law enforcement must be an integral part of that movement. The status quo policing approach (reactive) will not work anymore. "People have clearly begun to recognize that our strict law enforcement arrest approach isn't getting the job done," notes Darrel Stephens (2006), former executive director of the Police Executive Research Forum. Progressive criminal justice executives and communities realize that crime has multiple and complex causes and that police departments are not the first nor the only line of defense. If crime is to be controlled, there must be a community alliance or partnership and the causes must be attacked on multiple fronts.

Generic Community Resources and Programs

Community resources and programs that are available or can be established include:

- ***Victims' hotline:*** Similar to those available for domestic violence and rape victims and suicide prevention. The staff is trained to provide victim assistance in terms of compassion, advice, referrals, and a prepared information package.

- ***Human relations commission:*** The staff provides assistance to victims of hate crimes or incidents, holds hearings, and provides recommendations for problem resolution.

- ***United States Department of Justice Community Relations Service:*** The CRS, with headquarters in Washington, D.C., has 14 regional and field offices and provides services to every state. The Justice Department has trained staff who, when notified of a problem, will participate in and mediate community meetings in an attempt to resolve conflicts. Many states have similar justice agencies that perform these services.

- ***Conflict resolution panels:*** Specially trained staff of a city or county who can assist agencies and/or victims (including groups) in the resolution of conflict, such as that caused by hate or bias.

- ***The media:*** Cooperation in building public awareness of the problem of hate/bias violence via articles on causes and effects, resources, and legal remedies is essential.

- ***Multilingual public information brochures:*** These can be provided by government agencies on the rights of victims, services available, and criminal and civil laws related to hate and bias.

- ***Police storefronts:*** Police substations, established in the neighborhoods of communities with high concentrations of ethnic minorities, which are staffed by bilingual officers and/or civilians. The staff takes reports and provides assistance to the members of that community.

- ***Community resource list:*** List of organizations that specialize in victim assistance. Examples are the Anti-Defamation League of B'nai B'rith, Black Families Associations, Japanese-American Citizens Leagues, the NAACP, and the Mexican-American Political Association, to name a few. National organizations that might be contacted as a resource are listed in Appendix C. The importance of establishing networks with minority leaders and organizations cannot be overstressed. These leaders are extremely important for criminal justice agencies and should be identified and cultivated in advance so they will be available and willing to assist in a timely fashion with investigations, training, victim aid, and/or rumor control. If an agency experiencing serious hate/bias problems does not react quickly and effectively, victims and their community groups gain media attention when they publicly question an inadequate response or resolution. When a system involving trust and respect is already in place, such a network proves its worth if violence occurs in the agency's community. A good relationship with representatives of diverse communities is essential because it can help broaden the department's understanding of different cultures, ethnicities, and races. The same is true of members of gay and lesbian groups. When community members are utilized within departments, they can also help convince reluctant victims and/or witnesses to cooperate with investigators. Furthermore, they can encourage more victims to report incidents.

The key to a successful law enforcement response to hate crimes is building a partnership with victimized communities. There are many components and processes in building such a partnership. Other activities and events characterizing such a joint effort would include educating the public at large, providing organizational networking opportunities, monitoring the media, and implementing federal, state, and county programs. The activities for each are described in the following sections.

Educating the public at large. Prejudice and bias, which can ultimately lead to violence, are often the result of ignorance. In many cases the biased individual has had little or no firsthand exposure to the targeted group; thus the bias may be due to learned stereotypes and negative media images.

One key to combating ignorance is to educate the public as well as criminal justice system employees about the history, diversity, cultures, languages, and issues of concern of the various groups within the community. This can be accomplished through neighborhood forums, workshops, and speakers' bureaus. The speakers' bureaus should be composed of people who are well versed on the issues and are available to speak at community meetings, schools, and other forums. Criminal justice employees, of course, would be trained in the workplace and/or through in-service or academy-based training courses. Most cities and counties have organizations that represent community groups that can assist in developing and implementing such education at local elementary and secondary schools, in churches, and on college and university campuses. To check the accuracy of material presented, organizers of educational programs should have at least two or three minority community members provide input on the content of the program to be delivered. Preferably, they would represent the different subgroups within the community. Neighborhoods and community residents should be encouraged to observe their various heritages through the celebration of holidays and other special days via fairs and festivals. Calendars show that there are more holidays for different religions and cultures in the United States than anywhere else in the world.

Organizational networking. National and local organizations must network to share information, resources, ideas, and support regarding crimes motivated by hate. The list of potential organizations would include the NAACP, the ADL, the Committee against Anti-Asian Violence, the NGLTF, the SPLC, and the National Institute against Prejudice and Violence. Such advocacy organizations can construct an invaluable bridge to victim populations and assist in urging citizens to come to the police with information about hate crimes. Most of these organizations have publications and reports covering such topics as how to respond to bigotry, trends in racism, and community organizing.

Through networking, organizations or groups learn who their allies are, increase their own resources and knowledge about other minority groups, and form coalitions that make a greater impact on the community and the criminal justice system. They can also assist criminal justice agencies in dealing with community reactions to hate violence and help the victims of violence cope with the experience.

The Phoenix, Arizona, Police Department offers a good example of organizational networking. In 1994, a hate crimes advisory board with representation from most of Phoenix's ethnic groups was created. The knowledge that members have and share about their communities, cultures, and potential hot spots is highly beneficial. The organization expanded into the Central Arizona Hate Crime Advisory Board to reflect its growth and more recently changed its name to Arizona Citizens Hate Crime Advisory Board. The board has become Arizona police departments' conduit to their many different communities. These partnerships between human rights groups, civic leaders, community leaders, and law enforcement can advance police–community relations by demonstrating a commitment to be both tough on those responsible for hate crimes and aware of the special needs of hate crime victims.

Monitoring the media. Minority organizations and the criminal justice system must monitor the media, which can be a foe or an ally. The media must be used strategically for education and publicity about hate/bias crimes and incidents, about multicultural and multiracial workshops, and about festivals and other cultural events. They must be monitored in terms of accuracy of reporting and must be asked to publish corrections when warranted. Negative editorials or letters to the editor pertaining to an affected group should be countered and rebutted by an op-ed piece from management within the involved criminal justice agency. Organization leaders or their designated spokespersons should make themselves available as the primary sources of information for reporters to contact.

Federal, state, and county programs. Police executives should seek out every source of federal, state, and county law enforcement assistance programs and make the information available to investigators and/or task forces investigating or preventing hate crimes.

Churches, mosques, and synagogues. Where the usual support organizations (e.g., ACLU, NAACP, ADL) do not exist and sometimes even where they do, churches, mosques, and synagogues often are advocates for people facing discrimination and/or who are victims of a hate incident or crime. For example, the Concord (California) Hispanic Ministry acts frequently as an advocate for Latinos with tenant–landlord problems in addition to providing Spanish-language masses, family counseling, and religious classes.

Communities with Special Programs

Some jurisdictions have used a community approach to decrease the numbers of crimes and incidents of all types, including those motivated by hate/bias. Some exemplary programs include the following:

- ***Block watch volunteers program:*** The Northwest Victim Services (NVS), a nonprofit organization created in 1981 in Philadelphia, formed a partnership with police in the city's highest-crime-rate districts (the 14th and 35th) that utilizes an organized block watch program. Carefully selected, screened, and trained block watch volunteers not only perform the usual functions of neighborhood watch (crime prevention) but also perform a vital victim assistance role. The volunteer program has expanded and now provides assistance to citizens throughout the city. They provide emotional support for victims who are often frightened or unfamiliar with the criminal justice process and volunteers accompany the victims to the courtroom for the various stages of the trial.

- *Task force on police–Asian relations:* In localities that have large Asian populations, task forces have been created that consist of criminal justice members, educators, victim/refugee advocates, volunteer agency representatives, and representatives from each Asian group living or working in the community. The purposes are several: to train criminal justice employees on communication techniques that improve relations and make them more effective in dealing with the Asian community; to prepare Asians on what to expect from the various criminal justice components, especially the police; to open lines of communication between law enforcement and Asians; and to encourage Asians to report crimes and trust the police. Agencies in California that have created such task forces and could be contacted for additional details are the San Francisco, Westminster, Garden Grove, Anaheim, Fresno, San Jose, and Huntington Beach Police Departments. These task forces could certainly be adapted to other ethnic and racial groups as well. The city of Boston and other cities have effectively used the task force approach to resolve neighborhood problems, and have found them to be effective for exchanging information and curtailing rumors; identifying problems and working on solutions; and, perhaps most important, allowing citizens to help with and approach problems on a joint basis.

- *Network of Neighbors:* The Office of the Human Relations Commission (OHRC) in Montgomery County, Maryland, has a "memorandum of understanding" with the police that when a hate crime occurs, the police department immediately notifies the commission. The commission in turn contacts the volunteer of the Network of Neighbors who lives closest to the victim. The network member visits the victim as soon as possible to assure the person of community support and to assist with other needs. The volunteers receive training on victim assistance and referrals. The New York City Police Department modeled a similar Good Neighbor Program after Montgomery County's. The county also has three other networking programs established by mutual agreements between the police department and the OHRC: (1) Network of Teens; (2) Partnership Board; (3) Committee on Hate Violence. All are linked to the police department and hold monthly briefings reviewing hate incidents and crimes. The Network of Teens includes the STOP program, which educates juvenile perpetrators of hate violence about the impact of their behavior on both victims and the entire community. The program, which began in 1982, sends first offenders to the STOP program instead of through the court system. The OHRC staff requires that juvenile perpetrators and their parents attend five 2.5-hour sessions. Sessions include written and experiential exercises, discussions, films, and homework relating to their specific incident and the impact of hate and violence in general. Juveniles are also required to perform 40 hours of community service.

- *School Programs:* The Maine Office of the Attorney General's Civil Rights Team Project, created in 1996 with the help of a U.S. Department of Justice, Bureau of Justice Administration grant, uses teams of students and faculty members to promote awareness of bias and prejudice in its public high schools, middle schools, and elementary schools. Their stated mission is that no students in the state should have to experience anxiety, fear, or terror in school because of the color of their skin, their religion, their gender, their sexual orientation, their disability, or any other aspect of themselves that makes them different from other students. Law enforcement works together with teachers and administrators to empower students to stand up for civility and respect. The teams are made up of three or four students per grade, plus two or three faculty advisers. The teams have two formal responsibilities: (1) to promote awareness of bias and prejudice within their schools and (2) to organize forums for students to talk about harassment. If a team receives information about harassment, it is charged with forwarding that information to a responsible teacher or administrator. The Attorney General's office assigns a community adviser to each team to serve as liaison between the team and the Office. Annually, the Attorney General's office provides full-day training for new and returning civil rights teams and for faculty and community advisers. This training includes:

  - a presentation on the type of hate crimes committed in Maine schools
  - interactive exercises on the role of degrading language and slurs in escalating a situation to serious harassment and violence
  - a presentation by a Holocaust survivor or a victim of bias and prejudice
  - role-playing exercises on how to run effective civil rights team meetings
  - small-group work using real-life scenarios

  All participating schools agree to host Attorney General's office staff for a half-day workshop for faculty, administrators, and staff. The workshop gives teachers and other school staff a better understanding of the destructive impact of degrading language and bias-motivated harassment and teaches them how to intervene when students engage in such behavior. A similar project within the schools was created in Massachusetts.

Such community models, including those of churches and synagogues, can play a vital role in reducing violence in neighborhoods, schools, and the workplace. Successfully implemented programs can reduce individual violence, ranging from street crime to domestic abuse to drug-related crimes. Civil unrest, which can often include gang violence and open confrontations between various segments of society, can also be reduced. Building bonds of trust between the police and the community also allows community-oriented policing to contribute to the goal of promoting color-blind policing, where citizens and their police form new partnerships that offer the promise of reducing the potential for civil unrest.

Stephen Wessler, for the Bureau of Justice Administration (BJA), prepared a research paper, "Addressing Hate Crimes: Six Initiatives That Are Enhancing the Efforts of Criminal Justice Practitioners." The monograph highlights six BJA-funded projects that demonstrate the creativity and deep commitment of local, state, and federal law enforcement agencies in leading the nation's effort to combat bias-motivated crime. It identifies projects that support police and prosecutorial agencies in responding to hate crimes and supplies sources for additional information. To obtain a copy of this monograph (NCJ 179559), contact the National Criminal Justice Reference Service at www.ncjrs.gov.

SUMMARY

The changing demographics of our communities, coupled with a bleak economic environment, constitute significant factors resulting in an increase in crimes motivated by hate or bias. It is clear that a national, standardized data collection process is essential so that the representatives of the criminal justice system and the communities they serve can grasp the scope of the problem and allocate resources accordingly. Such a system would enhance the prospects for developing an effective response to crimes motivated by hate or bias. Similar monitoring approaches must also be utilized by schools and businesses to ensure that acts of bigotry are tracked and resolved quickly and effectively.

The degree to which the criminal justice system, especially law enforcement agencies, responds to acts of hate and bias intimidation, violence, or vandalism sends a message to victims, communities (especially the groups to which the victims belong), and perpetrators that racism, discrimination, and crimes motivated by hate will not be tolerated. If the criminal justice system reacts swiftly and effectively or is proactive, perpetrators will know their actions will result in apprehension and prosecution. Those sympathetic to perpetrators may be deterred from similar hate/bias actions. Such responses will calm the fears of the victims' groups and aid in establishing trust of the criminal justice system. Other members of the community who are sensitive to the impact of hate/bias crimes and incidents will also react favorably when state and federal laws are vigorously enforced, leading to long-term benefits for all.

DISCUSSION QUESTIONS AND ISSUES

1. ***Hate Crimes Monitoring Systems:*** Does your law enforcement agency (where you work or in the community in which you reside) have a system in place for monitoring hate/bias crimes and incidents? If yes, obtain a copy of the statistics for at least the past 5 years (or as many years as are available) of the hate/bias crimes and determine the following:

    a. What trends are noticeable in each category?

    b. Do the categories measure essential information that will assist your law enforcement agency in recognizing trends?

    c. What would improve the data collection method to make it more useful in measuring trends and making predictions?

    d. Has your law enforcement agency actually used the data to track the nature and extent of such crimes and incidents? Did it deploy resources accordingly? Provide the class with examples.

2. **Trend Monitoring:** Make a list of specific community social, economic, and political conditions and events occurring within the law enforcement jurisdiction in which you work or live. Which ones, if any, could potentially be connected to crimes motivated by hate? For each condition listed, make a "Comments" column. Suggest what specific factors a peace officer or criminal justice practitioner should look for in the community that would assist the agency in forecasting trends and events.

3. **Resources:** Find out what resources exist in your community to assist victims of hate/bias crimes.
   a. Which groups provide victim assistance?
   b. Which coalition groups exist, and what types of community outreach programs are offered?
   c. What types of pamphlets or other written materials are available?
   d. Which groups have speakers bureaus?
   e. Which groups are working with local law enforcement agencies with regard to response programs or cultural awareness training?
   f. Which groups are working with the district attorney's or prosecutor's office?

4. **Role of Your District Attorney's Office:** Assess the role of your district attorney's or prosecutor's office by determining the following:
   a. Does it have a special hate crimes or civil rights unit?
   b. Do hate crimes cases receive special attention?
   c. Are misdemeanor and felony hate crimes prosecuted differently?
   d. How does the office determine if it will prosecute a hate crime case?
   e. What types of training do assistant district attorneys receive regarding hate crimes?
   f. What types of community outreach does the office provide regarding hate crimes?

5. **Victim Assistance:** Identify avenues of victim assistance in your area. Research and document the following:
   a. Does your state have a crime victims' assistance program? Does it offer victim compensation? What about a victim's bill of rights?
   b. What services does the local department of mental health staff offer?
   c. Do any community groups, rape crisis centers, or crime victim services agencies in the area offer counseling to hate crimes victims?
   d. Are any mental health care professionals willing to donate their services to victims of hate crimes?

6. **Human Relations Commission:** What is the role of the human relations commission (HRC), if one exists in your area?
   a. Does it have a specific task force on hate crimes?
   b. Does it have any type of tracking system for recording statistics on hate crime?
   c. What is its relationship with local law enforcement agencies and district attorneys' offices regarding hate crime?

  d. What is its relationship with community organizations concerned with hate crimes? Has it produced any brochures, pamphlets, or other materials on hate crimes?

  e. Does it provide multicultural workshops or sensitivity training regarding different ethnic, racial, or lifestyle groups?

  f. Have there been occasions when the HRC has gone beyond the scope of its charter or stated goals that resulted in negative exposure or media attention? Describe the circumstances.

WEBSITE RESOURCES

Visit these websites for additional information about hate crimes and victim assistance:

American-Arab Anti-Discrimination Committee (ADC): http://www.adc.org

is a resource for information about civil rights efforts and includes useful summary data about cases and complaints regarding hate crimes and discrimination involving Arab Americans.

Anti-Defamation League (ADL): http://www.adl.org

This website is a resource for information on organized bigotry. The League collects and assesses a vast amount of information on anti-Semites, racists, and extremists. After carefully evaluating information, ADL disseminates that information through books, periodicals, reports, and other materials. The ADL pioneered the development of a model statute with enhanced penalties for bias-motivated crimes.

National Asian Pacific American Legal Consortium: http://www.napalc.org

The Consortium monitors and documents hate-motivated incidents, publishes an annual anti-Asian violence audit, represents victims of hate-motivated violence, advocates for the passage of strict hate crime laws, and educates the Asian Pacific American community, law enforcement, policy makers, and the general public about the problem of hate-motivated violence.

The National Association for the Advancement of Colored People (NAACP): http://www.naacp.org

The NAACP is the oldest and largest civil rights organization in the United States. Its principal objective is to ensure the political, educational, social, and economic equality of minority group citizens in the United States.

The National Conference for Community and Justice (NCCJ): http://www.nccj.org

This organization, founded in 1927 as The National Conference of Christians and Jews, is a human relations organization dedicated to fighting bias, bigotry, and racism in America. NCCJ promotes understanding and respect among all races, religions, and cultures through advocacy, conflict resolution, and education.

The National Organization for Women (NOW): http://www.now.org

NOW is the largest feminist organization in the United States, with over 500,000 contributing members. Since NOW was founded in 1966, it has struggled to end the injustice and inequality women face daily.

The National Council of La Raza (NCLR): http://www.nclr.org

NCLR is a private, nonprofit, nonpartisan, tax-exempt organization established in 1968 to reduce poverty and discrimination, and to improve life opportunities for Hispanic Americans. NCLR is the largest constituency-based national Hispanic organization, serving all Hispanic nationality groups in all regions of the country.

The Southern Poverty Law Center (SPLC): http://www.splcenter.org

The SPLC combats hate, intolerance, and discrimination through education and litigation. It tracks the activities of hate groups in the United States.

REFERENCES

"ADL Reports Resurgence of Racist Skinheads in U.S. and Launches New Online Racist Skinhead Project." (2006, February 7). Anti-Defamation League. New York, N.Y.

Berkowitz, Howard. (1999, September 14). Hate on the Internet, Congressional Testimony.

Bureau of Justice Statistics – Special Report. (2005, November). "Hate Crime Statistics, 2004" U.S. Department of Justice, Office of Justice Programs, Washington D.C.

Center for Democratic Renewal. (1992). *When Hate Groups Come to Town: A Handbook of Effective Community Responses.* Atlanta, Ga: Author.

DeGeneste, Henry I., and Sullivan, John P. (1997, July). "Policing a Multicultural Community." *Fresh Perspectives.*

Parker, Patricia A. (1991, December). "Tackling Unfinished Business: POP Plays Valuable Position in Racial Issues." *Police, 19,* pp. 5–9.

"Report says race factors into most hate crimes." (2005, November 15). *Contra Costa Times,* p. A15.

"Riots break out in Ohio after white supremacists' march." (2005, October 16). *Contra Costa Times,* p. A16

Ross, Loretta. (1995). "White Supremacy in the 1990s." *Public Eye,* pp. 1–12.

Southern Poverty Law Center. (2003, Summer). "In Sheep's Clothing," *Intelligence Report,* Issue 110, pp. 20–24.

SPLC Report. (2003, March). "Maine town's diversity rally outdraws hate-group gathering." Vol. 33, No. 1, p. 8.

SPLC Report. (2006, March). Volume 36, Number 1, p. 1.

Stephens, Darrel W. (2006). Chief of Police, Charlotte-Mecklenburg Police Department, Charlotte, North Carolina. Personal communication.

"World Church of the Creator - America's most dangerous supremacist group." (1992, September 21). Southern Poverty Law Center Newsletter, pp. 42–44.

Chapter 14

Racial Profiling

OVERVIEW

This chapter addresses the topic of racial profiling, a current, central, and controversial area of law enforcement. It provides the core knowledge important to students and professionals within the criminal justice system, including a conceptual definition of racial profiling, profiles, and profiling. The chapter also presents historical and background information on the effects of racial profiling on minorities as well as on various other ethnic, cultural, and religious groups as a consequence of the current war on terrorism. The chapter contains a discussion on and examples of manifestations of racial profiling and associated elements such as bias-based policing. There is, additionally, an examination of diverse points of view and perceptions of racial profiling and its impact upon minority communities, citizens, and law enforcement agencies along with statistical data from research on the issues. The chapter includes a section comparing profiling as a legitimate tool of law enforcement with racial profiling as a bias-based aberration of the tool. These conceptualizations of profiling are defined and presented with field examples and illustrations from several different law enforcement agencies. The chapter includes suggestions for preventing racial profiling in law enforcement.

COMMENTARY

Actual or perceived racial profiling by law enforcement officers affects blacks, Hispanics, Arab Americans, and other minority groups from every walk of life, every vocation, and every level of the socioeconomic ladder. The extent to which race, ethnicity, and/or national origin can be used as factors in targeting suspects for stops, searches, and arrests has been a concern of citizens and law enforcement for some time. The controversy over racial profiling is compounded by the unsupported assumption that the officer making traffic and field-interrogation stops of nonwhite citizens is making a race-based decision rooted in racial prejudice. These concerns became even more critical since the "War on Terrorism" began on September 11, 2001. Consider these excerpts from the media and how their content impacts law enforcement in general:

Bush issues ban on racial profiling by federal authorities

President Bush issued the first broad ban on racial profiling by federal law enforcement agencies but included exceptions permitting use of race and ethnicity to combat potential terrorist attacks. The new policy covers about 120,000 officers at 70 federal agencies with law enforcement powers. It prohibits the use of "generalized stereotypes" based on race or ethnicity, and allows officers to consider them only as part of a specific description or tip from a reliable source. ("Bush Bans Racial Profiling," 2003, p. A14)

ACLU of New Jersey wins $775,000 for Victims of Racial Profiling by State Troopers

Newark, N.J. The State of New Jersey has agreed to pay more than $775,000 to motorists who were victims of racial profiling to settle lawsuits brought by the American Civil Liberties Union of New Jersey. ("Racial Profiling," January 13, 2003)

Racial-profiling class-action suit is settled by California Highway Patrol

The California Highway Patrol settled a racial-profiling lawsuit yesterday by agreeing to extend a ban of some car searches and require officers to specify the reason for each drug-related traffic stop beyond just a hunch about wrongdoing. The settlement, filed in federal court, also requires the highway patrol to track all stops and constantly review that database to spot whether any officer is pulling over a disproportionate number of black or Hispanic motorists. The highway patrol also must pay $875,000 in legal fees and damages. (Contra Costa Times, 2003, p. A4)

Black and Hispanic drivers in large cities in [Illinois] are pulled over by police at a rate that far exceeds their share of the local population, according to an analysis of data from more than 2 million traffic stops last year. Springfield had the biggest gap: 42 percent of its traffic stops involved minorities even though its population is only 16 percent minority. It was followed by cities such as Peoria, Rockford, and Joliet. An Associated Press analysis of the traffic study also found that after being pulled over, minorities were more likely to be ticketed than white drivers. And minority drivers were more likely to have their cars searched and to be found with drugs and weapons, the numbers show. (Associated Press, 2005)

U.S. Border Patrol agents have arrested more than 150 suspected illegal immigrants during a major sweep in Riverside and San Bernardino counties . . . The sweeps came after a change in policy at the Border Patrol . . . similar "interior check points" and related activities have occurred in parts of Texas and elsewhere in the Southwest . . . In August, Border patrol officials rescinded a 4-year-old policy prohibiting agents from pursuing or arresting suspected illegal immigrants except near the border and at highway checkpoints. Federal agents said they were relying on intelligence to identify places with suspected illegal immigrants, stopping people as they stepped off buses and walked along the streets. Agents are questioning and arresting people based on their nationality only, said Tomas Jimenez, senior patrol agent in San Diego. . . . Abel Medina, director of Hermanidad Mexicana Nacional in Ontario, accused Border Patrol agents of racial profiling, which he said is improper and discriminatory. "It's one thing to arrest people; it's another thing when they are targeting by race," Medina said. "This is harassment and totally aggressive. And who are they stopping? They're stopping Latino people, people with brown skin, that's who." (*Los Angeles Times,* 2004, p. A18)

DEFINITIONS

Since the issues of biased policing came to the attention of the public and to law enforcement in the 1990s, racial profiling has been discussed and defined in hundreds of articles and publications. However, no single definition dominated the national conversation about this issue. The debate troubled not only those involved in the criminal justice system, but also concerned citizens and communities, scholars, researchers, civil rights organizations, and legislators. With no agreed-upon criteria for what does or does not constitute racial profiling, it was difficult to clarify, address, and develop approaches to prevent the practice. Variation among definitions means interested parties are often talking at cross-purposes, unwittingly discussing different types of police practices, behavior, and stops. For this reason, proposals to prohibit racial profiling were difficult to develop and carry out. Eventually, the U.S. government, federal and state legislatures, law enforcement organizations, and community advocacy institutions addressed the problem of definition and reached some agreement, This textbook utilizes the following definitions.

Racial Profiling

The authors will use the definition developed by the U.S. Department of Justice and the National Organization of Black Law Enforcement Executives (NOBLE). According to these organizations, racial profiling is any police-initiated action that relies on the race, ethnicity, or national origin rather than the behavior of an individual or on information that leads the police to a particular individual who has been identified as being, or having been, engaged in criminal activity. Racial profiling, also known as Driving While Black or Brown (DWB), has been ruled illegal by the courts and is considered improper police practice by law enforcement officers and agencies.

Profile: Formal and Informal

A formal profile is typically a document that contains explicit criteria or indicators that is issued to officers to guide them in their decision-making. It is usually based on data collected and interpreted to signify a trend or suggest that, given a particular set of characteristics (behavioral or situational commonalties), a person could believe that something may result based on that particular cluster of characteristics. A profile relies upon expert advice provided to law enforcement agencies to identify perpetrators of criminal activities. It can be an outline or short biographical description, an individual's character sketch, or a type of behavior associated with a group. It is a summary of data presenting the average or typical appearance of those persons or situations under scrutiny. Officers use these indicators of behavioral or situational commonalties to develop reasonable suspicion or probable cause to stop subjects. An informal profile represents the "street sense," personal experiences, and strongly held beliefs of the officers who use them (Harris, 2002). Informal profiles are more common in law enforcement than formal.

Profiling

Any police-initiated action that uses a compilation of the background, physical, behavioral, and/or motivational characteristics for a type of perpetrator who leads the police to a particular individual who has been identified as being, could be, or having been engaged in criminal activity.

Racially Biased Policing

Racially biased policing occurs when law enforcement inappropriately considers race or ethnicity in deciding with whom and how to intervene in an enforcement capacity (PERF Report, 2001). Racially biased policing is illegal. The authors will use the term *racial profiling* throughout this chapter instead of racially biased policing because it is a more commonly recognized term, although "racially biased policing" is a much better description of the phenomenon.

Bias-Based Policing

The act (intentional or unintentional) of applying or incorporating personal, societal, or organizational biases and/or stereotypes in decision making, police actions, or the administration of justice.

Race, Ethnicity, and Minority

Race, ethnicity, and minority refer to individuals of a particular descent, including Caucasian, African, Hispanic, Asian/Pacific, or Native American. In the text, the term *black* is used to describe all individuals with black skin, regardless of their national origin or ethnicity and includes African Americans. The term *Hispanic* is used to describe an individual's ethnicity. The use of the terms *minority* or *minorities* within the text are used to describe groups of individuals who represent a numeric minority within a racial or ethnic population.

Reasonable Suspicion

A police officer may briefly detain a person for questioning or request identification only if the officer has a reasonable suspicion that the person's behavior is related to criminal activity. The officer, however, must have specific facts that must be articulated to support his or her actions; a mere suspicion or "hunch" is not sufficient cause to detain a person or to request identification. Reasonable suspicion can be based on the observations of a police officer combined with his or her training and experience, and/or reliable information received from credible outside sources.

Suspect-Specific Incident

An incident in which an officer is lawfully attempting to detain, apprehend, or otherwise be on the lookout for one or more specific suspects who have been identified or described in part by national or ethnic origin, gender, or race.

HISTORICAL BACKGROUND OF THE TERM *RACIAL PROFILING* IN LAW ENFORCEMENT

During the 1990s, concerns about police use of racial profiling as a pretext to stop, question, search, and possibly arrest people became a major focus of minority individuals and communities, politicians, law enforcement administrators, scholars, and researchers. National surveys in the last decade revealed that the majority of Americans, white as well as black, believed racial profiling was commonly used in the United States, but 80 percent of those surveyed opposed the practice. They believed that police were routinely guilty of bias in their treatment of racial and ethnic minorities, and also that such behavior had been going on for a long time.

What is the source of racial profiling as both a term and as a law enforcement practice? Before addressing that question, it is useful to examine how people use prior events or information to make decisions in everyday life.

People routinely form mental images or tentative judgments about others and the surrounding circumstances or situation, both consciously and subconsciously, which is also a form of stereotyping. This sort of stereotyping, or looking for what one perceives to be indicators, provides a preliminary mental rating of potential risk to a person encountering a particular event or person.

It involves conscious and unconscious thought processes whereby an individual: (1) makes observations and selects data born out of that person's past experiences, (2) adds cultural and personal meaning to what he or she observes, (3) makes assumptions based on the meanings that he or she has attributed to the observation, (4) draws conclusions based on his or her own beliefs and, finally, (5) takes action (see Senge's "Ladder of Inference" discussed later in this chapter). This process comprises basic decision making in their lives by all people and it guides a person's interpretation of events. A person's socialization, including the person's upbringing by his or her parents, plays a major role in determining decisions and the actions taken as a result of these decisions in both professional and personal settings.

Profiling in law enforcement is used by officers to look for characteristics that indicate the probability of criminal acts or factors that tend to correlate with dangerous or threatening behavior. For officers, most of these characteristics have been internalized based on experience and training. If they have had dangerous encounters while on duty, these experiences prepare them for future, similar events—as the old saying goes, *better safe than sorry!* The professional training that leads to the development of indicators or common characteristics comes from many sources, beginning with the police academy and in-service training under the supervision of a field-training officer. Informal education may include mentoring by an older partner and pressure from peers on how to do the job, and more formal training continues via advanced officer courses on various subjects. All of these help establish the common practice of profiling. If an official profile of a suspect is used by an agency, and the perpetrator is caught, we say, "He or she fits the profile," thus validating this perspective. When serial bombing suspect Eric Robert Rudolph was finally apprehended in June 2003, for example, FBI profiling experts immediately confirmed that the notorious fugitive did indeed *fit their profile.* Training and experience provide officers with indicators to look for not only to prevent harm to themselves, but also to identify those people or events that are suspicious and warrant closer attention. This attention then helps civilians and police officers decide what action is prudent to take when confronted by a similar person or situation. This doesn't necessarily mean the person using profiling in this way is biased or prejudiced. Fulbright professor Ira Straus, in an article for United Press International, suggests that some degree of profiling can be appropriate and even necessary as long as it is not abusive. In the article, he is not using the term profiling to mean the same as the definition used in this textbook, but using "profiling" to mean stereotyping.

> Profiling is universal. Every person relies on it for a preliminary rating of their risks with each person they run into. If people do not profile explicitly, they do it implicitly. If they do not do it consciously, they do it unconsciously. But they go on doing it. They could not live without it.
>
> Do police do it too? Of course they do. All police and investigative efforts involve working from two ends, direct and indirect. The direct end means following the trail of specific leads and informants. The indirect end means profiling; that is, finding a social milieu or pool to look in and ask around in—a milieu where there are more likely to be informants, leads, and criminals answering to that crime.
>
> To profile is morally risky. The dangers of unfair and unreasonable profiling—that is, profiling based on unfounded prejudices such as racism—are well known. They are widely discussed, guarded against, and proscribed. (Straus, 2002, pp. 1–2)

Professor Straus implies that profiling (or in his context, stereotyping) is not always based on accurate information or data. When the meanings placed on observations are faulty or biased, the assumptions and conclusions, therefore, may be incorrect, thereby leading to inappropriate attitudes, behavior, and actions.

Law enforcement officers, airport security personnel, customs and border patrol agents, and members of some other occupations use profiles because, in the absence of conclusive, specific details, it is the only way to narrow the amount of information from which to make decisions, including whether or not to stop a person for further investigation.

Although there are other historical examples of racial profiling, the first use of the term appears to have occurred in New Jersey, where troopers were trying to stem the flow of illegal drugs and other contraband into and across their state. In the early 1990s, the Drug Enforcement Administration (DEA) and the New Jersey State Patrol (NJSP) developed a relationship. The DEA provided training to the NJSP on what it had determined to be common characteristics of drug couriers along Interstate 95 from Miami through New Jersey. The characteristics included the types of cars preferred (Nissan Pathfinders), the direction of travel, and the use of rental vehicles from another state. In addition, it was common to find that a third party had rented the vehicle, that the driver was licensed in a different state than the one where the rental took place, and that there were telltale behavioral cues (such as nervousness or conflicting stories). The profile also noted that the national origin of many of those involved in drug-trafficking organizations was predominantly Jamaican.

The NJSP used "pretextual stops" (that is, using some legal pretext, such as failing to signal a lane change or having a missing license plate or faulty brake light) on I-95 to determine the potential criminality of a car's driver and occupants. The officer(s) would then attempt to establish a legal basis to search for illegal drugs. Many argued, and the courts agreed, that these pretextual stops were also based on the fact that the cars' drivers and occupants were black or dark-skinned. In other words, they had been racially profiled—targeted because of the color of their skin. The resultant studies determined that blacks and Hispanics on I-95 were stopped with a frequency disproportionate to their numbers on that road. Due to the controversy, and the subsequent court decision and punitive judgment against the NJSP, they no longer distribute a typical felony offender profile to their officers "because such profiles might contribute to what the state's attorney general calls 'inappropriate stereotypes' about criminals" (Will, 2001). New Jersey, like other states, has also created legislation making racial profiling illegal, with criminal sanctions for officers using the practice.

PROFILING CHALLENGES IN THE WAR ON TERRORISM

Prior to September 11, 2001, the use by law enforcement agencies of profiles that included race, ethnicity, or national origin, or the act of profiling using the same criteria, had come to be generally frowned upon, or even condemned, in the United States. But an attitude change occurred after the horrendous attacks on the World Trade Center in New York City and the Pentagon. One outcome of that event was the establishment of the U.S. DHS and the attempt to coordinate law enforcement agencies and the military in defense of the nation's citizenry and infrastructure. The scope of the state of emergency created by the hijackers altered both public opinion and government policy concerning profiles and profiling based on national origin and ethnicity, especially regarding both the legitimacy and necessity of the practices. Given the ongoing and complex conflicts in the Middle East, plus the global terrorist threat from al-Qaida and other Islamic extremists, the issue became more charged and complicated. Police at the national and local level had to develop strategies for detecting and apprehending terrorists. Tentative profiles were quickly developed on the basis of obvious characteristics and experience.

Since all the terrorists involved in the September 11 incidents were Islamic males from the Middle East, the issue became whether law enforcement and security personnel could target or profile suspicious men with similar backgrounds for stops, searches, or increased questioning. Profiling, using those criteria, began to be employed on the basis of several factors common to these particular terrorists, who were:

- young males who were Arab in appearance;
- primarily citizens of Saudi Arabia;
- trained in fundamentalist religious and/or al-Qaida training camps in Afghanistan or Pakistan;
- adherents of Islam who had been inspired to religious extremism by fundamentalist clergy, especially with regard to *jihad* (see Glossary); and
- harboring a deep hatred, in general, of Western decadence, materialism, and immorality, which they perceived as undermining the values and stability of their societies, and, in particular, of America for its interference in Middle Eastern affairs.

In the aftermath of September 11 and the emergency federal legislation enacted in response to it, there were mass round-ups of individuals of Middle Eastern origin and descent in the United States and abroad based on profiles. In many cases, the rights of those apprehended may have been violated. Instances of persons of Middle Eastern or South Asian descent (or who appeared to be Arab or Muslim) removed from planes and subjected to detention, questioning, and search have been reported where there was no reasonable suspicion or probable cause that they might have harbored criminal intentions. ("ADC Fact Sheet," 2002) This subject is covered in more detail in Chapter 8, Law Enforcement Contact with Arab Americans.

Initially, there was little outcry among the general public against these actions and others. Recall that prior to September 11, 80 percent of Americans opposed racial profiling. After that day, however, "there [was] an immediate reversal of public opinion," says Michelle Alexander of the American Civil Liberties Union (ACLU) of Northern California. Polls taken soon after the attack showed 70 percent of Americans believed that some form of profiling was necessary, and acceptable, to ensure public safety. It is apparent that the public was willing to give up certain freedoms in exchange for helping the government reduce the opportunity for terrorists to operate in the United States. Members of the American Association for Public Opinion Research, at a May 2002 meeting, offered a historical perspective. They said that while civil liberties usually have broad public support, the public has been willing to tolerate substantial limits on those freedoms when there are serious threats to security and safety within the United States and to Americans abroad. Their report cited the decline in support for civil liberties after Pearl Harbor and again at the height of the Cold War. Other than the ACLU and the National Association of Arab Americans, there were few who spoke out against detentions of Middle Easterners and South Asians at security areas in airports and elsewhere after September 11. These organizations questioned the use of what appeared to them to be racial profiling and abuse of civil rights, generally and specifically. However, many citizens argued that proactive law enforcement and enhanced security measures at airports were necessary to prevent or reduce opportunities for terrorist acts and to investigate and bring to justice those involved. Discovering terrorists and their missions, prior to another attack, became a matter of urgency.

The researchers added, however, that support for civil liberties has always resumed when the threat subsides. This certainly was the case as time passed after September 11 without additional terrorist acts in the United States. Between 2001 and 2003, membership in the ACLU *increased* 15 percent (2003, p. A23). The increase suggests that despite the war on terrorism and the potential for terrorist acts, many Americans remain troubled by the potential for federal government overreaching that is embodied in such antiterrorism measures as the Patriot Act (increasing the FBI's wiretapping and search powers), which expands the powers of the criminal justice system.

The use of profiles and profiling in law enforcement requires a balancing of morality, legality, efficiency, equality, liberty, and security concerns. It has the potential to affect millions of innocent people in the United States who are or may appear to be of Muslim, Arab, Middle Eastern, or South Asian descent, or Sikh. It is important that law enforcement officials and security agents avoid hasty judgments and not condemn all Muslims, those of the Islamic faith, or Middle Easterners for the crimes of a few. Officers, agents, and those who protect airports and other public facilities should seek to learn more about both Islam and Arab civilization (see Chapter 8).

Reality Check

How does law enforcement balance the need to reduce crime, and especially terrorism, against the potential for accusations of discrimination, race biased policing, and stereotyping? It is a challenging and complex problem for officers, especially for those strongly committed to nonbiased practices who believe in proactive policing. The real issues with any type of law enforcement profiling or the development of profiles are: (1) Who is doing the profile construction and on what basis? Does that person have some expertise (for example, in behavioral science)? Is the profile creator objective, unbiased, and nonjudgmental in formulating a particular profile? (2) Who is interpreting the profile? Is that person sufficiently trained in its application? (3) Is the officer who is using profiling doing so legally? Is it based on departmental policy rather than his or her acting on personal biases, attitudes, and beliefs?

Criminal justice agencies are facing major challenges regarding the issue and impact of the use of profiles and profiling, especially after September 11. Law enforcement personnel are charged with (1) protecting the rights of those who are the subject of stereotyping, harassment, and discrimination (i.e., those who are *misidentified* as a result of profiles or profiling); (2) identifying and bringing to justice those who are terrorists and criminals (i.e., those who are *correctly identified*); (3) not missing terrorists and/or criminals who do not fit a particular profile or stereotype; and (4) not being so hampered by their personal stereotypes, attitudes, beliefs, perceptions, and knowledge (or lack thereof) that innocent people are detained and terrorists are not apprehended in the course of law enforcement.

POLICE AND CITIZEN PERCEPTIONS OF RACIAL PROFILING

Myth, Misperception, or Reality?

There are some police officers, government administrators, and others who maintain that racial profiling is a myth or a misperception. They argue that the majority of officers do not stop or detain people based on their race, ethnicity, or national origin, but on their behavior, location, circumstances, and other factors. Officers contend that those who are stopped often do not understand police procedures, or are overly sensitive, or are using the allegation that bias was involved in their stop, questioning, search, and/or arrest to cast aspersion on the action taken in an attempt to nullify it.

Although these observers claim that racial profiling doesn't exist, an abundance of anecdotes and statistics document that it does. As mentioned, national surveys have indicated that the majority of white, as well as black, Americans believe that racial profiling is widespread across the nation. The complaints about racial profiling now extend to Arab and Middle Eastern people or those who appear to be from that region of the world. Research completed in 2005, seems to document, using statistical analysis, that nonwhite citizens are still being stopped disproportionately to their numbers, even after public, media, and minority advocate organizations in the late 1990s and early 2000s decried the appearance of racial profiling. While acknowledging that a disparity exists, experts explain that decisions as to the cause of the disparity cannot be appropriately made from the data available in most cases.

Researchers studying allegations of racial profiling must also explore discretionary decision-making of individual officers, a subject that has long been the object of study by those doing research in the criminal justice field.

Most of the research on criminal justice has documented that the impact of racial prejudice on criminal justice agents' decision-making has been decreasing in prevalence and importance for at least 30 years. Prior to the 1970s, racial prejudice was still the basis for many state and local laws. Since that time, police departments have made continuing serious managerial efforts to reduce and eliminate prejudicial behavior by police officers, and recent research is no longer consistent with earlier research on the extent to which race per se directly influences police decisions. This recent research suggests that police officers' behavior is predicted primarily by legal and situation-specific factors and that the influence of race and other extra-legal factors is diminishing. (Engel, 2002, pp. 251–252)

Police Perceptions

What are the police officers' perceptions of allegations that all race-based decision-making by them is motivated by their own prejudice?

Most law enforcement officers would maintain they are not biased, prejudiced, or using racial profiling in their policing methods. Proactive policing sometimes involves using legitimate profiling based on officer experience and training or using profiles provided by their agency. Sometimes, however, officer experience can mean a lot of things. If the experience leads to faulty assumptions and conclusions, then the officer might engage in inappropriate behavior and take the wrong action. (See the "Education and Training" section of this chapter for a discussion of the sources of officers' beliefs and attitudes.)

Officers use profiling (behavioral commonalities or indicators) or written profiles to identify those whom they should investigate to determine if they are committing or about to commit a crime. Profiling is done on a daily basis by police officers, not just in high crime areas where gangs congregate or highway corridors where drug runners operate, but in all communities. It also takes place in predominantly white communities when officers see out-of-place or suspicious-looking members of minority groups. The officer in this situation would argue that he or she would find reason to check out anyone, regardless of color, who did not seem to fit the area or time of day, especially if he or she were acting suspiciously. Profiling also takes place when an officer sees a white person in a predominantly minority area, especially if the area is one in which drug sales or prostitution take place. The officer checks out the individual if reasonable suspicion is present that a crime might be taking place. Most officers would emphatically deny they are biased or prejudiced when using such profiling.

Officers also insist that both their agency and the community in which they work pressure them to reduce crime in the neighborhoods, and that profiling (not racial profiling) is a tool to accomplish a reduction in some crimes. If officers believe that their agency supervisors and managers want them to be aggressive on the streets by stopping vehicles and pedestrians to determine if there is potential criminal activity leading to a search and arrest, officers will do so, especially if this behavior is rewarded within their organization. Reward structures within agencies include such things as favorable evaluations, shifts, and assignments, and even promotions. Unfortunately, if officers come to believe that minority citizens are more likely to be involved in criminal activity of some sort and that aggressively stopping their vehicles will result in more searches and arrests, they are more likely to stop them (referred to as the expectancy theory), especially if the department encourages and rewards the practice.

Sometimes, however, departments targeting criminal activity can cause a backlash. Take, for example, the Oakland, California, "Riders" case. During a 3-week period ending July 3, 2000, four officers of the Oakland Police Department were accused of beating and framing suspects by planting drugs and writing false police reports. The officers' attorneys used the defense that top Oakland police brass promoted the practice of "attacking" suspects and having a "hostile" relationship with suspected drug dealers because of one program implemented by the department—Project SANE (Strategic Application of Narcotics Enforcement). The program involved redirecting about 57 officers, particularly during overnight hours, to target drug dealing. In his courtroom testimony, Police Chief Richard Word defended his department's aggressive policing policy and maintained that the effort to target street-level drug dealing did not cause the behavior of the officers who became known as The Riders. He added that officers should know the difference between proactive police work and violating civil rights and that the Riders had exceeded directives. Reducing crime in Oakland had become Word's top priority soon after he was promoted to chief. He, along with the city's mayor and manager, set a goal of a 20 percent reduction in crime. The officers were cleared in eight police misconduct counts and a mistrial was declared September 30, 2003, on 27 more charges. They had denied all charges but, according to one defense attorney, "they acknowledge they were aggressive on the job and say their behavior was rewarded. They were told push the line, stretch the law, but don't break it . . . [A] lot of stops were questionable, but these guys were told to push it" ("Oakland's Police Chief Angry," 2003, p. A5). There was a civil settlement of $10.9 million with the 119 plaintiffs, and the City of Oakland had to pay $3.6 million to contract with an independent monitoring agency that will oversee police reforms over a 5-year period ("Oakland to Analyze," 2003, p. A4). The three Oakland officers were retried and the attorneys for two of the three fired told the jury that "their clients were being prosecuted and vilified for merely doing their jobs. . . . The former officers, known as the Riders, had been made the scapegoats for a failed police department strategy of aggressive, drug-focused law enforcement" ("Riders' Followed Department Line, (2005), p. A5). In June of 2005, after two lengthy trials with no convictions and consistent jury deadlock, the Alameda County District Attorney moved to dismiss the criminal charges against two of the former Oakland police officers.

As indicated, some police officers and city or county administrators deny the existence of racial profiling. They claim that those who believe that they are the victims of racial profiling may not be aware of other factors that the officer may have considered. Traffic stops are the most common situations leading to complaints of racial profiling. A 2002 nationwide survey regarding police contact with the public by the U.S. Bureau of Criminal Justice Statistics determined that speeding was the most common reason for being pulled over, accounting for 54.8 percent of all traffic stops. The majority of drivers stopped by police (83.7 percent) felt they had been stopped for legitimate reasons ("Characteristics of Drivers, 2002," 2006).

The PERF undertook an extensive study of racial profiling. They chose to avoid the term *racial profiling,* preferring *racially biased policing.* They indicate in the report that racial profiling was defined so restrictively that the term does not fully capture the concerns of both police and citizens. For example:

> Racial profiling is frequently defined as law enforcement activities (e.g., detentions, arrests, searches) that are initiated *solely* on the basis of race. Central to the debate on the most frequently used definitions is the word "solely." In the realm of potential discriminatory actions, this definition likely references only a very small portion. Even a racially prejudiced officer likely uses more than the single factor of race when conducting biased law enforcement. For example, officers might make decisions based on the neighborhood and the race of the person, the age of the car and the race of the person, or the gender and the race of the person. Activities based on these sample pairs of factors would fall outside the most commonly used definition of racial profiling. ("Racially Biased Policing," 2001, p. 3)

Using this common definition of racial profiling, then, provides a very narrow meaning for the term. "Those who define the practice so narrowly (i.e., race as the only reason for stopping, questioning or arresting someone) that we can imagine only the most extreme bigots engaging in it. Using such a definition, racial profiling is easy to both denounce and deny" (Barlow & Barlow, 2002).

In the PERF study, staff conducted meetings around the country with citizens and police line and command staff regarding occurrences and perceptions of biased policing. (Note: PERF has produced a video and guide to facilitate police–citizen discussions on racially biased policing. To order free copies, see the "Website References" section of this chapter for their address. The subsequent report, *Racially Biased Policing: A Principled Response,* revealed that the police in the study were using the narrow definition of racial profiling (stops based *solely* on race or ethnicity) and thus could declare vehemently that police actions based solely on race, national origin, or ethnicity were quite rare. The citizens in the study, however, were using a broader definition, one that included race as one among several factors leading up to the stop of the individual.

> Many of our law enforcement participants did express skepticism that "racial profiling" was a major problem, exacerbating some citizens' frustration. It became clear to staff that these differing perceptions among citizens and police regarding racial profiling's pervasiveness were very much related to the respective definitions they had adopted. The citizens equated "racial profiling" with all manifestations of racially biased policing, whereas most of the police practitioners defined "racial profiling" as stopping a motorist based *solely* on race. Presumably, even officers who engage in racially biased policing rarely make a vehicle stop based *solely* on race (often ensuring probable cause or some other factor is also present). ("Racially Biased Policing," 2001, p. 15)

Other factors in police stops. Those concerned about racial profiling must also recognize that when a stop or detention by officers is not self-initiated, it was most likely to have been generated because a witness or victim had provided a description of a person or event that they felt required police action—a suspect-specific incident or one due to computer-generated information. This is the case in the majority of contacts police make with citizens. If the complainant describes a suspect of a certain race, ethnicity, or national origin, that is what the officer will search for. For example, if police receive a report of possible criminal activity, and reliable information indicates that he is 5 foot 8 inches, lean, long-haired, and Asian, then "Asian" may be considered, along with the other demographics, in developing reasonable suspicion or probable cause to detain. If, however, the citizen is reporting the activity of a minority because of his or her own biases, the police should attempt to ensure the legitimacy of the complaint and not be an agent of what might be racially charged paranoia. In Brooksfield, Wisconsin, dispatchers were trained to gather more information from callers to determine if the call is legitimate. If not, they then can explain this fact to the caller and not trigger a potentially volatile police–citizen encounter.

Some allegations of racially motivated stops are clearly not reasonable. In some cases, officers cannot discern the race or ethnicity of the driver and/or occupant(s) prior to the stop. For example, some cars have tinted or darkened windows or a head rest on the back of the seats. When officers use radar, it is another example of an electronic device determining which vehicle to stop and not the race, ethnicity, or national origin of the driver. Obviously at nighttime, it is challenging to identify drivers or passengers in detail. (Readers of this textbook should try to identify the occupants of a vehicle in front of them to test this argument.)

Policing during the 1990s and into the present day has been driven by two forces: (1) data developed and analyzed by specialists (crime analysts) that provides officers with predictions on where crimes might occur (including time of day and even generalized suspect information), and (2) POP or COP approaches, wherein neighborhood representatives tell officers about problems, including potential suspects, in their communities. In the latter case, members of the community demand that officers take enforcement action against drug dealers, prostitutes, gang members, those disturbing the peace, and suspicious persons regardless of their race or ethnicity. Take, for example, the following case study:

MINI CASE STUDY: CULTURE AND CRIME

Arlington County, Virginia

Ed Flynn, chief of police for Virginia's Arlington County, responded to the demands of his city's black community for stricter drug enforcement. "We had a series of community meetings. The residents said to us, 'Years ago, you had control over the problem. Now the kids are starting to act out again.' They even asked us, 'Where are your jump-out squads [officers who observe drug deals from their cars, then jump out and nab the participants]?'" So Flynn and his local commander put together an energetic strategy to break up the drug trade. They instituted aggressive motor-vehicle checks throughout the problem neighborhood, stopping and questioning those who were driving too fast or who had cracked windshields, too-dark windows, or expired tags. "We wanted to increase our presence in the area and make it quite unpleasant for the dealers to operate," Flynn says. The Arlington officers also cracked down on quality-of-life offenses like public urination, and used undercover surveillance to take out the dealers.

By the end of the summer, the department had cleaned up the crime hot spots. Community newsletters thanked the cops for breaking up the dealing. Chief Flynn observed, however, "We had also just generated a lot of data showing 'disproportionate' minority arrests. We are responding to heartfelt demands for increased police presence," he says. "But this places police department's in the position of producing data at the community's behest that can be used against them" (MacDonald, 2001).

The above facts in mind, should the police continue aggressive crime suppression activities in known high crime areas? The strategy often results in an overrepresentation of minorities in police stops—are the risks worth it? In what ways could the police improve and maintain good relations with such a community?

Another example of urban policing using race-neutral, data-driven methods is New York's innovative COMPSTAT (Computerized Statistics) program. COMPSTAT involves computer-generated crime analysis that allows police commanders to focus enforcement strategies on specific crimes and problem areas in the city. Officers are held accountable for reducing the specific crime in that area. If robberies are up in a certain precinct, officers are deployed to locate and arrest those responsible. If the neighborhood they are assigned to is a minority part of the city, those contacted will likely be members of minority groups. Race is irrelevant to this sort of policing. When Russian immigrants in New York dominated the Ecstasy trade, law enforcement efforts targeted (profiled) them, and ultimately their illegal activities were reduced. Arrests are most often the result of criminal intelligence, computer-generated data, and good police work, not racism.

There are some who argue that the use of racial profiling is justified and should be legal because the demographics of crime demonstrate a relationship between the numbers of blacks and Hispanics stopped, searched and arrested, and incarcerated and the numbers of crimes committed—that is, members of those minority groups do commit more crime than whites or Asians (MacDonald, 2001). Others argue this sort of rationalization perpetuates the problem through a vicious cycle. Studies have been used to both prove and disprove this hypothesis. It is open to question whether officers stop minorities because they believe this hypothesis, because they are biased, or both.

Victim and Civil Rights Advocates' Perceptions

The claims and counterclaims about the existence and prevalence of racial profiling have been made for years, and they should not be dismissed as misperceptions or misunderstandings. We have to regard them as indicators of a very real social phenomenon. There have been a few attempts to reliably estimate the degree to which blacks, Latinos, Arabs, and Asians have been victims of the practice.

There have been numerous studies over the years that have attempted to prove or disprove that minorities are stopped disproportionately to non-minorities. (See "Website Resources" in this chapter.) One such national study by Richard Lundman and Robert Kaufman, professors of sociology at Ohio State University, found that black men are 35 percent more likely than white men to report being stopped by police for a traffic violation. The researchers analyzed data from the National Crime Victimization

Study conducted by the U.S. Department of Justice in 1999. The study indicated that "African Americans who are stopped for traffic violations are less likely than whites to believe the police had a legitimate reason to stop them, and more likely to believe they were mistreated" (Lundman & Kaufman, 2003).

Other studies, past and present, have discovered almost parallel findings: that minorities allege that they are singled out by the police, stopped more frequently, and detained for longer periods of time than nonminorities (Tomaskovic-Devey, 2004). A Montgomery County, Maryland, traffic stop study showed that black drivers were stopped at a rate higher than their proportion of the county population or registered drivers ("Most Recent Traffic Stop Data," 2002, p. T3). Studies conducted by and reported in the *Boston Globe* had the same findings ("Boston to Track," 2003).

The *Boston Globe* studies included a three-part, investigative report series. The investigation involved an analysis of Massachusetts state records of traffic stops for speeding wherein clear disparities regarding race, gender, and age were documented. Police officers tended to give a ticket to some and a written warning to others. The *Globe*'s investigative analysis "found clear patterns in who gets a break and who does not when it comes to traffic enforcement":

- In cities and towns across the state [Massachusetts], Latino and black men were most likely to be ticketed. In Boston, for example, 42 percent of white women, 53 percent of white men, 58 percent of minority women, and 68 percent of minority men were ticketed when cited for speeding 15 m.p.h. over the limit in a 30 m.p.h. zone. Whites and women enjoyed an even larger advantage, on average, in suburbs and small towns.

- Older drivers are less likely to get ticketed—especially if they are white. The records show that, as drivers age, their chances of getting a warning increase. But this deference to age tends to be denied to blacks and other minorities.

- The racial and gender disparities persist no matter how egregious the speeding offense. For example, when local police cited drivers for going 25 m.p.h. over the speed limit, 89 percent of minority drivers were ticketed, versus 82 percent of whites ("Race, Sex, and Age," 2003, p. A1; "Troopers Fair," 2003, p. A1).

The report indicated, however, that disparities in tickets and warnings do not prove intentional bias or racial profiling by police.

Blacks are not the only Americans who say they have been the targets of racial or ethnic profiling by law enforcement. Hispanic men reported they were more likely than white men to question why they were stopped and how they were treated (Lundman & Kaufman, 2003). Also, just as DWB has been used by civil rights advocates to demonstrate racial profiling of African Americans or Hispanics, in recent years, "flying while Arab" has been used to describe the targeting of Arabs, South Asians, and Middle Easterners. The complaints of racial profiling are most often heard at airports and other places where there is a concern about the potential for terrorist attack. Civil rights advocates say that Arabs, South Asians, and Middle Easterners, most of them loyal American citizens, have become victims of the new war on terrorism. It is a difficult issue and one in which officers and security agents are damned if they do and damned if they don't. Minorities complain that they are not only more likely to be stopped than whites, but they are also often pressured to allow searches of their vehicles.

A special report published in 2006 by the Bureau of Justice Statistics (Characteristics of Drivers, 2002," 2006) regarding nationwide traffic stop data collected in 2002 contains the following highlights:

- In 2002, an estimated 8.7 percent of drivers age 16 or older were stopped by police, representing nearly 17 million of the 193 million drivers in the United States.
- Males were more likely than females to be pulled over by police, and young drivers more likely than their older counterparts to be stopped.
- White drivers were more likely than black and Hispanic drivers to be stopped by police for speeding. Subsequent to being stopped for speeding, blacks (78 percent) and Hispanics (85 percent) were more likely than whites (70 percent) to receive a ticket.
  - Whites were 76.2 percent of U.S. drivers and 76.5 percent of drivers stopped by police.
  - Blacks were 10.5 percent of persons who drive and 11 percent of stopped drivers.
  - Hispanics accounted for 9.7 percent of drivers and 9.5 percent of stopped drivers.
  - Drivers of other races were a smaller percentage of stopped motorists (2.9 percent) than of the driving population (3.6 percent).
- Among traffic stops of young male drivers in 2002, 11 percent were physically searched or had their vehicle searched by police. Among these young male drivers who were stopped, blacks (22 percent) and Hispanics (17 percent) were searched at higher rates than whites (8 percent).

The study includes the caveat: racial differences in traffic stops may not signal racial profiling.

To form evidence of racial profiling, survey findings would have to demonstrate (all other things being equal):

- Blacks and/or Hispanics were no more likely than whites to violate traffic laws, and
- Police pulled over blacks and or Hispanics at a higher rate than whites.

Because the survey has information only on how often persons of different races are stopped, not on how often they actually break traffic laws, analysis of data from the 2002 Police–Public Contact Survey has no basis for determining whether or to what extent racial profiling exists. ("Characteristics of Drivers, 2002," 2006, p. 2–3.)

There are many accounts by people who have been stopped by police on questionable grounds and subjected to disrespectful behavior, intrusive questioning, and disregard for their civil rights. In fact, a study by Amnesty International (AI) USA estimates there are 32 million victims of racial profiling and that 87 million individuals are at high risk of victimization during their lifetimes (AI, 2004). The study involved a series of nationwide hearings and public testimony from individuals alleging to be victims of racial profiling while driving, walking, shopping, traveling through airports and during other activities. These accounts lend credibility to the reality of the practice. Data collected by police departments to refute such claims often reveal that, without further analysis and interpretation, minority drivers are stopped in numbers out of proportion to their presence on the road.

The PERF report mentions the reactions of non-Hispanic white officers upon hearing their fellow officers, who are minority and within the study group, describing their own experiences:

> After a white officer in the group downplayed the scope of the problem, a minority officer would speak up and describe his or her personal experience with being pulled over by police. In several cases, it was clear to the facilitators that white officers were surprised by these stories. Their peers' experiences seemed to impact them in a way that the citizens' stories conveyed in press accounts did not. ("Racially Biased Policing," 2001, p. 15)

A study by professors David and Melissa Barlow surveyed African American police officers of the Milwaukee Police Department to determine if they felt they had been racially profiled at any time in their life, and if so, to what extent. The researchers wanted to discover the opinions of black officers on the legality of the circumstances under which they had been stopped by police. Because the subjects of the survey were themselves police officers, their views could not be easily dismissed.

> The personal experiences of people of color who have been victims of racial profiling are often rejected as being anecdotal, uninformed or overly sensitive. . . . [P]olice executives attempting to address the problem of racial profiling suggest that many incidents are simply problems of perception, because the public does not understand the intricacies, strategies and techniques of law enforcement. What appears to be racial profiling to the general public may be nothing of the sort. (Barlow & Barlow, 2002, p. 2)

The survey defined racial profiling as "when race is used by a police officer or a police agency in determining the potential criminality of an individual" (Barlow & Barlow, 2002, p. 14). Of the 2,100 sworn personnel of the Milwaukee Police Department, 414 were designated as black. The response rate to this survey was 38 percent (158 officers). Over 99 percent were over 25 years of age and had been sworn police officers for at least 1 year. The percentage of male respondents was 83.5 while the percentage of female respondents was 16.5.

Exhibit 14.1 shows that the majority of those who responded to the survey believed that they had been racially profiled. Note that the percentages drop off rapidly as the survey proceeded from questions about being stopped and questioned to questions about being arrested. The researchers suggest that the numbers fall off rapidly because the officers would have identified themselves as such upon being stopped and thus avoided further action. It should be noted that some of those surveyed reported that they were on duty but in plain clothes when they were stopped. From their findings, the Barlows conclude that black men are more likely to be the victims of racial profiling than black women by a ratio of three to one.

In their research, the Barlows also asked the sworn police officers of the Milwaukee Police Department whether they personally used racial profiling in the performance of their job. They found most (90 percent) of the respondents do not use racial

Question: In your professional opinion, do you believe you have ever been stopped, questioned, searched, ticketed, or arrested as a result of racial profiling?

	YES	NO
Stopped	69%	31%
Questioned	52%	60%
Searched	19%	81%
Ticketed	21%	79%
Arrested	7%	93%

Exhibit 14.1   Racial Profiling Survey.
(*Source:* Barlow & Barlow, 2002, p. 14.)

profiling nor believe it is a necessary or legitimate tool for law enforcement. The researchers concluded "Although many white Americans, members of law enforcement and government officials deny the existence of racial profiling or racially biased policing, the findings from the study suggest it is a reality" (Barlow & Barlow, 2002, p. 15).

The following mini-case studies involve descriptions of fictional events but are based upon similar, actual occurrences. The issues and implications of each should be discussed in class, especially the question of whether the police behavior is proper, justified, legal, or necessary.

MINI CASE STUDIES: CULTURE AND CRIME

You Decide—Racial Profiling?

A well-dressed young Hispanic male is driving through a predominantly white community early in the morning on his way to work in a new BMW. He is pulled over for speeding and the officer, instead of simply asking for a driver's license and writing a speeding ticket, calls for backup and is joined by another officer. The young man is told to leave his vehicle and the officers search it. "Hey, where did you get the money for something like this?," one officer asks mockingly as he starts the process of going through every inch of the BMW. One of the officers pulls off an inside door panel, and more dismantling of the vehicle follows. They say they are looking for drugs, but in the end find nothing. After ticketing the driver for speeding, the two officers casually drive off. Sitting in his now-trashed BMW, the young man smolders in his anger and humiliation.

1. Do you believe police officers do in fact pull over and search the vehicles of minorities disproportionately to their numbers?
2. Are there racial or ethnic characteristics on which officers can legitimately focus during an investigation or to prevent criminal activity?
3. Should profiling only include the actions, behavior, and activities of the person(s) observed by the officer?

4. How can law enforcement leadership and trainers teach officers to distinguish between behavioral profiling and racial profiling?
5. Are those who argue that the "demographics of crime" justify racial profiling using data that is biased? Does this sort of rationalization perpetuate the problem through a vicious cycle?

Does the War on Terrorism Give License to Law Enforcement to Engage in Racial Profiling?

An Arab American says he was recently a victim of racially profiling at an airport in Washington, D.C., while on his way to Detroit. He was pulled out of line, questioned, and searched. He reported that this was done in front of everyone else in line and was humiliating. He thought that the authorities at the airport were doing this so non-Arab Americans could see that they are doing something about security. He felt he had been racially profiled.

Discuss the following:

1. Passengers who appear "Arab-looking," which has included South Asians and Latinos, have been asked to leave airplanes because fellow passengers and crew members refuse to fly with them. How can airline security and management justify these actions?
2. Sikh men have been denied the right to board aircraft because they refuse to fly without their turbans, which equates to asking an individual to fly without a basic article of clothing.
3. Has the war on terrorism or the conflict in the Middle East provided the opportunity for officers and security personal to use racial profiling tactics?
4. What options are available for officers and security personnel to provide security and safety to the public they serve?

Racial bias, or the perception of same, distorts attitudes toward civil authority. It also impacts the victims' quality of everyday life. In addition to actual bias, the perception of bias is a substantial barrier to good police–community relations. The victims of racial profiling maintain that police use this practice because there are officers who believe that having black or brown skin is an indication of a greater risk of criminality, and they therefore view minorities as potential criminals. The victims believe, therefore, that skin color becomes evidence every time they engage in the most common and prototypically American act—driving.

PROFILING AS A LEGAL TOOL OF LAW ENFORCEMENT

Profiling and profiles have long been used as legitimate law enforcement tools to look for signs of potential criminal activity. They are tools utilized by law enforcement in almost every country in the world, although the people profiled will vary by country. For example, the constabularies in Northern Ireland and England have profiles that help them identify extremists among members of the IRA. Religion and national origin would be factors in this profile, not race or ethnicity. In Israel, the police have profiles of

Palestinian terrorists. Now the criminal justice community in many parts of the world is using profiles to locate and arrest members of Al-Qaida. In the United States, airport and homeland security agents using a profile of a potential terrorist might include such factors as (1) a man in his 20s or 30s who comes from Saudi Arabia, Egypt, or Pakistan; (2) who is probably living in one of six states: Texas, New Jersey, California, New York, Michigan, or Florida; (3) and is likely to have engaged in some sort of suspicious activity, such as taking flying lessons, traveling in areas of possible targets, or getting a U.S. driver's license. Meeting some of these criteria—not necessarily having a certain skin color—is enough to instigate questioning by law enforcement authorities.

PERF created policy intended for adoption by police departments across the nation. The policy clearly delineates what is legal profiling. The policy discusses the U.S. Constitution Fourth Amendment provision that officers shall *not consider* race/ethnicity to establish reasonable suspicion or probable cause except when based on trustworthy, locally relevant information that links a person or persons of a specific race/ethnicity to a particular unlawful incident(s). The policy:

- disallows use of race as a general indicator for criminal behavior;

- disallows use of stereotypes/biases;

- allows for the consideration of race *as one factor* in making law enforcement decisions if it is based on trustworthy and locally relevant information;

- links specific suspected unlawful activity to a person(s) of a particular race/ethnicity;

- and relies on *descriptions* of actual suspects, not general *predictions* of who may be involved in a crime.

For example, an officer observes the following: (1) the tail light is burned out on a vehicle with a white driver; (2) it is midnight; (3) the car is in a minority neighborhood where drugs are known to be sold; (4) the driver pulls up to the curb and talks briefly to someone standing there; (5) an exchange takes place; (6) the driver drives away; (7) the driver makes furtive movements as if hiding something under the seat when police pull him over. Although not a representative example because the driver is white, race was used as a part of the decision to pull the driver over.

PERF recommends that the following principle be applied: "Race/ethnicity should be treated like other demographic descriptors. Police can use race/ethnicity as one factor in the same way that they use age, gender and other descriptors to establish reasonable suspicion or probable cause." The organization recommends the best test for officers to use includes two questions: (1) Would I be engaging this particular person but for the fact that this person is white? (2) Would I be asking this question of this person but for the fact that this person is [fill in the demographic descriptor] ("Racially Biased Policing," 2001).

What is necessary in assessing the use of profiles and profiling is a combination of common sense and fairness, a balance between effective law enforcement and protection of civil liberties. The authors believe that profiles and profiling must not upset such a balance if they are used judiciously, fairly, and within the law. Most officers understand that profiling, not racial profiling, is an acceptable form of proactive law enforcement, and the courts agree. The U.S. Customs Service, the U.S. Border Patrol, and the DEA have long used profiles as a tool to detain and investigate persons fitting the "drug courier profile." Such a profile is based on behaviors, actions, traits, demeanor, intelligence information, carrier routes, statistical evidence, and other factors (not just a single characteristic like race or ethnicity). The U.S. Border Patrol obviously links race to incidence of crime on the border with Mexico. It is only logical to assume that most people attempting to illegally enter the country are of Hispanic/Latino or Mestizo descent. The use of profiles in this context appears to be legal and acceptable. A border patrol profile, however, not only includes the ethnicity of the individual but also such factors as their proximity to the border, erratic driving, suspicious behavior, and the officers' previous experience with alien traffic.

Now airport police and security agents, and other officials within Homeland Security, use profiles to identify those who might be a threat to security in their respective jurisdictions. For example, the Computer Assisted Passenger Prescreening System (CAPPS II), developed in 1998 and first tested in 2003 by the Federal Aviation Administration, is a nationwide preflight computer system used to check personal information on every airline passenger. Under the program, an airline passenger provides name, birth date, address, and phone number when getting a flight reservation. That information is checked against commercial databases (credit reports and consumer transactions) and a score is generated indicating the likelihood that the passenger's identity is authentic. The personal information is also checked against a government database to determine if the person is on a terrorism watch list or represents a security risk. Those deemed to be an elevated or uncertain risk are required to undergo secondary screening with a handheld wand. Anyone deemed a high risk is supposed to be brought to the attention of law enforcement. The system also screens passengers based on where they're flying and how they purchase their tickets—not on how they look. None of the profile information, on face value, involves the race, ethnicity, or national origin of the persons checked. CAPPS II seeks to streamline the airport screening process by flagging only those passengers deemed potential security risks. That will benefit the vast majority of travelers by ensuring fewer are stopped. Critics of CAPPS II, however, see the system as having the potential for unconstitutional invasions of privacy and government snooping. They also are concerned people may be falsely identified as terrorists.

Legitimate Use of Race/Ethnicity

An important question is whether race can *ever* be a valid consideration when conducting law enforcement activity. In the *Travis* opinion, the majority concluded that "race or ethnic background may become a legitimate consideration when investigators have information on the subject of a particular suspect" (Travis, 62 F. 3rd at 54). Simply put: the suspect described and being sought is of a certain race or ethnicity (refer to the definition of suspect-specific incident in this chapter). Court decisions have allowed officers to consider the totality of the circumstances surrounding the subject of their attention in light of their experience and training, which may include "instructions on a drug courier profile" (*Florida v. Royer,* 460 U.S. at 525, note 6). Actually, many courts have upheld the use of drug courier profiles as the sole determinant of a stop or cause for suspicion. Therefore, profiles combined with other facts and circumstances can establish reasonable suspicion or probable cause. Race or color may be a factor to consider during certain police activity (*U.S. v. Brignoni-Ponce,* 442 U.S., 837, 887,1975). The *Whren* decision by the Supreme Court enhanced the already extensive power of police to detain individual citizens under the banner of the war on drugs by allowing pretext stops through the "objective" standard test (Bast, 1997; Harris, 1999).

Some see the Whren decision (*Whren v. United States*) "objective standard" ruling as opening the door for police abuse. They argue that in the *Whren* case, it did not matter to the court that the officers lied about their intent, that they were violating departmental policy to make the stop, or that they really wanted to stop the car because it contained two African American men who sat at a stop sign for 20 seconds in an area known for drug dealing. They are concerned that the *Whren* decision clearly opens the door for racial profiling because it allows police officers to stop anyone without reasonable suspicion or probable cause, thus providing a mechanism for circumventing the Fourth Amendment requirements of the U.S. Constitution. Because minor traffic violations are numerous, they argue, to limit stops to the observation of traffic violations is no limitation at all. If a police officer wants to stop a car, but does not have the legal authority to do so, all the officer has to do is to follow it until the driver gets nervous and at some point turns right without a turn signal, drifts across the center line, or simply fails to come to a complete stop at a stop sign. Upon observing a minor traffic violation, the police officer can stop the driver and attempt to pressure him or her into giving consent for the car to be searched. Under this "objective" standard, the motivation of the officer and previous enforcement patterns become irrelevant (Barlow & Barlow, 2000). It is important to note that the Court's decision in Whren did not create the practice of pretextual stops. Instead it validated this long standing police practice that is even encouraged by police administrators. Neither was the Whren decision unpredictable. It is the result of more than a decade of decisions wherein the courts were unwilling to consider the legality of the use of race in law enforcement decision making (Withrow, 2006).

The courts said the burden that "brief detentions" place on law-abiding minority citizens is a minor and necessary inconvenience in the war on crime, suggesting that little damage is done by the practice of profiling. However, those who advocate making the standard for brief detentions more restrictive insist that these court decisions have failed to acknowledge that these detentions grow into regular occurrences, breeding resentment and anger both in the citizens stopped and the police officers who confront hostile persons of color. Police officers who use race, ethnicity, gender, sexual orientation, or national origin as factors in criminal profiling based on presumed statistical probabilities then contribute to the very statistics upon which they rely.

The Supreme Court has made it clear that as long as the government can show that police searches and seizures are objectively reasonable (that is, based on probable cause or reasonable suspicion), they do not violate the Fourth Amendment, regardless of the officer's subjective (actual) motivation for the search or seizure. That does not mean, however, that objectively reasonable searches and seizures can never violate the Constitution. Officers motivated by prejudice who lawfully search or seize only members of certain racial, ethnic, religious, or gender groups are still subject to claims of constitutional violations (i.e., racial profiling).

Police officers who undertake searches of persons or vehicles not incident to an arrest must have reasonable suspicion or probable cause to perform such a search. An officer who does not have reasonable suspicion may ask for a consent to search (except in those states or localities where it is illegal) and even have the motorist sign a waiver to that effect. Sometimes, however, evidence of racial bias may be discovered when there is a repeated pattern of minorities being subjected to consent searches much more often than whites. Law enforcement agencies must monitor the data they collect on discretionary consent searches to ensure that the discretion is not applied more often to minorities. One explanation for the disparity, according to some researchers, is that minorities may be more nervous around police and officers may misinterpret that as suspicious behavior.

Far-reaching authority for searches was granted to law enforcement when, on October 26, 2001, President George W. Bush signed the Patriot Act Presidential Executive Orders into law. The law gave sweeping new powers to both domestic law enforcement and international intelligence agencies. The provisions of the law, aimed at terrorism, expanded surveillance capabilities (in effect, searches) and allowed for nationwide wiretaps under certain circumstances. Many aspects of the new law were questioned by those concerned about the potential for government intrusion into the lives and civil rights of innocent people. The Patriot Act was renewed by congress on March 9, 2006, following an intense debate regarding protection of civil liberties. Proponents were able to show that in the four years since the Act was passed, there were no verified civil liberties abuses, and the new bill added more than 30 new significant civil liberties safeguards. The USAPA is discussed more fully in Chapter 10.

Illegitimate Use of Race/Ethnicity

Courts have held that matching a profile *alone* is not the equivalent of the reasonable suspicion or probable cause necessary to conduct an investigative detention or arrest (see, for example, *Reid v. George,* 448 U.S. 438, 1980, and Royer at 525, note 6). There are no circumstances under which officers may stop citizens based solely on their race, ethnicity, gender, religion, national origin, or any other demographic feature. Officers must base their stops of persons, whether in a vehicle or on foot, on reasonable suspicion or probable cause that a violation of the law has been or is about to be committed based on facts and information that they can articulate.

Some states, via legislation, have banned consent searches where there is no clear reason for suspicion. The mere nervousness of the motorist or occupant(s) is not sufficient reason to ask for a consent search. The Fourth (banning unreasonable search and seizure) and Fourteenth (equal protection of the laws) Amendments to the U.S. Constitution provide a framework for the protection of drivers from being indiscriminately targeted by the police via traffic stops. To prove this type of claim, the claimant must produce facts or statistics showing that they were targeted solely because of their race, ethnicity, gender, religion, or national origin. The burden then shifts to the police to provide evidence that they did not act solely on the basis of any of these factors.

A bill called the End Racial Profiling Act of 2004 was introduced in both the U.S. Senate and House of Representatives during the 108th Congress. The legislation bans racial profiling by local, county, state, and federal law enforcement officers. It specifically bans the practice of relying on race, ethnicity, national origin, or religion in selecting which individuals to subject to traffic stops, pedestrian stops, or other routine investigatory activities. It authorizes the Attorney General to provide incentive grants to assist agencies with complying with this Act and conditions the release of federal funds to state and local law enforcement agencies on their compliance with such requirements. It also would require applicants to establish an administrative complaint procedure or independent auditor program. Additionally, it directs the Attorney General to carry out a demonstration project to collect data on hit rates for stops and searches. It also directs the Attorney General to report to Congress annually on racial profiling by law enforcement agencies. The bill, not passed by the 108th Congress, was reintroduced during the 109th in December 2005 and was referred to the Committee on the Judiciary. As of the time of this textbook revision, it had not been passed and signed into law (United States Senate on line: http://www.senate.gov). The U.S. Department of Justice in 2003, had issued guidelines banning all racial profiling by federal agencies, and many states have also enacted laws against it.

Weeding out the illegitimate uses of profiles or profiling by police officers is the only way law enforcement can maintain credibility within the communities they serve. The authors believe that the majority of officers know not to act on any prejudices they might hold.

PREVENTION OF RACIAL PROFILING IN LAW ENFORCEMENT

To formulate measures to prevent the practice of racial profiling and inappropriate behavior and actions on the part of officers, the criminal justice system should consider the following seven areas:

- Accountability and supervision
- Agency policy to address racial profiling
- Recruitment and hiring
- Education and training
- Minority community outreach
- Professional traffic stops
- Data collection on citizens' race/ethnicity

Accountability and Supervision

Preventing the use of racial profiling or biased policing in law enforcement is critical. Police executives must reflect seriously on this and respond to both the reality of, and the perceptions of, biased policing. Law enforcement executives, managers, and supervisors must send a clear message to all personnel that using race, ethnicity, or national origin alone as the basis for any investigative stop is not only unacceptable conduct but also illegal. It can lead to termination from employment and possibly prosecution. If convicted, the officer(s) could be fined and/or incarcerated depending on the laws of the particular state.

Police managers and supervisors, in order to identify officers who might be biased, should monitor such indicators as: (1) high numbers of minority citizen complaints; (2) high numbers of use-of-force or resisting incidents involving minorities; (3) large numbers of arrests not charged because prosecutors find improper detentions and/or searches; (4) perceptible negative attitude toward minorities; (5) negative attitudes toward training programs that enhance police–community relations or cultural awareness.

Prevention of racial profiling also involves other components of the criminal justice system such as prosecutors and courts. Legislators are also an integral part of the process. For example, the following took place in New Jersey:

> Nearly five years after New Jersey state troopers shot three unarmed minority men and ignited a furor over racial profiling, the State Legislature passed a bill making it a crime for the police to use race as the primary factor in determining whom to stop and search. The General Assembly passed a bill that would make such profiling punishable by five years in prison and a $15,000 fine. A similar bill has already cleared the Senate, and Gov. James E. McGreevey immediately announced plans to sign the bill. ("New Jersey Adopts Ban," 2003, p. A1)

Supervision, legislation, and logging the race/ethnicity of drivers stopped alone will not root out rogue officers who use racial profiling tactics. A program that reviews other contacts officers have with residents should also be instigated to help reduce such incidents. Law enforcement agencies must convey to their communities that they, the citizens, will be protected from such abuses and that abuse is not tolerated or advocated. Preventing the use of racial profiling by law enforcement officers not only is crucial to maintaining credibility within the community, but also reduces exposure to civil liability on the part of the departments and officers. Law enforcement managers might use the following self-assessment to evaluate their agency's policies and practices to determine if any of them could lead to a negative image of the department in the community or possible civil liability.

Self-Assessment

1. Has your law enforcement agency taken a proactive stance regarding bias-based traffic law enforcement?

2. How many civil rights complaints has your department received during the past year? What percentage is related to traffic stops?

3. Has your department been negatively portrayed in the media regarding community relations or biased traffic enforcement?

4. Do you collect data on race, ethnicity, gender, and national origin?

5. Have you authorized department-wide use of in-car video systems?

6. Is there an effective citizen complaint system in place and is the department responsive?

7. Do you have supervisory control that can identify (early alert) officers who may have patterns of bias-based traffic enforcement?

8. Does your agency have disciplinary policies and training established for officers with patterns of bias-based traffic enforcement?

9. Has your agency instituted proactive measures to build positive relations with the minority community (for example, meetings with community leaders and neighborhood associations) before problems surface? ("Understanding Bias-Based Traffic Law Enforcement," 2003)

The authors of this text believe the majority of law enforcement officers, supervisors, and managers within agencies across the country are hard-working men and women who are committed to serving all members of our communities with fairness and respect. These professionals know racial profiling is unacceptable and conflicts with the standards and values inherent in ensuring all people are treated equally regardless of their race or ethnicity. They know racial profiling can expose a police department to costly lawsuits and ruin minority relations. They are intolerant of the use of racial profiling and willingly partner with their communities to address the issues involved and to develop approaches to eradicate either confirmed acts of racial profiling or the perception that it is taking place within their agency.

Agency Policies to Address Racial Profiling

Law enforcement agencies must have clear policies and procedures to address racial profiling and the perceptions thereof. As of 2003, according to the Bureau of Justice Statistics, 63 percent of departments had written policies concerning racial profiling by officers (see Exhibit 14.2). This included about 9 in 10 agencies serving populations of 250,000 or more residents (Bureau of Justice Statistics Report, 2006). Many departments in the United States have developed such general orders to cover not only traffic stops but also the temporary detentions of pedestrians and even bicyclists. The policies usually address the Fourth Amendment requirement that investigative detentions, traffic stops, arrests, searches, and property seizures by officers must be based on a standard of reasonable suspicion or probable cause which officers can support with specific facts and circumstances. The policy must include the following: (1) no motorist, once cited or warned, shall be detained beyond the point where there exists no reasonable suspicion of further criminal activity; (2) no person or vehicle shall be searched in the absence of probable cause, a search warrant, or the person's *voluntary* consent. The policy should specify that in each case where a search is conducted, this information shall be recorded, including the legal basis for the search and the results. It is strongly recommended consent searches only be conducted with written consent utilizing the agency forms provided.

According to the International Association of Chiefs of Police (IACP), departments without a policy should look at as many models addressing racial profiling as possible before they select one that meets their needs. Agencies should also involve community members, especially minorities and civil rights advocates, in the development and implementation of the policy. The policy must communicate a clear message to law enforcement personnel and the people they serve that racial profiling and other forms of biased-based policing are not acceptable practices. The statement should include what discipline (including criminal prosecution where such laws exist) could result if officers violate the provisions of the policy.

The San Francisco Police Department created a general order that outlines their policy for policing without racial bias. It states that "To maintain that trust, it is crucial for members of our Department to carry out their duties in a manner free from bias and to eliminate any perception of policing that appears racially biased." It clarifies the circumstances in which officers can consider race, color, ethnicity, national origin, gender, age, sexual orientation, or gender identity when making law enforcement decisions.

Policy: Investigative detentions, traffic stops, arrests, searches, and property seizures by officers will be based on a standard of reasonable suspicion or

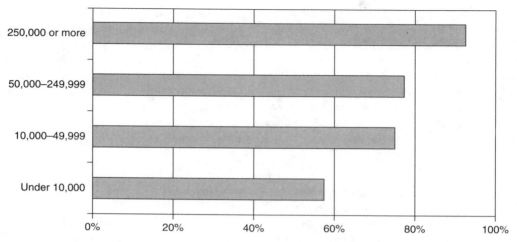

Exhibit 14.2   Local Police Departments with a Written Policy on Racial Profiling by Officers, 2003.
(*Source:* Bureau of Criminal Statistics, May 2006, NCJ 210118.)

probable cause in accordance with the Fourth Amendment of the U.S. Constitution. Officers must be able to articulate specific facts and circumstances that support reasonable suspicion or probable cause for investigative detentions, traffic stops, arrest, nonconsensual searches, and property seizures. Department personnel may not use, *to any extent or degree,* race, color, ethnicity, national origin, age, sexual orientation or gender identity in conducting stops or detentions, or activities following stops or detentions *except* when engaging in the investigation of appropriate suspect-specific activity to identify a particular person or group. Department personnel seeking one or more specific persons who have been identified or described in part by any of the above listed characteristics may rely on them in part only in combination with other appropriate identifying factors. The listed characteristics should not be given undue weight:

- Except as provided above, officers shall not consider race, color, ethnicity, national origin, gender, age, sexual orientation, or gender identity in establishing reasonable suspicion or probable cause.
- Except as provided above, officers shall not consider race, color, ethnicity, national origin, gender, age, sexual orientation, or gender identity in deciding to initiate even those consensual encounters that do not amount to legal detentions or to request consent to search. (San Francisco Police Department General Order 5.17, 07/17/03)

In 1979, the IACP, NOBLE, the National Sheriffs' Association, and the PERF created the Commission on Accreditation for Law Enforcement Agencies (CALEA). The primary purpose of the Commission is to improve law enforcement service by creating a national body of standards developed by law enforcement professionals. Furthermore, it recognizes professional achievements by establishing and administering an *accreditation* process through which a law enforcement agency can demonstrate that it meets those standards. "Participation in the CALEA accreditation program is voluntary, but successful completion provides a law enforcement agency with a nationally recognized award of excellence and professional achievement. Additional benefits of obtaining CALEA accreditation may include more favorable liability insurance costs and increased governmental *and community support*" (see CALEA website: www.calea.org.).

CALEA in 2001, issued Standard 1.2.9 regarding bias-based profiling. The standard requires that CALEA-accredited agencies have a written policy governing bias-based profiling and, at a minimum, include the following provisions: (1) a prohibition against bias-based profiling in traffic contacts, in field contacts, and in asset seizures and forfeiture efforts; (2) training agency enforcement personnel in bias-based profiling issues including legal aspects; (3) corrective measures if bias-based profiling occurs; and (4) an annual administrative review of agency practices including citizen concerns. CALEA does not require mandatory collection of traffic stop data even though there is a growing demand for such action. The Commission's position is that not all law enforcement agencies must collect traffic stop data when other successful measurement systems are in use and/or the situation in the community served does not indicate there is a concern about police bias (Bureau of Justice Statistics Report, 2006).

Recruitment and Hiring

Police agencies can reduce racial bias by recruiting and hiring officers who can police in a professional way. Within legal parameters, the department should hire a workforce that reflects the community's racial and ethnic demographics. Those hired should be expected to carry out their duties with fairness and impartiality. Having such a workforce increases the probability that, as a whole, the agency will be able to understand the perspectives of its racial/ethnic minorities and communicate with them effectively.

The officers that departments should be recruiting are those who are aware of and capable of managing their own ethnic, racial, and cultural stereotypes and biases in a professional way. These qualities are essential to reducing bias in policing. The multiple testing stages that applicants for law enforcement positions go through help weed out those who are unable to control their biases. Interviews, polygraphs, psychological tests, and background investigations are all intended to identify those who are biased to the point that they might act on their prejudices (see Chapters 1 and 3). It should be noted that the possibility of bias is not limited to white officers. Members of minority groups can have biases against white people, against members of other minority groups, or even against members of their own race/ethnic group. In 2003, the *Boston Globe* analyzed 20,000 citations by Boston police; it was discovered that "minority officers here are at least as tough as whites on minority drivers, and sometimes tougher" ("Minority Officers," 2003, p. A1). Police recruitment messages, verbal and written, must emphasize that those who are prejudiced, regardless of their race or ethnicity, and who cannot distinguish between appropriate and inappropriate behavior and actions, will not be hired. As mentioned earlier in this chapter, no one is completely free of bias, but the recruitment effort should be targeted at those who understand and control their biases.

Education and Training

Law enforcement agencies need to provide training and education to enable officers to utilize legal enforcement tools so they can perform their work professionally and effectively within today's multicultural communities. Some departments have utilized interactive simulation training exercises to train officers on professional traffic stop procedures, and especially those involving agitated citizens. Clearly, most law enforcement officers know not to act on the prejudices and stereotypes they might hold. However, the nature of prejudice is such that some people are not aware of their own prejudices or biases. Therefore, they make inferences and take actions toward certain groups based on these biased perceptions. Training that provides accurate information concerning groups about which officers might have prejudices and stereotypes is one of the approaches police departments should use to prevent racial profiling.

What is the mental process that takes place when an officer makes a stop based on race, ethnicity, or national origin? Officers who have a biased belief system observe and collect certain data that in turn reinforces that belief system. Meanings are added to make sense of the observations ("I notice minorities more and stop them more because of my biased beliefs about them"). Based on these meanings, assumptions are made that fill in for missing data ("This motorist is carrying drugs on him"). The officer draws conclusions (based on beliefs) and then takes action (decides to stop African American and Hispanic motorists much more frequently than whites). These steps in our thinking take place very quickly. Most of us are not aware that this process goes on all the time (see the section in Chapter 1 on prejudice in law enforcement).

In his book *The Fifth Discipline Fieldbook: Strategies and Tools for Building a Learning Organization,* management specialist Peter Senge and his coauthors provide a clear and simple model called the "Ladder of Inference" that illuminates most people's typical patterns (and flaws) of thinking. The authors discuss thinking and decision-making processes using the ladder to describe, from the bottom up, how people select data, add meanings, make assumptions, draw conclusions, adopt beliefs, and ultimately take action (see Exhibit 14.3). They maintain that:

> We live in a world of self-generating beliefs that remain largely untested. We adopt those beliefs because they are based on conclusions, which are inferred from what we observe, plus our past experience. Our ability to achieve the results we truly desire is eroded by our feelings that:
>
> - Our beliefs are the truth
> - The truth is obvious
> - Our beliefs are based on real data
> - The data we select are the real data (Senge, 1994, p. 242)

The authors explain that most people no longer remember where their attitudes and beliefs came from (i.e., what data or experiences led to their assumptions and conclusions). Therefore, they may not understand the basis of the actions they take. Senge and his coauthors discuss "leaps of abstraction" in which:

> our minds literally move at lightning speed . . . because we immediately "leap" to generalizations so quickly that we never think to test them. . . . [L]eaps of abstraction occur when we move from direct observation (concrete "data") to gen-

Exhibit 14.3   Ladder of Inference.
(*Source:* Senge, Roberts, Ross, & Smith, 1994, pp. 242–246. Reproduced with permission of Peter Senge.)

eralization without testing. Leaps of abstraction impede learning because they become axiomatic. What was once an assumption becomes treated as a fact. He says that we then treat generalization as fact. (Senge, 1994, pp. 192–193)

How do you spot leaps of abstraction? First, by asking yourself what you believe about the way the world works. . . . Ask "what is the 'data' on which this generalization is based?" Then ask yourself, "Am I willing to consider that this generalization may be inaccurate or misleading?" It is important to ask this last question consciously, because, if the answer is no, there is no point in proceeding. (Senge, 1994, p. 194)

In intensive training conducted by Senge nationwide, police and other corporate executives are able to learn about the models above and relate them to issues and challenges in their own organizations. The models provide some insight into what may be going on in officers' minds as they stop members of minority groups. Thus the models can help officers better understand their actions vis-à-vis racial profiling. It is natural for people to substitute assumptions for what is not known, but in the case of racial profiling, this is a very dangerous proposition. Officers have to recognize when they are converting their biases into "facts" and when their assumptions substitute for real data.

Training and education provide departments an opportunity to inform officers of the penalties for not adhering to policies and laws on the subject. Many state legislatures have created laws barring law enforcement officers from engaging in racial profiling. Such legislation also requires that every law enforcement officer participate in expanded training regarding racial profiling. This training is typically coordinated, monitored, and controlled by the Commission on Peace Officer Standards and Training, an agency that is found in every state. These state commissions should, if they haven't already, integrate the topic of racial profiling into their diversity training for both entry-level and in-service programs. Law enforcement agencies should consult local chapters of their community's minority group organizations to obtain accounts and examples of actual or perceived racially biased policing for use in training programs. Such programs should also cover:

1. Definitions of key terms involved, such as profile, profiling, racial profiling, racially biased policing, probable cause, and reasonable suspicion;

2. Identification of key indices and perspectives that signal cultural differences among residents in a local community;

3. The negative impact of biases, prejudices, and stereotyping on effective law enforcement, including examination of how historical perceptions of discriminatory enforcement practices have harmed police–community relations;

4. History and role of the civil rights movement and its impact on law enforcement;

5. Specific obligations of officers in preventing, reporting, and responding to discriminatory or biased practices by fellow officers;

6. Various perspectives of local groups and race-relations experts regarding cultural and police–community relations.

Training should also involve constitutional law and ethics. Every state will have different requirements, but here is an example from the Commission on POST of Missouri:

1. All commissioned, licensed peace officers, who have the authority to enforce vehicle/traffic laws, must attend a minimum of one hour of racial profiling training each year.

2. Individuals who have *no authority* to make traffic stops are *exempt* from this annual requirement.

3. All racial profiling training used to meet the requirement must be obtained from a licensed training center, an approved provider of continuing education, or a course approved by POST.

The law enforcement community is more capable than ever of effectively addressing biased policing. In the past few decades, there has been a revolution in the quality and quantity of police training, the standards for hiring officers, and accountability.

Minority Community Outreach

Every police and community interaction requires a strong, ongoing link to community groups and civil rights organizations. Links might be established when community-oriented policing, which became popular in the 1990s, is used to address neighborhood problems. A link is also established when community task forces are assembled to address issues, especially of racial profiling and the perception thereof. These steps demonstrate respect for the minority community and create shared responsibility for whatever action is taken. The police hold primary responsibility for community outreach on every level, but the community is also responsible for becoming involved in activities that form positive relationships with the police. Policing within the community can function only in an environment of mutual engagement and respect. In the context of racial profiling or biased policing, outreach to the community is imperative. For constructive dialog to take place, therefore, police executives must remain open to discussions of racial profiling or the perception thereof within their jurisdictions.

Although there are many examples of police departments collaborating with the minority community to discuss and resolve issues pertaining to racial profiling or racially biased policing, the Chicago Police Department could serve as a positive example. In 2000, Chicago's police superintendent sponsored a series of meetings between the police and residents of the minority community to address racial tensions and concerns about police racial bias. The forums included community activists, and staff of all ranks represented the police department. Prior to the first meeting, participants were surveyed for their opinions, perceptions, and observations about racial profiling and racially biased policing. The questionnaire also asked them to rate the department's strengths and weaknesses regarding minority outreach and solicited their ideas about how to improve police–minority relations and resolve issues. The forums were moderated by an independent facilitator. At the first meeting, community members shared their thoughts, experiences, and concerns, and police staff was asked to listen but not respond. Later in the day, the police shared their thoughts and reactions to the morning session, and the citizens were instructed to listen and not respond. During the final session of the day, all participants joined in a discussion of the issues and ideas raised earlier. The meetings continued over a period of time until the participants identified specific actions to be taken by both the police and community members to address the issues that had been raised ("Racially Biased Policing," 2001).

PROFESSIONAL POLICE TRAFFIC STOPS

The reason for every stop made by a law enforcement officer must be legally defensible and professional. Professional traffic stops involve four key elements:

- *Organizational/agency policy.* Agencies must develop a well-structured policy concerning professional traffic stops, outlining the conduct of officers and the prohibition of discriminatory practices.
- *Officer training.* Agencies should include a component on racial profiling into existing in-service training programs. Special workshop discussions on the issue of racial profiling can also be scheduled.

- *Data collection.* Agencies must collect traffic stop data when the situation in the community served indicates that there is a concern about police bias.

- *Accountability/supervision.* Law enforcement supervisors and managers must hold officers accountable for adhering to the policy. They must personally take the message to employees, as well as to the public, that biased policing will not be tolerated and could result in discipline, possibly including prosecution or termination. Managers, supervisors, and the entire workforce must embrace and adhere to the policy.

Deputy Chief Ondra Berry (Reno, Nevada, Police Department), now retired, in diversity training he conducts nationwide (and as he formerly did in communications with his own officers), offers the following advice: "When contemplating stopping a motorist, ask yourself, 'Is there a possibility that I may be making an assumption about this driver based on race? Am I moving from my own personal "data" and making a leap of extraction about this vehicle or about this person?'" Officers must recognize that this is a possibility. Berry further advises, "Do not take race into account when deciding who to stop. Use your good policing skills. Again, if you are normal, you have unbalanced views about people who are different from you" (Berry, 2006). The IACP, after significant study, identified the components that consititue a "professional traffic stop." The organization's publication, *Recommendations from the First IACP Forum on Professional Traffic Stops*," (2003) should be referred to for additional information.

DATA COLLECTION ON CITIZENS' RACE/ETHNICITY

When racial profiling became an issue throughout the United States, many law enforcement jurisdictions began collecting data on the race/ethnicity of people stopped and/or searched by police. Some did so voluntarily while others did so because of court decrees or community pressure. The purpose of collecting data is to address racially biased policing and the perceptions thereof and to determine whether it is taking place. The use of data collection requires officers to complete a form following each traffic stop.

Research by PERF ("Racially Biased Policing," 2001) examined the arguments for and against data collection:

Arguments in Favor of Data Collection

Data collection helps agencies:

1. Determine whether racially biased policing is a problem in the jurisdiction.
2. Convey a commitment to unbiased policing.
3. "Get ahead of the curve."
4. Effectively allocate and manage department resources.

Collecting data and interpreting them, if done correctly, reflects accountability and openness on the part of the agency. The process helps to improve police–community relations. Departments doing so identify problems and search for solutions. The data can be informative to department management about what types of stops and searches officers are making. Managers and supervisors can then decide not only if these practices are the most efficient allocation of department resources but also if biased policing is taking place. Without the collection and analysis of data, departments can have a difficult time defending their practices if challenged in court.

Arguments against Data Collection

1. Data collection does not yield valid information regarding the nature and extent of racially biased policing.

2. Data could be used to harm the agency or its personnel.

3. Data collection may impact police productivity, morale, and workload.

4. Police resources might be used to combat racially biased policing and the perceptions thereof in more effective ways.

Many departments still resist record keeping. They argue, for one, that the mere collection of "racial" statistics may imply that biased policing is taking place. These agencies maintain that the raw data, when first collected and before analysis and comparison with benchmarks, could reinforce or increase the public's negative perceptions of the agency at the cost of both the morale and effectiveness of officers. At the same time, some departments have expressed concern that any data they do collect could be used against them in court. These law enforcement executives question the ability of data collection systems to provide valid answers about the nature and extent of racially biased policing within their departments. The simple collection of data will neither prevent racial profiling nor accurately identify if it is taking place. The process alone does not protect agencies from public criticism, scrutiny, and litigation because the data collected is open to interpretation. The raw data collected represent meaningless numbers unless put into a relevant context using statistical benchmarks (to be discussed later) to provide a legitimate means of comparison. Standing alone, the data collected can be used to make or defend any position that someone may adopt about racial profiling. Law enforcement agencies, therefore, must take additional steps to ensure that the numbers they collect accurately reflect reality. Each department must evaluate its specific circumstances. For agencies that have had no community complaints and/or already closely monitor officer behavior in other ways, undertaking data collection may not be the most efficient use of resources.

Another argument used against data collection has been the observation that, within some law enforcement agencies, officers discontinued or reduced the number of self-initiated traffic stops and pedestrian contacts they made when data collection became a requirement. Officers, resentful or concerned about being monitored, ceased to initiate stops in order to avoid the possibility of being perceived as racially biased. Some agencies do not require the officer to reveal his or her identity on the data form. The identity of the individual(s) detained is never documented on the form. Some city/county administrators and law enforcement executives are also concerned about the time and costs associated with the collection and analysis of data.

Thus, data collection has its advantages, disadvantages, and limitations. PERF recommends that police agency executives, in collaboration with citizen leaders, review the pros and cons of the practice. They must factor in the agency's political, social, organizational, and financial situation to decide whether or not to either initiate data collection or to allocate available resources to other approaches to address racially biased policing and the perceptions thereof.

Data collection elements. PERF, COPS, and the U.S. Department of Justice have developed protocols and guidelines for the collection, analysis, and interpretation of vehicle stop data. These detailed how-to guides should be referred to by those involved in developing a system or methods of tracking vehicle stops and trying to measure racial bias in policing. The materials available from these agencies (see Website Resources at the end of this chapter) provide information upon what activities to target for data collection.

Most agencies collect data only on traffic stops (moving or mechanical violations) because of their frequency and also because this is where there is the greatest potential for police racial bias (or perception thereof) to occur. Another source of data is vehicle stops or general investigative stops of drivers. This sort of stop involves officer discretion (wherein the officer should have reasonable suspicion or probable cause to conduct an investigative stop) and is also an important source of information to analyze. Collecting data on *detentions* encompasses not only traffic and vehicle stops, but also pedestrian or bicyclist stops. A fourth source of data is *nonconsensual encounters,* in which an officer is not detaining the citizen, but is questioning him or her. PERF recommends that agencies collect data on all vehicle and traffic stops. Their recommendation does not include pedestrian stops or nonconsensual encounters that do not amount to detentions. Exhibit 14.4 shows a series of concentric circles that represent the types of activities police departments might target for data collection.

Data collection would be different for municipal and highway policing. The job of city police and county sheriffs is mostly responsive in nature in that they answer to calls for service from victims or witnesses to events. The officers' enforcement patterns depend on the character of the neighborhoods in which they serve, and thus the race/ethnicity of the persons they contact will vary accordingly. This must be taken

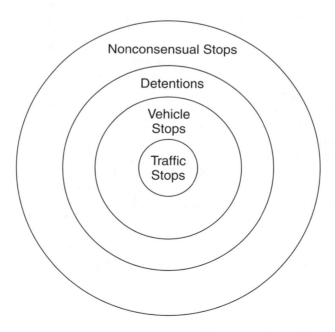

Exhibit 14.4   Activities That Could be Targeted for Data Collection.
(*Source:* PERF report, 2001, p. 121.)

into account during data analysis and interpretation. Comparative benchmarks must be utilized for each differing community and area of the city or county. Highway policing, in contrast, involves more self-initiated activity and more discretion on the part of officers. Moreover, it may prove useful for the collection and analysis to distinguish between low and high discretion stops.

The Montgomery County, Maryland, Police Department, as part of an agreement with the Fraternal Order of Police and the Department of Justice in 2000, began to collect data on all traffic stops, using electronic media rather than paper. All traffic stops result in the officers' entering specific information into a handheld computer (with special software); the information is later downloaded into the department's central database.

The Bureau of Criminal Statistics reported that, as of October 2004, 29 of the nation's 49 state law enforcement agencies required their officers to record the race or ethnicity of motorists stopped for traffic violations. Twenty-two state agencies required officers to record race or ethnicity data for all officer-initiated stops, and seven in more limited circumstances. The 22 state police agencies collecting race or ethnicity data for all traffic stops represent an increase of six states since 2001 and 13 states since 1999. Among the 20 agencies that did not require traffic patrol officers to collect race or ethnicity data in 2003, 14 agencies previously reported collection of race or ethnicity data in 2001. The report indicates that most agencies (27) relied on their officers' observations of the driver's race or ethnicity as the method of determining the race or ethnicity of the motorist ("Traffic Stop Data, 2004," 2005).

Statistical benchmarks or base rates. Statistical benchmarks or base rates are the comparative populations or groups against which the data collected are going to be analyzed and interpreted. Racial profiling analysis requires developing an appropriate benchmark, and this is the most important methodological decision made by researchers. The selection and development of benchmarks is a very complicated process often requiring the assistance of specialists in the field so the correct interpretation of the data is achieved. There is no agreement on what constitutes a reliable benchmark. Research on the subject of benchmarks identified three different methods:

1. ***Resident population of the community*** that is policed by the department under consideration—probably the most common method.

2. ***Field observation of drivers*** at randomly selected sites during randomly selected times. Normally field observers attempt to identify the race or ethnicity and approximate age of each driver.

3. ***Accident records for not-at-fault drivers*** to estimate the qualitative features (e.g. racial composition) of actual roadway users. Information arising from accident statistics is commonly used by traffic engineers to develop qualitative benchmarks of actual road users.

There are advantages and disadvantages to each of the types of benchmarks mentioned. None of these benchmarks are universally adaptable to every racial profiling evaluation and the advantages and disadvantages of each must be taken into consideration when deciding which one to use. However, one criminal justice researcher, Brian Withrow (2004, p. 23) maintains that:

> A benchmark comparison alone cannot measure the factors that influence a police officer's decision to initiate a traffic stop. We cannot even determine

whether or not the officer even knew the race of the individual prior to the stop. In other words, benchmark comparisons only tell us who gets stopped, not why.

The benchmarks selected must be able to help measure if individuals are being stopped on the basis of their race, ethnicity, or national origin. One question to be asked is, in a similar situation, would a person who was not a member of a minority group have been stopped? In other words, the correct comparison is not to the people living in the neighborhood or driving on the highway who did not engage in the same conduct as the person stopped, but to those who did engage in the same conduct but were not stopped because they were not of a minority race (U.S. Department of Justice, 2000). One can see how difficult a task it is to develop statistical benchmarks.

Unfortunately, most research and analysis of collected data on traffic and field interrogation stops (detentions) do not take into consideration the decision-making processes of the officers involved. Most data collection efforts have neglected the need to explain how and why officers make decisions pertaining to traffic or other stops when studying racial profiling. Research designs should also allow for the investigation of officers' decision-making after stops have been initiated (Engel, Calnon, & Bernard, 2002, p. 261).

Data analysis and interpretation. Once the data have been collected, what do they show? The most difficult part of the process is the analysis and interpretation of the statistics compiled. Ultimately, the problem with interpreting results is that these traffic and field-interrogation data have been collected without the guidance of any theoretical framework. Researchers have simply counted things such as the number of traffic stops, citations, and searches conducted by police against white and nonwhite suspects. Instead, the research should be conducted under the larger theoretical context of explaining behavior. Problems with the interpretation of empirical data are caused, in part, by data collection efforts that have not addressed why officers might engage in decision making based on citizens' race (Engel, Calnon, & Bernard, 2002).

Robin Engel and her coauthors state in their report that research on racial profiling should include consideration of three dependent variables:

1. ***The behavior of the individual police officer.***
    a. Why do police officers in general stop more black citizens than white citizens? How and why do officers make decisions?
    b. Why do some officers exhibit more racial disproportionality, while others exhibit less?
    c. Have there been changes in racial disproportionality over time?
2. ***The behavior of different police departments.*** Do some police departments have high rates of racial profiling and others have low rates? If so, what explains these differences?
3. ***The aggregate rates of officer and departmental behavior.*** Has race-based decision making been transformed in the past 40 years from one based primarily on individual racial prejudice to one based mainly on race-based departmental policies? (p. 261)

As explained, statistical benchmarks must be developed for comparison with the raw data collected by agencies. Among the decisions that must be made are:

1. Are the statistics collected compared with the city's racial makeup as determined by the nationwide census?

2. Are they compared with licensed drivers living in the city's jurisdiction?

3. Are they compared with the racial composition of the drivers on the roads, if that could be determined?

4. Are situational characteristics (e.g., suspects' characteristics, characteristics of the police–citizen encounter, and legal characteristics) considered and collected?

5. Are officers' characteristics (e.g., sex, race, experience, and attitudes) considered and collected?

6. Are organizational characteristics (e.g., formal and informal policies and attitudes and preferences of administrators and first-line supervisors) considered and collected?

7. Are community characteristics (e.g., demographic, economic, and political) considered and collected?

Data interpretation can be done internally by the law enforcement agency involved if the community political climate is good and there is trust that the analysis will be credible. However, since a positive community political climate is not usually the case, and to avoid the perception that the findings are suspect, most agencies obtain the services of an independent analyst. It is important that the analyst not only have some general knowledge of law enforcement procedures, but also be knowledgeable on the selection and development of statistical benchmarks or base rates. COPS, in conjunction with the Department of Justice (DOJ), produced a document entitled "How to Correctly Collect and Analyze Racial Profiling Data: Your Reputation Depends on It." This provides recommendations on the methodology for data collection and analysis. This 2002 document can be downloaded from their website at *www.cops.usdoj.gov*. Another helpful document, published in 2005, by PERF in collaboration with COPS and DOJ, is "Understanding Race Data from Vehicle Stops: A Stakeholder's Guide," by Lorie Fridell. (See the Website Resources under PERF at the end of this chapter).

Community task forces for development and implementation. Citizen input is critical to the success of data collection and interpretation. Community group representatives must be involved with police personnel of all ranks to form a task force. The task force members, including in most cases an independent analyst, work together to decide: (1) if data will be collected about the race/ethnicity of persons contacted by officers, (2) the design of benchmarks to utilize in the interpretation of the data, and (3) the response or action to be taken based on the interpretation. Representatives might include members of local community groups such as the NAACP, the Urban League, the ACLU, the Latino Unity Coalition, and Pan Pacific Asian representatives. Police departments should take their input and implement the appropriate recommendations in subsequent phases of the project. Task forces and community-oriented policing are beneficial to a department's efforts to investigate and solve problems associated with allegations of racial profiling. Task forces not only help ensure that the process addresses specific concerns of the community, but also help improve police–community relations. PERF suggests how to get started:

1. Unless mandated, decide, with citizen input, whether data collection should be one component of the jurisdiction's overall response to racially biased policing and the perceptions thereof.

2. Communicate with agency personnel as soon as a decision is made to start collecting data. The executive should provide a rationale for data collection and address anticipated concerns.

3. Set up a process for listening to the concerns of personnel, and have personnel help to develop constructive ways to address them.

4. Develop a police–citizen group to serve in an advisory capacity.

5. Develop the data collection and analysis protocol. Ensure that the interpretations will be responsible based on sound methodology and analysis.

6. Field test the data collection system for three to six months, and use that test to make modifications before implementing the system jurisdiction-wide. ("Racially Biased Policing," 2001, pp. 143–144)

Unintended results of data collection. In some agencies, when mandatory data collection was instituted, the number of traffic tickets dropped precipitously as officers, wary of being accused of racial profiling, stopped fewer people. This occurred in Houston and in Cincinnati. In other agencies, officers refused to fill out the forms or made mistakes, which made the data unusable. The officers complained that the collection process was a waste of time and that the data collected might be used against them. Some argued that officers who use racial profiling because they are prejudiced will never fill out the form. There are examples of cities in which police officers are so fearful of the possibility of being accused of being racist if they stop a person of color that they avoid making contact even if a violation or minor crime is being committed. If accusations begin to control policing, public safety suffers. Some agencies have equipped their patrol vehicles with video cameras and audio recording devices to provide evidence of the actions of their officers in the event of complaints.

SUMMARY

Citizen discontent and lawsuits against law enforcement can originate as a result of racial profiling or the use of profiles or profiling that appears to have been based on bias. Law enforcement professionals must be critical and introspective when analyzing this problem of racism and prejudice in the profession. They need to reflect seriously on the issues involved and respond to both the reality of, and the perceptions of, biased policing. It is imperative that members of the criminal justice community and government officials understand the strong feelings about racial profiling, especially the feelings of those who have been targeted. Racial profiling or racially biased policing must stop, not only because it is illegal, but also because it leads to distrust by the minority community and litigation with expensive settlements, and the results are not worth the negative public opinion. No one should have to fear being stopped or detained by police purely on the basis of skin color, ethnicity, or national origin.

Law enforcement executives should review complaints of racial profiling covering a period of time (5 to 10 years) to get a handle on the existence and/or perception of the problem and its scope. They should also conduct a series of meetings with community spokespersons and representatives of civil rights groups to elicit and listen to stories and accounts of racial profiling and perceptions of the same. If there is evidence that racial profiling has occurred and it appears to have been carried out by one or any number of officers, departments should take immediate and appropriate action—instigating an investigation that results in either confirming or refuting claims. The problem should be acknowledged and the public informed that it has been corrected. If a larger problem is identified, then other processes must be set into motion to study its scope and how it can be resolved. This is often accomplished through the use of a police–community task force, because racial profiling is not solely a law enforcement problem, but rather one that can be solved only through partnerships that are based on mutual trust and respect. Data collection and its proper interpretation can be one part of a police response to determine if biased policing is taking place and to what degree. The agency executive must work with community leaders to develop a multifaceted response tailored to the needs of the jurisdiction. Resolution would not only include data collection and analysis, but also training, education, supervision, monitoring, and recruitment within the agency. Every law enforcement agency must adopt a policy that specifies the circumstances in which race or ethnicity can be used as a factor in making enforcement decisions. That policy should indicate not only that officers are to patrol in a proactive manner, to investigate suspicious person(s) and circumstances aggressively, and to enforce the motor vehicle laws actively, but also that citizens will only be stopped or detained when there exists reasonable suspicion to believe they have committed, are committing, or are about to commit an infraction of the law.

DISCUSSION QUESTIONS AND ISSUES

1. ***Law Enforcement Agency Policy on Racial Profiling.*** The student can determine if a police department in the area meets recommended standards regarding policies pertaining to racial profiling:

    a. Does the policy clearly define acts constituting racial profiling using the definition provided at the beginning of this chapter?

    b. Does the policy strictly prohibit peace officers employed by the agency from engaging in racial profiling?

    c. Does the policy provide instructions by which individuals may file a complaint if they believe they were a victim of racial profiling by an employee of the agency?

    d. Does the agency provide public education relating to the complaint process?

    e. Does the policy require appropriate corrective action to be taken against a peace officer employed by the agency who, after an investigation, is shown to have engaged in racial profiling in violation of the agency's policy? What benchmarks are utilized and who interprets the data?

    f. Does the agency require the collection of data relating to traffic stops in which a citation is issued and to arrests resulting from those traffic stops, including information relating to:

        1. The race or ethnicity of the individual detained?

2. Whether a search was conducted and, if so, if it was based on the consent of the person detained?

g. Does the agency's policy require it to submit a report on the findings and conclusions based on the data collected to a governing body of the county or state for review and monitoring purposes?

2. ***Actual Incident for Discussion:*** In a city in Indiana, an African American police officer driving an unmarked police car was pulled over by an officer not from his agency. The officer was wearing a uniform at the time, but he was not wearing his hat, which would have identified him as a police officer when viewed from outside the car. According to a complaint filed, the trooper who pulled the man over appeared shocked when the officer got out of the car. The trooper explained that he had stopped the man because he had three antennas on the rear of his car. Discuss the following:

a. Do you think the officer who pulled over a colleague was guilty of racial profiling?

b. Do you think the officer was being honest when he said the reason for the stop was the multiple antennas? Is having multiple antennas a crime?

c. Can complaints of being racially profiled be dismissed as the exaggerations of hypersensitive minorities or people who do not understand the job of a police officer?

WEBSITE RESOURCES

Visit these websites for additional information about racial profiling and related issues:

American-Arab Anti-Discrimination Committee (ADC): http://www.adc.org

This website provides information about the ADC's civil rights efforts and useful summary data about cases and complaints regarding discrimination involving Arab Americans.

American Civil Liberties Union (ACLU): http://www.aclu.org

This website contains multiple locations for information about many issues, including racial profiling.

Americans for Effective Law Enforcement (AELE):
http://www.aele.org/traffic.html

This website offers publications, research, and education on a variety of criminal justice issues. Available online is an article, "Specimen Directive," which prohibits discriminatory stops, searches, and enforcement action.

Asian American Legal Defense and Education Fund (AALDEF):
http://www.aaldef.org

This website provides information about civil rights issues concerning Asian/Pacific Americans and highlights issues of immigration, family law, government benefits, anti-Asian violence and police misconduct, employment discrimination, labor rights, and workplace issues.

Commission on Accreditation for Law Enforcement Agencies (CALEA): http://www.calea.org

> CALEA was conceived in 1979 by the International Association of Chiefs of Police, the National Organization of Black Law Enforcement Executives, the National Sheriffs' Association, and the Police Executive Research Forum. The website contains information about the organization and the standards law enforcement agencies must adopt in order to be accredited.

Institute on Race & Poverty: http://www1.umn.edu.irp

> This website, affiliated with the University of Minnesota, provides access to various studies, including those dealing with race and poverty, components of racial profiling legislation, and racial profiling. The website offers two studies of particular interest. "Report on Traffic Stop Data in St. Paul" (2001, May 24) documents the University's analysis data on traffic stops—a study requested by the St. Paul Police Department. The report confirmed a disproportional number of minorities being stopped and searched and against whom action was taken. "Components of Racial Profiling Legislation" (2001, March) is a research paper presenting the essential elements of effective racial profiling legislation.

International Association of Chiefs of Police (IACP): http://theiacp.org

> This website provides a resource for law enforcement issues publications, including "Bias-Free Policing" by the 2001 Civil Rights Committee, which contains a policy statement for agencies concerning the prohibition of bias-based policing, and "Condemnation of Bias-Based Policing" by the 2001 Narcotics and Dangerous Drugs Committee.

Mexican American Legal Defense and Education Fund (MALDEF): http://www.maldef.org

> This website is a good source of information on Latino civil rights issues and publications.

National Organization of Black Law Enforcement Executives (NOBLE): http://www.noblenatl.org

> This website is a good source of information on many subjects, including recommended police policy and procedure, NOBLE publications, press releases and training material, resources, and classes. "Perspective: Racial Profiling—A Symptom of Bias-Based Policing" is an online primer on the subject of racial profiling.

Police Executive Research Forum (PERF): http://policeforum.org

> This website provides an abundance of information about racial profiling and model programs. PERF produced a free video and guide to facilitate police-citizen discussions on racially biased policing. They also produced a helpful guide, "Racially Biased Policing: A Principled Response."

REFERENCES

"ADC Fact Sheet: The Condition of Arab Americans Post-9/11." (2002). American-Arab Anti-Discrimination Committee.

Amnesty International USA. (2004). "Threat and Humiliation: Racial Profiling, Domestic Security and Human Rights in the United States." New York: Amnesty International USA.

Barlow, David E., and Melissa Hickman Barlow. (2002). "Racial Profiling: A Survey of African American Police Officers." *Police Quarterly,* 5(3), 334–358.

Barlow, David E., and Melissa Hickman Barlow. (2000). *Police in a Multicultural Society: An American Story.* Prospect Heights, IL: Waveland Press.

Bast, Carol M. (1997). "Driving While Black. Stopping Motorists on a Subterfuge." *Criminal Law Bulletin. 33,* 457–486.

Berry, Ondra. (2006). Retired Deputy Chief, Reno, Nevada, Police Department, personal communications.

Bureau of Justice Statistics Report. (2006, May). NCJ 210118.

"Bush Bans Racial Profiling." (2003, June 18). *Washington Post,* p. A14.

"Boston to Track All Stops by Police." (2003, July 20). *Boston Globe,* p. A1.

"Characteristics of Drivers Stopped by Police, 2002." (2006, June). U.S. Department of Justice, Office of Justice Programs, Bureau of Justice Statistics, NCJ 211471, by Erica Smith and Matthew Durose.

Engel, Robin S., Jennifer M. Calnon, and Thomas J. Bernard. (2002). "Theory and Racial Profiling: Shortcomings and Future Directions in Research." *Justice Quarterly, 19*(2), 249–273.

Harris, D.A. (2002). "Profiles in Injustice: Why Racial Profiling Cannot Work." New York: New York Press.

Harris, David A. (1999). "Driving While Black. Racial Profiling on Our Nation's Highways." American Civil Liberties Union. Available: www.aclu.org/prfiling/report/index.

Lundman, Richard J., and Robert Kaufman. (2003, February). "Driving While Black: Effects of Race, Ethnicity, and Gender on Citizen Self-Reports of Traffic Stops and Police Actions." *Criminology, 41,* 195–220.

MacDonald, Heather. (2001, Spring). "The Myth of Racial Profiling." *City Journal, 11*(2) pp. 1–5.

"New Jersey Adopts Ban on Racial Profiling." (2003, March 21). *News India-Time,* New Jersey, p. A1.

"New Study Shows Minorities Face More Stops on Some Illinois Roads." (2005, July 15). *Associated Press.*

"Oakland to Analyze Police Reform Deal." (2003, July 15). *Contra Costa Times,* p. A4.

"Oakland's Police Chief Angry with Rider Story." (2003, May 2). *Contra Costa Times,* p. A5.

"Race, Sex, and Age Drive Ticketing." (2003, July 20). *Boston Globe,* p. A1.

"Racially Biased Policing: A Principled Response." (2001). Police Executive Research Forum Washington, D.C.

"Racial Profiling." (2003, January 13). American Civil Liberties Union. Available: http://www.aclu.org.

"Recommendations from the First IACP Forum on Professional Traffic Stops." (2003). International Association of Chiefs of Police. Available: www.theiacp.org.

"Riders' Followed Department Line, Defense Says." (2005, March 29). *Contra Costa Times,* p.A5

"Sample Professional Traffic Stops Policy and Procedure." (2003). International Association of Chiefs of Police. Available: www.theiacp.org.

Senge, Peter, Art Kleiner, Charlotte Roberts, Richard Ross, and Bryan J. Smith. (1994). *The Fifth Discipline Fieldbook: Strategies and Tools for Building a Learning Organization.* New York: Currency Doubleday.

Straus, Ira. (2002, October). "Commentary: Profile to Survive." United Press International. Available: www.upi.com.

"Sweeps Far from Border Rouse Anger." (2004, June 11). *Los Angeles Times,* p. 3.

Tomaskovic-Devey, D., M. Mason, and M, Zingraff. (2004). "Looking for the Driving While Black Phenomena: Conceptualizing Racial Bias Processes and Their Associated Distributions." *Police Quarterly, 7*(1): 3–29.

"Traffic Stop Data Collection Policies for State Police, 2004." (2005, June). U.S. Department of Justice, Bureau of Justice Statistics Fact Sheet, NCJ 209156.

"Troopers Fair, Tough in Traffic Encounters." (2003, July 22). *Boston Globe,* p. A1 & A19.

"Understanding Bias-Based Traffic Law Enforcement." (2003, July). National Highway Traffic Safety Administration. Available: http://*www.nhtsa.dot.gov.*

U.S. Department of Justice. (2000). *A Resource Guide on Racial Profiling Data Collection Systems: Promising Practices and Lessons Learned.* Washington D.C.

Will, George F. (2001, April). "Exposing the 'Myth' of Racial Profiling." *Washington Post,* p. A19.

Withrow, Brian. (2004, March). "A Comparative Analysis of Commonly Used Benchmarks in Racial Profiling: A Research Note." (Unpublished paper submitted to the Academy of Criminal Justice Sciences by Brian Withrow, Wichita State University, School of Community Affairs, Wichita, Kansas).

Withrow, Brian. (2006). *Racial Profiling from Rhetoric to Reason.* Upper Saddle River, New Jersey: Pearson-Prentice Hall.

Part 5

CULTURAL EFFECTIVENESS FOR PEACE OFFICERS

15 Emerging Roles and Technology for Peace Officers in Multicultural Law Enforcement

Part Five concludes this text by highlighting some of the themes from previous chapters, while discussing broad concepts on the emerging role of peace officers within a twenty-first-century multicultural society.

Chapter 15 considers all the emerging and changing issues confronting the peace officer in his/her peacekeeping roles and in the use of high technology in multicultural law enforcement. Peace officers need to be competent to deal with their increasing roles in multi-jurisdictional crime-solving efforts (beyond homeland security and terrorism to incidents such as the D.C. sniper, identity theft, and multi-state crime scams). Moreover, the role of peace officers in assisting and communicating with multicultural communities regarding disasters and terrorism, and controlling rumors resulting from regional events (e.g., Hurricane Katrina recovery) requires additional resources, skills, and the use of new law enforcement tools and technology. Modern law enforcement requires an operating value and culture of improved intra-agency communication, as well as supportive relations with multicultural communities.

In addition to the Instructor's Manual for this text, further resource material is provided in the form of four appendices. These supplementary aids correspond to various chapters in the book. They include assessment instruments as well as a listing of consultants and services related to the content of this text.

Chapter 15

Emerging Strategies, Roles, and Technology for Peace Officers in Multicultural Law Enforcement

OVERVIEW

This chapter focuses on emerging and changing issues in the strategies and roles confronting the peace officer in multicultural law enforcement today. Peace officers now need to be able to manage and adapt to innovations and advanced technology within their increasing roles in local community policing and in multijurisdictional crime-solving efforts such as terrorism, homeland security, and disaster preparedness. The role of peace officers has increased in functions to encompass assistance to and communication with multicultural communities in disasters, terrorism, and controlling possible community confrontations resulting from global/regional events. The emerging roles for peace officers are highlighted as they pertain to working with multicultural special populations such as minority and immigrant youths, unauthorized migrants, and people with mental health problems. Curtailing litigation against law enforcement agencies is a key challenge for law enforcement leaders and officers, requiring changes in police policies, training, and practices. Training and preparation of future law enforcement personnel will require changes in the curriculum of the police academies, as well as the ongoing and continuing education of law enforcement officers.

COMMENTARY

Perhaps the biggest challenge facing law enforcement officers and leaders of the 21st century will be to develop law enforcement organizations and services that can (1) effectively recognize, relate to, and operate within the multicultural and global shifts in culture, (2) utilize technological advances, and (3) adapt to community/governmental expectations. As highlighted by the First Leadership Conference of the International Association of Chiefs of Police (IACP, 1999):

> Forces in the community, the police agency, local government, and global trends are profoundly altering expectations and requirements for leading police agencies successfully.

Today's law enforcement organizations must embrace innovations and technological advances through appropriate organizational change, training, education, and preparation of its officers. This is particularly important in the training curricula and processes within the police academies. Emphasis is critically needed in the area of working with multicultural communities and in the overall knowledge bases of diversity, basic psychology, interpersonal relations, and communications.

> Numerous current studies clearly demonstrate that the training of American police is deficient. Many police academies have a training curriculum consisting of approximately 400 hours. . . . Even when an academy is well structured . . . the curriculum concentrates on the law enforcement task, which occupies a relatively small portion of the police officer's time. Although most of the officer's time is devoted to service activities, training in the service function is, for the most part, de-emphasized or ignored at police academies. . . . Dedicated and responsible officers may be placed on the street unprepared for the experience they will face. They do not have a clear understanding of the true attitudes of the public they are policing. They may not have an appreciation of the historical factors that shaped the larger community and its neighborhoods. They may not understand the sources of the fears and prejudices of the people in the community, including themselves. They may not be trained in the techniques necessary to defuse dangerous situations with finesse or to seek alternatives to arrest. Unfortunately, they are too often taught to respond to threats or hostility with force. Lack of training in such subjects as introduction to social theory, basic psychology, human development and behavior, constitutional law, minority history, ethnic studies, interpersonal relations and communications skills allows communication blocks to remain intact. (Hunter, Mayhall, & Barker, 2000, pp. 194–195)

New models for law enforcement officers' training and education may need to be developed and implemented. As noted by Buerger (2004), current criminal justice education has developed a three-step program for law enforcement officers: (1) high school diploma or GED, (2) police training academy, and (3) 2- or 4-year undergraduate college education focusing upon the basic law enforcement certification curricula (2-year programs) and the criminal justice major for the undergraduate degree (4-year programs).

> The future will create new training needs not currently standard in either college programs or police training academies. New developments in technology will create a need for investigators who can cope with the criminal uses of those technologies. The sheer volume of financial crimes perpetrated via computer hacking and identity theft will exceed the capacity of federal agencies to investigate. If local police do not adapt to the need, private resources likely will fill the gap or leave local jurisdictions and their constituents without legal recourse. . . . With all of these factors in mind, what can the law enforcement and academic communities do to improve the balance between educating and training future police officers? Three main models—creating a new model of interdisciplinary criminal justice degree; modifying the existing social science curricula to similar effect; and placing greater emphasis at the point of hiring upon the course of study, rather than on mere possession of a degree—demonstrate some possible approaches. (Buerger, 2004)

Law enforcement officers and their organizations will need to continually update and increase their sophistication with advanced technology and scientific innovation to work within multicultural communities.

As criminals become more sophisticated in their use of advanced technology to perpetrate crime, criminal justice professionals must have equally sophisticated tools to prevent, investigate, and prosecute those crimes, to better track and manage offenders, and to protect the public. (Office of Justice Programs , 1999)

THE FUTURE OF PEACEKEEPING STRATEGIES IN MULTICULTURAL COMMUNITIES

Those who would uphold law and order in the 21st century will need to be more proactive and less reactive (Thibault, Lynch, & McBride, 2001). The new generation of peace officers must not only increase their knowledge in such matters but also promote positive law enforcement innovations, as noted in this chapter. In this section, we focus on a few strategies for agencies to consider in their efforts to keep community peace in a multicultural society.

Within multiracial communities facing the myriad challenges of transition and integration, economic constraints, and rising crime, representatives of the justice system need to act proactively, sensitively, and knowledgeably. If social order is not to be replaced by chaos, law enforcement representatives of all types not only need to be culturally sensitive but also must actively avoid racist, sexist, and homophobic behavior that may trigger violent social protest. Police researcher Neil Lingle (1992), in his futurist study more than a decade ago on ethnic groups and culture, identified programs that can promote a cooperative and interactive relationship between peace officers and the community that are still applicable today. His recommendations for law enforcement include the following:

- More cultural awareness and sensitivity training of personnel
- More recruitment and promotion of minorities and ethnics with the help of police unions
- More information to officers on external factors affecting their performance (e.g., influence of wealth and economic power, as well as racial or ethnic and political power)
- More study of institutional racism, organizational diversity, and the impact of minority employment and promotion on police policies and practices in the future

The recommendations from the President's First Leadership Conference of the International Association of Chiefs of Police reinforced similar emphases for the future (IACP, 1999):

The influx of new ethnic groups and sizable increases in the population of present groups require police leaders to possess and operationalize heightened degrees of cultural awareness and an ability to tailor leadership behavior to a richer and more varied set of subcultures. They must also ensure that these ethnicities are properly represented in the workforce. Population shifts are creating pressures on executives in suburban jurisdictions, urbanizing counties, sheriffs, and state police. The comparative tranquility of rural areas can no longer be taken for granted. (pp. 9–10)

Community-Based Policing

The last two decades of the 20th century brought problems to law enforcement that forced strategic changes within agencies. Because of greater population diversity in many communities, reduced budgets, increased unauthorized migration, social disorder, and domestic terrorism, criminal justice entities were subject to increased scrutiny and public review. Progressive law enforcement executives embraced a strategy of community-based policing to meet many of these challenges (see Chapters 1 and 14, this volume; Bucqueroux, 2004; IACP, 1999; Peak & Glensor, 1999). The Philadelphia Police Commissioner's Council vigorously first voiced the transition to this strategy in 1987, and its application has emerged with ever-increasing importance to multicultural law enforcement:

> A key concept . . . is that the police abandon the image of themselves as a "thin blue line," standing between the "good citizens" of the community on the one hand, and the "bad guys" on the other. Rather, they should favor an image of themselves as partners to the community in a joint effort to produce freedom from fear and victimization. . . . Finally, this concept acknowledges that unless the police work at establishing and maintaining a proper relationship with the community, they themselves can be seen as victimizers and troublemakers, rather than as peacekeepers. (pp. 4–5).

Law enforcement agencies adopting the community policing strategy have not only become partners within a community but advocates for public well-being. As a result, the role of the peace officer, especially at the line level, changes dramatically in those cities and counties using community-based policing. In addition, with increased contact between community members and police, there will be opportunities to educate the public as to the difficult practices and decisions that police have to make continually. The following example illustrates the community's review of racial profiling within local police citation practices for traffic violations:

> The Northeastern researchers cautioned that traffic tickets cannot identify the motives of police officers. But records can show patterns and identify disparities that should be discussed. "The goal here is to have police departments and communities discuss whether the level of disparity is explainable," said Jack McDevitt, director of the Northeastern's institute. . . . The state task force—composed of police officials, minority community leaders, and civil liberties groups—has met for six months without any consensus on what level of disparity should result in a community being monitored by the state. The lead researcher said despite that, communities should begin carefully reviewing patterns in ticketing in their own departments. "Police departments have had two opportunities to review their data now: the *Boston Globe* study, and our study," McDevitt said. "Those with the greatest disparities, I would think it would be in their interest to look at this issue now, instead of waiting for community members to ask why it took so long. You can't eliminate this behavior overnight." ("Profiling Study," 2004, p. A1)

Critical to the success of any community-based policing program is the resolution of two issues: (1) How willing are citizens to accept some responsibility for community law enforcement? and (2) How willing are police officers to relinquish the social isolation of police cars to become involved with neighborhood citizens in police–community programs? These issues must be a part of a strategic, long-term plan by the chief executive desiring to implement community policing (CP) in his or her community. Chief Darrel W. Stephens of Charlotte-Mecklenburg, North Carolina, maintains that community- or problem-oriented policing is the future of law enforcement and one of the most important next stage in the evolution of this profession.

Changing Organizational Work Culture

Part of the move to community policing involves changing the traditional law enforcement agency cultures from the more rigid military and bureaucratic cultures of the past to more flexible, corporatelike, proactive, and high-tech cultures (Benson, 2001). Law enforcement leaders have become change agents in this twenty-first century process.

Exhibit 15.1 differentiates between perceptions of the disappearing law enforcement work culture and the emerging culture. Contrasting the two views helps to explain why, within the criminal justice field, a different culture of public safety and law enforcement must be created by police officers and then communicated to the public. This is but a synopsis of the transition underway in the world of work and law enforcement, which in turn alters our views of various community service roles. The shift and trends seem to be away from the traditional approaches (i.e., reactive involving solely effective responding) toward a proactive approach (i.e., community-oriented policing focused upon prevention). The shift is toward preserving the public well-being and community service, and toward protecting life and property. In addition, it is a shift from solely public-sector law enforcement to synergistic multiagency teams by both public and private sectors working in cooperation (Gehl, 2004).

How is this transition for cultural change and to community orientation to be made? Typically, it takes an agency 5 to 7 years to go from traditional policing to community policing. As a start, some departments have created citizen police academy programs that provide knowledge of the Community Policing partnership between the community and the law enforcement agency (see Chapters 5 and 7 for several examples). As part of the citizen's program, community members also learn some of the requisite skills and resources to do problem solving. Other communities hold neighborhood forums to accomplish the same objectives. As with change for most people, it takes time to transform the attitudes of typical officers toward such modern policing. Some have the mistaken notion that there are community-oriented police officers—and then there are all those other real cops (Benson, 2001).

For long-term community policing success, departments must recruit people who exhibit compassion, have good communication skills, and are problem-solvers. Job descriptions and evaluations should be rewritten to emphasize and reward such abilities. Furthermore, community policing also requires obtaining personnel, whether sworn or not, who have the local foreign-language skills to reach out to new ethnic communities.

This law enforcement approach is not incident or technology driven. Officers work in the neighborhoods on a decentralized basis, stressing regular contacts with citizens. They report back to their supervisor, who in turn transmits the information to the chief executive and his or her staff so that additional resources can be deployed as necessary. In addition to tactical plans, the agency should have a plan that calls for consulting with key community leaders before merely reacting in the event of a major crisis. Too often, police reaction has been the stimulus event for riots. Obviously, community policing cannot function in a vacuum. It needs the support of not only the public but also other government agencies. Eldrin Bell, an African-American and the chief of police for Atlanta, Georgia (at a conference hosted by the National Organization of Black Law Enforcement Executives), declared, "We cannot get to community-oriented policing until we have community-oriented government." Chief Bell suggested that

TRADITIONAL WORK CULTURE	EVOLVING WORK CULTURE
Attitude	
Reactive; preserve status quo	Proactive; anticipate the future
Orientation	
Law enforcement as dispensers of public safety	Law enforcement as helping professionals
Organization	
Paramilitary with top-down command system; intractable departments and divisions; centralization and specialization	Transitional toward more fluid, participative arrangements and open communication system; decentralization, task forces, and team management
Expectations	
Loyalty to your superior, organization and buddies, then duty and public service; conformity and dependency	Loyalty to public service and duty, and one's personal and professional development; demonstrate leadership competence and interpersonal skills
Requirements	
Political appointment, limited civil service; education—high school or less	Must meet civil service standards; education—college and beyond, lifelong learning
Personnel	
Largely white males, military background and sworn only; all alike, so structure workload for equal shares in static sharply defined slots	Multicultural without regard to sex or sexual orientation; competence norm for sworm and non-sworn personnel; all different, so capitalize on particular abilities, characteristics, potential
Performance	
Obey rules, follow orders, work as though everything depended on your own hard efforts toward gaining the pension and retirement	Work effectively, obey reasonable and responsible requests; interdependence means cooperate and collaborate with others; ensure financial/career future
Environment	
Relatively stable society where problems were somewhat routine and predictable, and authority was respected	Complex, fast-changing, multicultural society with unpredictable problems, often global in scope, and less emphasis upon authority, with importance of leadership and community input.

Exhibit 15.1   Organizational Work Culture Transitions

government be decompartmentalized, cleaned up, and made more community-directed through use of community councils. He contended that in doing so community members and government employees work together to solve problems. Police senior leadership needs to be a driving force in the process, "Community policing is forcing executives to develop a new knowledge base, perfect change management skills, and, most profound for some, to jettison a number of historical fundamental professional beliefs and values. The evolution of community-oriented policing is far from complete. As it continues to evolve, the leadership role is destined to evolve with it. The role must always be viewed as dynamic" (IACP, 1999; Oliver, 2004). Community-oriented policing has brought about key changes in multicultural communities as is highlighted by the following example:

> Last week two veteran New York City police detectives, well-liked by their colleagues and well-respected in the community they served, were shot to death while responding to a mother's pleas to prevent her 28-year-old son from repeatedly taking her car without her permission. News reports pointed out that the officers were mourned not only by their fellow police officers but also by numerous community residents. The murder of partners Detective Robert Parker and Detective Patrick Rafferty sadly emphasizes the enormous mental tension police officers must endure on the job: they can never be sure that even a seemingly routine performance of their duty of public service will not escalate to the highest level of violence. However, the grief expressed by community residents—the only silver lining in this despairing story—is a measure of the trust they placed in those officers, a measure of their feeling they could count on them. From its beginning a decade ago the federally sponsored Community Oriented Policing Services program has had that as its twin goals reducing crime, and building the trust of citizens in the police officers; and in that time it has reaffirmed the old wisdom about policing: that citizens' trust in the police is an essential ingredient to preventing as well as solving crime. (Morial, 2004)

Community-oriented policing is proactive, and it is based on the neighborhood and the police identifying problems within the community and directing resources to solve them. For example, as the police move more into the world of high technology, we see officers with laptop computers using them to collect information and to analyze what is occurring in their neighborhood (e.g., recording and analyzing hate/bias crimes). Community-based policing involves additional expenses in cities or counties with already tight budgets. Public administrators and legislators must support ongoing CP efforts, lest they experience the dilemma of "pay me now" (providing budget for such strategies) or "pay me later" (the aftermath of lawsuits, riots, disturbances, distrust, and so forth).

A key, continuing learning process and role function in community-based policing is the ongoing monitoring of important local and global events that might affect multicultural law enforcement. Public events such as the anniversary of September 11, Earth Day, Double Ten Independence Day, Israeli Independence Day, Pakistan and Indian political demonstrations, and Israeli or Palestinian political rallies all have the potential for multicultural community conflicts and confrontation (although the majority of these events have been peaceful). Police presence is required at such events, but as with other situations, excessive police presence can escalate hostilities and decrease community partnership efforts. Law enforcement officials need to be well informed about current events around the globe, as conflicts outside the United States often have a ripple effect across the world and may have an impact on local events. The monitoring of world events and community trends will help police officers take a preventive posture that can ultimately help to avoid confrontation between various multicultural groups in this country (also see Chapter 13).

CRIME PREVENTION AMONG MINORITY AND IMMIGRANT YOUTH

If it is to succeed, community-oriented policing must focus on positive relations, contact, and communications between young people and peace officers. This approach not only counters but actually prevents juvenile delinquency (Bartol & Bartol, 1999; Goode, 2001). A related challenge today is how to train officers to be successful role models for the benefit of young people, especially those from immigrant or "ghetto" groups (for example in Chapter 1, the Bosnia Youth and IRCO programs). One aspect of this effort should be to make the case for equal justice in law and order from the perspective as perceived by minority and immigrant young people, so as eventually to attract some of these youth into law enforcement careers (Jahn, 2006).

According to the Justice Policy Institute's Report, *Ganging Up on Communities? Putting Gang Crime in Context,*

> Even at a time when the several leading national crime indicators suggest that serious and violent crimes are on the decline, many communities still experience unacceptable levels of crime, including youth crime and gang crime. However, the public safety issues affecting distressed neighborhoods in our big cities are not the same as those impacting other neighborhoods and communities. The places that are most impacted by crime tend to be the places with large investments in policing, detention, jails, prisons and law enforcement—which, according to the Bureau of Justice Statistics, now represents a $167 billion investment in criminal justice infrastructure. Fostering a national culture of fear concerning gangs only diverts our attention from the real problem and real solutions. . . . Multiple studies show that incarcerating young people only increases the likelihood that they will recidivate, whereas alternative programs could facilitate the process of aging out of normative delinquent behavior. On a number of measures, including public safety, efforts to incarcerate youth have proven unsuccessful. (Ziedenberg, 2005)

However, to facilitate the goals of community policing and equal justice with youth, some law enforcement and police officers may have to change how they perceive deprived or disturbed youth and how they deal with them as human beings. David Cole, a professor of law at Georgetown University, in his book about examining how the criminal justice system handles troubled youth from the underclass, provided an example of an African American youth's reactions to his encounters with law enforcement:

> Equal justice? How would you feel if the police regularly stopped you, for no apparent reason, demanding to know who you are and where you are going? Further, suppose they often search your car or belongings without sufficient cause because they consider your ethnic group more prone to criminality. How would you feel as the target of such frequent questioning and suspicion, especially if you can ill afford a lawyer to protect your rights? To make matters

worse when charges are leveled against you, you may spend months languishing in jail, until an often incompetent, public attorney is assigned to you; then he or she usually advises you to plead guilty. Should you get a jury trial, it will not be composed of your peers or those from your ethnic group. In reality, if I am a young man from my ethnic group, the statistics prove that in the U.S., our rate of imprisonment is seven times that of the general population, for my kind are automatically thought by police as inclined to violence and crime. People of color like me are arrested, convicted and killed more often than other citizens. In fact, among young persons within my group from the age of 20–29 years, one in three is in prison, on parole or probation. And who am I?—a black youth supposedly living in a democracy lauded as the home of the free and the brave. . . . Even when members of my group have an education and a job, we may be stopped by officers for "walking or driving while black." If white citizens were treated like we are by law enforcement, there would be a public outcry! For the vast majority of our people who have been stopped by police are subsequently proven innocent. There are no equal rights for my kind when it comes to search and seizure! (2000, p. 31)

Cole provides some sobering thoughts for planned change with respect to the way the criminal justice system treats youth from diverse racial and ethnic groups. But how about young people in general, what is the situation and what is working? Consider two cases:

Schools. Some law enforcement agencies contract with school districts to provide officers on a daily basis for security purposes, as well as to offer role models. Many officers get involved in educating youth on a voluntary basis in a variety of ways. Sworn officers are rightly proud of sponsoring projects such as the Police Athletic League (PAL), which involves neighborhood kids in constructive teamwork, or the Police Explorer Scout programs. Studies by police executives propose a variety of youth strategies for this purpose, ranging from a police high school curriculum to police cadet programs (Office of Justice Programs, 1999). So far, police in schools and increased security in these facilities have not deterred violence in random actions by alienated students against classmates, as occurred at Columbine High School in Littleton, Colorado, in 1999. It would seem that more preventative programs to identify violence-prone youth have to be developed by both police and educators through cooperative efforts (see Ziedenberg, 2005; Meadows, 2001).

Gangs. Perhaps the biggest challenge would appear to be in preventing or counteracting rising youth violence, especially among males between the ages of 12 and 24 in the nation's inner cities, where unemployed, disadvantaged youths seek identity and support through destructive gang participation (Britz, Rush, & Barker, 2001). As such, gangs declare truces and work together among the different ethnic, racial, and cultural communities, or link up with gangs in other cities for criminal activity. They can become a real threat to community stability if members' energies are not redirected.

Effective management of gang activities include improved educational opportunities, job training, and gang prevention programs. Organizational system planning and interventions are also needed (Britz, et al., 2001):

1. Develop a countywide master plan for helping youth at risk of joining gangs, especially among minorities and immigrants.

2. Overhaul the juvenile justice system, which often serves as a recruitment and training program for the gangs.

3. Focus on the 10 to 15 percent of gang members who are hard-core criminals.

4. Develop cooperative, private-industry programs to provide training and jobs for inner-city youth.

Law enforcement studies, such as those cited earlier, point out a number of antigang and youth-oriented strategies:

- Cooperation with the local clergy who maintain effective relations with gang members. For example, a coalition of Protestant and Catholic churches have formed the Southern California Organizing Committee, which promotes a Hope in Youth campaign. This is a 5 year, public–private investment in a $20 million fund. With it, teams were formed in their church congregations to work with youth. One team member would be an outreach worker with a caseload of 25 youths at risk, leading them away from gang involvement to alternative education or training and drug rehabilitation; a second team member would work with individual parents of gang members, while a third would develop parent unions to empower them with respect to their children's education. Each church then would sponsor and mentor gang members in transition to a more mature way of life.

- Assistance to local ethnic business organizations that wish to work with gangs in community ventures and job development. One such association was formed between the Korean-American Grocers Association and two Los Angeles African American gangs, the Bloods and the Crips. Gangs will increasingly occupy law enforcement time, and agencies must be creative in devising nonarrest approaches to a community's disadvantaged youth, particularly in conjunction with other community organizations.

- Creation of ethnic police benevolent associations to provide role models and programs for disadvantaged youth of similar cultural heritage who are in gangs or who are potential recruits. Hence, the African American police groups are involved with young, male African Americans, while the Hispanic police officers' groups focus on young Latino males, and the Asian American officer's groups direct services toward young males from Chinese, Vietnamese, Korean, and Japanese backgrounds. The same strategy can be extended to ethnic police organizations for Italian Americans, Irish Americans, Polish Americans, and so forth.

  Forward-looking officers encourage and participate in a community task force that "gangs up" on the problem by brainstorming on how to defuse the danger by providing positive places and group experiences for local youth. Social activities, sports, voluntary service, and other constructive mechanisms are emphasized. The goal should be to divert present-day gangs into team programs engaging in community rebuilding, while offering a gang alternative to youth who have not yet joined gangs but seek some group identity.

Community conservation or ecology corps provide one example of how young adults can be involved constructively in their communities. The plan for the annual National Youth Service Day (NYSD) is another. NYSD is the largest service event in the world, mobilizing millions of young people to identify and address the needs of their communities through service. NYSD is also an opportunity to recruit the next generation of volunteers and educate the public about the role of youth as community leaders. Junior Achievement has already proved what businesspersons can do to involve youth positively in productive ways. Even bored, middle-class or affluent youth would benefit from such outlets for their energies, in contrast to "hanging out" or "mall hopping." Such endeavors take a combination of public and private investment and personnel, and peace officers could provide needed leadership in this area.

- Counteracting hate groups that reach out to a troubled generation of alienated white youth from urban, suburban, and even rural areas. White supremacists groups often become surrogate families to angry, disaffected young men and women, some of whom are from the underclass, and may have parents in jail as well (1.5 million U.S. parents are in prison). Often their members are products of dysfunctional families and perceived of as outside mainstream activities. Skinheads are enlisted to engage in hate crimes against racial, ethnic, religious, or gay groups that these dysfunctional youth have learned to despise. Many of these young people have themselves already been in prison, where they were recruited by such gangs as the Nazi Low Riders (NLR). Some, too, are frustrated middle-class kids who use the Internet Web hate sites to absorb neo-Nazi propaganda. Others are lower-middle-class youths discontented with society because of socioeconomic conditions. Wanting to protest, they may begin by getting together for something like graffiti tagging but end up engaging in hate crimes against their scapegoats. The problem is global in scope. Europe has its own violent, young skinheads who attack immigrants. To undercut the white supremacists gangs (sometimes fueled by drugs and alcohol abuse) schools and colleges have begun programs to teach tolerance. What is needed is for both active and retired members of law enforcement to reach out in positive endeavors to help redirect the energies of these hate-filled youth into constructive enterprises.

- Apprenticeships or internships for youth in law enforcement have long involved interested young people on a part-time basis or during summer vacations (Taylor, 1999). Some have been at the high school level, organized through traditional police youth groups. However, with the increase of criminal justice studies in colleges and universities, innovative projects attempt to give these students some on-the-job, real-world experience in police, corrections, and justice activities. As a case in point, the criminal justice internships at New York's St. John's University are highly organized under a supervisor, Professor John McCabe, formerly chief of patrol in the New York Police Department. Those who have completed a majority of their criminal justice studies courses and meet the criteria can become interns. Student interns get hands-on experience and gain valuable insights into segments of the justice system, from juvenile justice and the district attorney's office to the U.S. marshals or drug enforcement agencies. The program to jump-start criminal justice careers provides three academic credits if successfully completed and has proved invaluable to the participants. St. John's University students (juniors or seniors) who qualify are required to complete 120 hours, or 8 hours a week, at the internship sponsor site. The program runs for 15 weeks, or one semester. The youth also must attend orientation sessions, as well as keep a daily log of their intern activities, verified and signed by their site supervisor. At the end of the process, participants prepare a term paper on their field experience and receive a letter grade. Some interns who work for a police department or federal agency are offered full-time positions upon graduation. Obviously, these internships not only facilitate the transition to a criminal justice job but also help the person to determine whether this is his or her preferred career field. The benefits to the law enforcement entities that employ such interns are numerous.

POLICE ENCOUNTERS AMONG PEOPLE WITH MENTAL ILLNESS

This chapter emphasizes the need for more cultural awareness and sensitivity training when it comes to law enforcement contact of various groups. One of the groups that law enforcement officer representatives encounter frequently is people with mental illness. Approximately 5 percent of U.S. residents have a serious mental illness and an estimated 7 percent of police contacts in jurisdictions with 100,000 or more people involve the severe mentally ill (U.S. Department of Justice, 2006). Sadly, at the time of the writing of this text's fourth edition, the average number of classroom hours that recruits spend nationally in the police academy on mental illness issues is a shockingly low 6.5 hours and sometimes (and it is not guaranteed) 1 hour of in-service training (Hails & Borum, 2003). The Police Executive Research Forum recommends a minimum of 16.0 hours of training on mental illness issues at the police academy level.

It is critical that law enforcement acquire knowledge and skills in the area of mental health. The following study reflects the volume of contacts two different police departments had in 2002:

> The Lincoln (Nebraska) Police Department found that it handled over 1,500 mental health investigation cases in 2002, and that it spent more time on these cases than on injury traffic accidents, burglaries, or felony assaults. The New York City Police Department responds to about 150,000 "emotionally disturbed persons" calls per year. (Kelly, 2002)

Mental illness is not just a police problem but a medical and social services problem, with major impact upon the local community, as well. Unfortunately, a number of the problems caused by or associated with people with mental illness often do become incidents where the police get involved. Police interactions with people with mental illness have the potential of being dangerous, but usually are not. According to the U.S. Department of Justice, there were 982 police officers assaulted and 15 police officers feloniously killed between 1993 and 2002 by "mentally deranged" assailants. These assaults and murders are tragic, but these attacks by people with mental illness represent one out of every 59 assaults on officers and one out of every 42 officers killed; and for the person with severe mental illness, it is estimated they are four times more likely to be killed by the police (U.S. Department of Justice, 2006).

Law enforcement officers encounter people with mental illness in many different types of situations. These types of incidents include roles that include criminal offenders, disorderly persons, missing persons, complainants, victims, and persons in need of care (U.S. Department of Justice, 2006). This information highlights the importance of training in mental illness recognition as well as using the appropriate technique in stabilizing the situation.

Crime Prevention among People with Mental Illness

In June 1999, the White House convened the first Conference on Mental Health to address ways of reducing the stigma of mental illness and discrimination against people with mental disorders. The Attorney General chaired a session on mental health and the criminal justice system to address the recurring cycle of people with mental disorders being incarcerated for crimes (often having only committed minor offenses) and receiving only minimal or no treatment for their underlying mental health problems. The session focused on legislative proposals to address these issues, including a mental health court proposal and other proposed legislation to improve services to the mentally ill within correctional settings.

Following up on the White House conference, the Office of Justice Programs and the Department of Health and Human Services (DHHS) Center for Mental Health Services hosted a July 1999 conference on the treatment of people with mental disorders within the justice system. Issues included the challenges of integrating criminal justice and mental health systems, diverting mentally ill offenders to appropriate treatment through mental health court programs, improving mental health services in the juvenile justice system, and creating community partnerships to respond to the needs of people with mental disorders.

The Bureau of Justice study, released at the time of the July conference, estimated that 283,800 mentally ill offenders were held in the nation's state and federal prisons and local jails at mid-year 1998, and an additional 547,800 mentally ill people were on probation in the community. Other findings included:

- Offenders identified as mentally ill were more likely than other offenders incarcerated or on probation to have committed a violent offense. Nearly 1 in 5 violent offenders in prison or jail or on probation were identified as mentally ill.

- When compared with other inmates and probationers, the mentally ill inmates and probationers reported higher rates of prior physical and sexual abuse and higher rates of alcohol and drug abuse by a parent or guardian while they were growing up.

- Since admission, 61 percent of the mentally ill state and federal prison inmates and 41 percent of the local jail inmates said they had received treatment for a mental condition in the form of counseling, medication, or other mental health services. Fifty-six percent of mentally ill probationers had received treatment since beginning their sentences.

- More than three-quarters of the mentally ill inmates had been sentenced to prison, jail, or probation at least once prior to their current sentence. Half reported three or more prior sentences. The mentally ill inmates were more likely than other prisoners to have a prior sentence for a violent offense.

- While incarcerated, the mentally ill were more likely than other inmates to be involved in fights and to be charged with breaking prison and jail rules (Office of Justice Programs, 1999).

Law enforcement strategies to deal with the problems of people with mental health issues within the criminal justice system include:

- Cooperation with the cultural leadership, local clergy, and other community-based agencies (e.g., homeless shelters, food banks, social services) to provide a network of support for people with mental health problems.

- Assistance to local ethnic business organizations that wish to work voluntarily with mental health issues within the community.

- Creation of specific police training and educational materials for working with people with mental health problems.

- Development of procedures and policies within the law enforcement agency for dealing with mental health problems.

Professional officers encourage the development of and participation in community task forces and committees on mental health issues. Brainstorming on how to defuse the stigma of mental illness and promote the well-being of people with mental health problems through positive support, services, and community connectedness is critical in task force effectiveness (Sentencing Project, 2002; Human Rights Watch, 2003).

CURTAILING LITIGATION AGAINST POLICE AGENCIES AND OFFICERS

Much innovation is necessary so that police responses will satisfy citizens rather than provoke them to lawsuits against officers and their departments, especially in multicultural communities. Nonviolent peacekeeping is particularly critical in ethnic, immigrant, and racially diverse communities, where misperception and miscommunication may occur because of language barriers, along with differences in body language and nonverbal interactions. Moreover, "mounting local, state, and federal legislation complicates analytical and planning decisions processes and multiplies the workload required to ensure that policies, protocols, training, and workforce behaviors are consistent with new legislative initiatives" (IACP, 1999). The principal problem in this regard relates to the use of force by law enforcement at the time of arrest; that is, whether it is perceived as excessive or deadly. Agencies that analyze citizen complaints against officers usually find that this area receives the most negative community feedback, especially from persons who feel disenfranchised.

America is a very litigious society. Throughout the United States, the last two decades of the 20th century witnessed a dramatic increase in individual and class-action suits against law enforcement agencies for mistreatment and killing of citizens by police officers. The scope of this national problem can be appreciated by citing statistics from one other city, Detroit. Between 1997 and 2000, that municipality had to pay $32 million because of lawsuits brought against the police. A city council analysis showed that 78 percent of the money so expended involved cases with only a small number of officers; 261 officers were named in more than one suit. The issue is what the city administration should do with such repeat offenders. Furthermore, are the officers guilty of unprofessional behavior and maltreatment or simply the victims of legal strategies by lawyers?

The City of Los Angeles had to pay $14,658,075 in 1991 as a result of settlements, judgments, and awards related to excessive force litigation against its police. Then, in 1994, a jury awarded Rodney King $3.8 million to compensate for police actions. A federal judge ruled on August 28, 2000, that the Los Angeles Police Department (LAPD) can be sued as a racketeering enterprise in the so-called Rampart corruption scandal. This unprecedented decision, subject to judicial review by higher courts, could open this municipality to scores of lawsuits capable of bankrupting the city. U.S. District Judge William Rea ruled from the bench on a civil suit brought against the LAPD by a man who claims he was beaten and framed in 1997 for a crime by rogue police officers in the LAPD's Ramparts Division. Such illegal actions by officers within the Ramparts Division caused 100 cases to be dismissed, resulting in five officers being charged with both conspiracy and even attempted murder. This latest ruling cleared the plaintiff to pursue the case under the federal racketeering statutes against conspiracies. His lawyers maintain the innocent man was a victim of a police conspiracy to deny him of his lawful rights as a citizen.

Many lawsuits against police agencies and their members are frivolous or unsubstantiated and are thus thrown out of court or are decided in favor of law enforcement. However, too many lawsuits result from inadequately screened or trained officers whose behavior on the job is not just unprofessional and unethical but outright biased and criminal. With greater public access to improved communications technology and increased information, citizens are fighting back when police abuse their human or civil rights. When they win these legal suits, taxpayers ultimately have to pay for the insufficiencies or mistakes of their public servants in the criminal justice system.

Some analysts believe the problem is exacerbated because personnel in too many agencies operate more like soldiers than like peace officers (e.g., growth of Special Weapons and Tactics [SWAT] teams in departments). For 150 years, police departments have been organized based on the military model. As noted in the Police Leadership in the 21st Century Conference, "The transition to participatory management seems irreversible. It is, less and less, a choice that the chief executive can control. In the empowerment environment of contemporary organizations, chiefs are less able to function entirely through hierarchical structures, especially to effect change" (IACP, 1999). In the 21st century the move to organizations in which power is increasingly shared and accountability required at all levels of the law enforcement agency will continue to be emphasized because of increasing public dissatisfaction with law enforcement agencies, highlighted by legal settlements against officers. Public dissatisfaction, in turn, is reflected in jury decisions, as exemplified by the following excessive force case:

> Ventura County must pay more than $2 million in damages to a Fillmore man shot in the back by a rookie sheriff's deputy two years ago as the man tried to disarm his intoxicated son at a wedding reception, a jury ruled Monday. The verdict came after a day of deliberations in U.S. District Court in Los Angeles, where retired Fillmore police officer Anthony Morales, 54, sued the county for violating his civil rights and demanded compensation for injuries sustained in the May 2000 shooting. In July, jurors held Deputy Tonya Herbst, 31, liable for

battery, negligence and civil rights violations after concluding that she used excessive force when she shot Morales as he wrestled a gun away from his son, Chad. The panel awarded $2,073,000 in compensatory damages following a separate damages phase that began last week. . . . "They were not pleased with this officer," Williamson said. "They did not find her credible. They specifically told us afterward that they did not believe her story." During the trial, Oxnard defense attorney Alan Wisotsky told jurors that Herbst believed her life and the safety of others were in danger when she saw the younger Morales raising the gun. He argued that Morales had not disarmed his son and had moved into the path of the bullet during a struggle for control of the weapon. He also noted that Herbst's actions were deemed justified by the Ventura County district attorney. But Williamson told jurors that Herbst ignored instructions from a training officer and recklessly fired her weapon after Morales had defused the situation. Attorneys sought about $3 million in compensation. (Wilson, 2003, p. B1)

On the other hand, what of the officer's rights when accused of misconduct during a legal action? Brian Harris, a homicide detective of the Houston Police Department, noting that in our judicial system the accused is presumed to be innocent until proven guilty, argued that under such circumstances, the public should afford sworn officers the same rights as the supposed victim. Until the evidence is presented and an inquiry commission or court has rendered a verdict, the public and media should not presume guilt. Furthermore, there is the issue of intent. When an officer's life or well-being is threatened, he or she may not intend to hurt a perpetrator while defending himself or herself. Again, this is where training comes in, so that discipline and control are maintained in very difficult situations that police increasingly find themselves in while patrolling and seeking to ensure law and order in the community. Detective Harris concludes that training in basic police practice and its implementation by supervisors are the keys to effective performance on patrol: "When police create time and distance between themselves and the suspect, then they can conduct a safer encounter."

EMERGING TECHNOLOGY AND MULTICULTURAL LAW ENFORCEMENT INNOVATIONS

Attempts are being made by the new generation of law enforcement leaders to develop innovative strategies, structures, and services that meet the changing needs of communities (Taylor, Caeti, Loper, et al., 2006; Foster, 2005; IACP, 1999; Office of Justice Programs, 1999). As noted by Buerger (2004), "Most police training curricula and most traditional, social science-based criminal justice programs lack the ability to prepare students to deal with technology-based crime or with financial crime. Those skills are taught in business and computer science programs in universities and elsewhere." These skills need to be incorporated within law enforcement curriculum. Moreover, each year new technologies emerge, such as using biometric procedures for rapid computerized identification of possible terrorists through their fingerprints at U.S. borders (the Immigration and Customs Enforcement's US-VISIT Program) and the identification of people by their eyes, smell, and other body characteristics ("New Ways," 2000, pp. 85–91), as well as DNA profiles as evidence (Dwyer, Neufeld, & Scheck, 2000). As these new opportunities for improved law enforcement unfold, the importance of government and law enforcement agencies working in parallel becomes even more critical. As highlighted by Boyd, Melis, and Myers (2004), "To build a stronger, more seamless, and more supportive partnership between all facets of law enforcement and the FBI, the Futures Working Group (FWG) formed on April 2, 2002. The FWG represents a partnership between the FBI and the Society of Police Futurists International (PFI), with its noble and ambitious goals that include the development of forecasts and strategies to ethically maximize the effectiveness of local, state, federal, and international law enforcement bodies as they strive to maintain peace and security in the 21st century."

Many innovative peacekeeping strategies have already been described in this book. Nevertheless, advancement in technology may require law enforcement agencies to abandon some of their tried-and-true methods. For example, the delay in information dissemination and communications to multicultural communities in the Washington, D.C., snipers' case affected not only those who became suspects, but also citizens of multicultural communities with fears and apprehensions about being possible victims in the case:

> After panic erupted over the first shootings, FBI trainees were brought in to staff the telephone tip lines at the Montgomery County, Md., police headquarters. The FBI, scorning the technological revolutions of the last half-century, relied on the same tried-and-true methods the bureau used to catch targets like John Dillinger in the 1930s. The *Washington Post* reported: "Authorities said information is taken down by hand on forms that make multiple carbon copies. Copies are sorted and marked 'immediate,' 'priority' or 'routine.' Tips that concern Montgomery County are put in one pile, Fairfax in another, Richmond in a third. FBI employees then drive the paperwork out to police in those locations." The *Post* noted complaints by numerous lawmen that "the FBI's problems handling thousands of phone tips are slowing and hampering the probe." When the FBI trainees were not laboriously scrawling down the latest tip, they were busy hanging up on the snipers. In a note attached to a tree after the ninth shooting, the snipers complained that tip line operators had hung up on them five times. The note denounced police "incompitence" [sic] and declared: "We have tried to contact you to start negotiation. These people took [our] calls for a hoax or a joke, so your failure to respond has cost you five lives." Shortly after the arrest of the two suspects, D.C. Police Chief Charles Ramsey publicly confessed: "We were looking for a white van with white people, and we ended up with a blue car with black people." (Bovard, 2003, p. A21)

Foster (2005), in his book *Police Technology,* highlights the following areas as emerging and future technologies:

1. Personal Locator Beacon (PLB) will allow people to be able to find each other in public places and under emergency conditions.

2. Transponder technology will facilitate greater numbers of house arrest arrangements, which could lessen the use of prison by 20 percent at a cost savings of up to $8 billion per year.

3. Magnetic Gradient Measuring and Passive Millimeter Wave (PMW) Imaging, which will improve the technology for detecting metal objects and contrabands in people and will allow for security screening in places such as airports and governmental facilities.

4. "Dataviellance" includes technology that will allow for better use of the massive amounts of data collected in homeland security monitoring efforts and activities.

5. Biometrics will enhance individual identity confirmation and improve access technologies.

6. Less-Lethal Use of Force Devices will focus on a variety of tools and technologies that can be used to incapacitate offenders without causing injuries.

Some agencies have established an innovation task force made up of the most creative officers from all units of a department. In this approach, the chief asks the group to discover ways for police to encourage a "climate of understanding within the community, and combat a climate of fear." To that end, the innovation team, along with community focus groups (described next), might together study new ideas of promise and develop action plans to implement them. The following are some examples of such innovations:

- Ongoing contact (in the form of both structured and unstructured meetings) with members of all minority and immigrant community organizations (including church leaders, business and civic leaders, school officials, and so forth). The ongoing nature of the program must be emphasized because, typically, law enforcement only meets with community leaders after a crisis.

- Bicycle or scooter bike patrols in problem and recreational areas; officers then interact with community members, especially where there are large concentrations of minority and immigrant youth.

- Crises management strategies not only for emergencies and disasters, but also for homeland security and working with neighborhoods at risk (see Chapters 10 and 11).

- Neighborhood or shopping mall storefront police substations.

- Police concentration on repeat offenders and repeat locations for criminal activities.

- Law enforcement strategies with the homeless and those with mental health problems.

- Teams consisting of officers from diverse backgrounds regularly meeting with inner-city youth, engaging them in such activities as sports, mentoring, and finding new ways to become role models.

- Preventative programs with schools to reduce school violence. For example, a Federal Bureau of Investigation (FBI) report (O'Toole, 2000), "The School Shooter: A Threat Assessment Perspective," lists personal traits in teenagers that may lead to violence. Police and educators need to use this profile to help identify high-risk youth who manifest poor coping skills, access to weapons, drug and alcohol abuse, alienation and narcissism, inappropriate humor, and no parental or guardian monitoring of television or Internet use. In addition to these characteristics, be alert to dysfunctional family situations, as well as poor interactions in school on the part of the troubled youngsters.

- Development of neighborhood child protection plans to reduce incidents of child abuse. Such plans should include constructive opportunities for youth to network with each other and with positive adult role models in their community. Such plans should also include business, civic, and religious organizations and the adoption of a particular high-risk neighborhood in which the police, community leaders, and family members make a commitment to protecting their youth. Such efforts would include collaboration in proactive research efforts, as noted in the following example:

> Research into child abuse and neglect needs to address parents' day-to-day concerns and try to solve them, J. Robert Flores, a U.S. Department of Justice administrator, said yesterday . . . most research into social problems comes too little, too late to be used to formulate policy, as he must do, he said. The result is that many policy makers, police officers and judges believe that "research just tells you about the problem after it happens," he said. "It doesn't contribute to solving the problem in the future." Flores spoke at the eighth annual International Family Violence Conference. Flores said a lot of current research proves its critics right. Even the most recent studies cover statistics from at least three to four years ago, despite the fact that the situation already may have changed. Meanwhile, his office must make policy on a "minute-to-minute basis," he said. "At the end of the day, if there's a vacuum of information, policy still needs to be set," Flores said. As an example, Flores highlighted the summer of 2002, when a number of widely reported child abductions occurred. People wanted to know if there was a trend towards this kind of crime, and how to protect their children if there was, he said. But research had not yet explored those topics, he said, leaving parents struggling for answers. (Yates, 2003, p. A3)

- Innovative strategies by police to counteract hate crimes within their communities (see Chapters 12 and 13).

Police supervisors in their departments should be actively encouraging the innovations described in this chapter, as well as police innovators who contribute to cultural synergy and peacekeeping. For example, agencies might have an award for the Innovative Officer of the Month and display the person's picture in the squad room with a description of his or her innovative practice on or off duty. Central to the use of innovation in multicultural law enforcement is the ability of officers and leaders to manage the forces of change (IACP, 1999):

> The nature and implications of the forces that are changing police leadership are only partially understood. Further dialogue and eventual consensus must top the leadership research agenda. Unfortunately, practitioners do not have the luxury of awaiting the results of scholarly study. Every day they must manage the impacts of and seize the opportunities presented by changing forces. (p. 11)

SUMMARY

Law enforcement officers and leaders of the 21st century will have to develop criminal justice organizations and services that can effectively recognize, relate to, and operate within the multicultural and global shifts in culture, technological advances, and community/governmental expectations. This chapter has highlighted the emerging issues confronting the peace officer in adapting innovations and advanced technology to changing strategies and roles in multicultural law enforcement. Law enforcement officers in the 21st century will need to be more proactive and less reactive. The new generation of peace officers must not only increase their knowledge bases, but also promote positive law enforcement innovations, as noted within this chapter, to include (1) increasing awareness and skills within multicultural communities and special populations like minority and immigrant youths, elderly, and people with mental health problems; (2) embracing and using community-oriented policing practices; (3) curtailing litigation against law enforcement agencies; and (4) utilizing the innovations and advanced technology available to law enforcement agencies. The functional role of peace officers has increased to involve assistance to and communication with multicultural communities in disasters and terrorist events, as well as controlling possible community confrontations resulting from global or regional events. Training and preparation of future law enforcement personnel for services to multicultural communities will require changes in the curriculum of the police academies, as well as the ongoing and continuing education of law enforcement officers.

In this final chapter, as throughout *Multicultural Law Enforcement*, the authors have shared information and insights about improving public service in diverse communities. Our intention has been to help readers become more proactive with regard to the changing population, while anticipating future developments in both the law enforcement agency and society. The basic premise is that the personal and professional development of modern peace officers requires cultural awareness training that reinforces creative agency policies and practices on this diversity or multicultural issue. Part One of this book was devoted to the impact of increasing cultural diversity on the community, peacekeeping, and the law enforcement agency. Part Two centered on cross-cultural training and communication for peace officers. Part Three reviewed cultural specifics relevant to officers when they interact with people from Native American, African American, Asian/Pacific Islander, Hispanic/Latino, or Middle Eastern backgrounds. Part Four examined the matter of culturally and racially motivated hate crimes and response strategies (as well as the issues involved with profiling and racial profiling).

Finally, in Part Five, we have offered an overview of how peace officers can improve their effectiveness in a multicultural workforce and community by practicing greater cultural sensitivity. Numerous concepts, methods, and anecdotes were provided to promote innovative, futuristic professional development of sworn officers and their associates. With the human family in profound transition during the 21st century, futurists expect further social disturbances. Thus, our analysis focused on planned changes in the image, operations, services, and skills of law enforcement practitioners within rapidly changing workforces and societies.

Readers are challenged to examine the concepts and techniques presented in these pages, as well as to implement those that are feasible within local agencies and communities. If the strategies proposed here are adopted, the law enforcement field will indeed provide more professional, diverse leadership within the public sector, while presenting positive models in that regard to the private sector. For the professionally minded who will go beyond the content of this book, several appendixes and the Instructor's Manual complement the main content of this text.

DISCUSSION QUESTIONS AND ISSUES

1. *Increase Awareness and Skills with Multicultural Communities Involving Special Populations:* The chapter emphasized the importance of training and education for skills in working with multicultural communities involving special populations (e.g., minority and immigrant youth, elderly, people with mental health problems). What are the groups or individuals in your multicultural community that might be considered as special populations? What are some of the specific skills and resources for law enforcement needed to address these special populations in your community?

2. *Emerging Technology and Multicultural Law Enforcement Innovations:* Law enforcement officers and agencies need to embrace and to utilize the innovations and emerging advanced technologies that are available for effective work in multicultural communities. Using the list of innovations as a starting point, brainstorm other innovations and advanced technology that you think would be important to multicultural law enforcement. In what ways will the items in your brainstormed list have a positive impact on multicultural communities? Would there be any negative impact on those communities?

3. *Curtailing Litigation against Police Agencies and Officers:* The authors noted that much innovation is necessary so that a police response will satisfy citizens rather than provoke them to lawsuits against officers and their departments, especially in multicultural communities. Select one or more multicultural groups that are part of your community (or a part of a nearby community) and discuss how nonviolent peacekeeping is particularly critical in ethnic, immigrant, and racially diverse communities. What does it mean to say that police officers should do their duties with honor and integrity?

WEBSITE RESOURCES

Visit these websites for additional information about strategies and roles related to emerging innovation and technology issues in multicultural law enforcement:

The Center for the Study of Technology and Society: http://www.tecsoc.org

This website provides information on the application of technology for law enforcement organizations, including the implication that the use of such technology has on multicultural communities and the diverse society as a whole.

International Association of Chiefs of Police (IACP): http://www.iacp.org

This website provides information and reports by the IACP highlighting emerging law enforcement issues and technology that might have an impact on multicultural communities.

National Alliance on Mental Illness (NAMI): http://www.nami.org

This website provides information and reports by the National Alliance on Mental Illness, which is a nonprofit, self-help, support, and advocacy organization of consumers, families, and friends of persons with mental illness.

National Mental Health Information Center (NMHIC):
http://www.mentalhealth.samhsa.gov/

> This website provides information related to the U.S. Department of Health and Human Services (HHS) mental health research, programs, policies, and media campaigns and highlights the latest research findings and policy efforts.

Police Executive Research Forum (PERF): http://www.cpdny.org/Chief/police.html

> This website provides information for improving policing and advancing professionalism through research and involvement in public policy debate.

Social Technology Future Consortium: www.socialtechnologies.com

> This website provides information for keeping up with and anticipating new developments in science and technology as these affect organizational strategies.

REFERENCES

Bartol, C. R., and A. M. Bartol. (1999). *Delinquency and Justice: A Psychosocial Approach.* Upper Saddle River, N.J.: Prentice-Hall.

Bell, E. (1992, September 28). Keynote speech at the conference sponsored by the National Organization of Black Law Enforcement Executives (NOBLE), the Police Executive Research Forum (PERF), and the Reno Police Department, Reno, Nev.

Benson, R. W. (2001). "Changing Police Culture: The Sine Qua Non of Reform." *Loyola of Los Angeles Law Review, 34*(1), pp. 681–690.

Bovard, J. (2003, October 3). "Concrete Lesson of the Snipers." *Washington Times,* p. A21.

Boyd, S., A. Melis, and R. Myers (2004). "Preparing for the Challenges Ahead" *FBI Law Enforcement Bulletin, 73(1),* pp. 2–11.

Britz, G. S., Rush, J., and T. Barker. (2001). *Gangs: An International Approach.* Upper Saddle River, N.J.: Prentice-Hall.

Bucqueroux, B. (2004). *Restorative Community Justice: A Comprehensive Approach to Reducing Crime and Violence in Our Culture.* Mason, Mich.: Police.com Publishing.

Buerger, M. (2004). "Educating and Training the Future Police Officer." *FBI Law Enforcement Bulletin, 73*(1), pp. 26–32.

Cole, D. (2000). *No Equal Justice: Race and Class in the American Criminal Justice System.* New York: Free Press.

Dwyer, J., P. Neufeld, and B. Scheck. (2000). *Actual Innocence.* New York: Doubleday.

Foster, R. E. (2005). *Police Technology.* Upper Saddle River, NJ: Pearson Prentice Hall.

Gehl, A. R. (2004). "Multiagency Teams: A Leadership Challenge." *The Police Chief, 70*(10).

Goode, E. (2001). *Deviant Behavior.* Upper Saddle River, N.J.: Prentice-Hall.

Hails, J., and R. Borum. (2003). "Police Training and Specialized Approaches to Respond to People with Mental Illnesses." *Crime and Delinquency. 49:* 1. p. 52–61.

Human Rights Watch. (2003). *United States: Mentally Ill Mistreated in Prison—More Mentally Ill in Prison than in Hospitals.* Washington, D.C.: Human Rights Watch.

Hunter, R. D., P. D., Mayhall, and T. Barker. (2000). *Police Community Relations and the Administration of Justice.* Upper Saddle River, N.J.: Prentice-Hall.

Jahn, C. (2006, May 11). "New Officers Reflect Diverse Face of City: More Women, Ethnic Minorities Now Recruits." *Sacramento Bee,* p. B1

Kelly, T. A. (2002). "A Policymaker's Guide to Mental Illness." Washington, D.C.: The Heritage Foundation. Available: http://org/Research/HealthCare/BG1522.cfm.

Lingle, N. (1992). "People of Color and Culture: The Future of California Law Enforcement" (Order 13-0247). Sacramento, Calif.: POST Commission.

International Associations of the Chiefs of Police (IACP). (1999). *Police Leadership in the 21st Century: Achieving and Sustaining Executive Success.* Recommendations from the President's First Leadership Conference. Available: http://www.theiacp .org/document/.

Meadows, R. J. (2001). *Understanding Violence and Victimization.* Upper Saddle River, NJ: Prentice-Hall.

Morial, M. H. (2004, September 14), "A 21st-Century Model of Law Enforcement." *Copley News Service.*

"New Ways of Identifying People." (2000, September 9). *Economist,* pp. 85–91.

O'Toole, M. E. (2000). *The School Shooter: A Threat Assessment Perspective.* Washington, D.C.: FBI.

Office of Justice Programs. (1999). *Office of Justice Programs Annual Report for Fiscal Year 1999.* Available: http://www.ojp.usdoj.gov/99anrpt.htm.

Oliver, W. M. (2001). *Community-Oriented Policing: A Systemic Approach to Policing* (3rd ed.). Upper Saddle River, NJ: Prentice-Hall.

Peak, K. J., and R. W. Glensor. (1999). *Community Policing and Problem Solving: Strategies and Practices.* Upper Saddle River, N.J.: Prentice-Hall.

Police Executive Research Forum. (1997). *The Police Response to People with Mental Illness: Trainers Guide.* Washington D.C.: PERF.

"Profiling Study Cities Dozens of Locales." (2004, January 21). *Boston Globe,* p. A1.

Sentencing Project. (2002). *Mentally Ill Offenders in the Criminal Justice System.* Washington, DC: The Sentencing Project.

Taylor, R. W., T. J., Caeti, D. K., Loper, E. J., Fritsch, and J. Liederbach. (2006). *Digital Crime and Digital Terrorism.* Upper Saddle River, NJ: Pearson Prentice Hall.

Taylor, D. (1999). *Jump Starting Your Career: An Internship Guide for Criminal Justice.* Upper Saddle River, NJ: Prentice-Hall.

Thibault, E. A., L. M., Lynch, and R. B. McBride. (2001). *Proactive Police Management.* Upper Saddle River, N.J.: Prentice-Hall.

U.S. Department of Justice. (2006). Office of Community Oriented Policing Services: "People with Mental Illness." Available: http:www.cops.usdoj./gov.mimie/open.pdf.

Wilson, T. (2003, September 16). "Man Shot by Deputy Awarded $2 Million: Jury Finds the Rookie Officer Liable for Negligence and Civil Rights Violations." *Los Angeles Times,* p. B1.

Yates, R. (2003, July 16). "U.S. Official Says Child Abuse Research Trails Need." *Union Leader* (Manchester, NH), p. A3.

Ziedenberg, J. (2005). *Ganging Up on Communities: Putting Gang Crime in Context.* Washington, D.C.: Justice Policy Institute.

Appendix A

Multicultural Community and Workforce:

Attitude Assessment Survey*

The first set of questions ask for your opinions about how certain segments of the community view the police. Using the response sheets (Attitude Assessment Survey Response Sheet) on pages 501–504, put the number of the response that you think best describes each group's perception. Remember, give the response based on how you feel each group would answer the statements.

1. In your opinion, how would this group rate the job this police department does? (See response sheet.)

2. This group generally cooperates with the police.

3. Overall, this group thinks that police department acts to protect the rights of individuals.

4. This group feels that the current relationship between the police and the community is described by which of the following?

5. Overall, this group feels this department responds to citizen complaints about officers in an objective and fair manner.

6. This group thinks most contacts with police are negative.

The next questions ask for your opinions about procedures and practices within the police department.

7. Overall, police supervisors in this department respond to citizens' complaints about employees in an objective and fair manner.

8a. Most police officers in this department are sensitive to cultural and community differences.

8b. Most civilian employees in this department are sensitive to cultural and community differences.

9a. This department adequately prepares officers to work with members of the community who are of a different race or ethnicity than the majority of the population.

*Adapted with permission from the Alameda, California Police Department, March 1993.

9b.   This department adequately prepares civilian employees to work with members of the community who are of a different race or ethnicity than the majority of the population.

10.   The police administration is more concerned about police–community relations than it should be.

11a.   Special training should be given to officers who work with community members who are of a different race or ethnicity than the majority population.

11b.   Special training should be given to civilian employees who work with community members who are of a different race or ethnicity than the majority population.

12.   Special training should be given to assist officers in working with which of the following segments of the community?

13.   How often are racial slurs and negative comments about persons of a different race or ethnicity expressed by personnel in this department?

14a.   Persons of a different race or ethnicity in this city are subject to unfair treatment by some officers in this department.

14b.   Persons of a different race or ethnicity in this city are subject to unfair treatment by some civilian employees in this department.

15a.   Prejudicial remarks and discriminatory behavior by officers are not tolerated by line supervisors in this department.

15b.   Prejudicial remarks and discriminatory behavior by civilian employees are not tolerated by line supervisors in this department.

16.   Transfer policies in this department have a negative effect on police–community affairs.

17.   Citizen complaint procedures in this department operate in favor of the citizen, not the employee.

18.   Internal discipline procedures for employee misconduct are generally appropriate.

19.   The procedure for a citizen to file a complaint against a department employee should be which of the following?

20.   With regard to discipline for misconduct, all employees in this department are treated the same in similar situations, regardless of race or ethnicity.

21.   What kind of discipline do you think is appropriate for the first incident of the following types of misconduct? (Assume intentional.)

This section examines your views about police–community relations training and community participation. Please circle the response that best describes your opinion.

22.   Do you think training in police–community relations was adequate to prepare you to work with all segments of the community?

23.   How often do you have opportunities to participate in positive contacts with community groups?

24.   Do you think this department has an adequate community relations program?

25. What subject areas related to community relations would be helpful on an in-service training basis?

26. What do you think is the most important thing that citizens need to understand about the police?

27. How can the police department best educate the public about police policies and practices?

28. Listed are steps that police departments can take to improve police services as they relate to community relations.

Attitude Assessment Survey Response Sheet

Place the number that corresponds to your response in each column.

	Business community	Minority resident	Community leaders	Most residents	Juveniles
Question 1: (1) Very good (2) Good (3) Fair (4) Poor (5) Very Poor					
Question 2: (1) Most of the time (2) Sometimes (3) Rarely (4) Never					
Question 3: (1) Strongly agree (2) Agree (3) Disagree (4) Strongly disagree					
Question 4: (1) Very good (2) Good (3) Fair (4) Poor (5) Very poor					
Question 5: (1) Strongly agree (2) Agree (3) Disagree (4) Strongly disagree					
Question 6: (1) Strongly agree (2) Agree (3) Disagree (4) Strongly disagree					

Place check in column corresponding to your response for each question.

	Strongly agree	Agree	Disagree	Strongly disagree	Don't know
Question 7:					
Question 8a:					
Question 8b:					
Question 9a:					
Question 9b:					
Question 10:					
Question 11a:					
Question 11b:					

Check one response for each group.

Question 12:	Strongly agree	Agree	Disagree	Strongly disagree
African American/black (includes Caribbean, Haitian, and so forth)				
Asian				
Hispanic				
Homosexual				

Circle your response.

Question 13:	(1) Often	(2) Sometimes	(3) Rarely	(4) Never

Place check in column corresponding to your response for each question.

	Strongly agree	Agree	Disagree	Strongly disagree	Don't know
Question 14a:					
Question 14b:					
Question 15a:					
Question 15b:					
Question 16:					
Question 17:					
Question 18:					

Circle one response.

Question 19:

(1) Citizen sends complaint in writing to department.

(2) Citizen telephones complaint to department.

(3) Citizen comes to department.

(4) Any of the above are acceptable means.

(5) None of the above are acceptable means.

Please explain.

_____

_____

Question 20: (1) Strongly agree (2) Agree (3) Disagree (4) Strongly disagree

Check one response for each.

Question 21:

Type of misconduct	Verbal warning	Training/ counseling	Oral reprimand	Formal reprimand	Suspension	Termination
Excessive force						
False arrest						
Discrimination						
Use of racial slurs						
Criminal conduct						
Poor service						
Discourtesy to citizen						
Improper procedure						

Please circle the response that best describes your opinion.

Question 22: (1) Yes   (2) No   (3) Did not receive training
If no, please describe why the training was not satisfactory.
Please explain._____

_____

_____

Question 23: (1) Frequently   (2) Sometimes   (3) Rarely   (4) Never

Question 24: (1) Yes   (2) No   (3) Don't know
Please explain._____

_____

_____

Question 25: _____

_____

_____

Question 26: What do you think is the most important thing that citizens need to understand about the police?

_____

_____

_____

Question 27:

Circle one only.
(1) Through patrol officer contacts with citizens
(2) Through public meetings
(3) Through the media
(4) Selected combinations of the responses above
(5) Other (explain): _____

_____

_____

(6) Don't know

Please indicate how important you think each of the following should be to this administration by placing the number that best describes your response next to the appropriate question.

Question 28:	1 Somewhat important	2 Important	3 Not at all important
Hire more police			
Focus on more serious crime			
Improve response time			
Increase salaries			
Provide more training			
Raise qualifications for potential applicants			
Be more courteous to public			
Increase foot patrols			
Reduce discrimination			
Provide dedicated time for community involvement			

Appendix B

Cultural Diversity Survey: Needs Assessment*

ANONYMOUS QUESTIONNAIRE

There has been a great deal of discussion in recent years about whether the job of police officer has been changing. Some of the discussion revolves around issues related to contact with people from different cultural, racial, or ethnic groups. Please check or enter one answer for each question.

1. Comparing the job of officer today with that of officer a few years ago, I think that today the job is
   ( ) a lot more difficult
   ( ) somewhat more difficult
   ( ) about the same in difficulty
   ( ) somewhat easier
   ( ) a lot easier

2. When I stop a car with occupant(s) of a different racial or ethnic group than myself, I must admit that I am more concerned about my safety than I would be if I stopped a car with the same number of white occupant(s).
   ( ) strongly agree
   ( ) agree
   ( ) disagree
   ( ) strongly disagree

3. If an officer notices a group of young people gathering in a public place and the young people aren't known to the officer, they should be watched very closely for possible trouble.
   ( ) strongly agree
   ( ) agree
   ( ) disagree
   ( ) strongly disagree

*Adapted with permission: police department wishes to remain anonymous.

4. If an officer notices a group of young people from another racial or ethnic group gathered in a public place, the officer should plan on watching them very closely for possible trouble.

    (   ) strongly agree

    (   ) agree

    (   ) disagree

    (   ) strongly disagree

5. How often do you think it is justifiable to use derogatory labels such as "scumbag" and "dirtbag" when dealing with possible suspects?

    (   ) frequently

    (   ) some of the time

    (   ) once in a while

    (   ) never

6. When I interact on duty with civilians who are of a different race, ethnicity, or culture, my view is that

    (   ) they should be responded to a little more firmly to make sure that they understand the powers of the police

    (   ) they should be responded to somewhat differently, taking into account their different backgrounds

    (   ) they should be responded to the same as anyone else

7. When I encounter citizens of a different race, ethnicity, or culture who have committed a violation of the law, my view is that

    (   ) they should be responded to a little more firmly to make sure they understand the powers of the police

    (   ) they should be responded to somewhat differently, taking into account their different backgrounds

    (   ) they should be responded to the same as anyone else

8. When interacting on duty with civilians who have a complaint or a question and who are of a different race, ethnicity, or culture, I try to be very aware of the fact that my usual gestures may frighten or offend them.

    (   ) strongly agree

    (   ) agree

    (   ) disagree

    (   ) strongly disagree

9. When interacting on duty with offenders who are of a different race, ethnicity, or culture, I try to be very aware of the fact that my usual behavior may frighten or offend them.

    (   ) strongly agree

    (   ) agree

    (   ) disagree

    (   ) strongly disagree

10. How often have you run into a difficulty in understanding what a civilian was talking about because of language barriers or accents?

    (   ) frequently

    (   ) once in a while

    (   ) hardly ever

    (   ) never

11. How often have you run into difficulty in understanding what an offender was talking about because of language barriers or accents?

    (   ) frequently

    (   ) once in a while

    (   ) hardly ever

    (   ) never

12. How often have you run into some difficulty in making yourself clear while talking to a civilian because of language barriers or accents?

    (   ) frequently

    (   ) once in a while

    (   ) hardly ever

    (   ) never

13. How often have you run into some difficulty in making yourself clear while talking to an offender because of language barriers or accents?

    (   ) frequently

    (   ) once in a while

    (   ) hardly ever

    (   ) never

14. How important is it that the police department provide training to make its members aware of the differences in culture, religion, race, or ethnicity?

    (   ) extremely important

    (   ) very important

    (   ) fairly important

    (   ) not too important

    (   ) not important at all

15. Personally, I believe that the training I have received on group differences is

    (   ) far too much

    (   ) somewhat too much

    (   ) about the right amount

    (   ) too little

    (   ) virtually nothing

16. The training in the area of group differences has been
    - ( ) extremely helpful
    - ( ) very helpful
    - ( ) somewhat helpful
    - ( ) not too helpful
    - ( ) not helpful at all

17. My own view is that our department's quality of service could be improved by
    - ( ) placing greater emphasis on hiring on the basis of the highest score obtained on the entrance exam, making no attempt to diversify by race, ethnicity, or gender
    - ( ) placing greater emphasis on diversity by race, ethnicity, or gender and somewhat less emphasis on the numerical rank obtained on the entrance examination
    - ( ) giving equal weight to both the score obtained on the entrance examination and diversification by race, ethnicity, or gender

18. What percentage of civilian or internal complaints against employees are adjudicated equitably?
    - ( ) over 80 percent
    - ( ) between 60 and 80 percent
    - ( ) between 40 and 60 percent
    - ( ) between 20 and 40 percent
    - ( ) less than 20 percent

19. Some civilian or internal complaints are adjudicated more favorably toward people from diverse groups rather than toward the majority population.
    - ( ) strongly agree
    - ( ) agree
    - ( ) disagree
    - ( ) strongly disagree

20. I think that employees of a different race or ethnicity receive preferential treatment on the job.
    - ( ) strongly agree
    - ( ) agree
    - ( ) disagree
    - ( ) strongly disagree

21. The racial diversity of my coworkers has made it easier for me to see issues and incidents from another perspective.
    - ( ) strongly agree
    - ( ) agree
    - ( ) disagree
    - ( ) strongly disagree

22. To think that employees of a different race or ethnicity than myself receive preferential treatment on this job

    (   ) bothers me because I do not think it is justified
    (   ) does not bother me because I think it is justified
    (   ) is fair only because it makes up for past discrimination
    (   ) I do not believe minorities get preferential treatment

23. In certain situations, having a partner of a different race or ethnicity than myself is more advantageous than having a partner of my same race or ethnicity.

    (   ) strongly agree
    (   ) agree
    (   ) disagree
    (   ) strongly disagree

24. I have received negative feedback from members of the community regarding the conduct of other officers.

    (   ) strongly agree
    (   ) agree
    (   ) disagree
    (   ) strongly disagree

25. I have received negative feedback from members of the community regarding the conduct of officers who are of a different race or ethnicity in particular.

    (   ) strongly agree
    (   ) agree
    (   ) disagree
    (   ) strongly disagree

26. I have received more negative feedback from members of the community regarding the conduct of officers from different races and ethnic backgrounds than about the conduct of white officers.

    (   ) strongly agree
    (   ) agree
    (   ) disagree
    (   ) strongly disagree

27. In terms of being supervised

    (   ) I would much rather be supervised by a man
    (   ) I would somewhat rather be supervised by a man
    (   ) I would much rather be supervised by a woman
    (   ) I would somewhat rather be supervised by a woman
    (   ) It does not make a difference whether a man or a woman supervises me

28. In terms of being supervised by a man
    ( ) I would much rather be supervised by a nonminority
    ( ) I would somewhat rather be supervised by a nonminority
    ( ) I would much rather be supervised by a minority
    ( ) I would somewhat rather be supervised by a minority
    ( ) It does not make a difference to which group my supervisor belongs

29. In terms of being supervised by a woman
    ( ) I would much rather be supervised by a nonminority
    ( ) I would somewhat rather be supervised by a nonminority
    ( ) I would much rather be supervised by a minority
    ( ) I would somewhat rather be supervised by a minority
    ( ) It does not make a difference to which group my supervisor belongs

If this questionnaire is being used for a training class, please check the one answer in the following questions that best applies to you.

30. What is your sex?
    ( ) male
    ( ) female

31. What is your race?
    ( ) white
    ( ) African American or black
    ( ) Hispanic
    ( ) Native American
    ( ) Asian American
    ( ) other

32. How many years have you been employed by the police department?
    ( ) 0 to 5 years
    ( ) 6 to 10 years
    ( ) 11 to 20 years
    ( ) more than 20 years

33. What is your current rank?
    ( ) officer
    ( ) sergeant
    ( ) lieutenant
    ( ) captain or commander
    ( ) deputy chief
    ( ) chief

34. What is the highest academic degree you hold?

(   ) high school
(   ) associate's degree
(   ) bachelor's degree
(   ) master's degree

Appendix C
Listing of Consultants and Resources

The following is a partial list of professional consultants and resources that may be useful to law enforcement agencies (current as of August 2006). Please note that we are not endorsing the services of these consultants but are making our readers aware of their specialized multicultural and cross-cultural training and consultation. We recommend searching the Internet for a more detailed listing.

Cross-Cultural Diversity Consultants and Resources

Aaron T. Olson, Organization and Training Services Consultant, P.O. Box 345, Oregon City, OR 97045. Telephone: (971) 409-8135. Retired Oregon State Police Patrol Sergeant and Supervisor, and now a Criminal Justice Instructor at Portland Community College, Portland, Oregon. Coauthor of *Multicultural Law Enforcement: Strategies for Peacekeeping in a Diverse Society* (4th Edition), *Multicultural Law Enforcement: Concepts and Tools in Practice and Instructor's Manual* (2nd Edition), and *Multicultural and Diversity Strategies for Fire Services.* Provides communications, leadership, instructor development and multicultural training and consulting to business, government, and public safety organizations. Website: http://www.atolson.com. E-mail: information@atolson.com

The Backup Training Corporation. 421 E. Coeur d'Alene Avenue, Coeur d'Alene, Idaho. Telephone: (800) 822-9398 or (208) 765-8062. Provides CD-ROM training courses on cultural diversity, community policing, and other topics for law enforcement. Website: http://www.thebackup.com.

ChangeWorks Consulting (CWC). 28 South Main Street #113, Randolph, MA 02368. Telephone: (781) 986-6150. Website: http://www.changeworksconsulting.org

Deena Levine & Associates. P.O. Box 582, Alamo, CA 94507. Telephone: (925) 947-5627. Coauthor of *Multicultural Law Enforcement: Strategies for Peacekeeping in a Diverse Society* (4th edition). Provides cross-cultural consulting for businesses and organizations. Website: http://www.dlevineassoc.com. E-mail: deena_levine@astound.net

Elsie Y. Cross Associates, Inc. 7627 Germantown Avenue, Philadelphia, PA 19118. Telephone: (215) 248-8100. Provides organization development in planning and implementing diversity initiatives. Offers a quarterly e-journal, on a broad range of issues that affect anyone interested or

512

engaged in diversity initiatives and programs. While its focus is primarily on the workplace, it also covers topics such as health care and criminal justice, just to name a few. Website: http://www.eyca.com

George Simons International. 236 Plateau Avenue, Santa Cruz, CA 95060. Telephone: (831) 531-4706. Provides consulting, coaching, training, e-learning and customized tools to empower organizations and their people to work, communicate and negotiate effectively across cultures. Website: http://www.diversophy.com

The GilDeane Group, Inc. 13751 Lake City Way, NE, Suite 210, Seattle, WA 98125. Telephone: (206) 362-0336. A consulting and training firm that helps people and their organizations work effectively across cultural borders. They believe *"cultural intelligence"* is key to this effectiveness. Website: http://www.gildeane.com

Guardian Quest. 900 Lakewood Place, Aurora, IL 60506. Telephone: (630) 449-0958. Provides training and consulting on organizational assessments, diversity, ethics, leadership, and train the trainer to businesses, government and public safety agencies. Retired Deputy Chief Ondra Berry from the Reno Police Department is co-founder of the organization. Website: http://guardianquest.com

Herbert Z. Wong & Associates. 245 First Street, Suite 1800, Cambridge, MA 02142. Telephone: (781) 749-2997. Dr. Herbert Z. Wong is coauthor of *Multicultural Law Enforcement: Strategies for Peacekeeping in a Diverse Society* (4th Edition), *Multicultural Law Enforcement: Concepts and Tools in Practice* (2nd Edition), and *Multicultural and Diversity Strategies for Fire Services.* Herbert Z. Wong & Associates' consultants engage in organizational surveys, cultural assessments, and workforce diversity training. The consulting firm specializes in diversity training and the assessment of organizational culture for implementing the strategic advantages of diversity. Federal law enforcement and regulatory agency diversity assessment and training are also provided. Website: http://www.surveyreturn.com

Loden Associates, Inc. 140 Hacienda Drive, Tiburon, CA 94920. Telephone (415) 435-8507. Loden Associates takes a comprehensive approach to the design and implementation of diversity initiatives that maximize synergy with strategic business goals and support for organizational culture change. All client consultation and program development is based on proven behavioral science principles that facilitate broad acceptance of change as they minimize resistance. Website: http://www.loden.com

ODT, Inc. P.O. Box 134, Amherst, MA 01004. Telephone: (800) 736-1293. An online store and source of alternative information on maps, corporate diversity materials and books. Offers an array of fascinating and thought-provoking resources to expand your view of the world. Website: http://www.odt.org

San Diego Regional Training Center (RTC). 10455 Sorrento Valley Road, Suite 202, San Diego, CA 92121. Telephone: (858) 550-0040. Provides training classes, training development, and consulting services to public agencies in the southern California area. Training classes include cultural awareness, train the diversity trainer, and leadership courses for law enforcement agencies. Website: http://www.sdrtc.org

Simulations Training Systems. P. O. Box 910, Del Mar, CA 92014. Telephone: (800) 942-2900 and (858) 755-0272. Produces simulation training programs for businesses, schools, government agencies and non-profit organizations dealing with the areas of cross-cultural relations, diversity, empowerment, team building, the use and abuse of power, ethics, and sexual harassment. Website: http://www.simulationtrainingsystems.com

Sounder, Betances and Associates, Inc. 5448 North Kimball Avenue, Chicago, IL 60625. Telephone: 773-463-6374. Works with public and private organizations of all sizes in providing consultation and training services on diversity awareness, diversity competency, diversity mentoring, leadership, and many more areas. Has a specialized program customized for law enforcement agencies. Website: http://betances.com

Anti-Bias Organizations and Government Agencies

U.S. Commission on Civil Rights. 624 9th Street N.W., Washington, D.C. 20425. Telephone: (202) 376-8312. The U.S. Commission on Civil Rights: (a) investigates complaints alleging that citizens have been deprived of their right to vote resulting from discrimination, (b) studies and collects information relating to discrimination on the basis of race, color, religion, sex, age, disability, or national origin; (c) reviews federal laws, regulations, and policies with respect to discrimination and equal protection under the law; and (d) submits reports to the President and to Congress on civil rights issues. Website: http://www.usccr.gov

American-Arab Anti-Discrimination Committee (ADC)
4201 Connecticut Avenue, NW, Suite 500
Washington, D.C. 20008
(202) 244-2990
Website: http://www.adc.org

Anti-Defamation League (ADL)
442 Park Avenue South
New York, NY 10016
(212) 684-6950
Website: http://www.adl.org

U.S. Department of Justice
Bureau of Justice Statistics
810 Seventh Street, NW
Washington, D.C. 20531
(800) 732-3277
Website: http://www.ojp.usdoj.gov/bjs

Asian American Justice Center (Formerly the National Asian Pacific American Legal Consortium)
1140 Connecticut Avenue, NW, Suite 1200
Washington, DC 20036
(202) 296-2300
Website: http://www.advancingequality.org

Center for Democratic Renewal National Office (CDR)
P.O. Box 50469
Atlanta, GA 30302-0469
(404) 221-0025
Website: http://www.thecdr.org

Coalition against Anti-Asian Violence
c/o Asian American Legal Defense and Education Fund
99 Hudson Street, 12th Floor
New York, NY 10013
(212) 966-5932
Website: http://www.aaldef.org/

Congress on Racial Equality (CORE)
30 Cooper Square
New York, NY 10003
(212) 598-4000
Website: http://www.core-online.org

Equal Employment Opportunity Commission (EEOC)
1801 L Street, NW
Washington, D.C. 20507
(202) 663-4400
Website: http://www.eeoc.gov

Gay & Lesbian Alliance against Defamation (GLAAD)
150 West 26th Street, Suite 503
New York, NY 10001
(212) 807-1700
Website: www.glaad.org

Jewish Council for Public Affairs
443 Park Avenue South, 11th Floor
New York, NY 10016
(212) 684-6950
Website: http://www.jewishpublicaffairs.org

Museum of Tolerance
9786 W. Pico Blvd
Los Angeles, California 90035
(310) 553-8403
Website: http://www.museumoftolerance.com

National Association for the Advancement of Colored People (NAACP)
Washington Bureau
1025 Vermont Avenue, NW
Washington, D.C. 20009
(202) 638-2269
Website: http://www.naacp.org

National Conference for Community and Justice
328 Flatbush Avenue
Box 402
Brooklyn, NY 11217
(718) 783-0044
Website: http://www.nccj.org

National Congress of American Indians (NCAI)
1301 Connecticut Ave NW, Suite 200
Washington D.C. 20036
(202) 466-7767
Website: http://www.ncai.org

National Council of La Raza (NCLR)
Raul Yzaguirre Building
1126 16th Street, N.W.
Washington, D.C. 20036
(202) 785-1670
Website: http://www.nclr.org

National Gay and Lesbian Task Force
1325 Massachusetts Ave NW, Suite 600
Washington, D.C. 20005
(202) 393-2241
Website: http://www.thetaskforce.org

National Organization for Women (NOW)
1000 16th Street, NW, Suite 700
Washington, D.C. 20036
(202) 331-0066
Website: http://www.now.org

National Organization of Black Law Enforcement Executives (NOBLE)
Hubert T. Bell Jr. Office Complex
4609-F Pinecrest Office Park Drive
Alexandria, VA 22312-1442
(703) 658-1529
Website: http://www.noblenatl.org

The Prejudice Institute
2743 Maryland Ave.
Baltimore, MD 21218
(410) 243-6987
Website: http://www.prejudiceinstitute.org

Southeast Asia Resource Action Center (SEARAC)
1628 16th Street, NW, 3rd Floor
Washington, D.C. 20009
(202) 667-4690
Website: http://www.searac.org

Southern Poverty Law Center
400 Washington Avenue
Montgomery, AL 36104
(334) 956-8200
Website: http://www.splcenter.org

U.S. Department of Justice Community Relations Service Headquarters
810 Seventh Street, NW
Washington, D.C. 20531
(202) 305-2935
Website: http://www.usdoj.gov/crs

Appendix D

Self-Assessment of Communication Skills in Law Enforcement:

Communications Inventory

The following is adapted for law enforcement from Dr. Phil Harris's Communications Inventory in *High Performance Leadership* (1992). As you answer the questions, think about your cross-cultural communication with both citizens and coworkers in your department. (Many of these questions also apply to communication with people of the same background.) Find your areas of strength and your areas of weakness and make it a point to improve those areas. To check whether your perceptions of your communication are correct, have a coworker or partner fill out the questionnaire for you. Part of knowing where to improve involves self-awareness and an honest appraisal of your strengths and weaknesses.

Instructions: Circle the word that best describes your approach to the communication process.

1. In communicating, I project a positive image of myself (e.g., voice, approach, tone).
   Seldom   Occasionally   Often   Always

2. When appropriate, I try to show my "receiver" (the person with whom I am communicating—for example, victims, citizens making complaints, suspects, witnesses, and coworkers) that I understand what is being communicated from his or her point of view. I do this by restating this point of view and by showing empathy and concern.
   Seldom   Occasionally   Often   Always

3. I am sensitive to culturally different usages of eye contact and I establish eye contact where appropriate, but avoid intense eye contact with people for whom less eye contact is more comfortable.
   Seldom   Occasionally   Often   Always

4. I am aware of when my own emotions and state of mind affect my communication with others. (For example, I know my own needs, motives, biases, prejudices, and stereotypes.)
   Seldom   Occasionally   Often   Always

5. I refrain from using insensitive and unprofessional language while on the job (including language used in written and computer communications).
   Seldom   Occasionally   Often   Always

6. I try not to let the person with whom I am communicating push my "hot buttons," which would negatively affect my communication (e.g., cause me to go out of control verbally).
    Seldom   Occasionally   Often   Always

7. When speaking with individuals from groups that speak English differently from the way I do, I try not to imitate their manner of speech in order to be "one of them."
    Seldom   Occasionally   Often   Always

8. With non-native speakers of English, I try not to speak in an excessively loud voice or use incorrect English (e.g., "You no understand me?") in an attempt to make myself clear.
    Seldom   Occasionally   Often   Always

9. I am aware that many immigrants and refugees do not understand police procedures and I make special efforts to explain these procedures (including their rights).
    Seldom   Occasionally   Often   Always

10. I check in a supportive manner to see if people have understood my message and directions and I encourage people to show me that they have understood me.
    Seldom   Occasionally   Often   Always

11. With non-native speakers of English, I make a special point to simplify my vocabulary, eliminate the use of slang and idioms, and try to use phrases that are not confusing.
    Seldom   Occasionally   Often   Always

12. I make extra efforts to establish rapport (e.g., show increased patience, give more explanations, show professionalism and respect) with individuals from groups that have typically and historically considered the police their enemies.
    Seldom   Occasionally   Often   Always

13. I am sensitive to cultural or gender differences between me and the receiver.
    Seldom   Occasionally   Often   Always

14. I convey respect to all citizens while on duty regardless of their race, color, gender, or other difference from me.
    Seldom   Occasionally   Often   Always

15. When using agency communication channels or media, I communicate professionally, avoiding inappropriate or derogatory remarks.
    Seldom   Occasionally   Often   Always

Participant's initials _____

[Source: Adapted with permission from the Alameda, California, Police Department, March 1993.]

Glossary*

Acculturation: The process of becoming familiar with and comfortable in another culture. The ability to function within that culture or environment, while retaining one's own cultural identity.

Affirmative action: Legally mandated programs whose aim is to increase the employment or educational opportunities of groups that have been disadvantaged in the past.

Alien: Any person who is not a citizen or national of the country in which he or she lives.

Al-jihad: Struggle (literal translation in Arabic). The term has also been used by some to mean "holy war" against infidels or nonbelievers.

Al-Qaida: Also spelled al-Qaeda. A multinational group that funds and orchestrates the activities of Islamic militants worldwide. It grew out of the Afghan war against the Soviets, and its core members consist largely of Afghan war veterans from all over the Muslim world. Al-Qaida was established around 1988 by the Saudi militant Osama bin Ladin. Bin Ladin used an extensive international network to maintain a loose connection between Muslim extremists all over the Arab world, as well as in Europe, Asia, the United States, and Canada.

Anti-Semitism: Latent or overt hostility toward Jews, often expressed through social, economic, institutional, religious, cultural, or political discrimination and through acts of individual or group violence.

Assimilation: The process by which ethnic groups that have emigrated to another society begin to lose their separate identity and culture, becoming absorbed into the larger community.

Awareness: Bringing to one's conscious mind that which is only unconsciously perceived.

Bias: Preference or an inclination to make certain choices that may be positive (bias toward excellence) or negative (bias against people), often resulting in unfairness.

Bias-based policing: The act (intentional or unintentional) of applying or incorporating personal, societal, or organizational biases and/or stereotypes in decision making, police actions, or the administration of justice.

Bigot: A person who steadfastly holds to bias and prejudice, convinced of the truth of his or her own opinion and intolerant of the opinions of others.

B-NICE incident: An acronym for any terrorist incident involving Biological, Nuclear, Incendiary, Chemical and/or Explosive weapons of mass destruction.

---

*Glossary adapted in part from *Transcultural Leadership: Empowering the Diverse Workforce.* Houston, Texas: Gulf Publishing Company. Permission granted from authors: George Simons, Carmen Vazquez, and Philip Harris (1993).

Consent decree: An out-of court settlement whereby the accused party agrees to modify or change behavior rather than plead guilty or go through a hearing on charges brought to court. [Source: CSIS Project Glossary @ (http://csisweb. aers.psu.edu/glossary/c.htm)]

Cosmopolitan: Literally, "a citizen of the world." A person capable of operating comfortably in a global or pluralistic environment.

Cross-cultural: Involving or mediating between two cultures.

Culture: A way of life developed and communicated by a group of people, consciously or unconsciously, to subsequent generations. It consists of ideas, habits, attitudes, customs, and traditions that help to create standards for a group of people to coexist, making a group of people unique. In its most basic sense, culture is a set of patterns for survival and success that a particular group of people has developed.

Cultural competence: A developmental process that evolves over an extended period of time; both individuals and organizations are at various levels of awareness, knowledge, and skills along a continuum of cultural competence. Culturally competent organizations place a high value on the following: (1) Developing a set of principles, attitudes, policies, and structures that will enable all individuals in the organization to work effectively and equitably across all cultures; and 2) developing the capacity to acquire and apply cross-cultural knowledge and respond to and communicate effectively within the cultural contexts that the organization serves.[(Adapted from Cross, T., Bazron, B.J., Dennis, K.W., and Isaacs, M.R. (1989).) *Toward a culturally competent system of care. Volume 1: Monograph on effective services for minority children who are severely emotionally disturbed.* Washington, DC: CASSP Technical Assistance Center, Georgetown University Child Development Center].

Department of Homeland Security (DHS): The cabinet-level federal agency responsible for preserving the security of the United States against terrorist attacks. This department was created as a response to the 9/11 terrorist attacks.

Discrimination: The denial of equal treatment to groups because of their racial, ethnic, gender, religious, or other form of cultural identity.

Diversity: The term used to describe a vast range of cultural differences that have become factors needing attention in living and working together. Often applied to the organizational and training interventions in an organization that seek to deal with the interface of people who are different from each other. Diversity has come to include race, ethnicity, gender, disability, and sexual orientation.

Domestic terrorism involves groups or individuals whose terrorist activities are directed at elements of government, organizations, or population without foreign direction.

Dominant culture: Refers to the value system that characterizes a particular group of people that dominates the value systems of other groups or cultures. See also **Macroculture/majority or dominant group.**

Emigre: An individual forced, usually by political circumstances, to move from his or her native country and who deliberately resides as a foreigner in the host country.

Ethnic group: Group of people who conceive of themselves, and who are regarded by others, as alike because of their common ancestry, language, and physical characteristics.

Ethnicity: Refers to the background of a group with unique language, ancestral, often religious, and physical characteristics. Broadly characterizes a religious, racial, national, or cultural group.

Ethnocentrism: Using the culture of one's own group as a standard for the judgment of others, or thinking of it as superior to other cultures that are merely different.

Glass ceiling: An invisible and often perceived barrier that prevents some ethnic or racial groups and women from becoming promoted or hired.

Heterogeneity: Dissimilar; composed of unrelated or unlike elements.

Immigrant: Any individual who moves from one country, place, or locality to another. An alien admitted to the United States as a lawful permanent resident.

Homeland security: Federal and local law enforcement programs for gathering, processing, and application of intelligence to provide the United States with a blanket of protection against terrorist attacks.

International terrorism: Involves groups or individuals whose terrorist activities are foreign-based and/or directed by countries or groups outside the United States or whose activities transcend national boundaries.

Jihad: See **Al-jihad.**

Macroculture/majority or dominant group: The group within a society that is largest and/or most powerful. This power usually extends to setting cultural norms for the society as a whole. The term majority (also minority, see below) is falling into disuse because its connotations of group size may be inaccurate.

Microculture or minority: Any group or person who differs from the dominant culture. Any group or individual, including second- and third-generation foreigners, who is born in a country different from his or her origin and has adopted or embraced the values and culture of the dominant culture.

Multiculturalism: The existence within one society of diverse groups that maintain their unique cultural identity while accepting and participating in the larger society's legal and political system.

Paradigm shift: What occurs when an entire cultural group begins to experience a change that involves the acceptance of new conceptual models or ways of thinking and results in major societal transitions (e.g., the shift from agricultural to industrial society).

Parity: The state or condition of being the same in power, value, rank, and so forth; equality.

Pluralistic: The existence within a nation or society of groups distinctive in ethnic origin, cultural patterns, religion, or the like. A policy of favoring the preservation of such groups with a given nation or society.

Prejudice: The inclination to take a stand for one side (as in a conflict) or to cast a group of people in a favorable or unfavorable light, usually without just grounds or sufficient information.

Profile: A "profile" is typically a document that contains explicit criteria or indicators issued to officers to guide them in their decision making. It is usually based on data collected and interpreted to signify a trend or suggest that, given a particular set of characteristics (behavioral or situational commonalties), a person could believe that something may result based on that particular cluster of characteristics. A profile relies on using expert advice provided to law enforcement agencies to identify perpetrators of criminal activities. It can be an outline or short biographical description, an individual's character sketch, or a type of behavior associated with a group. It is a summary of data presenting the average or typical appearance of those persons or situations under scrutiny. Officers use these indicators of physical, behavioral, or situational commonalties to develop reasonable suspicion or probable cause to stop subjects.

Profiling: Any police-initiated action that uses a compilation of the background, physical, behavioral, and/or motivational characteristics for a type of perpetrator that leads the police to a particular individual who has been identified as being, could be, or having been engaged in criminal activity.

Race: A group of persons of (or regarded as of) common ancestry. Physical characteristics are often used to identify people of different races. These characteristics should not be used to identify ethnic groups, which can cross racial lines.

Racially biased policing: Occurs when law enforcement inappropriately considers race or ethnicity in deciding with whom and how to intervene in an enforcement capacity.

Racial profiling: Any police-initiated action that relies on the race, ethnicity, or national origin rather than the behavior of an individual or information that leads the police to a particular individual who has been identified as being, or having been, engaged in criminal activity.

Racism: Total rejection of others by reason of race, color, or, sometimes more broadly, culture.

Racist: One with a closed mind toward accepting one or more groups different from one's own origin in race or color.

Refugee: A person who flees for safety and seeks asylum in another country. In addition to those persecuted for political, religious, and racial reasons, "economic refugees" flee conditions of poverty for better opportunities elsewhere.

Scapegoating: The practice of blaming one's failures and shortcomings on innocent people or those only partly responsible.

Stereotype: To believe or feel that people and groups are considered to typify or conform to a pattern or manner, lacking any individuality. Thus a person may categorize behavior of a total group on the basis of limited experience with one or a few representatives of that group. Negative stereotyping classifies many people in a group by slurs, innuendoes, names, or slang expressions that depreciate the group as a whole and the individuals in it.

Subculture: A group with distinct, discernible, and consistent cultural traits existing within and participating in a larger cultural grouping.

Suspect-specific incident: An incident in which an officer lawfully attempts to detain, apprehend, or otherwise be on the lookout for one or more specific suspects identified or described, in part, by national or ethnic origin, gender, or race.

Synergy: The benefit produced by the collaboration of two or more systems in excess of their individual contributions. Cultural synergy occurs when cultural differences are taken into account and used by a multicultural group.

Terrorism: A violent act or an act dangerous to human life, in violation of the criminal laws of the United States or any segment to intimidate or coerce a government, the civilian population, or any segment thereof, in furtherance of political or social objectives (U.S. Department of Justice, 1997).

Terrorist attack Pre-Incidence Indicators (TAPIs): A term used by the intelligence community to describe actions and behaviors taken by terrorists before they carry out an attack (Nance, 2003).

Transgender: The term "transgender" covers a range of people, including heterosexual cross-dressers, homosexual drag queens, and transsexuals who believe they were born in the wrong body. This term includes those who consider themselves to be both male and female, or intersexed, as well as those who take hormones to complete their gender identity without a sex change.

Weapons of Mass Destruction (WMD): Three types of weapons are most commonly categorized as WMD: (1) nuclear weapons, (2) biological weapons, and (3) chemical weapons. The subcategories of WMD include activities that may be labeled as "agro terrorism," which is to harm our food supply chain and "cyber terrorism," which is to harm our telecommunication, Internet, and computerized processes and transactions.

White supremacist group: Any ongoing organization, association, or group of three or more persons, whether formal or informal, having as one of its primary activities the promotion of white supremacy through the commission of criminal acts.

White supremacy: Helan Page, an African American anthropologist, defines white supremacy in the United States as an "ideological, structural and historic stratification process by which the population of European descent . . . has been able to intentionally sustain, to its own best advantage, the dynamic mechanics of upward or downward mobility or fluid class status over the non-European populations (on a global scale), using skin color, gender, class or ethnicity as the main criteria" for allocating resources and making decisions [Source: Ross, Loretta (1995). *White Supremacy in the 1990s*. The Public Eye. Sponsored by the Political Research Associates. (www.publiceye.org/eyes/whitsup.html) Somerville, MA, p. 6].

Index

A

Accountability, racial profiling and, 451–52
Acculturation, of Native Americans, 277–79
Adolescent(s)
    African American, 182–83
    Asian/Pacific American, 155
    crime prevention and, 479–83
    Latino/Hispanic American, 215–16
Affirmative action, 89, 98–99
African Americans
    aggressive behavior and, 187
    culture, 172
    demographics, 174–76
    family, 180–83
    group identification terms, 177
    hate/bias crimes against, 363–64
    historical information, 172–74
    identity issues, 176–77
    language and communication, 114–15,
        183–87
    law enforcement issues, 179–80, 187–94
    myths and stereotypes, 177–79
    racial profiling of, 116–18, 189
African American Vernacular English, 183–84
Agencies. *See* Law enforcement agencies
Agency policies
    professional traffic stops, 459–60
    racial profiling, 428–67
Aggressive behavior, African Americans and,
    187
Alfred P. Murrah Federal Building bombing,
    306, 312, 315
al-Qaida, 308, 310, 312, 447

American Civil Liberties Union (ACLU), 435
American Indians. *See* Native Americans
Americanization, of Arab American children,
    249–50
Anti-Defamation League (ADL), 406, 409
Anti-semitism, 368–73
    crimes, prevalence of, 370
    groups and individuals, 371–72
Applicant screening, 94–97
Arab Americans
    approaching, 250–51
    cultural practices, 250–54
    defined, 236–38
    demographics, 239
    differences and similarities, 240–42
    family structure, 247–54
    hate crimes against, 257–59
    historical information, 238–39
    Islamic religion, 244–47
    law enforcement issues, 254–61
    post 9/11 backlash, 118–19
    racial profiling and, 116–18
    small business owners, 256–57
    stereotypes, 242–44
Arm of the Lord, 371
Aryan Nation, 371, 409
Asian Anti-Trafficking Collaborative (AATC),
    164
Asian/Pacific Americans
    anti-Asian laws, 141–43
    communication, 157–59
    defined, 136–39
    demographics, 143–48

Asian/Pacific Americans (*cont.*)
   family, 154–57
   historical information, 140–43
   key motivating perspectives, 145–48
   labels and terms, 149
   law enforcement issues, 141, 159–64
   myths and stereotypes, 149–54
   task force on police relations, 422
   typology of, 140
Assessment, terrorism, 342–43
Assignments based on diversity, 51–53
Authority, African Americans and, 189–90

B

Base rates, 463–64
Bias-biased policing, 431
Bias crimes. *See* Hate/bias crimes
Biometrics, 487, 489
Bisexuals. *See* Lesbian, gay, bisexual, and
   transgender (LGBT) individuals
Black English. *See* African American Vernac-
   ular English
Black Pride movement, 176
Blacks. *See* African Americans
Black separatists, 411
Block watch volunteers program, 421–22
B-NICE Incident, 305
Border security, 335
Brotherhood, 58–59
Brutality, 190–91
Bureau of Alcohol, Tobacco and Firearms
   (ATF), 312
Bureau of Indian Affairs (BIA), 273, 274–75
   tribal police and, 286–88
Bureau of Justice Statistics (BJS), 32, 44, 220,
   284

C

Canadian Association of Chiefs of Police, 46
Career *versus* family debate, 61–62
Casinos, Native American, 293
Catastrophic threats, 343
Chief executive, 73–77, 101
Children
   African American, 182–83
   Arab American, 249–50
   Asian/Pacific American, 155

   Latino/Hispanic American, 215–16
   Native American, 283–84
Chinese Exclusion Act, 141
Christian identity, 410–11
Christianity, Islam, and Judaism, similarities
   between, 247
Christian Patriots, 411
Churches, hate crime programs, 421
Citizen's Police Academies, 345
Civil Rights Act, 56, 89
Clustering theory, 366–67
Collaboration, Asian/Pacific Americans and,
   161–62
Commission on Accreditation for Law En-
   forcement Agencies (CALEA), 454–55
Commission on Peace Officer Standards and
   Training (POST), 91
Commitment
   of chief executive, 74–75
   recruitment strategies and, 89
Communication. *See also* Cross-cultural com-
   munication
   African Americans and, 114–15
   Arab Americans and, 251–52
   Asian/Pacific Americans and, 157–59
   high- and low- context of, 112–14
   inclusive workplace, 127
   interviewing and data-gathering skills,
      119–21
   Latino/Hispanic Americans and, 217–19
   Native Americans and, 114–15, 279–82
   nonverbal, 121–24
   plan, 333–34, 337
   post 9/11 backlash, 118–19
Community-based policing, 31–35, 475–76
   consortium (CPC), 96
   crime prevention and, 479–83
   extension of, 323
   peacekeeping strategies, 475–76
Community/Communities
   African American, 191–92, 193–94
   Jewish, 372
   Latino/Hispanic American, 226–27
   LGBT individuals, police relations with,
      383–84
   local issues and terrorism, 311–13
   minority outreach, 459

multicultural, 344–46
networks and resources, 321
profiling, 414
programs/resources, hate crimes, 418–21
recruitment strategies in, 92
relations service (CRS), 416
special programs in, 421–24
terrorism assessment of, 342–43
Community-oriented policing (COP), 33
Community Oriented Policing Services
   (COPS), 33
COMPSTAT program, 441
Conflicts, racially and culturally rooted,
   48–50
Conversational distance
   Arab Americans, 251–52
   communication and, 123
Counterterrorism, counter, 339–41
Covenant of the Sword, 371
Crime prevention
   among people with mental illness, 484–85
   among youths, 479–83
   community-based policing and, 479–83
Crimes. *See also* Hate/bias crimes
   anti-semitic, 370
   Asian/Pacific Americans and, 159, 163–64
   scene of, protecting, 317–18
   relating to sexual orientation, 380–81
Crisis management, 318
Cross-cultural communication
   attempts, 114–19
   language barriers and law enforcement,
     107–10
   law enforcement context, 111–14
Cross-cultural misinterpretation, 22–23
Cross-national family issues, 216
Cross-racial perceptions, 179–80
Cultural groups, police knowledge of, 26
Culture
   African American, 172
   definition of, 21
   Middle Easterners, 250–54
   organizational work, 476–79
   police incidents and, 19–24
   race, ethnicity, and, 8–9
Culture shock, Asian/Pacific Americans and,
   154

D
Data collection
   hate/bias crimes, 404
   on traffic stops, racial profiling and,
     460–66
Data-gathering skills, 119–21
"Dataveillance," 489
Demographics
   African Americans, 174–76
   Arab Americans, 239
   Asian/Pacific Americans, 143–48
   Latino/Hispanic Americans, 207–9
Department of Defense, 381
Deportation, 16–18
Desecration, 292–93
Differential treatment
   African Americans and, 187–88
   Asian/Pacific Americans and, 160
   Homeland Security and, 347
   Latino/Hispanic Americans and, 221
   women and, 61
Disaster preparedness, strategies, 332–43. *See
   also* Homeland Security
Discrimination
   definition of, 46
   gender, 57–58
   policies against, 70
District attorneys' office, hate crimes and,
   389
Diversity
   of Arab Americans, 240–42
   assignments based on, 51–53
   dimensions of, 24–26
   in law enforcement, 44–46
   measuring responsiveness to, 46
   reactions to, 6–7
   of society, 8–18
Domestic counterterrorism, 339–41
Domestic terrorism, 304
Domestic violence, immigrants and,
   16–18
Double standard, 60
Driving under the influence (DUI), 22
Driving While Black or Brown (DWB),
   430
Drug Enforcement Administration (DEA),
   433, 447

E

Earth, Native American philosophy, 276–77
Ebonics. *See* African American Vernacular English
Elders, respect for, Native Americans, 282–83
Emergency preparedness, 343
Emotional expressiveness, Arab Americans, 252–54
Emotionalism, of African Americans, 185–87
Employees, satisfaction level for, 93–94
End Racial Profiling Act, 450
English as a Second Language (ESL), 139
Environmental Protection Agency (EPA), 225
Environmental risk, 225–26
Equal Employment Opportunity (EEO) Act, 53
Ethnicity, 431
    bias, 392
    culture, race, and, 8–9
    illegitimate use of, 450–51
    legitimate use of, 448–50
Ethnocentrism, 21
Ethnoviolence, 365–66
Excessive force, 190–91
Extended family, Native Americans and, 283
Eye contact, 121, 123
    Native Americans and, 280–81

F

Facial expression, communication and, 122–23
Family
    African American, 180–83
    Arab American, 247–54
    Asian/Pacific American, 154–57
    career *versus,* 61–62
    Latino/Hispanic American, 213–16
    Native American, 282–84
Federal Emergency Management Agency (FEMA), 331, 343
Federal laws
    anti-Asian, 141–43
    hate crimes, 385, 404–5
Federal Response Plan (FRP), 349
First priority level, terrorism assessment, 342
First-response challenge, terrorism, 313–14
Fishing, Native American, 293–94

Foot position, communication and, 122
Fourth priority level, terrorism assessment, 342
Fraternal organizations, police, 50–51
Futures Working Group (FWG), 488

G

Gaming, Native American, 293
Gangs, crime prevention and, 480
Gay and Lesbian Liaison Unit (GLLU), 72
Gays. *See* Lesbian, gay, bisexual, and transgender (LGBT) individuals
Gender. *See also* Women
    communication issues, 125–27
    discrimination, 57–58
Gestures, 122, 252
Glass ceiling, 100
Greetings, Arab American, 250–51
Group identification terms
    African Americans, 177
    Asian/Pacific Americans, 149
    Latino/Hispanic Americans, 209
    Native Americans, 281–82

H

Harassment, policies against, 70
Hate/bias crimes
    African Americans, 363–64
    Arab Americans, 257–59, 347
    clustering theory of, 366–67
    data collection, 404
    definition of, 364–66
    historical perspective, 358–64
    incident control and, 414–16
    investigations, 386–89
    Jews and anti-semitism, 368–73
    laws, 385–86, 404–5
    lesbian, gay, bisexual, and transgender (LGBT), 373–84
    military and, 381
    monitoring, 405–6
    national scope of, 361–64
    organized groups and, 406–11
    prosecution, 389–93
    reporting, 404–5
    response strategies, 411–12, 418–24
    in schools, 381–83

STEEP typology, 416–18
targets of, 368
trends and predictions for, 412–14
Uniform Crime Report (UCR), 405
urban dynamics theories, 366–68
victimology and, 393–96
Hate Crime Statistics Act (HCSA), 361, 404
Hate groups
black separatists, 411
identity, 410–11
Internet and, 413–14
monitoring, 405–6
neo-Nazis and Klans, 408–9
organized, 406–11
racist skinheads, 409–10
response to, 411–12
in the United States, 407–8
trends and predictions for, 412–14
white supremacists, 407
Hate incident, 365–66
Hate violence, economy and, 367
Head of household, Arab American family, 248–49
High-context communication, 112–14
High school police academy, 92–93
Hiring in the Spirit of Service (HSS), 96–87
Hispanic Americans. *See* Latino/Hispanic Americans
Historical information
African Americans, 172–74
Arab Americans, 238–39
Asian/Pacific Americans, 140–43
Homeland Security and, 330–32
Latino/Hispanic Americans, 205–7
Native Americans, 269–72
racial profiling, 432–34
terrorism, 305–7
Homeland Security, 223, 323
communities working with, 344–46
goals of, 329–30
historical information, 330–32
law enforcement issues, 346–49
multicultural considerations in, 332–43
reluctance to participate with, 346
sensitivity to legislation, 259–60
Hospitality, Arab American, 251
Hostile environment, 55–56

Human relations commission (HRC), 415–16, 419, 422
Hurricane Katrina, 343
Hurricane Rita, 343

I
Identity
African American, 176–77
hate groups, 410–11
Native American, 272–73
Illegal aliens, 210–11
Immigrants, 10–14
defined, 139
undocumented, 14–17
women, 16–18
workshops for, 14
youth, crime prevention among, 479–83
Immigration and Customs Enforcement (ICE), 16, 110, 223–25
terrorism and, 336–39
Immigration and Naturalization Services (INS), 16, 110, 256
Incentives, recruiting, 92
Incident
command system, 318
control, hate/bias crimes, 386–87, 387–88, 393–96, 414–16
Indian Child Welfare Act (ICWA), 284
Indian Gaming Regulatory Act (IGRA), 285
Informal networks, for women, 62–63
Informants, false tips from, 322–23
Infrastructure systems, as terrorist targets, 341–42
Inner cities, addressing the needs of, 193
Institute for Women in Trades, Technology, and Sciences (IWITTS), 57, 61, 91
Intelligence
access to, 319–20
provided, using, 334–35
warning and, 333–35
Internal Revenue Service (IRS), 312
International Association of Chiefs of Police (IACP), 88, 100, 190, 453
International Association of Women Police (IAWP), 63
International terrorism, 305
Internet, hate groups and, 413–14

Interruptions, Native Americans and, 279
Interviewing skills, 119–21
Iranians, 237. *See also* Middle Easterners
Islamic religion, 244–47
Israelis, 237–38. *See also* Middle Easterners

J
Jewish community concerns, 372
Jews, anti-semitism and, 368–73
Jihad, 434
Job hazards, 225–26
Judaism, similarities between Christianity and Islam, 247
Jurisdiction, Native Americans, 285–86

K
Kerner Commission Report, 84
King, Rodney, beating of, 189
Kinship ties, Native American, 283
Klans, 408–9
Ku Klux Klan (KKK), 30, 306, 371, 407

L
Labels. *See* Group identification terms
Ladder of Inference, 457
Language
    African Americans and, 183–87
    barriers, law enforcement and, 107–10
    demographics, Latino/Hispanic Americans, 208–9
    English as a Second Language (ESL), 139
    limited-English or non-English speakers, 107, 109, 110–11
    Native Americans and, 279–82
    problems, Arab Americans, 254
    style, using, 114–15
Latino/Hispanic Americans
    communication, 217–19
    defined, 204–5
    demographics, 207–9
    family, 213–16
    historical information, 205–7
    labels and terms, 209
    law enforcement issues, 219–29
    myths and stereotypes, 210–13
    typology of, 209–10
    values and sentencing, 23–24

Law enforcement
    African Americans and, 171–94
    Arab Americans and, 235–61
    Asian/Pacific Americans and, 135–64, 159–64
    cross-cultural communication and, 111–14
    first-response challenge for, 313–14
    hate/bias crimes and, 418–24
    Homeland Security and, 328–50
    improving in multicultural communities, 35–36
    Jewish community and, 372–73
    language barriers and, 107–10
    Latino/Hispanic Americans and, 202–29
    LBGT individuals in, 64–73
    male-female communications in, 125–27
    Native Americans and, 268–94
    nonverbal communication and, 121–24
    prejudice in, 26–31
    profiling as tool of, 446–51
    technology and, 487–90
    terrorism and, 303–24, 315–18
    transgender protocol and, 378–80
    values in, 121
    victim and, 394–96
    women in, 41, 44–46
Law enforcement agencies
    changes in, 41–46
    chief executive in, 73–77
    curtailing litigation against, 485–87
    diversity in, 44–46
    ethnic and racial issues within, 46–53
    investigation of hate/bias crimes, 387–88
    racial profiling policies and, 453–55
    recruitment, 84–99
    retention and promotion, 99–101
    selection processes, 93–99
    women in, 53–64
Law enforcement environmental assessment tool (LEEAT), 92
Law Enforcement Management and Administrative Statistics (LEMAS), 54
Laws, hate/bias crimes, 374, 385–86
Leadership models, 76–77
Legal issues, recruitment and, 98–99

Lesbian, gay, bisexual, and transgender (LGBT) individuals
  controversy over, 66–67
  hate crimes against, 380–81
  issues, training on, 71–73
  in law enforcement, 64–73
  policies against discrimination, 70
  support groups for, 73
  transition into law enforcement, 69
  treatment of, 67–69
  victimization, 373–84
Lewiston, Maine, responses to hate groups, 412
Limited-English speakers, attitudes toward, 110–11
Litigation, curtailing against police, 485–87
Local laws, anti-Asian, 141–43
Looting, 292–93
Low-context communication, 112–14

M
Machismo, 214–15
Magnetic Gradient Measuring, 488
Male-female communications, in law enforcement, 125–27
Management, crisis, 318
Marianismo, 214
Media
  hate/bias crimes and, 419, 421
  monitoring, 421
Melting pot myth, 5–6
Mental illness
  crime prevention among people with, 484–85
  police encounters among people with, 483–85
Mentor programs, for women, 62–63
Middle Easterners
  defined, 236–38
  demographics, 239
  differences and similarities, 240–42
  family structure, 247–54
  historical information, 238–39
  Islamic religion, 244–47
  law enforcement issues, 254–61
  stereotypes, 242–44
Military, hate/bias crimes in, 381

Minority
  community outreach, 459
  defined, 431
  youth, crime prevention among, 479–83
Modesty, Arab Americans and, 255–56
Monitoring
  hate crime, 405–6
  the media, 421
Mosaic, 5–6
Mosques
  hate crime programs and, 421
  taboos in, 245–46
Movies, Arab American stereotypes, 242–43
Multicultural communities, 344–46
  improving law enforcement in, 35–36
  peacekeeping strategies in, 474–79
  trend monitoring in, 416
Multicultural considerations, Homeland Security, 332–43
  border and transportation security, 335
  catastrophic threats, 343
  community assessment, 342–43
  critical infrastructure, protecting, 341–42
  domestic counterterrorism, 339–41
  emergency preparedness and response, 343
  Immigration and Custom Enforcement, 336–39
  intelligence and warning, 333–35
  racial profiling, 336
Multiculturalism, 3–6
Multicultural media, as resource, 322
Multijurisdictional action, terrorism, 318–21
Myths
  about African Americans, 177–79
  about Asian/Pacific Americans, 149–54
  about Latino/Hispanic Americans, 210–13
  about racial profiling, 436–37
  about terrorism, 307–11

N
National Alliance, 409
National Association for the Advancement of Colored People (NAACP), 177, 179, 410, 412
National Association of Women Law Enforcement Executives (NAWLEE), 63

National Black Police Officers Association, 52

National Center for Women and Policing (NCWP), 45, 63, 88

National Coalition of Anti-Violence Programs (NCAVP), 374

National Hate Crimes Hotline, 395

National Incident-based reporting system (NIBRS), 361

National Mental Health Association (NMHA), 382

National Organization of Black Law Enforcement Executives (NOBLE), 51

Native American Church (NAC), 289, 291

Native Americans
  acculturation, 277–79
  casinos and gaming, 293
  family, 282–84
  fishing, 293–94
  historical information, 269–72
  identity issues, 272–73
  language and communication, 114–15, 279–82
  law enforcement issues, 284–94
  military service, 271–72
  peyote and, 288–91
  philosophy of, 276–77
  populations, tribes, and reservations, 273–79
  sacred lands and sites, 292–93
  similarities among, 276

Neo-Nazis, 408–9

Networking, organizational, 420–21

Network of Neighbors, 422

Neurolinguistic programming (NLP), 113

Non-English speakers, attitudes toward, 110–11

Nonverbal communication, 121–24
  African Americans and, 184–85
  Arab Americans and, 251–52
  Asian/Pacific Americans and, 157–59
  key points for, 124
  Latino/Hispanic Americans and, 217–19
  Native Americans and, 280–81

O

Offensive terms, Native Americans and, 281–82

Openness, Native American, 279

Organizational
  change, managing, 75
  culture, 476–79
  networking, 420–21
  policy, professional traffic stops, 459

Organizations, police fraternal, 50–51

P

Passive Millimeter Wave (PMW) Imaging, 488

Peacekeeping, strategies in multicultural communities, 474–79

Peace officers
  Asian/Pacific American, 162–63
  community-based policing and, 475–76
  multicultural, 348–49
  roles and strategies for, 472–91

Peer relationships, prejudice and, 29–31

Perception
  African American women and, 192–93

Perceptions
  Native American, 284
  of police, 254–55, 437–41
  racial profiling, 437–41

Perimeter control, in terrorist attack, 315–16

Personal Locator Beacon (PLB), 488

Peyote, 288–91

Philosophy, Native American, 276–77

Physical distance, communication and, 123

Pillars of Islam, 245

Planning, recruitment strategies and, 89–90

Police
  community partnerships, developing, 75–76
  encounters among people w/ mental illness, 483–85
  fraternal organizations, 50–51
  incidents, culture and, 19–24
  knowledge of cultural groups, 26
  neighborhood partnership with, 414–15
  perceptions of, 192–93, 254–55, 437–41
  prejudice, 28–29
  relations with gay/lesbian community, 383–84
  services to multicultural communities, 348
  tribal, Native Americans, 286–88

Police Executive Research Forum (PERF), 34

Police officers
curtailing litigation against, 485–87
gay *versus* lesbian, differences in treatment of, 67–69
Latino/Hispanic American, 227–29
Police traffic stops
data collection on, 460–66
Native Americans and, 288
professionalism of, 459–60
racial profiling, 439–41
Policing
bias-biased, 431
community-based, 31–35
problem-oriented, 31–35
racially biased, 431
Policy *versus* practice debate, 64–65
Politics, hate/bias crimes and, 417–18
Population
changes in, 9–10
Native Americans, 273–79
Posse Comitatus, 371, 411
Post 9/11 backlash, 108, 118–19, 239, 243–44, 260–61
Prejudice
definition of, 27, 46
influences, 27–28
in law enforcement, 28–29
peer relationships and, 29–31
President's Crime Commission Report, 84
Problem-oriented policing (POP), 33
Profile, 430
Profiling, 116–18, 189, 336, 414, 428–67, 431, 432–34, 436–37, 446–51, 451–52, 453–55, 460–66. *See also* Racial profiling
accountability, 451–52
Prosecution, of hate/bias crimes, 389–93
district attorneys' office, 389
objective evidence: bias motivation, 390–93
special problems in, 389–93
Protection by Tribes, 292
Proxemics, 123
Public relations *versus* recruitment, 65–66
Public safety, in terrorist attack, 316–17

Q

Questions, Native Americans and, 280
Qur'an (Koran), 245

R

Race, 431
culture, ethnicity, and, 8–9
illegitimate use of, 450–51
legitimate use of, 448–50
Racial bias, 391
Racially biased policing, 431
Racial profiling, 428–67
accountability, 451–52
accusations of, 116–18
of African Americans, 189
agency policies on, 453–55
definitions of, 430–31
historical information, 428–30, 432–34
Homeland Security and, 336
Latino/Hispanic Americans and, 221–23
Native Americans and, 288
perceptions of, 436, 437–41, 441–46
prevention of, 451–59
supervision, 451–52
as tool, 446–51
war on terrorism and, 434–36
Racism, law enforcement agencies and, 46–53
Ramadan, 246
Reasonable suspicion, 431
Recruitment, 84–93
applicant screening, 94–97
of Asian/Pacific Americans, 162–63
crisis in, 85–87
difficulties in, 87–88
of Latino/Hispanic Americans, 228–29
legal issues and affirmative action, 98–99
prevention of racial profiling and, 455
programs, successful examples of, 97–98
public relations *versus*, 65–66
strategies, 88–93
Refugees, 139
Religion, Islamic, 244–47
Religious bias, 391–92
Religious practices, knowledge of, 246–47
Reservations, Native American, 273–79
Resources, recruitment strategies and, 90–91
Response
emergency, 343
to hate groups, 411–12

Response strategies, terrorism, 314–22
  community networks and resources, 321
  crisis management, 318
  incident command system, 318
  law enforcement, role in, 315–18
  multicultural media, as resource, 322
  multijurisdictional action, 318–21
Right of Tribe, 292

S
Sacred lands, Native Americans, 292
Safe Trails Task Forces (STTF), 286
Satisfaction level for employees, 93–94
Schools
  bullying in, 382–83
  computers and hate crimes, 381–83
  crime prevention, 480
  hate crime programs, 423–24
Screening, applicant, 94–97
Second priority level, terrorism assessment,
  342
Selection
  processes, 93–99
  of recruiters, 91–92
Self-disclosure, Native American, 279
September 11, 2001 attacks, 306, 311, 314,
  330–32, 340, 407, 434
Sexual harassment, 55–56
Sexual orientation. *See also* Lesbian, gay,
  bisexual, and transgender (LGBT)
  individuals
  bias, 392
  crimes relating to, 380–81
Silence, Native Americans and, 279
Simpson, O.J., 189
Single mothers, African American,
  181–82
Skinheads, 409–10
Small business owners, Arab, 256–57
Society, diversity of, 8–18
Special weapons and tactics unit (SWAT)
  team, 52, 101
State laws
  anti-Asian, 141–43
  hate crime, 385
Statistical benchmarks, 463–64
STEEP typology, 416–18

Stereotypes
  African Americans and, 177–79
  Arab Americans and, 242–44
  Asian/Pacific Americans and, 149–54
  Latino/Hispanic Americans and, 210–13
  Native Americans and, 281–82
  terrorism and, 307–11
Storefronts, hate/bias crimes and, 419
Strategic Information Operations Center
  (SIOC), 334
Supervision, racial profiling and, 451–52
Support groups, for lesbian, gay, bisexual, and
  transgender (LGBT) individuals, 73
Suspect-specific incident, 431
Synagogues, hate crimes and, 421

T
Talking, Native Americans and, 280
Target zone theory, 366–67
Task force on police-Asian relations, 422
Technology, as tool, 487–90
Television, Arab American stereotypes,
  242–43
Terms. *See* Group identification terms
Terrorism
  definitions of, 304–5
  detection of, 309–11
  first-response challenge and, 313–14
  foreign groups, 308–9
  historical information, 305–7
  law enforcement issues, 322–23
  local community issues, 311–13
  myths and stereotypes, 151–52, 243–44,
    307–11
  response strategies, 314–22
Terrorist Attack Pre-incident Indicators
  (TAPI), 314, 344
Terrorist Threat Integration Center (TTIC), 334
Third priority level, terrorism assessment, 342
Threats, African Americans and, 187
Touching
  Arab Americans and, 250–51
  Native Americans and, 280–81
Toxic Release Inventory (TRI), 225
Training
  hate crimes and, 378
  Homeland Security issues, 344–45

multijurisdictional, 320–21
racial profiling and, 456–58
of recruiters, 91–92
terrorist-related, 323
traffic stops, 459
Transgender hate crimes, 378. *See also* Lesbian, gay, bisexual, and transgender (LGBT) individuals
tools for law enforcement, 378–80
Transition
management plans, 75
for women, 63–64
Transportation security, 335
Trespassing, Native Americans and, 292
Tribal police, 286–88
Tribes, Native American, 273–79
Turks, 237. *See also* Middle Easterners
Typology
Asian/Pacific Americans, 140
Latino/Hispanic Americans, 209–10
STEEP, 416–18

U

Underreporting crime
of antisexual orientation incidents, 376–80
Asian/Pacific Americans and, 159
Latino/Hispanic Americans, 219
Undocumented immigrants, 14–17
Uniform Crime Report (UCR), 361, 404, 405
Urban dynamics theory, 366–68
U.S. Citizenship and Immigration Services (USCIS), 16
U.S. Equal Employment Opportunity Commission, 56
USA Patriot Act, 340

V

Verbal expressiveness, of African Americans, 185–87
Victimization
of African Americans, 192
Homeland Security and, 346–47
of Latino/Hispanic Americans, 220–21

of lesbian, gay, bisexual, and transgender (LGBT) individuals, 373–84
of Native Americans, 284–85
Violence
African Americans and, 187
in Asian/Pacific American family, 156–57
move-in, 367–68
Violence Against Women Act (VAWA), 17
Violent Crime Control and Law Enforcement Act of 1994, 33

W

War on terrorism, racial profiling and, 434–36, 446
Warren Christopher Commission, 84
Weapons of mass destruction (WMD), 305, 343
We-they distinction, 116
White Aryan Resistance (WAR), 371
White supremacist movement, 407
Women
African American, 180–81, 192–93
Arab American, 255–56
barriers to advancement, 63
differential treatment of, 61
double standard and, 60
immigrant, 16–18
Latino/Hispanic Americans, role of, 214–15
in law enforcement, 41, 44–46, 53–64
mentor and informal networking for, 62–63
recruiting, 88
role in Asian/Pacific American family, 154–55
Workforce. *See* Law enforcement agencies
World Church of the Creator (WCOTC) movement, 408–9

Y

Youth
African American, 182–83
Asian/Pacific American, 155
crime prevention among, 479–83
Latino/Hispanic American, 215–16